# MAN
# CORN

# MAN
# CORN

*Cannibalism and Violence in the Prehistoric American Southwest*

Christy G. Turner II

Jacqueline A. Turner

THE UNIVERSITY OF UTAH PRESS
Salt Lake City

LIBRARY OF CONGRESS CATALOGUING IN PUBLICATION DATA

Turner, Christy G.
    Man corn : cannibalism and violence in the Prehistoric American
Southwest / Christy G. Turner 11, Jacqueline A. Turner.
        p.    cm.
    Includes bibliographical references (p.            ) and index.
    ISBN 0-87480-566-X (alk. paper)
    1. Indians of North America—Anthropometry—Southwest, New.
2. Indians of North America—Southwest, New—Antiquities.
3. Indians of Mexico—Anthropometry. 4. Indians of Mexico—
Antiquities. 5. Human remains (Archaeology)—Southwest, New.
6. Human remains (Archaeology)—Mexico. 7. Cannibalism—Southwest,
New. 8. Cannibalism—Mexico. 9. Southwest, New—Antiquities.
10. Mexico—Antiquities.    I. Turner, Jacqueline A., 1934–1996.
II. Title.
E78.S7T877    1999
979'.01—dc21                                                98-8856

To the memory of

Jacqueline A. Turner,

September 21, 1934–February 13, 1996

# CONTENTS

# Introduction

## *Studying Southwestern Cannibalism*

◆  To find a thing you have to believe it to be possible.
—Derek Ager, *The New Catastrophism*

THE WORD *cannibal* comes from the Carib Indian tribal name. It refers to a person who eats human flesh, as well as any other organism that eats the flesh of its own kind. Regardless of a few local, affirmative customs involving cannibalism, humans are usually enjoined not to eat one another, at least not their own family, friends, and neighbors (a practice usually referred to as *endocannibalism*). Eating strangers or enemies, called *exocannibalism,* is less strongly prohibited and sometimes is even expected. Aztec feasting on sacrificed enemy captives was permitted, for example, although supposedly only by members of the upper class.

The reasons given for cannibalism vary from place to place. They include starvation cannibalism in the Arctic; cannibalism as a ritual element in social control in Mesoamerica; cannibalism as an institutionalized means of showing love and respect for the deceased in China; cannibalism for obtaining the power and strength of a sacrificial victim in Brazil; and cannibalism associated with social pathology and psychopathology the world over.

Nevertheless, the primal command is, do not eat people. Worldwide folklore, oral traditions, sacred writings, anthropological narratives, war stories, urban police records, clinical psychology sources, and tales of lost or helpless wanderers and explorers tell of cannibal peoples and cannibal events. The moral is everywhere the same: eating someone is disruptive, inconsiderate, evil. Cannibalism is bad, and bad people are cannibals.

Yet despite the prohibitions, and despite the revulsion that most contemporary people feel for it, reports and claims of cannibalism have been made throughout the ancient and modern world. Only a handful of modern claims for each of the world's major geographic regions are eyewitness accounts, but even so, these are enough to propose that cannibalism has occurred everywhere at one time or another. Many reports of it can be found in Gary Hogg's useful survey, *Cannibalism and Human Sacrifice* (1966). An earlier book, Ewald Volhard's *Kannibalismus* (1939), is probably the most extensive—if not a very critical—review of the ethnographic literature on the topic. Volhard examined hundreds of articles and books dealing with the peoples and cultures of Africa, Oceania, Asia, and the Americas. (Not surprisingly, considering the year his work was published in Germany, he failed to cover northern and western Europe.) No matter how much one wishes to disbelieve it, the articles and books Volhard examined are real, and at least some of them must be truthful.

One well-known disbeliever is the social anthropologist William

Arens, whose book *The Man-Eating Myth* (1979) challenges the existence of institutionalized cannibalism. We find it incredible that out of all the reports Volhard reviewed, Arens accepted not one as a reliable account of institutionalized cannibalism somewhere in the world. Donald Forsyth (1983, 1985) has offered effective rebuttals of Arens's claim, as have many other scholars.

Without repeating prior reviews of the literature, then, we simply assert our acceptance that the act of cannibalism has been practiced on men, women, and children all over the world for a very long time. Cannibalism is a natural, cultural, and psychological phenomenon that is sometimes institutionalized, though usually not, and that paleoanthropologists have suggested goes far back in the prehistory of our own and closely related species (Gibbons 1997). We believe it is more productive to try to understand its existence and its motives than to deny them. Any phenomenon that is so encrusted with taboo, emotion, revulsion, sensationalism, and controversy must be worthy of understanding.

This book is the first to examine prehistoric Southwestern cannibalism on a regional scale rather than site by site. It has two goals. First, we define and illustrate the characteristics of damaged human bones that we believe reflect acts of cannibalism in the American Southwest. Second, we attempt to explain why cannibalism occurred there, offering a few working hypotheses about local, proximate causes. In order to be persuasive in arguing that cannibalism existed, we present all the evidence we have been able to amass, which makes up the largest part of this book—chapter 3.

The regional approach has produced five principal findings about cannibalism in the American Southwest: (1) Cannibalism can be differentiated from all other forms of bone damage and mortuary practice by a distinctive signature which matches that seen in the bone refuse of large and small game animals. (2) Cannibalism was practiced for almost four centuries, beginning about A.D. 900. It was most common in the Four Corners area, especially among people living in Chaco Canyon and in or near outlying Chacoan great houses. (3) Southwestern cannibalism appears to have originated in Mexico, where the practice was common and dates back at least 2,500 years. (4) Social control, social pathology, and some manner of ritual sacrifice, probably in that order of weighting, are provisionally the best combination of explanatory factors. (5) Although reports of prehistoric Southwestern violence and cannibalism have been published since the beginning of the twentieth century, they have been largely ignored. This is partly because the writings of previous generations are seldom read any more and because it is widely believed that prehistoric Southwestern Indians were generally peaceful people (see Woodbury 1959, 1993 for further considerations of this sentiment). Our study, however, shows that violence was common in the Southwest and can be recognized in human skeletal remains by A.D. 400.

In the United States, the Southwest includes all of Arizona and New Mexico, most of the southern third of Colorado, and, at least prehistorically, the southern third of Utah. On anthropological, linguistic, geological, and ecological grounds, the Southwest also extends into northern and northwestern Mexico, to near the city of Durango (Reed 1964). The area embraced by this most inclusive definition is referred to as the Greater Southwest.

The southern half of the U.S. Southwest is an arid, mountain-rumpled, low-elevation desert; the northern half is a higher, subhumid series of canyon-cut plateaus and mountainous and volcanic districts. The northern region belongs to what is often referred to as the Colorado Plateau. Winter snowfall generally occurs above 2,000 meters, and snow remains on the ground longer in the north than in the south. The U.S. Southwest has hot summers, generally mild winters, and two seasons of precipitation—summer and winter. Regardless of the number of times rain falls, reliable supplies of water for supporting large, stable human settlements and necessary crops are uncommon except in a few wide, alluvial river valleys such as the Gila in southern Arizona, the Little Colorado and Puerco in northeastern Arizona and northwestern New Mexico, and the Rio Grande in northern and central New Mexico.

The Southwest has been inhabited by humans for at least 11,000 years, most of that time by closely related but subregionally separated nomadic hunters and gatherers. By the beginning of the common era, three main, regionally distinct archaeological cultures—Anasazi, Hohokam, and Mogollon—had evolved, and the people of each were growing maize in addition to hunting and gathering. Over time, population size increased. By A.D. 1000 the farming of maize, with contributions from beans, squash, and, where possible, cotton, had become the dominant economic base almost everywhere in the Southwest, with a related socioreligious framework. Analyses of plant and animal remains, however, show that hunting and gathering continued (e.g., Akins 1984; Greene and Mathews 1976; Lincoln 1961). Intra- and interregional trade also continued and possibly grew, as is evidenced by an increase in quantities of marine shells and other trade items (Haury 1976). Nevertheless, in an unpredictable, arid environment, agriculture is a precarious economic lifeway, so various backup systems were needed. Most important must have been the retention of the hunting and gathering socioeconomic system—flexible, mobile, and kin-based—that had worked well for millenia.

As was the case in Mesoamerica, where the actual and figurative seeds of Southwestern agriculture originated, prehistoric Southwestern Indians both evolved and borrowed elements for their cultural and economic system—a system similar to but simpler than that of their Mesoamerican counterparts. The system emphasized year-round community ritual observances, ancestor idolatry, social conformity, priestly authoritarianism, communalism, intellectual conservatism, animal and human sacrifice, warrior societies, rainfall magic, and fertility rituals for nature, crops, and humans. These features were present in the Greater Southwest wherever environmental conditions permitted some semblance of an agricultural and sedentary lifeway.

Ethnohistoric accounts suggest that violence, if not cannibalism, occurred in all parts of the Southwest as we have defined it, as they most certainly did farther south in Mesoamerica. Indeed, the title for this book comes from the Nahuatl (Aztec) word *tlacatlaolli,* "man corn," a "sacred meal of sacrificed human meat, cooked with corn" (Fernández 1992). We have examined human skeletal collections varying in size, antiquity, and completeness from the entire region, but osteological evidence for Southwestern cannibalism turns up mainly in the Little Colorado and Rio Grande "provinces" (Riley 1987:10) of Arizona and

Table 1.1

Chronology and Culture Periods for the Anasazi Culture Area of the
American Southwest and the Valley of Mexico

| Southwest | | Valley of Mexico | | |
|---|---|---|---|---|
| DATE | PERIOD | DATE | PERIOD | CULTURE |
| A.D. 1600 to present | Pueblo | 1500 | | |
| 1300 to 1600 | Pueblo IV | | | Aztec |
| | | | Postclassic | |
| 1100 to 1300 | Pueblo III | | | |
| 900 to 1100 | Pueblo II | 900 | | Toltec |
| 700 to 900 | Pueblo I | 850 | | |
| 400 to 700 | Basketmaker III | | Classic | Teotihuacan |
| 250 B.C. to A.D. 400 | Basketmaker II | A.D. 1 | | |
| 7000 to 250 B.C. | San José (Archaic) | | Preclassic | |

SOURCES: For the Southwest, Woodbury (1979:29); for the Valley of Mexico, Weaver
1981.

New Mexico—the region whose prehistoric people are widely known
today as the Anasazi or, in a recently popularized term that concedes
some cultural affiliation, ancestral Pueblo. Because most of the Southwestern archaeological sites discussed in this book are from these two
provinces, we use only the chronology and cultural periods defined by
Richard B. Woodbury (1979:29) for the Anasazi culture area (table 1.1).

That there is no evidence for cannibalism among the Hohokam, who
were more clearly influenced by Mesoamerican culture than any other
prehistoric Southwestern people, may be simply because it has not been
looked for there. The archaeologists of yesteryear did not excavate as
well as those of today and could easily have overlooked or discarded
damaged human remains, mistaking them for animal bone refuse. Modern archaeologists, on the other hand, often try to avoid excavating burial areas for political and economic reasons, so they budget as little time
as possible for burial excavation. Although our literature survey turned
up no Hohokam examples of bone modification like that characteristic
of Anasazi cannibalism, this does not necessarily mean that violence and
cannibalism were unknown to the Hohokam.

This book's conception took place shortly after Edward B. Danson
invited us to join the staff of the Museum of Northern Arizona's Glen
Canyon Project in 1958. This was a large project sponsored by the National Park Service and shared with the University of Utah to rescue archaeological, biological, geological, and historical information in the
lake basin that would fill after the completion of Glen Canyon Dam.

In November 1959, in Salt Lake City, we examined the human skeletal remains excavated by the University of Utah's Glen Canyon field
crews. One series, recovered under the direction of Robert H. Lister at
the Coombs site in Boulder, Utah, included at least 14 variously complete skeletons. One of these, Burial 4, an adult female, had received
what appeared to be bone-breaking blows to her head, and cancellous
tissue in her lower right leg bones had somehow been reamed out.

"These features suggest that the bones had been altered by some agency other than natural decay or rodent and carnivore activity, and that the alterations may be the result of cannibalism" (Turner 1961a:118).

Nothing was made of this suggestion. Robert Lister and Florence Lister did not mention it in their final analysis of the Coombs site (1961), nor did Jesse D. Jennings (1966), who wrote the final project synthesis. It is probably just as well, because since 1961 our requirements for identifying cannibalism have become much more rigorous. In our view today, the damage to the leg and head of the Coombs woman is insufficient grounds for suggesting cannibalism, although it remains a mystery how the leg was damaged.

Earlier claims had been made for Southwestern cannibalism, but until 1968 we made no effort to learn about any of them. Except for doing some forensic work for law enforcement agencies in California and Arizona, we did not study any aspect of postmortem bone damage. We now know that the earliest empirically based, published claim for prehistoric Southwestern cannibalism was made in 1902 by the Smithsonian Institution anthropologist Walter Hough. It was based on his 1901 discovery of broken and burned human bones at Canyon Butte 3, a small pueblo in northeastern Arizona dating between A.D. 1000 and 1200. The earliest review of Southwestern cannibalism claims was made by Erik K. Reed (1949a), who did not include Hough's. Reed allowed that there were two possible cases, one in the Grand Canyon area found by Gordon Baldwin, and the other excavated by Watson Smith at House of Tragedy, a small site dated at A.D. 1100–1200 in Wupatki National Monument.

In 1967 the senior author examined prehistoric teeth in the human skeletal collections at the Museum of Northern Arizona as part of a worldwide study of dental morphology. One set of bones and teeth was severely broken and damaged. The remains had been excavated by Alan P. Olson and associates in 1964 at an isolated location on Polacca Wash, downstream and out of sight of the present-day Hopi mesa-top villages in northeastern Arizona (Danson 1965; Olson 1966). The Polacca Wash bones were well preserved, rather like those from dry caves, yet the site was located in the open. The good preservation hinted at an age much more recent than the Pueblo III date (A.D. 1100–1300) suggested by Olson. He interpreted the remains as a prehistoric secondary and ceremonial "mass burial" without any signs of violence.

In these bones, however, there were scores of breaks that looked like those in the bones of a violently battered victim found in the Oakland hills of northern California that the senior author had analyzed for police a few years earlier. Some of the Polacca Wash bones were burned, too. Altogether the assemblage looked strikingly like the bone refuse of game animals found in many archaeological trash deposits. The severely broken but well-preserved condition of the hundreds of Polacca Wash human bones, teeth, and skeletal fragments was too remarkable to ignore.

The series was borrowed and taken to Arizona State University, where the senior author and Nancy T. Morris, then a graduate student in physical anthropology, studied it over the course of a year. Because this was the first analysis of human bone damage and modification in the Southwest, we (Turner and Morris) had no existing procedure to follow and so did a great deal of improvising. The first order of business was to inventory the assemblage so that some plan of quantified characterization could be developed. This inventory eventually included counts of green bone breakage, cut marks, burning, bone preservation, and animal chewing and gnawing. Bone element counts suggested that at least 30 people were represented in the assemblage, almost half of them 18 years old or younger. Because of the severe breakage and total disarticulation, sex identification was difficult. Out of a minimum of 30 individuals, only three females and one male were tentatively recognized.

In searching for ways to explain the Polacca Wash mass burial, we followed several lines of inquiry. An ethnographic survey of Pueblo hunting parties and other groups away from a village produced nothing like the Polacca Wash demography. We searched for surface remains of dead animals in the Hopi area, which we examined on the spot for types of damage, weathering, scatter, and completeness to see how well they matched the Polacca Wash mass burial. Because of the lack of associated cultural items that could be dated, we had a direct radiocarbon assay made on a sample of ribs. It produced a historic date of A.D. 1580 ± 95. In the end, we hypothesized that these people had been the captives who, according to legend, were killed in historic times after a Hopi attack on the large town called Awatovi.

Although we were unaware of the term at the time, we had performed a *taphonomic* analysis—that is, we had attempted to explain how the assemblage was deposited and damaged after death. We concluded that most of the damage had been done by humans. The archaeological context was minimal—a simple, isolated bone pile near the dry Polacca Wash, miles from the nearest Hopi village. But this was exactly the context and location that fit the legendary killing of Awatovi captives following that town's destruction by other Hopi Indians (Fewkes 1893a).

Nancy Morris delivered the Polacca Wash report at the 1969 meeting of the Society for American Archaeology in Santa Fe. The large meeting room was packed. Because the methodological approach was so novel and the interpretation of violence and cannibalism so contrary to prevailing concepts of the peaceful Pueblo Indians, few archaeologists in the audience voiced acceptance. One who did was Alan P. Brew.

Brew had excavated human remains that year from the floor of a pithouse dating about A.D. 950 on Burnt Mesa in northwestern New Mexico. He thought the Burnt Mesa human remains had been damaged in the same way as the Polacca Wash assemblage. Subsequently, Brew examined the Burnt Mesa series with Lynne Flinn and the senior author, using the Polacca Wash procedures but with refinements and additions. Again, the bone damage clearly pointed to a depositional situation that was chaotic, disordered, and not a result of environmental processes. By exclusion, the cannibalism interpretation was reached again (Flinn, Turner, and Brew 1976). The 11-person Burnt Mesa assemblage had the added advantage of being in an archaeological context that enabled Brew to suggest that the cannibalism occurred during a time of stress. This lent support to an emergency cannibalism hypothesis.

In retrospect, the Polacca Wash and Burnt Mesa studies were flawed in both method and theory. First, observation was limited to macroscopic damage—that which could be seen with the unaided eye. The possibility of routinely finding slighter damage was not considered. Although polishing marks were observed on Burnt Mesa bones, they were not recorded in a systematic fashion. It was not until 1982 (Turner 1983) that we (Turner and Turner) began routine microscopic examination with at least a ten-power hand lens for each piece and surface of bone in a mass burial. Thus, only in later studies and reanalyses did we look systematically for tiny anvil or hammerstone abrasions and polished surfaces.

Second, these early studies had no theoretical framework for explaining Southwestern cannibalism or any other process that might have produced the damaged bone deposits. Mass burials were rare in Southwestern archaeology and completely unknown in the Southwestern ethnographic literature. Explanation for them was all ad hoc. Soon after the Polacca Wash report was in print (Turner and Morris 1970), a spate of other reports followed describing mass burials that suggested cannibalism—for example, studies by Peter Pilles (1974), Dana Hartman (1975), and Paul Nickens (1975). Still, too little information was available to enable us to identify any typological, temporal, or spatial patterning of occurrence. Moreover, the reports tended to show that bone deposits were not being excavated and mapped with as much contextual detail as was needed, so theoretical development was possible only on a site-by-site basis. General hypotheses could not be proposed that were testable with the mass burial assemblages, although starvation was the most common suggestion.

Following Olson's (1966) precedent, we retained the term *mass burial,* probably unwisely. In a way Olson was correct, because some days or weeks after scavengers had added to the bone damage (without widely scattering the bone), humans had covered the Polacca Wash bone pile with sand. The Burnt Mesa people, however, had been left on a pithouse floor and buried naturally—patently not as a planned or considerate burial. By 1980 it had become clear that additional terms such as *charnel deposit, perimortem,* and *anvil abrasions* were needed to describe more precisely the contextual and osteological features of such skeletal assemblages, because some of these unusual sites were not in any sense burial sites. Their human contents were much more likely discarded body parts—in short, refuse. Some assemblages graded into others where the damage, disarticulation, and scattering were probably caused by very different mechanisms. And in some sites, different combinations of mechanisms operated together on a single assemblage. Simply concluding that cannibalism had occurred was frustratingly insufficient.

Although with experience it became easier to explain how bone was damaged, we made little progress in explaining why these damage episodes occurred. Consequently, after 1980 we began to study Southwestern mass burials on two fronts—first, with better observational methods, some experimentation, and further field observations of dead animals; and second, with greater effort at explanation. The archaeological community's awareness of mass burials eventually led to a few very careful skeletal excavations.

Stimulated by an invitation to present a paper in a Canadian symposium dealing with taphonomy in 1983 we began a long-term regional project to relocate and reexamine Southwestern sites and skeletal collections that had been reported as evidencing cannibalism, other forms of violence, or both. This book constitutes our primary report for that →

study, which ended in 1995.]At the same time, we assembled data on a large number of formal, considerate Southwestern burials where there were no indications of cannibalism, violence, or ritual bone modification. Table 3.1 lists the collections for which claims of cannibalism or violence have been made and which we have reexamined or think should be reexamined.

A major theoretical advance took place in 1993, when it became clear that sites with hypothesized cannibalism were not randomly distributed. Almost all were in or very near the Anasazi culture area. None had been found in the Mogollon region, where more severe winters should have produced some cannibalized assemblages if starvation had been the primary cause. Hence, we were able to rule out emergency cannibalism as the principal cause, and our thinking shifted to cultural and behavioral rather than environmental explanations. Environment had never topped our list as the single best explanation anyway, especially after the Polacca Wash study, in which the damaged human remains could be connected with the Hopi attack on Awatovi. Nevertheless, until 1993 we could never rule out environmental factors as the primary explanation.

Although we had already developed a research design for the National Geographic Society that included study of comparative material in Mexico, our new realization of the restricted distribution of cannibalized assemblages in the Southwest led us to a much greater appreciation of the importance of extraregional comparisons. These might help demonstrate that cannibalism had caused the bone damage and explain why the cannibalism had occurred. We concentrated our direct extraregional studies in Mexico, where cannibalism had without question occurred prehistorically, and limited our other extraregional investigations to searching through the bioarchaeological literature on the adjacent areas of California, the Great Basin, the Rocky Mountains, and the Great Plains, which in the end turned out to be largely unproductive.

Research on cannibalism has not been free of controversy or political and professional censuring. We have felt pressure in various forms, most often as statements of disbelief that cannibalism could ever have occurred in the Southwest or as undertones that our work should stop because it was offensive to one group or another. The most common form of censureship is being ignored (e.g., Martin 1994), but it also includes being dismissed (Bahn 1992) or urged to "concentrate possibly on something more positive in the history of Native Americans," as William Arens put it during a 1994 interview in a television documentary on Anasazi cannibalism ("Archaeology," The Learning Channel).

In attempting to understand Southwestern cannibalism, it is certainly not our intent to shame, ridicule, or belittle any prehistoric American Indian people—the great majority of whom were given considerate, formal burials—or their possible living descendents. Our analysis of prehistoric human skeletal remains is but one of many studies that need to be conducted if cannibalism is ever to be understood as a human phenomenon.

Toward that understanding, we turn in the next chapter to the characteristics of human bone deposits that we interpret as resulting from cannibalism. The kinds of damage seen in these human remains bear striking similarities to damage in nonhuman animal bone caused by butchering and cooking. At the same time, the presumably cannibalized bones are quite different from human remains left by all known South-western mortuary practices or by violence alone. The lengthy chapter 3—the heart of this book—encompasses our documentation and discussions for 76 Southwestern sites where claims for cannibalism, other violence, or both have been made, or where we think such a claim should be made. We include examples of violence there to show the differences between cannibalized and traumatized human remains. Chapter 4 provides comparative information from Mexico, where human sacrifice and cannibalism were established practices. Finally, chapter 5 lays out our hypotheses for explaining Southwestern cannibalism.

# Interpreting Human Bone Damage

## *Taphonomic, Ethnographic, and Archaeological Evidence*

◆  Fractured bone, like fractured stone, is cultural data
for archaeologists.
—Hind Sadek-Kooros, "Primitive Bone Fracturing: A Method
of Research"

HUMAN BONE CAN be damaged by both human and nonhuman means, before and after the bones are deposited in archaeological or geological contexts. Human-caused damage may involve, among other things, trauma, accident, mortuary practices, ritual, fabrication, reburial, desecration, and cooking. Our purpose in this chapter is to demonstrate that a particular constellation of damage characteristics in human bone can be identified as having resulted from cannibalism and not from animal scavenging, burial customs, violence without cannibalism, or some other cause. The evidence is, first, that the damage pattern of cannibalized human remains matches that found in the bones of large and small game animals that were processed as food. Second, the human damage pattern does not match that produced by animal or other environmental forces. And third, deposits of cannibalized human bones look nothing like skeletal remains that received what we call considerate burial or that were damaged around the time of death by violence alone, without cannibalism.

## Taphonomy

THE RUSSIAN paleontologist I. A. Efremov (1940) coined the term *taphonomy* to mean the study of postmortem bone distribution and modification ("processes of embedding"). Efremov was explicitly concerned with how terrestrial and aquatic fossils came to be associated in their geological matrices. Although Efremov did not specifically mention human behavior as an embedding mechanism, it is clear that he intended taphonomy to involve all relevant mechanisms, agents, conditions, and processes of the biosphere and lithosphere (see also Binford 1981; Lyman 1994; Noe-Nygaard 1977).

The taphonomic process begins with death and the initiation of *diagenesis*, the physical and chemical breakdown of the organism. Figures 2.1 and 2.2 illustrate stages in this process for two large animals whose diagensis occurred on the ground surface and ended in remnant bone scatters. A human cadaver passes through the same stages when left unprotected.

Taphonomy can be considered *death history*, the history that comes after an individual's *life history*. Death histories can be obtained only by examining tissues, usually bones, and their placement on the landscape, whether they are confined to a burial pit, hung up on a skull rack, partly reburied, or scattered and burned as waste across a room or trash mound. Life history can affect death history, particularly if death is preceded or soon followed by various damaging processes. The variably

10

brief transitional phase at or around the time of death we call the *peri-mortem* phase, to distinguish it from *postmortem* events or conditions.

Bone from an archaeologically derived skeleton that appears fresh, green, or vital has been stopped or slowed down in its decay, or diagenic track. Bone that has not been arrested in its natural diagenesis will continue its physical and chemical breakdown. Weathering, disintegration, bleaching, cracking, loss of organic components, and chemical and mineral replacement are some of the physical features of postmortem bone (for more, see Koch 1989; Morlan 1984, 1987).

In an archaeological context, conditions can be reconstructed to include antemortem, perimortem, and postmortem moments in life or death histories. For example, a bone wound such as a traumatic compound fracture that shows bone reaction and surrounding infection had to have been an antemortem wound, a life history event. The bone had live cells that reacted to the trauma, and it must have contained its full organic component if it was prevented from shattering the way weathered bone does. A trauma break that shows neither reaction nor shattering is a perimortem wound. Finally, an impact that shatters a bone into multiple small rectangular to subrectangular pieces, indicating that the binding organic component of the bone was low, would be interpreted as a postmortem break, a death history event.

These phases, of course, can vary. An ancient bone in a dry cave that has been protected from weathering can retain much of its organic component, and when hit, broken, cut, or burned it can behave physically as if it were fresh or perimortem bone. Context is as important as bone condition in reconstructing life and death histories. Efremov envisioned taphonomic research as more than laboratory study of bone modification. It must include contextual study at the time of excavation (Morlan 1987).

*Animal Damage to Bone*

Environmental processes that can affect skeletal death history begin immediately upon biological death with an increase in microbial number and activity due to the cessation of the body's immune system. Bacteria, fungi, and other saprophytic organisms metabolize soft and hard tissues and are joined in their decomposition activity by organic chemical and physical breakdown processes, accelerated, as most chemical reactions are, by warmth and moisture.

Mechanical and physical breakdown accompanies scavenger activity, mainly in the form of hard tooth chiseling, chewing, puncturing, and gnawing of bone for nutrients. Southwestern scavengers range from tiny annelid worms, fly larvae, and beetle-sized boring and chewing insects to larger invertebrates, small mammals including mice and wood rats, larger mammals such as skunks, badgers, and porcupines, and, finally, the better-known large scavengers such as crows, buzzards, coyotes, dogs, wolves, and bears. Some of these scavengers leave distinctive marks, but many do not. Figures 2.3–2.5 show examples of rodent gnawing and carnivore tooth puncturing of various pronghorn antelope skeletal elements. The amount, location, type, and degree of damage done to a human skeleton by animal scavengers provide information on events and conditions around the time of death.

During diagenesis, many small invertebrate and vertebrate species such as flies, carrion beetles, and maggots invade the carcass to feed and

Figure 2.1. The major remains of a highway kill (beef) near Alta Vista, Mexico. Natural on-surface breakdown differs considerably from that of human bone assemblages thought to have been cannibalized. Vertebrae remain a long time at the death site, as do whole crania. Bone bleaching is negligible here, indicating recent death. Odor was very strong (CGT neg. 4-14-94:34).

Figure 2.2. Breakdown is further along in a sheep skeleton near the abandoned Hopi village of Chokovi, Arizona. Note total bone bleaching, longitudinal cracking, and chewed ends of vertebral spines and ends of pelvic bones. The vertebrae remain articulated. There was no odor (CGT neg. 8-10-68:44).

Figure 2.3. Wupatki Ruin. Pronghorn antelope bone fragment with rodent gnawing (at arrow) (CGT neg. 7-15-93:28).

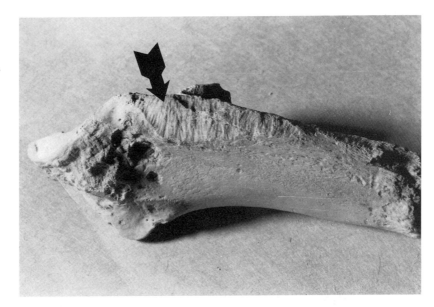

Figure 2.4. Wupatki Trench L. Pronghorn bone fragment with an edge about 3.0 cm long with rodent gnawing marks (CGT neg. 7-16-93:24).

Figure 2.5. Wupatki Trench L. Pronghorn distal femur fragment with carnivore tooth puncture marks (CGT neg. 7-16-93:27).

reproduce. Once most of the soft tissue has been consumed or carried away by these species or larger carnivores, primary or secondary scavengers then seek the fat and protein contained in the bones. This skeletal reduction leaves puncturing tooth marks in softer and flatter bones such as vertebral bodies, articular ends of long bones, and rib surfaces. Horned mammals often have their horns chewed away early in the carnivore feeding sequence.

Carnivore damage occurs only when a carcass or scattered bones are on the ground surface. Rodent damage can occur when bones are on the surface, in natural rock crypts, or buried and encountered by a burrowing mouse, squirrel, or other chisel-toothed animal. Throughout this book, we use *gnawing* to refer to rodent activity and *chewing* to refer to carnivore activity.

In addition to the ends of bones, where chewing produces scooped-out areas of removed cancellous bone, scavengers concentrate their chewing and gnawing at locations of spongy bone where the overlying cortex is thin. Carnivore chewing and bone breaking are more common on the ends of long bones than nearer their centers. Few Southwestern carnivores can break a bone as heavy as an adult human femur, but given enough time they can chew away much of a long bone from one or both ends well into the central shaft. Tooth scratches can occur everywhere on a large bone that has been well worked over by a carnivore.

Not all carnivore activity can be recognized as such, and caution is in order. We agree with Eileen Johnson (1985), who studied perimortem bone damage in an effort to distinguish between carnivore and hominid modification, that it is not always easily and reliably done. Carnivore tooth scratches can often be differentiated from stone tool cut marks by their U-shaped cross section, shallow depth, meandering random track, and concentration near the ends of long bones or on the processes and projections of flat or irregularly shaped bones. Stone tools usually leave straight cut marks that are V-shaped in cross section and further characterized by internal ridging or gouging.

A carnivore may "play" with a human bone or skull on a gritty surface such as a sandstone ledge, where bodies were sometimes placed in crevices. The play can leave striations. Those we have personally seen, such as the striations on the Verdure Canyon skeleton (Fink 1989), are distributed over much of the surface of the bone and are crisscrossed, circular, and unpatterned. The depth and fineness of such striations are generally fairly uniform, unlike cut marks, which can vary considerably in depth and width. Moreover, carnivore striations are seldom concentrated or parallel and rarely grade from deep to shallow in a discrete group, as occurs with anvil abrasions.

If a heavy human bone such as a femur or humerus has been cracked or fully broken by a large carnivore, the damage can almost always be classified as animal inflicted because of the presence of tooth *cusp scars* near the fracture site. Cusp scars are produced when the opposing teeth "dig in" as the crushing jaws close, much like the scars that form on an object twisting in a vice until it is tightened sufficiently to prevent any further movement. However, we have often been unable to decide whether finger and toe bones were broken by carnivores, humans, or natural mechanical-physical agencies.

Carnivore damage by itself has been well characterized, and it differs dramatically from damage due to cannibalism. William D. Haglund, Donald T. Reay, and Daris R. Swindler (1988, 1989) reviewed the types of bone damage known to be caused by carnivores. The types ranged from simple tooth marks, damaged margins, scooping of ends, and missing or broken pieces to heavy fractures and complete absence of entire bones. These authors reiterated that Gary Haynes (1983) and Lewis R. Binford (1981) had recognized four types of carnivore tooth marks: punctures, pits, scoring, and furrows.

Haglund and colleagues then described carnivore damage in remains from 37 recent human deaths discovered between 1979 and 1987 around Seattle, Washington. The individuals had been identified, so the date of each death could be closely estimated. Very careful collection methods were used to recover all possible skeletal elements and associated cultural materials at the death sites. Bone recovery was 100% for crania, which had only tooth punctures in the mastoid areas. Mandibles had high recovery (83%) but were damaged more often than crania. The least frequently found bone was the clavicle (25%), and all were damaged. Long bone recovery varied from the radius, the least frequent (35%), to the femur, the most frequent (65%). All long bones were damaged.

Haglund and colleagues could not completely assess the damage to ribs, sternum, sacrum, or vertebrae, although they managed to obtain counts of recovered elements. Rib recovery was 62%; vertebra recovery ranged from 61% for the cervical to 70% for the lumbar and 73% for the thoracic. The authors also determined that about 70% of all skeletal elements were recovered when the elapsed time from death to discovery of the body was 4.5 months or less. After six months, bone loss increased notably.

Carnivore damage to skeletons in the Seattle area was roughly inversely proportional to human population density. Bones recovered from areas inhabited by dogs were more damaged than those from areas presumably inhabited by coyotes. Rodent damage was identified by parallel incisor furrows. *Spiral fractures,* which resemble the curvilinear breakage pattern characteristic of shattered homogeneous materials such as glass or plastic, were limited to the fibula, radius, and ulna, the smallest of the six types of long bones.

A year later, George R. Milner and Virginia G. Smith (1989) published a similar sort of taphonomic study. Unlike Haglund and colleagues, Milner and Smith found that carnivore damage to crania was 25% (3 of 12 individuals) in a series of 30 Oneota Indian skeletons. The Oneotas had been killed and mutilated in a battle in west-central Illinois about A.D. 1300, and their remains had subsequently been placed in a burial mound. Another interesting difference between Milner and Smith's findings and those of Haglund, Reay, and Swindler is that although facial bones were damaged, mandibles were not (0 of 10). Carnivore damage to skulls reported in both studies was much less than that found in Anasazi skeletal remains believed to have been cannibalized.

Milner and Smith reported that carnivore damage to vertebrae was relatively slight. Only 4.3% of cervical vertebrae were damaged (5 of 117), 12.3% of thoracic (31 of 252), and 10.9% of lumbar (12 of 110). For 30 individuals the expected normal number of cervical vertebrae would be 210 (7 × 30), of thoracic vertebrae, 360, and of lumbar

vertebrae, 150. In fact, 55.7% of the expected number of cervical vertebrae were preserved, 70% of the thoracic, and 73.3% of the lumbar—
values very similar to those observed by Haglund and colleagues (1988).
These examples demonstrate that vertebra loss due to carnivore activity
is much less than that characteristic in sites with probable cannibalism,
as we discuss later in this chapter.

Milner and Smith (1989:48) concluded that "the areas most frequently affected include the ends of long bones, where there is generally
little covering soft tissue, and the bones in the vicinity of the facial, ab-
dominal, and gluteal regions." The carnivore damage was attributed to
coyotes, dogs, and/or wolves. There was also some rodent damage.

Rodent gnawing is distinctive: it consists of multiple and largely parallel gouged grooves that appear rather like saw marks in rough-cut
lumber (figs. 2.3 and 2.4). Rodents seem to prefer to gnaw on bone
edges such as the orbital border of the frontal and maxillary bones,
presumably for salt and other nutrients. Their gnawing does not
always appear to be nutritionally motivated, however. We collected
newly gnawed sticks, plastic objects, and other materials near our residence on the grounds of the Museum of Northern Arizona, where we
daily provided birds, squirrels, and chipmunks with grain and other
sorts of feed.

Birds also scavenge. Dan Morse (1984:124) reported: "All the flesh
can be removed from a dead [human] body by a flock of black vultures
in a few hours. It takes a little more time for the same result to be
achieved by a pack of dogs and/or other animals." Scavenging by birds
seldom leaves distinctive minutiae on bone surfaces. We have observed
one possible example made by a crow, a buzzard, or some similar large
species; it was a wide circular puncture in a thin scapular fossa. Even
though avian scavengers cannot chew a carcass apart, they can tear and
rip and contribute to widespread small bone scatter and loss from the
death site of any carcass. Human-caused damage is quite the opposite—
a great deal of breakage but less distant scattering.

Trampling on skeletons by large animals is an uncommon but real
source of bone breakage, scratching, and scattering, especially around
ponds where animal presence is concentrated. Deer, cattle, and presumably other grazers and browsers will chew and eat bones, possibly because of a need for phosphorus. Bone loss also occurs when animals
transport bones away from a carcass site. The next most common cause
of surface bone scatter and loss is water movement from heavy rains and
stream flooding. Buried bones can be moved about by the burrowing activities of fossorial mammals such as badgers. Dan Morse (1984:128)
provides some observations on the scattering of human bones by nonhuman agents at various intervals after deposition (table 2.1).

*Physical and Chemical*
*Damage to Bone*

Breakdown of bone by physical and chemical agents can often be recognized. Prehistoric bone surfaces and interiors are commonly eroded by
plant roots, which leave characteristic tracks, and large rootlets of trees
are often found perforating and breaking skeletal elements. Some invertebrates leave telltale scarifying minutiae, but in the arid Southwest they
are only minor contributors to diagenesis. Their activity, however, is
difficult to recognize, as are the effects of molds, fungi, and bacteria.

Acid or other chemical erosion of bone surfaces occurs most often

Table 2.1

Observed Scattering of Human Skeletal Remains over Time

| SEX/AGE | TIME SINCE DEPOSITION | SCATTERING |
|---|---|---|
| F/80 | 3 weeks | Articulated; no scatter |
| M/27 | 3 weeks | Disarticulated, minimal scatter |
| F/22 | 5 weeks | Slight scatter; some articulation |
| M/18, M/20 | 4 months | All bones in area 10 feet in diameter |

SOURCE: Morse (1984a).

NOTE: Other cases involving more time have more scatter and much bone loss.

when bone is buried in a damp setting. Soil acidity (pH < 7.0) is the most common source of chemical erosion and dissolution. Humic acid can be weakly concentrated near the ground surface. Bones that are buried or covered naturally in pits where groundwater percolation is slowed down are often poorly preserved. This seems to be due to the retention of water in the pit, which magnifies microbial and acid activity. Poor preservation is also common in coarse, sandy deposits. Because they retain moisture poorly, such deposits expose bone to drying and wetting phases, a situation that permits salt crystal growth during the drying phase. The formation and expansion of salt and calcium carbonate crystals (caliche), like ice in stone cracks, causes buried bone to exfoliate and burst, producing flaky, crumbly, chalky, and granular residues. This contrasts markedly with the condition of human-damaged bone, which often is hard, dense, and solid. Caliche formation is probably the major cause of buried bone destruction in the arid Southwest.

Unburied bone alters rapidly, both physically and chemically, under the hot Southwestern sun. Once bone is sun-bleached from ivory to white, it stays white for a long time. Our simple experiments show that bone bleaches white in a matter of a few days under exposure to bright summer desert sunlight. Surface cracking, presumably from dehydration, soon follows. Bleached *exfoliation flakes* characterize bone breakdown on the ground surface. Surface-exposed bone becomes externally chalky, like weathered house paint. Part of this physical and chemical damage is attributable to ultraviolet destruction of organic polymers, and part is simple oxidation reaction.

Staining and discoloration of bone surfaces and interiors occur through several chemical agents and are highly variable, even within a single skeleton. Surface patination forms with time, but irregularly, depending on depositional context. Scientific stain analysis is poorly developed in taphonomic research.

Most analysts of human bone assemblages believed to have been cannibalized have remarked on the bones' excellent state of preservation, which often contrasts markedly with very poor preservation of skeletal elements in considerate burials in the same site or in sites with similar conditions. This is true of archaeofaunal remains as well (S. James 1994). The better preserved human and animal bones represent cooking and the removal of flesh and fat—organic materials that would have served microorganism metabolism, with resulting bone-leaching acidic by-products.

*Human Damage to Bone*

*Evidence that could be looked for at every site*

Human perimortem modification of animal and human bones in the Southwest includes three primary direct forms—*breaking, cutting,* and *burning.* Burning includes cremation, and as Emil Haury (1976:171) noted, intentional breaking of cremated bones into very small pieces seems to have been practiced by the Hohokam in central Arizona, at least at Snaketown. Unlike carnivores, humans do not cause much bone penetration, although weapon points are occasionally found embedded in bone (fig. 2.6).

Breaking can occur in various ways. It was commonly caused by hammering or *impact blows.* These produce *spiral fractures, double fractures* ("butterfly breaks" [Ubelaker and Adams 1995]), longitudinally *splintered* long bones, and, in the case of vertebrae, finely crushed bone meal or powder. *Bone powder* is rarely found archaeologically except with the very best of excavation procedures under rare conditions of preservation (Dice 1993a; Sullivan and Phippen 1994). Bone breaking can also be done by leveraging, twisting, or snapping. With ribs, sometimes a *peeled* fracture occurs; it resembles the breakage of a fresh wooden branch that has been snapped, with the bark peeling away on one or both halves rather than shearing neatly at the breakpoint. Impact breakage can fail to separate the fractured pieces completely, leaving one or more fragments, often semicircular, partially adhering at the impact site. Impact breakage is a strong clue that human activity has been involved, especially if the breakage is near the midshaft of a long bone.

When bone damage indicates that impact breakage was done with a percussion stone (hammerstone, chopper or chopping tool, heavy core, natural cobble, etc.) used in conjunction with an anvil stone, the probability of human involvement increases greatly, especially if there is patterned multiple breakage. *Hammer-and-anvil* use frequently leaves abrasions, here referred to as *anvil abrasions,* that are formed mainly when a bone slips on a stone anvil at the moment of impact. A rough hammerstone can produce abrasions too, but our experience suggests hammerstone impact slippage leaves a crushed, smeared, or even dented surface more often than it leaves the fine, multiple, parallel striations of anvil abrasions (see examples in chapter 3, especially figs. 3.21, 3.25, and 3.49).

Prehistoric cutting of bone is distinctive and can be recognized by a number of features (Walker 1989). Stone tool *cut marks* are almost always V-shaped in cross section, and under 20-power magnification, ridging can be seen within the cut, owing to the imperfect cutting surface of the tool. Metal tool cut marks only rarely show such internal ridging. Stone tool cut marks on animal and human bone not only look similar but also occur in similar locations, usually near joints such as the mandible, shoulder, elbow, hip, and knee, where dismemberment apparently took place. Another similarity that indicates butchering in both humans and animals is that joint and flesh-stripping cut marks are frequently multiple. Cut marks are accidents of motion, caused by limited butchering skills or haste. They are not planned, so their similarities in location and multiplicity on human and animal bones can be due only to the application of game butchering skills to humans.

Figure 2.6. Wupatki Ruin. Pronghorn left humerus with tip of stone point embedded in the bone (at arrow). Humerus shaft also has perimortem breakage (CGT neg. 7-15-93:22).

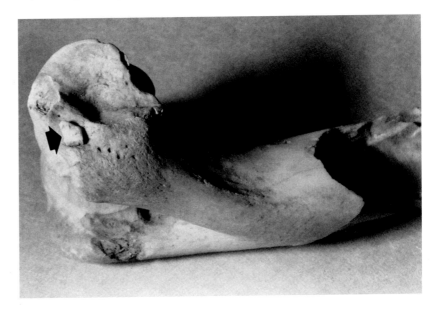

Cut marks vary in length and depth. Very fine prehistoric cut marks can be duplicated with fine-grained or glasslike stone tools such as obsidian blades. Coarser cut marks with substantial internal ridging are produced with less fine-grained stones such as cherty limestone, quartzite, and andesite. There is an uncommon form of cut mark that can best be characterized as a *chop mark*. One form of weapon that could produce this type of damage is the *tchamahia*, a large ground-stone knife that the Hopis once made. A specimen made of fine-grained stone that we photographed at Second Mesa was about 20 cm (8 inches) long. It had a precision-ground cutting edge and a short, indented handle area. Its shape brought to mind a modern butcher's bone-cutting meat cleaver.

Burned bone indicates human activity whether the burning was purposeful, as in cremation and cooking, or haphazard, as when bones were discarded into a fire pit or burned during the firing of trash. Bone, like any other organic material, can be oxidized by natural processes that may not always be recognizable in isolated bones. Indeed, the biophysical threshhold of burning is difficult to recognize. The degree of surface and internal burning can vary from slight scorching (light brown in color) and charring (dark brown)—sometimes with thermal flaking of the outer cortex, especially in crania—to charcoaling or carbonizing (black) and finally calcining (gray, blue-gray, chalky white). Burning can occur on an entire bone or be restricted to a single area. The range of burning depends not only on the amount and duration of thermal exposure but also on the degree of insulation by soft tissue or other material, water content, temperature gradients, and other factors.

At the lower end of the thermal alteration range there may be very little color or hardness change within or upon the surface of a bone. The sole change may be oxidation and loss or degradation of the organic component. The organic component helps significantly to hold bone together, so that with time, an area of a bone that has been exposed to fire may be soft, crumbly, and flaky (i.e., *thermal flaking*), whereas another area of the same bone may remain hard, dense, and ivorylike (see figs. 3.32 and 3.94 and Hegler 1984). Environmental preservation situations not related to heat can produce similar crumbly, discolored surfaces.

Pat Shipman, Alan Walker, and David Bichell (1985:58–62) identified the regular changes that take place in bone when it is heated. With respect to color changes, they found that from 20° to 285° C (92° to 887° F), bone remains neutral white, pale yellow, or yellow. From 285° to 525° C (887° to 1,607° F), changes begin with reddish brown, very dark gray-brown, neutral dark gray, and reddish yellow. From 525° to 645° C (1,607° to 1,967° F), color becomes neutral black with medium blue and reddish yellow. From 645° to 940° C (1,967° to 2,852° F), color lightens to neutral white with light blue-gray and light gray. At temperatures greater than 940° C (2,852° F), bone remains neutral white with some medium gray and reddish yellow. Shipman and colleagues (1985:314) noted that natural fires burn for shorter periods and at lower temperatures than controlled burning by humans, so the degree of burning is useful for detecting human activity. The pattern of burning of particular elements "provides strong circumstantial evidence of dietary practices."

*Evidence* →

Physical changes occur as the heated collagen is dehydrated and denatured. At 350° to 400° C the organic content is driven off so that cracking occurs. Additional microscopic changes occur with higher temperatures, including progressivly increased melting and vitrification of the bone surface.

Other thermal damage studies undertaken by Shipman, Giraud Foster, and Margaret Schoeninger (1984), along with the work of Michael Schultz, Carmen Pijoan Aguadé, and Peter Schwartz (1993) and others, report on histological changes in heat-damaged bone. Their scanning electron or polarized light micrographs show many differences between burned and unburned bone. Taphonomic analysts who lack such microscopes and slide-making facilities and who are confronted with the possibility of burned bone must be cautious in their visual identifications at the lower end of the thermal alteration range.

One final modification of animal or human bone indirectly related to heat occurs when bone fragments are placed in pottery cooking vessels and simmered for their grease or oil. Stirring the contents of the vessel rubs and polishes the ends of some of the fragments against the gritty surface, much the same as when bone splinters are rubbed against a stone to polish the point of a bone arrow, awl, or needle (figs. 2.7 and 2.8). Tim D. White (1992) proposed this mechanism and verified by experiment that fragment end-polishing, which he termed *pot-polishing*, can occur very quickly. A 20-power hand lens and strong side-lighting are needed to reliably detect pot-polishing. It is less tiring on the eyes if pot-polishing is looked for with a dissecting binocular microscope, again with strong and tightly focused side-lighting.

Bag-boiling with heated stones has been used to extract grease from bones. Stirring bone in this type of heated container may produce end-polishing on some fragments, although the sides of fragments could also make contact with the stones. We use the term *end-polishing* interchangeably with White's pot-polishing. Polishing may also occur with transporting, laboratory cleaning, storage in plastic bags, and other sorts of postexcavation handling, all of which can probably be recog-

Figure 2.7. Scanning electron micrograph of the pot-polished tip of a human bone fragment from Burnt Mesa. Specimen has polishing around the external aspect of the bifurcated tip but none within the notch; the latter would have been expected if the piece had been used as a probe, pick, or other makeshift tool (SEM by Mary M. Dytrych, neg. 9-15-92:28B).

Figure 2.8. Pronghorn bone fragment with polished tip about 2.0 cm in extent, from Wupatki Ruin. This makeshift tool has much more polishing than the 1.0 mm area of pot-polishing on the fragment shown in figure 2.7 (CGT neg. 7-15-93:24).

nized by the presence of polishing on the sides as well as the ends of bone fragments.

In the U.S. Southwest, modification of human bone was almost all destructive. People rarely modified human bones for utilitarian or ritual purposes—unlike the situation in prehistoric Mexico, where thousands of human bone artifacts such as long-bone rasps have been excavated. Consequently, perimortem and postmortem human bone damage in the Southwest can seldom be justifiably attributed to this sort of fabrication. Paul H. Ezell and Alan P. Olson (1955) provided the only literature review we know of on Southwestern artifacts made from human bone. Drawing from their review and our own literature search, we have found references only to the few objects listed in table 2.2. In addition,

Table 2.2
Artifacts Made of Human Bone Reported from the U.S. Southwest

| ARTIFACT | SITE | REFERENCE |
|---|---|---|
| Splinter awl with handle made from unmodified human coccyx bone | Hawikuh, NM | Hodge (1920) |
| Hooklike object made from a human ischium | Hawikuh, NM | Hodge (1920) |
| Cranial fragment with one edge ground smooth (scraper or polishing tool) | Shumway Ruin, AZ | Ezell and Olson (1955) |
| Fragment possibly from a human skull that likely had inlay | Pecos Pueblo, NM | Kidder (1932:270) |
| Flesher made from the distal two-thirds of a femur | Amoxiumquaa, NM | Reiter (1938:85) |
| "Gouge-shaped" object made from a human femur | Chaco Canyon Bc-51, NM | Whittemore (1939:138) |
| Perforated human tarsal | Pine Lawn Valley, NM | Martin, Rinaldo, and Antevs (1949:176) |
| Two cut bone tubes, polished at the ends, apparently made from human femurs | Shabik'eshchee Village, Chaco Canyon, NM | Roberts (1929:144) |
| Artifact of unknown function made from a human skull fragment | LA4473 (Basketmaker III pithouse), NM | Peckham (1963:79) |
| Modified human bone, undescribed | Largo-Gallina burial, NM | Chase (1976:79) |
| Human frontal bone used as a scoop or ladle | Burnt Mesa pithouse, NM | Flinn, Turner, and Brew (1976:312) |

we turned up references to painted human bones at five Southwestern sites (see Fink and Schroeder 1994; Hagberg 1939:197). Because of the rarity of these kinds of items, we believe that human charnel deposits represent neither work stations for nor the debris of artifact production.

## The Minimal Taphonomic Signature of Cannibalism

IN 1983 THE senior author (Turner 1983:233–234) published a list of taphonomic features believed to be characteristic of Southwestern "human butchering and cannibalism (or flesh removal and disposal of osseous remains)":

1. A single, short-term depositional episode can be discerned from stratigraphy and bone quality. Interment in the desert and plateau environment has to be rapid to prevent bone weathering and animal scavenging.
2. Bone preservation is good to excellent. Unmodified formal burials often have poor bone preservation, suggesting that soft tissue decay processes are absent in cannibalism.
3. Total whole bone and bone fragment count ranges between 400 and 3,500 elements in a given episode. Body reconstruction shows a high rate of unaccounted-for bone element loss.
4. All or most body segments are disarticulated.
5. Vertebrae are usually missing.
6. Massive perimortem breakage occurs in 40–100% of the skeletal elements.
7. Breakage is by percussion hammering against some form of anvil, with spiral and compression fracturing very common. Reaming of the marrow cavity is evident in a minority of long bones.
8. Head, face, and long bone breakage is almost universal.

9. Burning after butchering and breaking is evident in 2–35% of all elements.

10. Butchering and skinning cut marks occur on 1–5% of all whole and fragmentary elements, and usually in appropriate locations for muscle tissue or scalp removal. Microscopic examination of the cut marks can reveal perimortem bone condition as well as directionality, pressure, slicing, sawing, chopping and other kinesthetic considerations.

11. Animal gnawing and chewing occurs on only a small proportion of all elements, usually less than 5%. Some gnawing may have been done by humans and/or their dogs.

12. Bone and body reconstruction shows that the damage sequence was mainly (a) cutting, (b) breaking, and (c) burning or, if evident, gnawing.

13. Pseudo-tools or "accidentals" made of human bone may occur in the frequency range of 1 per 10,000+ pieces.

14. The frequency of human and other alteration in cannibalized bone lots is 95% for perimortem breakage, 20% for burning, 3% for cut marks, and 2% for possible gnawing or chewing.

Since 1983, additional prehistoric Southwestern channel deposits have been analyzed by several workers. Their results show much the same qualitative characteristics and correspondingly similar quantitative values. As might be expected, as more sites are added to the data base, the ranges of the values increase. For example, the number of pieces per site (point 3) now ranges from 118 to 5,015. The range for the percentage of elements broken (point 6) remains similar to the 1983 range, but the range for elements showing cut marks (point 10) has increased, owing chiefly to one site, Houck K; the upper limit now stands at 32.4% of all pieces. Gnawing (point 11) remains about the same; one site has an upper limit of 28.0%, but some of this is probably misidentified.

More or less independent studies by Shane Baker (1990), Michael Dice (1993a), Nancy Malville (1989), Penny Minturn (1994), and Tim White (1992) have shown these 14 characteristics to be present, and in much the same proportions, in seemingly cannibalized deposits recovered from, respectively, Rattlesnake Ruin (Utah), Leroux Wash (Arizona), Yellow Jacket (Colorado), Sambrito Village (New Mexico), and Mancos Canyon (Colorado).

Only for item 9, the sequence of processing, has there been enough difference of opinion to warrant additional evaluation. White (1992) felt that the Mancos Canyon human channel deposit exhibited significant burning before butchering and was thus doubtful about the foregoing sequence. The senior author (Turner 1992:10) agreed with White that the Mancos Canyon sequence looked the way he described it, but in most other Southwestern channel deposits, which have less burning, the sequence was more likely as characterized in item 9 and as suggested by Micozzi (1991:85): "The typical stages of animal butchery and processing include skinning, evisceration, disarticulation, filleting, fracture (marrow consumption) and possible burning."

When considering a human channel deposit for candidacy as a cannibalized assemblage, all of the foregoing characteristics should be considered whenever conditions and available documentation permit.

Southwestern assemblages in museum collections excavated before 1983, when the possibility of cannibalism in sites became generally known to most archaeologists, will not have a full contextual record, and analysts will have to depend chiefly on skeletal remains for taphonomic purposes. Nevertheless, it is our theoretical position that bone alone can generate a reliable reconstruction of the death history of a burial or charnel deposit.

In order to hypothesize that cannibalism occurred, we require that a minimal taphonomic signature consisting of the following six key perimortem damage features be present in human bones from a charnel deposit: (1) breakage, (2) cut marks, (3) anvil abrasions, (4) burning, (5) many missing vertebrae, and (6) pot-polishing. Occasionally polishing might be absent, owing to the location of the skeletal assemblage—for example, in an isolated campsite without pottery or at a site occupied before pottery began to be manufactured—but otherwise all the criteria should be present in the skeletal assemblage. Although it is theoretically possible that some unknown form of natural, nonhuman taphonomic agency could produce an assemblage of human skeletal remains with these six features, it is unreasonable to believe that such a thing ever happened. Moreover, if the six features are present in a human bone assemblage found in a cultural context such as on a structure floor, then the possibility that the damage was caused by natural, nonhuman agency seems very farfetched.

## Butchering and Cooking of Nonhuman Animals and Humans

ONE OF THE key reasons for believing that certain taphonomic features signal cannibalism is that they are similar or even identical to the types and frequencies of damage seen in nonhuman animal bones that clearly were processed and cooked for food. Michael Dice (1993a), Tim White (1992), Paola Villa (1992), and Villa et al. (1986) have shown in painstaking detail that the taphonomic signature of cannibalism is effectively the same as the signature for the butchering and cooking of medium-sized to large game animals. We need not repeat their efforts. Instead, in this section we offer some additional observations on artiodactyl processing, a new set of data on small mammals—prairie dogs, jackrabbits, and cottontails—and some comparisons among samples of artiodactyl, small mammal, and presumably cannibalized human bones.

Table 2.3 gives the frequencies of the six key perimortem damage types—impact breakage (as measured by the percentage of smashed fragments), anvil abrasions, cut marks, burning, pot-polishing, and animal gnawing or chewing—in antelope and deer bones from Wupatki Ruin, a site 25 miles northeast of Flagstaff, Arizona. (Ribs and long bone fragments are lumped for the two species.) Breakage is very high: more than 96% of the sample consists of smashed fragments. Anvil abrasions, burning, cutting, and polishing are much less frequent, occurring on 10.1–14.4% of the total number of pieces. There is surprisingly little evidence of animal damage, and only carnivore at that.

Table 2.4 provides long bone fragment lengths and data on polishing for the Wupatki artiodactyls, and table 2.5, data on artiodactyl ribs. In chapter 4, the mean lengths of these samples are compared with the means for human bone assemblages from the U.S. Southwest and Mexico. As will be seen there, the differences between the means of some samples are statistically significant, but we believe the statistics hold

Table 2.3

Perimortem Damage in Artiodactyls and Pronghorn Antelope (*Antilocapra americana*), Wupatki Ruin

| SKELETAL ELEMENT | | WHOLE | SMASHED FRAGMENT[a] | ANVIL ABRASION | CUT | BURN | POLISH | CHEW[b] |
|---|---|---|---|---|---|---|---|---|
| Antelope crania (n = 5) | n | 0 | 5 | 0 | 0 | 0 | 1 | 0 |
| | % | 0.0 | 100.0 | 0.0 | 0.0 | 0.0 | 20.0 | 0.0 |
| Antelope mandibles (n = 10) | n | 2 | 8 | 0 | 4 | 1 | 2 | 0 |
| | % | 20.0 | 80.0 | 0.0 | 40.0 | 10.0 | 20.0 | 0.0 |
| Artiodactyl long bone fragments (n = 172)[c] | n | — | 172 | 19 | 19 | 33 | 18 | 10 |
| | % | — | 100.0 | 11.0 | 11.0 | 19.0 | 10.5 | 5.8 |
| Artiodactyl ribs (n = 111) | n | 8 | 103 | 18 | 7 | 9 | 14 | 6 |
| | % | 7.2 | 92.7 | 16.2 | 6.3 | 8.1 | 12.6 | 5.4 |
| TOTAL (n = 298) | n | 10 | 288 | 37 | 30 | 43 | 35 | 16 |
| | % | 3.4 | 96.6 | 12.4 | 10.1 | 14.4 | 11.7 | 5.4 |

NOTE: Pronghorn antelope and deer bones came from excavations conducted at various Wupatki Ruin locations by Harold S. Colton, Lyndon L. Hargrave, and others in 1934. Bone identifications were made by Edward P. Lincoln (1961).

a. Only two examples of peeling breakage were found.
b. Most damage appears to have been done by carnivores, not rodents.
c. In order to make the sample of artiodactyl long bone fragments consistent with samples of human long bone fragments used in later comparisons (chapter 5), only unidentifiable fragments (i.e., no ends or obvious anatomy) were examined and measured.

little behavioral importance because the average length difference is not large relative to overall body size. Sampling differences due to excavation procedures and bone identification lie as much at the heart of the statistical differences as processing considerations do. Where rib and long bone fragment lengths are concerned, we believe that humans were being processed in the same way antelopes were.

In the Wupatki antelope rib sample, about a dozen fragments exhibit pot-polishing, but whole ribs do not—good evidence that the end-polishing was caused by stirring of the fragments in cooking vessels too small to hold whole ribs. The frequencies of polished rib and long bone fragments are about the same.

In comparing human with nonhuman animal body processing, scholars have so far focused their attention on large mammals such as deer and antelope. In order to add some samples of small mammals to the comparative data base, we examined two archaeological collections: prairie dog bones excavated at Juniper Terrace (NA1814A), located 23 miles northeast of Flagstaff, and rabbit and rodent bones from the fill of Room 2 at Houck K (NA8440), near the Puerco River in northeastern Arizona. Table 2.6 gives the frequencies of perimortem damage types in these collections, and figures 2.9–2.11 illustrate the damage observed in the prairie dog bones.

There are strong similarities in the frequencies of damage types in the two classes of small mammals. As might be expected on the basis of their size, there was less processing of these animals than of pronghorn,

Table 2.4
Lengths (cm) of Artiodactyl Long Bone Fragments from Wupatki Ruin

| | | | | | | |
|---|---|---|---|---|---|---|
| 11.2 | 5.7 | 11.9 | 4.4 | 8.5 | 12.0 | 7.1P |
| 6.4 | 6.4 | 8.4 | 8.3 | 7.6 | 8.4 | 15.3 |
| 8.8 | 7.4 | 6.9 | 6.9 | 6.2 | 7.6 | 8.6 |
| 5.2 | 6.6 | 7.8 | 8.4 | 5.5 | 7.6 | 6.8 |
| 6.5 | 6.9 | 5.1 | 6.2 | 2.5 | 4.8 | 4.5 |
| 9.5P | 8.1 | 8.9P | 10.1 | 6.2 | 9.1 | 10.1 |
| 13.5 | 9.5P | 13.0 | 8.6 | 7.1 | 8.3 | 6.5P |
| 9.1 | 7.1 | 14.4 | 9.9P | 10.2 | 8.9 | 10.5 |
| 7.3P | 9.5 | 8.0 | 6.7 | 10.4 | 7.1P | 6.5 |
| 6.5 | 6.7 | 3.9P | 9.4 | 7.9 | 8.4 | 8.0 |
| 6.0P | 8.2 | 7.7 | 13.0P | 12.9 | 11.2P | 11.7 |
| 11.7 | 8.9 | 10.3 | 11.8 | 8.4 | 10.6 | 10.6P |
| 8.9 | 14.7P | 11.3 | 15.0 | 12.2P | 8.3 | 13.1P |
| 10.2 | 12.4 | 11.2 | 13.5 | 6.5 | 6.8 | 7.9 |
| 9.0 | 7.4 | 7.4 | 7.4 | 7.9 | 7.0 | 11.4 |
| 10.1 | 6.5 | 10.3 | 15.7 | 7.9 | 12.5 | 11.8 |
| 19.1 | 6.8 | 8.8 | 8.9 | 11.7 | 16.1 | 6.9 |
| 6.5 | 6.2 | 9.6 | 7.0 | 10.5 | 10.0 | 7.7 |
| 10.6 | 8.2 | 9.8 | 10.3 | 8.0 | 16.7 | 9.1 |
| 8.8 | 9.5 | 14.3 | 14.0 | 8.9P | 5.3 | 4.5 |
| 5.5 | 5.4 | 4.3 | 4.7 | 4.6 | 9.3 | 6.2 |
| 10.5 | 7.0 | 9.4 | 8.0 | 8.6P | 7.3 | 3.6 |
| 3.4 | 7.3 | 7.2 | 7.9 | 4.0 | 4.1 | 4.5 |
| 10.2 | 8.1 | 8.4 | 4.0 | 5.9 | 4.6 | 4.9 |
| 3.9 | 5.1 | 10.0 | 5.7 | | | |

N = 172.   Range = 2.5–19.1.   Mean = 8.5.   S.D. = 2.9.
Polished fragments = 10.5% (18 of 172).

NOTE: "P" denotes end-polishing.

Table 2.5
Lengths (cm) of Artiodactyl Whole Ribs and Rib Fragments from Wupatki Ruin

| | | | | | | |
|---|---|---|---|---|---|---|
| 11.3 | 9.4 | 7.4P | 15.5 | 6.5P | 9.6 | 7.3 |
| 8.9 | 8.9 | 11.6 | 10.8W | 11.5 | 9.5 | 4.4 |
| 3.5 | 5.1 | 9.6 | 12.6 | 16.0 | 10.8 | 8.4 |
| 9.9 | 13.2 | 16.1 | 21.5 | 22.2 | 7.2 | 13.5 |
| 9.2 | 10.7P | 14.2 | 15.0 | 8.9P | 4.9 | 22.0W |
| 10.4P | 9.4 | 13.0 | 7.0 | 11.7 | 8.2 | 8.8 |
| 8.7 | 6.8 | 5.9 | 10.3 | 17.6 | 8.0 | 6.6 |
| 8.3 | 18.9W | 3.8 | 10.4 | 7.5 | 24.0W | 17.5 |
| 20.1 | 9.8 | 15.3 | 12.1 | 14.5W | 13.0 | 13.0 |
| 14.2 | 6.9 | 11.5 | 15.6 | 9.9 | 11.6 | 7.9 |
| 12.9 | 15.2 | 6.4 | 13.9 | 16.6 | 19.0 | 11.5 |

*Continued on next page*

*Table 2.5 Continued*

| | | | | | | |
|---|---|---|---|---|---|---|
| 18.1 | 19.0 | 9.7P | 9.2 | 13.0P | 11.4 | 20.0 |
| 9.7P | 11.2 | 15.4P | 13.8 | 14.4P | 12.3 | 8.0P |
| 11.6W | 4.5 | 11.8 | 10.4P | 10.9 | 12.6 | 5.5 |
| 14.3 | 10.0 | 16.2W | 18.2W | 13.9 | 10.6P | 18.9 |
| 18.1 | 10.5 | 6.9 | 7.1 | 8.5 | 10.7P | |

Whole: N = 8 (7.2%).   Range = 3.5–22.2.   Mean = 11.3.   S.D. = 4.1.
Broken: N = 103 (92.8%).   Polished fragments: N = 14 (12.6%).

NOTE: "P" denotes end-polished fragments; "W" denotes whole ribs.

Table 2.6
Perimortem Damage in Prairie Dogs from Juniper Terrace and in Rabbits and Rodents from Houck K

| SKELETAL ELEMENT | WHOLE | SMASHED FRAGMENT | ANVIL ABRASION | BURN | CUT | POLISH | GNAW |
|---|---|---|---|---|---|---|---|
| Prairie dogs | | | | | | | |
| Cranium | 0 | 31 | 0 | 0 | 0 | 2 | 0 |
| Mandible | 13 | 11 | 0 | 0 | 0 | 1 | 0 |
| Scapula | 0 | 1 | 0 | 0 | 0 | 0 | 0 |
| Humerus | 7 | 8 | 1 | 0 | 0 | 0 | 0 |
| Ulna | 8 | 2 | 0 | 0 | 0 | 0 | 1 |
| Radius | 4 | 6 | 0 | 1 | 2 | 0 | 0 |
| Pelvis | 1 | 19 | 2 | 1 | 1 | 1 | 0 |
| Femur | 5 | 17 | 1 | 0 | 2 | 2 | 0 |
| Tibia | 8 | 10 | 1 | 0 | 0 | 1 | 0 |
| TOTAL (151) | 46 | 105 | 5 | 2 | 5 | 7 | 1 |
| PERCENTAGE | 30.5 | 69.5 | 3.3 | 1.3 | 3.3 | 4.6 | 0.7 |
| Rabbits and rodents | | | | | | | |
| Cranium | 0 | 20 | 0 | 0 | 0 | 0 | 0 |
| Mandible | 10 | 4 | 0 | 0 | 0 | 0 | 0 |
| Scapula | 2 | 11 | 0 | 0 | 0 | 0 | 0 |
| Long bones | 28 | 170 | 4 | 1 | 1 | 8 | 2 |
| Vertebrae | 16 | 17 | 0 | 0 | 0 | 0 | 0 |
| Ribs | 3 | 5 | 0 | 0 | 0 | 0 | 0 |
| Pelvis | 17 | 13 | 0 | 0 | 1 | 0 | 0 |
| TOTAL (316) | 76 | 240 | 4 | 1 | 2 | 8 | 2 |
| PERCENTAGE | 24.0 | 76.0 | 1.3 | 0.3 | 0.6 | 2.5 | 0.6 |

NOTE: Juniper Terrace (NA1814A) is located 14 km (9 miles) west-southwest of Wupatki Ruin, in T 25N, R 8E, Secs. 34 and 35. The site was excavated in 1931 by Harold S. Colton, Katherine Bartlett, and Lyndon L. Hargrave. Prairie dog bones came from midden, rooms 1 and 2, and unknown provenience. Bone identifications were made by Milton A. Wetherill, February 1957. Missing skeletal elements were probably not identifiable. The site is pottery-dated at A.D. 1125–1175 (Pueblo III), according to Colton (1946). For the Houck K site (NA8440), room 2 fill, bone identification was by C. G. Turner, July 2, 1997.

Figure 2.9. Prairie dog (*Cyno-mys* sp.) crania and mandibles with perimortem breakage. Mandible half in lower left is 3.8 cm long. Refuse excavated from midden at Juniper Terrace Pueblo (NA1814A), a site north-east of Flagstaff, Arizona, dating A.D. 1125–1175 (CGT neg. 7-16-93:5).

although breakage was again much more frequent than other damage types. Burned bones were much less frequent in the small mammal series than in the antelope series, suggesting either that the prairie dog bones identified do not represent the actual amount of burning that occurred or that prairie dogs were prepared differently for consumption. Both suggestions are likely correct, as a few ethnographic examples that we describe later suggest.

Table 2.7 summarizes the frequencies of perimortem damage types for pronghorn and small mammals from tables 2.3 and 2.6 and compares them with figures for human remains from four archaeological sites. We chose these four sites because they were among the first ones excavated for which cannibalism was claimed—by Walter Hough, George Pepper, Earl Morris, and Frank Roberts, respectively (see chapter 3)—and because they show that statistically significant differences occur between human assemblages as well as between human and non-human animal assemblages (table 2.8). We believe such differences reflect the kinds and amounts of processing that occurred, the post-

Figure 2.10. Prairie dog front leg bones and one scapula with minor amounts of midshaft perimortem breakage. Burned radius in upper left is 3.4 cm long. Juniper Terrace Pueblo (CGT neg. 7-16-93:1).

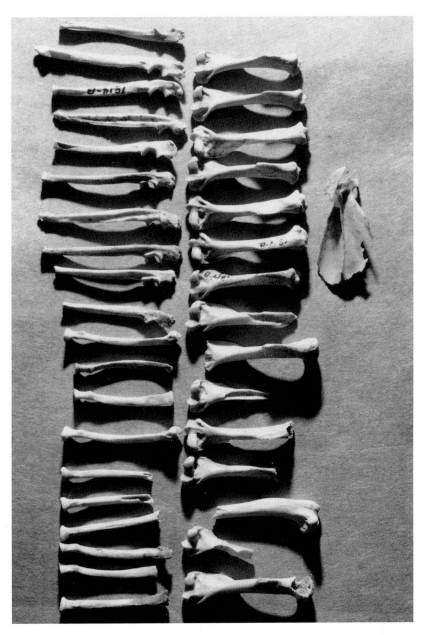

Figure 2.11. Prairie dog back leg bones and pelves with some midshaft and other perimortem breakage. Innominate in upper right has cut marks in addition to breakage and is 3.8 cm long. Juniper Terrace Pueblo (CGT neg. 7-16-93:2).

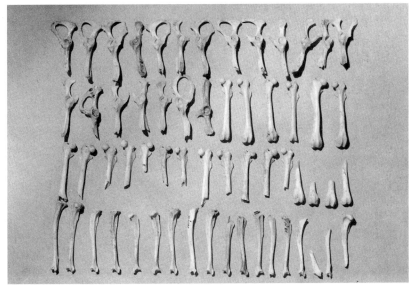

Table 2.7
Percentages of Perimortem Damage in Large and Small Animals and
Selected Human Examples

| SERIES | TOTAL PIECES | BREAKS | ANVIL ABRASIONS | BURNS | CUTS | POLISH |
|---|---|---|---|---|---|---|
| Prairie dog | 151 | 69.5 | 3.3 | 1.3 | 3.3 | 4.6 |
| Rabbit-rodent | 233 | 76.0 | 1.3 | 0.3 | 0.6 | 2.5 |
| Artiodactyl | 298 | 96.6 | 12.4 | 14.4 | 10.1 | 11.7 |
| Human (Canyon Butte 3) | 247 | 87.9 | 2.4 | 4.5 | 4.0 | 41.3 |
| Human (Peñasco Blanco) | 247 | 84.1 | 9.3 | 3.1 | 8.1 | 5.4 |
| Human (La Plata 23) | 350 | 73.7 | 1.1 | 17.7 | 2.6 | 0.3 |
| Human (Small House) | 152 | 58.5 | 6.6 | 3.9 | 7.9 | 10.5 |
| Nonhuman animal weighted average | 682 | 83.6 | 6.6 | 6.7 | 5.3 | 7.0 |

Table 2.8
Chi-Square Comparisons of Perimortem Damage Types in Large and
Small Animals and Some Human Collections

| PAIR | 4 D.F. | $P$ | 3 D.F. | $P$ |
|---|---|---|---|---|
| Prairie dog + Artiodactyl | 17.40 | <.002 | 3.47 | ns |
| Prairie dog + Peñasco Blanco | 5.67 | ns | 2.01 | ns |
| Prairie dog + La Plata 23 | 34.88 | <.001 | 37.89 | <.001 |
| Prairie dog + Small House | 10.29 | <.040 | 0.06 | ns |
| Prairie dog + Canyon Butte 3 | 30.86 | <.001 | 16.29 | <.001 |
| Artiodactyl + Peñasco Blanco | 30.62 | <.001 | 17.30 | <.001 |
| Artiodactyl + La Plata 23 | 63.34 | <.001 | 57.50 | <.001 |
| Artiodactyl + Small House | 5.94 | ns | 5.92 | ns |
| Artiodactyl + Canyon Butte 3 | 85.41 | <.001 | 83.30 | <.001 |
| Peñasco Blanco + La Plata 23 | 107.46 | <.001 | 108.63 | <.001 |
| Peñasco Blanco + Small House | 11.66 | <.025 | 5.54 | ns |
| Peñasco Blanco + Canyon Butte 3 | 130.7 | <.001 | 92.38 | <.001 |
| La Plata 23 + Small House | 67.68 | <.001 | 57.97 | <.001 |
| La Plata 23 + Canyon Butte 3 | 138.34 | <.001 | 130.11 | <.001 |
| Small House + Canyon Butte 3 | 28.70 | <.001 | 29.32 | <.001 |

mortem contexts, the skills of excavators and analysts, and the methods of excavation.

Table 2.8 gives the results of chi-square comparisons between pairs of assemblages for four and three degrees of freedom, respectively. In the former, breakage is included. In the latter it is excluded because to some extent breakage frequency is dependent on the number of bones collected by the excavator. Since there is no mention of screening for bone fragments in any of the reports on human charnel deposits excavated before 1990, some breakage frequencies could be considerably underrepresented.

In the four-degrees-of-freedom comparisons, which include breakage, most pairs are significantly different. Canyon Butte 3 is different mainly because of its great amount of fragment polishing. La Plata 23 clearly has an excess of burning. Peñasco Blanco and Small House do not stand out with any marked excess or paucity of a perimortem damage type. Whether this reflects their geographic proximity, both being in Chaco Canyon, or simple chance cannot be evaluated.

In the three-degrees-of-freedom comparisons, which exclude breakage, the same remarks apply, except that the prairie dog–antelope comparison becomes nonsignificant, as does the Peñasco Blanco and Small House comparison.

Altogether, inspection of the foregoing tables shows that small mammals, pronghorn antelope, and humans were treated much the same way in terms of types and amounts of perimortem damage, even though many individual pairs of interspecies and intersite data sets have significantly different chi-square values. It is clear that small mammal and antelope food refuse and all sets of human remains hypothesized to have been cannibalized exhibit the six perimortem damage criteria for proposing consumption. Moreover, despite the significance of some of the chi-square values, the proportions of the damage types are reasonably similar considering the several sources of variation possible—excavation procedures, depositional conditions, site location, experience and skill of the processors, and so forth.

In both nonhuman and human cases, breakage is the most common type of processing damage (table 2.7). The antelope breakage frequency is probably a bit inflated because of some selection on our part for heads, jaws, ribs, and long bone fragments—basically an identification problem. In both the nonhuman species and the representative human samples, anvil abrasions, burning, cutting, and polishing occur less often than does breakage. Processing marks occur more often in pronghorn than in small mammals—a not-unexpected finding considering their size differences. Ignoring breakage, the human bones were otherwise processed only slightly less than antelopes and generally more than small mammals. When weighted averages are calculated for the nonhuman animals in table 2.7 and then compared with the figures for humans, Peñasco Blanco comes closest to the animal average for breakage and polishing, Small House comes closest for anvil abrasions, and Canyon Butte comes closest for burning and cutting.

*Ethnographic Accounts of Animal Processing*

Differences in processing between species and between sites likely arise in part from butchering and cooking practices specific to local places and times. The Southwestern ethnographic record reveals a range of variation in such practices for nonhuman animals, and we believe it is safe to assume that a similar range existed prehistorically as well. Marie E. Brown (1993) assembled a lengthy review of ethnographically recorded Southwestern animal food and its methods of preparation. Table 2.9 summarizes her review of the literature. It demonstrates that roasting was used for cooking animals more often than boiling, but both methods could be used. Circumstances, rather than animal type or cultural tradition, determined which cooking method was employed. That humans, as we show in chapter 3, were processed somewhat less variably than nonhuman animals suggests ritualization of some sort or, more likely—since most of the cannibalized remains have been found in

Table 2.9
Southwestern Indian Methods of Preparing Animal Foods

| | | Method of Cooking | | | | |
|---|---|---|---|---|---|---|
| ANIMAL | TRIBE | ROAST | BOIL | OTHER | PAGE[a] | REFERENCE |
| Raven | Yavapai | A | | | 300 | Gifford 1936 |
| Robin | Zuni | ? | | | 301 | Ladd 1963 |
| Cottontail | Tepehuan | OF | + | | 302 | Pennington 1969 |
| | Havasupai | A, OF | | | 303 | Spier 1928 |
| | Yavapai | A | + | 1 | 303 | Gifford 1936 |
| Jackrabbit | Navajo | | | 2 | 304 | Hill 1938 |
| | Hopi | | + | | 304 | Beaglehole 1936 |
| | Havasupai | A | | | 304 | Spier 1928 |
| Chipmunk | Yavapai | EO | | | 306 | Gifford 1936 |
| Squirrel | Yavapai | EO | | | 306 | Gifford 1936 |
| | Havasupai | + | + | | 307 | Spier 1928 |
| | Great Basin | + | + | 3 | 308 | Fowler 1986 |
| | Tepehuan | A, OF | | | 309 | Pennington 1969 |
| Prairie dog | Navajo | A | | | 309 | Hill 1938 |
| | Yavapai | A | | | 309 | Gifford 1936 |
| Gopher | Tepehuan | OF | + | | 310 | Pennington 1969 |
| Kangaroo rat | Hopi | ? | | | 312 | Beaglehole 1936 |
| Wood rat | Yavapai | A | + | | 316 | Gifford 1936 |
| | Tepehuan | OF | | | 316 | Pennington 1969 |
| Porcupine | Yavapai | EO | | | 317 | Gifford 1936 |
| | Navajo | EO | | | 317 | Hill 1938 |
| Dog | Yavapai | EO | + | | 317 | Gifford 1932, 36 |
| Coyote | Yavapai | EO | + | 4 | 318 | Gifford 1932, 36 |
| Grizzly bear | Navajo | ? | | 5 | 320 | Hill 1938 |
| | Yavapai | ? | | 6 | 321 | Gifford 1932, 36 |
| | Puebloan | ? | | 7 | 321 | Tyler 1975 |
| Badger | Yavapai | EO | | | 322 | Gifford 1936 |
| Bobcat | Yavapai | EO | + | | 323 | Gifford 1932, 36 |
| Deer | Hopi | ? | | 8 | 325 | Beaglehole 1936 |
| | Laguna | | + | | 325 | Goldfrank 1954 |
| | Navajo | ? | | 9 | 325 | Hill 1938 |
| Mtn. sheep | Hopi | ? | | 8 | 326 | Beaglehole 1936 |

SOURCE: Brown (1993).

Key to methods of roasting:
A   Animal placed in ashes, with or without preparation
OF  Roasted over a fire, not in ashes
EO  Skinned and cooked in earth oven

Key to "other" forms of cooking:
1 Preserved a few days by skinning, charring, and drying; bones not cracked for marrow extraction
2 Hunted sometimes with fire surrounds and clubbed to death
3 Ground squirrels sometimes boiled whole and then crushed
4 Coyote bone marrow not eaten
5 Bear bones saved after meat removed, not broken, and, along with hide, deposited in special location
6 Small piece of raw bear heart eaten by men only
7 Bones and skull not scattered; hide treated like human scalp
8 Marrow not extracted; all bones placed on shrine
9 All bones broken

a. Page number in Brown (1993).

a restricted geographic and cultural region—a lesser degree of cultural and behavioral variation.

Some other references we have found in the ethnographic literature shed useful light on animal processing. Frank H. Cushing (1979:314), for example, described how wood rats were cooked by his Zuni informants: they tossed the bodies onto a bed of embers to burn away the tails, legs, and ears; then, after being skinned, the carcasses were hammered into a pulp between two stones. The resulting mass of meat, bones, teeth, and intestines was added to water and boiled into a soup. In another ethnographic example, four Mohave informants told Kenneth M. Stewart (1968:36) how rabbits were prepared during the nineteenth century. After skinning the animal, "they buried him in the ashes. Folded his limbs under and broke his legs and stuck them in the flesh. Tied him up good. When it was done they pounded the meat and bones together on a round stone. Then they kind of roasted and ate it. Nothing was left; the bones were good, too."

W. W. Hill (1938:155) explained how Navajos dressed out pronghorn antelope, which must have been about the same way humans were butchered, judging from the perimortem bone damage described in the next chapter:

> An incision was made in the hide from the belly toward the head, then from the belly toward the tail. Next he slit the hide on the inside of the fore and hind legs. . . . Then a cut was made around the skin of the neck and the hide removed in the most convenient manner. The hoofs were left attached to the hide. The heads were not skinned at this time. . . . When butchering, the joints were first broken. Next the front quarters were cut off, followed by the hind quarters. Then the intestines were taken out and immediately cleaned. . . . Following this the head, lungs, and liver were removed in one piece. Finally the ribs were cut from the backbone to complete the butchering.

Hill (1938:156) observed that after the killing and butchering and certain ritual activity, the pronghorn head was skinned and roasted by the side of the fire, whereas other meat was broiled directly on the coals.

Matilda Coxe Stevenson stayed among the Zunis for several years in the late 1800s, collecting mythology and ritual information. She recorded numerous day-to-day events (Stevenson 1904:368–369) and mentioned both roasting and boiling of meat: "In camp, meat is roasted before the fire. . . . Most game is stewed, if served in the village." Wilson D. Wallis and Mischa Titiev (1945:524–525) learned a Hopi recipe for preparing coyote, in which a "very hot fire was made, over which was set a cooking pot containing water and cedar needles. Into this were thrown the legs and large pieces of the coyote's body. A cover was put on the pot, and the meat allowed to cook for an entire day."

Two ethnographic descriptions from outside the U.S. Southwest demonstrate how the extraction of marrow from animal bones can account for a great deal of perimortem breakage. We think a similar process was employed on cannibalized human bones. Douglas Leechman (1951:355) provided a brief history of the extraction and use of "bone grease" by North American Indians, including his own observations among the Loucheux in the northern Yukon. There, caribou and moose bones were allowed to dry for a day after the meat had been re-moved. The bones were smashed into pieces "as big as fingernails" on an anvil stone that sat in the middle of a hide. The pieces were then placed in a vessel filled with simmering water. The rendered grease floated to the top and was skimmed off for cooking, eaten alone, or made into sweet pemmican.

Norman W. Zierhut (1967), following his stay among the boreal for-est Cree Indians at Calling Lake, Alberta, described their practice of marrow extraction. They discarded the bones of smaller animals unbro-ken, but broke open moose and deer bones for their marrow. Meat was first stripped from a marrow bone, which was then heated on burning coals for a short while. When it was cool enough to handle, the bone was placed across two large stones, eight to ten inches apart. It was then struck at midshaft with the blunt end of an ax or a hammer. In the past, a hammerstone was used. Two major pieces resulted, along with some small bone chips.

The marrow was extracted with the aid of a stick and placed in a con-tainer. Then the bones were broken into smaller pieces. "The only recog-nizable portions of the bone that remain are the distal and proximal ends" (Zierhut 1967:35). Other bones were broken up and placed in a pot of slowly boiling water. The fat rose to the surface and was col-lected. Ribs were broken into pieces two to six inches long. All of the pelvis was broken up. The vertebrae might have the spinous processes removed. The base of the skull was broken to expose the brain, which was either eaten or saved for tanning skins. The maxilla and nasal region were also broken.

Zierhut observed breakage for marrow in the humerus, radius, ulna, metacarpals, femur, tibia, metatarsals, body of the mandible, and verte-bral canal. Anticipating later discussion, we note that one of the tapho-nomic characteristics of cannibalized bone deposits is that most of the human mandibles are broken, something that rarely appears in consider-ate burials. The breakage of mandibles of moose, deer, and humans may be fortuitous, but we doubt it.

Finally, we want to mention some animal yield values compiled by the Food and Agriculture Organization (FAO) of the United Nations (1991:50), because they provide a crude baseline for estimating how much usable meat a human-sized carcass might produce. According to the FAO's figures, the average live weight of an 8- to 12-month-old sheep is 45 kg (99.2 lb.), and its yield values are as follows: dressing percentage (sheep carcass/live weight), 50%; carcass weight, 23 kg (50.7 lb.); lean meat, 55%; fat, 28%; and bone, 17%. These values do not include other edible elements such as heart, liver, tripe, skin, tongue, lungs, kidneys, blood, and brain. We apply the FAO's sheep figures to humans because sheep weight is closer to the weight of an average hu-man than are the weights of pigs or cows. Anthony Smith (1969:326) re-ports that the weight of the average adult American male is 168 pounds, and the average female, 142 pounds. Extrapolating from the figures for sheep, a 100-pound person would at a minimum provide roughly 30 pounds of meat from muscle and connective tissue, about 15 pounds of fat—along with whatever amount could be extracted by bone boiling—and several pounds of organs, blood, and skin. A similar estimate was made by Richard A. Diehl (n.d.) in his analysis of the faunal remains at

Tula, Mexico. He calculated that an average human adult would provide about 66 pounds of edible meat. We note these estimates in order to make the point that in a cannibalized assemblage containing five, ten, or more individuals, a great deal of edible tissue and fluids was at hand.

*Archaeological Accounts of Animal Processing*

A few archaeological reports can also be mentioned that augment the analogy between animal and human body processing. For example, the 10,000-year-old Olsen-Chubbuck bison kill and butchering site, involving 190 animals that had been driven and plunged into a gulley in northeastern Colorado by Paleo-Indian hunters, provides interesting similarities and contrasts with processed human remains. One similarity is that the excavator, Joe Ben Wheat, himself asked whether the meat had actually been eaten (1972:116)—a concern commonly expressed about human charnel deposits. Wheat observed that "aside from the knowledge that the kill was made to provide meat, the evidence for the actual utilization of that meat is meager." He thought (as we do about human charnel assemblages) that the evidence of butchering based on considerable disarticulation and certain missing skeletal elements was sufficient to warrant the inference that consumption had occurred. Second, Wheat (1972:117) argued that marrow extraction was the cause of the many smashed or missing vertebrae and the breakage of most other marrow-containing bones—conditions strikingly like those of human charnel deposits.

On the other hand, there were two conspicuous differences. Sixty stone butchering tools, projectile points, and other artifacts were found at the Olsen-Chubbock bison kill site, whereas almost no artifacts have been recovered in association with Anasazi charnel deposits. Moreover, burned bone was apparently not found at Olsen-Chubbuck, whereas it is present in the human bone assemblages.

Gwen Young (1980:114–117) analyzed faunal remains from a site in Tijeras Canyon, New Mexico, providing bone counts, species identifications, and minimal number of individuals (MNI). She believed that spoilage dictated consumption soon after butchering:

> There is one bit of evidence against the regular storage of meat during any period. The breast meat surrounding the ribs is the optimal meat for storage. Once a rib, or any bone, is broken, the meat around it spoils within a short time. If the head ends of ribs were, in fact, left attached to the vertebral column at the kill site, the ribs would certainly have been broken immediately, leading to the rapid putrification of the meat. The broken ribs, then, indicate that meat was generally consumed soon after the animal was killed. . . . Consistent spiral fracture patterns, evidence of marrow cracking, were noted on these shaft fragments, on some of the long bone ends, and on the elements lower in marrow content. Jagged, splintered edges, probable evidence of smashing, were also noted on all types of long bones.

Edward P. Lincoln (1961) classified the mammalian skeletal remains from eight archaeological sites in Wuptaki National Monument. Rabbits, pronghorn, rodents, and deer were the most common animals he identified from site refuse. Lincoln (1961:78–80) suggested how the animals had been prepared:

The method of cooking appears to have been boiling rather than roasting over an open fire, as very few of the bones show charring. Those that do are charred thoroughly and evenly over their entire surface. Evidently they had been exposed to fire after the meat had been removed rather than cooked with the flesh still covering them. Most of the larger long bones, including those of the jack rabbits, had been broken in the middle of the shaft. It is interesting that the only human limb bone, the femur of an adolescent male, had been broken in the same way.

That rabbits and antelope were the most commonly recovered animal remains from the Wupatki area may reflect food preparation techniques as much as frequency of capture. Smaller animals such as prairie dogs may have been crushed into small pieces, as cited earlier, making their recovery and identification difficult. Of special interest is Lincoln's suggestion (1961:802) that a smashed human skull and the just-mentioned femur, broken the same way as the animal bones and found in the refuse, represent cannibalism. However, Lincoln did not consider possible alternatives for this particular damage.

Faunal analysts Marie E. Brown and Kenneth L. Brown (1993) provided useful hints about prehistoric hunting practices across the entire northern Southwest as sampled by the Transwestern Pipeline project, which ran from the San Juan Basin in northwestern New Mexico across all of northern Arizona, ending in California's Mojave Desert. Along this transect, the majority of the identified archaeological taxa were lagomorphs and other small mammals. These authors allowed that rodent remains in the archaeological sites were sometimes the result of natural factors but sometimes were "culturally occurring (as evidenced by differential skeletal burning)" (Brown and Brown 1993:349). Lincoln (1961) also identified many rodents in his study of the Wupatki area. Their breakage and other perimortem damage indicated that the Wupatki people commonly ate them. One site of special interest to Brown and Brown (1993) was occupied in Basketmaker III times (A.D. 400–700). Of the deer and pronghorn remains found there, only limb elements were recovered, suggesting off-site butchering. The authors proposed that a large quantity of burned bone "raises the possibility that intensive bone processing occurred at the site" (Brown and Brown 1993:357).

※ Coprolites

Karen Clary (1984:267–269) analyzed the contents of 45 specimens of human fecal matter from Chaco Canyon, mainly from rooms in Pueblo Alto and Pueblo Bonito. She extracted 1,305 small cooked and uncooked bones from 71% of the feces. Of the identifiable taxa, all body parts of cottontail, prairie dog, and deer mice were eaten: "In some samples, abundant cranial, axial, and limb fragments and small articulated sections such as wrist joints suggest that entire rabbits were eaten. . . . Discolored or 'cooking brown' bone indicates that some were boiled or heat treated. Heat softens bone and permits easier chewing and breakage, and an abundance of discolored bone in some samples may be due to easier consumption."

Theodore E. White (1952) reconstructed butchering techniques based on antelope bone fragments excavated at an archaeological site (39FA83) in the Angostura Reservoir basin, South Dakota. On the basis of the occurrence of distal left tibia fragments, he judged that at least 31 animals had been butchered. Using this MNI as an expectation baseline, he found that fewer than half the expected skulls were present and fewer than 10% of the expected vertebrae (64 of 744), but that the number of long bones, scapulae, and pelves were much closer to expectations. Disallowing that preservation alone was responsible for the various bone element frequencies, White (1952:337) concluded: "It is difficult to escape the inference that the parts either were not brought into camp, as with the thoracic vertebrae, or that they were mutilated beyond recognition while cutting up the carcass, i.e., the proximal end of the humerus [only 3 specimens out of an expected 62]." In addition to the damaged humerii, the presence of almost two-thirds (19 of 31) of the expected left mandibles led him to suspect that much of the carcass processing took place at the site. The missing vertebrae, ribs and skulls, may have been broken up, boiled for oil, and discarded.

Kent Flannery (1967) reported on his zoological surveys and analyses of animal bones from archaeological excavations in the Tehuacan Valley, Mexico. He noted that animal remains in the early phases were less badly smashed than later ones. Deer bones of El Riego phase were particularly and inexplicably damaged: "Hundreds of fragments are no larger than a toothpick, and all have been splintered by heavy percussion blows" (Flannery 1967:159). The deer butchering sequence was reconstructed as follows: (1) The entire animal was carried back to the cave site. There, the hide and intestines were first removed. (2) Butchering then proceeded with the cutting of meat off the bones. (3) The long bones were then roasted and thoroughly pounded into splinters so that the marrow could be completely extracted. This is the processing sequence that also seems to characterize Anasazi human charnel deposits. The human skeletal remains show not only similar kinds of butchering but also a similar butchering sequence.

(A final group of archaeological studies sheds light on the complex issue of determining whether or not animal bones (and, by extension, human ones) were burned during cooking.)In one of the rare archaeological reports that discusses refuse taphonomy—Emil W. Haury's (1976) report on the reexcavation of Snaketown—Haury described how 100 fine-screened tests of Hohokam mound refuse each recovered many broken bones and crushed freshwater clamshells ranging in length or diameter from one to ten millimeters. Although some of the charring and scorching of the tiny bone fragments may have been caused by roasting, Haury (1976:119) thought more of it was likely due to the intentional or accidental firing of the refuse mounds, which were dumps for latrine wastes as well as household sweepings:

> An unusually high percentage of bones, whether of large or small animals, is burned. Coloration ranges from scorched black through deep brown to calcined white. Roasting parts of animals might produce charred bone-ends, but not the whole bone, and boiling would not yield the results observed. In short, food processing appears not to have been the main cause for this condition. However, the analysis of burned bones representing the principal meat producers reveals that almost half of the Artiodactyla bones were burned, while the effects of fire are seen in only about 20% of the rabbit bones [see table 2.10].

Table 2.10

Burned Bones of Major Meat-Producing Animals at Snaketown and
Pueblo Grande

| | Snaketown | | | Pueblo Grande | | |
|---|---|---|---|---|---|---|
| ANIMAL | TOTAL BONES | NO. BURNED | % BURNED | TOTAL BONES | NO. BURNED | % BURNED |
| Cottontail rabbit | 149 | 27 | 18.1 | 400 | 134 | 33.5 |
| Blacktail jack rabbit | 940 | 171 | 18.2 | 2,637 | 645 | 24.5 |
| Antelope jack rabbit | 122 | 24 | 19.7 | 3 | 0 | 0.0 |
| Mule deer | 355 | 150 | 42.3 | 31 | 10 | 32.3 |
| Bighorn sheep | 30 | 14 | 46.7 | 1 | 0 | 0.0 |

SOURCES: Snaketown data, Greene and Mathews (1976); Pueblo Grande data, S. James
(1994)

This difference is doubtless related to the methods used in preparing
the meat. Periodic removal of the organic cover of trash mounds by
fire may be held partly responsible, particularly in scorching the fine
bones that were components in human waste. However, trash-filled
pits exhibit no in situ burning, yet they produce heat-altered bones,
indicating that the condition was acquired before disposal. In all
probability the Hohokam threw bones in the hearth after the meat
was cleaned off, thereby taking advantage of the grease in them as a
little extra fuel.

Haury did not consider every aspect of taphonomy, such as the possibility that burned bone survived better than unburned bone or that a
large burned bone preserved better than a small one. Such factors might
have created a statistical illusion rather than a reliable sampling record
of human activity. We could have the same burned bone ratio sampling
problem in our own study of prairie dogs and pronghorn antelope.
However, the observation that there are roughly similar burning patterns at desert Snaketown (table 2.10) and in the Wupatki basin sites
(table 2.7)—that is, lower percentages of burned bones in small animals
and higher percentages in large animals—with differing refuse deposition patterns is more indicative of a real phenomenon than of a statistical quirk. The 20–40% frequency of bone burning at Snaketown and at
Pueblo Grande, a Hohokam site in Phoenix, Arizona (S. James 1994),
lends support to the possibility that the numbers reflect reality (table
2.10).

Jerry L. Greene and Thomas W. Mathews (1976:373) examined one-
third of the Snaketown mammal bones, identifying 1,688 specimens
with an MNI of 656. The frequency of burned bones in the larger and
most common meat-producing mammals is given in table 2.10. These
counts suggest that deer and bighorn sheep were roasted more often
than cottontails and jackrabbits. Greene and Mathews did not discuss
bone processing, however, so even this low-level interpretation should
be viewed cautiously. Some roasting occurred in all of the more commonly eaten species at Snaketown. The most interesting thing about
these frequencies of burned bones is that they are relatively high and

similar in the two large species, and relatively low and nearly identical in the three small species.

At Arroyo Hondo Pueblo, near Santa Fe, New Mexico, Richard Lang and Arthur Harris (1984:84–85) identified 256 charred artiodactyl and large mammal bones. Altogether they identified 14,125 mammal bones, which, if we understand their report correctly, suggests that large burned mammal bones made up only only 1.8% (256 of 14,125) of the total, a surprisingly low frequency compared with the frequencies of burning reported from other sites we have reviewed. They note, however, that "in a sample of 559 burned mammal bones, 46% to 53% represented large mammals, a percentage about twice that of large mammal bones in the total mammal bone collection from the site." In other words, it appears that at Arroyo Hondo, too, large mammal bones were selected for in some process that left them burned.

Last, we mention an interesting study dealing with the burning of small mammal bones, once more at Pueblo Grande. To test for whether or not the Hohokam ate rodents, Jennifer Waters (1995) experimented with rodent roasting to see how the burning compared with that on prehistoric rodent remains. She observed that bones of the experimental animals' extremities were always burned, whereas bones of the torso never were (recall Cushing's comment on Zuni rodent cooking). She found that rodent remains from the trash and midden areas of Pueblo Grande were burned as her experimental animals were, whereas burned rodent bones from other features did not have the experimental roasting pattern. Hence, food and nonfood rodents can often be distinguished. Judging from Waters's study and many other reports, it appears that rodents were regular items in trash middens and on aboriginal menus.

## Characteristics of Considerate Human Burials

THE MINIMAL taphonomic signature of cannibalism looks convincingly like the pattern of damage observed in animal bones excavated from food refuse deposits. Equally convincing to us is that it looks nothing like the condition of human bones excavated from deliberate burials, despite variation in mortuary customs geographically and over time in the Southwest. In this section we want to show that the cannibalism signature lies far outside the range of all considerate mortuary practices reported for the Anasazi area of the prehistoric Southwest.

We limit our discussion largely to the Anasazi area because so far, with only one exception, all the sites we know of for which convincing claims of cannibalism have been made are Anasazi. The exception is Ash Creek, a Salado site in the Tonto basin of central Arizona (see chapter 3). Salado mortuary practices were quite similar to those of the Anasazi, except that extended burial was more common there than flexed (Mitchell 1992:195). Another site where we think cannibalism occurred is Fence Lake, in the region of overlap between the Anasazi and Mogollon cultures. Again, these two areas were quite similar in burial customs, although cremations—reflecting Hohokam influence—were much more common among the Mogollon (Robinson and Sprague 1965).

Along a continuum from undisturbed, considerate burial to human charnel deposits, archaeological human bone assemblages can be placed in seven taphonomic categories:

Figure 2.12. Considerate, or formal, Southwestern burials (those showing concern for the dead) can usually be recognized by any of four defining characteristics, all of which are shown in this view of inhumations at Inscription House, Arizona (NA2160): (1) patterned body position, here flexed; (2) a defined or protected space where the dead are kept safe by burial, here in refuse and talus below the cliff dwelling (Ward 1975); (3) grave goods, here ceramic vessels that may have contained food or water; and (4) full articulation of skeletons. Museum of Northern Arizona Archive photograph by George J. Gumerman (June 1966).

Figure 2.13. A considerate single burial beneath the floor of a small room in Lake Canyon, Utah (42Sa544, Horsefly Hollow, Burial 2). The three defining characteristics are grave goods, position, and complete articulation. Photograph courtesy Floyd W. Sharrock, Department of Anthropology–Glen Canyon Project, University of Utah (March 1961).

1. *Normal, considerate burial with only minimal disturbance.* No perimortem skeletal modification. Only minor postmortem damage by plant roots, chemical decay processes, and some weathering—the baseline breakdown for archaeological and nonarchaeological subsurface bone deposits, human and nonhuman. There can be some loss or disturbance of small bones because of rodent and burrowing insect activity or other forms of natural bioturbation. No intentional human damage. Examples: Inscription House, Lake Canyon, and Curtain Cliff burials (figs. 2.12–2.14).

2. *Normal considerate burial with moderate environmental disturbance.* Definite disturbance by small animals such as rodents or badgers—for example, a few missing vertebrae or a missing mandible. An arm or a leg may have been moved from its normal anatomical position by animals or shifted by collapsed roofing in a crypt or other burial setting. Some animal modification present,

Figure 2.14. Considerate multiple Basketmaker burial at Curtain Cliff dune site (NA7114), near Chilchinbito, Arizona. Nothing in the skeletal remains explains why these three adults and five children were buried at one time. The single remaining mortuary item is the sandstone grinding slab at upper right. Excavated by Paul V. Long, Jr., and Bruce Baldwin, August 1958. Museum of Northern Arizona Archive photograph by Paul V. Long, Jr., 1958:5.

such as chewing or gnawing. No identifiable human modification. Example: Pueblo del Arroyo (fig. 3.272).

3. *Abnormal deposit with major environmental disturbance.* Considerable damage, disturbance, chewing and gnawing, disarticulation, scatter, and element loss are evident, caused largely by dogs, coyotes, or other carnivores. Skeletal material from one or more individuals in this condition may have been gathered up and buried following the animal despoilment. Example: Wupatki Room 59 (figs. 3.228 and 3.229).

4. *Abnormal deposit without environmental disturbance.* Normal burials may have been disturbed by humans engaged in building activities or in burying other individuals. Bones will be mixed up in reinterment, but there is no intentional perimortem damage. One example is B.57A at Turkey Creek Pueblo (AZ:W:10:78), Point of Pines, Arizona. Our examination of this assemblage determined that all the damage was postmortem, caused by disturbance and reburial of originally considerate burials. For another example, see Kidder (1958:fig. 70).

5. *Normal considerate burial with perimortem human-inflicted damage.* With or without a minor amount of environmental damage. A small amount of human modification can be identified in the form of a perimortem breakage wound or scalping cuts. Body position, location, and occasional grave goods indicate considerate burial or possible sacrifice, not abandonment. The taphonomic signature of cannibalism is not present. Example: Pueblo Bonito, Room 33, Skeleton 3 (figs. 3.65–3.67).

6. *Abnormal burial or abandoned bodies with perimortem human-inflicted damage.* With or without minor environmental damage. Human modification in some form or other is extensive—cut marks, disarticulation, missing elements, or burning. Some breakage may be present. This type may have resulted from trophy taking,

raiding, violence, human sacrifice, entrapment in a burning structure, secondary burial, or undefined mortuary or ritual behavior.
Human skulls and long bones may have been simply or elaborately
modified for display purposes in shrines or public places. There may
be no modification, but the bone is strangely located. For example,
Edgar L. Hewett (1936:68–69) wrote: "I have found examples [of
kiva ventilator shafts] in the San Juan valley with diagonally crossed
sticks with a skull resting thereon, inside the shaft." Minor to indis-
cernible breakage may occur when individuals have been placed on
the floors of pit structures whose roofs are then intentionally collapsed, as in the type of abandonment of Pueblo I Anasazi proto-
kivas in southwestern Colorado proposed by Richard Wilshusen
(1986). Obviously, there is a large degree of behavioral variation
within this class, a sure sign that with detailed study of several different cases, it could probably be subdivided. Example: Battle Cave
(figs. 3.83–3.92).

7. *Nonburial floor or pit deposit with perimortem human-inflicted
   damage.* With or without environmental damage. Human modification, disarticulation, and other processing is extreme and includes
   the minimal taphonomic signature of cannibalism with its high
   proportion of intentional bone breakage. Example: Leroux Wash
   (figs. 3.137–3.142).

*[handwritten margin note: close to the min. taph. sig. and six key criteria, but not not close]*

In this section we are mainly concerned with the first four of these
categories—those representing deliberate, considerate burials, whether
disturbed or undisturbed. The next section deals briefly with human
bones showing the effects of perimortem violence, and chapter 3 item-
izes and contrasts the assemblages we believe represent categories 6
and 7—those bearing the taphonomic signatures of violence and cannibalism.

Hundreds of publications contain information on Southwestern burials. Attempts to generalize about them have been less common. Elizabeth Boies Hagberg (1939) and Peggy Carle (1941) wrote their Master
of Arts theses on the subject of Southwestern Indian burial practices,
and there are a few topical mortuary studies such as Michael Stanislawski's (1963) work on extended burials and Michael Fink's (1996)
recent thesis on cremations.

A well-regarded regional summary was published in 1965 by John C.
McGregor. In general, he found that prehistoric Southwestern mortuary
practices were relatively simple. There was almost no perimortem treatment of the corpse, such as defleshing for secondary burial or mutilation
during sacrificial rites. Cremation and unmodified inhumation were the
main types of burial—the former among the Hohokam and the latter
everywhere else. Associated grave goods were correspondingly simple
and few, suggesting only minor development of classes or ranks of persons. The use of a distinct cemetery location seems to appear earlier in
the Hohokam area than elsewhere in the Southwest. Some use of subsurface mortuary architecture developed after 200 B.C., but no surface
or underground structures such as masonry charnel houses, crypts, or
tombs came into use.

As an overview of temporal and regional variation, McGregor's review can be condensed into the following list:

200 B.C.–A.D. 1. Mogollon: burials partly flexed in trash and in house subfloor pits. Hohokam: cremations in pits and trenches. Cemetery areas. Basketmaker I: no information.

A.D. 1–500. Mogollon: no changes. Hohokam: no changes. Basketmaker II: burials flexed, in stone-lined cists.

A.D. 500–700. Mogollon: no changes. Hohokam: shallow pit cremations. Basketmaker III: no changes.

A.D. 700–900. Mogollon: not discussed. Hohokam: not discussed. Pueblo I: flexed like Basketmaker, but in caves and rubbish heaps and under room floors.

A.D. 900–1100. Mogollon: in various villages, both inhumations and cremations. Hohokam: mainly pit cremations, but a few extended inhumations with head to east. Pueblo II and III: burial flexed and on side, placed in trash or other places where digging was easy. Sinagua: cremations and extended inhumations on back. Cohonina: only three burials known. Rio Grande: flexed inhumations.

A.D. 1100–1300. Pueblo III: burial in trash heaps, under room floors, and in sealed and abandoned rooms—anywhere digging was easy. Bodies flexed in western San Juan, flexed or straight in eastern San Juan. In southwest, where Hohokam influence occurred, inhumations were extended. Cremation rare but known for Flagstaff and Mesa Verde, suggesting contact or even population movement from the Hohokam area. Hohokam: cremation still dominant, but some inhumations known, buried with red-on-buff and polychrome pottery. Mimbres (Mogollon-derived): flexed inhumations. Salado: semiflexed and extended burials in trash mounds and in houses. Patayan (Cohonina): only three burials. Rio Grande: flexed burials.

A.D. 1300–1600. Pueblo IV: flexed and extended burials under room floors, in sealed rooms, and mostly in cemeteries within trash mounds or more distant sand dunes. Rio Grande: flexed burials. At late Pecos (historic?), burials were extended. Southern Pueblo (i.e., Gila Pueblo): extended burials and a few cremations. Hohokam (now called Hohokam-Salado or western Pueblo): extended inhumation, some cremations.

Turning specifically to the Anasazi, many reports on prehistoric burials provide details helpful in assessing the demographics of human charnel deposits as well as distinguishing considerate burials from cannibalized assemblages. We begin with a recent demographic analysis and then move on to a few examples from the ancestral Basketmaker culture.

Debra L. Martin and colleagues (1991) analyzed nearly 200 variously complete human skeletons excavated in northeastern Arizona by the Black Mesa Archaeological Project under the leadership of George Gumerman. Of adults whose sex could be determined, there were 37 males (45.5%) and 48 females (56.5%). There were 69 children (38.5%) ranging from newborn to age 10, and 20 (11.2%) whose ages were between 11 and 20 years. Mature adults numbered 87 (48.6%), and there were 3 individuals (1.7%) whose ages could not be determined. These values are close to those of cemetery populations known from other Anasazi settlements as well as from large Mogollon cemetery populations such as those recovered from Point of Pines and Grasshopper Ruin.

Arthur H. Rohn (1989:154) summarized mortuary practices during

Basketmaker II times (500 B.C.–A.D. 450) in the northern San Juan River area—a statement that can serve as a description of the typical, flexed Basketmaker burial. "Deceased members of society were regularly buried in abandoned storage cists, crevices in rock shelters, beneath house floors, or in general refuse areas. The pattern of folding the legs and arms against the body and adding items of clothing, adornment, and utilitarian utensils presaged a tradition of burial practices that changed very little throughout Puebloan prehistory." Like Rohn and others, Stanislawski (1963:308) believed that "prior to A.D. 1000, the common Southwestern burial pattern is seen to be that of flexure of the dead, with a few rare extended burials known." Later, extended burials became more common.

Thus, Basketmaker and later Puebloan conventional burials could never be confused with human remains suggesting cannibalism because the burials are almost always fully articulated and were placed in regardful locations and positions with mortuary offerings and other indications of consideration and care for the deceased. Cannibalized assemblages never show these attributes. Moreover, the considerately treated dead never exhibit the cannibal pattern of body destruction and processing, which minimally includes dismemberment, bone smashing, cooking, and eventual discard as waste. Despite these conspicuous differences, a few anomalous Basketmaker burials have been discovered, as the following examples illustrate.

In a survey of Basketmaker burial practices, George J. Gumerman and Jeffrey S. Dean (1989:113) noted: "An unusual aspect of BMII culture is indicated by the frequent postinterment removal of heads and long bones from corpses, apparent attempts to protect the heads of the deceased from vandalism, . . . and by the common association of fires and burned human bones in BMII burial caves." Alternatively, they suggested that missing body parts and burned bone might have been attributable to witchcraft practices. Less esoteric possibilities include prehistoric grave-robbing and cave reuse with unintentional burning of previously buried individuals by the cooking or camp fires of later occupants. Whatever the cause, there is no reason to believe that either missing skeletal elements or burned bones alone represent cannibalism. The six features of the minimal taphonomic signature need to appear in tandem for that interpretation to be warranted.

The effects of prehistoric grave-robbing on Basketmaker burials are well illustrated by some disturbed burials excavated by Earl H. Morris in 1931 from a series of ten caves situated between Carrizo Mountain and the Lukachukai Mountains in northeastern Arizona. Tree-ring dates of A.D. 620–670, material culture, house forms, and cranial shape indicated that most of the burials found in four of the caves were Basketmaker people. Postmortem grave-robbing was abundant and severely damaging. Earl Morris described the damage for Cave 4, which had been used only for interment, where he found the remains of 12 individuals: "The graves had been looted in ancient times, presumably in a search for beads and ornaments. The skeletons had been ripped out of their rough pits and the bones and wrappings scattered. The baskets that had accompanied them had been thrown out on the surface and were tramped to pieces. . . . The bead hunters had dug down to the body [of

Burial 1], twisted off the head, and thrown it out of the pit" (E. A. Morris 1980:52).

Another unusual characteristic of Basketmaker mortuary behavior was the interment of nonviolent multiple burials. In Sayodneechee burial cave (NA4164) in northeastern Arizona, for example, A. V. Kidder and Samuel Guernsey (1919:29) found four cists containing Basketmaker skeletons. Cist A contained 4 adults and 3 children; Cist B, 8 adults and 11 children under 5 years of age. Baskets and other burial goods were placed with both adults and children:

> There is no possibility of this remarkable deposit [Cist A] having been an ossuary, or repository for bones stripped of their flesh, for all the skeletons lay in order. . . . It appeared to us that the cist must have been filled at one time, perhaps to hold the dead from some particularly virulent epidemic. The bodies could hardly have been packed in so tightly, and yet show so little disturbance, if they had been put in one by one and the cist closed up between times. . . . No signs of violence, no crushed or cut skulls, no bones apparently broken before death, were noted; a massacre theory seems untenable. . . . It was noticed in Cist A that the skeletons were most badly rotted where they came in contact with others; those in Cists C and D, on the other hand, which were not crowded and did not touch one another, were excellently preserved, some so well that portions of the hair and tendons still adhered to the bones.

Ann Axtell Morris (1933:200) described a multiple Basketmaker burial she and Earl Morris found in Tseahatso Cave, downstream from Mummy Cave in Canyon del Muerto, Arizona: "At the bottom of a cist was an enormous basket packed with the bodies of four children, and above it lay fourteen more babies and infants. It did not mean war, for there were no signs of violence. Clearly some terrible contagious children's disease had swept the cave, dealing death within a single day or two to what must have represented most of the children in the community."

Other examples include the Curtain Cliff site, a probable Basketmaker III (A.D. 500–700) multiple burial in a sand dune northwest of Rough Rock Trading Post, Arizona (Long 1960; Turner 1960). With the three partly flexed adults and five children there were no grave goods other than a slab metate, and no signs of violence (fig. 2.14). The largest Basketmaker skeletal assemblage ever found was discovered in 1923 by Earl Morris in Canyon del Muerto. His American Museum of Natural History field party worked for days in a charnel deposit of burned and calcined Basketmaker remains said to be of all ages packed into a deep recess near Mummy Cave. Morris (1925:272) thought that there were "more than 100 bodies in the original heap." Although we searched for these remains, we were unable to locate them. Since Morris made no claim for violence or cannibalism, we did not include this assemblage in chapter 3.

It appears, then, that burying numerous individuals together was a common Basketmaker custom. Such multiple burials, if left undisturbed over the centuries, show all the hallmarks of considerate treatment of

the dead. Bones are not smashed into pieces, and they show no butchering marks, burning, or pot-polishing. The simple presence of multiple
skeletons in a grave does not signal cannibalism.

As the Basketmaker period phased into the later Pueblo period,
Anasazi burials continued to consist mostly of flexed interments (Mc-
Gregor 1965). Their common locations, however, shifted from cists inside rock shelters to trash middens and underneath the floors of rooms.
During the Pueblo III and IV phases, bodies were occasionally buried in
an extended position, rather than flexed. What is of interest here is not
these undisturbed, considerate burials—with their complete, undamaged
skeletons and accompanying grave goods—but the atypical, disturbed,
or hard-to-interpret Anasazi burials that we have encountered in the literature. They help to demonstrate the range of variation within "normal" mortuary practices and the kinds of bone damage that can be
subsumed under the term "disturbed burial."

Among the most exceptional sets of human remains reported for the
Anasazi-Pueblo area are those excavated in 1928 by Harold S. Gladwin
(1945) in rubbish mounds along the rim of a low plateau in the Red
Mesa Valley, north of Coolidge, New Mexico. "Three burials have been
found in which the soft parts of the body seem to have been encased in
adobe. . . . Five burials were found in which the skull was missing, although other bones were well preserved. One burial of a skull alone was
discovered, also in good state of preservation; no other bones were
found within a radius of five feet" (Gladwin 1945:58). After making
these tantalizing remarks, Gladwin said nothing else about the human
remains, including their dating. Nor did he provide a total number of
burials that would have told whether five burials without heads was the
majority or only a small number of a larger sample. If the remains still
exist, it would be worthwhile to examine the headless skeletons for perimortem cut marks.

There are scores of archaeological site reports and reams of unpublished field notes containing references to disturbed burials, although
few provide information on the taphonomic concerns that interest us
here. Apparently, the universal concern for the dead in the prehistoric
Southwest (as we infer from ethnographic reports for the historic period) was that they be buried or cached and remain undisturbed for as
long as they were remembered and, in turn, did not disturb the living.
Surface scatters of disturbed bones belonging to forgotten individuals
seem for the most part not to have been feared and to have lacked much
psychological or cultural significance. The released "spirit" and the de-
caying, potentially infectious physical body were more dangerous at the
time of death than years later when the defleshed dry bones resurfaced.

One early example of what was probably a disturbed burial was
found by J. W. Fewkes (1904:128) at the site of Kintiel in northeastern
Arizona; Fewkes believed it to be a secondary burial:

One of the most instructive burials at Kintiel was found in the east
cemetery. This was interpreted as a secondary interment. It consisted
of human bones stripped of flesh and deposited in the earth with customary mortuary vessels. The reason for the belief that these bones
were not covered with flesh when the bowls were placed upon them is

that their position was not that which they would have had if articulated. The femurs were placed in the reverse of the natural position, and a humerus was found crossing the femur. No skull or pelvis was found in the grave.

In a more recently excavated example, poor preservation and animal damage characterized the human remains Alan Olson (1971) recovered at the Cross Canyon group of sites northeast of Ganado, Arizona. At site NA8013, a Pueblo I–III site, Olson recovered two burials: "The skulls were missing from both burials and about the only positive thing that can be stated is that they appeared flexed. The amount of disturbance is probably balanced between human and rodent activity" (1971:39). At nearby PII–III Kinlichee Ruin (NA8022), "a large fragment of skull was found in the fill of Kiva 1. This did not seem to be associated with the two higher burials" (Olson 1971:40).

We examined these remains at the Museum of Northern Arizona on June 23, 1995, and found rodent and carnivore damage. Among the nine or so individuals from the two sites, the most interesting fact was the near total absence of crania and no sign of human damage to any of the cervical vertebrae.

Although inhumation was the usual Pueblo mortuary practice, a few cremations have also been found in Pueblo period sites. They caution us not to construe bone burning alone as evidence of cannibalism. Again, Fewkes (1911) provides one of the earliest examples. Writing about his excavation in Cliff Palace at Mesa Verde, he stated that he found one room with a large quantity of phosphate ashes that had calcined human bone and mortuary objects in them. He also found an unstated number of circular, thermally stressed stone enclosures on the mesa top that were filled with ash and "more or less burned" human bones (Fewkes 1911:39). Similar enclosures were said to be present at Spruce Tree House and Step House. Fewkes noted that Gustaf von Nordenskiöld had credited Richard Wetherill for having first found cremations at Mesa Verde.

In 1921, Jean Allard Jeançon found cremations at Chimney Rock Pueblo, a Chacoan outlier in southwestern Colorado. Chimney Rock Pueblo was occupied from A.D. 1075 to 1125, when it burned (Eddy 1977, 1993). Jeançon (1922:29) described the cremation area on the mesa slope: "There are indications that before the cremation was completed, earth was thrown over the whole mass, and only partial cremation occurred. Not a single case was found where there was enough left of the bones to determine anything more than that they were human bones. Accompanying these were masses of broken pottery and remains of artifacts all more or less showing the marks of fire. Each cremation had a fairly well defined area and did not seem to overlap any other area, as would have been the case if this had been a dumping ground."

In 1974, Museum of Northern Arizona archaeologists found burned bone at NA12,641 on the northwest side of Bullet Canyon, about two miles upstream from where it joins Grand Gulch. A study of the bone led Dana Hartman (1974) to believe that it had been cremated. Although these were thought to be Basketmaker remains, there was some uncertainty, because the site may also have been occupied later. We examined these remains, which are stored in the MNA physical anthropology collections. We agree with Hartman that the person had probably been cremated. There was no perimortem damage other than burning.

Finally, we want to discuss at some length a case that illustrates the importance of context in interpreting unusual burials—in this instance, its importance in distinguishing mortuary custom from the effects of violence, and both from cannibalism. At the Duckfoot site (5MT3868), a late Pueblo I (A.D. 750–900) settlement in the Montezuma Valley about five miles west of Cortez, Colorado, Ricky R. Lightfoot excavated burned but not pyre-cremated skeletal remains. They were analyzed by J. Michael Hoffman (1990, 1993), who worked out an MNI of 16. Males and children had been left in burned, abandoned pit structures, presumably upon their deaths. Hoffman (1990:44–45) noted: "One obvious difference between the burials in the midden area and the pitstructures is the burning of structures and bodies in the latter burial sites. . . . None of the burials from pitstructures [7] or midden show evidence of recent interpersonal trauma. . . . Midden burials . . . virtually without exception, show varying degrees of disturbance and direct alteration by carnivore chewing and gnawing. Direct evidence of canid tooth marks— canine and carnassial tooth punctures—is widespread."

Hoffman (1990:48–49) found no sign of cannibalism at the Duckfoot site but interpreted the burials this way:

> None of the skeletons, regardless of place of interment, whether burned or not, and whether complete or not, shows evidence of butchering which might support a notion of cannibalism, among other things. Turner's (1988) trio of cannibalism signs—butchered, burned, and broken bones—are not all present here. Although most of the pitstructure burials are burned and several of these are broken, there is no evidence of cut marks on any of the bones to support the notion of dismemberment prior to burning (i.e., cooking). All burned and broken bones can more parsimoniously be explained as the natural result of cremation in a burning structure with fragmentation mostly due to falling roof timbers or animal disturbance when direct fire damage alone is an insufficient cause in particular cases.

William M. Ferguson and Arthur H. Rohn (1987:69) interpreted the human remains at the Duckfoot site quite differently—as the result of violence or warfare. They wrote: "The skeletons represent bodies thrown into a burning pithouse. Their sprawled position indicates that this was not a formal burial." They also noted that at least one of the burned pit houses held an abundance of household items, including more than 20 pottery vessels, indicating that the "structure had been inhabited up to the moment fire consumed it" (1987:131). This room contained two human skeletons, "one sprawled across the hearth, the other along the north wall. Neither had been accorded a proper Anasazi burial; both had died violently. The burning roof material had charred very small portions of their bones, indicating their flesh was still present when the burning occurred. Yet both bodies lay atop some charred poles and the knee of one was elevated by the debris below. . . . It is certain that these bodies are evidence of violence that occurred 1,200 years ago" (Ferguson and Rohn 1987:135).

The context and scorched content of the Duckfoot pit houses, including burned sagebrush flowers and tree-ring wood that together signaled a date in the fall of A.D. 880, led Lightfoot (1993:298) to believe that abandonment had been catastrophic, but not in Ferguson and Rohn's sense:

> In all three burned pit structures, human skeletons covered or overlapped the hearths, yet the bones were burned only on the top, where they were exposed to the heat of the burning roof or of fires set inside the structure to ignite the roof. Although it is not clear why so many bodies were deposited in structures at abandonment, it appears that abandonment was rapid, with no intent to return. Structures were destroyed with usable tools and containers left inside. These details of abandonment suggest that the site may have been abandoned rapidly as the result of some catastrophe that caused the death of six or more individuals, including men, women, and children, and that the structures were destroyed as part of a funerary and abandonment ritual.

Although in this case archaeological context and taphonomic analysis are each inconclusive alone, together they indicate mortuary treatment at the Duckfoot site rather than violence. The Duckfoot remains could represent a case of food poisoning, viral infection, or something similar. Because these "burials" are sufficiently unusual, it might also be profitable to consider the possibility that these people died because of social deviance (including sorcery, wizardry, or witchcraft) or social pathology (in themselves or others), instead of from physical illness.

In summary, Anasazi burial practices (and Southwestern ones in general) were relatively simple in form and content, although intrasite, interregional, and temporal variation is evident—consistent with A. L. Kroeber's view (1927) that mortuary practices are as subject to fashion as are dress and manners. There is no evidence that any significant amount of postmortem processing of soft tissue or bone took place for secondary burials or any other identifiable purposes. There are no sets of human bones that could be attributed to bone curation (ancestor worship).

The taphonomic characteristics of human remains thought to have been cannibalized are altogether different from the characteristics of any of the other six classes of burials we proposed earlier and from all the forms of considerate burials reviewed here. The taphonomic signature of cannibalism is entirely different from bone damage associated with considerate burials. Neither Hagberg (1939), Carle (1941), nor McGregor (1965), in their literature reviews on Southwestern burial practices, turned up any examples of body treatment that might be confused with cannibalism.

[In closing this section, we want to emphasize that skeletal recovery techniques need to be improved in Southwestern archaeology, at the very least by adding procedures that allow taphonomic information to be collected systematically. These contextual and osteological procedures should be designed to help distinguish between intentional perimortem processing of the dead and unintentional disturbance by human and environmental agencies.]The term *disturbed burial*, although it sounds authoritative, has about as much explanatory power as the terms *cere-*

*monial object* and *environmental stress.* Taphonomic issues require identifying whether the disturbance was perimortem or postmortem, natural or anthropogenic, intentional or accidental, rapid or drawn out over time.

## Human Bone Damage Caused by Violence

ONE LAST CATEGORY of human-caused damage to human bone is that stemming from interpersonal violence. The osseous record of conflict and violence takes many forms, but we believe it looks quite different from the minimal taphonomic signature of cannibalism. Much of the comparative data for the two conditions will emerge in the site-by-site descriptions in chapter 3, but here we offer a few general remarks and some examples of sites evidencing violence that we discovered only after 1995, when we formally stopped collecting data for this book.

 All interpretations of prehistoric violence depend on the use of analogy, but because written and visual documentation of contemporary violence is so extensive, and because humans seem rather unimaginative in the ways they violently harm others, we believe analogic reasoning is a safe method for interpreting prehistoric human taphonomy when conflict is suspected. The forensic and bioarchaeological literature teems with cases of contemporary and historic violence. An excellent example is the forensic study by Clyde C. Snow and John Fitzpatrick (1989) of human remains recovered from the Battle of the Little Bighorn.

Essentially, there are three kinds of weapons—projectile, cutting, and percussion—that can leave characteristic marks on bone. Arrow and spear points have been found embedded in prehistoric Southwestern skeletons dating as far back as Basketmaker II times (Hurst and Turner 1993; Morris n.d.*b*; Wetherill 1893a, 1893b, 1894). Certainty of conflict is greater if the point is embedded in a bone rather than lying loose within the rib cage or near some other part of the body. We know of no instances of cannibalized bone assemblages in the Southwest in which projectile points were left embedded in the bones. If the victims had been killed in this fashion, the projectile points were removed sometime during body processing.

Unlike arrow and spear points, the knives that produced cut marks on bone were not commonly left in or near the victim. Although slicing and penetrating wounds may occasionally be detected on the bones of victims of violence, the most common cut marks are those left by trophy taking, particularly the taking of scalps. Trophy taking was one form of physical documentation that was often demanded in proof of warrior success. It might also have been valued in terms of acquiring the victim's "power." Ernest Beaglehole and Pearl Beaglehole (1935:23) noted that Hopis took scalps only of the bravest enemies; Alexander M. Stephen said the same thing (Parsons, ed., 1936:xxix). In the Southwest there are numerous ethnographic accounts and archaeological examples of scalping. For one, the Beagleholes (1935:23), describing the actions of Hopi warriors, wrote that "at times the whole head was severed; usually the hair was held in the left hand and the scalp removed by cutting across the forehead, above the ears, and across the base of the skull."

Douglas W. Owsley (1994:335) used scalping as the basis for estimating the frequency of violent death in South Dakota during late prehistoric to early historic times. The most common purpose of scalping there was to obtain a trophy that documented the taker's bravery in warfare. Scalps were removed mainly from the heads of young adults of both sexes—from males (7.1%, 23 of 324 individuals) slightly more often than from females (5.5%, 18 of 327). From this single perimortem mutilation, Owsley demonstrated that warfare was common on the Great Plains, sometimes escalating to the murdering of entire villages, as in the case of the infamous Crow Creek massacre. Owsley concluded that scalp taking (and warfare) was prehistoric and was not due to contact with Europeans (see also, e.g., Gilmore 1933; Neumann 1940).

Perhaps the most famous Southwestern archaeological scalp was found by Alfred Kidder and Samuel Guernsey (1919:190) in Cave 1, Kinboko Canyon (House Canyon), near Marsh Pass and Kayenta, Arizona. It was the skin of an entire Basketmaker head, including the face, found under the shoulders of a mummy. "In its preparation the scalp proper, including the ears, was removed from the skull in one piece; the face to the mouth in another; and the chin with the lower cheeks in a third." These were sewed back together and painted with greenish white, red, white, and yellow pigments. Kidder and Guernsey suggested that the specimen was a trophy of some enemy.

Other body parts that ethnographers report as having been taken as trophies among the Pueblo Indians include heads and hearts (Parsons, ed., 1936:xxxix; Parsons 1939:424; Voth 1905:60, 245, 264) and brains (Parsons 1939:627). We learned that one of an Awatovi woman's breasts was cut off and saved. Archaeologically, heads and hands have been observed to be missing from skeletons in a number of Anasazi sites. They are presumed to have been trophies, and examples will be detailed in chapter 3.

In contrast to the multitude of cut marks left on human bone by body processing for consumption—marks that have been found on practically every human skeletal element—cut marks left by trophy taking are rare and appear primarily on the cranial vault, where they are the results of scalping. Simple violence-related cut marks are even less common, although there are rare instances of knife wounds (fig. 3.10).

The last kind of damage suggesting prehistoric violence is the traumatic breakage of heads in general and faces in particular. Percussion wounds to crania are common in the skeletal assemblages discussed in chapter 3 (see figs. 3.4–3.6 and 3.8 for examples). Any single percussion wound (or cut mark, for that matter) can occur by nonviolent accident, such as a fall, and is not alone definitive evidence of violence. Moreover, stone, wood, and antler clubs, like knives, are seldom left at the scene of the violence. The probability that conflict happened increases when there is additional perimortem trauma, when there are multiple individuals with trauma, and when there is a context of violence, such as many traumatized skeletons of young adult males sprawled or heaped on the floor of a burned room.

[Percussion wounds occur in cannibalized and noncannibalized bone deposits and present no distinctive qualities in either situation. It is this lack of distinctiveness that allows us to hypothesize that the victims of cannibalism were beaten, possibly tortured, and then killed before they were dismembered, defleshed, and broken up for cooking purposes. This additional perimortem damage can be readily seen by turning to chap-

ter 3 and comparing the simple violence evident in the Cave 7 victims
(figs. 3.2–3.10) with the victims of both violence and cannibalism found
at Leroux Wash (figs. 3.136–3.153)).

Taphonomic examination of the remains of victims of violence often
yields evidence that their lives ended differently from those of people
who died of natural causes. If the dead were left on the ground surface at
the scene of a massacre, for example, there will usually be bone damage
caused by animal scavenging. If they were buried, bodies may have been
dumped unceremoniously into the grave pit without any ritual body
placement or other consideration for the dead.

A study from outside the U.S. Southwest nicely illustrates the differences between the proposed minimal taphonomic signature of cannibalism and the signatures of simple conflict and secondary burial. Sandra
Olsen and Pat Shipman (1994) examined 85 specimens of modified bone
surfaces in 38 individuals from 12 northern Great Plains sites ranging in
date from A.D. 400 to 1832. They found not only that bone damage in
victims of conflict differed from damage in secondary burials—which
were customary among some groups in Nebraska and Kansas, unlike in
the Southwest—but also that after the arrival of the Arikaras in Mandan
lands, the frequency of "battle-related injuries and perimortem mutilation dramatically increased" (1994:377). These mutilations included
defleshing, dismemberment, damaged foramen magnums, scalping, head
blows, and knife or arrow wounds. Comparing secondary burials with
remains from conflicts, they observed that the former had partial skeletons, many cut marks, defleshing marks on skull, mandible, and postcranial skeleton, cut marks with patterned orientations, scraping marks,
and sometimes enlarged foramen magnums. Instances of conflict left a
mostly complete skeleton, usually fewer than 20 cut marks, scalping,
rare mandibular and postcranial cuts, and variable orientation of cut
marks. Olsen and Shipman's perimortem damage types are compared
with the Southwestern cannibalism signature in table 2.11.

Finally, we mention a specific kind of violence—the killing and mutilation of witches—that some scholars believe could account for the bone
damage that we interpret as evidence of cannibalism. Do any ethnographic or legendary accounts support this contention? We believe they
do not.

The Southwestern Pueblo Indian dread of witches and witchcraft is
well known. Although Florence Hawley Ellis (1950) suggested that
witchcraft had increased in historic times as a reaction to acculturation
pressures, there is no doubt that she believed it to be an ancient and
widespread belief. Some ethnologists have suggested that fear of witches
is stronger and more pervasive among the Rio Grande Indians than
among the Hopis or Zunis, because of the former's greater amount of
cultural exchange with witchcraft-believing Hispanics (Beaglehole and
Beaglehole 1935; Ellis 1950; Simmons 1974; Titiev 1943, 1956). Considering the Hopis' substantial retention of their prehistoric culture, perhaps their treatment of witches is a better estimate of Anasazi practices
than those of the eastern Puebloans. Witch mutilation would run contrary to deep-seated feelings among the Hopis: "So great is the fear of a
witch's revenge that it is considered fool-hardy to attempt to kill one or
to betray his identity" (Titiev 1943:554). Whether the story is true or
not, only the legendary attack on Awatovi stands as a historic account of

Table 2.11
Condition of Human Bone in Three Contexts: Secondary Burials,
Conflict, and Hypothesized Cannibalism

| VARIABLE | SECONDARY BURIAL[a] | CONFLICT[a] | CANNIBALISM |
|---|---|---|---|
| Skeleton | Partial | Mostly complete | Very incomplete |
| Cut marks | 100s | Few (<20) | Several |
| Skull | Defleshed | Scalped | Scalped + broken |
| Mandible | Cutting | Cutting rare | Cutting occurs |
| Postcranial cuts | Many | Few | Several |
| Cut orientation | Patterned | Variable | Patterned |
| Cut types | Scraping, cuts | Chops, cuts, wounds | Cuts, few chops |
| Foramen magnum | Enlarged | Not affected | Not affected |
| Burning[b] | — | — | Present |
| Anvil abrasions[b] | — | — | Present |
| Pot-polishing[b] | — | — | Present |
| Vertebrae[b] | — | — | Destroyed |
| Perimortem breakage[b] | — | — | Massive |

a. After Olsen and Shipman (1994).
b. Not discussed by Olsen and Shipman (1994).

a killing justified because the victims were said to be witches—but those killed at Awatovi were not processed like game animals. And the mutilation of the captives at Polacca Wash, after the surprise attack on the town, happened not because the captives were witches but because the captors disagreed over possession of them.

Marc Simmons (1974) recorded a few stories of Pueblo witch execution in historic times. These accounts usually involve only a single person, not a group as the charnel deposits do. Examples include an execution at Sandia Pueblo in 1796, when a man accused of witchcraft was hung by his hands and lashed repeatedly until he died (Simmons 1974:33). At Isleta Pueblo the treatment was to keep the witch in a squatting position until he died (Simmons 1974:85). At Zia Pueblo in the 1880s, two witches were clubbed to death; this is one of only two accounts involving more than one person (Simmons 1974:85).

Witches were sometimes accused of eating children, as in a case in 1854 at Nambé Pueblo involving two men said to have been seen pulling their victim's bones from their mouths and noses. They were executed with a single blast from a shotgun (Simmons 1974:96). At an unstated time, a Nambé woman accused of extensive witchcraft was burned to death in her house (Simmons 1974:103). At Zuni the usual method of executing witches was to draw the arms back and hang the accused by the elbows until dead. If the accused failed to die within a certain length of time, he was clubbed to death in the head by a member of the Bow priesthood (Simmons 1974:111).

In short, our review of the ethnographic literature yielded no parallels between prehistoric multiple-body charnel deposits and accounts or legends of Puebloan witch killings. Nothing we have found in the ethnographic literature on witch execution even begins to approach the taphonomic characteristics of the prehistoric charnel deposits. We have found no mention anywhere of witches being eaten. Belief in witchcraft might well have been a powerful mechanism for prehistoric social control, but we see no way to tie the oral traditions of witch killing to the perimortem condition of the prehistoric skeletal remains evidencing the taphonomic signature of cannibalism.

This review of prehistoric human skeletal damage attributable to violence shows that it possesses various degrees of identifiability. Perimortem violence ranges from the irrefutable embedded knife, obvious cutting wounds caused by scalping, and face- and vault-smashing trauma delivered by blunt clubs to less clear-cut damage in the form of solitary wounds that could have resulted from accidents instead of intentional injury. The types of bone damage caused by violence occur also in human skeletal deposits evidencing cannibalism, enabling us to propose that these victims were brutalized as well as consumed.

## The Sum of the Evidence

PAUL BAHN (1991, 1992) proposed that the human-animal butchering similarity was fortuitous and therefore meaningless, because there are only a few ways in which to butcher either an animal or a human. As we have seen, however, butchering is only one aspect in the perimortem history of a carcass. There are other processing considerations, different cooking traditions, and, in the end, different ways in which waste was disposed of. The hypothetical butchers of human carcasses made mistakes in cutting and performed other processing "errors" on humans similar to those they made when butchering game animals. They broke human bones in the same ways and into pieces about the same sizes as larger game animal bones. They roasted and boiled human and large nonhuman parts in similar ways. Indeed, if it were not possible to distinguish human bones from those of large animals in archaeological deposits, cannibalism would not be an issue, because the perimortem processing for the two is qualitatively and quantitatively similar. All bone in archaeological refuse would simply be identified as the residue of meals.

The ethnographic literature on Southwestern Indian methods of butchering and preparing animal food shows that cooking methods for the same or similar animals varied considerably among communities and tribes. However, roasting *and* boiling were commonly used for the same individual large animal, whereas one method or the other was generally used for smaller animals. Because deer, bighorn sheep, and pronghorn antelope were both boiled and roasted, it can be suggested that the same held for humans if they were cannibalized. Also, it seems that roasting was often limited to the heads of large game animals. Thus, if the analogy holds, human heads should show burning more often than other parts of the body.

Archaeological descriptions of nonhuman animal bone modification and damage, combined with ethnographic accounts of butchering and cooking, provide a powerful means for reconstructing the types of activities and processing that led to the damaged human bone assemblages we and others have argued represent acts of cannibalism. Keeping these animal-butchering scenes and processing facts in mind should help readers understand the prehistoric human death, dismemberment, and cooking to be described in the next chapter—episode after episode.

# 3

## Taphonomic Evidence for Cannibalism and Violence in the American Southwest

### Seventy-Six Sites

♦   Our intense abomination for cannibalism is a food taboo.
—William Graham Sumner, *Folkways: A Study of the Sociological Importance of Usages, Manners, Customs, Mores,
and Morals*

SINCE THE BEGINNING of scientific archaeology in the American
Southwest, many researchers, including ourselves, have made
claims for prehistoric violence and cannibalism (table 3.1). For this
study we have directly evaluated other scholars' claims by examining the
relevant skeletal collections ourselves whenever possible. When we
could not do so, we appraised claims on the basis of descriptions written
by the original discoverer or other analysts. Whereas in chapter 2 we
showed that the damage pattern of presumably cannibalized human remains matches that found in large and small game animals, here we include human skeletal assemblages showing evidence of violence so that
the taphonomic signature of cannibalism can be appreciated for its
uniqueness with respect to other human assemblages.

[Presented in chronological order, the claims arise from 76 prehistoric
sites (fig. 3.1), starting with the late-nineteenth-century discoveries of
Richard Wetherill in southeastern Utah. We chose to organize the chapter chronologically by date of claim instead of, say, geographically or by
date of site because we want to make the point that from the very incep-
tion of Southwestern archaeology, violence and cannibalism have been
recognized by open-minded individuals of every generation. In a way,
the chronology is a historical monument to those past workers whose
observations and interpretative skills are often overlooked or deliberately ignored today.

In order to help readers make intersite comparisons, we present information in this chapter in a standardized, reference handbook style, using
data categories derived from worksheets we developed for this study.
The categories are explained in the appendix, where the data forms are
also reproduced. Every claim for cannibalism or violence is evaluated in
site-specific discussion sections. Whenever possible, the perimortem
damage for each bone assemblage is quantified and tabulated and photographic documentation is provided. As might be suspected, the information for each assemblage could be expanded into a full monograph in
its own right, like Tim White's (1992) monograph on the Mancos
Canyon site. Our intent, however, is to describe and characterize many
sites in a uniform fashion so that they can all be evaluated with maximal
comparability under one cover.

Although our purpose in this chapter is to present data and analysis
for individual sites, at the end of the chapter we offer a few brief statistical analyses of the entire data set. Tables 3.77–3.82 provide comparisons
by age, sex, time period, and depositional context. Altogether, we see or
agree with evidence for cannibalism in 286 individuals at 38 sites.

Table 3.1
Claims for Cannibalism or Violence in Southwestern Sites, by Date of Claim

| NO. | DATE | SITE | STATE | CLAIMANT | TYPE | AGREE[a] |
|---|---|---|---|---|---|---|
| 1 | 1893 | Cave 7 | UT | R. Wetherill | Violence | Yes (P) |
| 2 | 1893 | Long House | CO | G. Nordenskiöld | Violence | ? |
| 3 | 1893 | Awatovi | AZ | J. Fewkes | Violence | Yes (P) |
| 4 | 1894 | Snider's Well | CO | R. Wetherill | Violence | Yes (OK) |
| 5 | 1902 | Canyon Butte Ruin 3 | AZ | W. Hough | Cannibalism | Yes (P) |
| 6 | 1919 | Hawikuh | NM | F. Hodge | Cannibalism | ? |
| 7 | 1920 | Peñasco Blanco | NM | G. Pepper | Cannibalism | Yes (P) |
| 8 | 1920 | Pueblo Bonito | NM | G. Pepper | Cannibalism | Yes (OK) |
| 9 | 1929 | Comb Wash | UT | E. Morris (field notes) | Cannibalism | Yes? |
| 10 | 1929 | Battle Cave | AZ | E. Morris (field notes) | Violence | Yes (P) |
| 11 | 1929 | Charnel House Tower | CO | P. Martin | Violence | Yes (OK) |
| 12 | 1934 | Jack Smith's Houses | AZ | K. Bartlett | Violence | ? |
| 13 | 1939 | La Plata 23 | CO | E. Morris | Cannibalism | Yes (P) |
| 14 | 1939 | La Plata 41 | NM | E. Morris | Cannibalism | Yes (OK) |
| 15 | 1939 | Whitewater District | AZ | F. Roberts, Jr. | Violence | Yes (OK) |
| 16 | 1946 | Alkali Ridge | UT | J. Brew | Violence | Yes (P) |
| 17 | 1949 | Grand Canyon | AZ | E. Reed | Cannibalism | ? |
| 18 | 1952 | House of Tragedy | AZ | W. Smith | Cannibalism | Yes (P) |
| 19 | 1953 | Te'ewi | NM | F. Wendorf, E. Reed | Violence | Yes (P) |
| 20 | 1955 | Turner-Look | UT | M. Wormington | Cannibalism | ? |
| 21 | 1957 | Small House, Chaco | NM | F. Roberts, Jr. | Cannibalism | Yes (P) |
| 22 | 1961 | Coombs Site | UT | C. Turner | Cannibalism | No (P) |
| 23 | 1964 | Mesa Verde 499 | CO | R. Lister | Violence | Yes? |
| 24 | 1966 | Sambrito Village | NM | A. Dittert et al. | Cannibalism | Yes (P) |
| 25 | 1970 | Polacca Wash | AZ | C. Turner & N. Morris | Cannibalism | Yes (P) |
| 26 | 1974 | Leroux Wash | AZ | P. Pilles (Pecos Conf.) | Cannibalism | Yes (P) |
| 27 | 1974 | Casas Grandes, Mexico | — | C. Di Peso | Cannibalism | No |
| 28 | 1974 | Mancos Canyon | CO | P. Nickens (& T. White) | Cannibalism | Yes (OK) |
| 29 | 1976 | Burnt Mesa | NM | L. Flinn et al. | Cannibalism | Yes (P) |
| 30 | 1976 | Huerfano Mesa | NM | J. Chase | Cannibalism | ? |
| 31 | 1976 | Llaves-Alkali Springs | NM | J. Chase | Cannibalism | ? |
| 32 | 1976 | Llaves-Alkali Spr. 2 | NM | J. Chase | Cannibalism | ? |
| 33 | 1976 | Llaves-Alkali Spr. 12 | NM | J. Chase | Cannibalism | ? |
| 34 | 1979 | Largo-Gallina Bg2 | NM | R. Mackey & R. Green | Cannibalism | No (P) |
| 35 | 1979 | Largo-Gallina Bg3 | NM | R. Mackey & R. Green | Cannibalism | No (P) |
| 36 | 1979 | Largo-Gallina Bg20 | NM | R. Mackey & R. Green | Cannibalism | No (P) |
| 37 | 1979 | Largo-Gallina Bg51 | NM | R. Mackey & R. Green | Cannibalism | No (P) |
| 38 | 1979 | Largo-Gallina Bg88B | NM | R. Mackey & R. Green | Violence | Yes (P) |
| 39 | 1979 | Grinnell | CO | P. Nickens | Cannibalism | Yes (OK) |
| 40 | 1980 | Mariana Mesa | NM | C. McGimsey | Violence | Yes (OK) |
| 41 | 1982 | Monument Valley | UT | G. Nass & N. Bellantoni | Cannibalism | Yes (OK) |
| 42 | 1983 | Jones Ranch Road 7 | NM | R. Anyon | Violence | ? |
| 43 | 1983 | Chi Chil Tan 108A | NM | R. Anyon | Violence | ? |
| 44 | 1983 | Ash Creek | AZ | C. Turner | Cannibalism | Yes (P) |
| 45 | 1984 | Chaco 1360 | NM | P. McKenna | Violence | Yes (P) |
| 46 | 1988 | Cottonwood Wash | UT | T. White | Cannibalism | Yes (P) |

*Continued on next page*

*Table 3.1 Continued*

| NO. | DATE | SITE | STATE | CLAIMANT | TYPE | AGREE[a] |
|---|---|---|---|---|---|---|
| 47 | 1988 | Marshview Hamlet | CO | C. Turner | Cannibalism | Yes (P) |
| 48 | 1988 | Rattlesnake Ruin | UT | S. Baker | Cannibalism | Yes (OK) |
| 49 | 1989 | Fence Lake | NM | S. Grant | Cannibalism | Yes (P) |
| 50 | 1989 | Yellow Jacket 5MT-1 | CO | N. Malville | Cannibalism | Yes (OK) |
| 51 | 1989 | Yellow Jacket 5MT-3 | CO | N. Malville | Cannibalism | Yes (OK) |
| 52 | 1989 | Teec Nos Pos | AZ | C. Turner | Cannibalism | Yes (P) |
| 53 | 1991 | Lake Roosevelt | AZ | C. Turner et al. | Violence | Yes (P) |
| 54 | 1992 | Ram Mesa Kiva | NM | M. Ogilvie & T. Hilton | Uncertain[b] | No (OK) |
| 55 | 1992 | Ram Mesa Pithouse | NM | M. Ogilvie & T. Hilton | Uncertain[b] | No (OK) |
| 56 | 1992 | Aztec Wash I 5MT10207 | CO | C. Turner & J. Turner | Cannibalism | Yes (P) |
| 57 | 1992 | Aztec Wash II 5MT10206 | CO | C. Turner & J. Turner | Cannibalism | Yes (P) |
| 58 | 1993 | Aztec Wash III 5MT7723 | CO | M. Dice | Cannibalism? | Yes (OK) |
| 59 | 1993 | Hanson Pueblo | CO | J. Morris et al. | Cannibalism | Yes (OK) |
| 60 | 1993 | La Plata Hwy LA37592 | NM | C. Turner et al. | Cannibalism | Yes (P) |
| 61 | 1993 | La Plata Hwy LA37593 | NM | C. Turner et al. | Cannibalism | Yes (P) |
| 62 | 1993 | La Plata Hwy LA65030 | NM | C. Turner et al. | Cannibalism | Yes (P) |
| 63 | 1993 | Coyote Village | CO | C. Turner et al. | Cannibalism? | Yes (P) |
| 64 | 1993 | St. Christopher's Mission | UT | C. Turner et al. | Cannibalism? | Yes (P) |
| 65 | 1993 | Salmon Ruin | NM | C. Turner et al. | Cannibalism | Yes (P) |
| 66 | 1993 | San Juan River | UT | C. Turner et al. | Cannibalism | Yes (P) |
| 67 | 1993 | Kin Klethla | AZ | J. Haas & W. Creamer | Violence | Yes (OK) |
| 68 | 1993 | Brown Star | AZ | J. Haas & W. Creamer | Violence | Yes (OK) |
| 69 | 1995 | Wupatki | AZ | C. Turner & J. Turner | Violence | Yes (P) |
| 70 | 1995 | Bc51 Chaco[c] | NM | C. Turner & J. Turner | Violence | Yes (P) |
| 71 | 1995 | Guadalupe Ruin | NM | C. Turner & J. Turner | Problematic | ? |
| 72 | 1995 | Mesa Verde 875 | CO | C. Turner & J. Turner | Problematic | ? |
| 73 | 1995 | Betatakin Kiva | AZ | C. Turner & J. Turner | Violence | Yes (P) |
| 74 | 1995 | Houck K | AZ | C. Turner & J. Turner | Cannibalism | Yes (P) |
| 75 | 1995 | Pueblo del Arroyo | NM | C. Turner & J. Turner | Violence | Yes (P) |
| 76 | 1995 | Black Mesa D:7:262 | AZ | C. Turner & J. Turner | Uncertain | Yes (P) |

a. This column denotes whether or not we agree with the original claim. The notation (P) indicates that we have personally examined the human remains in question, and (OK) indicates that the analyst's descriptions and illustrations are so convincing that we feel restudy is unnecessary. A question mark means that we believe study or restudy is desirable.

b. At Ram Mesa the analysts reached no conclusion but the archaeologists involved believed the bone damage was due to cannibalism.

c. Includes other Casa Rinconada–area sites Bc50, Bc53, Bc57, and Bc59.

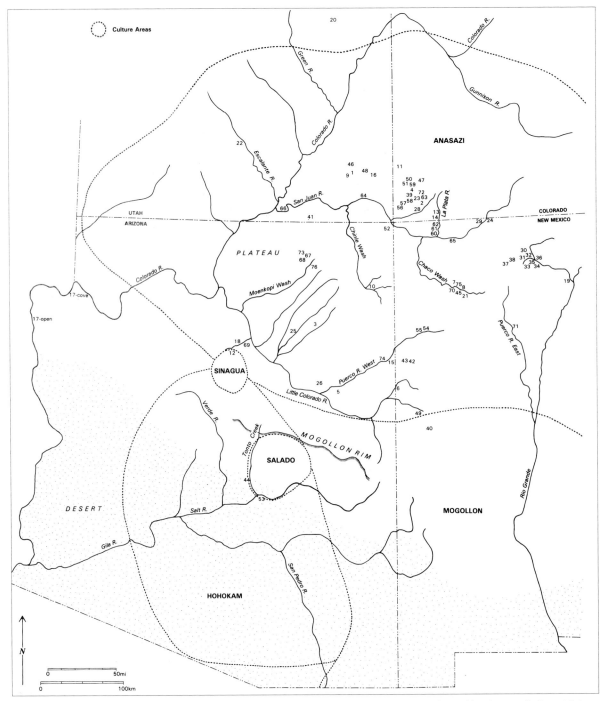

Figure 3.1. Locations of Southwestern sites reviewed in chapter 3, for which claims of violence and/or cannibalism have been made. Numbers are keyed to those in text and in table 3.1. Map by Alison Dean.

**1**
**Cave 7**

**Claim Date.** 1893.

**Claimant.** Richard Wetherill (see fig. 3.60).

**Claim Type.** Violence.

**Other Designations.** 42Sa22180.

**Site Location.** North fork of Whiskers Draw, southeastern Utah, 1,720 m elevation (5,640 feet). USGS Cream Pots quadrangle (provisional edition 1985), T 36S, R 21E, NW ¼ of Sec. 29.

**Site Type.** Dry alcove in vertical-cliffed sandstone canyon.

**Cultural Affiliation.** Anasazi, Basketmaker II stage.

**Chronology.** Preceramic, perhaps ca. A.D. 400.

**Excavators and Date.** Richard Wetherill and associates for the B.T.B. Hyde Exploring Expedition, 1893.

**Institutional Storage.** Department of Anthropology, American Museum of Natural History (AMNH), New York.

**Site Reports.** Wetherill (1893a, 1893b); "H" (1894); Hurst and Turner (1993).

**Osteological Reports.** Turner (1983); Hurst and Turner (1993).

**Skeletal Evidence of Stress.** Nothing substantial. Some subadults have mild or healed porotic hyperostosis.

**Burial Context.** Bodies laid near one another in sterile sand beneath later Puebloan structure and occupation.

**Associated Artifacts.** Stone dart points, knife blades, and a few personal items including pendants, beads, pipes, and "awls."

**Figures.** 3.2–3.10.

**Taphonomy.** CGT and JAT.

*MNI.* Wetherill reported excavating 92 individuals, but we located and studied parts of only 61 in the AMNH. The location of most of the postcranial elements is unknown; according to a letter from Richard Wetherill to Talbot Hyde, dated September 4, 1894, they were not included in the initial shipment of crania belonging to 96 skeletons sent from Mancos, Colorado, to New York (Blackburn and Atkins 1993:86).

*Age and Sex.* Nine subadults and 52 adults. Among the 61 individuals there are 40 males, 15 females, and 6 whose sex could not be determined (hereafter abbreviated "sex?").

*Preservation.* Generally good. Small amounts of soft tissue remain on a few individual bones. Some groundwater damage.

*Bone and Fragment Number.* Not calculated due to missing elements.

*Breakage.* Breakage of cranial and facial bones is extensive. Exact frequency not counted because of missing elements. Most of the damaged crania have one or more perimortem fractures due to severe impact blows from clubs, stone mauls, or axes.

*Cut Marks.* Cut marks are mostly limited to the head region, although a few postcranial bones have cut marks as well. Presumably these bones were sent to New York because Wetherill or someone else recognized the cut marks and the value they might have.

*Burning.* None.

*Anvil Abrasions.* Very few.

*Polishing.* None.

*Vertebrae Number.* Not determinable.

*Scalping.* Yes.

### Richard Wetherill

Historians are seldom neutral in their appraisal of pioneers, and their assessment of Richard Wetherill is no exception. Some Southwestern archaeologists have branded him nothing more than a pot hunter, but it is evident now that this is an unbalanced judgment. We acknowledge this multifaceted rancher, pioneer in archaeology, and Indian trader for his findings and sound interpretations.

In the winter of 1893 Wetherill's outfit was prospecting for antiquities north of Bluff, Utah. In "Cave 7" their venture hit paydirt, some of it scientific. They unearthed stratigraphic, artifactual, and cranial evidence showing the relationship between early Basketmaker and later Puebloan culture. Morever, Wetherill recognized wounds resulting from conflict in some of the 94 predominantly male Basketmaker skeletons, an insight that has seldom been acknowledged.

This scientific bonanza was made possible by support from Talbot Hyde and Fred Hyde, Jr., wealthy brothers whom Wetherill met at the Chicago World's Fair in the summer of 1893. Wetherill had been bitten by the treasure-hunting bug at the age of 30 after discovering Mesa Verde by a guest at his ranch, amateur archaeologist Gustaf E. A. von Nordenskiöld. The Hyde brothers continued to aid Wetherill's wide-ranging Anasazi diggings, including the 1893 excavation of 90 skeletons—now lost—massacred at Snider's Well kiva, the 1895 discovery of Kiet Siel, and his last excavations in 1897–1899 at Pueblo Bonito with young, Harvard-trained George H. Pepper.

Considering Wetherill's broad experience and two discoveries of extraordinary prehistoric violence, we wonder whether he might have influenced Pepper's thinking about cannibalism as the cause of broken and burned bones in Pueblo Bonito and Peñasco Blanco. Seemingly always a gentle man, Wetherill met a violent end, killed by gunfire from a Navajo waiting in ambush.

Life history: b. June 12, 1858, Chester Co., Pa.; d. June 22, 1910, Chaco Canyon, N.M. Attended primary and secondary schools in Fort Leavenworth, Kansas. Married Marietta Palmer, 1896. See McNitt (1966); Blackburn and Williamson (1997).

Figure 3.2. Cave 7 excavation by Hyde Exploring Expedition, Utah, December 1893. Blackburn and Atkins (1993:79) identify these men as, from left to right, Wirt Jenks Billings (front), James Ethridge (rear), Harry French, Al Wetherill, Robert Allen, and John Wetherill. Photographer probably was Charles B. Lang. Courtesy University Museum, University of Pennsylvania (neg. S4-139872).

Figure 3.3. Cave 7. Perimortem trauma breakage of cranial vault, maxilla, and mandible. AMNH 99/7339 (CGT neg.6-25-78:16).

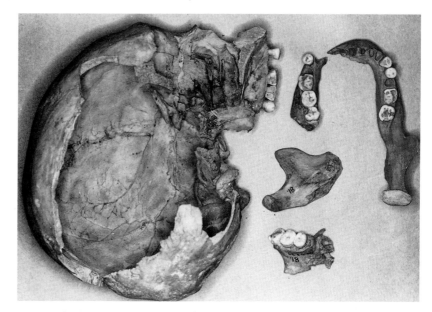

Figure 3.4. Cave 7. Face showing complete loss of cranial vault due to perimortem trauma breakage. AMNH 99/7381, male (CGT neg. 6-25-78:11).

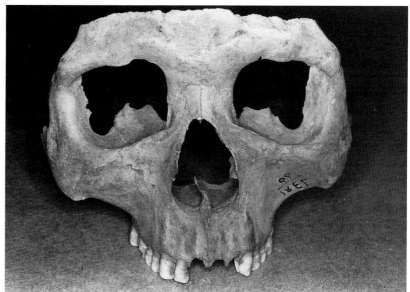

Figure 3.5. Cave 7. Same cranium as that in figure 3.4, showing circular impact blow to left rear aspect of vault. AMNH 99/7381, male (CGT neg. 6-25-78:9).

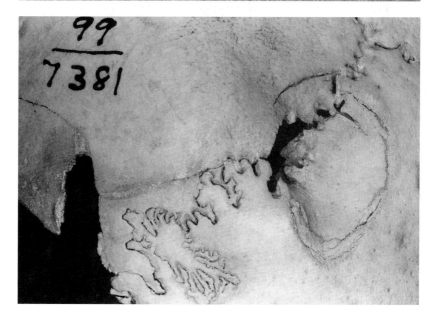

Figure 3.6. Cave 7. Marked fragmentation of head and face caused by repeated blows. AMNH 99/7335, male (CGT neg. 6-25-78:7).

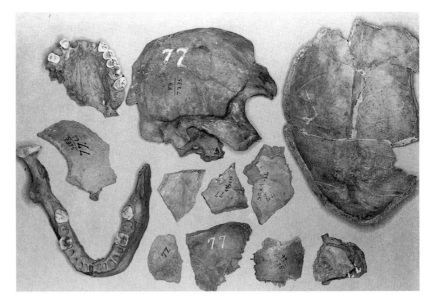

Figure 3.7. Cave 7. Circular penetration wound in left maxilla attributable to pointed, daggerlike wooden or bone weapon. A second facial wound is represented by the smashed right central incisor socket. AMNH 99/7338, male (CGT neg. 6-25-78:14).

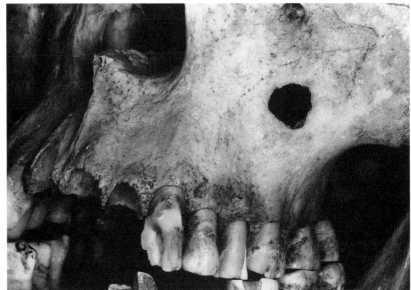

Figure 3.8. Cave 7. Maxilla showing blown-out anterior teeth caused by smashing of the mouth region with a blunt weapon such as a club or baton. AMNH 99/7375, male (CGT neg. 6-25-78:16).

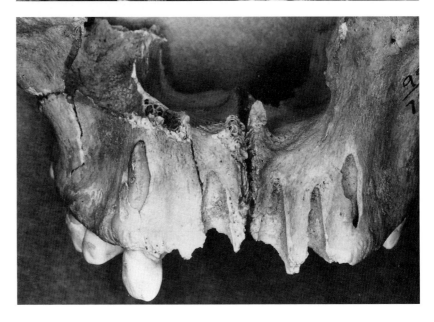

Figure 3.9. Cave 7. Mastoid process with deep cut marks that could have been made with a chopping blow from a large stone knife, presumably in an effort to decapitate this person. AMNH 99/7447, male (CGT neg. 6-25-78:20).

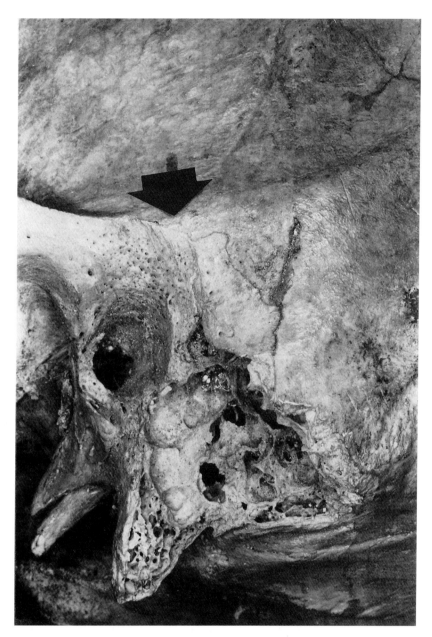

Figure 3.10. Cave 7. A stone point penetrated the ventral surface of this left first rib of an adult male, suggesting a frontal attack by a knife-holding, right-handed assailant. This is the same individual shown in figure 3.7, whose maxilla had been pierced. Both wounds would have been painful but not immediately lethal, suggesting hand-to-hand combat or torture. AMNH 99/7338 (CGT neg. 6-25-78:19).

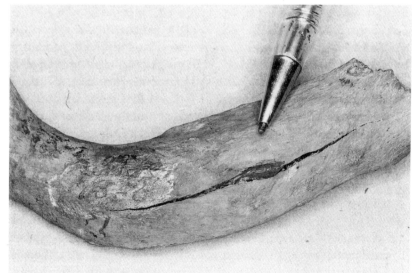

*Gnawing, Rodent.* None.

*Chewing, Carnivore.* None.

*Insect Parts.* None.

*Other Modification.* Various embedded stone points, according to Wetherill; however, we found in the collection only one example, a rib with an embedded stone point tip (fig. 3.10). There was no sign of bone reactivity.

**Archaeologist's Interpretation.** Richard Wetherill (1893a) recognized the importance of the Cave 7 discoveries, as is evident in his letter of December 17, 1893, to Talbot Hyde from "First Valley Cottonwood Creek, 30 Miles North Bluff City":

> [Many skeletons were being found] at a depth of 5 and 6 feet in a cave in which there are cliff dwellings and we find the bodies *under* the ruins, three feet below any cliff dweller sign. They are a *different* race from anything I have ever seen. They had *feather cloth* and baskets, no pottery. Six of the bodies had stone spear heads in them, and what I consider the most valuable find in the History of America is the finding in one joint of the backbone of *skeleton 103* a spear point of stone sticking into the bone at least an inch. . . . One has an arrow shot through the breast bone.

Wetherill (1893b) wrote to Gustaf van Nordenskiöld: "We have back bones with stone spear points still sticking in them and several breast bones shot through with arrows and many broken heads and arms. With these we have not less than (70) seventy stone spear heads." A writer identified only as "H" (1894) reported: "The number of skeletons found at one level and in one place would suggest a sudden and violent destruction of a community by battle or massacre." Winston B. Hurst and C. G. Turner (1993) believe that the article by "H" was Talbot Hyde's submission of Wetherill's remarks.

Recognition of Basketmaker violence at Cave 7 is evident in Richard Wetherill's "First Hyde Collection" field catalog entries (AMNH Anthropology Archives): "Article 89, spear head, found in ribs of [skeleton] 81; article 101, spear head, found in ribs of 100 right side; article 103, skeleton, spear head sticking in back bone; article 106, spear head, found inside of ribs of 76; article 114, spear head, in ribs of 113 point down; article 115, spear head, found with skeleton 117 in ribs point down; article 118, skeleton, head broken; article 136, spear head, in head of 137; article 137, skeleton, head badly broken; article 140, point of spear head, section of back bone of 103; article 198, spear point, found between ribs of right breast."

**Other Interpretations.** None known.

**Discussion.** Our examination of the skeletal remains fully supports Wetherill's interpretation of violence. Figures 3.3–3.10 show the kinds of trauma and wounds the Cave 7 Basketmaker people received. Although a few archaeologists had credited Wetherill for recognizing the Basketmaker-Pueblo chronological sequence—for example, E. H. Morris (1939) and J. O. Brew (1946)—no one had acknowledged his discovery of extreme violence until Hurst and Turner (1993) reviewed the Cave 7 findings.

The pattern of bone damage revealed by the Cave 7 victims, and by others from sites still to be reviewed, shows foremost that violence can cause perimortem breakage in just about any bone, although arms, legs, and heads receive the heaviest damage. Bone surfaces near the fractures generally lack anvil abrasions. Faces receive the most identifiable damage, and mutilation such as stabbing the face (fig. 3.7) or smashing the mouth (fig. 3.8) can sometimes be inferred. There are frequent "blown-out," or ruptured, upper anterior tooth sockets (fig. 3.8), indicating heavy blows directly to the mouth region. We have found experimentally that hitting the crown of a tooth with a hammer breaks the alveolar bone as shown in fig. 3.8 and elsewhere. Stone tool cut marks occur most often on the head and suggest trophy taking of scalps, ears, and sometimes the entire head. A few embedded weapon points are found, but the surrounding bone usually shows no infection or healing, indicating that death occurred relatively soon after the trauma.

The next three sites—Long House, Awatovi, and Snider's Well—also yielded human remains for which claims of violence were proposed. The claims are reasonable, but the types and amounts of evidence available for independent evaluation fall far short of the evidence provided by the extraordinary Cave 7 assemblage, regardless of its incompleteness.

| | |
|---|---|
| **2**<br>**Long House, Mesa Verde** | **Claim Date.** 1893. |

**Claimant.** Gustaf Eric Adolf von Nordenskiöld.

**Claim Type.** Violence and warfare.

**Other Designations.** Ruin 15 (Nordenskiöld 1973); 1200 (Hayes 1964:34); Gila Pueblo survey MV:154 (Hayes 1964:34).

**Site Location.** In a shallow cave about 30.5 m (100 feet) below the canyon rim on the west side of Wetherill Mesa, southwestern Colorado. Cave faces south down Long House Draw, a tributary of Rock Canyon. Longitude 108°30'9" west; latitude 37°11'13" north.

**Site Type.** Cliff house with more than 150 rooms, 21 kivas, a "great kiva," and a defensive wall.

**Cultural Affiliation.** Mesa Verde Anasazi.

**Chronology.** Tree-ring dates of A.D. 1200–1280 (Pueblo III).

**Excavators and Dates.** G. Nordenskiöld (John Wetherill, foreman), 1891; George S. Cattanach, Jr. (with others), 1958–1962.

**Institutional Storage.** National Museum, Helsinki, Finland; Archaeology Research Center, Mesa Verde National Park, Colorado.

**Site Reports.** Nordenskiöld (1973); Cattanach (1980).

**Osteological Reports.** Retzius (1973); Cattanach (1980:ch. 3); Miles (1975).

**Skeletal Evidence of Stress.** None indicated.

**Burial Context.** Human remains found in rooms, kivas, and trash areas. No cemetery exists at the site. There were several "disturbed" burials that we find suspicious, and two burials consisting only of skulls.

Most suspicious is Burial 40 (cat. no. 23685), an adult male (29 ± 1 year) studied by C. F. Merbs, although without forensic or taphonomic considerations. Cattanach (1980:145–146, fig. 125) reported that the head appeared twisted off. The remains were found in the fill and on the floor of Kiva M, mixed with fallen wall and roof materials. Only the torso was found on the kiva floor. The use of Kiva M was abruptly ended by a fire (Cattanch 1980:92).

Burial 38 (cat. no. 23679) is correspondingly of interest. Merbs identified it as an adult male (31 ± 4 years). It was found in the fallen wall debris of Kiva O and was thought to have been a disturbed burial. On page 146 of his report, Cattanach (1980) says that Burial 38 consisted only of one skull. On the same page he notes that two other skulls were found with Burial 38 but were not assigned burial numbers. On page 141, Burial 38 is said to consist of bones of four individuals. Everything considered, there is an interesting taphonomic challenge waiting here.

Burial 39, identified by Merbs as a 1.5- to 2-year-old child, is represented only by a skull found in the trash fill of Kiva K. There are several other burials with missing body parts at this site.

**Associated Artifacts.** None.

**Figures.** None

**Taphonomy.** None.

*MNI.* "Forty occurrences of human remains were designated as 'burials'" (Cattanach 1980:141), but there is no identifiable taphonomic workup for MNI.

*There is no information for Age and Sex, Preservation, Bone and Fragment Number, Breakage, Cut Marks, Burning, Anvil Abrasions, Polishing, Vertebrae Number, Scalping, Gnawing, Chewing, or Insect Parts.*

*Other Modification.* Some body parts were removed at some time during individual burial histories.

**Archaeologists' Interpretations.** Nordenskiöld (1973:29) wrote: "Though the inhabitants of Long House [on the basis of their defensive architecture], were admirably prepared for defence, still there are indications to suggest that they eventually succumbed to their enemies. Human bones—ribs, vertebrae, etc.—are strewn in numbers here and there among the ruins. . . . Perhaps too [because of the low yield of artifacts in Long House] the place had been entirely plundered of any articles of special value by victorious enemies."

Nordenskiöld (1973:35) remarked that Richard Wetherill had found a mummy in Ruin 16, north of Long House: "It had not been buried, but lay in an estufa [kiva], half within the tunnel which I have spoken of [earlier]. It was the body of a man, probably one of the ancient inhabitants of the cliff-dwelling who had fallen in defence of his hearth and home. The position seemed to indicate that he had tried to escape from the estufa by the said passage."

Cattanach (1980:141) felt that the evidence for violence at Long House was inconclusive: "It is possible to speculate that the later occupants of Long House moved into the rock shelter for defensive purposes, as suggested by the apertures . . . in the breastworks. However, there is no evidence in the relatively few burials from Long House that an attack had ever been made directly upon the pueblo."

**Other Interpretations.** James S. Miles (1975:24), writing of the Long House skeletal conditions, noted that "none of the fractures appeared to be the result of warfare. There were no depressed skull fractures, and no arrowheads or other foreign bodies imbedded in bone."

Cattanach (1980:147) included a fascinating but noninterpretive 1964 FBI report, part of which said that "a microscopic examination of eight hair specimens screened from human feces . . . [shows that] all of the hairs are human head hairs of Mongoloid origin. Most of them are dark reddish-brown and a few are black." Tim White (1992:340), in discussing the criteria he and others used to hypothesize cannibalism, wrote: "The only higher level of inference would be that in which cannibalism was only to be inferred upon the recovery of human bones such as terminal phalanges from within demonstrably human coprolites." We wonder how often human hair has been identified in archaeologically derived human feces and whether White would allow hair as well as bone for preeminent testimony—probably not, considering how often hair is found in food.

**Discussion.** Although the human remains from Long House were studied by human biology specialists Merbs, Miles, and, additionally, Frederick S. Hulse and Kenneth A. Bennett (Cattanach 1980:141), only Miles seems to have attended to taphonomic or forensic considerations. For this reason, we believe that a systematic reexamination of the Long House skeletal remains along taphonomic lines would be useful. At this writing, however, local representatives of the U.S. Department of Interior–National Park Service have decided to disallow human skeletal research on Mesa Verde National Park collections.

# 3
# Awatovi

**Claim Date.** 1893.

**Claimant.** Jesse Walter Fewkes (fig. 3.11).

**Claim Type.** Violence.

**Other Designations.** NA820.

**Site Location.** About 4.5 km (3 miles) southwest of Keams Canyon, northeastern Arizona. USGS Egloffstein Butte quadrangle (1966), T 27N, R 19E, SW ¼ of SW ¼ of Sec. 23.

**Site Type.** Large prehistoric and historic multistoried village.

**Cultural Affiliation.** Western Pueblo (Hopi).

**Chronology.** Occupied from late prehistoric times to 1700. According to Hopi oral tradition, Awatovi was sacked during a secretly planned massacre of the town's inhabitants by Hopi warriors from other villages at the request of Awatovi's chief. F. W. Hodge (1912:119) stated that Awatovi numbered 800 people at that time, a number in line with the 1664 counts for Oraibi (1,236) and Shungopovi (830) cited by J. O. Brew (1949:17).

**Excavators and Dates.** J. W. Fewkes, 1892, 1895 (Fewkes 1899). In the 1930s, J. O. Brew led excavations for the Peabody Museum, Harvard University, but they were not focused on the massacre issue (Brew n.d., 1937, 1939, 1941, 1949; Smith 1992).

**Institutional Storage.** The small amount of skeletal material from Awatovi that Fewkes saved is curated at the Department of Anthropology, National Museum of Natural History (NMNH), Smithsonian Institution, Washington, D.C. The more extensive Peabody Museum finds—largely irrelevant to this study—are at Harvard University, Cambridge, Massachusetts.

**Site Report.** Fewkes (1899). Fewkes (1893a) earlier published a short

## Jesse Walter Fewkes

J. W. Fewkes started his scientific career as an assistant in Harvard University's Museum of Comparative Zoology, having studied to be a taxonomic marine biologist. He eventually published some 70 papers in that field. In 1887 he crossed the continent for a collecting trip on the coast of California, stopping on the way to see Pueblo Indians. They must have impressed Fewkes immensely because two years later he had abandoned marine biology and was conducting ethnological fieldwork among the Zunis as director of the Hemenway Southwestern Archaeological Expedition.

In 1891 he began fieldwork among the Hopis, which led to many discoveries, including his parallel ethnographic and archaeological investigations that corroborated Hopi legends about the surprise attack on Awatovi and its 800 inhabitants in 1700. Fewkes was well received by the Hopis, even being initiated into the Walpi Antelope and Flute societies. On First Mesa he was called Nakwipi (Boiled Medicine), according to Harry C. James (1974:194).

By May 1895 Fewkes had been appointed ethnologist in the Bureau of American Ethnology, and he became chief in 1918. He remained with the Smithsonian Institution until his retirement in 1928, publishing some 200 monographs, articles, and comments in ethnography and archaeology. Among his extensive travels and writings were trips to Casas Grandes, Chihuahua, and pioneering and lasting contributions to the study of Mesoamerican sources of Southwestern Indian culture.

Fewkes met Richard Wetherill in 1895, along with Columbia University's T. M. Prudden, whom Wetherill had escorted to the Hopi Snake Dance that summer at Walpi. Fewkes had resumed his Awatovi excavations and conceivably discussed them with Wetherill and Prudden. His last fieldwork, at age 75, took place during the summer of 1926 at Elden Pueblo near Flagstaff; his wife and constant field companion, Harriet Olivia (Cutler), accompanied him.

Life history: b. November 14, 1850, Newton, Mass., d. May 31, 1930, after an operation in April 1925 from which he never fully recovered. Educated Harvard University, natural history, with honors, 1875; M.A. and Ph.D., 1877; additional study with Louis Agassiz; two years postdoctoral study in Europe. See Hough (1932), Swanton and Roberts (1931).

Figure 3.11. Jesse Walter Fewkes and Harriet Olivia Cutler Fewkes (both seated), at Elden Pueblo (NA142), near Flagstaff, Arizona, 1926. Fewkes was still actively pursuing archaeological research a quarter-century after his initial 1892 Awatovi excavations. Standing are J. P. Harrington and Mrs. J. C. Clarke; the woman in the background is not identified. Photographer unknown. Museum of Northern Arizona Archive photograph, original negative in Smithsonian Institution National Anthropological Archives (Arizona 360-C).

paper on the destruction of Awatovi and the killing of most of the captives, based on his 1891 and 1892 archaeological and ethnographic fieldwork.

**Osteological Report.** The Awatovi skeletal remains have been used in many topical physical anthropology reports, but we know of no taphonomic analysis of the skeletons found by Fewkes or Brew. Although we examined the Awatovi collection, we decided not to do a detailed taphonomic study because few of the most important remains, those excavated under Fewkes's direction, were saved, and the mission skeletons found by the Peabody Museum expedition represent deaths from before the massacre in 1700.

**Skeletal Evidence of Stress.** Porotic hyperostosis is evident in some crania. By late Pueblo III times, porotic hyperostosis is common in most Anasazi skeletal series. Hence, it has little value as an indicator of inter- or intrasite differences in nutritional or health stress.

**Burial Context.** Fewkes reported finding many human bones at the eastern end of Awatovi. Brew and associates recovered several burials from the mission and mission buildings. The skull and facial shape of one of the Peabody mission skeletons looked European to us.

**Associated Artifacts.** Unknown.

**Figures.** 3.12–3.14.

**Taphonomy.** We did not systematically examine the remains for reasons already indicated.

*MNI.* 3. Fewkes did not save all of the skeletal material he excavated at Awatovi. Moreover, it is uncertain precisely where in Awatovi these individuals were found.

*Age and Sex.* A young adult female and two adult males.

*Preservation.* Poor to good.

*Bone and Fragment Number.* Not determined.

*Breakage.* Yes, in all three individuals.

*Cut Marks.* On the female only.

*Burning.* Yes.

*Anvil Abrasions.* Yes, on the female.

*Polishing.* None.

*Vertebrae Number.* Not determinable.

*Scalping.* Yes. At the very least the female was scalped, as is evidenced by cut marks on her frontal and left temporal bones (fig. 3.13).

*Gnawing, Rodent.* None.

*Chewing, Carnivore.* None.

*Insect Parts.* None.

*Other Modification.* None.

*Individual Damage.* SI 156324, female, has cut marks on right half of frontal including cuts or abrasions along the upper border of the right orbit. The left side of the frontal has two patches of abrasions (10 x 8 mm and 10 x 5 mm) between temporal border and temporal suture. Face was not mutilated. SI 156325, male, has sockets of upper incisors and right canine broken, probably by a blow to the face. SI 156326, male, has breakage of nose, right mastoid, and skull base.

**Archaeologist's Interpretation.** Fewkes's original field notes are curated in the National Anthropological Archives, Smithsonian Institu-

70

Figure 3.12. Awatovi, Arizona. Young adult female skull NMNH 156-324, excavated by J. W. Fewkes, showing perimortem cuts and abrasions on right half of frontal bone (CGT neg. 4-27-94:32).

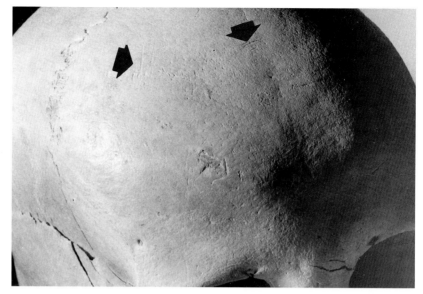

Figure 3.13. Awatovi. Close-up of skull shown in figure 3.12 (NMNH 156-324), showing in detail the frontal bone cuts (upper right) and abrasions (left and lower right). Actual width of the area in the image is 3.5 cm. The woman likely had her scalp removed before she received the blow to her forehead; otherwise the soft tissue would have interfered with the direct stone-to-bone contact attested to by the abrasion marks (CGT neg. 4-27-94:29).

Figure 3.14. Awatovi. Adult, sex?, NMNH 156-326, excavated by J. W. Fewkes, showing perimortem damage to skull base and right mastoid. The mastoid process has been largely broken off by what appears to have been a crushing rather than a severing blow. There are no identifiable cut marks or abrasions (CGT neg. 4-27-94:26).

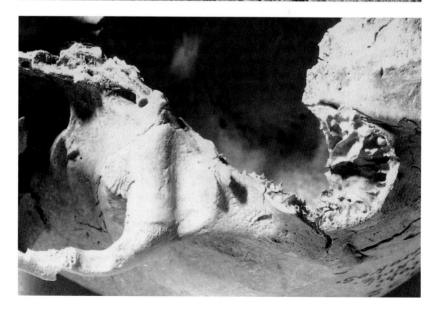

tion. We examined them on November 18, 1993, and May 26, 1995, a century or so after they had been penned. In file 4408(11), field notes titled "Moqui, 1891" (Fewkes 1895:134) contain his earliest known comment on Awatovi:

> June 3. Visited *O-wa-to-be* which lies about 9 miles from Keam's Canon, and the same or about the same from Wal-pi. The legend is that this town was destroyed by the Oraibes, middle mesa and first mesa. The Mi-shuno-ves took prisoners of women, and consider themselves related to *O-wa-to-be*. Walpis did not take women. Alosekas from Owa-to-be. Mishunnis [unreadable word] them. Tom [Keam?] thinks trouble between O-wa-to-be and other mesas arose because O-watobes adopted Mexican religion prevented rain. He has heard that the three mesas combined, to [unreadable] went to each home and killed the males. He also thinks trouble arose on account of rabbit hunt fracas.

In one of the earliest uses of archaeology to test Southwestern ethnographic information and folklore (if not *the* earliest), Fewkes in the following year, on June 7, 1892, began digging in the legendary massacre area of Awatovi, aided by hired Hopi workmen. The spelling in the following description is his (Fewkes 1895[13], un-numbered page):

> The Po-wa-ka (wizard) kibva is a square structure in the enclosure near mission. It is a square structure subterraneaous/Excavated part in pit and found ashes and human bones, thus substantuating the traditional account. Excavated to floor. Indians recognized this as the Po-wa-ko kibva. Made a section through middle of the kib-va and found good skulls, leg bones etc. Also evidences of fire in abundance // Skull found in the middle of the excavation on the floor // A great number of skeletons at the S.E. corner of the rec-tangle beyond the missi[o]n.

One of Fewkes's several rough sketch maps of Awatovi shows the village as a rectangular area with a gateway on the east side and a church outline in the southeast corner. The south wall of the church is near a cliff edge. There are no more 1892 Awatovi notes and sketches after June 25, suggesting that Fewkes spent about two weeks digging there.

Three years later he was back digging at Awatovi once more (NAA file 4408(21), July 1895, unnumbered page):

> No more bones found in these rooms. Evidently no slaughter here but in the corner of the court at East of Church; the hum[an] long bones the hum[an] bones—these were all thrown together promis-cously [*sic*]—And the Hopi workman said this must be the place where the slaughter occurred. A reexamination of the south East of the court shows hum[an] bones thrown in; At that point if any-where the slaughter occurred—Bone not regularly thrown in there, no pottery etc. Evidently here was holocaust.

In a separate notebook (Fewkes n.d.:22), he made the briefest of
notes on what two Hopis told him in 1895 about Awatovi (unnumbered page):

Masiumptiwa's story of Awatobi—*Honani Badger.* Oraibi, Mi-
cunovi and Walpi joined together. Sitcomovi & Hano not on the
first mesa when event happened.
Phratries

| Awata nynim | Owakulti | These three came |
| Honan    " | Mamzranti | from Awatovi |
| Pakut | Mirmtcumli | |
| Piba | | |
| Patki | Tcino remembered an old man who when a | |
| Pikas | boy remembered an old man who was a boy | |
| Flute | when Awato—destroyed 60 + 60=120 + 60=180 | |
| Tcua | | |

Oraibi came to Walpi at four o'clock. Micañ came to Walpi at
night fall.

The numbers are Fewkes's assumptions for the spans of the three
generations since Awatovi was destroyed. This estimate of 180 years
earlier placed the event at 1715—close to 1700, the date of destruction that scholars would later agree upon. Fewkes obviously was intrigued by the Awatovi legend and ruin, although, as can be sensed
from the foregoing quotations, his note taking and record keeping
were minimal. Nevertheless, seven years after he began digging in
Awatovi, Fewkes (1899:610–612) published the following account:

There is good evidence that a massacre of Awatobians occurred in
the southeastern angle of the eastern part of the pueblo, just east of
the mission. If so, it is probable that many of the unfortunates
sought refuge in the outbuildings of the church. Suspecting that
such was the case, I excavated a considerable space of ground at
these places and found many human skulls and other bones
thrown together in confusion. The earth was literally filled with
bones, evidently hastily placed there or left where the dead fell.
These bodies were not buried with pious care, for there were no
fragments of mortuary pottery or other indication of burial objects. Many of the skulls were broken, some pierced with sharp implements. . . . According to the legends, the hostiles entered the
pueblo through the adjacent gateway; their anger led them especially against those of the inhabitants who were regarded as
*powako* or sorcerers, and their first acts of violence would naturally have been toward those who sought refuge in the buildings
adjacent the church. Near this hated "Singing-house" the slaughter
began, soon extending to the kivas and the whole of the eastern
section of the village. There was no evidence of murderous deeds in
the rooms of the western section of the old pueblo, and the legends
agree in relating that most of the men were in kivas, not far from
the mission, when the village was overthrown.

In 1892, while removing the soil from a depression about the

middle of the eastern court of Awatovi, about 100 feet north of the
northern wall of the mission, I laid bare a room 28 by 14 feet, in
which were found a skull and many other human bones which,
from their disposition, had not been buried with care. The discovery of these skeletons accorded with the Hopi traditions that this
was one of the rooms in which the men of Awatobi were gathered
on the fatal night, and the enclosure where many died. I was de-
terred from further excavation at that place by the horror of my
workmen at the desecration of the chamber. In 1895, however, I
determined to continue my earlier excavations and to trace the
course of the walls of the adjacent rooms.

Although Fewkes's notes and published accounts do not indicate
from whom he gathered all the oral traditions relative to Awatovi's
destruction (we suspect that one source was A. M. Stephen), there is
no doubt that his empirical findings are consistent with the Hopi oral
tradition. That tradition continues with an account of what happened
to most of the Awatovians taken captive and their maltreatment at
another location that we think is the Polacca Wash charnel deposit
(site number 25 in this chapter) where at least 30 individuals were
killed and mutilated (Turner and Morris 1970).

**Other Interpretations.** The 43 human skeletons that Brew (n.d.) found
were burials under the floor of what he called Spanish Church B.
These would have predated the destruction of Awatovi in 1700. In his
1937 progress report, Brew made no mention of human skeletons either in or outside of the kivas that were excavated. In 1949, he mentioned church burials but said nothing about finding any individuals
who might have died during the sacking of Awatovi.

Many years later, Watson Smith (1992) recalled some of the work
done by the Peabody Museum Awatovi Expedition of 1936–1939, of
which he was a permanent staff member. Prior to Smith's narrative it
was uncertain whether the expedition had made any attempt to relocate and reexcavate Fewkes's burned and bone-littered kiva. Smith
(1992:150) said that they did find "evidences of burning and also a
few human bones, but hardly enough evidence to warrant Fewkes'
conclusion." There are two points that undermine this remark. First,
it was published only a year before Smith died at the age of 96, a half-
century after the Peabody Museum excavations were conducted. A
50-year-old recollection has to be weighed against observations written down at the time of, or soon after, excavation, as Fewkes's were.
Second, the limited quantity of human remains found by the Peabody
Museum workers could reflect either Fewkes's having already removed most of the skeletons or the two parties' not having excavated
in the same area—a possibility, considering that Fewkes did not publish an excavation map and his field drawings were sketchy at best.

The various reports and monographs that resulted from the
Peabody Museum Awatovi Expedition make no mention of trauma-
tized human skeletal remains such as Fewkes (1899) reported. Ac-
cordingly, in February 1993 the senior author searched through the
Awatovi skeletal collection at the Peabody Museum, with help from
Lane Beck and her assistants. Two sets of remains were found with

perimortem damage. Burial 90 (N3227), an adult male, had cut marks on his mandible and all over the top of his skull. Burial 122, an individual of unknown sex found in room 444, had cut marks on the forehead. Both indviduals seem to have been scalped, and the former shows every indication of having had at least his head defleshed. Because Brew did not report on Awatovi burials, it remains unknown—at least until time-consuming archival research in Brew's field notes can be done—whether these two individuals were victims of the probable Hopi attack on Awatovi in 1700 or of some earlier conflict.

Notes written by Fray José Narváez Valverde (1937:386) in 1732 identify 1700 as the year when the Hopis attacked Awatovi, an attack Narváez said involved more than 100 warriors led by an Indian named Espeleta. All the Awatovi braves were killed, the women were taken captive, and the town was left "desolate and unpeopled." The dating for the Awatovi massacre, secure in Brew's time (1949:89) with a final tree-ring date of 1700, continues to be strengthened. John P. Wilson (1972) found a Spanish historical document (dated at Santa Fe, September 18, 1701) in the Biblioteca Nacional in Madrid supporting the oral tradition of a Hopi attack on Awatovi that was responsible for its destruction. He points out that this document is also the earliest one known dealing with the destruction of Awatovi and that it confirms the year of attack.

Albert Yava (1978:92–93) was told much the same legend about the destruction of Awatovi, with some details that Fewkes may have left unpublished:

The chief of Awatovi said, "I promised that the Oraibis can take all the women. You Walpi Reed Clan people, you can have all the land and the fields, because they are too far away from the Oraibis. The land is yours, the women are theirs. . . . [The attackers from Oraibi, Walpi, and Mishongnovi waited outside Awatovi until the signal to attack was given by the Awatovi chief.] They stormed into Awatovi, and the first thing they did was to pull the ladders out of all the kivas, trapping the men who were sleeping or having ceremonies down there. They threw burning cedar bark, firewood and crushed chili peppers into the kivas, so that everyone down below was suffocated. They also did this to many of the houses, which had their entrances through the roofs. They killed anyone they caught, men or old women. They herded the young women and children out of the village and took them to a place that is now called Skull Ridge or Skull Mound. There they killed quite a few of their captives. This spot is called Skull Mound because after the Awatovi affair people used to find a lot of skulls there. . . . After leaving Skull Mound, the war party marched its captives to another place. There was some more killing there. They killed any old men or old women who happened to be among the prisoners. . . . There are long stories about this destruction containing a great many details, but I have indicated the main events.

Ekkehart Malotki and colleagues (1993:399–403) collected a version of the Awatovi story that went this way:

The attackers climbed to the top of the mesa and began the assault.
There were many of them, so many in fact that they filled the village of Awat'ovi. They exactly followed the orders they had received. Running from kiva to kiva, they found that the men were
inside. Immediately, they pulled out the ladders . . . [and] lit the [ju-
niper bark] . . . which they hurled into the kivas. Next, they set the
wood stacks on top of the kivas aflame and threw them down
through the hatches. Then they shot their arrows down on the
men. . . . Now the raiders stormed into all the houses. Wherever
they came across a man, no matter whether young or old, they
killed him. Some they simply grabbed and cast into a kiva. Not a
single man or boy did they spare. . . . [The raiders] once more,
went from house to house. Wherever they found an old man they
cut him down. Old women they killed too. Younger women and
girls they herded together. . . . [The raiders then] attacked the
houses themselves. Whatever would burn, they set aflame, the
buildings and their wood stacks. Awat'ovi presented a terrible
sight. It had been turned into a ruin.

Peter Whiteley (1988:21–22) learned of the same story, with a focus on the planning of the massacre at the Awatovi chief's behest:

Tapolo, the *Kikmongwi* [chief] [of Awatovi] was convinced that it
was now beyond his power to re-create harmony among his
people. Those people who favored the Kastilam [Spanish mission-
aries] were obviously *popwaqt,* 'witches,' and would have to be
eradicated. So he visited secretly at night with Espeleta and with
the leaders of Mishongnovi, Shongopavi, and Walpi. With each
leader, he sat and smoked and told them of his plan: "My children
(meaning his people) have become evil. They are engaging in
witchcraft and conspiring with the Kastilam [Castilians]. I have
been thinking about it for a long time and can see no other solu-
tion. My village must be destroyed—razed to the ground, so that
Awat'ovi will be no more." The other leaders pondered his suggestion. They knew that this was how other villages had been destroyed—Pivanhonkyapi, Palatkwapi, Sikyatki, and even the third
world below—but still this, though a chief's prerogative, was an
extreme measure, to be undertaken only in the direst of circumstances. Tapolo himself would have to die in the process, as well as
his sons—this was how such matters were arranged in the Hopi
way. So this was an act of great sacrifice on his part, to benefit the
rest of the Hopi people. The evil would be rooted out and mankind
purified.

Yava (1978:37–38) provided additional information that enables
us to view Awatovi's destruction not as unique but as one of several
incidents in a long-standing tradition of repeated conflict and violence: "The people of Sikyatki had to go away because of evil things
that had occurred, and because of enmity with Keuchaptevela, the old
Walpi. . . . The Snake Clan had to leave Tokonave because of friction
with other people in the village. The chief of Pivanhonkapi had his

village destroyed because, as in the case of Awatovi, the people had turned away from decent living. The Payupkis abandoned their village because of quarrels with nearby Tsikuvi. Oraibi was broken in two by dissension."

Cosmos Mindeleff (1891:25) recorded the story of the destruction of Sikyatki, in which "nearly all of the Sikyátki men were killed, but some of them escaped to Oraibi and some to Awatubi [sic]. A number of the girls and younger women were spared, and distributed among the different villages, where they became wives of their despoilers." H. R. Voth (1905) independently collected legends about the destruction of both Sikyatki and Awatovi. His accounts are very much like those cited.

It takes little imagination to envision the sort of quarrelsomeness that Yava, Mindeleff, and Voth describe for the Hopis as having been common in the prehistoric Southwest, given the description of the Cave 7 Basketmaker massacre and several more to follow. The motivation described in legend for the nighttime massacre of the Awatovi townspeople and the subsequent killing and mutilation of captives provides an analogue for understanding other, earlier charnel deposits and mass burials.

Discussion. Legends of the destruction of Awatovi and Fewkes's pioneering method of verification by direct archaeological investigation in the appropriate part of the ruins represent two independent lines of evidence that he developed in the course of his Tusayan research. Fewkes's findings are undeniable, despite his failure to save all skeletal remains and his Victorian decision to publish a mild version of the Awatovi captive story. Ancillary evidence of an extremely violent episode is provided by the perimortem trauma on Awatovi crania and by the Polacca Wash charnel deposit discussed later (see figs. 3.121–3.135). We suspect that one of Fewkes's unpublished versions of the Awatovi captive story, in addition to telling about the mutilation, killing, and dismemberment of women and children, also mentioned that victims were burned and that cannibalism had occurred. We suspect that Yava likewise recognized Anglo abhorrence of cannibalism and refrained from telling about the cooking of the captives. Moreover, we are not entirely dependent on Fewkes or the others cited for the legendary account. George Wharton James (1901, 1917) agreed with Fewkes because he had heard the same legend several times from different Hopis. In 1967 we, too, were told the Awatovi story by a Hopi woman who, along with other Hopis, pointed out to us the direction of Skeleton Hill. The Polacca Wash charnel deposit was in the general direction they indicated.

The legendary attack on Awatovi was neither unique, as Yava and others have noted, nor due solely to the presence of Europeans at Awatovi, as has been claimed by recent Indian apologists and historic revisionists. There was no mission at Sikyatki, which, according to James (1917:92–93), received a similar attack just before or shortly after the arrival of Spanish explorers in northeastern Arizona. This attack, too, involved taking the pueblo by surprise, overwhelming and killing the males, laying waste to the village, and making captives of the women and children.

In regard to the Peabody Museum's reexcavation of Fewkes's

burned kiva and to Smith's rejection of Fewkes's claim for having found a great deal of human bone, it must be asked, how much burning and and how much bone is needed to demonstrate that a violent act occurred? There is no question that Fewkes's work was not up to the technical standards of his time. Richard Wetherill was already keeping stratigraphic and spatial records, doing field inventorying of artifacts and skeletons, and making photographs. Fewkes's accomplishments, like those of many other pioneers in science and exploration, can be ignored or negated owing to his faults. But it was not Fewkes who claimed that Awatovi had been sacked and captives massacred; it was, and continues to be, Hopis themselves who keep this oral tradition alive.

Scientific reconstruction of prehistoric events, however, almost always demands physical evidence; oral traditions are rarely considered sufficient. Despite the good register of the combined lines of evidence for the Awatovi–Polacca Wash massacre, we recognize that our acceptance of it is not shared by all Southwestern scholars. Notwithstanding the several versions of the legendary destruction of Awatovi and related killing of the captives, not a single rock art scene, kiva drawing, or painted hide is known to depict this event. But perhaps the scientific requirement should be tempered in recognition that prehistoric Indians did not live in a world of written words as we do today. R. C. Padden (1967:xiii–xiv) made this incisive point regarding the Aztecs: "The imperial Aztecs were meticulous keepers of records, a fact more remarkable when one considers that beyond the glyph they were entirely dependent upon the sense of hearing and the power of memory. . . . The entire realm of Aztec intellect was one primarily associated with vocal sounds rather than written words." The prehistoric emphasis on memory and oral tradition instead of written records suggests that we should not expect to find many glyphs, drawings, designs, or other nonoratory sources to help us comprehend Anasazi cannibalism. In the context of the nearly pure sound-and-memory form of record keeping in North American prehistory, we should be prepared to give folklore more credence as a source of information about prehistoric events than is currently done. This is not to argue for a return to the ways of Fewkes and his often literal acceptance of Pueblo Indian migration myths. Instead, we propose that legendary accounts of violence be accepted as evidence complimentary to the physical finds we have described.

Taken together, the Awatovi–Polacca Wash multiple associations—bioarchaeological, chronometric, taphonomic, locational, contextual, historic documentary, and legendary—provide the preeminent standard against which to assess by taphonomic means other reconstructions of probable violence and cannibalism in the archaeological record of the American Southwest. The Cave 7 and Awatovi victims demonstrate that large-scale violence occurred even in the preceramic days of Anasazi history and continued into historic times. At best, Fewkes and later workers found skeletal elements representing far fewer individuals than the presumed 800 villagers at Awatovi. Perhaps 50 women and children survived the horror. This crude ratio should be kept in mind when considering how many traumatized skeletons need be recovered before a massacre can be proposed. Even in an extensively excavated village, a few bodies in certain contexts can signal large-scale violence.

## 4
## Snider's Well

**Claim Date.** 1893 (letter by Richard Wetherill to B.T.B. Hyde); 1894 (note by Wetherill published in *Archaeologist*).

**Claimant.** Richard Wetherill.

**Claim Type.** Violence.

**Other Designations.** Aztec Springs; Yucca House; NA3299; 5MT5006.

**Site Location.** In the Yucca House group of ruins in Montezuma Valley, southwestern Colorado. USGS Towaoc quadrangle (1966), T 35N, R 17W, NE ¼ of Sec. 35.

**Site Type.** Large Chacoan outlier pueblo. Human remains found in painted kiva about 6.4 m (21 feet) in diameter and 3 m (10 feet) or more deep.

**Cultural Affiliation.** Architecturally similar to Mesa Verde.

**Chronology.** Later Pueblo period, based on the presence of cranial deformation, large corrugated pots, and large deep circular kiva. Yucca House has three tree-ring dates of A.D. 1163, 1229, and 1263, according to William J. Robinson and Bruce G. Harrill (1974:38), who suggest that "occupation in the 13th century is indicated by these few dates."

**Excavators and Date.** Richard Wetherill, his brothers Al and John Wetherill, and probably others of the Hyde Exploring Expedition, April 1893.

**Institutional Storage.** Unknown. Three years of searching has failed to locate the skeletal assemblage.

**Site Reports.** Wetherill first wrote to B.T.B. Hyde on March 20, 1893, briefly describing the find at Snider's Well. On June 24, 1894, Wetherill sent a letter about the excavation to Warren K. Moorehead, editor of *Archaeologist* (Ohio Archaeological and Historical Society), who published it in the September 1894 issue of the magazine.

**Osteological Report.** None known.

**Skeletal Evidence of Stress.** Unknown.

**Burial Context.** Skeletons lying on and near kiva floor.

**Associated Artifacts.** One excavation photograph shows pottery vessels arranged with skeletons for photography.

**Figure.** 3.15 (see also Blackburn and Atkins 1993:84).

**Taphonomy.** RW.

*MNI.* Possibly as many as 90 individuals. In Wetherill's letter to Hyde in March 1893 he wrote:

> Our last trip out up to Blue Mountain has been very successful having found a pair of war clubs, one looks like a baseball bat. The other a policeman's billet of elk horn, very heavy and strung on small end. Another back bone with one leg attached, with spear point in it yet. . . . On the way home I will stop at Snyder's in Montezuma Valley. They have started a well there and dug down about *twelve feet* and *struck a layer of skeletons* and have now taken out about fifty and many more in sight. I will finish the work then.

Figure 3.15. Completed excavation of Snider's Well kiva at Yucca House (Aztec Springs), Colorado. Numerous human bones were stacked between James Ethridge and Wirt Jenks Billings for photography, but not enough to represent 90 individuals. The ground surface, barely distinguishable at skyline, suggests the kiva was 3.0 to 3.5 m (10 to 12 feet) deep. Photograph probably taken by Charles Lang, 1894. B. T. B. Hyde gift, 1923–31, courtesy American Museum of Natural History (acc. no. 67) (CGT copy neg. 5-3-94:16).

The caption of one excavation photograph in the AMNH Department of Anthropology archives says that 90 skeletons had been found. The bone pile shown in figure 3.15 is substantial. Like Cave 7, Snider's Well contained a very large charnel deposit. If Wetherill was correct about the number of individuals, then the kiva contained the largest number of bodies ever found in a single prehistoric Southwestern architectural unit.

*Age and Sex.* The bones that can be safely identified in the excavation photographs are those of adults and near-adults.

*Preservation.* Excavation photographs suggest good preservation.

*Bone and Fragment Number.* Hundreds of bones were found, judging from the bone pile in one of the excavation photographs (fig. 3.15).

*Breakage.* Yes, but articulation was evident, and most of the bones in the excavation photographs appear complete.

*There is no information for Cut Marks, Burning, Anvil Abrasions, Polishing, Vertebrae Number, Scalping, Gnawing, Chewing, or Insect Parts.*

*Other Modification.* Wetherill reported that some crania had stone axe impact holes.

Archaeologist's Interpretation. Wetherill's published letter (1894:288) stated:

> In the fore part of April [1893] we worked out what was known as Snider's Well . . . on a long, narrow ridge, southwest of Aztec Springs, near the site of the large ruins in Montezuma County, Colorado. . . . At a depth of ten feet we came upon a mass of skeletons that had originally been thrown into the room in a haphazard manner. All of the skulls saved had each a hole in it such as would be made by striking it with a stone axe. Of the twenty-five specimens examined, all proved to be of the cliff dweller's type, having the perpendicular [cradle board] flattening at the back of the head. The skulls from the regular burial mounds in the vicinity have the oblique flattening upon the back of the head, showing there must be some distinction between the races. We infer from this discovery that these skeletons must have been prisoners or captives killed and thrown in this estufa.

Other Interpretations. None known.

Discussion. The Yucca House group of ruins was recognized early in the history of scientific exploration of the Southwest as one of the major prehistoric site complexes in Colorado. William M. Holmes (1878) first described it, noting that the region was important prehistorically. Frank McNitt (1966:74) is the only other writer we know of for Snider's Well. He remarked that near Yucca House, in 1893, a rancher named Snider was digging a well in a natural depression when he encountered human bone at two feet, then more bone two feet deeper. He quit digging when he realized he was in a "mass burial pit." Snider wrote to Wetherill, who was in or near Bluff, Utah. Wetherill replied, suggesting that Snider stop digging until he could get to Snider's ranch. He arrived shortly and completed the skeletal excavation and examination of the kiva's wall paintings.

Because the Snider's Well charnel deposit was as large as any other known for the Southwest, we tried to learn everything possible about it. Although the bone assemblage seems to be lost, we accept Wetherill's interpretation of extensive skull damage as having been caused by violence, since we found his claim for violence valid at Cave 7. Despite the limited amount of contextual information that might explain why the bodies were deposited in the kiva, the extensive cranial damage suggests that these individuals were victims of conflict, if not of warfare.

It should be noted that Wetherill's astute distinction between the two kinds of cranial deformation is another of the original observations for which he never received credit by later archaeologists and physical anthropologists (Reed 49b, 1963; Stewart 1937). Wetherill's 1894 note in the *Archaeologist* says that at least 25 of the Snider's Well crania had what is today referred to as occipital deformation.

Wetherill proposed that these individuals had been captives who were killed, not only because of their wounds and unique context but also because the crania from burial grounds in the vicinity differed, having what is now called lambdoidal deformation. T. D. Stewart (1937) believed the latter was intentional, in contrast to the unintended occipital condition, implying differences in affiliation, as would any of a numer of other cultural practices.

## 5
## Canyon Butte Ruin 3

**Claim Date.** 1902.

**Claimant.** Walter Hough.

**Claim Type.** Cannibalism.

**Other Designations.** None known. The name comes from the large, prominent butte east-southeast of Holbrook, Arizona, which can be seen from the group of four sites that Hough named Canyon Butte 1, 2, 3, and 4. Lee Young provided us with a copy of an 1884 Rand, McNally map of Arizona showing the name "Canon Butte" at the location of what is today called Woodruff Butte.

**Site Location.** About 4.0 km (2.5 miles) west of the Petrified Forest National Park boundary, northeastern Navajo County, Arizona, on the ranch property of Raymond Fitzgerald. USGS Padilla Tank quadrangle (1982), T 17N, R 23E, NE ¼ of NW ¼ of Sec. 22.

**Site Type.** Multiple-room masonry pueblo.

**Cultural Affiliation.** Canyon Butte 3 is located on or near the Anasazi-Mogollon boundary; according to A. E. Dittert, Jr., pottery used there included types associated with both cultures (Turner and Turner 1992a).

**Chronology.** Dittert dated surface sherds mainly to A.D. 1000–1200. This is earlier than the 1200–1300 "safe placement" proposed by Roberta Jewett and accepted by Tim White (1992:367) on the basis of the former's identification of pottery vessels illustrated in Hough (1903). As will be seen, the earlier date is more likely, because it fits with the Chacoan territorial expansion.

**Excavator and Date.** Walter Hough, May 1901.

**Institutional Storage.** Department of Anthropology, National Museum of Natural History, Smithsonian Institution, Washington, D.C.

**Site Reports.** Hough (1902, 1903) briefly but usefully described the site, its locality, and the excavation.

**Osteological Report.** Turner and Turner (1992a).

**Skeletal Evidence of Stress.** None.

**Burial Context.** Charnel pit in cemetery area. Previously unpublished excavation photographs taken by Hough (fig. 3.16) show the cemetery setting.

**Associated Artifacts.** None.

**Figures.** 3.16–3.28.

**Taphonomy.** CGT and JAT. Skeletal inventory is in table 3.3.

    *MNI.* 4 (table 3.2).

    *Age and Sex.* One adult male; one old adult female; one adult?, sex?; and one subadult 15 to 17 years.

      *Preservation.* Good.

      *Bone and Fragment Number.* 247 (30 whole).

      *Breakage.* 87.9%.

Table 3.2
Minimal Number of Individuals (MNI) at Canyon Butte 3

| SKELETAL ELEMENT | AGE | SEX | NOTES |
|---|---|---|---|
| Maxilla, left | Adult | ? | |
| | Old adult | F | |
| Maxilla, right | Subadult | ? | |
| | Old adult | F | Belongs with old adult F left |
| Mandible, left | Subadult | ? | |
| | Old adult | F | |
| | Adult | ? | |
| Mandible, right | Subadult | ? | Belongs with subadult left |
| Extra UP1 | Adult? | ? | Does not fit in any maxilla |
| Pelvis fragment | Adult | M | |
| Pelvis fragment | Adult | ? | |
| Femur | Adult | M | |
| Ulna, left | Adult A | ? | |
| | Adult B | ? | |
| | Adult C | ? | |
| Ulna, right | Adult A | ? | Belongs with adult A left |
| | Adult B | ? | Belongs with adult B left |
| | Adult C | ? | Belongs with adult C left |

SUMMARY: Four individuals. One adult male; one old adult female; one adult?, sex?; one
subadult (15–17), sex?.

*Cut Marks.* 4.0%.
*Burning.* 4.5%.
*Anvil Abrasions.* 2.4%.
*Polishing.* 41.3%.
*Vertebrae Number.* 7.3% of expected (MNI = 4 × 24 vertebrae
per individual = 96 expected vertebrae).
*Scalping.* Yes.
*Gnawing, Rodent.* None.
*Chewing, Carnivore.* 0.4% possible (1 of 247).
*Insect Parts.* None found.
*Other Modification.* None.

**Archaeologist's Interpretation.** Within a year of his excavation at
Canyon Butte Ruin 3, Hough (1902:901) wrote in *Harper's Monthly*
magazine:

> In the cemetery, among other orderly burials, was uncovered a
> heap of broken human bones belonging to three individuals. It was
> evident that the shattered bones had been clean when they were
> placed in the ground, and some fragments showed scorching by
> fire. The marks of the implements used in cracking the bones were
> still traceable. Without doubt this ossuary is the record of a can-
> nibal feast, and its discovery is interesting to science as being the
> first material proof of cannibalism among our North American
> Indians.

The following year Hough (1903:312–313) wrote a similar note
about this exceptional find, adding that "there was no evidence that
with them had been interred any organic material. . . . Undoubtedly

Table 3.3
Bone Elements and Perimortem Damage at Canyon Butte Ruin 3

| SKELETAL ELEMENT | WHOLE | FRAGMENT | IMPACT BREAK | ANVIL ABRASION | CUT MARK | BURN | POLISH | CHEW |
|---|---|---|---|---|---|---|---|---|
| Cranial | | | | | | | | |
| Maxilla | 0 | 3 | 3 | 0 | 0 | 0 | 6 | 0 |
| Mandible | 0 | 3 | 3 | 0 | 0 | 1 | 4 | 0 |
| Parietal | 0 | 2 | 2 | 0 | 2 | 0 | 2 | 0 |
| Occipital | 0 | 3 | 3 | 0 | 0 | 0 | 1 | 0 |
| Temporal | 0 | 3 | 3 | 0 | 0 | 0 | 5 | 0 |
| Teeth (1 extra) | | | | | | | | |
| Fragments | — | 48 | 48 | 0 | 0 | 2 | 24 | 0 |
| Postcranial | | | | | | | | |
| Vertebrae fragments | — | 15 | 15 | 1 | 3 | 0 | 9 | 0? |
| Scapula | 0 | 3 | 3 | 0 | 1 | 0 | 1 | 0? |
| Clavicle | 0 | 3 | 3 | 0 | 1 | 0 | 1 | 0 |
| Rib | 0 | 32 | 32 | 0 | 1 | 0 | 10 | 0 |
| Humerus | 2 | 5 | 5 | 0 | 0 | 0 | 2 | 1? |
| Radius | 2 | 8 | 8 | 0 | 0 | 0 | 1 | 0 |
| Ulna | 1 | 9 | 9 | 0 | 0 | 0 | 1 | 0 |
| Hand & foot | 22 | 0 | 0 | 0 | 0 | 0 | 2 | 0? |
| Pelvis | 2 | 11 | 11 | 0 | 0 | 0 | 0 | 0 |
| Femur | 0 | 11 | 11 | 1 | 2 | 0 | 4 | 0 |
| Tibia | 1 | 9 | 9 | 1 | 0 | 2 | 3 | 0 |
| Fibula | 0 | 5 | 5 | 0 | 0 | 0 | 3 | 0 |
| Long bone fragments | — | 38 | 38 | 3 | 0 | 0 | 23 | 0 |
| Bone type unknown | 0 | 6 | 6 | 0 | 0 | 6 | 0 | 0 |
| TOTAL (247) | 30 | 217 | 217 | 6 | 10 | 11 | 102 | 1? |
| PERCENTAGE | 12.1 | 87.9 | 87.9 | 2.4 | 4.0 | 4.5 | 41.3 | 0.4? |

Percentage of expected vertebrae = approx. 7.3 (7 of 96; MNI = 4).[a]

NOTE: Only elements that were present are listed. Impact breakage, anvil abrasions, cut marks, burning, and polishing represent perimortem damage. Chewing is postmortem damage.

a. Fragmentation size suggests that about two fragments could represent one whole vertebra.

here was evidence of cannibalism, but as the find is unique so far in this region it probably only indicates anthropophagy from necessity. Ceremonial cannibalism among the North American Indians was not unknown, however, as references in the early writers bear witness."

Other Interpretations. Although White (1992:367) did not examine the Canyon Butte 3 skeletal remains, he allowed that the assemblage was similar in "many ways [to] other cases" where cannibalism had been proposed on a more detailed basis. In White's judgment, Hough's find was once unique in the Southwest but now "stands as an early discovery in a series." White accepted Hough's claim for cannibalism at Canyon Butte 3 independently of our taphonomic study of the skeletal remains.

Discussion. We analyzed the skeletal assemblage Hough found in the Canyon Butte 3 charnel pit and later relocated the site with the generous help of M. Lee Young of Holbrook, Arizona, who knew the location of the site from his younger years cowboying in the area (Turner and Turner 1992a). We agree with Hough's claim because the Canyon Butte assemblage has all six of the minimal perimortem taphonomic requirements for proposing cannibalism. The types and amounts of perimortem damage were different from those seen in the Cave 7 and

Walter Hough

Although Walter Hough had earned his M.A. in 1884, he began a lifetime of government service with the U.S. National Museum and the Bureau of American Ethnology in 1886 at the bottom of the ladder—as a copyist in the Division of Ethnology. He received his doctorate in 1894 and moved through the ranks to eventually become head curator of anthropology in 1923. His first professional fieldwork, at age 37, came during an 1896 trip to New Mexico and Arizona, when he served as J. W. Fewkes's assistant.

Their Arizona work commonly started from the Atlantic and Pacific railroad station at Holbrook. From there they traveled by wagon and horseback to the Hopi villages or into the Mogollon high country. Hough's time in Holbrook, however, was not all spent on business. On December 29, 1897, he married Myrtile Zuck, daughter of a prosperous Holbrook family.

Hough returned time and again to the Holbrook-Hopi area. One of these trips, the 1901 Museum-Gates Expedition, led to his excavations of small sites west of Petrified Forest. In one of these, Canyon Butte Ruin 3, he and his workmen discovered a small deposit of burned and broken human bones in the cemetery area. Hough interpreted the find as the remainder of a cannibal feast. He announced this discovery the next year in *Harper's Monthly,* making it the first published claim for cannibalism in the American Southwest.

Hough would have been aware of Fewkes's Awatovi massacre findings, and he probably knew something of Richard Wetherill's discoveries at Cave 7 and Snider's Well. He may well have known of Pepper's thoughts on cannibalism in Chaco Canyon, although we cannot find a direct personal link between Hough and Pepper until many years later.

Life history: b. April 23, 1859, Morgantown, W. Va.; d. September 20, 1935, Washington, D.C., of heart failure. Educated Morgantown Academy, Preparatory School of West Virginia Agricultural College, B.A., 1883; M.A. 1884; Ph.D., 1894, West Virginia University. See Judd (1936).

Figure 3.16. Excavation in Canyon Butte 3 cemetery by local laborers hired by Walter Hough, 1901. The original print of this photograph has "Cannibal Ruin" written on the back. National Anthropological Archives photograph (Hough papers 94-7834).

Figure 3.17. Rock art panel on the western cliff edge of Canyon Butte 3. The slump boulder, about 3 m across, has toppled over and now rests upside-down. The style of these designs dates around A.D.1200. All the designs at Canyon Butte 3 fit into a widespread western Anasazi style that terminates around 1300, adding some support to the ceramic date for the cannibal event—close to 1200 and certainly before 1300 (CGT neg. 6-13-90:2).

Figure 3.18. In the vicinity of Canyon Butte 3 is a deep box canyon containing rock art. Shown to us by Lee Young, the site has many separate panels containing hundreds of individual petroglyphs, making it one of the larger groups of Pueblo II–III rock art in northeastern Arizona. This scene of threatening violence, along with the apparent horned serpent facing to the right, was done in a style dating from late 1200 to 1300 or later (CGT neg. 6-13-90:12).

Figure 3.19. Canyon Butte 3. Entire charnel assemblage sent to the Smithsonian Institution after Hough's 1901 excavation. Fortunately, it was misaccessioned as an archaeological specimen and stored in the archaeology division, so it escaped the sorting by skeletal element that happened to human skeletons in physical anthropology. In sorting, the unidentifiable pieces would likely have been discarded. Scale is 15 cm (CGT neg. 5-16-96:7).

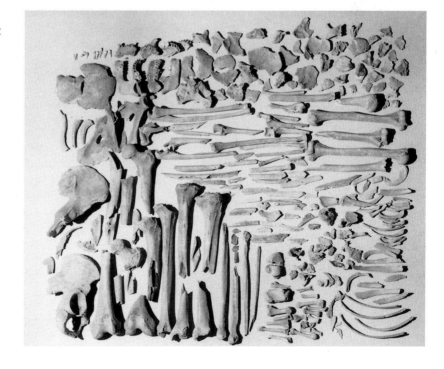

Figure 3.20. Canyon Butte 3. Cranial and mandibular pieces, all with perimortem breakage. Two adults and one subadult are represented by the pieces of maxilla and mandible. A fourth adult? is represented by the maxillary premolar shown in the lower right. Burning and thermal flaking of external surfaces show in four pieces (CGT neg 7-19-89:5; reprinted with permission from *American Antiquity*).

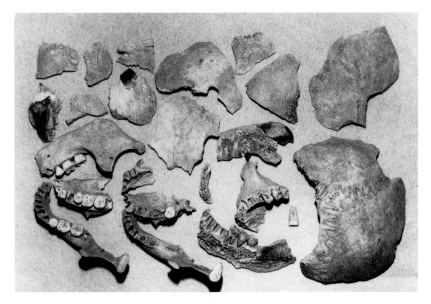

Figure 3.21. Canyon Butte 3. External surface of adult parietal with about 25 striations, each 3.0 cm in length, caused by an anvil or hammerstone (CGT neg. 7-18-89:19; reprinted with permission from *American Antiquity*).

Figure 3.22. Canyon Butte 3. Adult first cervical vertebra, cranial view, fractured at both anterior and posterior arches. Cut marks are shown at arrows (CGT neg. 7-18-89:22; reprinted with permission from *American Antiquity*).

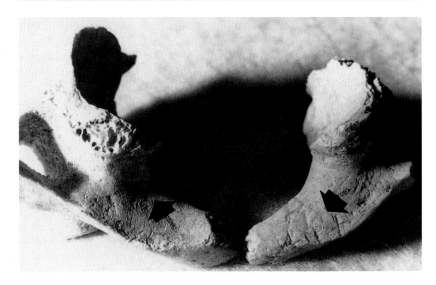

Figure 3.23. Canyon Butte 3. Lumbar vertebral fragment with cut marks on ventral surface—an indication of body processing exceeding simple dismemberment (CGT neg. 7-18-89:21; reprinted with permission from *American Antiquity*).

Figure 3.24. Canyon Butte 3. Rib fragment with relatively deep, V-shaped cut marks on interior surface. Their location suggests that much more body processing occurred than simple dismemberment. Cut marks are about 1.0 cm long. NMNH 212185 (CGT neg. 7-18-89:18).

Figure 3.25. Canyon Butte 3.
Rib with anvil abrasions and
plant root tracks on external surface. Notch in lower area caused
by smashing blow (CGT neg.
7-18-89:26; reprinted with permission from *American
Antiquity*).

Figure 3.26. Canyon Butte 3.
Rib fragment with long diagonal
cut marks on external surface
(CGT neg. 7-18-89:17; reprinted
with permission from *American
Antiquity*).

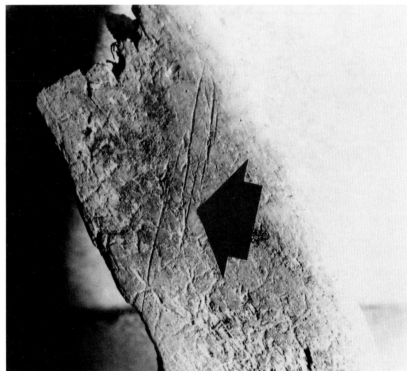

Figure 3.27. Canyon Butte 3.
Midshaft perimortem breakage
of matched pair of adult femurs.
Both were broken by hammer
blows to the bone resting on
an anvil (CGT neg. 7-18-89:35;
reprinted with permission from
*American Antiquity*).

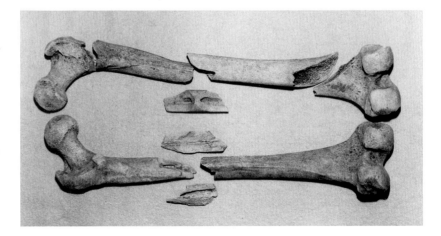

Figure 3.28. Canyon Butte 3. Perimortem flake and spiral breakage of a femur midshaft area, reassembled to show that the breakage occurred before burning of the smashed pieces. This damage sequence is common in Anasazi skeletal assemblages with apparent cannibalism. NMNH 212185 (CGT neg. 7-18-89:30; reprinted with permission from *American Antiquity*).

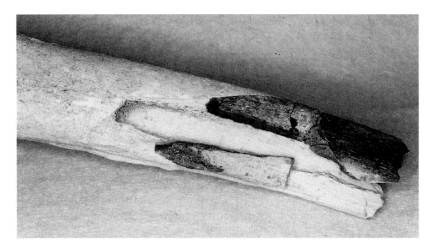

Awatovi remains, although collecting procedures undoubtedly differed in all three cases. Still, two readily distinguishable perimortem bone damage signatures exist. One resulted from violence alone. The other is mixed, exhibiting signs of violence, butchering, and cooking.

Because Hough is the earliest published claimant for prehistoric Southwestern cannibalism based on empirical evidence, more recognition should have been given him in the scholarly history of American archaeology. One reason there are so few references to Hough's claim may be that he presented no supporting evidence in the form of photographs or line drawings. It is more likely, however, that his claim was ignored because interest in human taphonomy was minimal prior to 1952, when Watson Smith (1952) proposed cannibalism on the basis of a pit full of disarticulated human bones, or even 1976, when Flinn, Turner, and Brew (1976) made note of Hough's cannibalism claim. His published claim was never evaluated until our study 90 years later.

As part of that evaluation, we examined the Hough papers in the Anthropological Archives of the National Museum of Natural History. Curiously, we found that Hough's notebooks for the 1901 Museum-Gates expedition had information for the days prior to and after his excavation of the three Canyon Butte sites, but nothing about them turned up. Moreover, Hough's photographic log for the expedition begins right after his May excavations, but we could find no notes for the photographs taken of the Canyon Butte 3 charnel pit excavation. The only information is written directly on one of the three original prints (see fig. 3.16).

Hough missed seeing the many petroglyphs that are present in the boulder talus along the low mesa edge on which Canyon Butte 3 is located (fig. 3.17). Their style tends to support a date for the site of around A.D. 1200. There are other panels in the vicinity as well, one depicting the threat of violence (fig. 3.18)—a rare iconographic theme in the Southwest. Patricia McCreery and Ekkehart Malotki (1994) published an extensive compilation and interpretation of rock art in nearby Petrified Forest National Park. Although they discovered almost every icon and theme imaginable, including the rare one of violence just mentioned, they did not come upon any scene that could be interpreted as decapitation or butchering of humans, let alone as a

cannibal feast. However, one petroglyph panel in Petrified Forest
National Park known to rock-art student McCreery portrays a pros-
trate horned kachina image showing ribs and intestines. McCreery
(personal communication, November 7, 1989) related that a young
Hopi man, upon seeing the glyph, remarked: "Ah! The starvation
story!" The design and several other elements on the panel appear to
be Glen Canyon Style 3, maybe even Style 2 (Turner 1963). If the former, a date of late Pueblo III (A.D. 1200–1300) is suggested—more
recent than the rock art and pottery at Canyon Butte 3. The panel de-
picted in figure 3.18 probably dates to late Pueblo III as well.

We suggest that the historical and theoretical importance of
Hough's find and claim for cannibalism lies in the fact that the cannibal episode was one of several such prehistoric events and activities
that were never discovered by historians and ethnographers because
the reasons for cannibalism had largely ceased by A.D. 1300. Hence,
the Canyon Butte and other, similar human skeletal assemblages
demonstrate that ethnography cannot be the sole or decisive test of an
interpretation or reconstruction of prehistoric events, contrary to
what Arens (1979) and others insist upon.

## 6
## Hawikuh

**Claim Date.** 1919.

**Claimant.** Frederick Webb Hodge.

**Claim Type.** Cannibalism.

**Other Designations.** NA960.

**Site Location.** About 24 km (15 miles) southwest of Zuni Pueblo,
northwestern New Mexico. USGS Ojo Caliente Reservoir quadrangle
(1972), T 8N, R 20W, SE ¼ of SW ¼ of Sec. 7.

**Site Type.** Large, multistoried, masonry pueblo.

**Cultural Affiliation.** Western Pueblo (Zuni).

**Chronology.** Pueblo III and IV; the A.D. 1275–1475 time period applies
to the cannibalism claim. Hawikuh continued as a major town into
historic times. The historic "discoverer" of the Southwest, a native
African named Esteban, was almost certainly murdered there, and a
Franciscan church and friary were built and used until 1672, when
Hawikuh was sacked and burned by Apaches. It burned again during
the Pueblo Revolt of 1680 (Smith et al. 1966:100). The human bone
assemblages that were claimed to have been cannibalized were in the
deeper layers of Hawikuh and were associated with pottery types that
today are called Heshotauthla Polychrome (1275–1400) and
Kechipawan Polychrome (1375–1475) (Smith et al. 1966:304–308,
321–324).

**Excavator and Date.** F. W. Hodge, 1917–1923. The excavations were a
joint undertaking of the Bureau of American Ethnology, Washington,
D.C., and the Museum of the American Indian, Heye Foundation,
New York.

**Institutional Storage.** Some of the Hawikuh skeletons recovered during the field seasons of 1917 and 1918 were accessioned January 30,
1919, in the Department of Anthropology, National Museum of Natural History, Washington, D.C. (accession no. 63196). The where-
abouts of skeletons found between 1920 and 1923 have not been
determined.

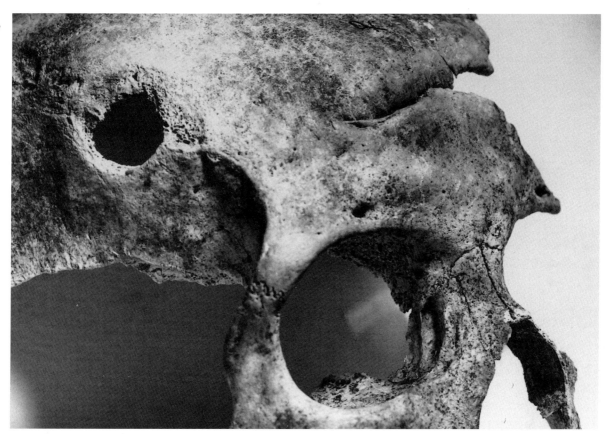

Figure 3.29. Hawikuh, New Mexico. Adult skull with two severe wounds on frontal bone that seem to have been in different stages of healing at the time of death. The bone bordering the older linear cut across the forehead was largely inactive. The more recent circular wound was in the process of healing at the time of death. The circular wound resembles surgical trephining but was more likely due to the missing bone plug's having exfoliated or been absorbed with antemortem decay of covering soft tissue (see Hamperl and Laughlin 1959). Nothing in the nature of the pathology helps determine whether the wounds were caused by repeated violence or separate accidents. NMNH 308755 (CGT neg. 1-9-89:18).

**Site Reports.** Hodge (1918); Smith et al. (1966).
**Osteological Report.** Hrdlička (1931).
**Skeletal Evidence of Stress.** None known.
**Burial Context.** Field notes indicate that 996 individuals were excavated; 679 were inhumations (I), 317 cremations (C). These individuals were assigned to the following six time periods: A.D. 1200–1300: 2 I, 0 C; 1300–1400: 15 I, 11 C; 1350–1475: 20 I, 13 C; 1475–1650: 165 I, 88 C; 1630–1670: 100 I, 0 C; no dates: 337 I, 205 C.

According to Watson Smith and colleagues (1966:192), "cremation was most probably introduced sometime in the years from about 1400 to 1450." Smith et al. (1966:193) provided a complete breakdown for age and sex as determined in the field for 996 individuals, and age and sex was later identified by Aleš Hrdlička for 261 nonrepresentative individuals sent to the National Museum.

One set of bones said to have been cannibalized was discovered in the western refuse area, perhaps at a depth of 15 feet. The remains were well below more recent burials. Similarly disarticulated human remains were found in Hodge's room 223, Group B roomblock

(Smith et al. 1966:pl. 8, fig. *c*). No information is provided about the excavation of room 223.

**Associated Artifacts.** Many burials contained offerings, but the disarticulated assemblages apparently had none.

**Figure.** 3.29.

**Taphonomy.** FWH.

>    *MNI.* Not reported for the disarticulated bone sets.
>
>    *Age and Sex.* Not reported for the disarticulated bone sets.
>
>    *Preservation.* The remains claimed to have been cannibalized were said to be in better condition than the more recent burials.
>
>    *There is no information for Bone and Fragment Number, Breakage, Cut Marks, Burning, Anvil Abrasions, Polishing, Vertebrae Number, Scalping, Gnawing, Chewing, Insect Parts, or Other Modification.*

**Archaeologist's Interpretation.** According to Smith et al. (1966:181), Hodge wrote to Hrdlička on January 2, 1919, relating that he would revise as soon as possible a paper on Hawikuh burial customs. The paper was never published, so Smith et al. (1966) included it word for word in their monograph. This decision was most fortunate, for it was in this unpublished paper that Hodge recorded his Zuni workmen's belief in cannibalism and dismemberment (Smith et al. 1966:184):

> Elsewhere in the debris [on the western slope], usually at its lower levels, were found other old burials, only in exceptional cases being accompanied with artifacts. . . . In a number of cases only parts of skeletons were found, rarely with accompaniments. This lack was not owing to decay, for in most instances the bones were in even better condition than those of remains interred long subsequent to them. . . . In one case the bones of the skeleton had been broken to pieces, not on account of disturbance by burrowing animals, but deliberately. In this case the bones were not scattered beyond the normal limits of the grave. All these unusual burials were very old, although in a number of instances it was possible to save at least a part of the skeleton. . . . It is difficult to offer a reasonable conjecture in explanation of these anomalies. In the case of the last mentioned the Zuni insisted that these bones were the remains of a human feast, their ancestors having practiced cannibalism at times under the stress of famine. In explanation of the occurrence of only parts of skeletons, especially those unaccompanied with mortuary vessels or other objects, it was urged by the natives that they were the remains of enemies who had been killed, and this may possibly have been the case.

Hodge found a few multiple inhumations (Smith et al. 1966:198), but these were articulated individuals with mortuary goods, completely different from the assemblages resulting from supposed cannibalism, wherein multiple individuals were disarticulated and broken up and lacked burial goods. Hodge ended his paper with a comment from his Zuni workmen that may well illustrate how witches were treated (Smith et al. 1966:199): "Burial 118—adult, headed E. Flexed tightly, on back, knees drawn up to chest, elbows raised & hands clasped on right side of head. Left elbow higher than head (see photo). Indians think this person buried alive. No objects. Depth 10 feet."

In 1918 Hodge wrote that the "skeletons in most of these older graves were usually incomplete, as if purposely dismembered at the time of burial (fig. 64) [which shows an armless and headless flexed burial without grave goods]; and in one instance the bones almost without exception had been deliberately broken (fig. 65)" (1918:64). Hodge's figure 65 shows some 50 to 60 bones, only two of which, a femur and a mandible, appear to be whole.

Smith et al. (1966) included another unpublished Hodge paper, one that dealt with ceremonial deposits in the Hawikuh cemetery. These items consisted largely of "sacrifices" of artifacts such as pottery and perishable materials, including food items. Hodge classified these ceremonial deposits as mortuary deposits, deposits probably mortuary, sacerdotal deposits ("strictly religious"), and animal burials. It was in this last class, which consisted mainly of turkey and dog burials, that Hodge included some human remains (Smith et al. 1966:293): "A strange deposit consisted of a mass of broken human and animal bones, 6 feet 4 inches deep, as if the remains of a feast. The Zuni reluctantly stated that in ancient times their ancestors, under stress of hunger, ate human flesh. Among the bones were part of a knife made from a deer's rib."

**Other Interpretations.** None known.

**Discussion.** Hodge and his field supervisors must have been strongly impressed with the disarticulated sets of human remains, because two of them were among only 63 burials photographed out of a total of 996 inhumations and cremations (Smith et al. 1966:176).

We are unable to tell from the clear but small photograph of the "human, deer and other animal" remains scattered on the floor of Room 223—one of the possibly cannibalized bone assemblages— what sort of damage the bones might have been subjected to (Smith et al. 1966: pl. 8, fig. *c*). Figure 65 in Hodge (1918:65), however, which illustrates a "pre-Hawikuh burial" found in 1917, shows quite clearly the sort of long bone breakage that characterizes bone assemblages with the taphonomic signature of probable cannibalism.

It is unclear exactly how many deposits of disarticulated human remains Hodge recovered. If our reading and evaluation of him as presented in Smith et al. (1966) and his 1918 paper are correct, there may have been as many as five assemblages of anomalous human remains, including the two already mentioned (those in Room 223 and Hodge's fig. 65):

1. The assemblage at the "ancient" level of Room 223, House Group B. This is shown in figure *c* of plate 8. The caption reads: "Human, deer, and other animal bones are scattered on floor" (Smith et al. 1966). The "ancient level" seems to equate with a date of roughly 1275–1400.

2. A dismembered body illustrated in Hodge (1918:64, fig. 4). It was said to have been found at a depth of 4 feet during the 1917 excavation of the western cemetery.

3. The remains illustrated in Hodge (1918:65, fig. 65): a "'pre-Hawikuh' [1275–1400] burial almost every bone of which had

been deliberately broken." There were no grave goods, and the remains were found at a depth of 6 feet 4 inches in the western refuse deposit, excavated in 1917. There are no identifiable animal bones in Hodge's figure 65.

4. Deposit 226, described by Hodge (Smith et al. 1966:293) as "a mass of broken human and animal bones, 6 feet 4 inches deep as if the remains of a feast." Although this example has the same depth as our number 3, it seems to differ in that it had part of a knife made from a deer's rib. It was not reported when or where 226 was excavated.

5. Remains noted by Smith et al. (1966:184), quoting from Hodge's manuscript written in the winter of 1918–1919; they say that "in a number of cases," disarticulated skeletons were found.

On January 9, 1989, and November 19, 1993, the senior author examined the Hawikuh skeletal series housed at the NMNH. Only one cranium was found with antemortem and perimortem damage (fig. 3.29). Apparently none of Hodge's aberrant cases was saved by him or Hrdlička. On May 28, 1994, we made a second search of Hawikuh records and skeletons. We found the 1917–1919 records (SI accession numbers 63,196, 64,296, and 71,050) and Hawikuh skeletons, but neither notes nor bones were related to possible cannibalism.

In sum, the published photographs are suggestive of cannibalism, but we have no direct taphonomic means to evaluate Hodge's claim. Nevertheless, we are inclined to accept it, because (1) he learned from Zuni workmen their beliefs about ancestral cannibalism and mutilation; (2) having excavated 1,000 burials and studied as many bone objects, Hodge was so familiar with both that he would have reacted like any modern bioarchaeologist upon seeing a cannibalized assemblage for the first time; and (3) Zuni oral tradition maintains that their chiefs had their first Old World visitor, the African Esteban, dismembered. Hodge (1937:26) accepted Spanish accounts of Esteban's gruesome ending, recounting that "his body was cut into a great many pieces, which were distributed among all the chiefs, in order that they might know that he was surely dead." Given what is now known about prehistoric human body processing within a 40-mile radius of Zuni (see sites 49, 54, 55, and 74 in this chapter), it implies neither barbarism nor irrationality to suggest that Esteban was cut up and eaten in a demonstration of malice and disrespect. Indeed, the act might have been politically astute if it served to intimidate the Indians who accompanied Esteban and warn potentially sympathetic Zunis to avoid the new foreigners.

As was the case with Long House and Snider's Well, we were unable to locate the relevant Hawikuh remains in order to independently assess Hodge's claim for cannibalism. On the other hand, our research turned up nothing that provided a basis for rejecting the claim. Because there is not even a minimal physical description of the bones in question, we prefer to make no judgment at this time.

7
Peñasco Blanco

**Claim Date.** 1920.

**Claimant.** George H. Pepper.

**Claim Type.** Cannibalism.

**Other Site Designations.** 29SJ410; Bc250; White Rock Point (Lister and Lister 1981:235).

**Site Location.** In Chaco Canyon, about 4.8 km (3 miles) west of Pueblo Bonito, on top of a mesa 100 m above the junction of Chaco and Escavada washes, San Juan County, northwestern New Mexico. USGS Kin Klizhin Ruin quadrangle (1966), T 21N, R 11W, SW ¼ of NW ¼ of Sec. 3.

**Site Type.** A great house described by Lister and Lister (1981:235) as containing more than 150 ground-level rooms and nine or more kivas and as having stood three stories high.

**Cultural Affiliation.** Anasazi, Chaco branch.

**Chronology.** Stephen H. Lekson (1986) identified five stages of construction at Peñasco Blanco, begining at A.D. 900 and continuing to 1120–1125.

**Excavator and Date.** In 1898, while George Pepper and Richard Wetherill were excavating at Pueblo Bonito, a Navajo member of their crew named Waylo (also spelled Wylo) excavated skeletal remains, along with perishable and nonperishable refuse, in a single room at Peñasco Blanco. Pepper (1920:378) provided the only known written description of the Peñasco Blanco charnel assemblage based on direct observation: "During the period of our work in Pueblo Bonito some of our Navajo workmen cleaned out a number of rooms in Peñasco Blanco and in one of these a great many human bones were found. Some of these, including portions of the skull, were charred, and the majority of long bones had been cracked open and presented the same appearance as do the animal bones that have been treated in a similar way for the extraction of the marrow."

**Institutional Storage.** Department of Anthropology, American Museum of Natural History, New York.

**Site Report.** None.

**Osteological Report.** None.

**Skeletal Evidence of Stress.** We found four occipital fragments with grade 1–2 porotic hyperostosis and a frontal bone with grade 1 cribra orbitalia. One individual had active bone inflammation.

**Burial Context.** From a single room, although Pepper did not say whether Waylo found the bones on the floor or in the room fill. There are no known photographs by Pepper or Wetherill showing this or the other rooms Waylo dug into at Peñasco Blanco. Because of the nearly complete lack of contextual information, we have been skeptical of the claim for cannibalism and have spent an extraordinary amount of time and effort examining the skeletal remains to make certain that the damage was truly perimortem.

**Associated Artifacts.** AMNH Anthropology catalog H, vol. 7, pp. 71–72, 80, lists entries 8958 through 9004 as having been found by Waylo in one room at Peñasco Blanco. Entries include what is usually regarded as refuse—matting fragment, pottery bowl fragment, bone awl, piece of cord, corn husk, bark fragment, wooden stick, turkey feathers, and so forth. We have no reason to suspect that any

Table 3.4
Minimal Number of Individuals (MNI) at Peñasco Blanco

| SKELETAL ELEMENT | AGE | SEX | NOTES |
|---|---|---|---|
| Maxilla, whole | Adult | ? | Blown-out anterior teeth |
| | Adult | ? | Blown-out anterior teeth |
| Maxilla, left | Adult | ? | Blown-out anterior teeth |
| Maxilla, right | Adult | ? | |
| | Adult | ? | |
| | 2–3 | ? | |
| Mandible, whole | 17–18 | ? | |
| | Adult | ? | |
| | Adult | ? | |
| | Adult | ? | |
| | Young adult | F | |
| Mandible, left | Adult | M | Does not fit with R mandibles |
| Mandible, right | 2–3 | ? | |
| | Adult | ? | Blown-out anterior teeth |

SUMMARY: Eight individuals. One adult male; one young adult female; four adults, sex?; one 17- to 18-year-old, sex?; one 2- to 3-year-old, sex?.

of these items was in direct association with the human skeletal remains.

**Figures.** 3.30–3.59.

**Taphonomy.** CGT and JAT, May 27, 1993, and May 3–5, 1994. Skeletal inventory is given in table 3.5.

*MNI.* 8 (table 3.4).

*Age and Sex.* One adult male, four adults, sex?, one young adult female, one 17- to 18-year-old, sex?, and one 2- to 3-year-old child.

*Preservation.* Good. Bone is mainly hard and creamy white in color.

*Bone and Fragment Number.* 578 (49, or 8.5%, whole). There are also 86 whole and 6 fragmented teeth.

*Breakage.* 84.1%.

*Cut Marks.* 8.1%.

*Burning.* 3.1%.

*Anvil Abrasions.* 9.3%.

*Polishing.* 5.4%.

*Vertebrae Number.* 2.6% of expected (5 of 192).

*Scalping.* Yes.

*Gnawing, Rodent.* 0.2%.

*Chewing, Carnivore.* 2.1%.

*Insect Parts.* None found at time of skeletal examinations.

*Other Modification.* None.

**Archaeologist's Interpretation.** Pepper (1920:378) suggested cannibalism as the reason for the condition of this assemblage: "It would therefore seem that these Pueblo Indians [referring to both Peñasco Blanco and Pueblo Bonito], either through stress of hunger or for religious reasons, had occasionally resorted to the eating of human flesh."

**Other Interpretations.** Tim White (1992:337–338) noted that Pepper suggested cannibalism because the human bone exhibited damage similar to that of game animals. White, however, did not include

Table 3.5
Bone Elements and Perimortem Damage at Peñasco Blanco

| SKELETAL ELEMENT | WHOLE | FRAGMENT | IMPACT BREAK | ANVIL ABRASION | CUT MARK | BURN | POLISH | GNAW/ CHEW |
|---|---|---|---|---|---|---|---|---|
| Cranial | | | | | | | | |
| Maxilla | 2 | 4 | 6 | 0 | 0 | 1 | 0 | 0 |
| Mandible | 5 | 4 | 8 | 2 | 6 | 1 | 1 | 1? |
| Frontal | 1 | 2 | 2 | 0 | 2 | 1 | 1 | 0 |
| Parietal | 0 | 7 | 4 | 0 | 1 | 4 | 1 | 0 |
| Occipital | 0 | 10 | 10 | 1 | 2 | 0 | 0 | 0 |
| Temporal | 2 | 18 | 19 | 2 | 5 | 1 | 0 | 0 |
| Base | 0 | 2 | 1 | 0 | 0 | 0 | 0 | 0 |
| Teeth (not in total) | (86) | (6) | (2) | 0 | 0 | 0 | 0 | 0 |
| Fragments | — | 35 | 35 | 2 | 3 | 1 | 0 | 0 |
| Postcranial | | | | | | | | |
| Cervical vertebrae | 1 | 0 | 1 | 1 | 0 | 0 | 0 | 0 |
| Thoracic vertebrae | 1 | 0 | 0 | 0 | 0 | 0 | 0 | 0 |
| Vertebrae fragments | — | 16 | 16 | 1 | 1 | 0 | 0 | 0 |
| Sacrum | 0 | 1 | 0 | 0 | 0 | 0 | 0 | 0 |
| Scapula | 4 | 7 | 11 | 2 | 1 | 1 | 0 | 0 |
| Clavicle | 3 | 2 | 1 | 0 | 1 | 0 | 0 | 0 |
| Rib | 0 | 84 | 84 | 5 | 7 | 1 | 3 | 0 |
| Humerus | 0 | 9 | 9 | 0 | 4 | 0 | 1 | 0 |
| Radius | 2 | 8 | 1 | 1 | 0 | 0 | 0 | 2 |
| Ulna | 3 | 10 | 4 | 2 | 0 | 2 | 1 | 5 |
| Hand & foot | 23 | 14 | 4 | 0 | 1 | 0 | 0 | 0 |
| Pelvis | 0 | 7 | 4 | 0 | 1 | 0 | 0 | 1 |
| Femur | 0 | 20 | 19 | 4 | 2 | 0 | 6 | 2 |
| Tibia | 0 | 27 | 27 | 4 | 1 | 0 | 7 | 2 |
| Fibula | 2 | 13 | 11 | 3 | 0 | 0 | 1 | 0 |
| Long bone fragments | — | 196 | 176 | 24 | 7 | 2 | 9 | 0 |
| Bone type unknown | — | 33 | 33 | 0 | 2 | 3 | 0 | 0 |
| TOTAL (578) | 49 | 529 | 486 | 54 | 47 | 18 | 31 | 13 |
| PERCENTAGE | 8.5 | 91.5 | 84.1 | 9.3 | 8.1 | 3.1 | 5.4 | 2.3 |

Percentage of expected vertebrae = approx. 2.6 (5 of 192; MNI = 8).[a]

NOTE: Only elements that were present are listed. Impact breakage, anvil abrasions, cut marks, burning, and polishing represent perimortem damage. Gnawing and chewing are postmortem damage.

a. Fragmentation size suggests that about five fragments could represent one whole vertebra.

Peñasco Blanco in his literature survey on Southwestern cannibalism, because there were no published details on the condition of the bones.

**Discussion.** We provide extensive photographic documentation of the Peñasco Blanco bone damage (figs. 3.30–3.59) and measurements of fragment lengths (tables 3.6 and 3.7) in anticipation of both lay and professional criticism of Pepper's generally overlooked claim that the bone appearance in this assemblage resembled game animal processing. With respect to the fragment measurements, note how small the standard deviations are, which suggests that the relatively uniform size was intentional, not caused by random factors. The means for long bone and rib fragments are nearly identical (8.3 cm and 7.3 cm, respectively). As the record now stands, Pepper should be credited with having made this pioneering taphonomic observation. We wonder, however, whether the similarity between the human bone damage and game animal processing might have been brought to Pepper's at-

Table 3.6
Lengths (cm) of Unidentifiable Human Long Bone Fragments from
Peñasco Blanco

| | | | | | | |
|---|---|---|---|---|---|---|
| 9.9 | 15.0 | 14.9 | 13.9 | 11.2 | 10.1 | 11.2 |
| 7.2 | 9.0 | 5.1 | 2.9 | 6.0 | 5.6 | 7.8 |
| 6.6 | 7.8 | 8.4 | 4.9 | 6.0 | 8.7 | 3.8 |
| 13.3 | 9.8 | 7.7 | 5.2 | 9.1 | 7.5 | 13.1 |
| 10.8 | 15.5 | 12.3 | 10.7 | 12.9 | 8.2 | 3.5 |
| 8.5 | 9.9 | 6.5 | 9.7 | 12.0 | 3.4 | 7.1 |
| 7.0 | 5.1 | 10.6 | 3.5 | 7.2 | 6.1 | 7.9 |
| 2.6 | 21.6 | 17.3 | 16.4 | 15.2 | 9.8 | 12.6 |
| 11.3 | 9.0 | 7.7 | 7.4 | 5.1 | 10.6 | 8.2 |
| 10.9 | 4.2 | 8.1 | 6.0 | 8.1 | 4.2 | 5.3 |
| 3.6 | 11.1 | 6.2 | 7.2 | 3.8 | 10.1 | 12.1 |
| 8.5 | 7.1 | 10.1 | 5.2 | 10.6 | 6.8 | 8.5 |
| 9.8 | 6.5 | 9.3 | 7.5 | 6.8 | 12.0 | 5.5 |
| 2.8 | 10.1 | 9.1 | 10.1 | 3.1 | 11.1 | 6.6 |
| 4.3 | 17.2 | 4.0 | 7.1 | 5.2 | 7.7 | 7.7 |
| 8.2 | 6.3 | 5.6 | 10.0 | 4.6 | 5.5 | 3.6 |
| 10.1 | 8.2 | 13.3 | 4.4 | 7.7 | 8.9 | 9.2 |
| 9.9 | 7.9 | 12.6 | 6.2 | 5.6 | 18.3 | 8.6 |
| 13.0 | 7.3 | 8.7 | 7.4 | 8.5 | 6.4 | 7.9 |
| 5.6 | 9.0 | 4.0 | 6.6 | 7.4 | 11.9 | 10.1 |
| 5.2 | 11.1 | 8.1 | 11.6 | 10.5 | 5.5 | 7.2 |
| 7.0 | 8.5 | 16.0 | 6.9 | 6.3 | 3.5 | 4.4 |
| 5.4 | 10.0 | 6.2 | 7.9 | 5.7 | 6.4 | 2.7 |
| 9.7 | 12.9 | 7.6 | 6.7 | 6.3 | 7.0 | 10.6 |
| 4.8 | 12.4 | 5.1 | 12.5 | 9.1 | 6.0 | |

N = 147.   Range = 2.6–21.6.   Mean = 8.3.   S.D. = 3.4.

NOTE: Measurements are for a sample of 174 out of 176 fragments. Identification is slightly different from that in table 3.5. Damage is perimortem.

Table 3.7
Lengths (cm) of Broken Human Rib Fragments from Peñasco Blanco

| | | | | | | |
|---|---|---|---|---|---|---|
| 8.7 | 8.3 | 6.4 | 4.5 | 4.3 | 6.6 | 5.5 |
| 5.4 | 7.5 | 6.5 | 11.0 | 10.3 | 5.1 | 4.6 |
| 5.1 | 3.5 | 5.2 | 11.7 | 10.9 | 5.9 | 4.3 |
| 6.0 | 5.6 | 4.2 | 11.9 | 11.6 | 11.4 | 12.1 |
| 8.9 | 4.4 | 6.4 | 13.1 | 11.5 | 7.0 | 5.6 |
| 6.5 | 4.8 | 5.3 | 14.0 | 10.6 | 8.0 | 9.4 |
| 3.0 | 6.2 | 3.0 | 11.6 | 9.3 | 5.0 | 6.9 |
| 3.8 | 5.3 | 7.1 | 11.5 | 9.2 | 4.0 | 10.8 |
| 4.1 | 4.9 | 3.9 | 14.0 | 12.1 | 6.5 | 5.2 |
| 4.4 | 3.4 | 5.1 | | | | |

N = 66.   Range = 3.0–14.0.   Mean = 7.3.   S.D. = 3.1.

NOTE: Identification is slightly different from that in table 3.5. Damage is perimortem.

Figure 3.30. Peñasco Blanco, Chaco Canyon, New Mexico. All of the cranial, mandibular, and 13 vertebral pieces for the MNI of eight. There are five burned cranial pieces in upper right. Perimortem breakage, burning, thermal flaking, and severe damage to vertebrae can be seen. More than half the burned pieces in the assemblage are skull parts, suggesting head roasting. Many years ago the assemblage was assigned two catalog numbers and stored in two different areas of the American Museum because, as the catalog indicated, the labels from some storage containers had been eaten by mice. Catalogers were uncertain whether the bones with missing labels were from Peñasco Blanco. In lower right are two vault pieces that conjoin perfectly, as did other pairs, for catalog numbers H/11801 and H/9155. Scale is 15 cm (CGT neg. 5-4-94:16).

Figure 3.31. Peñasco Blanco. Cranial fragment with perimortem breakage, anvil abrasions, and cut marks. Actual width of image in photograph is 3.3 cm. AMNH H/11801 (CGT neg. 5-3-94:34).

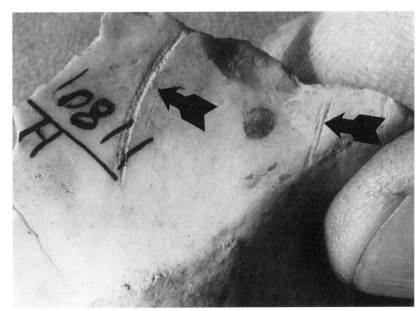

Figure 3.32. Peñasco Blanco. Burned cranial vault fragment, 6.5 cm in diameter, showing exfoliation of heat-damaged external cortex. AMNH H/9155 (CGT neg. 5-4-94:13).

Figure 3.33. Peñasco Blanco. Left temporal bone with cut marks above the external auditory meatus. These could have been caused by scalping, butchering, ear-trophy taking, or all three. AMNH H/9155 (CGT neg. 5-4-94:5).

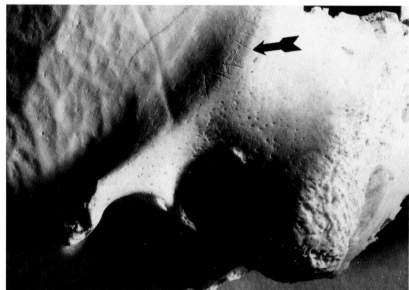

Figure 3.34. Peñasco Blanco. Tooth-bearing maxillary pieces. Breakage was more frequent for anterior teeth and sockets than for posterior teeth. This difference suggests that facial trauma took place while jaw musculature was still present and could protect the posterior teeth. Subadult in lower left had been burned. AMNH H/9155 and H/11801 (CGT neg. 5-4-94:21).

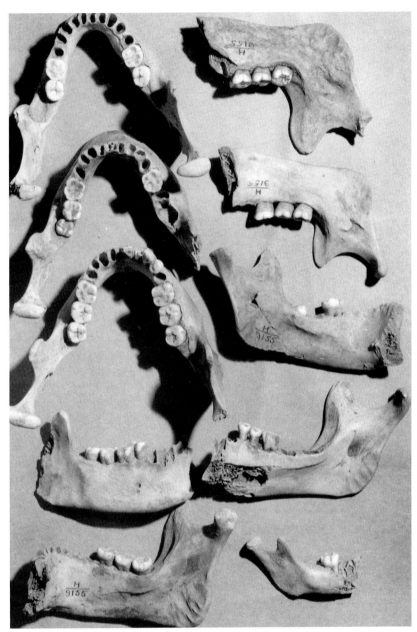

Figure 3.35. Peñasco Blanco. Mandibles belonging to eight individuals, all with some form of perimortem breakage. Middle right subadult was burned. AMNH H/9155 and H/11801 (CGT neg. 5-4-94:19).

Figure 3.36. Peñasco Blanco. Horizontal cut marks on right ascending ramus of mandible, complete except for torn-off tip of coronoid process (both left and right tips are missing). Breakage of the tips could have been done by twisting the jaw off the cranial base or by smashing it loose after the muscles had been severed. AMNH H/11801 (CGT neg. 5-27-93:36).

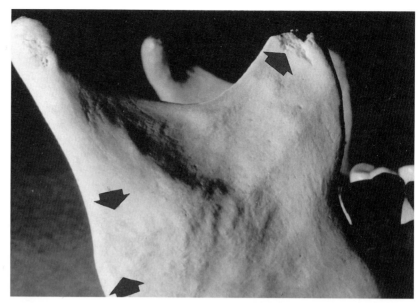

Figure 3.37. Peñasco Blanco. Detail of cut marks on right ascending mandibular ramus of figure 3.36. AMNH H/11801 (CGT neg. 5-27-93:35).

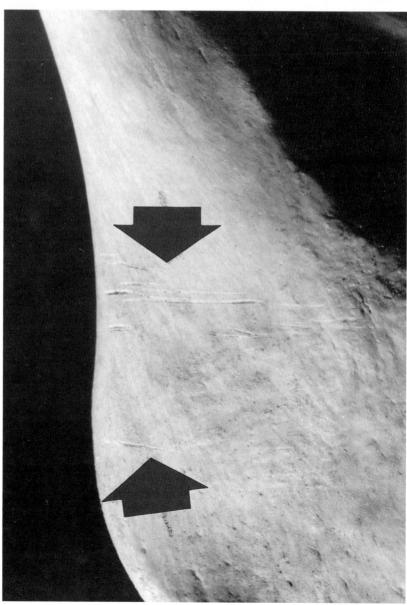

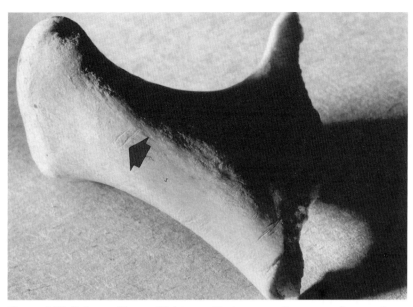

Figure 3.38. Peñasco Blanco. Right mandibular ascending ramus fragment. Short, horizontal cut marks are present all along the distal ramus border. Length of cut mark at arrow is 1.5 mm. Horizontal cut marks of the mandibular ascending ramus are characteristic of Anasazi human bone deposits for which cannibalism has been proposed. AMNH H/11801 (CGT neg. 5-27-93:13).

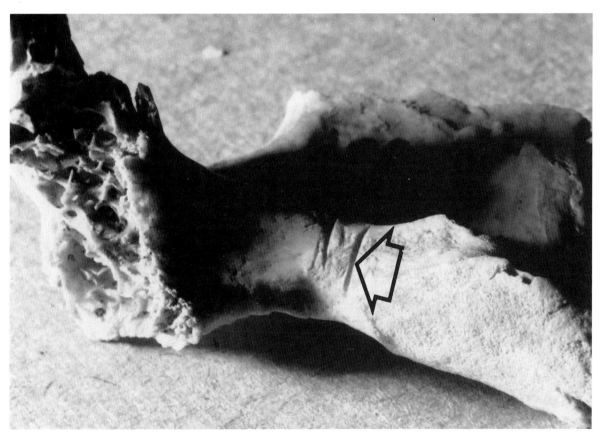

Figure 3.39. Peñasco Blanco. Vertebral fragment with two deep, V-shaped cut marks 5.0 mm in length. The location of these cut marks would have had little to do with simple dismemberment. Actual width of image in photograph is 3.3 cm. AMNH H/11801 (CGT neg. 5-27-93:10).

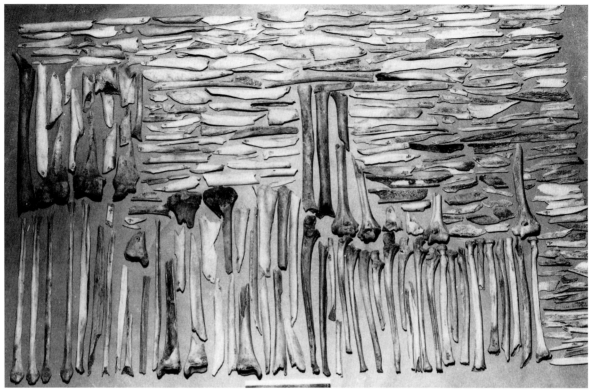

Figure 3.40. Peñasco Blanco. All of the long bones, whole and fragmentary, for the MNI of eight. Readily identified elements are arranged vertically; horizontally, the pieces are less certain. Only three long bones were not broken. The large amount of intentional breakage of these bones is another characteristic shared by all Anasazi sites for which cannibalism has been proposed. Scale is 15 cm. AMNH H/9155 and H/11801 (CGT neg. 5-5-94:24).

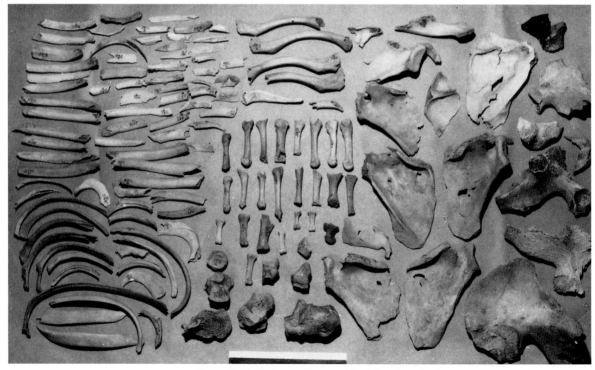

Figure 3.41. Peñasco Blanco. All of the ribs, clavicles, scapulae, pelves, and hand and foot bones for the MNI of eight. Note the general uniformity of rib fragment length, which is similar to the average length of long bone fragments. Scale is 15 cm. AMNH H/9155 and H/11801 (CGT neg. 5-5-94:19).

Figure 3.42. Peñasco Blanco. A closer view of representative perimortem long bone breakage. The complete radius included for comparison at top is undamaged. Pencil at bottom is 13.5 cm long. Most of these long bone fragments cannot be readily identified as to bone element. Spiral breaks are present in many of the heavier fragments. The preservation of these and most other pieces is excellent. The bone is hard, dense, and creamy white or ivory in color, and it retains sharp edges along the fracture planes. Many of the thin pieces are translucent, a quality that can be found in most cooked bone. AMNH H/11801 (CGT neg 5-27-93:7).

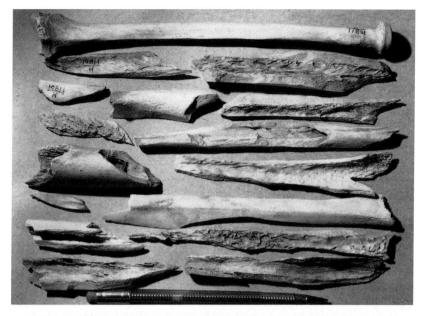

Figure 3.43. Peñasco Blanco. Rib fragment with perimortem breakage and polishing of tip (at left). Actual width of image in photograph is 3.3 cm. AMNH H/11801 (CGT neg. 5-27-93:31).

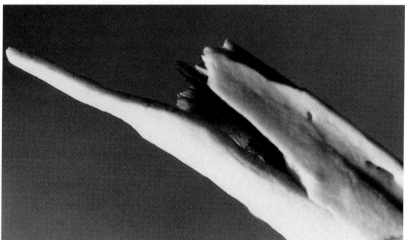

Figure 3.44. Peñasco Blanco. Three minute perimortem cut marks (about 1.0 mm long) on the inferior and internal surface of rib 1. Such cut marks indicate that the rib cage had been forced open for butchering of the intercostal muscles. This interpretation is supported by the perimortem breakage of the proximal rib end, which attaches to the vertebral column. AMNH H/11801 (CGT neg. 5-27-93:18).

Figure 3.45. Peñasco Blanco.
Proximal femur fragment
with perimortem breakage and
cut marks at arrow, below
trochanter. AMNH H/11801
(CGT neg. 5-3-94:36).

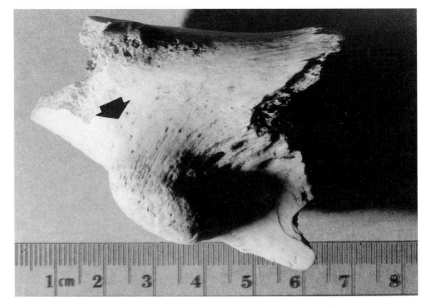

Figure 3.46. Peñasco Blanco.
Humerus fragment with perimortem breakage and at least
six chop marks. Arrows point to
anvil abrasions, which suggest
that the bone had been turned
over at least twice as the
butcher tried to break it open.
Actual width of image in photograph is 4.4 cm. AMNH H/9155
(CGT neg. 5-4-94:2).

Figure 3.47. Peñasco Blanco.
Humerus fragment with perimortem breakage and chop and
cut marks. AMNH H/9155 (CGT
neg. 5-4-94:36).

Figure 3.48. Peñasco Blanco. Long bone fragment with peri-mortem breakage and anvil abrasions. Cuts are 3.0 mm long. AMNH H/11801 (CGT neg. 5-27-93:25).

Figure 3.49. Peñasco Blanco. Long bone fragment with peri-mortem breakage and anvil abrasions along fracture. Actual width of image in photograph is 3.3 cm. AMNH H/11801 (CGT neg. 5-3-94:32).

Figure 3.50. Peñasco Blanco. Fibulae fragments with peri-mortem anvil abrasions (upper) and cut marks (lower). Actual width of image in photograph is 3.3 cm. AMNH H/9155 (CGT neg. 5-4-94:8).

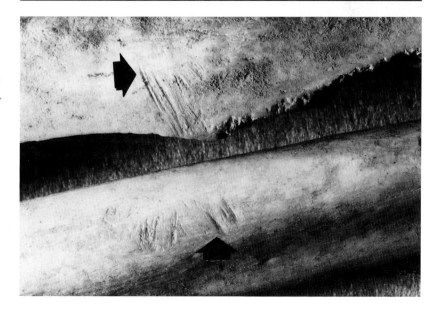

108

Figure 3.51. Peñasco Blanco. Tibia fragment with perimortem breakage and pot-polishing (at arrow). Actual width of image in photograph is 3.3 cm. AMNH H/11801 (CGT neg. 5-3-94:29).

Figure 3.52. Peñasco Blanco. Long bone fragments with perimortem breakage and pot-polishing at ends. Actual width of image in photograph is 3.3 cm. AMNH H/11801 (CGT neg. 5-3-94:23).

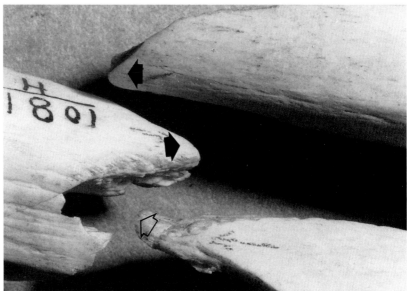

Figure 3.53. Peñasco Blanco. Femur fragment with perimortem breakage and carnivore chewing tooth pits. AMNH H/9155 (CGT neg. 5-4-94:14).

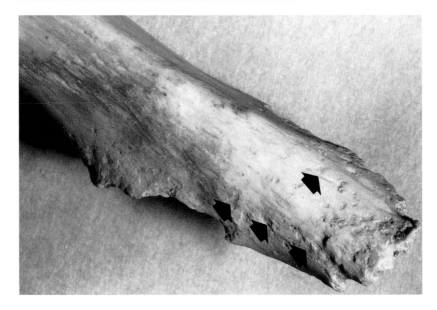

Figure 3.54. Peñasco Blanco. Perimortem carnivore-chewing tooth pits on two radius fragments (lower); extensive perimortem rodent gnawing on tibia fragment (upper). Animal damage indicates open discard after human processing was finished. Scale in cm. AMNH H/9155 (CGT neg. 5-4-94:18).

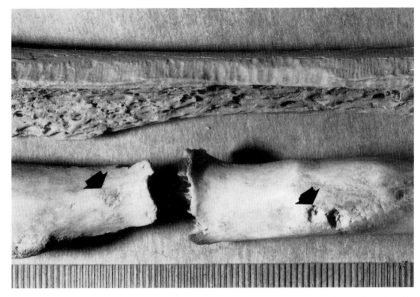

Figure 3.55. Peñasco Blanco. Five proximal ulna fragments with probable carnivore perimortem chewing damage. Specimen in lower right was undamaged. AMNH H/9155 (CGT neg. 5-4-94:15).

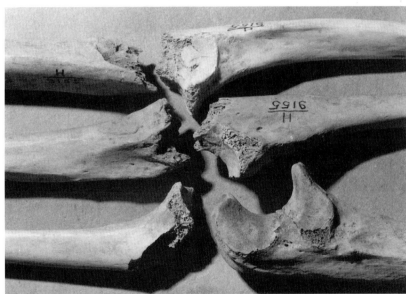

Figure 3.56. Peñasco Blanco. At the time of death of the person represented by the scapula and long bone fragment, prior breakage and infection was advanced on both bones. This unhealed condition suggests that the shoulder flesh might have smelled bad (necrotic or sickly) and possibly was considered inedible by the assailants. Both pieces, however, have perimortem breakage, but no discernable polishing. AMNH H/11801 (CGT neg. 5-27-93:22).

Figure 3.57. Peñasco Blanco. Scapula fragment with multiple sets of anvil abrasions. Striations are each about 3.0 mm long. AMNH H/11801 (CGT neg. 5-27-93:27).

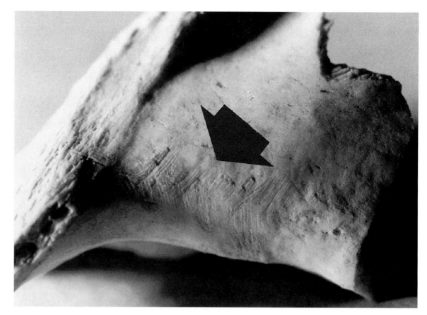

Figure 3.58. Peñasco Blanco. Charred rib (upper) and burned long bone fragment (length, 7.5 cm). AMNH H/11801 (CGT neg. 5-27-93:21).

Figure 3.59. Peñasco Blanco. End-polishing of nonhuman long bone splinter in collection with human bone. Identification of this small fragment as nonhuman is based on its very smooth surface and high density. Actual width of image in photograph is 3.3 cm. AMNH H/11801 (CGT neg. 5-27-93:15).

tention by the more broadly experienced rancher and lay archaeologist Richard Wetherill.

In 1898 Pepper (1920:378) noted on empirical grounds the possibility of prehistoric Chaco Canyon cannibalism. This was a few years before Hough's 1901 discovery at Canyon Butte 3 in Arizona. Still, it was Smithsonian scientist Hough who promptly made public his discovery and interpretation of cannibalism in 1902. Privately supported Pepper was eventually pressured by AMNH officials in 1920 to publish at least his field notes, which contained only the few brief remarks quoted earlier.

Inasmuch as cannibalism was not then practiced by living Southwestern Indians but was well known by early Spaniards to have been ritually practiced in central and northern Mexico, it is understandable that both Pepper and Hough attributed their discoveries to starvation or ritual events instead of to deliberate, nonreligious practices. Working at a time of blind romanticism about the "noble American Indian savage," they may have found any other possibility inconceivable. It might be all right to eat someone in an emergency, as Eskimos did on occasion, but it was too much then, and seems still to be so today, even to think that ancient Indians might have eaten human flesh for some reason other than starvation.

We have moved from cases of violence to two episodes of probable cannibalism. The Canyon Butte episode took place some distance from a major prehistoric population center, which provides an excuse for attributing it to some anomalous manner of uncivilized life often found in rural folk. The episode at Peñasco Blanco, however—at the very center of prehistoric Southwestern architectural development—forces us to sit up and pay attention. Although one might blindly dismiss a single case of cannibalism in Chaco Canyon, table 3.1 shows that there are other cases in the canyon proper—too many to dismiss as anomalies. Our next episode comes from Pueblo Bonito, the ultimate architectural icon of the prehistoric Southwestern Indian.

## 8
## Pueblo Bonito

**Claim Date.** 1920.

**Claimant.** George H. Pepper.

**Claim Type.** Cannibalism in Rooms 61 and 80. In addition, our skeletal analyses have turned up several cases of violence and possible human sacrifice.

**Other Designations.** 29SJ387; Bc253 (Lister and Lister 1981:237).

**Site Location.** Chaco Canyon, San Juan County, northwestern New Mexico. USGS Pueblo Bonito quadrangle (1966), T 21N, R 11W, SE ¼ of SW ¼ of Sec. 12.

**Site Type.** A great house that Lister and Lister (1981:237) report as having more than 300 ground-level rooms and at least 32 kivas, including two great kivas, and that may have stood five stories high.

**Cultural Affiliation.** Anasazi, Chaco branch.

**Chronology.** A.D. 900–1200.

**Excavators and Dates.** George H. Pepper, field director, and Richard Wetherill, foreman, for H.B.H. Hyde Exploring Expedition, 1896–1899. Later, Neil M. Judd (1954) directed excavations from 1921 to 1927 for the Smithsonian Institution and National Geographic Society. National Park Service archaeologists continue to conduct research on and stabilization of the great house. Although Pepper claimed cannibalism at Pueblo Bonito and Judd claimed violence, no skeletal analyst or archaeologist has since touched on these subjects.

**Institutional Storage.** With the help of Anibal Rodriguez, we searched for skeletal collections and accession records over the years at the American Museum of Natural History, Department of Anthropology. On May 5, 1994, we determined that the bones from Pepper's Room 80, which he claimed had been cannibalized, had reached New York and been cataloged (nos. 6850–6860). According to a handwritten note in the catalog, however, all the Room 80 bones except one entry that we could not locate were discarded at a later date. There seems to be no paper trail that would help to explain why the human remains from Peñasco Blanco that Pepper claimed to have been cannibalized were saved, whereas those for which he claimed cannibalism at Pueblo Bonito were not. There are no records for the Room 61 bones. Human remains from various other rooms were deposited at AMNH by Pepper and at NMNH by Judd.

**Site Reports.** Pepper (1920); Douglass (1935); Judd (1954); Judge (1989); others.

**Osteological Report.** There is none that deals with the human remains on which Pepper based his cannibalism claim. Studies of other Pueblo Bonito skeletons include those of Akins (1984, 1986), Akins and Schelberg (1984), Hrdlička (1931), and Palkovich (1984). The remains have been used for many topical studies.

**Skeletal Evidence of Stress.** Unknown for target remains.

**Burial Context.** Pepper (1920:378) remarked in his conclusions for the Pueblo Bonito excavations in the 1890s: "There was no evidence of human bones having been employed in the preparation of ornaments or implements. The finding of cracked and calcined human bones in some of the rooms brings up the question of the eating of human flesh by the people of this pueblo. There was no evidence of human bodies having been buried in rooms above the first floor and only portions of skeletons were in evidence in Rooms 61 and 80 which contained broken and charred bones."

**Associated Artifacts.** An unusual painted stone mortar, 21.6 cm (8.5 inches) in height, was found in Room 80 at a depth of 1 m (3 feet 6 inches) near the west wall where Navajo workmen found broken and burned human bone. A close-up of the elaborately painted vessel is shown in Lister and Lister (1981:44). The mortar was earlier illustrated in place by Pepper (1920:266). Figure 3.62 gives an idea of the depth of room fill below the nearby Navajo workman, and it possibly shows some of the human bone fragments near the mortar.

**Figures.** 3.60–3.81.

**Taphonomy.** GHP; CGT and JAT.

*MNI.* Rooms 61 and 80: at least two cannibalized individuals, ages and sexes unknown. Room 33: two adult males and one adult female evidencing violence. Contrary to Pepper, who believed that running water during rainstorms was responsible for disturbing various burials, we found that a minimum of three individuals recovered from Room 33 had met with violence (table 3.8, numbers 3, 10, and 14).

Table 3.8
Notes on Crania from Pueblo Bonito Room 33

| FIELD NO. | AMNH NO. | SEX | AGE | NOTES |
|---|---|---|---|---|
| 1 | H.3659 | M | Mid-age adult | No damage; occipital deformation; grade 2 palatine torus; grade 1 mandibular torus. |
| 2 | H.3660 | M | Old adult | No damage; lambdoidal deformation; grade 2 palatine torus; grade 3 mandibular torus. |
| 3 | H.3661 | M? | Young adult | Broken occipital, nose, left mandibular coronoid process (figs. 3.66–3.68); no tori; lambdoidal deformation. |
| 4 | H.3662 | M | Old adult | No damage; cranial deformation; grade 1 palatine torus. |
| 5 | H.3663 | F | Old adult | No damage, cranial deformation; grade 2 mandibular torus; mummified head. |
| 6 | H.3664 | M | Very old adult | No damage; lambdoidal deformation; grade 1 palatine torus; grade 3 mandibular torus. |
| 7 | H.3665 | F? | Young adult | No damage; lambdoidal deformation; grade 1 palatine torus; grade 0 mandibular torus. |
| 8 | H.3666 | M? | Old adult | No damage; no deformation; no tori. |
| 9 | H.3667 | ? | ? | "Exchanged with Dr. Broom, 1914." |
| 10 | H.3668 | F? | Old adult | Broken right temporal, maxilla, smashed mandible (figs. 3.69–3.70); lambdoidal deformation; grade 1 palatine torus; grade 0 mandibular torus. |
| 11 | H.3669 | M | Old adult | No damage; lambdoidal deformation; no tori. |
| 12 | H.3670 | M | Old adult | No damage; lambdoidal deformation; no tori. |
| 13 | H.3671 | M | Adult | No damage; most of skeleton present except pelves and C1, C2 vertebrae; tall; L femur = 44.8 cm; R femur = 45.6 cm.; L tibia = 39.2 cm; R tibia = 39.4 cm |
| 14 | H.3672 | M | Adult | Several cuts and breaks on head (figs. 3.71–3.80); cuts on C1 vertebra; most of postcranial skeleton present and without damage; lambdoidal deformation; grade 2 porotic hyperostosis; grade 0 cribra orbitalia; grade 1 palatine torus; tall; L femur = 43.8 cm; R femur = 44.7 cm; L tibia = 38.4 cm; R tibia 38.1 cm. |

NOTE: Considerable numbers of postcranial bones from about ten individuals are stored as mixed and disassembled H.3658. Some humeri have carnivore chewing on ends; one proximal end of ulna has been chewed. No obvious human damage was observed for scapulae, hands and feet, vertebrae, pelves, legs, and most ribs.

Figure 3.60. Pueblo Bonito, Chaco Canyon, New Mexico, May 1896. Setting up field kitchen. AMNH Anthropology Archives (CGT copy neg. 5-4-94:32).

Figure 3.61. Pueblo Bonito, May 1896. From left: E. C. Cushman, Clayton Wetherill, George H. Pepper, Hatch, and Richard Wetherill—the group Pepper called the "quintet." Photograph was set up by R. Wetherill; Pepper worked the camera shutter with a long string. Note that all the men's hats are tilted back, a photographic trick Wetherill must have learned to overcome the usual hat shadowing of faces. AMNH Anthropology Archives (CGT copy neg. 5-4-94:34).

Later excavations by Judd turned up several individuals in Rooms 320A and 330 that we recognize as having perimortem cranial breakage and cut and abrasion marks.

*Age and Sex.* Catalog lacks age and sex information for the remains from Rooms 61 and 80. The Room 33 remains evidencing violence, which we examined, were two males and one female, each more than 18 years of age.

*Preservation.* Unknown, but Pepper's remark about burning suggests that the overall condition may have been poor, possibly explaining the subsequent discarding.

*Bone and Fragment Number.* Although Pepper (1920) did not indicate the amount of bone recovered, the AMNH catalog entries for Room 80 include the following 17 or more human skeletal elements, all from within room fill at the same level, with the majority discovered in the northwest corner of the room: "6850 80 Tibia, Femur Hu-

Figure 3.62. Pueblo Bonito, 1896? Pepper proposed that the human remains found in Rooms 61 and 80 (arrow, lower right) had been cannibalized. These two rooms were separated from one another by at least ten others, making it unlikely that the human remains in the rooms were the result of a single episode of cannibalism. Photographer uncertain. AMNH Anthropology Archives (CGT copy neg. 5-4-94:5).

man Against N. wall 13'-6" from E. wall; 6851 80 Ribs (3) Southeast Corner; 6852 80 Fibula, etc. East central part; 6853 80 Scapula, etc. Same position as 6850; 6854 80 Clavicle and Rib 14' W of E. wall near N. Wall; 6855 80 Radius calcined 7'-8" E. and 1'-5" from S. wall; 6856 80 Radius 14' W. from N.E. corner 3' S. of N. wall; 6857 80 Rib 7'-2" E. of S.W. corner 1' N of S. wall; 6858 80 Rib 10'-6" E. of S.W. corner 2'-6" N. of S. wall; 6859 80 Scapula From centre of room; 6860 80 Rib 16' W. of N.E. corner 3' S. of N. wall."

Handwritten notes in the typed catalog indicate that the foregoing bones were subsequently discarded, except for item 6854, which was transferred to AMNH Anthropology catalog 99.

*Breakage.* Yes.

*Cut Marks.* Unknown.

*Burning.* At least one radius was cataloged as calcined.

*There is no information for Anvil Abrasions, Polishing, Verte-*

Figure 3.63. Pueblo Bonito, Room 80, 1896? The painted stone mortar in center of view is located near the human charnel deposit, some pieces of which may be in the foreground. AMNH Anthropology Archives (CGT copy neg. 5-4-94:3).

*brae Number, Scalping, Gnawing, Chewing, Insect Parts, or Other Modification.*

Judd's Human Remains. Our examinations were systematic, but we did not develop element inventories for lack of time. The following are individuals at NMNH with some perimortem damage, disarticulation, or other item of interest: Catalog no. 327058 (FS1392), Room 320A, female. Catalog no. 327059 (FS1393), Room 320A, female. Catalog no. 327059 (FS1382), Room 320A, parts of 5 other individuals. Catalog no. 327060 (FS1380), Room 320A, skeleton in NE corner. Catalog no. 327072, female with two cuts on frontal, 5 mm and 11 mm long, respectively. Has lambdoidal deformation. Catalog no. 327077, enlarged R lower I2 without R lower C. Defect pits in other teeth. Upper teeth normal but have defect pits. Catalog no. 327083 (FS1946), Room 330, adult male. Skull breakage, blown-out socket L

Figure 3.64. Pueblo Bonito, 1896? The location of Room 61 (arrow, center), where burned and broken human bone was found that Pepper suggested represented cannibalism. Photographer uncertain. AMNH Anthropology Archives (CGT copy neg. 5-4-94:7).

Figure 3.65. Pueblo Bonito, 1897? Looking westward and down into Room 61. There is no known record that the human remains found in this room were shipped back to New York. Photographer uncertain. AMNH Anthropology Archives notation for this photograph (no. 212, Pueblo Bonito 171-226) indicates that two of the Navajos are "Klioliga and son" (CGT copy neg. 5-4-94:11).

118

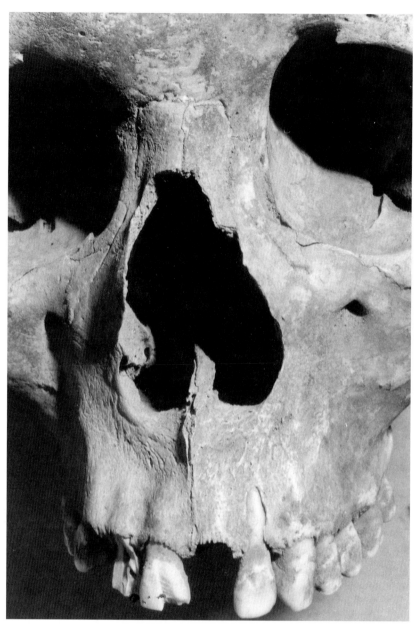

Figure 3.66. Pueblo Bonito, Room 33, Skeleton 3. Young adult male? showing perimortem breakage of the nasal bones. This room contained several "disturbed" burials. Our taphonomic analysis suggests that bone damage in these burials was more likely caused by perimortem violence than by postmortem disturbance. G. H. Pepper series. AMNH H/3661 (CGT neg. 5-6-94:21).

Figure 3.67. Pueblo Bonito, Room 33, Skeleton 3. Perimortem impact breakage of posterior vault. G. H. Pepper series. AMNH H/3661 (CGT neg. 5-6-94:20).

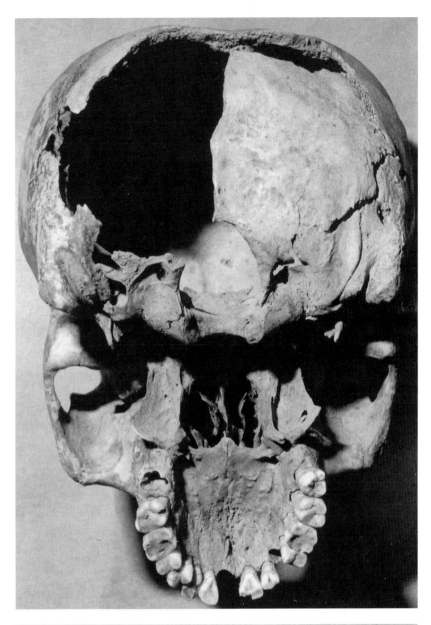

Figure 3.68. Pueblo Bonito, Room 33, Skeleton 3. Perimortem breakage of left mandibular coronoid process. Compare with figure 3.36. G. H. Pepper series. AMNH H/3661 (CGT neg. 5-6-94:22).

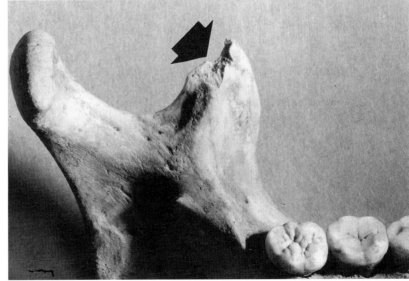

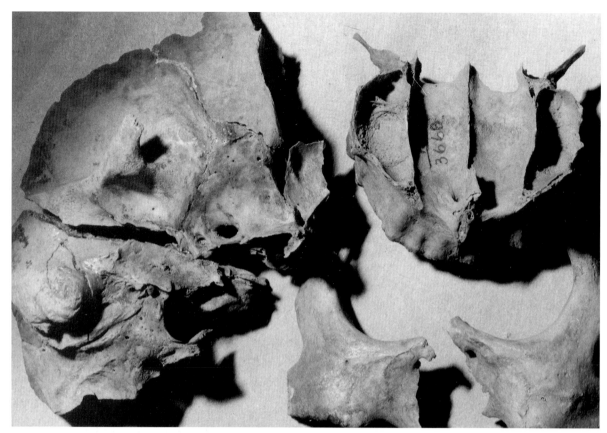

Figure 3.69. Pueblo Bonito, Room 33, Skeleton 10. Old adult female? showing perimortem breakage of entire head. Shown are right temporal bone, maxilla, and left and right zygomatic bones. G. H. Pepper series. AMNH H/3668 (CGT neg. 5-6-94:24).

Figure 3.70. Pueblo Bonito, Room 33, Skeleton 10. Perimortem breakage of anterior and inferior mandibular symphysis region. G. H. Pepper series. AMNH H/3668 (CGT neg. 5-6-94:25).

Figure 3.71. Pueblo Bonito, Room 33, Skeleton 14. Adult male with perimortem breakage of right side of skull and frontal bone. Face has been broken away from vault. Back of head is up and to the left. Arrow points to cut marks. G. H. Pepper series. AMNH H/3672 (CGT neg. 5-6-94:16).

Figure 3.72. Pueblo Bonito, Room 33, Skeleton 14. Detail of right lateral perimortem vault breakage shown in figure 3.71. Arrows point to cut marks. G. H. Pepper series. AMNH H/3672 (CGT neg. 6-29-89:18).

Figure 3.73. Pueblo Bonito, Room 33, Skeleton 14. Deep perimortem cut mark on anterior border of left temporal bone. Orbit of left eye is at upper left. G. H. Pepper series. AMNH H/3672 (CGT neg. 6-29-89:16).

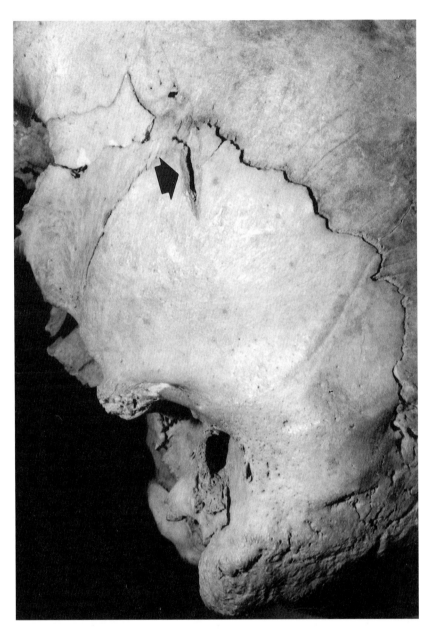

Figure 3.74. Pueblo Bonito, Room 33, Skeleton 14. Detail of perimortem cut marks in the left temporal-frontal junction area. G. H. Pepper series. AMNH H/3672 (CGT neg. 5-6-94:13).

Figure 3.75. Pueblo Bonito, Room 33, Skeleton 14. Perimortem breakage and chopping marks on a cranial fragment. Illustrated bone area is 3.4 cm wide. G. H. Pepper series. AMNH H/3672 (CGT neg. 5-6-94:10).

Figure 3.76. Pueblo Bonito, Room 33, Skeleton 14. Perimortem cut marks on the right lower orbital border. G. H. Pepper series. AMNH H/3672 (CGT neg. 5-6-94:12).

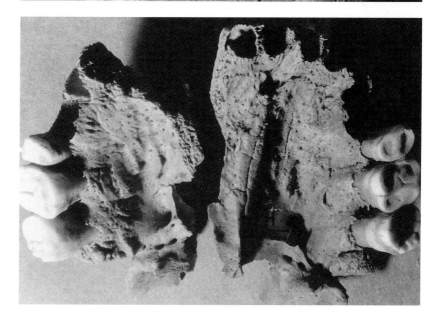

Figure 3.77. Pueblo Bonito, Room 33, Skeleton 14. Perimortem breakage of the maxilla, which has an unusually large palatine torus for an Anasazi cranium. G. H. Pepper series. AMNH H/3672 (CGT neg. 5-6-94:17).

124

Figure 3.78. Pueblo Bonito, Room 33, Skeleton 14. Perimortem cutting of the superior surface of the first cervical vertebra lateral to the articular surface. G. H. Pepper series. AMNH H/3672 (CGT neg. 5-6-94:9).

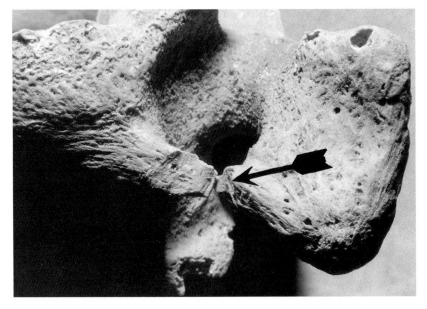

Figure 3.79. Pueblo Bonito, Room 33, Skeleton 14. Perimortem cutting of left orbital border of frontal bone. G. H. Pepper series. AMNH/3672 (CGT neg. 5-6-94:14).

Figure 3.80. Pueblo Bonito, Room 33, Skeleton 14. Perimortem cutting of right temporal bone. Illustrated bone area is 2.5 cm wide. G. H. Pepper series. AMNH/3672 (CGT neg. 5-6-94:11).

Figure 3.81. Pueblo Bonito, 1896. Sifting Room 33 fill for turquoise beads. From left: unidentified Navajo, O. Buck, G. Pepper, R. Wetherill. AMNH Anthropology Archives (CGT copy neg. 5-4-94:1).

upper I1 and I2, perimortem breakage of upper crowns of RI1, LR M1, lower M2. Maxilla adjacent to nasal opening has breakage. Catalog no. 327096 (FS1943), Room 330, female, 15–18 years, blown-out L upper I1. Catalog no. 327097 (FS1933), Room 330, cut mark 5 mm long on left mandible near anterior border ascending ramus, and possible anvil abrasions. Five to six years old. Unnumbered maxilla in box labeled "Pueblo Bonito 327095," which is skeleton FS1931 from Room 330. FS1931 is a 12- to 15-year-old skull together with an adult maxilla and postcranial bones without arms and most vertebrae. Adult maxilla has notched teeth and is about the right age to belong to postcranials numbered 327095. Catalog no. 327127 (FS1880), Room 329, skull, 6-year-old child. Cut marks on occipital bone. Abrasions on right side of frontal. Two adult skulls were found above a jar placed with this child.

**Archaeologist's Interpretation.** Pepper (1920:378) suggested that cannibalism had occurred at both Pueblo Bonito and Peñasco Blanco. He based his proposal for Pueblo Bonito on the damaged condition of the human bones in Rooms 61 and 80, which resembled those from Peñasco Blanco. Coupled with what Pepper believed to have been the remains of cannibal feasts was the curious scarcity of human skeletons in Pueblo Bonito. Pepper and Wetherill recovered not many more than 18 skeletons in five other Pueblo Bonito rooms; 14 of them came from Room 33. Most of the 14 had disarticulated lower jaws. The Hyde Exploring Expedition added only about 30 other, variously complete skeletons, all from rodent-disturbed shallow graves in burial mounds at some distance from Pueblo Bonito. Like later Chaco Canyon archaeologists, particularly Edgar L. Hewett (1936) and Judd (1954), Pepper was puzzled by the scarcity of human skeletons, considering the grand size of Pueblo Bonito and other standing ruins in Chaco Canyon.

Pepper (1920:223) described the situation in Room 61 (figs. 3.63 and 3.64) this way: "Most of the specimens found in this room were in the debris covering the floor; fragments of a human skull, scattered about in the southeast corner; pieces of a jaw with teeth and fragments of the cranium, blackened and charred to such an extent that it seems hardly possible that it could have been accidental. There was no evidence of there having been a fire in this room. . . . The pieces of skull lay as if they had been scattered by hand. . . . There were a few fragments of human bones beside the skull, but these showed no evidence of having been burnt."

In Room 80, several rooms west of Room 61 at a depth of 1.06 m (3 feet 6 inches), Pepper (1920:267) observed that "a number of human bones were found. They were scattered throughout the debris and had evidently fallen from one of the upper rooms. These bones show evidences of having been burned and they were broken, as is the case with other human bones found in the pueblos of this group; from the fact that they had been in one of the upper rooms, it may be that they had been used for some ceremonial purpose, as it was not the custom to bury even portions of bodies in the upper rooms."

**Other Interpretations.** Judd (1954:337) mentioned only that Pepper had found broken and burned human bone in Rooms 61 and 80. He said nothing about Pepper's cannibalism suggestion. Neither did Robert Lister and Florence Lister (1981:36). Nancy Akins's (1986) Chaco Canyon mortuary study is especially conspicuous in its lack of discussion of Pepper's cannibalism claim for Pueblo Bonito and Peñasco Blanco and of a third claim for Chacoan cannibalism, one made by Frank H. H. Roberts for damaged bones found in a site he called Small House, which we review later in this chapter.

**Discussion.** Because our direct taphonomic examination of the 578 whole and fragmented human skeletal pieces from Peñasco Blanco supports Pepper's claim for their having been cannibalized, we accept his interpretation for the cracked and burned human bones from Pueblo Bonito Rooms 61 and 80 as well, even though we did not see them and he did not recognize all six of our minimum taphonomic criteria for proposing cannibalism. In addition, our acceptance of Pepper's Pueblo Bonito claim rests with the fact that Pueblo Bonito is within easy walking distance of Peñasco Blanco and Small House, downstream and upstream in Chaco Canyon, respectively, where there were other human charnel deposits that do evince the taphonomic signature of cannibalism. We would, of course, be more secure in our acceptance of Pepper's claim had there been even a small amount of additional documentation—if the catalog had given estimates of the ages for the bones from Room 80, for example, or if the unpublished photograph of the room had shown the bones instead of just an X marking the spot from which they had been removed.

Explaining the Pueblo Bonito and other hypothesized Chacoan cannibalism may be facilitated by taking into account the overall mortuary record in Chaco Canyon—a record that has both biological and cultural components. For example, the disturbance of many of the surprisingly few burials in Pueblo Bonito has been interpreted in two primary ways by the principal excavators. Pepper (1920) reported skeletons from only seven rooms: Room 32 (1 partial skeleton); Room 33 (12 of 14 skeletons disturbed; at the least, the mandibles were detached in most cases); Room 53 (at least two disturbed skeletons); Room 56 (at least two completely disturbed skeletons, possibly disordered by Warren K. Moorehead, the Ohio archaeologist Pepper allowed to dig in 1897); Room 61 (one of the cannibalism claims); Room 79 (one subfloor child burial); and Room 80 (again, cannibalism). Pepper (1909:248) attributed the disturbances, particularly those of the numerous Room 33 skeletons, to the "havoc wrought by the inflow of water."

Given the generally good recovery of perishable organic materials, Judd (1954:339–340) did not accept Pepper's explanation. Judd, like Pepper, discovered only a few burials, and most were disturbed. Judd thought the disarticulations were caused by grave robbers who had ransacked at least four of the burial rooms: "It seems clear that the [skeletal] disorder could have been caused by human agency only and not natural forces. . . . [With near abandonment of Pueblo Bonito] a relatively small band of raiders, striking with speed and ruthlessness, could so paralyze the broken community that its store of maize, its womenfolk, and even the jewels on its shallowly buried dead might be seized at little risk."

Theodore R. Frisbie (1978:213) believed Pepper's explanation to be unsatisfactory, reluctantly siding with Judd, but manifestly he would have been delighted if his hypothesis that the "majority of individuals [had been] sacrificed to accompany the primary burials" could somehow have been proven.

Akins (1986:125) was unimpressed by the arguments of Pepper, Judd, or Frisbie for the Pueblo Bonito burial disturbances. She believed that such disturbance was a common "natural" problem in the canyon: "Secondary burial combined with a variety of phenomena such as rodent and carnivore activity, trash deposition, and the effects of rain is at least as plausible as previous explanations."

We found no perimortem damage to Pepper's Room 32 skeletal remains. However, as figures 3.65–3.77 and table 3.8 show, perimortem breakage and cut marks occur on at least the crania of burials 3, 10, and 14 from Room 33—damage that cannot be attributed to rainwater rushing into the room. The cutting and breaking is not all easily blamed on turquoise-seeking grave robbers, either, although the possibility exists that it was the looters' way of denigrating the dead. If grave robbers were solely responsible for the disturbance and damage, it is surprising that in the two-by-two meter "above floor" room containing 12 bodies, vandals left behind 30,000 turquoise, shell, and jet beads, ornaments, and carvings, and that 30 or more bowls, jars, and pitchers were not trampled and broken to bits.

We reject raiding and associated grave robbing as the cause of the disturbance because there is perimortem damage that is more likely due to antemortem events than to postmortem grave robbing, and there is no positive evidence for raids on Pueblo Bonito. To argue for raiding, one needs independent evidence such as structural burning, abandoned bodies on floors, and other persuasive signs like those found by Fewkes at Awatovi, Wendorf at Te'ewi, Di Peso at Casas Grandes, and McGimsey at Mariana Mesa—all sites discussed in this chapter.

The perimortem condition of the Room 33 skeletons suggests human sacrifice with later carnivore disturbance. Skeleton 14 had a wealth of grave goods and had received a great deal of cranial trauma and cutting, as well as cutting of his neck—which looks more like Mesoamerican sacrificial burials evidencing mutilation (see Alta Vista in chapter 4) than like any other known rich burial in the Southwest, such as the Sinagua "Magician" (McGregor 1943) or the Hohokam "Mexican" (Bair, Turner, and Turner n.d.).

In addition to the perimortem skeletal trauma we have illustrated and tabulated here, there are other puzzling aspects about the Pueblo Bonito mortuary assemblages. Judd completely excavated about 175 rooms and kivas, yet found skeletons in only four. (A few isolated human bones and teeth were recovered in other rooms and in at least one kiva.) Clearly, there was no regular practice of intramural burial at Pueblo Bonito, regardless of how many of its rooms were occupied at any one time. Like the few skeletons found by Pepper and Wetherill in the 190 rooms they dug, Judd's finds and their context were unusual. In Room 320 Judd (1954:325–326) reported finding 10 skeletons—9 females and a fetus—largely disarticulated and scattered on the room floor. (Actually, there were more individuals represented.) In Room 326, at least 9 of the 10 or 11 adults were also females, and again some were disarticulated and scattered. Females accounted for most of the 24 individuals found in Room 329—17 women, 1 man, and 6 children. All of the adults were disarticulated and scattered.

Room 330 had 23 skeletons. Judd (1954:329 and elsewhere) believed this room had been built during his "Old Bonito" construction phase, which occurred during Pueblo II times (A.D. 900–1100). In it, the 4 women were in the minority; the majority was made up of 13 men plus 6 children. Only four of the corpses had escaped perimortem damage: "The others had been callously pulled and kicked about" (Judd 1954:333). One of the human lumbar vertebrae in this room had an arrowhead embedded in it—lethal, judging from the lack of periosteal reaction. One of the females (NMNH 327096), 15 to 18 years old, has a blown-out alveolar socket for her left upper central incisor, and a 5- to 6-year-old child has a 5-mm-long cut mark and possible anvil abrasions on the anterior border of the left ascending ramus.

Judd's skeletal numbers are lower than those determined by Ann Palkovich (1984) from her osteological examinations at the NMNH. She found that Room 320 contained 21 individuals (1 male, 13 female, 7 unknown); Room 326, 18 (4 male, 10 female, 4 unknown); Room 329, 24 (2 male, 10 female, 12 unknown), and Room 330, 32 (16 male, 9 female, 7 unknown).

Room 330 also produced a provocative dental finding. Accessioned November 20, 1924, the Room 330 skeletal remains were assigned catalog numbers 327079–327101. In the wooden storage tray containing catalog no. 327095 is the skull of a 12- to 15-year-old subadult along with an unnumbered, tooth-bearing older adult maxilla and numbered leg bones. Some of the teeth in the adult maxilla had been intentionally chipped (see fig. 5.7). Chipping is present on the mesial and distal borders of the right upper first incisor and the left upper second incisor. It is also present on the mesial border of the right upper second incisor and right upper canine, which are developmentally fused into one large tooth (another rare instance of canine fusion occurs in an individual from Room 320A, suggesting a genetic relationship). The distal border of the left upper first incisor is broken, so it is impossible to say whether chipping had been present on that surface, which is also the case for the mesial borders of the left upper first incisor and the left upper canine. In addition, there is an interproximal (toothpick) groove at the crown-root junction of the mesial surface of the left upper first premolar. Intentional modification of anterior teeth is a diagnostic feature of Mexican Indian rather than Southwestern teeth. Chipping, seemingly with a punch and hammer, is one of the common ways in which teeth were modified in Mexico. It is possible that Room 330 at Pueblo Bonito contained the remains of a prehistoric Mexican.

The burial excavations in Room 330 were well recorded by Frans Blom, whose field notes are curated in the National Anthropological Archives. Even though the burials were unearthed during a four-day digging blitz in July 1924, Blom managed to record their locations, condition, and associations. Most had what he termed "crushed or smashed skulls." Skulls were frequently detached and positioned in clusters of two or three. There were at least five instances in which small arrowheads lay near or upon skulls. For skeleton 22, he recorded that its "vertebrae were found in a circle, as if they had been strung on a string and laid down in a ring" (Blom 1924:62). O. C. Haven's photographs of the charnel deposit in Room 330 (Judd 1954:pl. 98, 99) show the skeletons wildly scattered, awkwardly positioned, and sometimes face down.

From the visual disarray one senses some amount of time compression, such that one stratigraphic level contained a mix of earlier, deliberate, formal burial events and later postmortem disturbances, just as Judd proposed. However, we also get a subjective impression of haphazard disposal and dumping of some bodies or body parts onto the floor of Room 330. The fractured heads can be seen in Judd's photographs of this and other charnel rooms. In the absence of regular intramural burying of dead adults in Pueblo Bonito, both formal burials and the haphazard dumping of whole bodies or parts could have been linked to unnatural deaths, perhaps killings for sacrifice or other motives. A hypothesis of human sacrifice can be entertained because of the unusual sex ratios in these rooms. Where else in the Southwest does a large ruin have evidence for very little intramural burial, possible cannibalism, very unequal sexual representation, perimortem trauma, disarticulated bodies, very few subfloor infant burials, the skeletal remains of a possible Mexican, and evidence of direct trade and ideological contact with Mesoamerica?

In some instances Judd felt he was able to determine that the scattered and mutilated Pueblo Bonito bodies had first been buried, because there were ceramic grave goods, other durable items made of common and semiprecious stone and animal bone, and an occasional preserved burial mat. He did not say, however, whether there were any signs of unnatural death. Judd (1954:334–335) based his grave-robbing thesis on the chaotic burial conditions in rooms 320, 326, 329, and 330, where two-thirds of 68 "interments" had been violated: "Of the other 45 bodies most had been dragged from their burial mats before decomposition was complete. Articulated limbs, a

torso here and there, skulls with part of the cervical vertebrae attached, all provide seemingly convincing evidence that the general
confusion in these four rooms was caused by irreverent hands."

Thus, we can view these skeletons as indicating two temporally
separated actions—the traumatic damage done to the living or dying,
and the later tearing apart of bodies by prehistoric Indians in search
of turquoise and other valuables, or else intent on desecrating the
graves with or without robbery. There is no temporally fine physical
evidence to help explain why the cutting and breakage occurred, although given the monumental setting of the Chaco great houses and
the rich deposits of turquoise and other items of wealth and prestige,
with and without human remains, it would be easy to continue specu-
lating about ritual sacrifices and special mortuary events along lines
well known for Mesoamerica.

It is not speculation, however, when we cite Judd (1954:129, pl.
28) concerning three large, bifacially chipped, leaf-shaped stone
knives found with other ritual items in a wall cache in Kiva Q, the
second largest great kiva at Pueblo Bonito: "They far excel in skill
and execution all other blades known to me from the main Pueblo
area. . . . I doubt that their better has been found elsewhere in the
United States. . . . The materials used are foreign to Chaco Canyon."
Judd made no comparisons with Mesoamerican ceremonial knives,
but they are similar to the large flint knives stuck in the noses and
mouths of decapitated skulls buried at the great Aztec Templo Mayor
and elsewhere—knives called *tecpatl,* the weapon of Huitzilopochtli,
the warrior god whose knife was used in human sacrifice (Matos
1984:161). Moreover, the human effigy vessels from Chaco Canyon
illustrated by Pepper (1906:pl. 29), especially the ecstatic-appearing,
tatooed male humpback with a possible quid in his left cheek, remind
us of west Mexican drug-linked effigy vessels. Pepper, too, recognized
a Mexican similarity.

From these comments, it can be seen that a very detailed taphonomic analysis of all the noncannibalized Pueblo Bonito and other
Chaco Canyon human remains is needed. It could be argued that the
scatter and disarticulation of bodies in Rooms 33, 320, 329, and 330,
and in other sites, represent the end results of human sacrifice and
special mortuary activity (i.e., Reyman), rather than grave robbing
(Judd) or natural bioturbation (Akins). In Mesoamerica, human sacrifice and cannibalism go hand in hand. Given that cannibalism has
been established for Chaco Canyon as far as circumstantial evidence
permits, then there is no reason for the sacrifice component not also
to have been practiced by those who dominated the Chacoan community. Akins (1986) has convincingly demonstrated with a number of
lines of independent evidence that there were high-status burials in
Chaco Canyon. The skeletons of these elites and any associated human remains need to be examined microscopically for taphonomic
details that might better explain why and under what circumstances
they died, and chemical assays are in order to see whether they originated outside the desert Southwest.

Until all the Chaco Canyon human skeletal remains are examined
from a taphonomic perspective, there is only one other possible mortuary problem left to consider, namely, determining whether age and

sex profiles meet any sort of a priori demographic expectation. This can be done, thanks to Nancy Akins's tremendous effort to track down and inventory through records and skeletal collections all known burials from Chaco Canyon (1986:table B.1). Using her compilation, and dividing the sample into children and adults to facilitate comparison, of the 490 individuals Akins identified, 33.9% (166 of 490) are children below the age of 12. Subtracting her 45 individuals of unknown age from the total of 490, the percentage of children rises to 37.3% (166 of 445).

Most large archaeological sites with relatively good preservation, such as Hawikuh, produce about 50% children, although the percentage can vary considerably. A marked difference from 50% is usually associated with small sample size. Because the Chaco mortuary sample approaches 500 individuals, the 10% or more "deficiency" in children is unlikely to be a simple sampling error. Nor can it be blamed on good infant health or on bad preservation. In the case of health, one of the more striking impressions given by the Chaco Canyon skeletons is that of the relatively large number of children who had porotic hyperostosis and cribra orbitalia in progress at the time of their deaths. Many of these children were likely anemic, and some severely so, raising their risk of infection. Palkovich (1984) has drawn the same conclusion. Bone preservation is no worse in the Chaco skeletal collections we have examined than in most other Southwestern collections of similar antiquity, and it is absolutely better than what is seen in burials from southern Arizona, such as those from Arizona State University's Lake Roosevelt project.

Thus, given Chaco Canyon's relatively good human bone preservation, the relatively poor health of Chaco children, which suggests an expected excess of childhood mortality, and the quite reasonable sample size, it would seem there are children missing from the Chaco mortuary population. Unusual burial location is just one of many possible factors that could have caused the lower-than-expected frequency of deceased children. Another factor is hinted at in Hopi and Zuni oral traditions about child sacrifice. Salmon Ruin, a great house to be discussed later, is linked by road with Chaco Canyon. There, at least 30 children were burned up in the flesh on top of Tower Kiva soon after two adults seemingly were cannibalized. Far to the south in Yucatan, but not irrelevant to the question, the number of Maya children sacrificed in the Chichén Itzá cenote was equal to that of adults and may even have been higher, if differential preservation could be measured. And again in Mexico, Robert B. Pickering (1985:309) identified more than 1,000 isolated bones of children in just part of the ceremonial area of Alta Vista in Zacatecas. Children were a significant part of the human skeletal element assemblage there that did not receive formal burial.

Were it not for the probable cannibalism in Chaco Canyon, other taphonomic riddles such as rampant burial "disturbance," and the unsolved problem of the canyon's missing cemeteries, there would be no compelling reason to ponder the question of possible missing child skeletal remains. But in the Chacoan taphonomic context, even the suspicion of missing children takes on a life of its own.

**9**

**Comb Wash**

**Claim Date.** 1929.

**Claimant.** Earl H. Morris.

**Claim Type.** Cannibalism.

**Other Designations.** None known.

**Site Location.** In Comb Wash on the first low ridge north of the mouth of Arch Canyon, Utah. USGS Brushy Basin Wash quadrangle (1957), T 37S, R 20E, NE ¼ of Sec. 25.

**Site Type.** Morris's (n.d.*a*:4) notes indicate that he dug in an "enormous amount of refuse" on the east and south sides of a "good sized site," one of many in the canyon bottom. Charles L. Bernheimer's notes (May 26, 1929) record that there were many ruins in the broad valley of Comb Wash.

**Cultural Affiliation.** Uncertain. Site location suggests Mesa Verde Anasazi.

**Chronology.** Morris's notes indicate that the ceramics were earlier than the ceramics he then called Mesa Verde Black-on-white. This would be sometime before A.D. 1200.

**Excavator and Date.** Earl H. Morris, May 27, 1929.

**Institutional Storage.** With the help of Anibal Rodriguez, we searched for this skeletal material on May 5, 1994, in the Department of Anthropology, American Museum of Natural History. Together we determined that there was no record that the bones had ever been cataloged or curated.

**Site Reports.** Morris's field notes for the 1929 Bernheimer Expedition, p. 4; Bernheimer's diary of the expedition, p. 10 (May 27, 1929).

**Osteological Report.** None known.

**Skeletal Evidence of Stress.** None known.

**Burial Context.** Morris said that in refuse two feet below the surface he encountered a layer of flat sandstone slabs under which were broken and burned human bones.

**Associated Artifacts.** One black-on-white ceramic vessel (Morris n.d.*a*:4).

**Figures.** None.

**Taphonomy.** EHM.

> *MNI.* 1.

> *Age and Sex.* Adult, sex unknown.

> *Breakage and burning were present. There is no information for Preservation, Bone and Fragment Number, Cut Marks, Anvil Abrasions, Polishing, Vertebrae Number, Scalping, Gnawing, Chewing, Insect Parts, or Other Modification.*

**Archaeologist's Interpretation.** Morris's notes (p. 4) indicate that he dug a 25-foot-long (7.6 m) trench in the site's refuse area. The refuse was 3–4.5 feet (0.9–1.4 m) deep. "About 8' farther up the slope, 2' from surface, were many flat sandstones forming a layer. Under these were the bones of an adult, the large ones cracked and broken. All were badly scattered. Many were partially burned, including the skull, which was broken apart, the pieces being scattered about. It seems not improbable that here was an indication of cannibalism. Mashed down under one of the stones was most of a very squat b-on-w pitcher" (Morris n.d.*a*:4).

**Other Interpretations.** Bernheimer's notes for May 27, 1929, say in part that "[John] Wetherill and Morris went to one of the many cliff

## Earl Halstead Morris

Stimulated as a boy by digging in Anasazi ruins with his father, Earl Morris, while still an undergraduate at the University of Colorado, joined Edgar L. Hewett's archaeological field parties, first in 1911 in New Mexico and then in 1912 and 1914 in Guatemala. In 1915 Morris obtained additional training under Nels C. Nelson in the Rio Grande area. On Nelson's recommendation, Clark Wissler, director of the American Museum of Natural History, persuaded Morris to excavate Aztec Ruin, which he did intermittently for the next ten years, finding much skeletal evidence of violence.

Morris's many-faceted career as a Southwestern and Mesoamerican archaeologist began with the University of Colorado, continued with the American Museum and the Carnegie Institution of Washington, and came full circle with a final career appointment at the University of Colorado and University of Colorado Museum. He excavated almost as many sites in the Southwest as Richard Wetherill (Lister and Lister 1968), but the two pioneers were separated by a critical generation of formal scientific education and emerging professionalism.

Morris proposed violence to explain human bone damage in Battle Cave, Arizona, and elsewhere. He claimed that cannibalism had occurred in sites in Utah, New Mexico, and Colorado. We emphasize La Plata 23 because it is Morris's only claim for cannibalism that we can directly assess—the skeletal remains from the other sites have been lost, mislaid, or discarded.

Life history: b. October 24, 1889, Chama, N.M.; d. June 25, 1956, Boulder, Colo., of a heart attack. Graduated valedictorian, Farmington High School, N.M.; B.A. 1914, M.A. 1916, University of Colorado. Additional graduate study 1917, Columbia University. Named first recipient of A. V. Kidder award, 1953. Married author-artist Ann McCheane Axtell in 1923 (d. 1945); Lucile Bowman, June 4, 1946. See E. A. Morris (1956), Burgh (1957), and Lister and Lister (1968).

houses to dig. They found two children's skeletons and one charred set of human bones which made them suspicious of cannibalism. They could explain it in no other way. The pottery found was post-basket-maker and pre-pueblo."

Discussion. Whenever we have been able to check Morris's interpretations of cannibalism or violence directly, we have found him to have been a keen, insightful, and reliable observer. For this reason we feel his claim for Comb Wash cannibalism is reasonable, even though we were unable to locate and study the damaged skeleton.

## 10
## Battle Cave

Claim Date. 1929.

Claimant. Earl H. Morris (fig. 3.82).

Claim Type. Violence. Morris and his wife, Ann Axtell Morris (1933:218), named this cave site Battle Cove because of its abundant record of violence and perimortem bone damage.

Other Designations. Battle Cove.

Site Location. In the south wall of Canyon del Muerto opposite Antelope House, Canyon de Chelly National Monument, northeastern Arizona. USGS Canyon del Muerto quadrangle (1955), T 5N, R 9W, center of projected Sec. 15.

Site Type. Large dry cave. The 120- to 150-meter-long cave had three areas: a western third with a level floor on which was a row of six to eight contiguous masonry rooms; a central third that was a sloping, uninhabitable ledge; and an eastern third containing several slab-lined cists and pot holes. It was in one of the eastern-area cists that Morris found the human remains in question.

Figure 3.82. Earl H. and Anne A. Morris (left), daughters Sarah Lane and Elizabeth Ann (holding "White Dog"), and nurse Pauline Miale (right). Location uncertain but may have been Awatovi in 1938 or 1939 (E. A. Morris, personal communication). Earl Morris excavated and named Battle Cave. Museum of Northern Arizona Archive photograph (Watson Smith scrapbook, p. 27).

**Cultural Affiliation.** Basketmaker II.

**Chronology.** Morris's notes indicate that the cave had a long occupation. Because he found only nonceramic waste in the cist, he assumed that the skeletal remains dated to Basketmaker II times. However, they seem to have been a secondary deposit, so the absence of pottery could be due to mortuary behavior instead of chronology.

**Excavators and Date.** Earl H. Morris, Ann Axtell Morris, and Edward M. Weyer, Jr., 1929.

**Institutional Storage.** Department of Anthropology, American Museum of Natural History.

**Site Report.** None. Field notes and catalogs are on file in the Department of Anthropology, AMNH.

**Osteological Report.** None.

**Skeletal Evidence of Stress.** None noted.

**Burial Context.** Dry "bone cist" 3.5 by 5 by 4 feet (1.07 by 1.52 by 1.22 m) deep. In addition to the human remains, the cist contained fragments of cultural and natural refuse, none identified by Morris as related to the human skeletal remains.

**Associated Artifacts.** Morris noted perishable waste materials including cordage, basket fragments, pieces of wood, fragments of cradleboards, cakes of pigment, etc.

**Figures.** 3.83–3.92.

**Taphonomy.** CGT and JAT, May 5, 1994. Skeletal inventory is in table 3.10.

　　*MNI.* 10 (EHM); 11 (CGT and JAT, table 3.9).

　　*Age and Sex.* Three children (4–5 years, 6, and 6–9 months); one 15- to 18-year-old male?; one young adult, male?; one middle-aged adult male; one old adult, male?; two old adult males; one old adult female; one old adult, sex?.

　　　*Preservation.* Good.

　　　*Bone and Fragment Number.* 180.

　　　*Breakage.* 5.5%.

　　　*Cut Marks.* 0.5%.

Table 3.9
Minimal Number of Individuals (MNI) at Battle Cave

| SKELETAL ELEMENT | AGE | SEX |
|---|---|---|
| Maxilla, whole | Old adult | ? |
| | Older adult | F |
| | Older adult | M |
| | Mid-adult | M |
| | 4–5 | ? |
| | Young adult | M? |
| Mandible, whole | 15–18 | M? |
| | Young adult | M |
| | Older adult | M |
| | Older adult | M |
| Mandible, right | Old adult | M? |
| Vault | <6 months | ? |
| | 6–9 months | ? |

SUMMARY: Eleven individuals. Two older adult males; one middle-aged adult male; one older adult female; one old adult, male?; one old adult, sex?; one young adult, male?; one 15- to 18-year-old, male?; one 4- to 5-year-old child; one 6- to 9-month-old infant; one infant less than 6 months old.

Table 3.10
Bone Elements and Perimortem Damage at Battle Cave

| SKELETAL ELEMENT | WHOLE | FRAGMENT | IMPACT BREAK | ANVIL ABRASION | CUT MARK | CHEWING |
|---|---|---|---|---|---|---|
| Cranial | | | | | | |
| Maxilla | 7 | 0 | 3 | 1 | 0 | 0 |
| Mandible | 3 | 3 | 2 | 0 | 0 | 0 |
| Frontal | 8 | 1 | 0 | 1 | 1 | 0 |
| Parietal | 15 | 2 | 1 | 0 | 0 | 0 |
| Occipital | 7 | 1 | 2 | 0 | 0 | 0 |
| Temporal | 14 | 0 | 2 | 1 | 0 | 0 |
| Base | 5 | 0 | 0 | 0 | 0 | 0 |
| Teeth (not counted) | | | | | | |
| Postcranial | | | | | | |
| Vertebrae | 50 | 0 | 0 | 0 | 0 | 0 |
| Rib | 35 | 0 | 0 | 0 | 0 | 0 |
| Humerus | 5 | 0 | 0 | 0 | 0 | 0 |
| Radius | 3 | 0 | 0 | 0 | 0 | 0 |
| Ulna | 6 | 0 | 0 | 0 | 0 | 0 |
| Hand & foot | + | 0 | 0 | 0 | 0 | 0 |
| Femur | 8 | 0 | 0 | 0 | 0 | 1 |
| Tibia | 7 | 0 | 0 | 0 | 0 | 0 |
| TOTAL (180) | 173 | 7 | 10 | 3 | 1 | 1 |
| PERCENTAGE | 96.1 | 3.9 | 5.5 | 1.7 | 0.5 | 0.5 |

Percentage of expected vertebrae = 18.9 (50 of 264; MNI = 11).

NOTE: Only elements that were present are listed. No burning or polishing was observed. Impact breakage, anvil abrasions, and cut marks represent perimortem damage. Chewing is postmortem damage.

Figure 3.83. Battle Cave, Canyon del Muerto, Arizona. Adult male skull with blown-out anterior tooth sockets and extensive perimortem breakage of cranial vault, left side of face, and nose. Arrow on forehead points to cut marks. AMNH 99/9572 (CGT neg. 5-5-94:32).

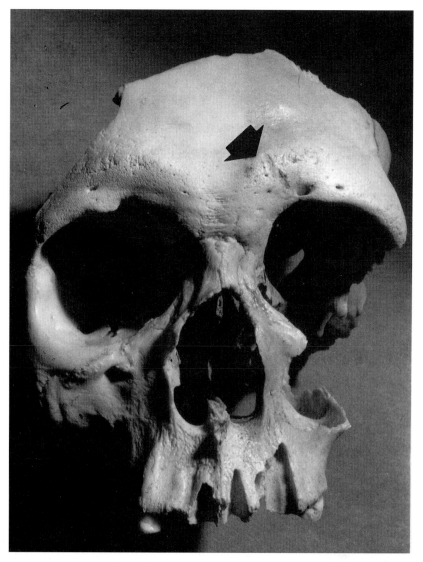

Figure 3.84. Battle Cave. Adult male of figure 3.83, showing perimortem breakage of cranium. Scale is 15 cm. AMNH 99/9572 (CGT neg. 5-5-94:34).

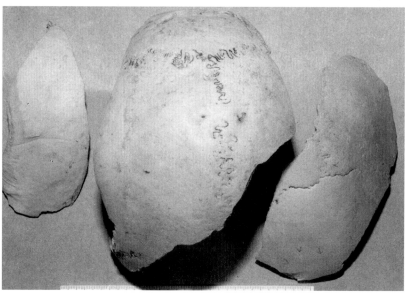

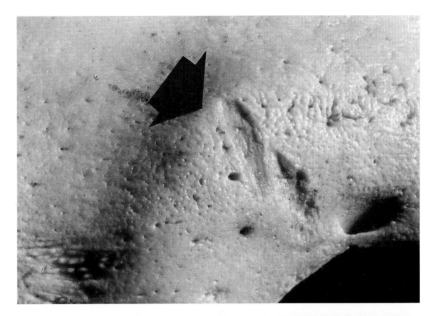

Figure 3.85. Battle Cave. Adult male of figure 3.83, showing perimortem cut mark on left supraorbital ridge. Actual width of image in photograph is about 3.3 cm. AMNH 99/9572 (CGT neg. 5-5-94:33).

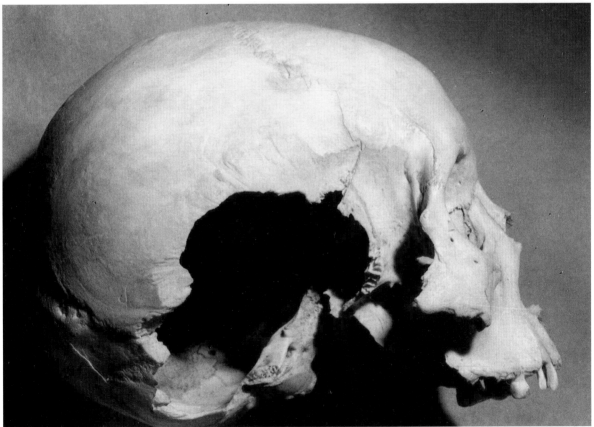

Figure 3.86. Battle Cave. Adult female skull with perimortem breakage of right temporal and zygomatic process. AMNH 99/9570 (CGT neg. 5-5-94:30).

Figure 3.87. Battle Cave. Adult female of figure 3.86, showing perimortem breakage of right maxillary alveolar bone and all three molar sockets. AMNH 99/9570 (CGT neg. 5-5-94:31).

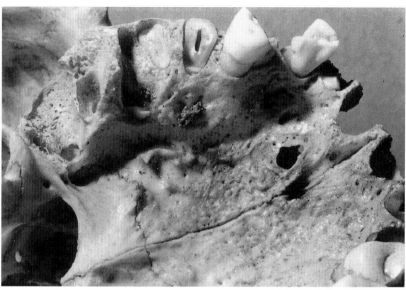

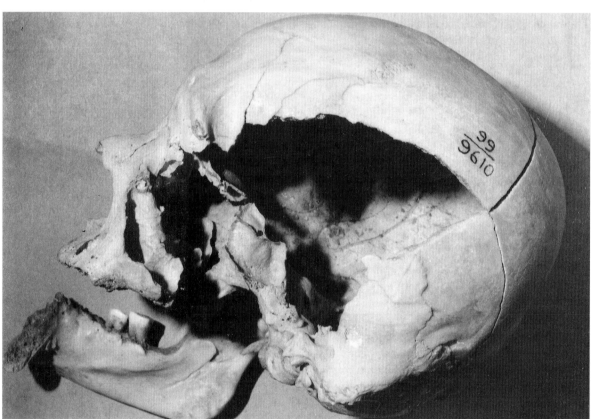

Figure 3.88. Battle Cave. Old adult male? with perimortem breakage of left side of cranial vault, face, and mandible. AMNH 99/9610 (CGT neg. 5-5-94:36).

Figure 3.89. Battle Cave. Adult male with perimortem breakage of cranial vault. Face and mandible are missing. AMNH 99/9577 (CGT neg. 5-5-94:35).

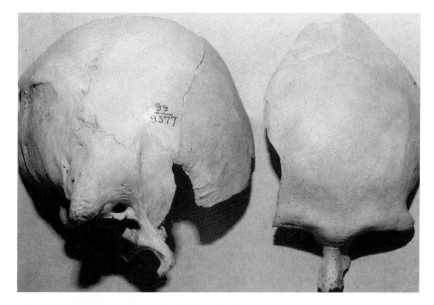

Figure 3.90. Battle Cave. Child (4–5 years old) with perimortem breakage of skull base. There are hammer or anvil abrasions at arrow, which suggests that the child was decapitated before the cranial base was smashed. AMNH 99/9569 (CGT neg. 5-5-94:29).

*Burning.* 0.0%.

*Anvil Abrasions.* 1.7%.

*Polishing.* 0.0%.

*Vertebrae Number.* 18.9% of expected (50 of 264).

*Scalping.* Probably not. Of the 66 cranial pieces, only one frontal bone has cut marks.

*Gnawing, Rodent.* 0.0%.

*Chewing, Carnivore.* 0.5%.

*Insect Parts.* None found during skeletal examination.

*Other Modification.* None noted.

Archaeologist's Interpretation. Morris (n.d.*b*:2) wrote: "In one cist, oval, some 3½ feet [wide] and 4 feet deep, there was a mass of disarticulated bones representing at least six adults, one child half grown, one smaller child, and two babies. These bones, and others to be mentioned, show that a great fight or massacre occurred here. Two adult skulls were entire; the whole face of one was crushed in; the right base

Figure 3.91. Battle Cave. Adult female with perimortem breakage of right mastoid process. Very faint anvil or hammer abrasions are present near the fracture. AMNH 99/9568 (CGT neg. 5-5-94:28).

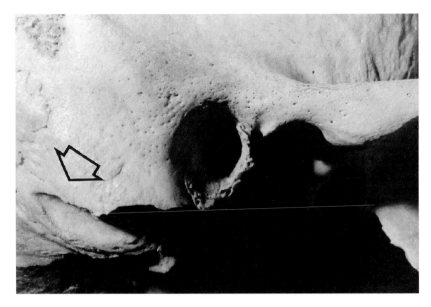

Figure 3.92. Battle Cave. Old adult mandible with perimortem breakage. Dark oblong hole near bottom of jaw (arrow) is a bone cancer site, not a trauma wound. AMNH 99/9578 (CGT neg. 5-5-94:27).

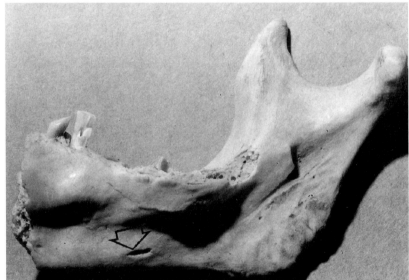

of another similarly treated and two smashed like egg shells. The larger child's skull was broken in around the foramen magnum and the entire base of the smaller one also knocked in. The heads of both babies were marked. Apparently these bones lay until after time and animals had weathered them, then were gathered up and thrown into the cist which was about a third full of dust and refuse."

Also in this end of the cave Morris (n.d.*b*:5–6) uncovered more evidence of violence in a mummy: "About 45 feet west of the bone cist under point of large stone another cist was visible. It sloped backward under the stone. In trash which filled it at depth of 2 feet was Burial 6, an adult [female, according to Lister and Lister (1968: 137)]. The body had lain on right side closely flexed, head to north, wrapped in two very heavy feather string blankets. The grave had been robbed, in the course of which process body was torn apart and torso turned over on left side. No accompaniments remained except the feather cloth. The body told an eloquent story. In the flesh of the left side was the foreshaft of an arrow. It had entered at the side above the eighth rib, and ranged upward between ribs and skin to emerge over the fifth rib. The reed shaft had been broken away and the stone point, which had come through the skin, was also missing excepting the tang, which remained in the slot in the foreshaft. This old person had been killed by a terrific blow on the left side of the head which broke the lower jaw at center and carried [caved?] in entire left side of skull."

**Other Interpretations.** James A. McDonald (1976:37) noted: "Only at Battle Cove was the Basketmaker II material unmixed with material from later stages (E. Morris 1929:1–6). A number of Basketmaker II cists were found in the southern portion of the alcove at the site, many of which contained burials. Some of the bodies showed signs of violent death, including one with an embedded arrowshaft."

**Discussion.** The type and amount of damage we found in the skeletal remains from the Battle Cave cist support Morris's interpretation of violence. We were unable to locate the mummy with the embedded arrow. Although the bones from the cist have some intentional perimortem breakage, lack most vertebrae, and show other signs of processing (table 3.10), the absence of identifiable burning and polishing means that the standards for proposing cannibalism cannot be met.

In 1992, David A. Breternitz and associates reexamined Battle Cave and, at our request, kept an eye out for signs of burned bone. None was found, nor was there anything else on the cave floor, owing to heavy tourist traffic in this part of Canyon de Chelly National Monument. Even if Breternitz had noticed a burned human bone, however, we still would not propose cannibalism for Battle Cave because all of the perimortem damage is limited to skull elements. None of the postcranial elements has any perimortem damage.

Our only disagreement with Morris is that we found little weathering and almost no animal gnawing of the human bone. The bones seem not to have remained on the ground surface as long as Morris implied. They are indeed very clean, however, and comparing them with another skeleton Morris found in the north section of Battle Cave, we understand why he felt they had been long exposed: "*Burial 8. . . . Old person, probably male. . . . Wrapped in feather string blanket. Stench so vile that remains were reburied*" (Morris n.d.*b*:7). Note that this is not the adult mummy with the arrow wound.

Like the more than 90 massacred people discovered in Cave 7 by Richard Wetherill, Earl Morris's 13 massacred Battle Cave individuals show that deadly conflict was part of the Basketmaker lifeway in both Utah and Arizona.

## 11
## Charnel House Tower

**Claim Date.** 1929.

**Claimant.** Paul S. Martin.

**Claim Type.** Violence.

**Other Designations.** Ray Ruins; Wright Ruins.

**Site Location.** About 51.5 km (32 miles) northwest of Cortez, southwestern Colorado, and about 4.0 km (2.5 miles) south of the junction of Cahone and Cross canyons, Montezuma County T 39N, R 19W, SW ¼ of SE ¼ of SW ¼ of Sec. 36 (per Martin 1929).

**Site Type.** Large, multiple-unit masonry buildings arranged in a crescent. A circular tower 8.5 m (28 feet) in diameter stands at the southeast corner of the site.

**Cultural Affiliation.** Mesa Verde Anasazi.

**Chronology.** Pueblo II (Martin found abundant black-on-white pottery of "proto–Mesa Verde" type and some "true" Mesa Verde ware.

**Excavator and Date.** Paul S. Martin, July–August 1928.

**Institutional Storage.** Uncertain. Martin (1929:2) said that the excavations were conducted as the "1928 archaeological expedition of the State Historical Society of Colorado." Our inquiries of Susan Collins, Carolyn McArthur, and Jeannie Brako at the Colorado Historical Society Museum, Denver, disclosed no human remains from this expedition. Nor did our inquiries of Robert B. Pickering at the Denver Museum of Natural History, even though Martin said that some cultural materials (a cradleboard, matting, and turkey eggshells) were deposited at the "Colorado State Museum," as it was then named.

We also queried Jonathan Haas about the possibility of Martin's Charnel House Tower materials having been sent to the Field Museum of Natural History in Chicago, where Martin was employed after the 1928 excavation. Haas and James Carucci determined that the series was not in their collections.

**Site Report.** Martin (1929).

**Osteological Report.** None known.

**Skeletal Evidence of Stress.** None known.

**Burial Context.** A mass burial under four feet of stones, earth, and charcoal in the southern half-room of the round tower (which was divided by a crosswall).

**Associated Artifacts.** None reported.

**Figures.** None.

**Taphonomy.** PSM.

> *MNI.* 14.
>
> **Age and Sex.** Eleven adults, three of them identified as females, and three infants.
>
> *There is no information for Preservation, Bone and Fragment Number, Breakage, Cut Marks, Burning, Anvil Abrasions, Polishing, Vertebrae Number, Scalping, Gnawing, Chewing, or Insect Parts. Other Modification (severed heads) is described in following quotation.*

**Archaeologist's Interpretation.** Martin (1929:26) wrote:

> In the northeast corner [of the tower floor] we came across a veritable mass of bones, which covered an area greater than six square feet. These bones represented individuals who had probably been killed or who had all died at the same time from other causes. However that may be, the bones were literally flung into this corner, one skeleton lying across another, in great confusion. One skull, to our great surprise, was covered with hair, which to all appearances, was thickly matted with blood. No other bones could be found for this skull nor for two others. There were in all eleven adults, three of which were females, and three infants. Mixed with these bones was much charcoal, although the bones themselves

were not at all calcined. . . . Directly under this mass burial (which suggested the name Charnel House) were three more burials. These last, however, were undoubtedly placed before the tragedy, for they were carefully flexed [and had associated grave goods; below them was yet another child burial].

Under the T-shaped doorway in the wall that divided the floor of the tower, Martin (1929:27) found two infant skulls that lacked postcranial elements and had no grave goods.

Martin (1929:27) suggested: "In later times [of the village's occupation], there may have been a massacre, at which time the fourteen people, found as a mass burial, were flung into the tower. Later the tower was fired, and with it possibly the whole village." He concluded (1929:31): "Houses were built in the open with little if any idea of protection from enemies. That this trust was rudely and tragically shattered is testified to by finding burned houses, kivas, and the mass burial of Charnel House Tower."

**Other Interpretations.** None known.

**Discussion.** It is unfortunate that Martin did not illustrate his mass burial with either a line drawing or a photograph; he wrote that "due to a high wind and excessive dust, a good photograph was not obtainable" (1929:26). After the human remains had been cleared away, however, he did manage to get a good photograph of the T-shaped doorway inside the tower (1929:pl. 8, fig. 2). Nevertheless, given his clearly written descriptions, we accept his interpretation that the Charnel House village had met a violent end.

If the Charnel House Tower human remains can ever be located (assuming that they were saved; except for the few items mentioned earlier, Martin does not indicate where any of the collections went), it would be easy to determine by chemical tests whether there actually was human blood on the severed head with hair. We have searched extensively for this assemblage and have eliminated the most likely museums—the Colorado State Historical Museum, the Denver Museum of Natural History, and the Field Museum of Natural History—and even some unlikely ones identified for the other skeletal series discussed in this book.

**12**
**Jack Smith's Alcove**
**Houses**

**Claim Date.** 1934.

**Claimant.** Katharine A. Bartlett.

**Claim Type.** Violence.

**Other Designations.** NA408 and NA1295A (Coconino National Forest AR-03-02-329).

**Site Location.** East side of San Francisco Peaks, near Flagstaff, Arizona. USGS Sunset Crater West quadrangle (1966), T 23N, R 8E, NW ¼ of SE ¼ of SW ¼ of Sec. 17. The two sites are near each other, 0.4 km (0.25 mile) east of U.S. 89 and approximately 122 m (400 feet) south of Jack Smith's tank.

**Site Type.** Alcove houses (surface structures with attached small rooms or alcoves for storage).

**Cultural Affiliation.** Sinagua.

**Chronology.** A.D. 900–950 (Pueblo II in the Anasazi chronology), based on tree-ring dates for NA408.

**Excavator and Date.** Lyndon L. Hargrave, 1930 and 1932.

**Institutional Storage.** Skeletal material from NA1295A is in the Department of Anthropology, Museum of Northern Arizona (MNA), Flagstaff. The burned NA408 skeletal fragments were apparently not saved.

**Site Reports.** Hargrave (1933); Colton (1946).

**Osteological Report.** Bartlett (1934).

**Skeletal Evidence of Stress.** None evident in unburned bones (CGT).

**Burial Context.** Skeletons found on floors of burned alcove houses. However, NA1295A photos in MNA photo archives indicate that the nearly complete burial in that room was intrusive.

**Associated Artifacts.** Five obsidian arrow points at NA408; jars and other artifacts on floor of NA1295A.

**Figures.** None.

**Taphonomy.** KAB.

*MNI.* 2 (KAB).

*Age and Sex.* One male?; one unspecified (KAB). CGT found a nearly complete middle-aged male skeleton (heavy tooth wear, but most teeth still present) and the skull of an older female (much antemortem tooth loss, alveolar resorption, and complete socket filling) in the skeletal material from NA1295A. There are no site records of the female's having been found, although the photo archives have several views of the whole skeleton in place.

*Preservation.* Both of the NA1295A individuals are in fair condition. Both were coated with shellac, so bone surfaces could not be rigorously examined for perimortem cuts or abrasions (CGT).

*Bone and Fragment Number.* Not recorded by KAB or CGT.

*Breakage.* No perimortem breakage (CGT).

*Cut Marks.* None.

*Burning.* Yes (KAB). The female skull shows separation of the outer external table of the frontal bone from the inner cancellous layer, in addition to charring. The male skeleton has no obvious burning but is moderately stained by soil (CGT).

*Anvil Abrasions.* None (CGT).

*Polishing.* None (CGT).

*Vertebrae Number.* Not counted, but many present (CGT).

*Scalping.* None (CGT).

*Gnawing, Rodent.* None (CGT).

*Chewing, Carnivore.* None (CGT).

*Insect Parts.* None (CGT).

*Other Modification.* None (CGT).

**Archaeologists' Interpretations.** Hargrave (1933:41) wrote that "the dwelling [NA1295A] had been destroyed by fire." Harold S. Colton (1946:63–65) wrote, "Between the firepit [of NA408A] and the west post was a burned human body."

**Other Interpretations.** Bartlett (1934:16) provided more details: "NA408 was an alcove house which was destroyed by fire. On the floor were found charred human bones, beside which these arrow points were lying all together. It appears that when the house was burned, perhaps by an enemy, a person was trapped inside and perished in the flames, and that at the time the man(?) had with him his bow and arrows, the only remains of which are these beautiful points." Elsewhere Bartlett (1934:72) noted: "Evidence of burned human bodies was found on the floors of NA408 and 1295A, an alcove house and a pithouse [actually an alcove house too] located close to each other. It appeared that one individual in each house had been killed just before, or was burned to death in the fires which destroyed these two dwellings."

Notes in the MNA site file for NA408, presumably made by Colton, are about the same as the foregoing, except for one additional interpretation: "Five finely made projectile points, bunched as though shafts were tied together or resting in quiver were found by body."

Discussion. Because the NA408 skeletal remains cannot be located, the only taphonomic observations possible are for NA1295A. The female skull from that site does evidence burning. There was no other perimortem damage. The nearly complete male skeleton has no convincing burning or other obvious perimortem damage. We believe that the MNA photo archive record is correct—namely, the adult male was an intrusive burial. The photographs suggest that it was found several centimeters above the floor. Thus, we are unable by taphonomic means either to support or refute the claim made by Bartlett that violence was involved in the deaths of the people found in these two sites. Hargrave, however, tested other structures in the immediate neighborhood and found two others that had burned. If these were all part of a contemporaneous community, a robust case for violence could be made. If the sites were not contemporaneous, then the discovery of burned bodies in burned buildings might instead represent an uncommon mortuary behavior in which the deceased's possessions were destroyed, including his or her dwelling, as was sometimes the case among the tribes of western Arizona (Hagberg 1939).

A burned adult female was found in a Sinagua pithouse (NA20,700) dating to about A.D. 800–850 (Fink and Turner n.d.). This site is located in the neighborhood of Jack Smith's Alcove Houses and is another example of a burned structure containing human remains on the floor. Michael Fink and Korri Dee Turner examined the remains carefully, finding no direct evidence of violence. Nevertheless, they proposed that the remains represented either an accidental death or a case of violence. Penny Minturn, the excavator, showed us the remains. We agreed with Fink and Turner that there was no identifiable perimortem damage other than burning. It may be that burned pithouses represent nothing more than prehistoric firetraps.

## 13
## La Plata 23

Claim Date. 1939.
Claimant. Earl H. Morris.
Claim Type. Cannibalism.
Other Designations. None known.
Site Location. Near junction of, and between, Pond's Arroyo and La

Plata River, southwestern Colorado, about 3.2 km (2 miles) north of New Mexico state line and 14.5 km (9 miles) north of La Plata, New Mexico. USGS Red Mesa quadrangle (1968), T 32N, R 12W, near center of Sec. 3.

**Site Type.** "A rock shelter about 4.5 m long, 2.1 m deep, and 1.8 m high at front, located 400 m north of Site 23 mounds" (Morris 1939:74–75).

**Cultural Affiliation.** Anasazi.

**Chronology.** A.D. 1100+.

**Excavator and Date.** Harry L. Shapiro, who accompanied Earl H. Morris on the 1927 Ogden Mills expedition.

**Institutional Storage.** Department of Anthropology, American Museum of Natural History, New York.

**Site Report.** Morris (1939).

**Osteological Report.** None.

**Skeletal Evidence of Stress.** None.

**Burial Context.** Human skeletal remains within and scattered around a firepit and filling a large corrugated jar (Morris 1939:75, pl. 35).

**Associated Artifacts.** Cooking jar.

**Figures.** 3.93–3.97.

**Taphonomy.** EHM; CGT and JAT, May 2, 1994. Skeletal inventory is in table 3.12.

*MNI.* 2 (EHM); 5 (CGT and JAT, table 3.11).

*Age and Sex.* One adult and one adolescent (EHM); one adult, female?, one adult, sex?, two subadults, sex?, and one infant (CGT and JAT).

*Preservation.* Good.

*Bone and Fragment Number.* 350 (65 whole; 285 fragments); also 34 whole teeth.

*Breakage.* Present (EHM). 73.7%.

*Cut Marks.* 2.6%.

*Burning.* Present (EHM). 17.7%.

*Anvil Abrasions.* 1.1%.

*Polishing.* 0.3%.

*Vertebrae Number.* 8.3% of expected (10 of 120).

*Scalping.* Possible; there are two cut marks on one skull.

*Gnawing, Rodent.* None.

*Chewing, Carnivore.* Yes. Most chewing occurred on hand and foot bones, some of which we may have confused with perimortem smashing by humans.

*Insect Parts.* None found at time of skeletal examination.

*Other Modification.* Heavy chop marks occur on one of the occipital fragments and on a left parietal.

**Archaeologist's Interpretation.** Morris (1939:75) described the rock shelter deposit of human bones as follows:

H. L. Shapiro noticed a few potsherds and bits of bone scattered upon the surface, which led him to dig into the earth between the wall and the head of the talus slope. There at a depth of 10–20 cm he found a shallow firepit with slab walls flaring outward. On all sides charcoal and ashes continued for some distance away from it, showing that at some time there had been a much larger fire than

Table 3.11
Minimal Number of Individuals (MNI) at La Plata 23

| SKELETAL ELEMENT | AGE | SEX | NOTES |
|---|---|---|---|
| Maxilla, whole | Adult | ? | |
| Mandible, whole | Adult | ? | Teeth and sockets not damaged |
| | Adult | ? | Teeth and sockets not damaged |
| Long bone | Infant | ? | |
| Femur | Subadult | ? | |
| Femur | Subadult | ? | |
| Femur | Subadult | ? | |
| Vault | Adult | F? | Burning and hack marks |

SUMMARY: Five individuals. One adult, female?; one adult, sex?; two subadults, sex?; one infant.

Table 3.12
Bone Elements and Perimortem Damage at La Plata 23

| SKELETAL ELEMENT | WHOLE | FRAG-MENT | IMPACT BREAK | ANVIL ABRASION | CUT MARK | BURN | POLISH | CHEW |
|---|---|---|---|---|---|---|---|---|
| Cranial | | | | | | | | |
| Maxilla | 1 | 2 | 3 | 0 | 0 | 0 | 0 | 0 |
| Mandible | 2 | 0 | 0 | 0 | 1 | 1 | 0 | 0 |
| Frontal | 1 | 0 | 0 | 0 | 0 | 0 | 0 | 0 |
| Parietal | 2 | 0 | 2 | 0 | 1 | 1 | 0 | 0 |
| Occipital | 0 | 2 | 2 | 0 | 1 | 0 | 0 | 0 |
| Temporal | 2 | 0 | 2 | 0 | 0 | 0 | 0 | 0 |
| Base | 0 | 2 | 2 | 0 | 0 | 0 | 0 | 0 |
| Teeth | 34 | 0 | 0 | 0 | 0 | 0 | 0 | 0 |
| Fragment | — | 3 | 0 | 0 | 0 | 0 | 0 | 0 |
| Postcranial | | | | | | | | |
| Vertebrae | 1 | 14 | 14 | 0 | 0 | 0 | 0 | 0 |
| Sacrum | 1 | 0 | 1 | 0 | 0 | 0 | 0 | 0 |
| Scapula | 2 | 2 | 4 | 0 | 0 | 0 | 0 | 0 |
| Clavicle | 1 | 4 | 5 | 0 | 0 | 0 | 0 | 0 |
| Rib | 0 | 68 | 68 | 0 | 1 | 4 | 1 | 0 |
| Sternum | 0 | 2 | 0 | 0 | 0 | 0 | 0 | 0 |
| Humerus | 1 | 5 | 5 | 0 | 0 | 0 | 0 | 3? |
| Radius | 0 | 5 | 5 | 0 | 0 | 0 | 0 | 3 |
| Ulna | 0 | 10 | 10 | 2 | 0 | 0 | 0 | 1 |
| Hand & foot | 50 | 30 | ? | 0 | 0 | 1 | 0 | 30[a] |
| Pelvis | 1 | 4 | 4 | 0 | 0 | 1 | 0 | 0 |
| Femur | 0 | 5 | 5 | 0 | 1 | 0 | 0 | 1 |
| Tibia | 0 | 6 | 6 | 1 | 1 | 0 | 0 | 0 |
| Fibula | 0 | 5 | 5 | 1 | 2 | 0 | 0 | 0 |
| Patella | 0 | 1 | 0 | 0 | 0 | 0 | 0 | 1 |
| Long bone fragments | — | 115 | 115 | 0 | 1 | 54 | 0 | 0 |
| TOTAL (350) | 65 | 285 | 258 | 4 | 9 | 62 | 1 | 39 |
| PERCENTAGE | 18.6 | 81.4 | 73.7 | 1.1 | 2.6 | 17.7 | 0.3 | 11.1 |

Percentage of expected vertebrae = 8.3 (ca. 10 of 120; MNI = 5).[b]

NOTE: Only elements that were present are listed. Impact breakage, anvil abrasions, cut marks, burning, and polishing represent perimortem damage. Chewing is postmortem damage.

a. All chewing is apparently by carnivores, and some of the "chewed" hand and foot bones may have been smashed instead.

b. Fragmentation size suggests that the 14 fragments could represent about nine whole vertebrae.

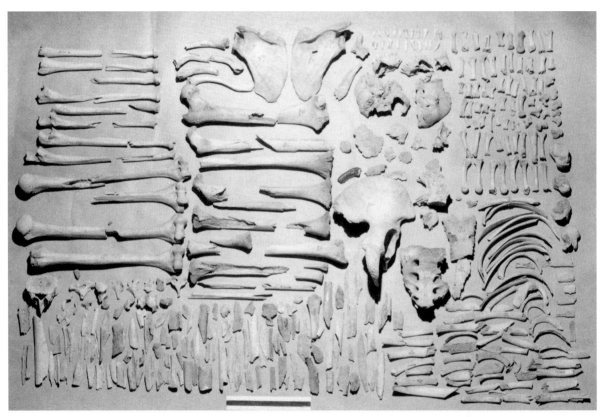

Figure 3.93. La Plata 23, Colorado. Most of the skeletal assemblage for an MNI of four. The few vertebral fragments are at lower left between the humerus and long bone fragments positioned vertically. Hand and foot bones are in the upper right. Rib fragments in lower right. As elsewhere, note their general uniformity in length. Cranial fragments and teeth are above the pelvic bones. Scale is 15 cm. AMNH 99/9328 (CGT neg. 5-2-94:24).

Figure 3.94. La Plata 23. Remainder of the skeletal assemblage, showing the crumbly and chalky heat-stressed top of a roasted adult female head, along with five pieces of mandible that can be reassembled into two almost complete jaws. The woman's cranium is also damaged by perimortem chop marks. The face is missing. AMNH 99/9328 (CGT neg. 5-3-94:8).

Figure 3.95. La Plata 23. Adult left mandible fragment with cut marks along interior-inferior border. Because there are no muscle attachments at the location of the cut marks, they must represent the cutting through of the skin and other tissue of the upper neck to gain access to the tongue. There was an abscess and bone inflammation at the root tip of the third molar. AMNH 99/9328 (CGT neg. 5-3-94:6).

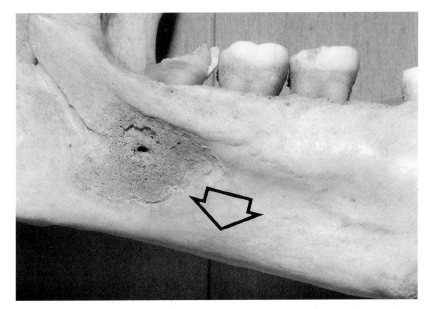

Figure 3.96. La Plata 23. Rib fragments illustrating three types of perimortem damage. The upper fragment has minute rounding from pot-polishing at the tip on right. The middle rib has cut marks at arrow. The lower rib has the breakage type called "peeling," which tears away the outer cortex as if it were the bark of a woody plant. AMNH 99/9328 (CGT neg. 5-2-94:30).

Figure 3.97. La Plata 23. Adult right humerus with perimortem percussion breakage at midshaft. The three pieces could be reassembled into nearly one complete bone. AMNH 99/9328 (CGT neg. 5-2-94:33).

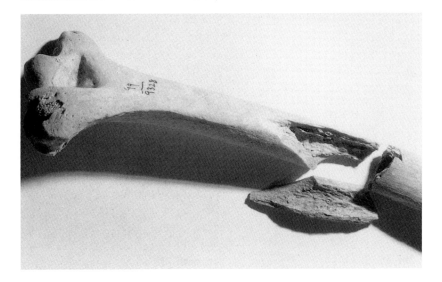

the pit could contain. Mixed through the burned layer were many
bones, principally human, most of them splintered and charred
wholly or in part. Just forward of the fire area a large corrugated
jar had been buried. It was full of human bones, all of them broken, and some blackened in spots by fire. Conspicuous among
them were parts of two skulls, leg and arm bones, ribs and vertebrae. Two individuals were represented; one a lightly framed
adolescent nearing maturity, the other an adult of massive proportions. Of the latter, the breast bone and lumbar vertebrae were the
largest and broadest that I have ever seen. There can be little doubt
that the two persons were cooked and eaten beneath the shelter of
the ledge. Both skulls had been broken open, and most of the long
bones splintered, just as would have been done to secure the brains
and marrow. Whatever the event, it cannot be attributed to the
[Basketmaker III] inhabitants of the dwellings at Site 23. The large
skull visible in plate 35 was short and strongly deformed at the
back; and the corrugated pot, as well as the varieties of black-
on-white and black-on-red wares represented by sherds found
among the debris, are all of highly evolved Pueblo wares and,
hence, date from a period much later than that represented by the
dwellings on the neighboring river terraces.

**Other Interpretations.** None.

**Discussion.** Although we identified three more individuals than Morris
did, we nevertheless agree with his interpretation of the perimortem
damage as representing cannibalism. That the La Plata 23 bone assemblage was found mainly in a pottery vessel, and a utilitarian
(cooking) jar at that, is extraordinarily suggestive. It cannot be argued that this bone-filled jar represents a cremation, because the bone
burning is relatively restricted, unlike the usual complete incineration
and extensive calcining characteristic of cremation. The burning of
only the top of one skull without thermal damage elsewhere indicates
head roasting rather than cremation (fig. 3.94).

Considering the association between the La Plata 23 bones and
cooking jar, we are puzzled by the near absence of pot-polishing in
this ideal context. Perhaps the victims were mainly roasted; the assemblage includes a relatively large percentage of burned bone,
mainly long bone fragments. Moreover, a great deal of bone is missing for an MNI of five; perhaps more polished pieces were in that
missing portion. As can be seen in the tables for bone elements and
perimortem damage in this chapter, there is considerable intersite
variation in the frequency of polishing. The rarity of bone polishing
at La Plata 23 is not fatal to White's (1992) pot-polishing hypothesis,
nor does it detract from the significance of the unique pottery-vessel
context. Whatever the reason for the bone fragments having been
placed or left in a cooking vessel, we are as confident as circumstantial evidence permits that the La Plata 23 perimortem damage signals
a cannibalism event.

La Plata 23 is the first of at least five sites in the La Plata River valley with probable cannibalism. This is one of the heaviest local concentrations of such sites outside Chaco Canyon. The next site, La

Plata 41, is a great house complex. Great houses are associated with apparent cannibalism along the La Plata River as well as in Chaco Canyon.

| | |
|---|---|
| **14**<br>**La Plata 41** | **Claim Date.** 1939. |

**Claim Date.** 1939.

**Claimant.** Earl H. Morris.

**Claim Type.** Cannibalism.

**Other Designations.** La Plata 41, Building XIV.

**Site Location.** On the right bank of the La Plata River, 2.4 km (1.5 miles) south of Colorado state line and 4.4 km (2.75 miles) north of La Plata, northwestern New Mexico. USGS La Plata, New Mexico–Colorado quadrangle (1963), T 32N, R 13W, NE ¼ of Sec. 22.

**Site Type.** Large multiple buildings. Great houses.

**Cultural Affiliation.** Anasazi.

**Chronology.** A.D. 1100 (Site 41 ranges from Basketmaker III to Pueblo III times).

**Excavator and Date.** Earl H. Morris, 1930.

**Institutional Storage.** Probably discarded by someone at Peabody Museum, Harvard University. In February 1993, with the help of Lane Beck, we found two La Plata 41 parietal fragments at the Peabody Museum. These belonged to burials 29 (Room 3, House 4) and 73 (Room 7, House 7). They were probably saved only as pathological specimens; both had severe porotic hyperostosis. It would appear that some sort of housekeeping event occurred at the Peabody Museum.

**Site Report.** Morris (1939).

**Osteological Report.** None.

**Skeletal Evidence of Stress.** Two severe cases of porotic hyperostosis.

**Burial Context.** Skeletal fragments in pit beneath two rooms of Building XIV.

**Associated Artifacts.** Large early Pueblo III bowl.

**Figures.** None.

**Taphonomy.** EHM.

> *MNI.* 6.
>
> *Age and Sex.* Four adults, one adolescent, and one small child.
>
> *Preservation.* Seemingly good.
>
> *Breakage.* Morris wrote that most of the long bones were broken and that burning had occurred.
>
> *There is no information for Bone and Fragment Number, Cut Marks, Anvil Abrasions, Polishing, Vertebrae Number, Scalping, Gnawing, Chewing, Insect Parts, or Other Modification.*

**Archaeologist's Interpretation.** Morris (1939:105, pl. 81) described and illustrated this find as follows:

> Occupying most of the area beneath Rooms 3 and 4, and continuing westward beyond their limits, was a pit 2.45 m in diameter and 90 cm deep. The earth fill contained some refuse and a quantity of human bones. The skulls of four adults, arm and leg bones of an adolescent, a clavicle and a radius of a small child showed that the bones were representative of at least six persons. The heads of

three of the adults had been split crosswise just forward of the coronal suture, the other from back to front in the median line. With few exceptions, the large bones and many small ones as well, had been split and cracked to pieces. They had the dead white appearance characteristic of bones that have been cooked, or freed from the soft parts before being covered with earth. This was not the bleach resulting from sunlight. A minor portion were browned, and some charred from exposure to fire. All facts considered, it would be difficult to regard this mass of human remains (pl. 81) as other than the residuum of a cannibalistic rite or orgy. In the bone-bearing stratum, which lay 15–38 cm above the pit floor, were most of the fragments of a large bowl (pl. 299*d*) of early Pueblo III ware, thus dating the event.

**Other Interpretations.** White (1992:368–369) listed La Plata 41, Building XIV, in his survey of Southwestern sites with cannibalism claims. He allowed that Morris's taphonomic descriptions were accurate, but he did not say whether he agreed with Morris's cannibalism interpretation.

**Discussion.** We accept Morris's cannibalism interpretation because burning, breakage, and good bone preservation were identified. Morris did not mention finding any vertebrae, so this criterion may have been met also. As remarked on previously, whenever we have been able to examine directly skeletal remains that Morris interpreted as damaged by violence or cannibalism, we have found him a reliable observer and hardheaded interpreter. Finally, there are skeletal assemblages exhibiting probable cannibalism from other sites in the vicinity of La Plata 41 that we have examined—Salmon Ruin, the La Plata Highway series, and La Plata 23.

Morris found other sets of human remains suggesting violence in La Plata 41 and nearby. In Site 41, Building VII, Room 11, he discovered a nonceremonial burial (30/77): "In west corner of room a bottle-necked pit, 76 cm in diameter at the mouth, 1.22 m at bottom, and 1.14 m deep, had been dug down into natural clay. In it were bones of five persons: a small child, an adolescent, two mature adults, one male, the other female, and an aged individual, apparently female, without a tooth in either jaw. Bodies had been thrown in a heap on pit bottom and covered with refuse earth" (1939:99).

In Site 41, Trench A, which yielded Pueblo II and early Pueblo III sherds, Morris found that "in a very shallow irregular hole scooped into natural earth, were the bones of an adult male who had lain until skeletonized before interment, or else had been dug up elsewhere and reburied where found. The bones had been thrown in an orderless heap (pl. 65), only the right femur and innominate suggesting from their relative positions that they might still have been articulated when laid down. Presumably the individual was killed by a blow which produced a round hole 3.18 cm in diameter in the left parietal" (1939:90–91, pl. 65). Inspection of Morris's plate 65 reveals that most of the long bones are whole, and there are only a few identifiable vertebrae. Although plate 65 is an excellent photograph, it is impossible to tell whether the parietal damage was perimortem or postmortem.

In Trench G, "where [it] passed over southeast arc of kiva, the scrambled skeletons of two adults had been thrown in against masonry" (Morris 1939:94). In our view, the Trench A and G deposits appear similar and could represent secondary burials. It would be highly desirable to locate and examine these and all other Site 41 skeletal remains for taphonomic considerations.

Finally, Morris (1939:82) reported on a traumatized burial he found in 1929 at Site 33 in the La Plata district, but closer to the Mancos River to the west than to the La Plata River itself. The find was made in Building IV (Pueblo III times), in a 5-meter-wide kiva that was constructed within a 14-room D-shaped pueblo:

> The [excavation] pit at the south laid bare the upper half of the skeleton of an adult, sprawled upon the [kiva] floor (pl. 45). It lay face downward with right arm flung forward beyond the head, and left outspread, but bent at the elbow. The bones were as hard and solid as oak staves. Notwithstanding, the skull was shattered and spread over an area more than 30 cm in diameter. There was no stone or log upon it to account for this breakage as the chamber went into ruin. Plainly enough, whoever struck down the individual further vented his rage by beating flat the head of the fallen victim. On the floor near that portion of the skeleton uncovered were four connecting sherds of a highly typical Mesa Verde bowl.

La Plata 41 was the first of the great houses outside of Chaco Canyon for which cannibalism was claimed on the basis of the condition of human skeletal remains recovered in rooms or pits. Moreover, there are several claims for cannibalism in sites within easy walking distance of great houses—for example, La Plata 23, which is only 5.6 km (3.5 miles) upstream. Finding probable episodes of cannibalism in Chacoan outliers as well as in Chaco Canyon great houses is powerful evidence of behavioral as well as architectural linkage.

## 15
## Whitewater District

**Claim Date.** 1939.

**Claimant.** Frank H. H. Roberts, Jr.

**Claim Type.** Violence.

**Other Designations.** NA4120; NA4597. Site area called "The Ruins" by local Navajos (Roberts 1939:xii).

**Site Location.** South of the Puerco River, west of Whitewater Creek, and 5.6 km (3.5 miles) south of Allantown, Arizona. USGS Lupton, Arizona–New Mexico quadrangle (1971), T 22N, R 30E, SW ¼ of Sec. 36.

**Site Type.** Great house with satellite community. The great house main structure sits atop a mesa ridge. The excavated structures that contained the relevant human remains were built on a talus slope below the great house.

**Cultural Affiliation.** Anasazi, Chaco branch.

**Chronology.** Pueblo I–II (Developmental Pueblo), A.D. 700–1100.

**Excavators and Date.** Frank H. H. Roberts, Jr., and Laboratory of Anthropology students, 1931–1933.

**Institutional Storage.** National Museum of Natural History, Smithson-

ian Institution, Washington, D.C., 15 skeletons; Laboratory of Anthropology, Santa Fe, New Mexico, 4 skeletons. The 15 NMNH
skeletons, which we examined in May 1995, included the following:

367839 19-32G. Adult female, complete, no perimortem damage.
Skull has symmetrical lambdoidal deformation. Illustrated in Stewart (1940:pl. 52).

367840 12-32G. Adult female, only clavicles missing, no perimortem
damage. Skull has symmetrical lambdoidal deformation and an
old healed depressed trauma wound on right side of frontal bone.

367841 7-32B. Adult male, most vertebrae missing but no perimortem damage. Skull has no deformation.

367842 4-32B. Adult female with some vertebrae missing but no perimortem damage. Skull has lambdoidal deformation.

367843 2-32B. Old female, complete, with no perimortem damage.
Skull has lambdoidal deformation. Nose has a healed break.

367844 1-32G. Adult male without skull, ribs, and vertebrae. No
perimortem damage.

367845 14. Adult male, proximal end of left fibula missing. Remaining part has a perimortem fracture and polishing of the fracture
tip. Left tibia is broken in the same area as the fibula. Nose and
right upper canine socket have perimortem breakage, as do right
orbit, maxilla, and zygomatic process. There are no cuts, abrasions, or burning. The bone is well preserved. The skull has lambdoidal deformation.

367846 7-32G. Old female, nearly complete, without perimortem
damage. Skull has lambdoidal deformation.

367847 17-32G. Adult female skull without postcranial elements. No
perimortem damage.

367848 8. Adult female?, nearly complete, without perimortem damage. No cranial deformation. Illustrated in Stewart (1940:pl. 56).

367849 3-32F. Adult female skull with lambdoidal deformation more
pronounced on right side. No postcranial elements, no perimortem
damage.

367850 1-32F. Adult male?, no postcranial elements, no perimortem
damage. Skull has lambdoidal deformation.

367851 X. Adult male? with lambdoidal deformation. No perimortem damage. Illustrated in Stewart (1940:pl. 53).

367852 Y. Adult male with only slight cranial deformation and no
perimortem damage.

368075 5-32F. Adult male, nearly complete, perimortem breakage at
left gonion, left temporal, and left mastoid. No other perimortem
damage. No cranial deformation. Illustrated in Stewart (1940:pl.
57), where perimortem damage shows.

**Site Reports.** Roberts (1939, 1940, n.d.).

**Osteological Report.** Stewart (1940). T. D. Stewart's identifications of
age, sex, and cranial deformation agree closely with ours. He believed
that the lambdoidal deformation was intentional. We agree.

**Skeletal Evidence of Stress.** There are minor degrees of porotic hyperostosis and cribra orbitalia.

**Burial Context.** Roberts reported finding 150 burials, mainly in refuse
mounds. A few were recovered from room, kiva, and storage pit loca-

Figure 3.98. Whitewater District. Frank H. H. Roberts's Burial 14, an adult showing perimortem damage of the upper right side of the face, the temporal region, and the mandibular coronoid process. NMNH 367845 (CGT neg. 5-23-95:8).

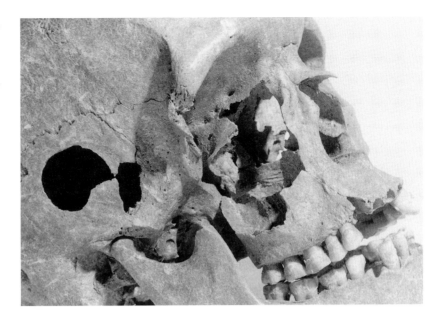

tions. One of two individuals whom Roberts interpreted as having been "captives" was dumped on a room floor, the other in a pit near a refuse mound. In addition, the upper body of one person was found within the fill of a kiva, and leg parts were found outside. The Whitewater skeletal series generally lacks disarticulation and perimortem breakage. Roberts's field notes, curated in the National Anthropological Archives, Smithsonian Institution, state that he recorded human skeletal information on "burial cards." These cards cannot not be located, and so the skeletons that reached NMNH cannot be matched up with the published reports, the field catalog, or Roberts's field notes.

**Associated Artifacts.** No artifacts were found in association with the "captives" or the isolated body parts. Other burials were sometimes accompanied by mortuary offerings. Apparently no artifacts were found in association with the 15 skeletons sent to Washington (Roberts 1940:145–152).

**Figure. 3.98.**

**Taphonomy.** FHHR and CGT.

*MNI.* Three with perimortem damage plus an unspecified number of skulls with "penetration" holes.

*Age and Sex.* Not reported for individuals evidencing violence. Skeletal population as a whole had 69 adults (23 male, 28 female, 18 sex indeterminable), 76 infants and children, and 5 of unknown age or sex due to poor preservation.

*Preservation.* Variable but mostly poor.

*Bone and Fragment Number.* One of the "captives" and one of the damaged normal burials were probably complete or nearly so; however, preservation was reported to have varied considerably.

*Breakage.* Roberts found "a number" of normal burials whose skulls had penetration holes and fractures. None of these skulls was sent to Washington. Because the skulls were parts of whole skeletons, the holes cannot represent the hanging or mounting of trophy heads.

*Cut Marks.* None.

*Burning.* None.

*Anvil Abrasions.* None.

*Polishing.* None.

*Vertebrae Number.* Not counted.

*Scalping.* None.

*Gnawing, Rodent.* None.

*Chewing, Carnivore.* Bones of at least one person (FHHR).

*Insect Parts.* None.

*Other Modification.* See following quotations regarding head penetration holes.

Archaeologist's Interpretation. Roberts (1940:136) claimed that violence was evident:

> A few individuals gave evidence of having met a violent end. . . . A number of the skulls had small, circular broken areas that apparently were produced by means of a comparatively sharp-pointed instrument. Others had larger more irregular places where the bone was crushed in but not punched out, wounds undoubtedly produced by a blunt object such as a maul or club. . . . Projectile points were associated with skeletons in several instances in positions suggesting they had been in the body of the person when it was interred. Several were found in the chest cavities and one was between the shoulder blade and the ribs, the inner surface of the scapula showing a scar such as might be produced by a point.

On the floor of Talus Unit Room 12, a Developmental Pueblo surface structure dated by reused beams at later than A.D. 918, Roberts (1939:204–205) encountered

> an adult, probably a male, [which] was peculiar in that the body had been placed front down with the face turned to one side. The legs were tightly flexed. The left arm extended along the side and the right was crossed over the back. The positions of the arm bones suggested that the person had been bound, his hands tied behind his back. The individual appeared to have been dumped on the floor and then covered with refuse, stones, and mud plaster. . . . The fact that there were no accompanying mortuary offerings and that the individual apparently was tied suggests a captive or prisoner of war. . . . One other skeleton exhibiting a similar position, sprawled face down with the arms crossed over the back and the left foot drawn up as though tied to the lashings that held the wrists, was uncovered in a shallow pit [without grave goods] beyond the limits of the refuse mound.

Concerning the fill of Kiva A, Roberts (1939:184–185) reported: "A portion of the skull rested on the bench. The remaining bones were just below that level and somewhat scattered, but not sufficiently disarticulated to indicate the burial of an already decomposed body. There were no leg or foot bones, however, the pelvic bones were present and in good state of preservation. They were normal in every respect. The acetabula. . . . were undamaged. All of the remaining fill was carefully sifted but not one additional bone was recovered."

He went on to hypothesize that the missing legs were the result of shallow grave despoiling by village dogs, because he found an isolated and gnawed femur and foot bones some 15 m (50 feet) away. Since the head of the femur was missing, he could not make a match except on the basis of general size.

**Other Interpretations.** None known.

**Discussion.** The two "captives" and the Kiva A torso belong to Talus Units 1 and 2, which Roberts dated as Developmental Pueblo (Pueblo I–II). Thus these individuals, whose burial descriptions surely document violence, may not have been associated with the great house, although we cannot be certain because Roberts did not test the great house due to lack of funds. As for the burials with perforated crania, Roberts did not indicate where they were found. We suspect they were all Developmental Pueblo in date, since this was Roberts's main research focus in the early 1930s. Some of the satellite structures, however, date later—that is, they were contemporaneous with the great house—and so some of the perforated crania could date to Pueblo III. Whatever their date, we found none of these perforated skulls in the NMNH series itemized earlier.

Although Roberts's violence interpretations seem reasonable for the perforated crania and the so-called captives (who possibly were witches), as does his scavenging scenario for the Kiva A missing legs, he provided no field photographs or line drawings of any of these traumatized individuals. Stewart's (1940) appended osteological study includes six photographic plates of standard cranial views. LA50-3 appears to have perimortem breakage of the vault. USNM 368075 has perimortem breakage as described earlier.

In sum, taphonomic analysis only partly verifies Roberts's claim for violence in the Whitewater District. During our examination of the skeletal remains in May 1995, we found only two individuals with perimortem damage (367845, 368075), one of which is shown in figure 3.98.

## 16
## Alkali Ridge

**Claim Date.** 1946.

**Claimant.** John Otis Brew.

**Claim Type.** Violence.

**Other Designations.** Sites 5 (Abajo:7:5) and 13 (Abajo:7:13).

**Site Location.** Sites 5 and 13 are about 5.6 km (3.5 miles) apart, each on Alkali Ridge (Alkali Mesa), southeast of the Abajo (or Blue) Mountains, about 12.9 km (8 miles) east of Blanding and 16.1 km (10 miles) south of Verdure, San Juan County, southeastern Utah. Site 5: USGS Bradford Canyon quadrangle (provisional edition 1985), T 37S, R 23E, SE ¼ of SE ¼ of Sec. 1. Site 13: USGS Devil Mesa quadrangle (provisional edition 1985), T 36S, R 23E, SW ¼ of NE ¼ of Sec. 23.

**Site Type.** Site 5 had slab and masonry houses, a refuse mound, and two kivas. Site 13 was a large pit-house village with kivas, plazas, and scores of contiguous storage rooms.

**Cultural Affiliation.** Site 5 is Mancos Mesa phase Anasazi; Site 13 is Mesa Verde Anasazi.

**Chronology.** Site 5 is Pueblo II; the Site 13 kiva is Pueblo III.

**Excavators and Date.** J. O. Brew (director), J. A. Lancaster, and others, 1931–1933.

**Institutional Storage.** Peabody Museum of Archaeology and Ethnology, Harvard University, Cambridge, Massachusetts.

**Site Report.** Brew (1946).

**Osteological Report.** Brues (1946).

**Skeletal Evidence of Stress.** "Generally poor health" (Brues 1946:328).

**Burial Context.** Burial N/922 was an 18-year-old male found flexed in a refuse mound at Site 5. Brew's illustration (1946:fig. 192*b*) shows clearly that N/922 was a formal, considerate burial. Burial N/933, a 40- to 44-year-old male, was buried on top of and in contact with another adult male (N/934) in the kiva fill of Site 13. The illustration of this double "burial" (Brew 1946:fig. 192*i*) suggests that the two men were unceremoniously dumped in the kiva. Burial N/932 was found without grave goods in Site 13, Pithouse D.

**Associated Artifacts.** N/922 was buried with three ceramic vessels. N/933 and the associated male had no mortuary goods.

**Figures.** None.

**Taphonomy.** JOB, Alice Brues (AB), and CGT.

     *MNI.* 3.

     *Age and Sex.* N/922: subadult male (AB), 18-year-old male (JOB). N/933: middle-aged male (AB), 40- to 44-year-old adult male (JOB). N/932: middle-aged male (AB).

     *Preservation.* Fair.

     *Breakage.* Slight.

     *Cut Marks.* Present.

     *There is no information for Bone and Fragment Number, Burning, Anvil Abrasions, Polishing, Vertebrae Number, Gnawing, Chewing, or Insect Parts.*

     *Scalping.* Yes.

     *Other Modification.* Arrowhead tip in unhealed vertebra of N/933.

**Archaeologist's Interpretation.** Brew believed Burial N/922 had met a violent death, because the right frontal bone and orbit were broken. He (and Brues) believed the same for N/933, because it had an embedded arrow point in one of the vertebrae and showed signs of having been scalped and beaten on the head. N/932 and N/933 had been buried together, but only the latter evidenced trauma.

**Other Interpretations.** Alice Brues (1946:327) identified the same two instances of Alkali Ridge violence that Brew had seen. At Site 5, burial 2 (N/922), a subadult male, had "the right frontal region broken in, apparently by a blow from some heavy cutting instrument before death." She suggested violence for skeleton 1 (N/933), a middle-aged male, from Site 13, Unit 3, kiva, because "the left side of the head is broken in; a crack extending across the face is apparently the result of the same force. Deeply stained scratches in a position indicative of scalping are also found. Since part of an arrow-head was found imbedded in one of the dorsal vertebrae . . . it seems certain that this individual met a violent death. . . . Apparently the settlements were by no means safe from hostile attack" (Brues 1946:328).

Discussion. In February 1993 the senior author briefly examined two Alkali Ridge individuals. Both had perimortem damage. The left humerus of N/933 had cut marks at the elbow. This individual also had scalping cut marks on the cranial vault. N/932, from Site 13, Pithouse D, also had cut marks on the skull. This adult was deposited without any grave goods, and the stratigraphy suggests the body was placed in the pithouse near the time of its abandonment (Brew 1946: 170). Brues (1946:328) considered N/932 to be a middle-aged male but mentioned no cut marks. Nevertheless, it is noteworthy that among the many physical anthropologists who have studied skeletal remains of prehistoric Southwestern Indians, Alice Brues was among the first to recognize cut marks on human bone.

Thus, 3 of the 18 Alkali Ridge adults recovered by J. O. Brew show some form of traumatic perimortem damage, including scalping, dismemberment or mutilation, one unquestionable arrow wound, and heavy blows to the face and head. If the second but seemingly undamaged male associated with N/933 is added to this group of males, then more than one-fifth (22.2%) of the excavated males died violent deaths over a period of several generations. The scalping suggests to us trophy or coup taking. We agree with Brew and Brues that there is taphonomic evidence for violence on Alkali Ridge.

## 17
## Grand Canyon

Claim Date. 1949.

Claimant. Erik K. Reed.

Claim Type. Cannibalism.

Other Designations. Sites uncertain. Neither Reed nor Gordon C. Baldwin was explicit. Cave candidates are "Nuav Caves" (Sloth Cave?), A:13:1, A:13:18, and A:13:22. Open site candidates are AZ F:6:8 and AZ F:6:22.

Site Location. Cave candidates: Area due west of the western boundry of the Hualapai Indian Reservation, lower Granite Gorge, near Columbine Falls/Cave Canyon, northwestern Arizona. USGS Columbine Falls quadrangle (1971), T 31N, R 15W, projected Sec. 8. Open site candidates: east (Arizona) side of the Colorado River, approximately 38.6 km (24 miles) and 40.2 km (25 miles), respectively, south of Boulder Dam, northwestern Arizona. USGS Mt. Perkins, Arizona-Nevada quadrangle (1959), projected T 26N, R 22W, NE ¼ of Sec. 31.

Site Type. Cave and sand dune settings.

Cultural Affiliation. Patayan.

Chronology. Uncertain. The major prehistoric occupation of this area took place about A.D. 1000–1200. If the sites were used by Pai speakers, then the occupation may have been later.

Excavator and Date. Gordon C. Baldwin, 1947.

Institutional Storage. Unknown.

Site Report. Baldwin (1948), from which Reed (1949a) suggested cannibalism.

Osteological Report. None.

Skeletal Evidence of Stress. Unknown.

Burial Context. Human bone fragments in firepit and burned human bones recovered from refuse areas.

Associated Artifacts. Unknown.

Figures. None.

Taphonomy. GCB.

>    *MNI.* 2 or more.
>
>    *Breakage.* Yes (perimortem?).
>
>    *Burning.* Yes.
>
>    *There is no information on Age and Sex, Preservation, Bone and Fragment Number, Cut Marks, Anvil Abrasions, Polishing, Vertebrae Number, Scalping, Gnawing, Chewing, Insect Parts, or Other Modification.*

Archaeologist's Interpretation. Baldwin (1948:81) wrote that "in several of the cave sites in the western Grand Canyon and at least one open site a number of burnt human bones were recovered from the refuse and the charred remains of parts of two skeletons from a large firepit. This may show that cremation was practiced to some extent."

Other Interpretations. Reed (1949a:2) wrote that "in 1947, working in Patayan sites along the Lower Colorado River between Pyramid Canyon and Black Canyon, Gordon Baldwin found burned human bones in refuse deposits and charred remains of two human skeletons in a large firepit at one of these sites. . . . There is no evidence of cannibalism in the Southwest, so far as I know, except perhaps Baldwin's suggestive finds of burned human bones in Patayan (Yuman) sites on the Colorado River, and possibly the broken and split human bones at a Big Hawk Valley site [House of Tragedy], and the striking La Plata instance [Morris's La Plata 23]."

Discussion. Reed's suggestion that there was cannibalism in one or more of Baldwin's sites cannot be evaluated without the human remains, which to date have not been located. Dating, pottery identifications (if any was found), and other research that would permit a better resolution of the cultural background need to be done if the skeletal remains are ever discovered. Gerald A. Bair (personal communication, 1995) has suggested that if Tizon Brown Ware sherds had been found with the burned human remains, then the individuals were probably Pai speakers or ancestral Pai (Cerbat), which would mean that cremation rather than cooking was the more likely explanation for the burned human bone.

In sum, we have been unable to produce any evidence that would either support or refute Reed's suggestion for cannibalism. The claim stands in need of further study.

## 18
## House of Tragedy

Claim Date. 1952.

Claimant. Watson Smith.

Claim Type. Cannibalism and violence.

Other Designations. NA682.

Site Location. In Big Hawk Valley, about 12.1 km (7.5 miles) west-northwest of Wupatki Pueblo and 2.4 km (1.5 miles) east of U.S. 89, northeastern Arizona.

Site Type. A four-room masonry surface pueblo with kiva and outdoor storage pits.

Cultural Affiliation. Klethla focus, Kayenta Anasazi.

Chronology. A.D. 1100–1200.

Excavators and Date. Watson Smith and field crew, including Milton Wetherill and Richard Shutler, Jr., 1948.

Institutional Storage. Department of Anthropology, Museum of Northern Arizona, Flagstaff.

Site Report. Smith (1952).

Osteological Reports. Ennis (1952); Turner and Turner (1990, 1992b).

Skeletal Evidence of Stress. None.

Burial Context. A partial skeleton on room floor (Burial 1), two partly disarticulated skeletons on kiva floor (Burials 2 and 3), and two fragmented individuals (Burial 4) in outdoor storage pit D. Only in the first two settings is there perimortem bone damage. None of the skeletal elements in pit D corresponds to those of Burial 1; they represent two additional individuals.

Associated Artifacts. An unworked knifelike basalt blade 5.5 cm long was found in Room 1 between the legs of Burial 1, which was represented only by hammerstone-fractured, burned leg bones with cut marks.

Figures. 3.99–3.105.

Taphonomy. CGT and JAT. Skeletal inventories are in tables 3.13–3.16.

   *MNI.* 5.

   *Age and Sex.* Burial 1: young to middle-aged adult male?; Burial 2: young adult male; Burial 3: young adult female; Burial 4A: adult female; Burial 4B: old adult, sex?.

   *Preservation.* Good to fair.

   *Bone and Fragment Number.* 378.

   *Breakage.* 4.8%.

   *Cut Marks.* 0.3%.

   *Burning.* 0.5%.

   *Anvil Abrasions.* 0.3%.

   *Polishing.* 0.0%.

   *Vertebrae Number.* 48.3% of expected (58 of 120).

   *Scalping.* None.

   *Gnawing, Rodent.* None.

   *Chewing, Carnivore.* 4.0%.

   *Insect Parts.* None.

   *Other Modification.* None.

Archaeologist's Interpretation. Smith thought that Burial 1, represented only by a pair of broken legs, indicated violence. He cautiously suggested that the fragmented bones of Burial 4 in storage pit D represented a cannibalistic event, although he allowed that they might just as well have been reburied bones.

Other Interpretations. None.

Discussion. In our original taphonomic study of the House of Tragedy assemblage (Turner and Turner 1990, 1992b), the long bones of Burial 3 and all the remains of Burial 4 could not be found and examined due to museum misplacement. In 1993 the missing bones were found. There were no cut marks, roof fall damage, or animal gnawing on either femur of Burial 3. It remains a mystery how the woman's entire articulated left leg moved 20 cm (8 inches) downward from her

Table 3.13
Bone Elements and Perimortem Damage at House of Tragedy, Room 1,
Burial 1

| SKELETAL ELEMENT | WHOLE | FRAG-MENT | IMPACT BREAK | ANVIL ABRASION | CUT MARK | BURN | CHEWING |
|---|---|---|---|---|---|---|---|
| Foot | 6 | 4 | 0 | 0 | 0 | 0 | 7 |
| Femur | 0 | 3 | 3 | 1 | 1 | 2 | 0 |
| Tibia | 0 | 2 | 0 | 0 | 0 | 0 | 0 |
| Fibula | 2 | 0 | 0 | 0 | 0 | 0 | 2 |
| Patella | 2 | 0 | | | | | |
| TOTAL (19) | 10 | 9 | 3 | 1 | 1 | 2 | 9 |
| PERCENTAGE | 52.6 | 47.4 | 15.8 | 5.3 | 5.3 | 10.5 | 47.4 |

Percentage of expected vertebrae = 0.0 (0 of 24).

NOTE: Only elements that were present are listed. No polishing was observed. Impact breakage, anvil abrasions, cut marks, and burning represent perimortem damage. Chewing is postmortem damage.

Table 3.14
Bone Elements and Perimortem Damage at House of Tragedy,
Kiva, Burial 2

| SKELETAL ELEMENT | WHOLE | FRAGMENT | IMPACT BREAK | CHEWING |
|---|---|---|---|---|
| Cranium | 1 | 0 | | |
| Maxilla | | | 1 | 0 |
| Mandible | | | 1 | 0 |
| Postcranial | | | | |
| Cervical vertebrae | 7 | 0 | 0 | 0 |
| Thoracic vertebrae | 12 | 0 | 2 | 0 |
| Lumbar vertebrae | 5 | 0 | 0 | 0 |
| Sacrum | 1 | 0 | 0 | 0 |
| Scapula | 0 | 2L+R | 2 | 0 |
| Clavicle | 2 | 0 | 0 | 0 |
| Rib/sternum | 25 | 5 | 5[a] | 0 |
| Humerus | 0 | 1L | 0 | 1 |
| Radius | 0 | 1L | 1 | 1 |
| Ulna | 0 | 1L | 1 | 1 |
| Hand | 2 | 0 | 0 | 1 |
| Pelvis | 0 | 1L | 1 | 0 |
| Femur | 0 | 1R | 0 | 1 |
| Patella | 1R | 0 | 0 | 0 |
| TOTAL (68) | 56 | 12 | 14 | 5 |
| PERCENTAGE | 82.4 | 17.6 | 20.6 | 7.4 |

Percentage of expected vertebrae = 100 (24 of 24).

NOTE: Only elements that were present are listed. No items showed anvil abrasions, cut marks, burning, or polishing. Impact breakage represents perimortem damage. Chewing is postmortem damage. L denotes left; R denotes right.

a. Five ribs (7.4%) have peel breaks.

Table 3.15
Bone Elements and Perimortem Damage at House of Tragedy,
Kiva, Burial 3

| SKELETAL ELEMENT | WHOLE | FRAGMENT | IMPACT BREAK | CHEWING |
|---|---|---|---|---|
| Cranium | 1 | 0 | 0 | 0 |
| Postcranial | | | | |
|   Cervical vertebrae | 7 | 0 | 0 | 0 |
|   Thoracic vertebrae | 12 | 0 | 0 | 0 |
|   Lumbar vertebrae | 5 | 0 | 0 | 0 |
|   Sacrum | 1 | 0 | 0 | 0 |
|   Scapula | 2LR | 0 | 0 | 0 |
|   Clavicle | 2LR | 0 | 0 | 0 |
|   Rib/sternum | 24/1 | 0 | 1Rib | 0 |
|   Humerus | 2LR | 0 | 0 | 0 |
|   Radius | 2LR | 0 | 0 | 0 |
|   Ulna | 2LR | 0 | 0 | 0 |
|   Hand & foot | 71 | 0 | 0 | 1 |
|   Pelvis | 1 | 0 | 0 | 0 |
|   Femur | 2LR | 0 | 0 | 0 |
|   Tibia | 2LR | 0 | 0 | 0 |
|   Fibula | 2LR | 0 | 0 | 0 |
|   Patella | 2LR | 0 | 0 | 0 |
| TOTAL (139) | 139 | 0 | 1 | 1 |
| PERCENTAGE | 100.0 | 0.0 | 0.7 | 0.7 |

Percentage of expected vertebrae = 100 (24 of 24).

NOTE: Only elements that were present are listed. No anvil abrasions, cut marks, burning, or polishing was observed. Impact breakage represents perimortem damage. Chewing is postmortem damage. L denotes left; R denotes right.

Table 3.16
Bone Elements at House of Tragedy, Pit D, Burial 4

| SKELETAL ELEMENT | WHOLE | FRAGMENT |
|---|---|---|
| Cranial | | |
|   Maxilla | 1 | 0 |
|   Frontal | 1 | 0 |
|   Parietal | 1L | 0 |
|   Occipital | 1 | 0 |
|   Temporal | 2LR | 0 |
|   Fragments | — | 15 |
| Postcranial | | |
|   Cervical vertebrae | 5 | 2 |
|   Vertebrae fragments | — | 9 |
|   Scapula | 0 | 4 |
|   Clavicle | 2 | 0 |
|   Ribs | 4 | 40 |
|   Humerus | 0 | 2 |
|   Radius | 1 | 1 |
|   Ulna | 2 | 0 |
|   Hand & foot | 35 | 3 |
|   Pelvis | 0 | 3 |
|   Femur | 0 | 6 |
|   Tibia | 0 | 4 |
|   Fibula | 0 | 6 |
|   Patella | 1L | 0 |
| TOTAL (152) | 56 | 96 |
| PERCENTAGE | 36.8 | 63.2 |

Percentage of expected vertebrae = 20.8 (10 of 48; MNI = 2).[a]

NOTE: Only elements that were present are listed. No impact breakage, anvil abrasions, cut marks, burning, polishing, or chewing was observed. L denotes left; R denotes right.

a. Fragmentation size suggests that the 11 fragments could represent about five whole vertebrae.

Figure 3.99. House of Tragedy, Wupatki National Monument, Arizona. View from the north into the kiva with two young-adult skeletons on the floor. The largely disarticulated male Burial 2 is in the upper center. The extended female Burial 3, with her left leg disarticulated from the pelvis, is in the center. Notice that her head and right arm are in and near the fire pit to the right of the upright deflector slab. Both individuals were found directly on the floor and without grave goods. Some dismemberment seems to have occurred along with the violence, at least to the male, because the amount of identifiable animal damage is too limited to attribute all the disarticulation to carnivores. Museum of Northern Arizona Archive photograph by Watson Smith (7-13-48).

Figure 3.100. House of Tragedy, Pit D. Stone slabs in place at bottom of pit containing the completely disarticulated Burial 4 (arrow), which on analysis turned out to contain skeletal elements of two persons. Smith thought that Burial 4 might have been cannibalized, but taphonomic evidence is not supportive. Burial 4 shows no sign of violence and there are no cut marks. Museum of Northern Arizona Archive photograph by Watson Smith (7-23-48).

166

Figure 3.101. House of Tragedy, Room 1, Burial 1. Represented only by fragments of leg and foot bones, which may have belonged to a man. Both femurs were broken in their midshaft areas, and only the distal halves were found. An unburned fragment fits with the burned half of the upper distal femur. The white flakey surface at left is modern damage due to the weakened bone structure following its perimortem burning. Analysis of Burial 1 suggests cannibalism.  (CGT neg. 6-14-90:31).

Figure 3.102. House of Tragedy, Burial 1. Left femur with anvil abrasions on distal end. Actual width of image in photograph is about 3.3 cm (CGT neg. 7-16-93:32).

Figure 3.103. House of Tragedy, Burial 2. Perimortem breakage of anterior maxillary and mandibular teeth and sockets of the largely disarticulated male found in the kiva. Posterior teeth unaffected. The oral damage is attributable to violence (CGT neg. 7-16-93:29).

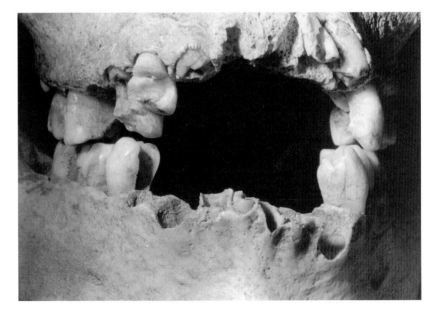

Figure 3.104. House of Tragedy, Burial 2. Perimortem peeled breaks on medial aspects of ribs. There are no recognizable tooth marks or scars that would suggest animal involvement in the rib damage (CGT neg. 7-16-93:33).

Figure 3.105. House of Tragedy, Burial 2. Perimortem midshaft breakage (parry or warding-off fractures?) of the radius and ulna (on left). Animal damage on ends of the distal humerus and proximal femur (on right). It is evident that this man suffered trauma and violence while in or near the kiva (CGT neg. 6-11-92:36).

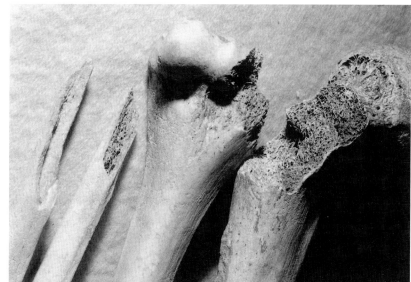

pelvis. Burial 2 had considerable impact damage but no other perimortem damage attributable to human action.

The storage-pit-deposited Burial 4, actually two incomplete skeletons, had no identifiable perimortem damage, so we must reject Watson Smith's tentative suggestion of cannibalism based on breakage and situational evidence. There is no suggestion from either the actual bones or Smith's detailed excavation notes why the two disarticulated and incomplete adults had been deposited in pit D. Burial 1, however, possesses telling signs of cannibalism and violence. Altogether, the presence of three perimortem-damaged adult male and female skeletons on room and kiva floors at House of Tragedy, and many more of both sexes and all ages in various rooms at nearby Wupatki Pueblo, cannot be a result of chance alone. Somebody was murdering, mutilating, and perhaps even feeding on victims from small and large settlements at the western edge of the twelfth-century Anasazi world.

Claim Date. 1953.

Claimants. Fred Wendorf and Erik K. Reed.

Claim Type. Violence.

Other Designations. LA252. The Tewa name, Te'ewi'onwikeji, means "little cottonwood gap pueblo ruin."

Site Location. On a high terrace overlooking the west side of the Chama River just below its confluence with the Rio Oso, and upstream several kilometers from the confluence of the Chama with the Rio Grande, north of Española, northwestern New Mexico. USGS San Juan Pueblo quadrangle (1953), T 22N, R 7E, SW ¼ of SW ¼ of Sec. 25.

Site Type. Six-hundred-room double-plaza pueblo.

Cultural Affiliation. Rio Grande.

Chronology. A.D. 1250–1500, based on tree-ring and ceramic evidence. Kiva I had a tree-ring date of 1410–1411.

Excavators and Dates. J. Lee Correll, 1950; Roscoe Wilmeth, 1951; both aided by University of New Mexico students under the supervision of Stanley A. Stubbs.

Institutional Storage. Maxwell Museum of Anthropology, University of New Mexico, Albuquerque, New Mexico.

Site Report. Wendorf (1953).

Osteological Report. Reed (1953).

Skeletal Evidence of Stress. Not reported.

Burial Context. Wendorf (1953:46) described the situation well: "Skeletal material—The remains of twenty-four or more individuals were found on the floor of the kiva [Kiva I]. Two, an infant and an adult, were near the center of the room. The remainder were around the edges, adjacent to the wall. All were burned. Fragments of another individual were also found in the ventilator. Scattered bones of six different individuals were found above the fallen and burned roof. Many of these had been burned or show other signs of violence."

Associated Artifacts. Kiva I contained pottery, pendants, beads, clay pipes, manos, metates, axes, a stone ball, bone, shell, antler, turkey-bone whistles, cordage, and cloth.

Figures. None.

Taphonomy. Although Reed made an osteological study, focusing on standard measurements, his special interest was cranial deformation and some pathology; therefore, he did not make taphonomic observations.

*MNI.* 30 (EKR).

*Age and Sex.* Infants and small children, 6; adult and subadult males, 24. No females were identified by Reed, who was quite a reliable osteologist.

*Preservation.* Reported to be poor because of burning.

*Breakage.* Yes.

*Cut Marks.* Yes.

*Burning.* Yes.

*There is no information for Bone and Fragment Number, Anvil Abrasions, Polishing, Vertebrae Number, Scalping, Gnawing, Chewing, Insect Parts, or Other Modification.*

Archaeologist's Interpretation. Linking his conclusion to the Kiva I holocaust, Wendorf (1953:93) proposed that "the abandonment of

Te'ewi may have been sudden, and possibly the result of attack by another group. The major evidence supporting this suggestion was found in the excavation of Kiva I. There the remains of twenty-four or more individuals were found, some on the floor of the structure, others lying above the fallen roof debris. The situation suggested that several individuals were caught in the burning of the kiva and others managed to get out of the kiva but were killed before they could escape from the area."

Other Interpretations. Reed (1953:104) wrote:

> The major part of the [skeletal] collection comes from the large burnt kiva excavated in 1950, "Room 6" or Kiva 1. At least twenty-four adult and sub-adult individuals, possibly more, are represented—all males, and mostly very young men. There are also six small children or babies. None of these are "burials" in the usual sense; they were not deliberately laid-out inhumations, flexed or extended, with accompanying offerings. Instead, they evidently are people who died where they were found, in the burning of the kiva—perhaps during a ceremony involving primarily young males (such as an initiation?), or possibly in the course of an enemy attack. The skeletons are irregularly dispersed through the fill, above as well as below the fallen roof layer; they are so fragmentary and disarranged, in most cases, that no clear picture can be obtained. Quite a number of the bones are charred, some very severely burned, even calcined; only a few in any one individual, however. A good many bones are broken and crushed, or appear chopped off—not, however, sufficiently frequently and definitely the latter, I believe, to justify a positive assertion that these people were killed by enemy action and flung into the kiva which then was fired. This intriguing thought is certainly a possibility, but I feel that the equally dramatic picture of the young men struggling to escape from the burning ceremonial chamber must also be suggested. The presence of fragmentary partial remains of a few very small children favors the former explanation, however. A possible compromise solution, combining both ideas and explaining the occurrence of skeletons both above and under the fallen roof, would be that the young men were caught in the kiva by an enemy raid and those who emerged before the structure was fired were killed and tossed back in.

Discussion. The timing of this event, when the townsmen seem to have been conducting some age-related activity in a kiva, is similar to that of the legendary Hopi attack on Awatovi. We assessed Wendorf and Reed's claim for violence by briefly examining part of the LA252 Room 6 skeletal series. Most skeletons were incomplete. Of the perimortem damage identified by Reed (burning, chopping, and breakage), we confirmed the burning, head smashing, and crushing. To this perimortem damage we can add one example of scalping and corpse exposure as identified by post-episodic carnivore chewing of various bones. We did not find any damage that we considered to be chopping. The following individuals curated in the Maxwell Museum of Anthropology have perimortem damage that supports Wendorf and

Reed's propositions about violence:

B.36. Adult, sex? Burned femur head, cranial breakage.

B.78 50/15. Adult male. Pelvis belongs to two different males. Distal end of right humerus chewed, and two tooth puncture marks present.

B.79 50/16. Three individuals. A subadult with more than half the vault broken. Frontal bone has a suite of 15 anvil abrasions, each about 3 cm long. A second subadult with cranial breakage. An adult male with impact breakage of the left temporal bone and maxilla.

B.92. Three individuals. An adult, sex?, with breakage of the maxilla, occipital base, right temporal, sphenoid, and left parietal. This adult's sternum was chewed and has a carnivore tooth puncture mark. The left humerus has both ends chewed off, and there are on the humerus several cutlike scratches attributable to carnivore chewing. An adult female has one proximal humerus fragment with tooth punctures. Three cranial fragments are broken. The frontal fragment has 2-cm-long cut marks. A third individual is another adult female with a frontal fragment having breakage.

B.94. Two individuals. Adult male? face with burning of the forehead. Another adult male, also with forehead burning.

B.105. Two adults with 17 cranial vault fragments.

## 20
## Turner-Look Site

Claim Date. 1955.

Claimant. H. M. Wormington.

Claim Type. Cannibalism and violence.

Other Designations. None known.

Site Location. About 26 km (16 miles) west of U.S. 50, on the Albert Turner ranch, about where Cottonwood Creek joins Diamond Creek, Grand County, east central Utah.

Site Type. Nine-room agricultural village of connected and freestanding circular structures.

Cultural Affiliation. Fremont Culture, Northern Periphery.

Chronology. A.D. 1050–1100 (ceramic date).

Excavator and Date. H. M. Wormington, 1939–1941, 1947–1948.

Institutional Storage. Denver Museum of Natural History, and Museum of Western Colorado, Grand Junction, Colorado.

Site Report. Wormington (1955).

Osteological Report. Reed (1955).

Skeletal Evidence of Stress. A young adult, possibly female, was mildly hydrocephalous (Reed 1955:40).

Burial Context. Marie Wormington (1955:15) described the Structure A burial setting as follows:

> To the north of the fireplace was a partially rock-lined ovate pit 38 inches long, 30 inches wide, and 14 inches deep, filled with sand and charcoal. It had been dug through both floors and continued into the underlying gravels. Resting on the fill in the pit was a human mandible. It was not burned. To the east of the fireplace lay the shaft of a robust human femur with a heavily marked linea aspera. The condyles had been broken off, leaving sharp, jagged

edges. The bone was hard and well preserved. A fragment of the left portion of an upper jaw containing 2 pre-molars was found in the trash outside the building at a depth of 30 inches.

In Structure E, Wormington (1955:19) found "a fragment of a human skull, that of an adult, [which] lay in the upper 8 inches of the fill, near the north wall." In Structure G she came across "a small fragment of a child's skull [that] lay on the floor. A fragment of the left portion of the maxilla of an adult, containing molars, pre-molars, and an incisor, was found in the first 8 inches of fill below a level of sterile adobe which overlay the southern portion of the structure" (1955:27).

In an "outdoor living area . . . a fragment of an adult human skull lay a foot to the east on the same level as the firepit" (Wormington 1955:34). Also outdoors, Wormington (1955:36) found four burials, one a double burial (her Burial I). Burial II was inexplicably incomplete.

**Associated Artifacts.** A carved circular slate plaque and a perforated shell were found with Burial I.

**Figures.** None.

**Taphonomy.** None.

*MNI.* Ignoring the burials, three individuals can be suggested as victims of violence: in Structure A, an adult (on basis of maxilla), possibly male (on basis of robust femur); and in Structure G, another adult maxilla and the fragment of a child's skull.

*Age and Sex.* Possibly two adults, one possibly male, and one child.

*Preservation.* Good to very poor.

*Bone and Fragment Number.* Seven pieces, ignoring the burials.

*Breakage.* Yes (HMW).

*Cut Marks.* Possible (HMW).

*There is no information for Burning, Anvil Abrasions, Polishing, Vertebrae Number, Scalping, Gnawing, Chewing, Insect Parts, or Other Modification.*

**Archaeologist's Interpretation.** In a thoughtful discussion about warfare that included consideration of the Fremont Culture rock-art shield figures, Wormington (1955:87) raised the question of cannibalism and violence:

If shields were used, some strife is indicated. There is also some evidence which suggests the practice of cannibalism and it is slain enemies or captives who are most likely to be eaten. A number of human bones which seem to have been deliberately cracked or broken were found in the vicinity of fireplaces. The human femur, from which the condyles appear to have been removed by chopping, which lay by the fire-pit in Structure B, is certainly suggestive. . . . The possibility that trophy heads were taken may also be considered. Pictographs in the Uintah Basin illustrated by Reagan show individuals wearing necklaces or collars such as are shown on Fremont pictographs and carrying what appear to be severed heads. In this connection the mandible found on the floor of Structure A is of interest. A number of fragments of human skulls which seem to have been intentionally broken were found in the refuse. Possibly the brains were eaten and the mandibles retained as trophies.

**Other Interpretations.** Erik Reed (1955:38–43) indicated that the Burial I adult was a middle-aged male that, according to medical and forensic experts in Denver, had a depressed fracture of the right temporal-parietal area with fracture lines extending into the occipital bone.

**Discussion.** Wormington readily accepted that Burial I (with the depressed cranial fracture) had met a violent death, but she was uncertain why an adult male was buried with a 4- to 6-year-old child.

Since most of the isolated bone fragments were parts of the head, Wormington's suggestion about the taking of trophy heads is not unreasonable, although a taphonomic study is needed, especially to assess her point about the eating of the victim's brains.

On September 7, 1993, we examined all of the Turner-Look site skeletal series in the Denver Museum of Natural History (the remainder is believed to be curated at the Museum of Western Colorado, Grand Junction.) The Denver Museum has the Burial I adult male and associated child. We agree with Reed's assessment of age and sex for both individuals, and we agree that the adult had received a perimortem blow to the right side of the head in the area of the parietal bone. The angle and severity of the head wound of the Burial I adult male is indicative of violence, although the damage could have happened after death if a large stone had accidently dropped on the head at the time of burial. There is no other form of environmental or human-induced perimortem damage to the adult male or the child. Until the isolated bone fragments from structures A, E, and G can be examined along taphonomic lines for evidence of violence or cannibalism, the claim for cannibalism should be put on hold.

## 21
## Small House

**Claim Date.** 1957.

**Claimant.** Frank H. H. Roberts, Jr.

**Claim Type.** Cannibalism.

**Other Designations.** 29SJ2385; LA42385.

**Site Location.** About 14.5 km (9 miles) east of Pueblo Bonito, near the left bank of Chaco Wash, Chaco Canyon, San Juan County, northwestern New Mexico. USGS Sargent Ranch quadrangle (1966), T 21N, R 10W, NW ¼ of NW ¼ of NE ¼ of Sec. 36.

**Site Type.** Small, roughly rectangular masonry pueblo with approximately ten rooms.

**Cultural Affiliation.** Chaco Anasazi.

**Chronology.** A.D. 900.

**Excavator and Date.** Frank H. H. Roberts, Jr., 1926.

**Institutional Storage.** Department of Anthropology, National Museum of Natural History, Smithsonian Institution, Washington, D.C.

**Site Report.** None. Roberts's 1926 field notes are on file at NMNH National Anthropological Archives; he also wrote a 1957 personal letter to Frank McNitt (1966).

**Osteological Report.** Turner (1993).

Table 3.17
Minimal Number of Individuals (MNI) at Small House

| SKELETAL ELEMENT | AGE | SEX | NOTES |
|---|---|---|---|
| Maxilla, whole | 15–18 | ? | Blown-out anterior teeth |
| Maxilla, left | 12–15 | ? | |
| | 15–18 | ? | |
| Mandible, whole | 12–15 | ? | Cut marks |
| | adult | ? | |
| Mandible, left | 12 | ? | |
| | 12–15 | ? | |
| Mandible, left ramus | Adult? | ? | Does not match any right part |
| Mandible, right | Adult | ? | Cut mark |
| Mandible, right ramus | >12 | ? | Does not match any left part |
| Mandible, fragment | 3–4 | ? | |

SUMMARY: Eight individuals. Two adults, sex?; one adult?, sex?; four juveniles 12–15; one 3- to 4-year-old child.

Table 3.18
Bone Elements and Perimortem Damage at Small House

| SKELETAL ELEMENT | WHOLE | FRAGMENT | IMPACT BREAK | ANVIL ABRASION | CUT MARK | BURN | POLISH |
|---|---|---|---|---|---|---|---|
| Cranial | | | | | | | |
| Maxilla | 0 | 3 | 3 | 0 | 0 | 0 | 1 |
| Mandible | 1 | 7 | 5 | 1 | 3 | 1 | 0 |
| Frontal | 0 | 3 | 3 | 0 | 1 | 1 | 0 |
| Temporal | 4 | 0 | 0 | 1 | 1 | 2 | 0 |
| Teeth | (56) | (0) | ? | 0 | 0 | ? | 0 |
| Fragments | — | 1 | 0 | 0 | 1 | 0 | 0 |
| Postcranial | | | | | | | |
| Cervical vertebrae | 2 | 0 | 0 | 0 | 0 | 0 | 0 |
| Lumbar vertebrae | 1 | 0 | 0 | 0 | 0 | 0 | 0 |
| Scapula | 2 | 0 | 0 | 0 | 0 | 0 | 0 |
| Rib | 0 | 1 | 1 | 0 | 0 | 0 | 1 |
| Humerus | 2 | 5 | 4 | 1 | 2 | 0 | 0 |
| Radius | 0 | 8 | 8 | 0 | 0 | 0 | 0 |
| Ulna | 2 | 2 | 0 | 0 | 0 | 0 | 0 |
| Hand & foot | 40 | 0 | 0 | 0 | 0 | 0 | 0 |
| Pelvis | 0 | 2 | 0 | 0 | 0 | 0 | 0 |
| Femur | 0 | 13 | 13 | 0 | 2 | 1 | 2?[a] |
| Tibia | 0 | 9 | 9 | 0 | 0 | 0 | 0 |
| Fibula | 0 | 6 | 6 | 0 | 0 | 0 | 0 |
| Patella | 1 | 0 | 0 | 0 | 0 | 0 | 0 |
| Long bone fragments | — | 37 | 37 | 7 | 2 | 1 | 14 |
| TOTAL (152) | 55 | 97 | 89 | 10 | 12 | 6 | 16 |
| PERCENTAGE | 36.2 | 63.8 | 58.5 | 6.6 | 7.9 | 3.9 | 10.5 |

Percentage of expected vertebrae = 1.6 (3 of 192; MNI = 8).

NOTE: Only elements that were present are listed. No gnawing or chewing was observed. Impact breakage, anvil abrasions, cut marks, burning, and polishing represent perimortem damage.

a. Not included in total due to uncertainty over whether polishing actually occurred.

Figure 3.106. Small House, Chaco Canyon, New Mexico. View down canyon. In 1926 Frank H. H. Roberts's workmen discovered the human charnel deposit that many years later he proposed had been cannibalized. Room 4, where the fragmented and burned remains of at least eight people were discovered in a subfloor pit, was probably on the right side of the photograph, near the Navajo boy. No screens are evident, so some of the smaller pieces of bone in the charnel pit were likely not recovered. Note that the masonry is coarse compared with the refined classic Chacoan styles. Masonry style and early types of ceramics form the basis for dating the charnel deposit at A.D. 900. Photographer presumed to be F. H. H. Roberts, Jr. National Anthropological Archives, Roberts Collection, no number.

Figure 3.107. Small House. Cranial pieces. Upper specimen has burning of frontal and mastoid bones, as does the temporal bone at middle left. Very few of the loose teeth arranged vertically along the left fit the tooth sockets of these upper and lower jaws, suggesting additional individuals had been processed. Scale is 15 cm. NMNH 334055 (CGT neg. 4-27-94:35).

Figure 3.108. Small House. Perimortem breakage of adult and subadult crania. Burning is present at arrows, locations with little overlying protective soft tissue. NMNH 334055 (CGT neg. 5-20-92:2; reprinted with permission from *American Journal of Physical Anthropology*).

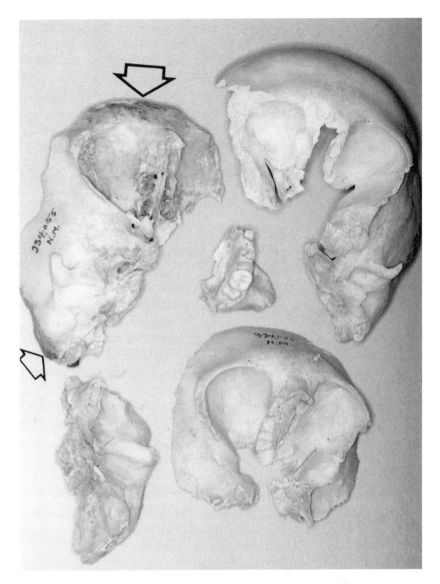

Figure 3.109. Small House. Facial damage was extensive, including violent smashing that resulted in blown-out anterior tooth sockets (arrow). Tooth on left was diseased, not damaged by violence. Actual width of image in photograph is 3.3 cm. NMNH 334055 (CGT neg. 5-20-92:31; reprinted with permission from *American Journal of Physical Anthropology*).

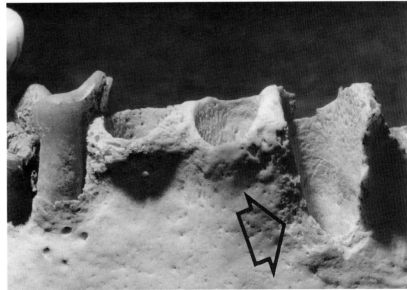

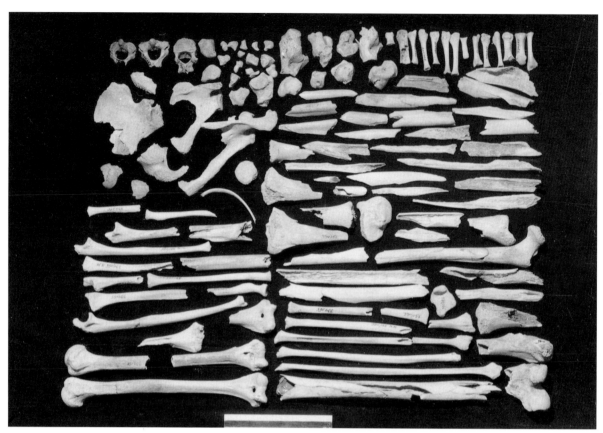

Figure 3.110. Small House. Postcranial assemblage representing an MNI of eight. Only three vertebrae were recovered (upper left). The long bone in lower right was reassembled many years ago by an unknown person. Scale is 15 cm. NMNH 334055 (CGT neg. 4-27-94:13).

Figure 3.111. Small House. Representative perimortem breakage of long bones. Burned piece at arrow. Bottom fragment is about 20 cm long. NMNH 334055 (CGT neg. 5-20-92:6; reprinted with permission from *American Journal of Physical Anthropology*).

Figure 3.112. Small House. Reassembled adult and subadult long bone shafts. Fragment at upper left (arrow) had burned after being broken from shaft by percussion—burning after breakage is the general sequence of damage in most of the human charnel deposits believed to have been cannibalized. NMNH 334055 (CGT neg. 5-20-92:4; reprinted with permission from *American Journal of Physical Anthropology*).

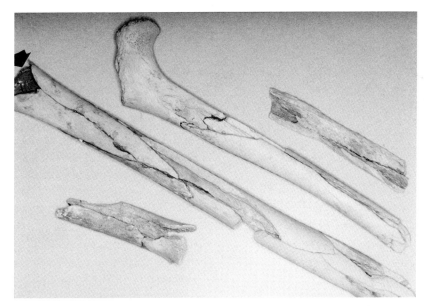

Figure 3.113. Small House. Detail of long bone perimortem percussion breakage with anvil abrasions at fracture (arrow). Actual width of image in photograph is 3.3 cm. NMNH 334055 (CGT neg. 5-20-92:8; reprinted with permission from *American Journal of Physical Anthropology*).

Figure 3.114. Small House. Detail of hammerstone or stone axe percussion crushing with adhering conchoidal bone chips (at arrow) in subadult femur. Actual width of image in photograph is 3.3 cm. NMNH 334055 (CGT neg. 5-20-92:18; reprinted with permission from *American Journal of Physical Anthropology*).

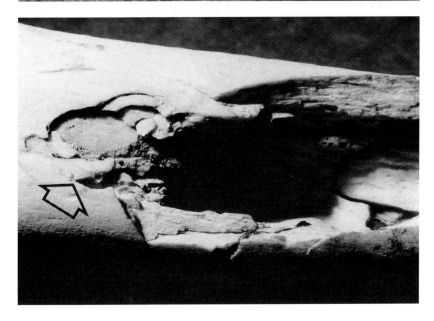

Skeletal Evidence of Stress. One subadult has cribra orbitalia.

Burial Context. Bone fragments found in pit under floor of Room 4.

Associated Artifacts. None indicated in Roberts's field notes.

Figures. 3.106–3.114.

Taphonomy. CGT, 1992. Skeletal inventory is in table 3.18.

    *MNI.* 8 (table 3.17).

    *Age and Sex.* One child; 4 subadults; 2 adults, sex?; one individual of indeterminable age and sex.

    *Preservation.* Generally good.

    *Bone and Fragment Number.* 152.

    *Breakage.* 58.5%.

    *Cut Marks.* 7.9%.

    *Burning.* 3.9%.

    *Anvil Abrasions.* 6.6%.

    *Polishing.* 10.5%.

    *Vertebrae Number.* 1.6% of expected (3 of 192).

    *Scalping.* Probably.

    *Gnawing, Rodent.* 0.0%.

    *Chewing, Carnivore.* 0.0%.

    *Insect Parts.* None found during skeletal examination.

    *Other Modification.* None.

Archaeologist's Interpretation. In Roberts's 1957 letter to McNitt, he speculated that the damaged Small House human remains might have resulted from ceremonial cannibalism or human sacrifice.

Other Interpretations. Elsewhere the senior author (Turner 1993) published a separate report on the Small House charnel deposit. There the idea was developed that Anasazi cannibalism could have been a form of terrorism used by the instigators of the rapid growth of the "Chacoan system." Tooth sockets were blown out in at least three individuals (two 12- to 15-year-old adolescents and a young adult), and without cut marks on internal mandibular surfaces there is no way to argue for any ritual treatment.

Discussion. Although we agree with Roberts's unexplained claim that cannibalism likely occurred at Small House, there is no taphonomic evidence in the osteological and dental remains that helps explain its occurrence except to suggest that violence was involved. If the estimated date of A.D. 900 is correct, then Small House is one of the earliest cases of Southwestern cannibalism.

**22**
**Coombs Site**

Claim Date. 1960 (RHL et al.); 1961 (CGT).

Claimants. Robert H. Lister, J. Richard Ambler, and Florence C. Lister; Christy G. Turner II.

Claim Type. Violence (RHL et al.); cannibalism (CGT).

Other Designations. 42GAa34.

Site Location. Within the city limits of Boulder, Garfield County, southern Utah, at 2,042 m (6,700 feet), on a hill slope overlooking Boulder Creek, a tributary of the Escalante River, 1.2 km (0.75 mile) to the west.

Site Type. Village of 83 structures (37 jacal/masonry habitation rooms, 10 pithouses, 35 storage units, and 1 ramada), and dune burials.

Cultural Affiliation. Kayenta Anasazi.

Chronology. Pueblo II to early Pueblo III (A.D. 1075–1275).

Excavators and Date. R. H. Lister (director), J. R. Ambler (foreman), and students, 1958–1959.

Institutional Storage. Natural History Museum, University of Utah, Salt Lake City, Utah.

Site Reports. Lister (1959), Lister, Ambler, and Lister (1960), Lister and Lister (1961).

Osteological Reports. Roberts (1991); Turner (1961a); Turner and Turner (1992a).

Skeletal Evidence of Stress. Porotic hyperostosis is present.

Burial Context. Skeletons and bone fragments on room floors, plus six roofed burial pits in the dunes to the south of the village. Turner (1961a) suggested that Burial 4, found in a dune pit on the southern edge of the site, had received a severe blow to the head and that one lower leg might have been cannibalized. The very incomplete and poorly preserved Burial 5, on the floor of Structure E, was thought by Lister, Ambler, and Lister (1960) to have been murdered.

Associated Artifacts. Formal burials were accompanied by pottery vessels and other grave goods. Flexed Burial 11, a young adult female, is noteworthy because she had a 74-piece turquoise necklace, 13 vessels, and several other small items. Burial 4 had a Tusayan Corrugated jar and part of a coiled basket with it. Burial 5 had three arrow points near the chest.

Figures. 3.115–3.116.

Taphonomy. RHL et al. and CGT.

*MNI.* 12.

*Age and Sex.* Three infants; 2 adolescent females; one 20-year-old female; one adult female; two adult males?; one old adult male. Burial 4: adult female (RHL et al.; CGT); Burial 5: adult (RHL et al.), adult male? (CGT).

*Preservation.* Fair to good.

*Bone and Fragment Number.* Not counted.

*Breakage.* Yes (CGT).

*Cut Marks.* Yes (CGT).

*Burning.* Uncertain (CGT).

*Anvil Abrasions.* Yes (CGT).

*Polishing.* Yes (CGT).

*Vertebrae Number.* Not counted.

*Scalping.* Yes (CGT).

*Gnawing, Rodent.* Uncertain (CGT).

*Chewing, Carnivore.* Yes (CGT).

*Insect Parts.* None observed (CGT and JAT).

*Other Modification.* Two lower leg bones from Burial 5 lack internal cancellous tissue, which seemingly was removed by reaming or scooping.

Archaeologist's Interpretation. There are two levels of analysis to consider for the Coombs violence and cannibalism—the sets of individual skeletal remains and the site as a whole. First, the remains. Lister, Ambler, and Lister (1960:268) suggested that Burial 5 "may have been a murder victim. The well preserved bones were sprawled on the floor of Structure E." They described the find (1960:28–29), starting with the clearing of a burned floor area. Then,

Figure 3.115. Coombs Site,
Utah. External view of perimortem percussion breakage
of Burial 4 vault. The person received at least two blows to the
top and back of her head. The
latter wound, shown here, suggests a hammerlike weapon
(CGT neg. 1959:17).

Figure 3.116. Coombs Site.
Detail of perimortem percussion
trauma to Burial 4, internal view,
showing classic form of fresh
bone impact trauma where
internal diameter of wound is
greater than outside diameter
(CGT neg. 1959:15).

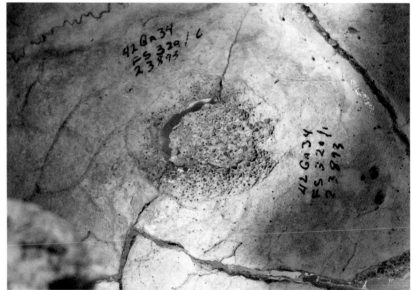

a few articulated human finger and lower arm bones came to light.
The right humerus, the right scapula, some of the right ribs, and a
few fragments of a skull were carefully cleared but the remainder
of the skeleton was not present. These bones were lying directly on
the floor, beneath the burned roof debris. As none of the bones
showed any sign of charring, it was obvious that the body had not
been buried after the room had been fire gutted, for any pit would
have removed some of the ash and charcoal remaining from the
former roof. The body must have been on the floor at the time the
conflagration swept the room. It also seems likely that at least
some flesh was still on the bones because when exhumed these
bones were articulated and none showed signs of having been
burned. The right arm was flung outward from the body, palm upward, as if the individual was sprawled out on the floor rather than
carefully laid away. Three hypotheses concerning the death of this
Coombs villager can be presented: (1) whatever the person's role

or status may have been, such as an unwelcome visitor or lover, bad shaman, or an enemy of any sort, he was murdered (three arrowpoints were found in the vicinity of the rib cage) and the house was burned down on top of him; (2) the house ignited accidentally and he was trapped by the fire; and (3) he died of natural causes and the dwelling was set afire as a funeral pyre. . . . Circumstantial evidence, particularly the arm position and presence of arrow points, implies prehistoric foul play. . . . Remaining portions of the rib cage were found lying in a position to suggest that most of the body must have occupied the same area taken up by the south wall of Room 14, Structure A. Probing under this wall failed to locate any more bones.

Second, the site. "Why the village was abandoned after a fairly short period of occupation is not apparent. The ultimate cause, or perhaps the last chapter of Coombs history, is associated with fire. The majority of the structures throughout the site had burned" (Lister and Lister 1961:8). Despite two years of excavation, no basis was found on which to determine whether the fire had been due to conflict, accident, or intent to destroy the village before abandonment.

**Other Interpretations.** Heidi Roberts (1991:73–74), who did a demographic study of the Coombs Site skeletal remains, including bone found in nonburial settings, remarked:

One male (Fs 1267), represented by a single mandible, was found at almost the exact center of a burned pithouse. The mandible was located in the fill of the structure and no evidence of burning was evident. A second individual, possibly male (Fs 776), consisted of a disarticulated and disturbed skeleton described as a case of "prehistoric foul play" (Lister, Ambler, and Lister 1960:29). This burial (5) was found in a jacal structure which had burned. The right arm, right scapula, some of the right ribs, and skull were articulated and "three arrowpoints were found in the vicinity of the rib cage" (Lister, Ambler, and Lister 1960:29). Excavators speculated that the rest of the skeleton was disturbed during the construction of Structure A. No evidence of trauma was found on any of the skeletal elements but a mandible fragment is slightly burned. Charring occurs on the surface around the margins near gnathion and probably supports the archaeologist's claim that the individual was in the structure when it burned. A third male also is an isolated mandible (Fs 28) found in a test trench with no associated artifacts and no evidence of a prepared grave. The fourth male (Fs 567) was found in midden filling a borrow pit and consists of the left pubic symphysis, 3 cranial fragments, and a left first rib. This last individual was identified as a possible male because only portions of a maxilla and left malar were found.

**Discussion.** There are problems in field and observation records for the skeletal remains. Moreover, the senior author's early proposal for cannibalism (Turner 1961a) was inadequately based. A subsequent half-day examination in 1988 of part of the Coombs collection curated at the Museum of Natural History, University of Utah, Salt Lake City, did not turn up all six of the key taphonomic criteria. Although more study of the Coombs series is needed, the second examination did establish that perimortem breakage, cutting, abrasions, and polishing were present. No burning was found in the two individuals examined, but if Roberts's example of a burned mandible is added, then all six key cannibalism criteria are present, although not in one individual or site location.

As things stand now, the perimortem-damaged Coombs skeletal remains and site burning surely signal violence. Whether the interpretation can be extended to include cannibalism is unclear. A complete reexamination is needed.

## 23
## Mesa Verde 499

**Claim Date.** 1964.

**Claimant.** Robert H. Lister.

**Claim Type.** Violence.

**Other Designations.** Part of the Far View group.

**Site Location.** About 6.4 km (4 miles) north of Mesa Verde National Park headquarters, Colorado, between the east fork of Navajo Canyon and Soda Canyon, near the north end of Chapin Mesa, just west of Far View House or Mummy Lake, at 2347 m (7700 feet) elevation. USGS Mesa Verde National Park quadrangle (1967), T 35N, R 15W, Sec. 27.

**Site Type.** A 12-room, possibly two-story masonry pueblo with tower and with a kiva in each of two courtyards.

**Cultural Affiliation.** Mesa Verde Anasazi.

**Chronology.** Early Pueblo III, A.D. 1100–1150 (two tree-ring dates of 1123).

**Excavators and Date.** Robert H. Lister and members of the University of Colorado Archaeological Field School, 1953.

**Institutional Storage.** Most materials went to the University of Colorado, Boulder. Some or all may have been returned to Mesa Verde National Park.

**Site Report.** Lister (1964).

**Osteological Report.** Wade and Armelagos (1966).

**Skeletal Evidence of Stress.** William D. Wade and George J. Armelagos (1966:109) found some degree of porotic hyperostosis in 3 of at least 13 individuals of varying degrees of completeness. In 1966 the cause of porotic hyperostosis was unknown, but anemias were implicated. Today, this relatively large amount of porotic hyperostosis in a skeletal sample alerts analysts to the possiblity of significant iron deficiency (excessive maize, insufficient meat), parasite load, or infective stress.

**Burial Context.** In Kiva B, Lister found a nearly complete adult sprawled on the floor between the firepit draft deflector and the entrance to the external air-intake ventilator tunnel.

**Associated Artifacts.** None.

**Figures.** None.

**Taphonomy.** None.

*MNI.* 1.

*Age and Sex.* Adult male.

*Preservation.* Fair to good.

*Breakage.* Yes, at least skull.

*Vertebrae Number.* Not reported, but line drawing (Lister 1964:81, fig. 12) and photograph of upper body and skull (Lister 1964:83, pl. 21) of Kiva B burial suggests that all 24 were recovered.

*Chewing, Carnivore.* Possible.

*There is no information for Bone and Fragment Number, Cut Marks, Burning, Anvil Abrasions, Polishing, Scalping, Gnawing, Insect Parts, or Other Modification.*

Archaeologist's Interpretation. Lister (1964:37) described the human remains: "An almost complete human skeleton (Burial 1) was found on the floor of the kiva between the deflector and the entrance to the ventilator tunnel. The position of skeleton, as well as other factors mentioned in the section on burials, indicates that the individual had been killed or wounded before being thrown or placed in the kiva. Five large slabs of stone had been thrown or piled on top of the body." He added (1964:79):

> It was not a burial in the normal sense, for there was evidence that the individual had been injured or killed before being thrown or placed on the kiva floor. A small bone awl was present in the chest cavity suggesting that the person had been stabbed. The skeleton rested on its left side with the right leg crossed over the left. The left arm was flung back over the head. The individual's back was bent backward and the neck so twisted that the head faced to the rear. The head had been crushed by large stones which appear to have been thrown upon the ill fated person. The corpse may have been mutilated by dogs or wild animals before it was completely covered by debris in the abandoned kiva because the right hand and the right radius were missing. No burial furnishings were associated with the skeleton.

> Lister (1966:88) elsewhere strengthened his case for violence by adding that burials never occurred in rooms at this settlement: "An adult male skeleton, found on the floor of one of the kivas at Site 499, obviously was not a normal burial. . . . All other primary burials were found in trash heaps." He added (1966:96): "The presence of the unusual human burial upon the floor of one kiva, and a dog skeleton in another, may have interesting implications. Such occurrences are not infrequent at Anasazi sites and may be found to be associated with socio-religious ceremonies related to the abandonment of a kiva."

Other Interpretations. Wade and Armelagos (1966:97) reported that "the calvarium is badly fragmented but the mandible is intact. The post-cranial skeleton is nearly complete and in fair to good state of preservation."

Discussion. Judging from Lister's written descriptions and excellent illustrations, we agree that there is a strong case for this adult male's having met a violent death. There is a definite need for taphonomic study to determine whether the missing hand had been cut off, instead of being removed by scavengers as Lister suggested, and to see whether the skull breakage involved any identifiable perimortem mutilation. Cutting off a hand as a war trophy was practiced by Zuni warriors well into the early part of historic contact. Frank Cushing (1896:328) wrote that around 1630, "thus speedily was slain the first resident priest of Zuni. . . . Then [the armed religionists] sallied forth to follow Fray Martin. They overtook him at night . . . cut off his hand and scalped him, they killed also this venerable friar and hastened back to their town. There the ceremonial of the scalp dances of initiation were performed over the scalps of the two friars."

## 24
## Sambrito Village

**Claim Date.** 1966.

**Claimants.** Alfred E. Dittert, Jr., Frank W. Eddy, and Beth L. Dickey.

**Claim Type.** Cannibalism.

**Other Designations.** LA4195.

**Site Location.** On right (west) bank of San Juan River just below its junction with Sambrito Creek, northwestern New Mexico. Today the Sambrito Village site is inundated by the waters of Navajo Reservoir.

**Site Type.** Large village of 37 pithouses with one kiva, 25 surface structures, and 28 exterior pits.

**Cultural Affiliation.** Anasazi.

**Chronology.** A.D. 400–1000, with most occupation concentrated during the later part of the Piedra phase, between 900 and 950. The human remains for which the cannibalism claim was made date to the Piedra phase.

**Excavators and Date.** Frank W. Eddy and Alfred E. Dittert, Jr., 1960.

**Institutional Storage.** Department of Anthropology, Arizona State University, Tempe.

**Site Report.** Dittert, Eddy, and Dickey (1966).

**Osteological Reports.** K. Bennett (1966); Jones (1972); Turner (1983); Minturn (1994).

**Skeletal Evidence of Stress.** None.

**Burial Context.** Scattered bone assemblages found in two pithouses, 6 and 25.

**Associated Artifacts.** None.

**Figures.** 3.117–3.120.

**Taphonomy.** The Sambrito Village assemblage has been examined by different people five times (Bennett, Dittert et al., Jones, Minturn, and Turner). Kenneth A. Bennett did not deal with taphonomy. Dittert, Eddy, and Dickey did field analysis for MNI, which was preliminary. W. P. Jones and, to a degree, Turner (CGT), were unable to correlate site features with storage boxes. Thus, Penny Dufoe Minturn's is the best study, and her findings are followed herein. Minturn determined that the human remains from Pithouse 6 were animal scavenged and archaeologically damaged. There was no identifiable prehistoric damage done by humans to the Pithouse 6 remains, so only the assemblage from Pithouse 25 is relevant. The skeletal inventory in table 3.19 is from Minturn (1994).

*MNI.* 11 (PDM).

*Age and Sex.* Eight adults, based on right temporal bones; three children, based on postcranial bones. The adults, based on mandibles and teeth: one 15- to 18-year-old female; one female over 30; one young adult male; one adult, sex?; one 15- to 18-year-old, sex?; three probable adults, sex?.

Figure 3.117. Sambrito Village, New Mexico. Left half of adult frontal and incomplete parietal with external thermal flaking and perimortem breakage. Black bar length is 3.0 cm (photograph by Korri Dee Turner 8-21-92:21, courtesy Penny Dufoe Minturn).

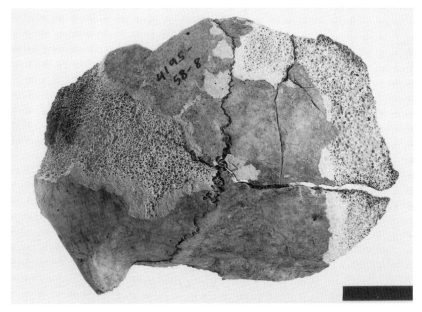

Figure 3.118. Sambrito Village. Perimortem impact damage showing how breakage does not necessarily follow bone element suture lines, even in subadults. Here, fragments of left parietal adhere to occipital (arrow). The right parietal and an Inca bone have been reassembled in this subadult. Black bar length is 1.0 cm (photograph by Korri Dee Turner 8-21-92:31, courtesy Penny Dufoe Minturn).

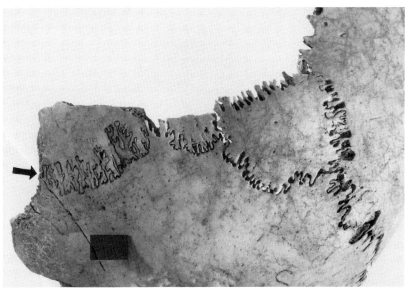

Figure 3.119. Sambrito Village. Adult right parietal with one or possibly two perimortem impact fractures and associated anvil or hammerstone abrasions. Black bar length is 1.0 cm (photograph by Korri Dee Turner 8-21-92:22, courtesy Penny Dufoe Minturn).

Figure 3.120. Sambrito Village. Adult mandibular right ascending ramus with multiple cut marks on external surface. Black bar length is 1.0 cm (photograph by Korri Dee Turner 8-21-92:18, courtesy Penny Dufoe Minturn).

*Preservation.* Good.
*Bone and Fragment Number.* 640.
*Breakage.* 95.6%.
*Cut Marks.* 2.8%.
*Burning.* 16.9%.
*Anvil Abrasions.* 2.5%.
*Polishing.* None found (PDM); present (CGT, May 1997).
*Vertebrae Number.* 12.9% of expected (34 of 264).
*Scalping.* Probable. Five cut marks occur on vault bones.
*Gnawing, Rodent.* None.
*Chewing, Carnivore.* 2.3%.
*Insect Parts.* None found.
*Other Modification.* None.

**Archaeologists' Interpretation.** Dittert, Eddy, and Dickey (1966:248) reported that scattered human bones belonging to at least 44 individuals were found in 17 locations, mostly in semisubterranean pithouses. One of the bone lots, from Pithouse 25, represented the remains of 12 individuals that had been deposited sometime before the roof collapsed. This assemblage contained many burned long bones that were split lengthwise. Impact percussion scars suggested the use of a stone hammer to open the shafts. The breaks were irregular but were not the shattered fracture type produced when dried bone is broken. This evidence indicated that the human bones were fleshed and broken open while the bone was still green. One or two long bones showed some scouring as if the interior marrow had been scraped out.

In general, the skeletal parts that were present were the long bones and skulls; other portions were missing. Apparently these people were killed, cannibalized, and tossed onto the house floor, after which the structure was burned down upon them. This may not represent the total size of the murdered group, since the pithouse was only trenched, and more individuals might have lain in the unexcavated portions. Three other sets of remains, showing similar kinds of dam-

Table 3.19
Bone Elements and Perimortem Damage at Sambrito Village,
Pithouse 25

| SKELETAL ELEMENT | WHOLE | FRAGMENT | IMPACT BREAK | ANVIL ABRASION | CUT MARK | BURN | CHEWING |
|---|---|---|---|---|---|---|---|
| Cranial | | | | | | | |
| Maxilla + zygomatic | 0 | 9 | 9 | 0 | 1 | 0 | 0 |
| Mandible | 0 | 5 | 5 | 0 | 1 | 1 | 1 |
| Frontal | 0 | 7 | 7 | 2 | 1 | 4 | 0 |
| Parietal | 0 | 16 | 16 | 2 | 1 | 8 | 0 |
| Occipital | 0 | 9 | 9 | 1 | 0 | 2 | 0 |
| Temporal | 0 | 15 | 15 | 2 | 3 | 1 | 0 |
| Base | 0 | 2 | 2 | 0 | 0 | 0 | 0 |
| Teeth (not counted) | | | | | | | |
| Fragment | — | 83 | 83 | 1 | 0 | 1 | 0 |
| Postcranial | | | | | | | |
| Vertebrae | 7 | 27 | 27 | 0 | 0 | 0 | 0 |
| Scapula | 0 | 2 | 2 | 0 | 0 | 1 | 1 |
| Clavicle | 2 | 6 | 6 | 0 | 1 | 0 | 1 |
| Rib | 12 | 42 | 42 | 0 | 0 | 1 | 1 |
| Humerus | 0 | 9 | 9 | 1 | 1 | 0 | 2 |
| Radius | 2 | 9 | 9 | 0 | 1 | 1 | 2 |
| Ulna | 1 | 8 | 8 | 0 | 0 | 0 | 0 |
| Hand & foot | 2 | 28 | 28 | 0 | 0 | 2 | 0 |
| Pelvis | 0 | 7 | 7 | 0 | 0 | 4 | 0 |
| Femur | 2 | 9 | 9 | 0 | 1 | 2 | 0 |
| Tibia | 0 | 19 | 19 | 2 | 0 | 1 | 1 |
| Fibula | 0 | 5 | 5 | 0 | 0 | 1 | 0 |
| Long bone fragments | — | 295 | 281 | 5 | 7 | 78 | 6 |
| TOTAL (640) | 28 | 612 | 612 | 16 | 18 | 108 | 15 |
| PERCENTAGE | 4.4 | 95.6 | 95.6 | 2.5 | 2.8 | 16.9 | 2.3 |

Percentage of expected vertebrae = 12.9 (34 of 264; MNI = 11).

SOURCE: Minturn (1994). Minturn's data and observations were reviewed by C. G. Turner, her M.A. advisor.

NOTE: Only elements that were present are listed. A minor amount of polishing was observed. Impact breakage, anvil abrasions, cut marks, and burning represent perimortem damage. Chewing is postmortem damage.

age, were found in the fill of Pithouse 6, making a total of fifteen unusually damaged skeletons from the site. Group burials were common at Sambrito Village (72% of sample, 25 articulated burials) (Dittert, Eddy, and Dickey 1966:243–249).

**Other Interpretations.** Bennett (1966) said nothing about the remains from Pithouses 6 and 25. Jones (1972) tried to deal with the problem of the skeletal remains having been bagged with "feature" numbers (7 and 58) that could not be matched with complete certainty to the pithouse numbers in the published site report. Jones came up with an MNI of 27 and found a little evidence for violence and cannibalism. The senior author (Turner 1983), like Jones, had trouble with the provenience and storage numbers and therefore tried to match the MNI of 12 that Dittert, Eddy, and Dickey obtained for Pithouse 25 by not using all the material that Jones did. Doing so produced an MNI of only five. Despite the underestimate, positive identifications were made of cut marks, burning, breakage, abrasions, and good bone preservation.

Minturn (1994) found the human bone assemblage from Sambrito Pithouse 25 to exhibit the minimal taphonomic signature of cannibalism. Her comparisons of Sambrito Village with other Anasazi assemblages suggesting cannibalism showed statistically significant differences. These she attributed to diverse and flawed archaeological collecting methods rather than to prehistoric processing or behavioral differences. She concluded that there was an Anasazi focus to Southwestern cannibalism but that its cause or causes remained obscure.

Discussion. Like Minturn, we still find nothing in the Sambrito taphonomy, archaeological field notes, or published site report that helps us understand how this bone assemblage came to be deposited or why these people were probably cannibalized. This assemblage, like almost all the others reviewed in this chapter, illustrates the need for specialized skeletal recovery procedures when charnel deposits are encountered, just as there are specialized routines for the recovery of archaeomagnetic, carbon-14, tree-ring, and other sorts of materials.

## 25
## Polacca Wash

Claim Date. 1970.

Claimants. Christy G. Turner II and Nancy T. Morris.

Claim Type. Cannibalism.

Other Designations. NA8502.

Site Location. Left (east) bank of Polacca Wash, 4.8 km (3 miles) downstream from Coyote Springs, 16.1 km (10 miles) south of Hopi villages, midway between Awatovi and Shungopovi, northeastern Arizona. USGS Tovar Mesa quadrangle (1966), T 26N, R 16E, SE ¼ of SW ¼ of Sec. 23.

Site Type. Isolated charnel deposit of disarticulated and severely damaged human bones with no material culture. Remains were found in red aeolian sand covering gray clays, silts, and sands through which cuts the 10-meter-deep Polacca Wash channel.

Cultural Affiliation. Historic Hopi.

Chronology. Uncorrected carbon-14 date on a sample of ribs: A.D. 1580 ± 95.

Excavators and Date. Alan P. Olson, Roger Kelly, and Carol Potter, March 11, 1964. After the senior author came across the charnel assemblage in the Museum of Northern Arizona physical anthropology collections, he, Roger Kelly, and Alexander J. Lindsay, Jr., visited the site on August 5, 1967. Their examination of the site area turned up a few scattered Tusayan pottery sherds that ranged in age from Basketmaker III to Pueblo IV, but no structure or any other form of habitation. All that remained of Olson's excavation were scattered small fragments of bone and broken teeth and some small pieces of fractured cherty stone. Although erosion was active in the aeolian sands, no ash or charcoal was found.

Institutional Storage. Department of Anthropology, Museum of Northern Arizona.

Site Report. Olson (1966). His field notes and related correspondence are in the site files, Museum of Northern Arizona.

Osteological Reports. Unpublished report by University of Arizona student Stephen I. Rosen (SIR), May 1964, in the MNA NA8502 site file. This report contains no taphonomic information. Other reports are Turner and Morris (1970); Turner (1983); Turner and Turner (1992a).

**Skeletal Evidence of Stress.** None.

**Burial Context.** Isolated mass burial or charnel deposit. There are no known habitation sites or any other activity or use areas in the vicinity.

**Associated Artifacts.** None.

**Figures.** 3.121–3.135.

**Taphonomy.** SIR; CGT and NTM, 1970; CGT and JAT reexamination, July 1993. The following description is based on the 1993 restudy except where noted. Skeletal inventory is in table 3.22.

*MNI.* 30 (CGT & NTM); 30 (SIR); 30 (CGT & JAT) (tables 3.20–3.21).

*Age and Sex.* Two 1- to 3-year-old infants; six 3- to 12-year-old children; four 13- to 17-year-old adolescents (one female); sixteen adults (two female, one male); two probable adults. These age and sex estimates are from Turner and Morris (1970), because there has been some skeletal element loss between 1970 and 1993. Given the extreme fragmentation, sex is very difficult to estimate; however, the number of male or malelike bones is very small. The following values were determined in 1993.

*Preservation.* Mainly good to excellent.

*Bone and Fragment Number.* 1,049.

*Breakage.* 92.8% (+ 0.8% peel breaks).

*Cut Marks.* 2.6%.

*Burning.* 18.6%.

*Anvil Abrasions.* 1.5%.

*Polishing.* 0.3%.

*Vertebrae Number.* 5.4% of expected (39 of 720).

*Scalping.* Yes.

*Gnawing, Rodent, and Chewing, Carnivore.* 6.5%.

*Insect Parts.* None.

*Other Modification.* A circular hole 2.5 cm in diameter is present in the right side of the head, centered on the coronal suture, of an adult female with occipital cranial deformation. Although the cause and method of production cannot be determined because of surface weathering, the cylindrical (rather than cone-shaped) hole suggests cutting rather than punching (fig. 3.126).

**Archaeologist's Interpretation.** Olson (1966) applied the term "mass burial" to this assemblage. He suggested, on the basis of four potsherds found in the burial area, that the remains were prehistoric. He believed that the burial was secondary, because of its disarticulation, and ceremonial, because crania seemed to be arranged around the edge of the deposit. He hinted at the possibility of cannibalism, because the bones were broken and charred, but at the same time he thought there was no evidence of violence. Neither Olson nor Rosen seems to have noticed the cut marks.

**Other Interpretations.** Jesse Walter Fewkes collected oral traditions about the destruction of the nearby town of Awatovi and its 800 inhabitants, as have others (for example, H. C. James 1974:62–64). As we described earlier in this chapter, Hopi warriors from other villages attacked at dawn, trapping many men in their kivas and killing other

Table 3.20
Minimal Number of Individuals (MNI) at Polacca Wash

| SKELETAL ELEMENT | AGE | SEX | NOTES |
|---|---|---|---|
| Maxilla, whole | Old adult | ? | Blown-out anterior teeth, some burning |
| | Old adult | ? | Blown-out anterior teeth |
| | Mid-adult | F? | Blown-out anterior teeth |
| | Adult | ? | All teeth smashed |
| | 15 | ? | No damage |
| | 12–15 | ? | Blown-out anterior teeth |
| | 12 | ? | Blown-out anterior teeth |
| | 2 | ? | Blown-out anterior teeth |
| Maxilla, left | Old adult | ? | |
| | Young adult | ? | |
| | 17–18 | ? | Blown-out anterior teeth, some burning |
| | 15–18 | ? | Blown-out anterior teeth |
| Maxilla, right | Old adult | ? | Smashed nose |
| | Old adult | ? | Blown-out anterior teeth |
| | Adult | ? | |
| | 3 | ? | Blown-out anterior teeth |
| | 1 | ? | |
| Mandible, whole | Old adult | F | Burned, broken at L horizontal ramus |
| | Old adult | ? | |
| | Adult | M | |
| | Young adult | F? | Broken at symphysis |
| | Young adult | ? | |
| | 17–18 | ? | |
| | 10? | ? | |
| | 6–8 | ? | |
| Mandible, left | Old adult | F? | Broken symphysis |
| | Adult | M | Broken symphysis, burned at gonion |
| | Adult | F? | Cut ascending ramus |
| | Adult | ? | |
| | 18 | ? | Broken at L horizontal ramus |
| Mandible, right | Old adult | F? | Broken at L horizontal ramus, burned |
| | Adult | ? | Broken at R horizontal ramus |
| | Young adult | ? | Broken at R horizontal ramus |
| | Young adult | ? | Broken at symphysis |
| | 15 | ? | Broken at R horizontal ramus |

NOTE: Since the 1970 Turner and Morris study, in which 30 individuals could be determined from maxillae, the number of maxillae and other bones has decreased, most likely because of misplacement. See table 3.21 for MNI summary.

Awatovians elsewhere in the town. What is important in terms of the Polacca Wash site is Fewkes's (1893a:366) recounting of the Hopi oral tradition about "Death Mound":

All who were capable of moving were compelled to travel or drag themselves till they came to the sand-hills of Mi-con-in-o-vi and there the final disposition of the prisoners was made. . . . All the women who had song-prayers and were willing to teach them were spared and no children were designedly killed, but were divided among the villages, and most of them went to Mi-con-in-o-vi. The remainder of the prisoners, men and women, were again tortured

Table 3.21
Polacca Wash MNI Estimate Based on Maxilla Count, Cranial Robusticity, and Dental Development

| | Individuals | | | | |
| AGE GROUP | NO. | % | MALE | FEMALE | SEX? |
|---|---|---|---|---|---|
| Infant (1–3 years) | 2 | 6.7 | — | — | 2 |
| Child (4–12 years) | 6 | 20.0 | — | — | 6 |
| Adolescent (13–17 years) | 4 | 13.3 | — | 1 | 3 |
| Adult (>18 years) | 16 | 53.3 | 1 | 2 | 13 |
| Probable adult | 2 | 6.7 | — | — | 2 |
| TOTAL | 30 | 100.0 | 1 | 3 | 26 |

SOURCE: Turner and Morris (1970).

Table 3.22
Bone Elements and Perimortem Damage at Polacca Wash

| SKELETAL ELEMENT | WHOLE | FRAGMENT | IMPACT BREAK | ANVIL ABRASION | CUT MARK | BURN | POLISH | GNAW/ CHEW |
|---|---|---|---|---|---|---|---|---|
| Cranial | | | | | | | | |
| Maxilla | 8 | 10 | 17 | 0 | 0 | 1 | 0 | 0 |
| Mandible | 4 | 37 | 39 | 1 | 2 | 18 | 0 | 0 |
| Frontal | 1 | 18 | 17 | 1 | 2 | 1 | 0 | 0 |
| Parietal | 10 | 21 | 25 | 3 | 0 | 3 | 0 | 0 |
| Occipital | 0 | 22 | 21 | 1 | 0 | 0 | 0 | 0 |
| Temporal | 6 | 27 | 27 | 1 | 1 | 2 | 0 | 0 |
| Base | 0 | 14 | 14 | 0 | 0 | 0 | 0 | 0 |
| Teeth (225) | | | | | | | | |
| Fragments | — | 217 | 218 | 0 | 0 | 50 | 0 | 0 |
| Postcranial | | | | | | | | |
| Cervical vertebrae | 8 | 10 | 10 | 0 | 0 | 1 | 0 | 0 |
| Vertebrae fragments | — | 36 | 36 | 0 | 0 | 2 | 0 | 0 |
| Scapula | 13 | 20 | 34 | 1 | 0 | 3 | 0 | 7 |
| Clavicle | 1 | 18 | 19 | 1 | 2 | 2 | 0 | 1 |
| Rib/sternum | 2 | 120 | 122 | 1 | 1 | 6 | 1 | 1 |
| Humerus | 2 | 19 | 19 | 2 | 3 | 1 | 0 | 2 |
| Radius | 1 | 22 | 21 | 0 | 3 | 3 | 0 | 2 |
| Ulna | 1 | 19 | 19 | 0 | 2 | 2 | 0 | 5 |
| Hand & foot | 14 | 29 | 2 | 0 | 0 | 2 | 0 | 28 |
| Pelvis | 0 | 28 | 28 | 0 | 1 | 6 | 0 | 5 |
| Femur | 2 | 28 | 27 | 1 | 6 | 1 | 0 | 3 |
| Tibia | 1 | 27 | 27 | 1 | 2 | 2 | 1 | 11 |
| Fibula | 0 | 5 | 5 | 0 | 0 | 0 | 0 | 0 |
| Patella | 0 | 1 | 0 | 0 | 0 | 0 | 0 | 1 |
| Long bone fragments | — | 226 | 227 | 2 | 2 | 89 | 1 | 1 |
| Bone type unknown | 0 | 1 | 0 | 0 | 0 | 0 | 0 | 0 |
| TOTAL (1,049) | 74 | 975 | 974 | 16 | 27 | 195 | 3 | 67 |
| PERCENTAGE | 7.0 | 93.0 | 92.8 | 1.5 | 2.6 | 18.6 | 0.3 | 6.5 |

Percentage of expected vertebrae = 5.4 (39 of 720; MNI = 30).[a]

NOTE: Only elements that were present are listed. Impact breakage, anvil abrasions, cut marks, burning, and polishing represent perimortem damage. Gnawing and chewing are postmortem damage.

a. Fragments of postcervical vertebrae represent about 21 whole vertebrae.

Figure 3.121. Polacca Wash, Arizona. The general isolation of the charnel deposit can be appreciated. In the foreground, to the right of the shovels and boxes, are the remains of an MNI of 30. Carole A. Potter (seated) and Alan P. Olson are shown. Museum of Northern Arizona Archive photograph by Roger E. Kelly (March 1964).

Figure 3.122. Polacca Wash. Final exposure of the charnel deposit. The presence of more complete crania at the edge of the deposit is a taphonomic feature attributable to rolling rather than a result of ritual placement. Very small bone fragments are visible, demonstrating that the body processing was done here. Museum of Northern Arizona Archive photograph by Roger Kelly (March 1964).

Figure 3.123. Polacca Wash. Completing the excavation of the mass burial. Carole Potter (left) and Roger Kelly are removing the remainder of the bones and bone fragments from the sterile and unburned fine aeolian sand matrix that held the charnel deposit. Museum of Northern Arizona Archive photograph by Alan Olson (March 1964).

Figure 3.124. Polacca Wash. Cranial vault fragments showing exfoliation of outer cortex. Whole parietal in lower left. This distinctive type of damage is now thought to be due to thermal stress, which causes cross-sectional differences in preservability. The remaining small amount of outer cortex is soft, chalky, and creamy white in color. The cancellous bone is harder and much less chalky. The inner cortex is hard, dense, and ivory colored (CGT neg. March 1968:18).

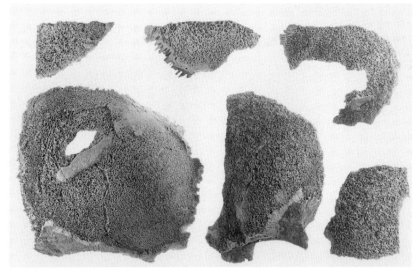

Figure 3.125. Polacca Wash. Cranial fragments showing carbonization, or charcoaling, on the interior (top) surface and decarbonization, or calcining, on the exterior. This demonstrates in cross section the difference in the degree of heating and the resultant lower preservability of the external surface, as seen in figure 3.124. Actual width of image in photograph is 3.3 cm (CGT neg. 7-16-93:34).

Figure 3.126. Polacca Wash. Right side of adult female skull with hole 2.5 cm in diameter centered on the coronal suture. Weathering of the surface and internal circumference has obliterated whatever cut marks might have been present. The vertical walls of the near-perfect circle indicate that the hole was not punched; rather it must have been scraped and cut. This is not trephining in the sense of a surgical procedure. There is no sign of infection, healing, or use wear (CGT neg. March 1968:22; reprinted with permission from *American Antiquity*).

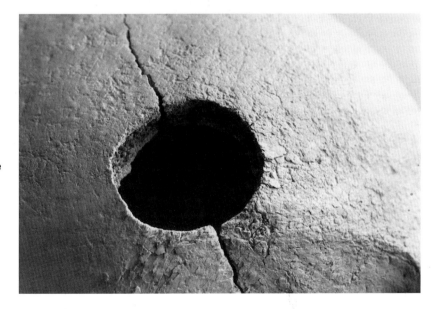

194

Figure 3.127. Polacca Wash. Frontal bone fragment illustrating the extensive damage inflicted on this individual. Four separate blows can be identified (indicated by arrows), and there are others not visible (CGT neg. March 1968:20; reprinted with permission from *American Antiquity*).

Figure 3.128. Polacca Wash. Six adult and subadult maxillae showing characteristic severe breakage from the cranial vault and greater amounts of perimortem damage to anterior than to posterior teeth. Such destruction of the face occurred in individuals of all ages, from children (lower left) to older adults (upper center). Most of the adult maxillae are relatively small, suggesting that more females were present than males, as is claimed in Hopi oral traditions about the Awatovi captives (CGT neg. March 1968:11; reprinted with permission from *American Antiquity*).

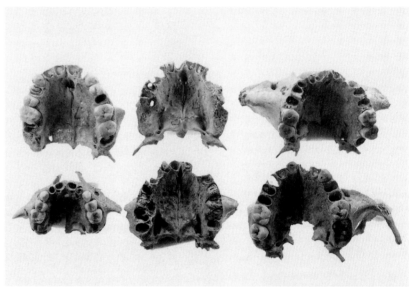

Figure 3.129. Polacca Wash. Representative maxilla with impact damage to teeth and sockets. The breaking out of the alveolar bone of the right canine has been replicated experimentally: a levering action occurs when force is applied to the anterior surface of the crown. The fulcrum then is located on the lingual border of socket near the crown-root junction. The result is a blowing or levering out of the labial wall of the tooth socket. The posterior teeth remain basically unharmed, indicating that the anterior socket damage occurred while the more distally positioned protective jaw musculature was still present (CGT neg. March 1968:15; reprinted with permission from *American Antiquity*).

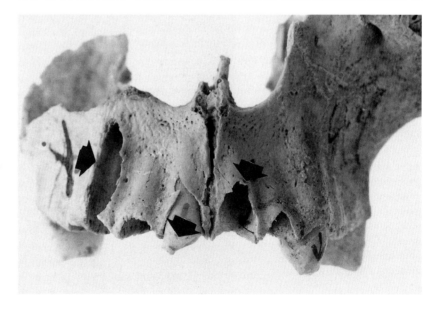

Figure 3.130. Polacca Wash. Representative adult and subadult mandible fragments illustrating the characteristic breakage pattern. The relatively small size and gracility of most of the mandibles suggest that they belonged to females (CGT neg. March 1968:9; reprinted with permission from *American Antiquity*).

Figure 3.131. Polacca Wash. Burned adult male? mandible with very fine cut marks at arrow (CGT neg. 11-10-94:10).

Figure 3.132. Polacca Wash. Only 5.4% of the expected number of vertebrae turned up in the charnel deposit, and most of those were fragments. Shown are four vertebrae fragments with characteristic damage to the vertebral bodies, even in the small-bodied cervical vertebrae (CGT neg. March 1968:30).

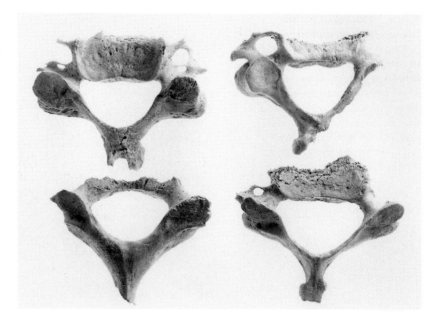

Figure 3.133. Polacca Wash. Representative rib fragments, showing snap, twist, and peel breakage and relatively uniform size. In the lower left is a randomly collected stew bone, 12.5 cm long, from a contemporary Hopi village trash dump to illustrate similarity in length. No animal tooth marks occur on any of these rib fragments (CGT neg. March 1968:3; reprinted with permission from *American Antiquity*).

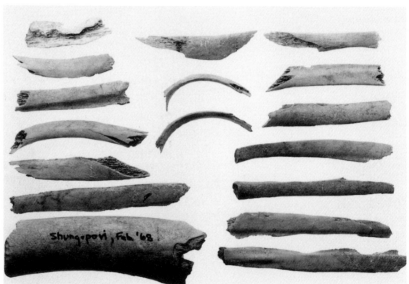

Figure 3.134. Polacca Wash. Representative long bone perimortem breakage (CGT neg. March 1968:1; reprinted with permission from *American Antiquity*).

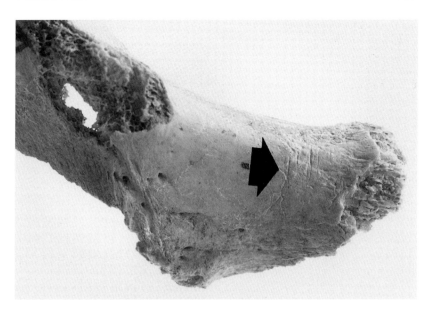

Figure 3.135. Polacca Wash. Cut marks on neck of adult femur (CGT neg. March 1968:39; reprinted with permission from *American Antiquity*).

and dismembered and left to die on the sand-hills, and there their bones are, and the place is called Mas'-tco-mo.

Fewkes reported that he had had the captive massacre site pointed out to him but did not excavate it. Had he done so, he might have found exactly what he described of the bloodbath (Fewkes 1893a: 369): "In some variants of the legend gruesome tales of the cruelties to which the women were submitted at Mas'-ki are told. Most horrible mutilations were made of the persons of those wretched ones who would not go with the captors, and, if the stories are correct, the final butchery at Mas-tco'mo must have been horrible."

Harold Courlander (1971:217–219) was also told the story of the Awatovi massacre—by six different Hopi informants. Courlander's version tells of three killing events after Awatovi was destroyed. The first occurred the following day when a few Awatovi warriors who had escaped followed and attacked the war party with its many captives. These Awatovi men were outnumbered and all killed. Each was decapitated. The place where this occurred was called Maskoteu (Skull Mound) and was said to be near what is now called Five Houses. The second event occurred near the wash that runs due east of Polacca village. There, a frenzy of killing and decapitation of captive Awatovians was caused by a dispute over who would get to keep the captives. The slain victims were said to have been thrown into a gully. Today this location is called Mastoeki (Place of the Dead Persons). It is this legendary location that is likely represented by the Polacca Wash charnel deposit. The third and final killing of captives occurred near Wepo Wash, west of Walpi. This place is known as Masjumo (Dead Person Hill).

Like Fewkes and Courlander, Ekkehart Malotki and Michael Lomatuway'ma (1987:10) wrote: "The place name *Mas-qoto* 'head of Maasaw/skull,' also attested as *Mas-qotnamuri* 'ridge of skulls,' refers to a location where Awat'ovi captives were slaughtered by the Hopi after the destruction of their village."

One detail of what happened to the captives of the Awatovi massacre that we learned about in August 1967 was the cutting off of some of the captive women's breasts. Not one of our three informants, however, mentioned cannibalism. We were also told accounts and locations of various other "death mounds" involved in unrelated instances of violence.

The Awatovi massacre story is still being told among the Hopis. A version collected by Malotki et al. (1993:399–403), after describing the attack on Awatovi at dawn, goes on to tell what happened afterward:

> Evidently, a handful of Awat'ovi men and boys had managed to hide somehow and had not been discovered. . . . Meanwhile, the Oraibis and Mishongnovis were getting ready to go home, taking the women, girls and children with them. Then [the surviving males] set out in pursuit of the enemies. At some place they came upon them and attacked. However, those on the Oraibi side far outnumbered them and quickly overpowered them, killing them all. Having killed them, they cut off their heads and gathered them in a pile. The place where this happened came to be known as Masqoto or "Skull." . . . [The attackers argued among themselves about dividing the captives.] The Walpis and Mishongnovis simply refused to give up their women. Thereupon one of the Oraibis exclaimed, "In that case no one shall have them. Let's get rid of them. If we kill them all, nobody can have them." . . . No sooner had this been proposed than they started slaughtering the women and girls. They would just grab one and kill her any old way, either by stabbing her or shooting her. Some of the women and girls, poor wretches, were crying, "Let me go with you. Don't kill me. I'd like to go with you." But they were pleading in vain, and a great number of them were killed. [Those] who they did not murder they injured severely by cutting off their arms or legs. Some men who interceded on behalf of the women they mutilated by severing their penises and testicles. In some cases they also cut off the women's breasts. . . . Those who had been wounded they left where they were. One after the other the poor things perished there miserably. This is how they dealt with their female captives. A large number of them, women and girls, were murdered. The children they did not harm.

Discussion. Turner and Morris (1970) eventually disagreed with all of Olson's interpretations of the charnel deposit. They suggested a historic date on the basis of good preservation and carbon-14 dating of rib fragments. They doubted that the assemblage was secondary, because so many tiny fragments of bone were found, whereas larger and much more easily gathered pieces such as pelves were mostly missing. They also doubted that the remains were a ritual or ceremonial deposit, because no grave goods were found and because close examination of the excavation photographs revealed cranial fragments in the interior of the assemblage, not just around the edges. Finally, Turner and Morris identified cut marks and game-animal-like breakage and burning, all of which could be fitted to a scenario of violence and con-

sumption of human flesh but to no other social or natural explanation. Their observation about the small and uniform size of rib fragments (mean = 10.4 cm; SD = 4.7) drew attention to the fact that
these fragments were about the same average length as fragments of
animal bone present as food refuse in modern Hopi village trash, a
length related to the size of modern Hopi cooking vessels.

Watson Smith (1992:150) remained doubtful about the
Awatovi–Polacca Wash relationship because the latter "is located
somewhat away from the pathway that would have been taken by
people walking from Awatovi to Second Mesa, [though] not so far
away as to cripple the hypothesis." We hasten to point out that there
is no reason to assume that the captors felt it necessary to take the
shortest route home, particularly if they were, as the legend says,
quarreling among themselves over possession of the captives. The extra distance in question amounts to less than one or two hours' walking time (5 km, or 3 miles). And if there were two post-attack
massacre sites near Awatovi, rather than just one, then there is even
more reason to disregard the minimal route objection. The captors
might have been taking evasive action in case other survivors attacked them.

Fewkes (1904) remarked in passing that he had collected several
versions of the legend about how the Awatovi captives were tortured,
mutilated, and killed and decided to present the "least horrible" one.
We searched Fewkes's notes in the Smithsonian Institution's National
Anthropological Archives, where his papers are preserved, and found
no additional stories relating to the Polacca Wash charnel deposit.
This does not necessarily mean that he obtained no other versions, for
the following reasons. (1) At his death most of his papers and notes
were located in his home, and NAA records indicate that not all of
them were saved. (2) Fewkes's style of note taking was to record
mainly difficult-to-remember things such as distances, measurements,
familial relationships, and Hopi words. A story that included a description of cannibalism would not be easily forgotten. (3) Fewkes
took notes on at least two unrelated Hopi stories that he subsequently
marked over with the word "private." These stories had to do with
female genital manipulation and odor, suggesting that Fewkes might
have been a bit straitlaced, concerned about how his notes would be
viewed by others, or cognizant of how his Smithsonian supervisors
would react. We speculate that the more terrible versions included
descriptions of cannibalism and that if they were available, they
would correspond to the taphonomic indications of roasting and
boiling.

On August 20, 1967, we returned to the Polacca Wash site area for
a final inspection. We came across the decomposed hide and greasy
bones of a dead horse—an excellent resource for assessing whether
the damage to the humans had been caused mainly by local scavengers. The horse skull was completely intact and had no recognizable damage. The ribs had been chewed at their distal ends and had
carnivore tooth puncture marks. The long bones were intact except
for chewing of one femoral trochanter. The vertebrae and pelvis were
untouched. The vertebral borders of the scapulae had been chewed
on. The carcass was largely held together by cartilage and ligament,

except for a back leg that was out of its hip socket and both front legs, which had separated from the body at the proximal ends of the humerus. One humerus and a rib fragment were located about one meter from the body. Hide and hair were present but largely decomposed. The carcass still smelled, but not much more than Southwestern dry cave mummy tissue. The hooves were present, as were the teeth, which were beginning to flake and crack.

It was quite evident that the horse was decomposing in a way very different from that of the humans excavated by Olson and associates in the same locality. The obvious big difference was in the small amount of breakage of the horse's skeleton compared with the massive breakage of the human skeletal elements. Carnivores could be ruled out as the principal cause of the Polacca Wash bone damage. Furthermore, there were very few fresh breaks in the human bones, so the damage was not caused by Olson and associates during excavation. The bone damage had to have been done by humans as part of some terrible bygone event.

## 26
## Leroux Wash

**Claim Date.** 1974–1975.

**Claimants.** Peter J. Pilles, oral field report at 1974 Pecos Conference, Mesa Verde National Park, Colorado; Dana Hartman, oral report at 1975 meeting of the American Association of Physical Anthropologists, Denver, Colorado.

**Claim Type.** Cannibalism.

**Other Designations.** NA12854.

**Site Location.** Near Leroux Wash, 13 km (8 miles) north of Holbrook, Arizona. USGS Holbrook quadrangle (provisional edition 1986), T 18N, R 20E, SW ¼ of NE ¼ of NW ¼ of Sec. 2.

**Site Type.** A medium-sized, 15- to 20-room isolated surface masonry pueblo with outlying rooms and a possible great kiva, according to Pilles's site photo identifications (Museum of Northern Arizona photo archives). The site overlooks several square miles of potentially excellent dry-farming land in nearby Leroux Wash.

**Cultural Affiliation.** Anasazi, Winslow Branch, according to surface sherds collected by Pilles. Michael H. Dice (1993a:28) allowed that the victims might have been Mogollon, on the grounds that such sites are known to exist as close as 50 km (31 miles) to the south.

**Chronology.** Late Pueblo III (A.D. 1250–1300), according to ceramic dating by Pilles. An uncorrected carbon-14 date obtained from rib fragments submitted by CGT to Robert Stuckenrath at the Smithsonian Insitution Radiation Biology Laboratory (SI-5790) is ±885 years before present (A.D. 1065), or late Pueblo II (Stuckenrath, personal communication, March 15, 1983).

**Excavators and Date.** Dana Hartman and Peter Pilles, July 24, 1974. This was a characteristic MNA public service operation, in response to a report of exposed human bones. The one-afternoon visit involved mainly picking up bone fragments on the ground surface of the charnel deposit, which had been dug up by a treasure hunter.

**Institutional Storage.** Department of Anthropology, Museum of Northern Arizona, Flagstaff.

**Site Report.** None, a common practice in MNA public service operations; however, oral reports were presented at professional meetings.

**Osteological Reports.** Turner (1983); Fay and Kline (1988); Turner and Turner (1992a); Dice (1993a).

**Skeletal Evidence of Stress.** None.

**Burial Context.** Two charnel pits next to the exterior wall of the masonry pueblo.

**Associated Artifacts.** None.

**Figures.** 3.136–3.153.

**Taphonomy.** MHD; CGT and JAT, July 1993 restudy. Skeletal inventory is in table 3.24. Tables 3.25–3.30 provide measurements for long bone and rib fragment lengths.

*MNI.* 35 (table 3.23). There have been more examinations of this cannibalized skeletal series than of any other in the Southwest: by Hartman and Pilles in 1974, by Turner in 1982 and 1993, by White in 1984, by Fay and Klein in 1988, by Dice in 1989 (1993a), by Willey in 1989 (for canid activity), and by Turner and Turner in 1993. Because of slightly different approaches, each of these workers obtained different MNI values. Dice (1993a) determined his MNI of 21 on the basis of the single most frequently occurring bone or bone area, the external occipital protuberance. The largest Leroux Wash MNI, that of our 1993 restudy, positively identified 35 individuals. This was done by painstakingly matching and segregating age, side, occlusion, and idiosyncratic aspects of maxillas, mandibles, and a few infant long bones of varying lengths for which no jaw elements were present.

*Age and Sex.* We identified two 3- to 4-year-olds; one 5- to 6-year-old; three 9-year-olds; one 10-year-old; one 11- to 12-year-old; one 12-year-old; three 12- to 15-year-olds; one 15-year-old; one 16- to 17-year-old; nine young adults; one adult; nine middle-aged adults; one middle-aged to old adult; and one old adult.

*Preservation.* Good to excellent.

*Bone and Fragment Number.* 3,203 (MHD); 3,367 (CGT and JAT), not counting about 100 rib fragments used for radiocarbon dating.

*Breakage.* 99.7% (3,193 of 3,203, MHD); 78.6% (2,646 of 3,367, CGT and JAT).

*Cut Marks.* 2.0% (65 of 3,203, MHD); 4.7% (157 of 3,367, CGT and JAT).

*Burning.* 2.9% (94 of 3,203, MHD); 3.7% (123 of 3,367, CGT and JAT).

*Anvil Abrasions.* 3.5% (113 of 3,203, MHD); 5.6% (189 of 3,367, CGT and JAT).

*Polishing.* Not observed (MHD); 5.0% (168 of 3,367, CGT and JAT).

*Vertebrae Number.* 15.3% of expected (77 of 504, MNI = 21, MHD, wherein a fragment was equivalent to a whole vertebra); 3.6% of expected (approx. 30 of 840, MNI = 35, CGT and JAT, wherein two or more fragments were estimated to be equivalent to a whole vertebra).

*Scalping.* Yes (MHD); yes (CGT and JAT).

*Gnawing, Rodent.* Very little (MHD); none (CGT and JAT).

Table 3.23
Minimal Number of Individuals (MNI) at Leroux Wash

| SKELETAL ELEMENT | AGE | SEX | NOTES |
| --- | --- | --- | --- |
| Maxilla, whole | 3–4 | ? | Does not fit any mandible |
| | 10 | ? | Does not fit any mandible |
| | Mid-adult | ? | Does not fit any mandible |
| | Mid-adult | ? | Does not fit any mandible |
| | Mid-adult | ? | Does not fit any mandible |
| | Mid-adult | ? | Does not fit any mandible |
| Maxilla, left | 3–4 | ? | Does not fit any mandible or maxilla |
| | 5–6 | ? | Does not fit any mandible or maxilla |
| | 9 | ? | Does not fit any mandible or maxilla |
| | 11–12 | ? | Does not fit any mandible or maxilla |
| | 12 | ? | Does not fit any mandible or maxilla |
| | 12–15 | ? | Does not fit any mandible or maxilla |
| | 16–17 | ? | Does not fit any mandible or maxilla |
| | Young adult | ? | Does not fit any mandible or maxilla |
| | Young adult | ? | Does not fit any mandible or maxilla |
| | Young adult | ? | Does not fit any mandible or maxilla |
| | Young adult | ? | Does not fit any mandible or maxilla |
| | Mid-adult | ? | Does not fit any mandible or maxilla |
| Maxilla, right | 9 | ? | Fits with whole 9-year mandible |
| | 9 | ? | Does not fit any mandible or maxilla |
| | 12–15 | ? | Fits with right 12–15-year mandible |
| | 12–15 | ? | Does not fit any mandible or maxilla |
| | 15 | ? | Does not fit any mandible or maxilla |
| | Young adult | ? | Does not fit any mandible or maxilla |
| | Young adult | ? | Does not fit any mandible or maxilla |
| | Young adult | ? | Does not fit any mandible or maxilla |
| | Mid-adult | ? | Does not fit any mandible or maxilla |
| | Mid-adult | ? | Does not fit any mandible or maxilla |
| Mandible, whole | 9 | ? | Fits with right 9-year maxilla |
| | Young adult | ? | Does not fit any maxilla |
| | Young adult | ? | Does not fit any maxilla |
| | Adult | ? | Does not fit any maxilla |
| | Mid-adult | ? | Does not fit any maxilla |
| | Mid-adult | ? | Does not fit any maxilla |
| | Mid-old | ? | Does not fit any maxilla |
| | Old adult | ? | Does not fit any maxilla |
| Mandible, left | 15 | ? | Unable to assess for fit |
| | Young adult | ? | Unable to assess for fit |
| | Mid-adult | ? | Unable to assess for fit |
| | Old? adult | ? | Unable to assess for fit |
| Mandible, right | 12–15 | ? | Fits with right 12–15-year maxilla |
| | 12–15 | ? | Unable to assess for fit |
| | Young adult | ? | Unable to assess for fit |
| | Adult | ? | Unable to assess for fit |
| | Old? adult | ? | Unable to assess for fit |
| Mandible, symphysis | Adult | ? | Unable to assess for fit |
| | Adult? | ? | Unable to assess for fit |

SUMMARY: 35 individuals. All sex?; two 3- to 4-year-olds; one 5- to 6-year-old; three 9-year-olds; one 10-year-old; two 11- to 12-year-olds; four 12- to 15-year-olds; one 16- to 17-year-old; nine young adults; one adult; nine middle-aged adults; one middle- to old-aged adult; one old adult.

Table 3.24
Bone Elements and Perimortem Damage at Leroux Wash

| SKELETAL ELEMENT | WHOLE | FRAGMENT | IMPACT BREAK | ANVIL ABRASION | CUT MARK | BURN | POLISH |
|---|---|---|---|---|---|---|---|
| Cranial | | | | | | | |
| Maxilla | 5 | 24 | 19 | 6 | 3 | 0 | 0 |
| Mandible | 6 | 30 | 14 | 8 | 9 | 1 | 1 |
| Frontal | 7 | 29 | 7 | 11 | 9 | 2 | 4 |
| Parietal | 12 | 52 | 23 | 12 | 22 | 1 | 0 |
| Occipital | 3 | 42 | 27 | 4 | 13 | 1 | 0 |
| Temporal | 13 | 48 | 30 | 8 | 16 | 1 | 0 |
| Teeth (299) | | | | | | | |
| Fragments | — | 227 | 174 | 18 | 8 | 24 | 3 |
| | | | | | | | |
| Postcranial | | | | | | | |
| Cervical vertebrae | 6 | 4 | 3 | 0 | 0 | 0 | 1 |
| Vertebrae | | | | | | | |
| fragments | — | 95 | 91 | 0 | 1 | 2 | 1 |
| Scapula | 3 | 41 | 34 | 2 | 3 | 0 | 2 |
| Clavicle | 0 | 13 | 7 | 1 | 5 | 0 | 0 |
| Rib/sternum | 2 | 218 | 183 | 6 | 3 | 3 | 17 |
| Humerus | 0 | 7 | 6 | 1 | 0 | 0 | 0 |
| Radius | 0 | 5 | 5 | 0 | 0 | 0 | 0 |
| Ulna | 0 | 10 | 7 | 2 | 1 | 0 | 0 |
| Hand & foot | 44 | 115 | 108 | 1 | 0 | 6 | 0 |
| Pelvis | 0 | 68 | 59 | 4 | 2 | 0 | 3 |
| Femur | 0 | 85 | 38 | 22 | 13 | 0 | 12 |
| Tibia | 0 | 59 | 32 | 7 | 8 | 0 | 12 |
| Fibula | 0 | 42 | 31 | 0 | 5 | 0 | 6 |
| Patella | 1 | 2 | 2 | 0 | 0 | 0 | 0 |
| Long bone | | | | | | | |
| fragments | — | 1,079 | 816 | 66 | 33 | 64 | 100 |
| | | | | | | | |
| Bone type unknown | 0 | 970 | 930 | 10 | 3 | 18 | 6 |
| | | | | | | | |
| TOTAL (3,367) | 102 | 3,265 | 2,646 | 189 | 157 | 123 | 168 |
| PERCENTAGE | 3.0 | 97.0 | 78.6 | 5.6 | 4.7 | 3.7 | 5.0 |

Percentage of expected vertebrae = 3.6 (30 of 840; MNI = 35).[a]

NOTE: Only elements that were present are listed. No gnawing or chewing was observed. Impact breakage, anvil abrasions, cut marks, burning, and polishing represent perimortem damage.

a. The 95 postcervical vertebral fragments represent about 20 whole vertebrae.

>    *Chewing, Carnivore.* None.
>    *Insect Parts.* None.
>    *Other Modification.* None.

**Archaeologists' Interpretation.** Both Pilles and Hartman proposed a cannibalism event. This included the cutting, breaking, burning, and depositing of the bones in two pits, notably with some cranial fragments placed in a nested or stacked arrangement (Pilles, personal communication, July 19, 1997). Pilles and Hartman found the human remains largely in the backdirt left by a treasure hunter. Only the small amount of bone shown in figures 3.137–3.142 remained in place, making behavioral interpretations based on context next to impossible.

**Other Interpretations.** All the analysts who have dealt with Leroux Wash have concluded that the massive bone damage is best explained by cannibalism. David A. Breternitz is reported (G. Alexander 1974:5) as having said that the cannibalized remains at Leroux Wash (and

Table 3.25
Lengths (cm) of Unidentifiable Human Long Bone Fragments with
Intentional Perimortem Breakage Only, Leroux Wash

| | | | | | | |
|---|---|---|---|---|---|---|
| 12.8 | 5.3 | 8.9 | 3.9 | 10.4 | 15.3 | 8.4 |
| 3.5 | 5.6 | 8.5 | 5.3 | 10.5 | 6.2 | 5.2 |
| 9.5 | 6.2 | 8.6 | 6.1 | 7.9 | 7.4 | 9.9 |
| 3.6 | 3.7 | 3.4 | 6.7 | 6.2 | 5.4 | 6.8 |
| 12.9 | 9.7 | 2.6 | 4.4 | 8.5 | 6.9 | 4.7 |
| 4.5 | 5.1 | 4.8 | 1.5 | 4.5 | 5.1 | 2.6 |
| 3.3 | 5.0 | 4.1 | 2.2 | 2.8 | 4.0 | 5.1 |
| 7.7 | 3.2 | 5.7 | 2.7 | 1.5 | 5.2 | 1.9 |
| 5.5 | 4.2 | 2.9 | 4.5 | 2.7 | 6.0 | 4.0 |
| 3.0 | 3.3 | 5.9 | 3.2 | 6.3 | 6.6 | 6.9 |
| 6.0 | 4.0 | 4.1 | 2.9 | 9.3 | 5.1 | 5.3 |
| 8.5 | 6.6 | 5.8 | 10.9 | 10.6 | 5.8 | 11.5 |
| 10.8 | 6.2 | 6.0 | 6.5 | 9.5 | 4.7 | 5.5 |
| 7.4 | 11.6 | 7.0 | 6.8 | 9.9 | 7.3 | 9.5 |
| 10.9 | 8.1 | 4.1 | 5.9 | 7.1 | 7.2 | 8.2 |
| 10.7 | 4.9 | 8.8 | 6.3 | 6.9 | 4.1 | 4.4 |
| 4.2 | 3.5 | 4.6 | 4.1 | 7.0 | 13.1 | 11.6 |
| 7.1 | 3.8 | 4.1 | 11.5 | 8.3 | 5.4 | 3.5 |
| 5.1 | 4.4 | 3.6 | 5.5 | 1.8 | 9.5 | 3.9 |
| 3.0 | 2.5 | 4.1 | 5.6 | 6.6 | 4.3 | 4.1 |
| 7.3 | 3.7 | 4.1 | 7.2 | 5.4 | 8.0 | 4.5 |
| 10.3 | 13.5 | 8.1 | 5.9 | 4.6 | 3.2 | 4.3 |
| 2.0 | 4.0 | 2.3 | 3.0 | 10.2 | 12.9 | 6.2 |
| 3.3 | 5.7 | 5.6 | 4.4 | 6.9 | 4.2 | 6.5 |
| 6.0 | 3.3 | 3.2 | 4.3 | 8.7 | 10.1 | 3.4 |
| 6.1 | 8.0 | 5.9 | 5.1 | 7.1 | 3.7 | 4.3 |
| 3.6 | 4.9 | 4.9 | 4.5 | 6.0 | 5.1 | 5.6 |
| 4.9 | 9.7 | 7.5 | 3.5 | 5.1 | 9.1 | 7.1 |
| 3.4 | 3.7 | 2.3 | 7.6 | 8.2 | 5.5 | 4.3 |
| 5.3 | 5.2 | 2.6 | 2.5 | 4.5 | 4.0 | 2.3 |
| 3.5 | 2.5 | 4.0 | 4.5 | 3.5 | 3.7 | 2.3 |
| 2.0 | 3.1 | 3.0 | 2.9 | 4.1 | 4.4 | 7.6 |
| 5.7 | 4.7 | 4.0 | 5.8 | 3.1 | 4.3 | 3.8 |
| 3.8 | 4.2 | 4.6 | 3.0 | 6.3 | 8.0 | 2.0 |
| 5.1 | 2.9 | 3.6 | 5.0 | 6.6 | 4.0 | 4.6 |
| 3.7 | 6.7 | 4.4 | 10.5 | 5.1 | 5.5 | 9.1 |
| 5.7 | 3.6 | 5.6 | 7.2 | 4.1 | 5.0 | 11.7 |
| 8.4 | | | | | | |

N = 260 (out of 816 possible).   Range = 1.8–15.3.   Mean = 5.7.   S.D. = 2.6.

Table 3.26
Lengths (cm) of Unidentifiable Human Long Bone Fragments with Perimortem Intentional Breakage and Polishing, Leroux Wash

| | | | | | | |
|---|---|---|---|---|---|---|
| 11.0 | 8.9 | 9.2 | 7.2 | 9.6 | 7.5 | 7.5 |
| 6.6 | 7.7 | 11.3 | 12.9 | 10.0 | 10.3 | 12.3 |
| 6.6 | 8.2 | 7.5 | 5.6 | 5.6 | 8.4 | 9.9 |
| 5.6 | 7.0 | 10.7 | 8.6 | 8.3 | 14.9 | 13.1 |
| 15.5 | 11.6 | 6.1 | 12.5 | 10.9 | 11.5 | 12.6 |
| 6.5 | 5.3 | 10.1 | 8.0 | 5.3 | 8.0 | 6.5 |
| 6.7 | 10.3 | 7.5 | 8.4 | 5.7 | 12.4 | 7.9 |
| 8.1 | 7.6 | 8.6 | 5.0 | 7.9 | 6.6 | 7.0 |
| 7.5 | 8.4 | 6.0 | 9.2 | 6.4 | 6.0 | 9.5 |
| 6.6 | 10.7 | 11.3 | 6.2 | 5.6 | 8.1 | 7.0 |
| 9.0 | 5.1 | 5.8 | 9.2 | 11.3 | 8.1 | 7.6 |
| 8.7 | 10.9 | 9.9 | 7.8 | 6.2 | 3.9 | 3.6 |
| 2.5 | 3.2 | 5.5 | 4.6 | 4.2 | 7.5 | 5.3 |
| 5.4 | 2.4 | 7.4 | 3.7 | 9.0 | 3.6 | 2.7 |

N = 98 (out of 100).    R = 2.4–15.5.    Mean = 7.9.    S.D. = 2.7.

Mancos Canyon) could have been due to starvation or ritual. Breternitz noted that there were no indications of ritual offerings in either site and that the well-dated Mancos incident occurred during a time of presumed environmental stress. On the other hand, Mesa Verde National Park superintendent Ronald R. Switzer felt that this Anasazi cannibalism was done for "ceremonial reasons" (G. Alexander 1974:5).

Dice (1993a:108–109) has spent the greatest amount of time working with this series. One of his objectives was to compare the bone damage with that found on abundant antelope remains from Wupatki Pueblo. He found that "the Wupatki antelope remains and the Leroux Wash human remains were similar in terms of the types of marks found and their location on the skeletons. . . . [Thus] it can be inferred that the Leroux Wash victims were used for food and/or other products."

Discussion. The Leroux Wash skeletal series has had a rather complex history, beginning with its initial recovery. The site was discovered in November 1973 by a "treasure hunter" who came across it accidentally. In 1974 the Museum of Northern Arizona learned of the charnel deposit (G. Alexander 1974:1). This stimulated Peter Pilles, Robert Crabtree, and Dana Hartman to visit the site on their own on July 24, 1974. Because the treasure hunter had badly disturbed the deposit, there was little else to do but gather up the remains and make standard on-site survey observations.

In the laboratory, the bones were promptly examined, and in August 1974 Peter Pilles gave an oral report on the Leroux Wash skeletal find at the Pecos Conference in Mesa Verde National Park, Colorado. On September 15, 1974, a news article by George Alexander, a *Los Angeles Times* science writer, appeared on cannibalism as reported at the Pecos Conference by Peter Pilles and by Paul R. Nickens for Mancos Canyon. On November 18, 1974, Pilles replied to an inquiry from

Table 3.27
Lengths (cm) of Unidentifiable Human Long Bone Fragments with Perimortem Intentional Breakage and Burning, Leroux Wash

| | | | | | | |
|---|---|---|---|---|---|---|
| 5.1 | 1.6 | 6.0 | 2.8 | 2.5 | 1.9 | 3.5 |
| 2.7 | 4.1 | 6.1 | 4.1 | 4.9 | 3.2 | 2.8 |
| 2.9 | 2.6 | 3.6 | 3.9 | 4.2 | 5.5 | 4.5 |
| 3.4 | 6.1 | 5.5 | 4.0 | 2.5 | 3.2 | 2.1 |
| 2.7 | 4.1 | 2.5 | 2.0 | 1.9 | 2.6 | 2.6 |
| 2.1 | 2.7 | 1.8 | 1.5 | 2.2 | 3.4 | 2.0 |
| 1.7 | 2.0 | 3.8 | 2.3 | 3.9 | 1.8 | 2.6 |
| 2.0 | 2.1 | 2.8 | 1.6 | 1.0 | 1.3 | 1.5 |
| 1.6 | 1.6 | 1.2 | 0.9 | 1.2 | 1.3 | |

N = 62 (out of 64).    Range = 0.9–6.1.    Mean = 2.9.    S.D. = 1.3.

Table 3.28
Lengths (cm) of Unidentifiable Human Long Bone Fragments with Peri-
mortem Intentional Breakage and Anvil/Hammerstone Abrasions,
Leroux Wash

| | | | | | | |
|---|---|---|---|---|---|---|
| 10.1 | 9.5 | 8.1 | 7.1 | 9.9 | 10.3 | 5.9 |
| 8.7 | 14.9 | 7.6 | 12.6 | 3.3 | 4.2 | 5.9 |
| 5.2 | 6.2 | 6.1 | 7.1 | 8.2 | 7.0 | 3.6 |
| 5.3 | 7.5 | 5.7 | 7.3 | 7.9 | 5.4 | 5.1 |
| 7.0 | 4.6 | 4.8 | 5.7 | 7.5 | 5.2 | 5.7 |
| 6.4 | 5.3 | 5.6 | 4.8 | 4.9 | 6.6 | 3.9 |
| 3.4 | 3.7 | 7.1 | 15.6 | 7.9 | 8.7 | 3.1 |
| 5.9 | 6.3 | 6.1 | 8.1 | 2.9 | 4.9 | 9.5 |
| 5.8 | 7.4 | 8.6 | 6.0 | 4.8 | 4.3 | 7.0 |
| 8.3 | 3.6 | 9.5 | | | | |

N = 66 (out of 66).    Range = 2.9–15.6.    Mean = 6.7.    S.D. = 2.5.

Rose Tyson (San Diego Museum of Man) about the cannibalism site. He described the site as having 15–20 rooms, several satellite rooms, a plaza-enclosing wall, a great kiva, and a date of late Pueblo III. He wrote that Dana Hartman had analyzed the skeletal material, finding 34 individuals of both sexes and all ages with shattered long bones, cut marks, and so forth. Hartman presented a paper on this and other cannibalized burials at the annual meeting of the American Association of Physical Anthropologists in April 1975 (copy of Pilles letter in NA12854 site file). Her published abstract (1975) dealt with cannibalized mass burials, suggesting environmental stress in late Pueblo III times as a primary cause, but she did not specifically mention the Leroux Wash assemblage.

There is no record of the assemblage's receiving further study until October 1982, when C. G. Turner examined it and proposed that some bone fragments be dated directly. A carbon-14 date of A.D. 1065 was obtained by Robert Stuckenrath, Smithsonian Institution, from a sample of rib fragments.

Table 3.29
Lengths (cm) of Unidentifiable Human Long Bone Fragments with Perimortem Intentional Breakage and Cut Marks, Leroux Wash

| | | | | | | |
|---|---|---|---|---|---|---|
| 7.7 | 6.3 | 8.5 | 10.6 | 6.9 | 4.5 | 12.5 |
| 8.9 | 9.9 | 6.6 | 4.8 | 6.4 | 4.8 | 4.2 |
| 3.9 | 6.4 | 5.5 | 3.8 | 3.8 | 6.0 | 3.0 |
| 3.1 | 2.9 | 3.6 | 4.5 | 3.7 | 4.1 | 4.9 |
| 4.8 | 2.2 | 4.2 | 4.1 | 6.2 | | |

N = 33 (out of 33). Range = 2.2–12.5. Mean = 5.5. S.D. = 2.4.

Table 3.30
Lengths (cm) of Human Rib Fragments with Intentional Perimortem Breakage, Leroux Wash

| | | | | | | |
|---|---|---|---|---|---|---|
| 10.4 | 17.3 | 14.8 | 17.0 | 12.9 | 6.6 | 8.5 |
| 11.4 | 9.5 | 12.4 | 12.4 | 11.6 | 13.4 | 6.8 |
| 6.9 | 5.0 | 4.9 | 9.2 | 9.7 | 10.5 | 7.7 |
| 2.6 | 5.0 | 4.7 | 5.4 | 7.6 | 8.5 | 6.8 |
| 4.8 | 7.1 | 9.7 | 6.9 | 10.5 | 10.8 | 7.4 |
| 6.9 | 6.5 | 6.8 | 4.8 | 6.8 | 4.5 | 7.0 |
| 3.7 | 5.4 | 6.9 | 4.5 | 4.6 | 6.0 | 6.4 |
| 7.4 | 5.0 | 6.1 | 7.8 | 5.7 | 5.0 | 7.3 |
| 5.2 | 2.9 | 4.7 | 5.0 | 9.1 | 6.0 | 5.6 |
| 6.7 | 6.2 | 4.1 | 5.9 | 4.8 | 2.5 | 4.1 |
| 4.2 | 7.2 | 10.0 | 9.0 | 6.9 | 4.3 | 3.7 |
| 6.6 | 3.5 | 3.0 | 4.1 | 4.5 | 6.1 | 3.2 |
| 4.7 | 5.5 | 3.8 | 5.5 | 6.6 | 6.6 | 4.5 |
| 4.8 | 3.4 | 3.9 | 3.2 | 3.5 | 6.1 | 3.7 |
| 3.4 | 3.9 | 4.5 | 3.3 | 3.2 | 4.9 | 6.5 |
| 6.1 | 4.7 | 6.8 | 5.6 | 3.2 | 4.7 | 5.4 |
| 3.9 | 3.7 | 3.7 | 2.2 | 2.8 | 3.6 | 4.3 |
| 5.2 | 4.8 | 3.3 | 4.4 | 3.3 | 4.9 | 4.7 |
| 3.5 | 5.1 | 3.3 | 5.3 | 4.6 | 4.9 | 4.9 |
| 3.4 | 5.2 | 3.5 | 2.9 | 4.9 | 5.9 | 5.2 |
| 4.8 | 4.5 | 3.6 | 3.9 | 3.1 | 4.3 | 5.1 |
| 4.9 | 4.5 | 4.3 | 2.6 | 3.1 | 5.1 | 2.0 |
| 3.9 | 3.5 | 4.1 | 2.7 | 5.7 | 7.5 | 4.5 |
| 6.3 | 3.4 | 1.9 | 3.6 | 3.5 | 3.6 | 3.2 |

N = 168 (out of 183).    Range 1.9–17.3.    Mean = 15.7.    S.D. = 2.7.

In 1983 Turner published his preliminary taphonomic analysis of Southwestern archaeological sites suggesting cannibalism, including the Leroux Wash human remains. In October 1984, the Leroux Wash series was briefly examined by Tim D. White, University of California, Berkeley, with Hartman's assistance.

In the summer of 1988, under Turner's supervision, Patricia M. Fay and Pamela Y. Klein studied the skeletal material and wrote a taphonomic report for David A. Wilcox.

Figure 3.136. Leroux Wash, Arizona. View of site area. The dark mound on horizon at left is the small masonry pueblo outside of which the human charnel deposit was excavated. Robert Crabtree and Dana Hartman are standing in a large shallow depression noted in the site photograph records as a great kiva. Leroux Wash is in the distant eastern background. Isolation and defenselessness are apparent in this picture. Museum of Northern Arizona Archive photograph by Peter J. Pilles, Jr. (July 1974).

Figure 3.137. Leroux Wash. Dana Hartman excavating the human skeletal remains from Leroux Wash "cluster 1." The eroding windblown sediments behind Hartman and above the skull, mandible, and other bones show that the bone exposure was due to downslope washing away of the overlying sands. There is no indication of a pit outline in this picture. Museum of Northern Arizona Archive photograph by Peter J. Pilles, Jr. (July 1974).

Figure 3.138. Leroux Wash. Detail of cluster 1 bone deposit showing cranial, mandibular, and long bone fragments dumped at random. The photo shows no identifiable outline of what must have been a shallow pit. Museum of Northern Arizona Archive photograph by Peter J. Pilles, Jr. (July 1974).

Figure 3.139. Leroux Wash. Dana Hartman holding a cluster 1 cranium that is warped, probably by the weight of the 25–50 cm of overburden, as shown in figure 3.137. Museum of Northern Arizona Archive photograph by Peter J. Pilles, Jr. (July 1974).

Figure 3.140. Leroux Wash. Bone fragments at the base of cluster 1. The bone distribution suggests the outline of a shallow pit. Unlike the warping of the previous cranium, this bone breakage has been determined to have been perimortem rather than postmortem. Museum of Northern Arizona Archive photograph by Peter J. Pilles, Jr. (July 1974).

Figure 3.141. Leroux Wash. Mainly cranial elements show in this view of Dana Hartman brushing dirt away from the charnel deposit in cluster 2. Pit stratigraphy cannot be identified in this picture. However, there seem to be small pieces of charcoal in the cluster 2 fill that were not evident in views of cluster 1. The nesting of the skull fragments may be more coincidental than intentional. Museum of Northern Arizona Archive photograph by Peter J. Pilles, Jr. (July 1974).

Figure 3.142. Leroux Wash. Final excavation view of cluster 2. Soil appears ashy (on left) and flecked with bits of charcoal, giving the charnel deposit the appearance of lenses of ash and trash commonly seen in prehistoric middens. Museum of Northern Arizona Archive photograph by Peter J. Pilles, Jr. (July 1974).

Figure 3.143. Leroux Wash. All of the whole and fragmentary maxillae. There was no complete cranium in this charnel deposit. Each maxilla has perimortem breakage, and most have impact breakage of the anterior teeth and sockets. Arrow points to specimen shown in figure 3.144 (CGT neg. 7-15-93:2).

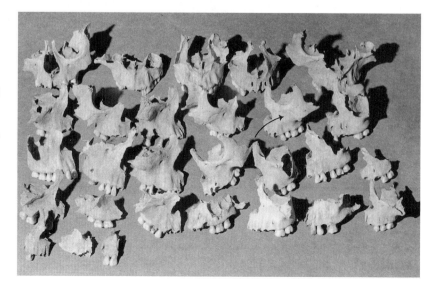

Figure 3.144. Leroux Wash. Detail of an adult left zygomatic bone still attached to a fragmentary maxilla. Anvil abrasions are present on the left, and cut marks on the right (CGT neg. 7-16-93:4).

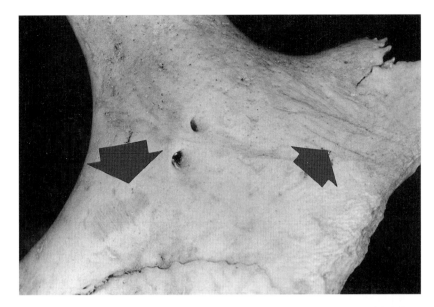

Figure 3.145. Leroux Wash. All of the whole and fragmentary mandibles. As with the maxillary fragments, each has bone or dental perimortem breakage. Because adult mandibles are among the strongest and best preserving bones of the human skeleton, the breakage must have been purposeful (CGT neg. 7-15-93:5).

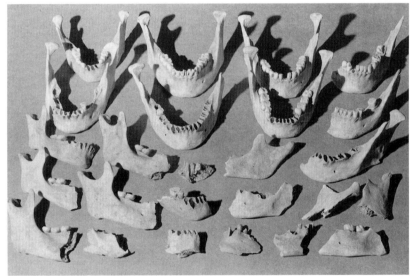

Figure 3.146. Leroux Wash. All the identifiable vertebrae. Given an MNI of 35, and combining pieces, less than 5% of the expected number of vertebrae (30 of 840) are represented. What fragments are present have been pounded into small pieces—hardly something anyone would do to 35 people if the intent was war-related postmortem mutilation or killing of alleged witches. The whole first cervical vertebra at upper left is 7.0 cm in diameter (CGT neg. 7-15-93:17).

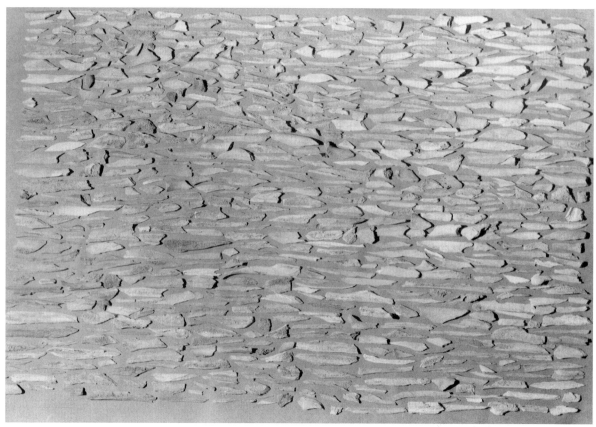

Figure 3.147. Leroux Wash. Long bone fragments that could not be readily identified. All represent perimortem fragmentation of whole long bones, and many have cut marks and anvil abrasions. There are about 800 pieces in the picture, and as arranged they cover an area 99.0 cm wide (CGT neg. 7-15-93: 11). The previous comment about mutilation and witchcraft applies here as well.

Figure 3.148. Leroux Wash. Femoral neck with circumferential perimortem cut marks. Actual width of image in photograph is 3.3 cm (CGT neg. 7-16-93:9).

Figure 3.149. Leroux Wash. Femur fragment with perimortem breakage and cut marks. Cut area is about 5.1 cm in length (CGT neg. 7-16-93:12).

Figure 3.150. Leroux Wash. Long bone fragment with at least three separate fields of perimortem anvil abrasions. Actual width of image in photograph is 3.3 cm (CGT neg. 7-16-93:2).

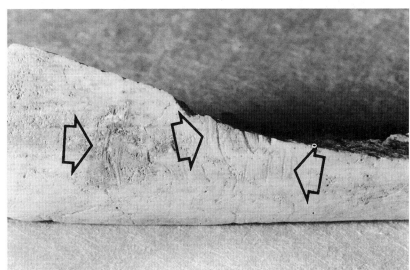

Figure 3.151. Leroux Wash. Long bone fragment with multiple perimortem cut marks. Actual width of image in photograph is 3.3 cm (CGT neg. 7-16-93:7).

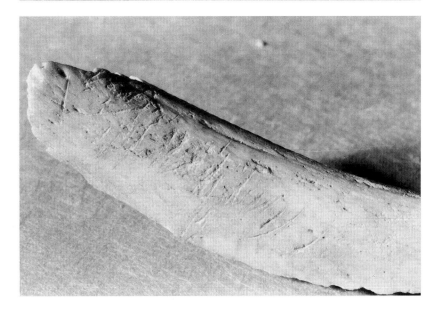

Figure 3.152. Leroux Wash. Long bone fragment with anvil abrasions on internal surface, indicating repeated impacts, even after bone had broken open exposing the cancellous tissue. Actual width of image in photograph is 3.3 cm (CGT neg. 8-6-86:30).

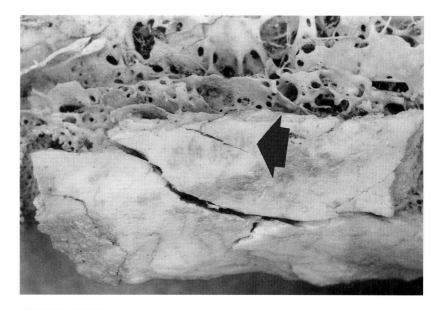

Figure 3.153. Leroux Wash. Rib fragments with relatively short, uniform lengths like those from Polacca Wash. Cut marks are present on all three; the upper specimen has been cut on the chest cavity (internal) side (CGT neg. 1-12-83:35).

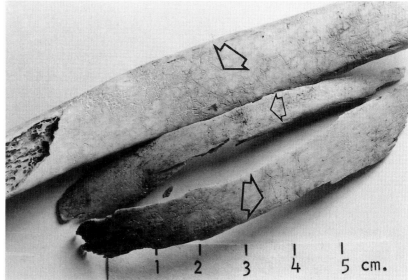

In August 1988, using the site and site area photographs taken by Peter Pilles, we located and examined the Leroux Wash site, finding the shallow basins of the charnel pits excavated by Hartman and Pilles, as well as bleached and friable human bone fragments, sherds, and a few stone chips scattered on the ground in the vicinity of the excavation area.

In February 1989, Patrick S. Willey studied the Leroux Wash and Polacca Wash series for carnivore damage. He reported to David Wilcox that carnivores might have been involved, but they were not known to produce the burning and cutting that he, too, observed in these assemblages.

In November 1989, Michael Dice interviewed Hartman and Pilles, studied the Leroux Wash material for his M.A. thesis, and visited the site. He completed his work in 1993 (Dice 1993a). In September 1992, Willey replied to our inquiries about his observations on both series. He indicated that no progress had been made in analyzing the

1989 observations. In July 1993, we reexamined the Leroux Wash skeletal material, doing another full taphonomic workup, the summary findings of which are reported here.

Inasmuch as Leroux Wash has the largest MNI of any Southwestern assemblage thought to have been cannibalized, future site excavation could determine whether there is more to the charnel deposit than the nested cranial parts that Pilles and Hartman found remaining in place after the damage done by the treasure hunter. Also, excavation might reconcile the difference between the dates obtained from carbon-14 and ceramics.

<table>
<tr><td>27<br>Casas Grandes</td><td></td></tr>
</table>

**27**
**Casas Grandes**

**Claim Date.** 1974.

**Claimant.** Charles C. Di Peso.

**Claim Type.** Violence and cannibalism.

**Other Designations.** CHIH:D:9:1; Paquimé.

**Site Location.** Approximately 125 km (75 miles) south of the international border between Mexico and the United States at the Arizona–New Mexico line, in Viejo Casas Grandes, Chihuahua, Mexico, at 30°22' N, 107°58' W, 1476 m above mean sea level.

**Site Type.** Large, multiperiod, adobe-walled pueblo with ceremonial structures including plazas, a serpent mound, a platform mound, ball courts, a reservoir and other water supply structures, and other specialized features.

**Cultural Affiliation.** Principal city of the Casas Grandes archaeological zone, Chichimecan culture.

**Chronology.** Di Peso's (1974b) historical sequence at Paquimé has three cultural periods dated mainly by tree-rings: Viejo, A.D. 700–1060; Medio, 1060–1340; and Españoles, 1660–1684. These dates are controversial, and a revision of the tree-ring dating has been published by Jeffrey S. Dean and John C. Ravesloot (1993).

**Excavators and Date.** Joint Casas Grandes Expedition, Amerind Foundation, Dragoon, Arizona (Charles C. Di Peso, director), and Instituto Nacional de Antropología e Historia (INAH), Mexico (Eduardo Contreras, official representative), 1958–1961.

**Institutional Storage.** INAH, Paquimé, Chihuahua.

**Site Reports.** Di Peso (1974a, 1974b); Di Peso, Rinaldo, and Fenner (1974). The entire set of reports constitutes eight volumes.

**Osteological Reports.** Benfer (1968); Butler (1971); Di Peso, Rinaldo, and Fenner (1974).

**Skeletal Evidence of Stress.** Harris lines were observed by X-ray in Medio-period long bones but not in those of the earlier Viejo-period people (Di Peso, Rinaldo, and Fenner 1974:341).

**Burial Context.** Di Peso, Rinaldo, and Fenner (1974) developed an elaborate classification of burials, involving 13 types with several subtypes. For considerations of violence and cannibalism the types are not especially useful, because they are tied as much to skeletal position and location as to numbers and completeness of individuals. Recomposing the types along anatomical and taphonomic lines, and ignoring the unaltered, articulated single or multiple burials, those of potential interest are (1) the formally buried disarticulated or mixed remains (complete, incomplete, extra elements, some articulation): Types 1C, 1D, 1E, 1G, 1H, 11D, 11E, 3C, 3D, 3E, 3G, 3H, 5, 6, 7C, 8 ("human sacrifice" of various subtypes); (2) the unburied bodies: Types 2, 9; and (3) the isolated bone(s) not formally buried: Types 13A, 13B, and 13C.

**Associated Artifacts.** Grave furniture, mostly pottery vessels, was found in 190 (42.5%) of the formal burials.

**Figures.** None.

**Taphonomy.** CCDP.

*MNI.* In Paquimé, Di Peso and associates found 576 prehistoric Casas Grandes individuals. Of these, 127 were thought to have been killed when the city was destroyed about A.D. 1340 (Di Peso, Rinaldo, and Fenner 1974:325).

*Age and Sex.* Robert A. Benfer, Barbara H. Butler, and coauthors Di Peso, John B. Rinaldo, and Gloria J. Fenner did a great deal of age and sex analysis. Benfer found no significant sex differences; Butler did, with a slightly significant excess of females. Age ratios varied considerably among Paquimé architectural and spatial units. Assuming that approximately 50% of all burials should be children below the age of 12, then Paquimé had a deficiency of children, since they made up only 33.4% of the burial population (Di Peso, Rinaldo, and Fenner 1974:359).

*Preservation.* Generally poor to very poor.

*Breakage.* Two unburied Diablo-phase individuals were reported as having been traumatized by a head and a limb fracture, respectively.

*Cut Marks.* None found.

*There is no information for Bone and Fragment Number, Burning, Anvil Abrasions, Polishing, Vertebrae Number, Scalping, Gnawing, Chewing, or Insect Parts.*

*Other Modification.* In a set of six skulls, four had the tops of their vaults drilled for suspension.

**Archaeologists' Interpretation.** Di Peso, Rinaldo, and Fenner devoted 90 pages in their volume 8 (1974:325–415) to Casas Grandes burials, mainly mortuary statistics, and 18 pages in volume 2 (Di Peso 1974b) to interpretation. Because the methodology had yet to be developed, they did not directly address human taphonomy. They did, however, make a convincing case for the violent end of the city.

Of the consultants and graduate students involved in Casas Grandes skeletal research—Benfer, Walter A. Birkby, Butler, Edward F. Harris, Thomas W. McKern, G. Richard Scott, and N. Ned Woodall—only Birkby was approached for his forensic expertise. He examined three crania for postmortem polishing and scraping, and these were only half of the six human skulls found in a room with more than 100 black-bear long bones and other objects and presumed to have been trophies (Di Peso, Rinaldo, and Fenner 1974:53–54). (The other three trophy crania had somehow disappeared while on loan to the University of Texas.) Birkby found signs of scraping but no polishing or cut marks. Di Peso, Rinaldo, and Fenner believed that four of the six original skulls had from one to four holes drilled in them for hanging.

Four artifacts made from human bone were found at Casas

Grandes. A fragment of an ascending mandibular ramus had been ornamented with turquoise mosaic (Di Peso, Rinaldo, and Fenner 1974: 10–11); the top of a skull had been made into a simple, undecorated bowl (1974:63); a presumed necklace made of perforated human hand and foot bones was found in a burial vault, but not placed on a burial (1974:65); and the distal end of a right humerus had "butchering scars." The illustration of the last shows the broken shaft, but we cannot tell whether the breakage was perimortem or postmortem.

In developing his hypothesis that Mesoamerican "*pochteca* [trader] contacts" were the main cause of culture historical changes at Casas Grandes and in the American Southwest, Di Peso (1974a:58) reviewed much of the Mesoamerican and Southwestern ethnohistoric and ethnographic literature. He recognized the symbolic representations of five southern Mexican cults or god-complexes at Casas Grandes in the Medio period (Di Peso 1974b:ch. 4)—those of Tezcatlipoca, Quetzalcoatl, Xiuhtecutli, Xipe Totec, and Tlaloc. To the south these cults were strongly linked with human sacrifice and, not rarely, cannibalism. Regarding the Xipe Totec cult, Di Peso (1974b:562–564) wrote that scalping, trophy heads, and cannibalism

> were all integral to this Mesoamerican cult, particularly as practiced by the Aztec, who paid special homage to Xipe during their festival of *Tlacaxipeualiztli,* the second month of their calendar, which occasioned the ceremonial scalping of certain of their sacrifical victims. Though very tentative, it may be suggested that residuals of this practice may still exist in the Chichimeca among the Western Puebloans. . . . Cannibalism, although not unique to Xipe Tótec cultists, was nonetheless a meaningful function of their sect.[81] Paquimian evidence of this practice was found in their trash[82] in the form of butchering marks on human bone; among the Western Pueblo the scalp-takers were required to nibble a newly acquired scalp so they could receive the Beast God's warrior and rain-making powers.

Di Peso's footnote 82, alluding to human skeletal evidence for Casas Grandes cannibalism, reads only, "See Type 13 human remains, vol. 8, p. 337, fractured human bone found in trash deposits along with similarly fractured animal bone" (Di Peso 1974b:713). The text for Type 13 burials is a definition for "miscellaneous human bone." Three subtypes were created. Type 13A was human bone from unsealed fill or floor proveniences. There were 223 fragments, mainly from unburied individuals who had died in the final destruction of Casas Grandes. (Type 13A is like Type 2, which was more or less complete bodies found on floors.) Type 13B consisted of 65 bone fragments from sealed fill settings: "None of these remains, obviously, could have been associated with the end of the city, and it was originally thought that they might offer evidence suggesting the practice of cannibalism during the Medio Period. The scarcity of their number and the complete lack of any traces of butchering scars, however, served to discredit this theory" (Di Peso 1974b:713). Finally, Type 13C consisted of seven bone fragments from construction trash in architectural features. "Again, it was hoped that this trash bone might be suggestive of the practice of cannibalism, but no evidence was found to indicate that this was the case" (Di Peso 1974b:713).

In sum, we found no evidence in the Casas Grandes reports for whole or fragmented bones that could be used to argue for cannibalism there. The texts concerning cannibalism in volumes 2 and 8 are incompatible. This does not mean that perimortem body processing was unknown. Di Peso did describe several examples of human sacrifice, murder, postmortem disarticulation, and death-linked ritual treatment of children and adults. For example, he tells of finding the skeleton of a child "whose body was carefully wrapped around the subsurface base of one of the upper pillars that supported the roof of a public room" (1974b:637). In the House of the Skulls, workmen found trophy heads "scraped and drilled for suspension" (Di Peso 1974b:638). And almost one-quarter of the men, women, and children whose remains were uncovered by the excavations had died at the hands of some enemy and were never buried (Di Peso 1974b:639).

The various burial types that included disarticulated remains have the potential for documenting violence. Although no taphonomic analysis was done for the Casas Grandes skeletal series, the 126 Medio-period unburied bodies found on terminal Diablo-phase floors are inarguable evidence of attack and violence, surely signaling an end to Paquimé (Di Peso, Rinaldo, and Fenner 1974:337). Among the 126 unburied people, trauma was recognized in two: a blow to the head in one, and a shattered limb in the other.

Other Interpretations. Although there has been much discussion about the dating of Casas Grandes, little attention has been given to the skeletal population to learn whether taphonomic data could be extracted to test Di Peso's various sociopolitical and cultural-historical interpretations—ritual sacrifice, warfare, and cannibalism. John C. Ravesloot (1988) has paid the greatest amount of attention to at least the mortuary data. He and Patricia M. Spoerl (1989:135) theorized about Casas Grandes warfare as it affected the development of status hierarchies:

> There is considerable direct and indirect evidence for warfare as an integral aspect of Casas Grandes society throughout the Medio period [reassessed by Dean and Ravesloot (1993) to date from A.D. 1200 to 1450]. The presence of trophy skulls and the association of objects made from human bone with a number of Casas Grandes burials suggests that warfare may have played a critical role in the emergence of a centralized structure. Once a hierarchical social structure was established as an adaptive choice, warfare may have been reinforced and manipulated by Casas Grandes elite because conditions of chronic warfare could have served to strengthen their position in the society.

Here Ravesloot, as he had earlier (1988), followed some of Di Peso's major interpretations—Casas Grandes was attacked and destroyed, trophy skulls were taken, and cannibalism was a possibility.

Beatrice Braniff (personal communication, March 22, 1994) felt that Tezcatlipoca ideology was present at Casas Grandes, because of human body processing and skull collections. But unlike Di Peso, she did not believe Quetzalcoatl was worshiped there, because there is only one possible iconographic example, a polychrome jar showing a painted snake whose head is capped with two apparent feathers. Braniff did not believe this portrayed Quetzalcoatl, but it seems to us that it does. Moreover, the jar is very similar to a complete polychrome vessel illustrated by Carl Lumholtz (1902, vol. 1, pl. 2) that was found among burials at a site called San Diego, about 13 km (8 miles) south of Casas Grandes. Lumholtz (1889:96) said that he excavated other mortuary vessels with the plumed serpent design at San Diego. Many of the San Diego pottery designs illustrated by Lumholtz are strikingly like those of Pueblo IV Hopi ceramics.

Braniff believes that cannibalism was practiced at Casas Grandes, but not for food. Instead, she thinks human flesh was consumed for ritual reasons, as was the case when human hearts or other types of human flesh were added to posole (hominy stew) and eaten by the Aztecs.

**Discussion.** We included Casas Grandes in this chapter instead of chapter 4, which deals with Mexico, because although the site has many cultural features that are intermediate between heartland Mesoamerica and the American Southwest, more of them resemble the latter than the former. It is also geographically closer to the Southwest than the most northerly Mexican sites with strong Mesoamerican qualities, such as Alta Vista, La Quemada, and Guasave. Moreover, the international boundary that falsely dichotomizes the American Southwest and Mexico did not exist when Casas Grandes was occupied.

Di Peso's claim for cannibalism is self-contradictory. On the basis of the published osteological descriptions, illustrations, and statements, we cannot agree that cannibalism has been demonstrated for Casas Grandes at any time period. Considering the strong probability of cannibalism in the American Southwest and its certainty in central Mexico, it is surprising that cannibalism cannot be taphonomically demonstrated for Casas Grandes, situated between the two. The absence of broken, burned, cut, abraided, and polished bone fragments could be a result of simple mechanical destruction due to the rocky, alkaline soil with its bone-shattering wet and dry cycles of salt crystal formation. Support for this possibility exists in the animal remains, which were not especially common at Paquimé from the beginning of the Viejo period (A.D.650) to the end of the historic Españoles period (1684). Despite the enormous amount of excavation, only 949 individual animals could be reconstructed. Bones of small animals, the preservation qualities of which probably correspond to those of small fragments of human bone, are less common than might be expected. Only 44 individual cottontails and 121 jackrabbits were recognized. Larger-boned antelope (276 individuals) and deer (110) were much more numerous (Di Peso, Rinaldo, and Fenner 1974:242).

Despite the eight highly detailed and magnificently illustrated volumes of descriptive data and analysis that were published for the Casas Grandes project, the claim for cannibalism is not based on adequate evidence. Di Peso's claim for violence, however, is richly documented and highly convincing. We hope that a restudy of the unburied Diablo-phase skeletons will be done someday for all forms of physical trauma, perimortem animal scavenging, and bone surface weathering exposure. These kinds of observations would shed additional light on the ruinous attack that finished off Paquimé. They would also provide a more complete bioarchaeological basis for theoretical predictions about what to expect taphonomically in other instances of Southwestern and Mesoamerican archaeology where raiding and warfare are suspected.

## 28
## Mancos Canyon

**Claim Date.** 1974.

**Claimants.** Paul R. Nickens and Larry V. Nordby; also Tim D. White.

**Claim Type.** Cannibalism (PRN, LVN, and TDW).

**Other Designations.** 5MTUMR 2346.

**Site Location.** South of Mesa Verde National Park on the Ute Mountain Indian Reservation, Montezuma County, southwestern Colorado, about 0.8 km (0.5 mile) west of the junction of Navajo and Mancos Canyons, on the north side of the Mancos River.

**Site Type.** Medium-sized masonry pueblo with kiva.

**Cultural Affiliation.** Mesa Verde Anasazi.

**Chronology.** Pueblo III (about A.D. 1100). Two short periods of occupation were recognized on archaeological grounds.

**Excavator and Date.** David A. Breternitz, general supervisor; J. A. Lancaster and Larry V. Nordby, field operations; summer 1973.

**Institutional Storage.** Mesa Verde National Park Research Center.

**Site Report.** Nordby (1974).

**Osteological Report.** Nickens (1974, 1975); White (1992).

**Skeletal Evidence of Stress.** Dental hypoplasia, porotic hyperostosis, cribra orbitalia, Harris lines, and periosteal reaction were identified by Nickens (1974) and White (1992).

**Burial Context.** Nordby (1974:243) and Nickens (1975:294) reported that the human remains were found in nine separate bone beds. White (1992:80) illustrated these as coming from about the same number of surface masonry rooms and interroom spaces, many with whole or discarded stone and ceramic artifacts, none specifically linked to the human remains. The pueblo had two construction phases, and it seems that all or at least most of the bone was deposited in the older rooms while the walls were still standing (Nordby 1974).

Nickens (1975:284) reported that he tried several times to match fragments from the nine bone units, but "the experiment provided no association between bones from separate rooms." White and associates spent scores of hours doing the same thing. It is unclear precisely how many pieces of bone White studied, but assuming the number was 2,100 (see "Bone and Fragment Number" below), then after 245 hours of matching attempts, only 1.5% of the assemblage (31 interroom pieces) fit together. White did not suggest how these few pieces were transported away from their breakage site. They could have been moved by scavengers, but bagging and labeling errors and provenience mixing in any phase of field and laboratory processing are always possibilities. Without point mapping of each bone fragment, there are too many sources of error to believe uncritically that their assumed resting places have site-specific behavioral significance. We, too, have attempted to reassemble bone fragments, although with very inadequately excavated and mapped skeletal elements. These tasks were primarily useful for demonstrating an occasional rare sequence of breaking and burning. However, we have dealt only with single-room floor assemblages and pit deposits, never with a multiroom series.

**Associated Artifacts.** Nickens (1974:13–18) provided counts for sherds, stone flakes, and stone and bone artifacts found in each of the bone clusters ("burials"). The stone items included "unutilized" flakes, cores, scrapers, hammerstones, mano and metate fragments, hammerstones, and one projectile point. Bone items included tube beads and an awl fragment. The pottery types included Mancos and Mesa Verde Corrugated, Mancos and McElmo Black-on-white, and Tusayan Polychrome. Apparently no cultural materials were found with the scattered bone fragments. White (1992:59) noted that in Room 23 there were "corrugated pottery sherds intimately associated with the skeletal remains." Like every other known Southwestern charnel deposit suggesting cannibalism, the Mancos Canyon assemblage included no fragmented or whole bone with an embedded weapon point.

**Figures.** None.

**Taphonomy.** PRN, 1975; TDW.

*MNI.* 33 (PRN 1974, 1975); 29 (TDW).

*Age and Sex.* Many adolescents and young adults (PRN). Five 0- to 6-year-olds; eight 6- to 18-year-olds, 15 adults; and one age? (TDW). Sex was not determined by TDW. Nickens (1974) originally suggested that there were 13 Mancos Canyon individuals whose sex could be determined, but he did not say how many of these were found at 5MTUMR 2346. The same remark applies to his age determinations.

*Preservation.* Good to excellent (PRN, TDW).

*Bone and Fragment Number.* A total of 1,814, not counting 85 loose teeth (PRN). White (1992:66) set up definitions for bone condition classes; a "specimen" was a fragmented or whole bone or tooth. He listed 2,100 specimens in his data base (1992, Appendix 2, p. 421). An element was an unbroken bone. Judging from the excellent photographs, there were not many whole bones in the Mancos Canyon series. A "piece" was a broken bone or a set of reassembled bones that fit together. There were 2,106 pieces (1992:69) and a total of 2,027 nondental specimens (1992:327).

*Breakage.* 86.6% (1,571 of 1,814). Whole bones, mainly those of hands and feet, totaled 243 (PRN). White defined a whole bone as at least 50% present, whereas we define a whole bone as at least 95% complete. Our procedures are not comparable. Nevertheless, breakage, according to White, was extensive.

*Cut Marks.* Yes (PRN); 11.7% (TDW).

*Burning.* Yes (PRN); 21.5% (TDW).

*Anvil Abrasions.* Not observed (PRN); 18.5% (TDW).

*Polishing.* Not observed (PRN); 6.0% (TDW).

*Vertebrae Number.* 9.9% of expected (78 of 793) (PRN; we assume that three of Nickens's fragments equal one whole vertebra).

White illustrated 143 whole and fragmentary specimens and inventoried 134 in his data base. Using White's MNI of 29, there should have been 696 vertebrae, or about 20.5% of the expected number—about 10% more than Nickens's count.

*Scalping.* Yes. Nickens (1975:289) indicated only that long bone fragments had cut marks, but White (1992:164–207) illustrated many vault cut marks that could have resulted from scalping.

*Gnawing, Rodent.* Not considered by PRN. White found none.

*Chewing, Carnivore.* None (PRN and TDW).

*Insect Parts.* None indicated by Nordby, Nickens, or White.

*Other Modification.* None indicated by PRN or TDW.

**Archaeologist's Interpretation.** Nordby (1974) found no archaeological or taphonomic support for secondary burial but allowed that cannibalism had been carried out either by assailants who attacked the Mancos site or by site inhabitants who attacked some other, larger pueblo. Nordby (1974:240–241) favored the latter interpretation because there were too many individuals for the small size of the Mancos site. He further proposed that the Mancos Canyon cannibalism was probably not caused by famine or disease but was instead some form of ritual.

**Other Interpretations.** Nickens agreed that there had been cannibalism in Mancos Canyon but disagreed with Nordby over the cause. Unknowingly anticipating an alternative suggestion for the bone condition raised many years later by Peter Bullock (1991, 1992), Nickens (1974:291) emphasized that the condition and context of the bone assemblage was due to "something beyond merely mutilation of individuals in a postmortem condition." He saw no evidence of violence or any sign of magical or religous meaning. By elimination, he offered famine as the underlying cause of the Mancos Canyon cannibalism. White (1992:363) seems to have agreed that the Mancos people were consumed because of hunger, although he cautiously noted that "there are no osteological markers reliably associated with starvation."

**Discussion.** The perimortem damage that Nickens, Nordby, and White found in the Mancos Canyon charnel deposit includes the minimal criteria we deem necessary before cannibalism can be hypothesized. If this or any other cannibalized series could be examined along lines currently under investigation by Smithsonian physical anthropologist Donald Ortner (personal communication), it is possible that scurvy, if not evidence of starvation, might be identified in the cranial bones of some of the children. We disagree with Nickens, and presumably also with White, about the absence of violence.

In any forensic case involving human death, cut marks on one or more of the victim's bones would be perfectly acceptable evidence for hypothesizing foul play, as would a bashed-in head. Add broken teeth and smashed and traumatized alveolar bone without anvil abrasions, and the forensic scientist is well on the way to establishing that violence occurred. Our taphonomic problem in recognizing violence here is much like a problem in the current national issue of battered wives and children—how does a medical doctor determine for reporting purposes whether a child or woman's wounds are accidental, self-imposed, or administered by a violent parent or spouse? The physical damage is generally the same. What differs most often is the *amount* of trauma. One or two burns on an infant's body might have been caused accidentally by the infant, but many burns, on different parts of the body, signal intent, not accident.

White's human-animal comparisons show a strong likelihood of violence against the humans at Mancos Canyon: the human bones were damaged much more than the comparative animal bone assemblages. Michael Dice (1993a) found the same differential in his comparisons of the Leroux Wash human remains with prehistoric Wupatki antelope bones. Although there may be little qualitative difference between the butchering of animals and the mutilation of humans, there is certainly a quantitative difference in these comparisons. Moreover, if one considers the probable context at the time of the Mancos Canyon deaths, one must ask how 29 to 33 people were controlled over a relatively short period of time before they were killed and butchered. These people were slaughtered either one after another or all at about the same time. Would anyone stand around waiting to be butchered and cooked? Surely someone balked.

White (1992:360) objected to workers using terms such as *violence* and *mutilation* when discussing cases of Southwestern human bone damage. What he seems not to appreciate is that there are powerful sanctions in all cultures against damaging and eating live and dead humans. Animals are routinely eaten, and most of their body parts are "mutilated" and manipulated into tools, other products, and scrap. To treat humans the same way as other animals, for whatever reason, means they are being mutilated and violated, whether for food or for ritual requirement.

We see nothing in the taphonomy or context of the Mancos assemblage by itself that would point to Nordby's suggested ritual activity. Nickens (1974:52) felt the same way: "In summary, the evidence points to the practice of cannibalism, albeit the type cannot be ascertained. No magico-religious connections are seen in the material." On the other hand, Nickens found no evidence that he believed pointed to violence. We believe that when the Mancos Canyon charnel deposit is plotted on a map of the Southwest along with all the other sites with cannibalized bone deposits (see fig. 3.292), a case for some manner of Anasazi ritual observance has to be considered. We examine this possibility in chapter 5.

## 29
## Burnt Mesa

**Claim Date.** 1976.

**Claimants.** Lynn Flinn, Christy G. Turner II, and Alan Brew.

**Claim Type.** Cannibalism.

**Other Designations.** LA4528.

**Site Location.** On Burnt Mesa, a plateau north of the San Juan River, south of the Pine River, northwestern New Mexico. USGS Pine River quadrangle (1954), T 30N, R 7W, W ½ of Sec. 7 and E ¼ of Sec. 8.

**Site Type.** Three pithouses and a paved-floor surface structure.

**Cultural Affiliation.** Anasazi, late Piedra phase.

**Chronology.** A.D. 950.

**Excavator and Date.** Alan Brew, 1969.

**Institutional Storage.** Arizona State University, Tempe.

224

Figure 3.154. Burnt Mesa, New Mexico. Concentration of human bones and pottery sherds directly on pithouse floor. The metate would have served well as an anvil upon which to crack open long bones with either of the two manos in this remarkable view. Scale is 1 m. Excavation and photograph by Alan P. Brew (APB neg. 8-27-69:12).

Figure 3.155. Burnt Mesa. Additional human bones with perimortem breakage on same pithouse floor as in figure 3.154. Photograph by Alan P. Brew (APB neg. 9-9-69:6).

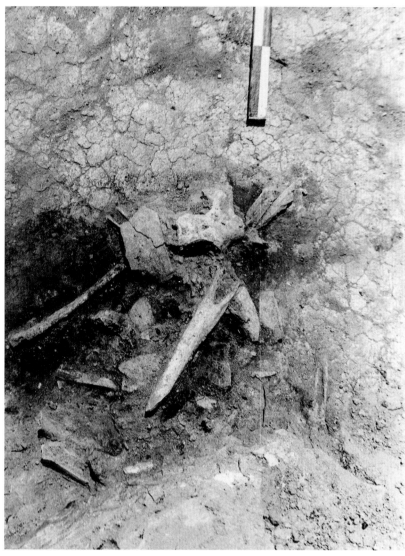

Figure 3.156. Burnt Mesa. Much of the charnel assemblage. Alan Brew at right (CGT neg. October 1970:30).

Table 3.31
Bone Elements and Perimortem Damage at Burnt Mesa

| SKELETAL ELEMENT | WHOLE | FRAGMENT | IMPACT BREAK | ANVIL ABRASION | CUT MARK | BURN | POLISH | GNAW/ CHEW |
|---|---|---|---|---|---|---|---|---|
| **Cranial** | | | | | | | | |
| Maxilla[a] | 3 | 14 | 10 | 1 | 0 | 2 | 0 | 0 |
| Mandible | 1 | 19 | 19 | 1 | 0 | 4 | 2 | 0 |
| Frontal | 2 | 110 | 110 | 3 | 1 | 42 | 1 | 0 |
| Parietal | 4 | 160 | 160 | 6 | 3 | 58 | 1 | 0 |
| Occipital | 1 | 21 | 21 | 4 | 0 | 6 | 2 | 0 |
| Temporal | 4 | 44 | 44 | 2 | 0 | 7 | 2 | 0 |
| Teeth (not counted) | | | | | | | | |
| Fragments | — | 224 | 224 | 18 | 0 | 83 | 14 | 0 |
| **Postcranial** | | | | | | | | |
| Vertebrae | 10 | 59 | 59 | 0 | 0 | 7 | 5 | 1R |
| Sacrum | 0 | 1 | 1 | 0 | 0 | 0 | 0 | 0 |
| Scapula | 2 | 37 | 37 | 1 | 0 | 7 | 0 | 0 |
| Clavicle | 5 | 6 | 6 | 2 | 0 | 7 | 1 | 0 |
| Rib | 8 | 72 | 72 | 1 | 1 | 5 | 14 | 1? |
| Humerus | 2 | 77 | 77 | 5 | 0 | 9 | 3 | 0 |
| Radius | 0 | 11 | 11 | 3 | 0 | 0 | 1 | 0 |
| Ulna | 1 | 15 | 15 | 0 | 0 | 4 | 6 | 0 |
| Hand & foot | 19 | 93 | 93 | 6 | 0 | 5 | 2 | 0 |
| Pelvis | 2 | 31 | 31 | 6 | 0 | 4 | 0 | 1R |
| Femur | 0 | 120 | 120 | 4 | 7 | 11 | 5 | 0 |
| Tibia | 1 | 68 | 68 | 5 | 4 | 9 | 3 | 1C |
| Fibula | 1 | 35 | 35 | 4 | 1 | 7 | 3 | 0 |
| Long bone fragments | — | 2,081 | 2,081 | 34 | 0 | 916 | 26 | 0 |
| TOTAL (3,389) | 67 | 3,322 | 3,322 | 106 | 17 | 1,200 | 91 | 4 |
| PERCENTAGE | 2.0 | 98.0 | 98.0 | 3.1 | 0.5 | 35.4 | 2.7 | 0.1 |

Percentage of expected vertebrae = approx. 8.3 (22 of 264; MNI = 11).[b]

NOTE: Only elements that were present are listed. Korri Dee Turner added the observations for abrasions, polishing, and gnawing in summer, 1993. Impact breakage, anvil abrasions, cut marks, burning, and polishing represent perimortem damage. Gnawing and chewing are postmortem damage.

a. Zygoma added to maxilla in this series since in most others the broken zygomata is usually found attached to the maxilla.

b. Fragmentation size suggests that about five fragments could represent one whole vertebra.

Site Report. None.
Osteological Reports. Flinn, Turner, and Brew (1976); Turner (1983).
Skeletal Evidence of Stress. Minor porotic hyperostosis.
Burial Context. Skeletal fragments scattered on pithouse floor.
Associated Artifacts. Metates on floor may have been used as anvils upon which bones were cracked open. An edge-polished human cranial vault fragment appears to have been used as a scoop.
Figures. 3.154–3.156.
Taphonomy. LF and CGT; Korri Dee Turner. Skeletal inventory is in table 3.31.

*MNI.* 11.

*Age and Sex.* One infant; 2 children; 1 subadult; 7 adults (4 male, 2 female, 1 sex?).

*Preservation.* Good.

*Bone and Fragment Number.* 3,389.

*Breakage.* 98.0%.

*Cut Marks.* 0.5% (2.8% in Korri Turner restudy).

*Burning.* 35.4%.

*Anvil Abrasions.* 3.1%.

*Polishing.* Present.

*Vertebrae Number.* 8.3% of expected (22 of 264).

*Scalping.* Uncertain.

*Gnawing, Rodent, and Chewing, Carnivore.* Yes.

*Insect Parts.* None found.

*Other Modification.* One skull fragment shows edge polishing as if it had served as a scoop or ladle.

Archaeologist's Interpretation. Brew felt that there was environmental stress at A.D. 950 on Burnt Mesa, so the bone damage could have been the consequence of emergency or starvation cannibalism. He found no evidence that the pithouse containing the human remains had burned or that the people had been assaulted or otherwise intentionally killed. His excavation showed that the "human remains were a single depositional event that coincided with the final occupation of the structure [Pithouse 1]. There was no evidence that the human remains might have been intrusive. The individuals were found directly on the floor surface and although there were some localized concentrations of bone fragments, most occurred randomly" (Flinn, Turner, and Brew 1976:310).
Other Interpretations. None.
Discussion. Since 1976 we have regarded damaged faces and anterior teeth and tooth sockets without anvil abrasions as evidence of violence. Such damage is present in the Burnt Mesa charnel deposit. Consequently, we are now less inclined to view the Burnt Mesa bone assemblage as due primarily to starvation cannibalism; it could just as well fit the social pathology or social control explanatory model that we outline in chapter 5.

The Burnt Mesa assemblage was restudied by Korri Dee Turner, with special emphasis on obtaining information on polishing and abrasion, information not collected in the original analysis. Her findings are incorporated in table 3.31.

**30
Huerfano Mesa**

**Claim Date.** 1976.

**Claimant.** James E. Chase.

**Claim Type.** Violence and cannibalism.

**Other Designations.** AR-03-10-02-03; AR-03-10-02-04.

**Site Location.** In the Gallina River district, 0.8 km (0.5 mile) east of Alkali Springs, Santa Fe National Forest, Rio Arriba County, northwestern New Mexico. USGS Llaves quadrangle (Provisional Edition 1983), T 25N, R 1E, S ½ of NW ¼ of Sec. 2.

**Site Type.** Pit and surface house settlement on a small mesa.

**Cultural Affiliation.** Largo-Gallina Anasazi.

**Chronology.** A.D. 1150–1250.

**Excavator and Date.** Herbert W. Dick, 1972–1974.

**Institutional Storage.** Colorado State University, Fort Collins.

**Site Report.** Dick (1976).

**Osteological Report.** Chase (1976) reported on the five burials from Huerfano Mesa. Two of these, numbers 3 (G-3-7) and 5 (G-4), had "striations"; Chase (1976:71) attributed those on Burial 3 to "a primitive cutting instrument." He described Burial 2 as follows (1976:70–71):

> The child was buried in an artificial rock pile 6–8 feet west of a burned, rectangular pit house. Burial was earth-filled and covered by a large sandstone slab. The child, tightly flexed, was placed on the right side with head to the north, the face to the west. No tibias were present, and the femora were reversed from their normal flexed position. . . . On the popliteal surface of the right femur, [are] numerous striations caused by a primitive cutting instrument, probably a thin flint knife. . . . There is little doubt that these were caused before burial and while the bone was green.

**Skeletal Evidence of Stress.** Chase (1976:90), referring to the entire skeletal series from Huerfano Mesa and the Llaves–Alkali Springs sites together (see sites 31–33), remarked that "deficiencies are indicated by osteoporosis being present in most individuals examined."

**Burial Context.** Burial 3 was a nine-year-old child buried in a rock pile. No tibias were present, and the femurs were reversed. Burial 5 consisted of a calvarium, right femur, and right tibia found in the fill three feet above the floor of surface house 4. In Site 2 (AR-03-10-02-02), a circular pithouse, Burial 6 was found in a west bin. Burial 6 consisted of four articulated lumbar vertebrae, a femur, and several carpals and phalanges. Extreme arthritic lipping indicated that it was an old adult. This individual, a male, had striations on his femur that Chase (1976:73) noted were "not the result of natural or root action."

**Associated Artifacts.** None.

**Figures.** None.

**Taphonomy.** JEC.

*MNI.* 3.

*Age and Sex.* One 9-year-old child; one 32- to 35-year-old adult male; one very incomplete old adult.

*Cut Marks.* Yes.

*There is no information for Preservation, Bone and Fragment Number, Breakage, Burning, Anvil Abrasions, Polishing, Verte-*

*brae Number, Scalping, Gnawing, Chewing, Insect Parts, or Other Modification.*

**Archaeologist's Interpretation.** Dick (1976:47) considered the house 4 structure to be unusual, deteriorating slowly, with some elements having been removed after abandonment and with a "disarticulated male, adult, human skeleton strewn on the floor on the west side of the room." The difference between Dick's and Chase's placement of burial 5 cannot be resolved, because the report does not indicate who actually excavated the burials. Dick (1976:18) also noted by way of comparison:

> Although not fully reported extensively in the scientific literature, a number of provocative traits are reported in the popular literature for the Gallina phase. Hibben (1944, p. 68) describes the material. "In addition, there was a woman bow person described as having the head hair braided into six strands gathered in a bun on the back of the head and red paint placed down the scalp line where the hair was parted. . . . In three towers excavated, one contained 16 people, . . . another tower contained five defenders, and in still another, 11 bodies."

**Other Interpretations.** Chase (1976:79) mentioned a "modified human bone" object. This item was not described but merely listed along with seeds, potsherds, bird bones, and concretions that were thought to be funerary offerings because they were found with four of the burials.

**Discussion.** Chase proposed violence and cannibalism as the causes of damage observed in human bones from a group of sites in the Llaves–Alkali Springs area, of which Huerfano Mesa was one. For the details of his interpretation, see the discussion section for site number 33, Llaves–Alkali Springs 12. Together these sites and others (Bahti 1949; Hibben 1944; Mackey and Green 1979; Turner, Turner, and Green 1993) indicate considerable violence and conflict in the Largo-Gallina area.

## 31
## Llaves–Alkali Springs

**Claim Date.** 1976.

**Claimant.** James E. Chase.

**Claim Type.** Violence and cannibalism.

**Other Designations.** Burial 2, AR-03-10-02-189.

**Site Location.** About 1.3 km (0.8 mile) northwest of the Llaves Post Office, Rio Arriba County, northwestern New Mexico. USGS Llaves quadrangle (Provisional Edition 1983), T 25N, R 1E, SE ¼ of SW ¼ of NE ¼ of Sec. 10.

**Site Type.** Isolated grave 10.7 m (35 feet) east of a surface and pithouse site.

**Cultural Affiliation.** Largo-Gallina Anasazi.

**Chronology.** A.D. 1150–1250.

**Excavator and Date.** Herbert W. Dick, 1972–1974.

**Institutional Storage.** Colorado State University, Fort Collins.

**Site Report.** Dick (1976).

**Osteological Report.** Chase (1976).

**Skeletal Evidence of Stress.** Chase (1976:70) reported that Burial 2 (G-189), a young adult male, had "medium osteoporosis."

**Burial Context.** Chase (1976:69) wrote: "Remains were disturbed but not in recent times. Conjecture is that the burial is a kill site with formal burial by the Indian, with possible post-mortem mutilation because no hands or feet were found." Body was buried in a flexed position with head facing north.

**Associated Artifacts.** A serrated projectile point was present in the pelvic region. No other artifacts were found.

**Figures.** None.

**Taphonomy.** JEC.

*MNI.* 1.

*Age and Sex.* 25 ± 3 years, male.

*Preservation.* Good.

*Bone and Fragment Number.* Not only were hands and feet missing, but only three vertebrae (lumbar) were found.

*Vertebrae Number.* 12.5% of expected (3 of 24).

*There is no information for Breakage, Cut Marks, Burning, Anvil Abrasions, Polishing, Scalping, Gnawing, Chewing, Insect Parts, or Other Modification.*

**Archaeologist's Interpretation.** None.

**Other Interpretations.** In addition to his remarks quoted under "Burial Context," Chase (1976:69) wrote: "A serrated projectile point was found in the pelvic cavity. Impact of the point may have been a contributing cause of death."

**Discussion.** This is one of the individuals on whom Chase constructed his thesis for Largo-Gallina cannibalism and violence.

---

## 32
## Llaves–Alkali Springs 2

**Claim Date.** 1976.

**Claimant.** James E. Chase.

**Claim Type.** Violence and cannibalism.

**Other Designations.** Burial 4, AR-03-10-02-81; Site 80, LA654, and Chupadero Ranger Station.

**Site Location.** Chupadero Spring Arroyo, 0.4 km (0.25 mile) north of the old Chupadero Camp Ranger Station, Rio Arriba County, northwestern New Mexico. USGS Llaves quadrangle (Provisional Edition 1983), T 25N, R 1E, NW ¼ of NE ¼ of Sec. 4.

**Site Type.** A circular building 3.7 m (12 feet) high, possibly a granary.

**Cultural Affiliation.** Largo-Gallina Anasazi.

**Chronology.** A.D. 1150–1250.

**Excavator and Date.** Herbert W. Dick, 1972–1974.

**Institutional Storage.** Colorado State University, Fort Collins.

**Site Report.** Dick (1976).

**Osteological Report.** Chase (1976).

**Skeletal Evidence of Stress.** None indicated.

**Burial Context.** Two individuals buried beneath a floor. Burial 4A (G-81A) was an adult female, and 4B (G-81B), an adult male.

**Associated Artifacts.** The adult male had a small side-notched stone point embedded in the upper tibia.

**Figures.** None.

**Taphonomy.** The female had received a "severe blow to the left side of the head causing a separation of the coronal suture which had not begun to heal" (Chase 1976:71). She also had a fractured left fibula.

*MNI.* 2.

*Age and Sex.* Adult male (burial 4B, G-81B); 22-year-old female (burial 4A, G-81A).

*Preservation.* The burials had been disturbed, and the male was very incomplete.

*Cut Marks.* The male's left femur had "striations caused by a sharp instrument 15 mm superior to the adductor tubercle on the popliteal surface" (Chase 1976:72).

*There is no information for Bone and Fragment Number, Breakage, Burning, Anvil Abrasions, Polishing, Vertebrae Number, Scalping, Gnawing, Chewing, Insect Parts, or Other Modification.*

Archaeologist's Interpretation. None.

Other Interpretations. Chase (1976:72) wrote that "one can only surmise that this female died of violent causes as did her companion, a male."

Discussion. Cut marks on the back of the femur near the knee suggest dismemberment, as was seemingly the case elsewhere in the Largo-Gallina area. Even more than the breakage of the female's vault and fibula, the embedded stone point in the male's tibia is secure evidence for proposing violence. Taken together, and considering the joint burial context, this evidence allows a secure hypothesis of violent and possibly simultaneous death.

**33**
**Llaves–Alkali Springs 12**

Claim Date. 1976.

Claimant. James E. Chase.

Claim Type. Violence and cannibalism.

Other Designations. Burial 12, no site number.

Site Location. Three km (1.9 miles) south of Alkali Springs, on west side of Capulin Creek, Rio Arriba County, northwestern Mexico. USGS Llaves quadrangle (Provisional Edition 1983) T 25N, R 1E, Sec. 10.

Site Type. Isolated grave 9.1 m (30 feet) northeast of a probable pit-house.

Cultural Affiliation. Largo-Gallina Anasazi.

Chronology. A.D. 1150–1250.

Excavator and Date. Herbert W. Dick, 1972–74.

Institutional Storage. Colorado State University, Fort Collins.

Site Report. Dick (1976).

Osteological Report. Chase (1976).

Skeletal Evidence of Stress. None reported.

Burial Context. Flexed burial of adult female and child.

Associated Artifacts. Potsherds and a round sandstone concretion.

Figures. None.

Taphonomy. JEC.

*MNI.* 2.

*Age and Sex.* Female, 25–35 years; child of unspecified years.

*Preservation.* Poor; burial had been disturbed by plowing.

*Cut Marks.* Chase (1976:77) reported that "striations appear on the anterior distal end of the femur. These are of the same nature and structure as those found on burial #3. The proximal end of the ulna is hollowed out and smooth on the inside. The modified ulna length is 12.75 cm."

*There is no information for Bone and Fragment Number, Breakage, Burning, Anvil Abrasions, Polishing, Vertebrae Number, Scalping, Gnawing, Chewing, or Insect Parts.*

*Other Modification.* See "Cut Marks."

Archaeologist's Interpretation. None.

Other Interpretations. Chase (1976:79) combined the various Llaves-area human skeletal remains to argue for violence and cannibalism:

> Evidence of dismemberment prior to burial exists as no burial is 100% complete. The tarsals and carpals are most often missing with tibias and lumbar vertebrae next. There are definite cutting striations of two burials (Nos. 3 and 12) and numerous suspicious marks on others. Most of these striations occur near or on the popliteal surface of the femur; however, an unusual modification occurred with the ulna of burial 12. Further indication of dismemberment is provided by the many isolated bones; for example, the four lumbar vertebrae found in burial 6, as well as many carpals and tarsals strewn about the houses and missing from burials. Some individuals were burned either accidentally or on purpose. This is supported by the presence of a charred mandible in burial 7. . . . Of seven fractures observed, four could only have been as the result of being struck by something blunt, wielded by someone. It is unlikely that a frontal or parietal fracture of the type seen would be caused by a fall as a femoral or fibular fracture could have. This alone is ample justification for a conclusion of hostile or violent cause; but the two projectile points, one in the pelvic cavity of No. 2 and one embedded in the tibia of 4-B, are conclusive. Ample evidence, therefore, does exist for a conclusion of altercations between individual households, clans, villages, or with some outside group. . . . Violence was evident in 38% of the total population studied and 60% of the adults. Of those definitely sexed as male (five), three exhibit evidence of violence for a 60 percentile. Two identifiable females were killed by severe blows to the head. Violence was the way of life for this population in the Gallina.

In Chase's (1976:90) concluding summary he wrote: "Partial burials occur in any part of the house with no definite organization. Complete interment is rare. In those interments which appear complete, there is always some part absent, most often parts of the hands and feet. Although at times, other parts are missing, notably tibias. In addition are the striations on the popliteal surface of femora and the proximal end of tibias. All of which suggests individual post-mortem dismemberment. I suggest anthropophagy as a reason for dismemberment; perhaps the four articulated lumbar vertebrae are the remains of a ceremonial meal."

Discussion. Chase's interpretation of violence in the Llaves area is quite reasonable. His case for cannibalism, however, is insufficient as it presently stands, because (1) missing bones and scattering can be caused by natural agencies, even subsurface bioturbation, and (2) no site has more than one or two of the criteria Chase offers to argue for cannibalism. Turner, Turner, and Green (1993) found a similar situation in other Largo-Gallina sites. Together the Llaves–Alkali Springs area sites might have all the criteria necessary for suggesting cannibalism, but no single site has all of them. Additional study is needed.

## 34
## Largo-Gallina Bg2

**Claim Date.** 1979.

**Claimants.** James Mackey and Roger C. Green.

**Claim Type.** Violence and cannibalism.

**Other Designations.** Cuchillo.

**Site Location.** On the southern bank of the Gallina River, 4 km (2.5 miles) from the junction of the Gallina and Chama Rivers. About 29 km (18 miles) east of Lindrith, New Mexico. USGS Laguna Peak quadrangle (1953), T 25N, R 2E, NW ¼ of Sec. 27.

**Site Type.** One pithouse and one single-unit house were excavated.

**Cultural Affiliation.** Gallina Anasazi.

**Chronology.** A.D. 1100–1300.

**Excavator and Date.** E. H. Blumenthal, Jr., and Carroll Burroughs, 1939.

**Institutional Storage.** Maxwell Museum of Anthropology, University of New Mexico, Albuquerque.

**Site Reports.** Blumenthal (1940); Mackey and Green (1979).

**Osteological Reports.** Lange (1940); Turner and Turner (1992a); Turner, Turner, and Green (1993).

**Skeletal Evidence of Stress.** None.

**Burial Context.** Skeletons in burned single-unit house.

**Associated Artifacts.** Pottery, stone artifacts, and woven material.

**Figures.** 3.157–3.158.

**Taphonomy.** CGT and JAT. Skeletal inventory is in table 3.33.

*MNI.* 16 (table 3.32). Determined by actual count of skeletons; this was not a disarticulated assemblage. In Turner, Turner, and Green (1993), a one-year-old infant was reported as present in Bg2, making the MNI 17. In rechecking our raw data sheets we cannot identify this infant, so we leave it out of this re-tally.

*Age and Sex.* Six adult males; one adult male?; one young adult female; three adult females?; four adults, sex?; one 15- to 18-year-old, sex?.

*Preservation.* Poor, largely burned.

*Bone and Fragment Number.* 2,687.

*Breakage.* 0.1%.

*Cut Marks.* 0.0%.

*Burning.* 86.4%.

*Anvil Abrasions.* 0.0%.

*Polishing.* None.

*Vertebrae Number.* 24.5% of expected (94 of 384).

*Scalping.* None.

*Gnawing, Rodent.* None.

*Chewing, Carnivore.* 1.1%.

*Insect Parts.* None.

*Other Modification.* None.

Table 3.32
Minimal Number of Individuals (MNI) at Largo-Gallina Bg2

| SKELETAL ELEMENTS | AGE | SEX | CATALOG NO. AND NOTES |
|---|---|---|---|
| Pelvis, L clavicle | Adult | M | 60/1 |
| Mandible, L humerus, fragment L clavicle | Adult | M | V (A45) |
| Maxilla + mandible | Adult | M | 60/6 |
| Maxilla + mandible | Adult | M | X Grade 2–3 mandibular torus |
| Skull + mandible | Adult | M | 60/13 |
| Mandible, pelvis | Adult | M | 60/13(?) 2–3 mandibular torus |
| Pelvis, humerus | Adult | M? | III |
| Maxilla, skull parts | 18–19 | F | VIII slight occipital deformation |
| Maxilla + mandible | YA | F? | V and XIV |
| Maxilla + mandible | Adult | F | XI slight occipital deformation |
| Mandible fragments | Adult | F? | XIV C2 + C3 vertebrae fused |
| Maxilla + skull parts | Adult | ? | A? I, + no number |
| Pelvis, femur, radius | Adult | ? | IV almost entirely calcined |
| Maxilla + mandible | Adult | ? | IX slight occipital deformation |
| Mandible, scapula | Adult | ? | XV |
| Maxilla + mandible | 15–18 | ? | XVI |

SUMMARY: 16 individuals. Six adult males; one adult, male?; one adult female; three adults, female?; four adults, sex?; one 15- to 18-year-old, sex?.

NOTE: MNI in this site is based on laboratory identifications and on archaeological recognition of in situ individuals.

**Archaeologist's Interpretation.** Blumenthal (1940:12) wrote: "The skeletal material from Cuchillo consists of portions of sixteen very badly charred individuals. Arrowpoints *in situ* give further proof that the inhabitants were destroyed by an enemy attack."

**Other Interpretations.** Mackey and Green (1979:146) listed Bg2 in their discussion of skeletons exhibiting evidence of violent death. They mentioned cannibalism in their concluding remarks (1979:153). Turner, Turner, and Green (1993:90) theorized: "The human remains from Bg2 on their own signal the consequences of a raid with some women and children taken as captives." This and the following Largo-Gallina sites (sites 35–38) are part of a series of some 116 skeletons, 36 of which Mackey and Green believed showed evidence of violent death (burning, crushed skulls, broken long bones, and projectile points in some skeletons). Five Largo-Gallina sites had multiple bodies on floors.

**Discussion.** The large amount of burning, large number of people in a room, small amount of other perimortem damage, full articulation, and profoundly obvious context favor a hypothesis of violent death without cannibalism.

There were other such sites evidencing violence in the Gallina area. One was described in a popular article by Frank C. Hibben (1944), who in 1934 excavated the first of several of the 500 Gallina sites with towers he had located in an area 56 by 80 km (35 by 50 miles). The tower was square, 7.6–10.7 m (25–35 feet) high, and 6 by 6 m (20 by 20 feet) in the interior. We know nothing else about the site or

Taphonomic Evidence

Table 3.33
Bone Elements and Perimortem Damage at Largo-Gallina Bg2

| SKELETAL ELEMENT | WHOLE | FRAGMENTS | IMPACT BREAKS | BURNING | CHEWING |
|---|---|---|---|---|---|
| Cranial | | | | | |
|   Maxilla | 1 | 11 | 0 | 11 | 0 |
|   Mandible | 1 | 31 | 3 | 29 | 0 |
|   Frontal | 1 | 7 | 0 | 7 | 0 |
|   Parietal | 4 | 2 | 0 | 4 | 0 |
|   Occipital | 2 | 6 | 0 | 5 | 0 |
|   Temporal | 2 | 6 | 0 | 4 | 0 |
|   Teeth (not counted) | | | | | |
|   Fragments | — | 240 | 0 | 215 | 0 |
| Postcranial | | | | | |
|   Cervical vertebrae | 23 | 9 | 0 | 4 | 0 |
|   Thoracic vertebrae | 19 | 19 | 0 | 3 | 0 |
|   Lumbar vertebrae | 10 | 7 | 0 | 3 | 0 |
|   Vertebrae fragments | — | 174 | 0 | 154 | 18 |
|   Sacrum | 2 | 2 | 0 | 1 | 0 |
|   Scapula | 1 | 25 | 0 | 15 | 0 |
|   Clavicle | 3 | 6 | 0 | 3 | 1 |
|   Rib | 13 | 245 | 0 | 154 | 1 |
|   Humerus | 1 | 39 | 0 | 36 | 1 |
|   Radius | 1 | 8 | 0 | 7 | 0 |
|   Ulna | 1 | 7 | 0 | 7 | 0 |
|   Hand & foot | 39 | 157 | 0 | 163 | 0 |
|   Pelvis | 1 | 72 | 0 | 67 | 1 |
|   Femur | 4 | 37 | 0 | 28 | 1 |
|   Tibia | 3 | 11 | 0 | 11 | 1 |
|   Fibula | 0 | 14 | 0 | 8 | 0 |
|   Patella | 7 | 1 | 0 | 3 | 2 |
|   Long bone fragments | — | 1,332 | 0 | 1,301 | 3 |
| Bone type unknown | 0 | 80 | 0 | 80 | 0 |
| TOTAL (2,687) | 139 | 2,548 | 3 | 2,323 | 29 |
| PERCENTAGE | 5.2 | 94.8 | 0.1 | 86.4 | 1.1 |

Percentage of expected vertebrae = approx. 24.5 (94 of 384; MNI = 16).[a]

NOTE: Only elements that were present are listed. No anvil abrasions, cut marks, or polishing was observed. Impact breakage and burning represent perimortem damage. Chewing is postmortem damage.

a. Fragmentation size suggests that about five fragments could represent one whole vertebra.

its exact location, but inside the tower were 16 burned bodies. Hibben described some of them. One woman had 16 arrows in her chest and stomach. She held a short oak bow. Two men had fallen from the roof and were found one on top of the other. One of the men held two bows in one hand and 27 arrows in the other. The second man had a stone axe still embedded in his cranium over the left eye. Another woman had an arrow in her shoulder. There were other "warriors," and in the ventilating shaft was a 15- to 16-year-old boy with one arrow in his hip. The boy was thought to have burned alive (Hibben 1944:68).

Hibben went on to say that in subsequent years of excavation, he and his helpers found another tower with a similar situation, but there were only five defenders. A third tower had 11 bodies, one again be-

Figure 3.157. Largo-Gallina area, site Bg2, New Mexico. Shown is perimortem burning of an abnormally developed mandible that belonged to an adult female?, one of 16 people found in a burned structure. In the background is another of her developmental anomalies—fused first and second cervical vertebrae. Individual no. 14, Maxwell Museum of Anthropology (CGT neg. 6-6-92:10).

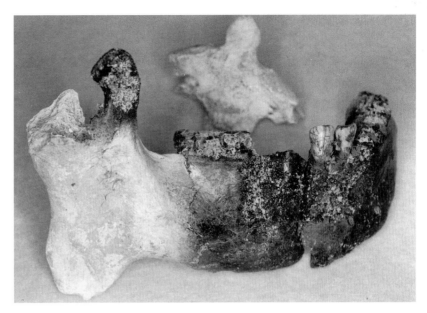

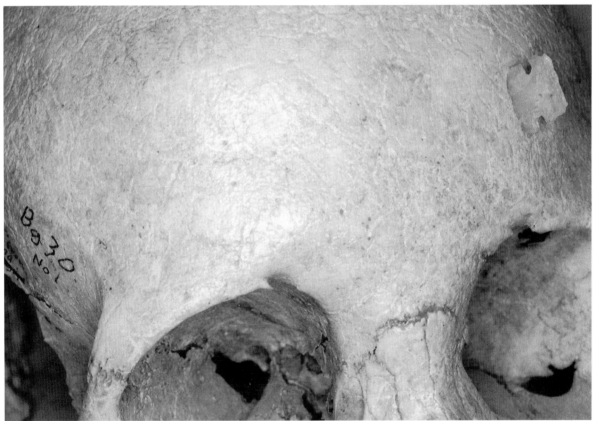

Figure 3.158. Largo-Gallina area. Perimortem arrow wound without bone reaction in the forehead of an adult female skull from Bg30, a site with few records. Bone condition, heavy coverage by root tracks, and cranial morphology correspond well to other, well-provenienced prehistoric remains in the Largo-Gallina area. The photograph is included here because of archaeological references to fatal arrow wounds at Bg2; all the Bg2 skeletal material with embedded arrows, however, has been lost. Individual no. 1, Maxwell Museum, University of New Mexico (CGT neg. 6-6-92:9).

ing a woman with a bow in her hand. By 1941 he had excavated 17 towers, all burned and all containing bodies. Tree-ring cutting dates placed construction of at least two towers at A.D. 1143–1248 (Hibben 1944:70).

| | |
|---|---|
| **35**<br>**Largo-Gallina Bg3** | **Claim Date.** 1979. |

**Claimants.** James Mackey and Roger C. Green.

**Claim Type.** Violence and cannibalism.

**Other Designations.** Nogales Cliff-House.

**Site Location.** About 21 km (13 miles) northeast of Lindrith, northwestern New Mexico, in a small side *rincon* off the larger Nogales (or "Spring") Canyon. We estimate the site to be located in USGS Llaves quadrangle (Provisional Edition 1983), T 25N, R 1E (Spring Canyon) in Sec. 6, 7, 18.

**Site Type.** Cliff dwelling. Eleven houses and 13 storage rooms or cists were excavated.

**Cultural Affiliation.** Largo-Gallina Anasazi.

**Chronology.** A.D. 1100–1300. Wooden beams from "Balcony House" provided a tree-ring date of 1264.

**Excavator and Date.** E. H. Blumenthal, Jr., and Carroll Burroughs, 1939.

**Institutional Storage.** Maxwell Museum of Anthropology, University of New Mexico, Albuquerque.

**Site Reports.** Blumenthal (1940); Mackey and Green (1979).

**Osteological Reports.** Lange (1940); Turner, Turner, and Green (1993).

**Skeletal Evidence of Stress.** None.

**Burial Context.** Unit House 5 contained nine individuals, mostly children. Seven burials were found in various locations near House 5.

**Associated Artifacts.** None reported.

**Figures.** 3.159–3.161.

**Taphonomy.** CGT and JAT. Skeletal inventory is in table 3.35.

    *MNI.* 11 (table 3.34).

    *Age and Sex.* Two adult males; two adults, male?; two adult females; one adult, sex?; one 15- to 18-year-old; three 4- to 6-year-olds.

    *Preservation.* Fair to good.

    *Bone and Fragment Number.* 303.

    *Breakage.* 6.9%.

    *Cut Marks.* 0.3%.

    *Burning.* 0.0%.

    *Anvil Abrasions.* 1.0%.

    *Polishing.* None.

    *Vertebrae Number.* 14.0% of expected (37 of 264).

    *Scalping.* Possible. One parietal bone has cut marks.

    *Gnawing, Rodent.* None.

    *Chewing, Carnivore.* None.

    *Insect Parts.* None found during skeletal examination.

    *Other Modification.* None.

**Archaeologist's Interpretation.** Blumenthal (1940:12) thought that the cliff house showed signs of abandonment rather than sacking.

**Other Interpretations.** Mackey and Green (1979:146–147) listed the

Table 3.34
Minimal Number of Individuals (MNI) at Largo-Gallina Bg3

| SKELETAL ELEMENT | AGE | SEX | NOTES |
|---|---|---|---|
| Maxilla, whole | Adult | M | Individual 60/14 |
| Mandible, whole + other | Adult | ? | Individual 60/7 |
| Postcranial | Adult | M | Individual 60/3 |
| Cranium | Adult | M? | Individual 60/11 |
| Skull | Adult | M? | Individual 60/8 |
| Skull + postcranial | Adult | F | 60/4 postcranial and 60/5 |
| Skull + postcranial | Adult | F | Individual 60/10 |
| Cranium | 15–18 | F? | Individual 60/? |
| Cranium | 4–6 | ? | Individual 60/3 |
| Skull | 4–6 | ? | Individual 60/4 |
| Whole skeleton | 4–6 | ? | Individual 60/9 |

SUMMARY: Eleven individuals. Two adult males; two adults, male?; two adult females; one adult, sex?; one 15- to 18-year-old female?; three 4- to 6-year-old children.

Table 3.35
Bone Elements and Perimortem Damage at Largo-Gallina Bg3

| SKELETAL ELEMENT | WHOLE | FRAGMENTS | IMPACT BREAKS | ANVIL ABRASIONS | CUT MARKS |
|---|---|---|---|---|---|
| **Cranial** | | | | | |
| Maxilla | 6 | 0 | 4 | 0 | 0 |
| Mandible | 3 | 1 | 1 | 0 | 0 |
| Frontal | 4 | 3 | 4 | 2 | 0 |
| Parietal | 13 | 3 | 8 | 0 | 1 |
| Occipital | 6 | 2 | 3 | 1 | 0 |
| Temporal | 11 | 0 | 1 | 0 | 0 |
| Fragments | — | 3 | 0 | 0 | 0 |
| **Postcranial** | | | | | |
| Cervical vertebrae | 7 | 0 | 0 | 0 | 0 |
| Thoracic vertebrae | 22 | 0 | 0 | 0 | 0 |
| Lumbar vertebrae | 8 | 0 | 0 | 0 | 0 |
| Sacrum | 1 | 1 | 0 | 0 | 0 |
| Scapula | 6 | 0 | 0 | 0 | 0 |
| Clavicle | 2 | 1 | 0 | 0 | 0 |
| Rib | 35 | 5 | 0 | 0 | 0 |
| Humerus | 6 | 0 | 0 | 0 | 0 |
| Radius | 5 | 0 | 0 | 0 | 0 |
| Ulna | 5 | 0 | 0 | 0 | 0 |
| Hand & foot | 116 | 0 | 0 | 0 | 0 |
| Pelvis | 7 | 0 | 0 | 0 | 0 |
| Femur | 6 | 0 | 0 | 0 | 0 |
| Tibia | 7 | 0 | 0 | 0 | 0 |
| Fibula | 5 | 0 | 0 | 0 | 0 |
| Patella | 3 | 0 | 0 | 0 | 0 |
| Long bone fragments | — | 0 | 0 | 0 | 0 |
| TOTAL (303) | 284 | 19 | 21 | 3 | 1 |
| PERCENTAGE | 93.7 | 6.3 | 6.9 | 1.0 | 0.3 |

Percentage of expected vertebrae = 14.0 (37 of 264; MNI = 11).

NOTE: Only elements that were present are listed. No burning, polishing, chewing, or gnawing was observed. Impact breakage, anvil abrasions, and cut marks represent perimortem damage.

238

Figure 3.159. Largo-Gallina area, site Bg3. This adult male? had been hit several times, which broke his front teeth and supporting alveolar bone. He had been struck additionally on the forehead, left parietal, and occipital area. There are scalping cut marks on the left parietal. Individual 60/8, Maxwell Museum of Anthropology (CGT neg. 6-6-92:14; reprinted with permission from *Journal of Anthropological Research*).

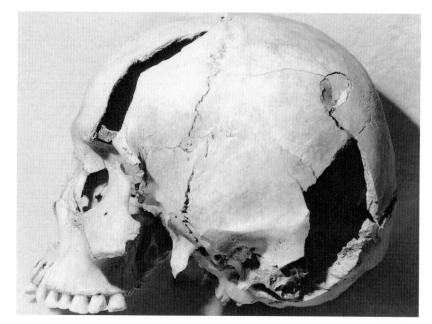

Figure 3.160. Largo-Gallina area, site Bg3. Another adult male? cranium with perimortem trauma. This man received two impact blows to the left and right parietals (external view) and another on the forehead (not shown). Individual 60/11, Maxwell Museum of Anthropology (CGT neg. 6-6-92:17; reprinted with permission from *Journal of Anthropological Research*).

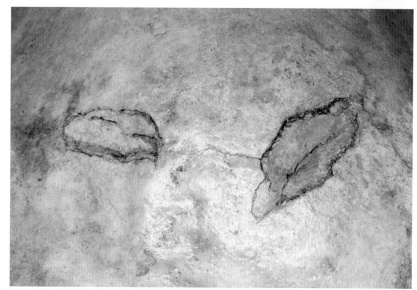

Figure 3.161. Largo-Gallina area, site Bg3. Internal cranial damage from the percussion wounds shown in figure 3.160. Individual 60/11, Maxwell Museum of Anthropology (CGT neg. 6-6-92:15; reprinted with permission from *Journal of Anthropological Research*).

Bg3 skeletons as among those evidencing violent death because they showed disarticulation and possibly embedded projectile points. In their summary (1979:153) they included Bg3 as a possibly cannibalized site.

**Discussion.** We believe cannibalism is not indicated because of the absence of burning and the minimal amount of postcranial damage. Our taphonomic analysis favors Mackey and Green's suggestion of violence rather than Blumenthal's suggestion of simple abandonment. The demographic profile and perimortem damage suggest that women and children could have been taken captive during the violent episode represented by this skeletal assemblage. We do not know the basis on which Blumenthal suggested the number of children. Possibly he and Burroughs were unable to recover all the skeletons. Nevertheless, there is still a deficiency of women and children. Turner, Turner, and Green (1993:91) proposed that "the Bg3 bodies were apparently not exposed to postmortem animal scavenging, suggesting an attack in winter with covering snowfall."

**36**
**Largo-Gallina Bg20**

**Claim Date.** 1979.

**Claimants.** James Mackey and Roger C. Green.

**Claim Type.** Violence and cannibalism.

**Other Designations.** Rattlesnake Point; Bloody Bucket.

**Site Location.** On south end of Rattlesnake Point, about 32 km (20 miles) northeast of Lindrith, New Mexico. USGS Cañada Ojitos quadrangle (Provisional Edition 1983), T 26N, R 1E, Sec. 15.

**Site Type.** Habitation site consisting of two pithouses, a tower with an exterior cist, a unit house, and a reservoir.

**Cultural Affiliation.** Largo-Gallina.

**Chronology.** A.D. 1100–1300; tower, 1085.

**Excavator and Date.** Frank C. Hibben, 1947 (tower); Thomas N. Bahti, 1948 (pithouse and surface structures).

**Institutional Storage.** Maxwell Museum of Anthropology, University of New Mexico, Albuquerque.

**Site Reports.** Bahti (1949); Mackey and Green (1979).

**Osteological Report.** Turner, Turner, and Green (1993).

**Skeletal Evidence of Stress.** None.

**Burial Context.** Eleven skeletons on pithouse floor and two on tower floor.

**Associated Artifacts.** Bahti found pottery, stone tools, and two bone awls in the pithouse. He made no claim that these objects were directly associated with the human skeletal remains.

**Figures.** 3.162 and 3.163.

**Taphonomy.** CGT and JAT. Skeletal inventory is in table 3.37.

*MNI.* 13 (table 3.36).

*Age and Sex.* Eight adult males; two adult females; one adult, sex?; two 11- to 12-year-olds. Bahti mentioned also finding a one-year-old infant.

*Preservation.* Good.

*Bone and Fragment Number.* 715.

*Breakage.* 14.3%.

*Cut Marks.* 1.0%.

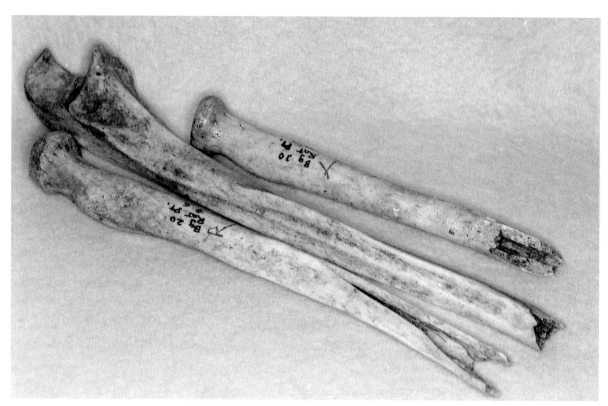

Figure 3.162. Largo-Gallina area, site Bg20. Parry fractures of lower arm bones of an adult male. Individual no. 6, Maxwell Museum of Anthropology (CGT neg. 6-6-92:1; reprinted with permission from *Journal of Anthropological Research*).

Table 3.36
Minimal Number of Individuals (MNI) at Largo-Gallina Bg20

| SKELETAL ELEMENT | AGE | SEX | NOTES |
|---|---|---|---|
| Mandible, left | Adult | M | Individual 2B |
| Right femurs, eight | Adult | M | Individuals without numbers |
| Skull + postcranial | Adult | M | Individual 1 |
| Skull + other fragments | Adult | M | Individual 1B |
| Skull + postcranial | Adult | M | Individual 2 |
| Postcranial | Adult | M | Individual 4 |
| Postcranial | Adult | M | Individual 5 |
| Postcranial | Adult | M | Individual 6 |
| Pelvis | Adult | M | Individual 7 |
| Cranium + postcranial | Adult | M | Individual 9 |
| Left + right femurs | Adult | M | Individual 10 |
| Postcranial | Adult | F | Individual 3 |
| Pelvis | Adult | F | Individual 7 |
| Cranium + postcranial | Adult | ? | Individual without number |
| Skull | 11–12 | ? | Individual 4 |
| Skull | 11–12 | ? | Individual without number |

SUMMARY: 13 individuals. Eight adult males; two adult females; one adult, sex?; two 11- to 12-year-old children.

Figure 3.163. Largo-Gallina area, site Bg20. Adult male left femur with impact breakage and associated chopping marks, more of which are present on left tibia. In addition, this man had percussion breakage of his mandible, forehead, both temporal bones, both clavicles, both scapulas, right humerus, and right fibula. Because there are no anvil abrasions with any of this breakage, he must have been hammered and mutilated in the flesh, possibly while alive. Individual no. 1, Maxwell Museum of Anthropology (CGT neg. 6-6-92:24; reprinted with permission from *Journal of Anthropological Research*).

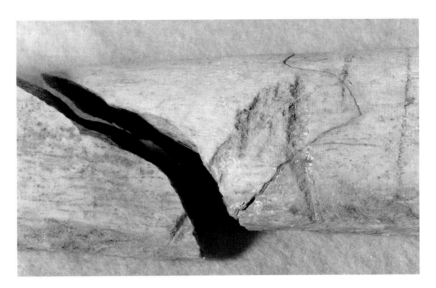

Table 3.37
Bone Elements and Perimortem Damage at Largo-Gallina Bg20

| SKELETAL ELEMENT | WHOLE | FRAGMENTS | IMPACT BREAKS | ANVIL ABRASIONS | CUT MARKS | CHEWING |
|---|---|---|---|---|---|---|
| Cranial | | | | | | |
|   Maxilla | 5 | 0 | 5 | 0 | 0 | 0 |
|   Mandible | 4 | 6 | 5 | 0 | 0 | 0 |
|   Frontal | 2 | 7 | 7 | 0 | 0 | 0 |
|   Parietal | 6 | 8 | 12 | 1 | 0 | 0 |
|   Occipital | 3 | 4 | 4 | 0 | 0 | 0 |
|   Temporal | 6 | 8 | 6 | 0 | 0 | 0 |
|   Fragments | — | 60 | 37 | 0 | 0 | 0 |
| Postcranial | | | | | | |
|   Cervical vertebrae | 42 | 4 | 0 | 0 | 0 | 0 |
|   Thoracic vertebrae | 66 | 0 | 0 | 0 | 0 | 0 |
|   Lumbar vertebrae | 27 | 4 | 0 | 0 | 0 | 0 |
|   Vertebrae fragments | — | 40 | 0 | 0 | 0 | 0 |
|   Sacrum | 6 | 3 | 1 | 0 | 0 | 0 |
|   Scapula | 4 | 7 | 2 | 0 | 0 | 0 |
|   Clavicle | 4 | 7 | 2 | 0 | 0 | 0 |
|   Rib | 30 | 144 | 10 | 0 | 0 | 0 |
|   Humerus | 10 | 3 | 2 | 0 | 3 | 1 |
|   Radius | 4 | 6 | 2 | 0 | 1 | 0 |
|   Ulna | 4 | 7 | 1 | 0 | 0 | 0 |
|   Hand & foot | 94 | 0 | 0 | 0 | 0 | 0 |
|   Pelvis | 10 | 4 | 0 | 0 | 0 | 1 |
|   Femur | 15 | 1 | 2 | 1 | 1 | 1 |
|   Tibia | 14 | 1 | 2 | 0 | 1 | 3 |
|   Fibula | 11 | 1 | 2 | 0 | 0 | 0 |
|   Patella | 8 | 1 | 0 | 0 | 1 | 0 |
|   Long bone fragments | — | 14 | 0 | 0 | 0 | 0 |
| TOTAL (715) | 375 | 340 | 102 | 2 | 7 | 6 |
| PERCENTAGE | 52.4 | 47.5 | 14.3 | 0.3 | 1.0 | 0.8 |

Percentage of expected vertebrae = approx. 46.5 (145 of 312; MNI = 13).[a]

NOTE: Only elements that were present are listed. No burning or polishing was observed. Impact breakage, anvil abrasions, and cut marks represent perimortem damage. Chewing is postmortem damage.

a. Fragmentation size suggests that about five fragments could represent one whole vertebra.

*Burning.* 0.0%.
*Anvil Abrasions.* 0.3%.
*Polishing.* 0.0%.
*Vertebrae Number.* 46.5% of expected (145 of 312).
*Scalping.* None.
*Gnawing, Rodent.* None.
*Chewing, Carnivore.* 0.8%.
*Insect Parts.* None found during skeletal examination.
*Other Modification.* None.

**Archaeologist's Interpretation.** Bahti (1949:55) reported: "Ten adult skeletons were found in a heap in the north portion of the pit house, and one infant's skeleton (about one year old) was located at the bottom of the ventilating shaft. All of the adult skulls exhibited premortem fractures; four contain arrow points. Six flint chips of unknown use were found in close association with the skeletons; one is embedded below the left eye of one of the skulls. One foot and one lower arm show indications of having been cut. No other tarsals or metatarsals were present. . . . From the position of the skeletons, it is apparent that the pit house had been abandoned for some time before the bodies were thrown in."

**Other Interpretations.** Mackey and Green (1979:146–147) proposed cannibalism for four of the skeletons based on the older and simpler three-criteria test (perimortem cutting, breakage, and burning) of Flinn, Turner, and Brew (1976).

**Discussion.** Because of the lack of bone burning at Bg20, it, like Bg3, fails both the older and the newer, more rigorous six-criteria test for proposing cannibalism. An acceptable scenario is that of a violent raid coupled with the taking of female and child captives at Bg20, as seen in the demographic profile and perimortem damage.

## 37
## Largo-Gallina Bg51

**Claim Date.** 1979.
**Claimants.** James Mackey and Roger C. Green.
**Claim Type.** Violence and cannibalism.
**Other Designations.** None known.
**Site Location.** On a ridge on the west side of the Continental Divide. Gavin Wash is to the east, Starve Out Canyon to the west. The site is also north of Cañada Larga, the eastern branch of Largo Wash, about 11 km (7 miles) west of Lindrith, New Mexico. USGS Billy Rice Canyon quadrangle (1963), T 24N, R 3W, NW ¼ of Sec. 10.
**Site Type.** Unit house associated with masonry tower.
**Cultural Affiliation.** Largo-Gallina Anasazi.
**Chronology.** A.D. 1100–1300.
**Excavator and Date.** Uncertain, but likely Frank C. Hibben, early 1930s.
**Institutional Storage.** Maxwell Museum of Anthropology, University of New Mexico, Albuquerque.
**Site Report.** Mackey and Green (1979).
**Osteological Report.** Turner, Turner, and Green (1993).
**Skeletal Evidence of Stress.** None evident.
**Burial Context.** Burned skeletons scattered on tower floor.
**Associated Artifacts.** Undetermined.

Table 3.38
Minimal Number of Individuals (MNI) at Largo-Gallina Bg51

| SKELETAL ELEMENT | AGE | SEX | NOTES |
|---|---|---|---|
| Cranium + postcranial | Adult | M? | Individual 60/45a |
| Skull fragments + other | Adult | ? | Individual 4 |
| Skull fragments + other | Adult | ? | Individual 22 |

SUMMARY: Three individuals. One adult male?; two adults, sex?.

Table 3.39
Bone Elements and Perimortem Damage at Largo-Gallina Bg51

| SKELETAL ELEMENT | WHOLE | FRAGMENTS | BURNING |
|---|---|---|---|
| Cranial | | | |
| Mandible | 0 | 2 | 2 |
| Frontal | 0 | 0 | 0 |
| Parietal | 0 | 2 | 2 |
| Occipital | 0 | 1 | 0 |
| Temporal | 0 | 3 | 1 |
| Fragments | — | 30 | 30 |
| Postcranial | | | |
| Cervical vertebrae | 3 | 0 | 3 |
| Clavicle | 0 | 1 | 1 |
| Rib | 0 | 4 | 4 |
| Hand & foot | 0 | 2 | 2 |
| Pelvis | 0 | 2 | 2 |
| Long bone fragments | — | 66 | 66 |
| Bone type unknown | 0 | 100 | 100 |
| TOTAL (216) | 3 | 213 | 213 |
| PERCENTAGE | 1.4 | 98.6 | 98.6 |

Percentage of expected vertebrae = 4.2 (3 of 72; MNI = 3).

NOTE: Only elements that were present are listed. No impact breaks, anvil abrasions, cut marks, polishing, gnawing, or chewing was observed. Burning represents perimortem damage.

**Figures.** None.
**Taphonomy.** CGT and JAT. Skeletal inventory is in table 3.39.

> *MNI.* 3 (table 3.38).
> *Age and Sex.* One adult, male?; two adults, sex?.
> *Preservation.* Poor due to extensive burning.
> *Bone and Fragment Number.* 216.
> *Breakage.* 0.0%.
> *Cut Marks.* 0.0%.
> *Burning.* 98.6%.
> *Anvil Abrasions.* 0.0%.
> *Polishing.* 0.0%.
> *Vertebrae Number.* 4.2% of expected (3 of 72); most loss attributable to burning.
> *Scalping.* 0.0%.
> *Gnawing, Rodent.* 0.0%.
> *Chewing, Carnivore.* 0.0%.

*Insect Parts.* None found during skeletal examination.

*Other Modification.* None recognized.

Archaeologist's Interpretation. Unknown.

Other Interpretations. Violence (Mackey and Green 1979).

Discussion. "There is no perimortem damage pointing to cannibalism, and were it not for the archaeological field observations, we would be on shaky grounds even to suggest violence in this case" (Turner, Turner, and Green 1993:104).

---

**38**

**Largo-Gallina Bg88B**

Claim Date. 1979.

Claimants. James Mackey and Roger C. Green.

Claim Type. Violence.

Other Designations. None known.

Site Location. Same as Bg51.

Site Type. Three ridge-top pithouses, one connected by tunnel to a large defensive tower.

Cultural Affiliation. Largo-Gallina Anasazi.

Chronology. A.D. 1100–1300.

Excavator and Date. Roger C. Green, 1957.

Institutional Storage. Maxwell Museum of Anthropology, University of New Mexico, Albuquerque.

Site Report. Mackey and Green (1979).

Osteological Report. Turner, Turner, and Green (1993).

Skeletal Evidence of Stress. None identifiable.

Burial Context. Multiple skeletons on pithouse floor.

Associated Artifacts. Green found an 18-by-25.4-cm (7-by-10-inch) stone object close to the left shoulder of skeleton 3. On his field map he called this object a *tiponi* stone—an artifact known ethnographically as "the most sacred fetish of the religious society associated with [a given] clan" (Ellis 1951:195).

Figure. 3.164.

Taphonomy. CGT and JAT. Skeletal inventory is in table 3.41.

    *MNI.* 11 (table 3.40).

    *Age and Sex.* Eight adult males; two 15- to 18-year-old males; one 12-year-old, sex?

    *Preservation.* Poor.

    *Bone and Fragment Number.* 1,592.

    *Breakage.* 0.4%.

    *Cut Marks.* 0.0%.

    *Burning.* 0.0%.

    *Anvil Abrasions.* 0.0%.

    *Polishing.* 0.0%.

    *Vertebrae Number.* 56.1% of expected (148 of 264).

    *Scalping.* 0.0%.

    *Gnawing, Rodent.* 0.0%.

    *Chewing, Carnivore.* 0.0%.

    *Insect Parts.* None found during skeletal examination.

    *Other Modification.* None seen.

Archaeologist's Interpretation. Violence. Excerpts from Green's field notes reveal the episodic violence that produced the charnel deposit:

Figure 3.164. Largo-Gallina area, site Bg88B. Remains of massacred adults and adolescents on pithouse floor. The infant that was discovered in the ventilating shaft is not in view. Photograph by Roger C. Green (July 1957).

Table 3.40
Minimal Number of Individuals (MNI) at Largo-Gallina Bg88B

| SKELETAL ELEMENT | AGE | SEX | NOTES |
|---|---|---|---|
| Cranium + postcranial | Adult | M | Individual 60/1 |
| Cranium + postcranial | Adult | M | Individual 60/2 |
| Vault + postcranial | Adult | M | Individual 60/3 |
| Cranium + postcranial | Adult | M | Individual 60/4 |
| Cranium + postcranial | Adult | M | Individual 60/5 |
| Cranium + postcranial | Adult | M | Individual 60/6 |
| Skull + postcranial | Adult | M | Individual 60/7 |
| Skull + postcranial | Adult | M | Individual 60/11 |
| Cranium + postcranial | 15–18 | M | Individual 60/8 |
| Cranium + postcranial | 15–18 | M | Individual 60/9 |
| Cranium + postcranial | 12 | ? | Individuals 60/7, 60/10, 60/11 |

SUMMARY: 11 individuals. Eight adult males; two 15- to 18-year-old males; one 12-year-

July 24, 1957. In afternoon worked in Bg88B-pithouse. I was working at 4–6' level in north end of pithouse attempting to work out relationship between tunnel and pithouse. At 6½ feet in depth—4 feet 8 inches out from wall was a large flat stone dipping in fill to the west. Just behind it I found what appear to be human bones. On the east side of tunnel a block of bench appears to have broken away and slopes foreward—Right at the break I found another bone. It looks to be an arm bone.

July 25, 1957—Thurs On bench 62" west from Stake 0 at north end of pithouse I found human patella. It appeared right below a rodent hole in that area, which probably explains its presence.

Table 3.41
Bone Elements and Perimortem Damage at Largo-Gallina Bg88B

| SKELETAL ELEMENT | WHOLE | FRAGMENTS | IMPACT BREAKS |
|---|---|---|---|
| Cranial | | | |
| Maxilla | 9 | 5 | 2 |
| Mandible | 10 | 3 | 0 |
| Frontal | 7 | 4 | 0 |
| Parietal | 15 | 4 | 0 |
| Occipital | 6 | 6 | 0 |
| Temporal | 18 | 2 | 0 |
| Fragments | — | 117 | 3 |
| | | | |
| Postcranial | | | |
| Cervical vertebrae | 24 | 28 | 0 |
| Thoracic vertebrae | 70 | 9 | 0 |
| Lumbar vertebrae | 19 | 3 | 0 |
| Vertebrae fragments | — | 135 | 0 |
| Sacrum | 7 | 5 | 0 |
| Scapula | 2 | 26 | 0 |
| Clavicle | 4 | 13 | 0 |
| Rib | 0 | 241 | 0 |
| Humerus | 16 | 10 | 0 |
| Radius | 9 | 11 | 0 |
| Ulna | 9 | 14 | 0 |
| Hand & foot | 505 | 3 | 0 |
| Pelvis | 13 | 18 | 0 |
| Femur | 20 | 4 | 0 |
| Tibia | 19 | 7 | 1 |
| Fibula | 10 | 21 | 0 |
| Patella | 10 | 0 | 0 |
| Long bone fragments | — | 50 | 0 |
| | | | |
| Bone type unknown | 0 | 51 | 0 |
| | | | |
| TOTAL (1,592) | 802 | 790 | 6 |
| PERCENTAGE | 50.4 | 49.6 | 0.4 |

Percentage of expected vertebrae = 56.1 (148 of 264; MNI = 11).[a]

NOTE: Only elements that were present are listed. No anvil abrasions, cut marks, burning, polishing, gnawing, or chewing was observed. Impact breakage represents perimortem damage.

a. Fragmentation size suggests that about five fragments could represent one whole vertebra.

Cleared rest of bench in NW quadrant and picked up part of good wall above height of bench. On the North-east quadrant of Bg88 were found a number of skeletons. The one below [sketch shows adult on back with head against bench, complete except for missing left foot] is skeleton #1; its head is 10'4" from stake D [noted on sketch is "(1) humerus is broken off, (2) right foot was under a large stone, and (3), it was 2'4" from the pelvis to skull of #4"]. It is oriented North 65 East. Its height was 5'7".

A sketch of adult skeleton 4, shown on its back with its right arm upon the bench, has various positional measurements and notes that the left ulna is broken and the left hand missing. Adult skeleton 5, also on its back, is shown in two views: one from before a large stone was removed from its chest, with other stones nearby, and one from afterward, with notes of a broken rib and broken left ulna. Adult skeleton 9 was on its stomach. Sketch notes indicate a broken left humerus lying over a large stone, a broken neck, and a broken left tibia and fibula. The sketch also records that all of the nine skeletons in the northeast quadrant were lying on fallen roof material that had been burned. The skeletons were probably thrown in after the roof had burned down. Skeleton 10, a child, was found in the east bin near the deflector.

By July 31, Green had exposed most of the skeletal assemblage and had begun to take the bones out. He recorded what was present, and we quote a few lines from his notes indicating missing and damaged elements to give a sense of the complex situation: "Skeleton No 1—Left foot only calcaneus. Rt Hand—most, but not all. Rt arm—humerus—radius & ulna—all broken. Clavicle—both broken and sticking up vertically. Skeleton No 4 Left leg—complete—broken. Left arm—complete except for hand no hand in evidence Rt leg—complete—femur broken. Skeleton No 3—Skull—badly smashed by stone on top Left arm—hand bones burned? Rt leg—phalanges on the s wall side of foot are missing."

**Other Interpretations.** In Linda S. Cordell's (1989:319) discussion of conflict in the northern and central Rio Grande region of New Mexico, she argued that "despite the widely shared notion that Gallina sites reflect an unusual amount of burning and carnage, the number of burned Gallina pithouses is not uncommon in comparison to other southwestern pithouse villages . . . and some recent observations on the skeletal collections have failed to confirm great evidence of violence and burning (Maria Mercer, personal communication, 1984)."

When we inquired about Mercer's finding, Cordell (personal communication, February 22, 1993) replied that it was a remark that a graduate student had made to her. Mercer, under the supervision of Stanley Rhine, was studying bone-muscle development in the Maxwell Museum collections, not taphonomy or warfare.

**Discussion.** A skeletal assemblage showing perimortem trauma and consisting only of adult males and one adolescent is strong evidence of an attack, seemingly for the purpose of destroying the houses, killing the men, and taking the women and children captive. Were it not for Green's field notes, we could not be sure whether the missing hands and feet were perimortem or museum curation losses. His direct field observations permit the secure conclusion that in addition to killing the men, the assailants took some of their slain victims' body parts. Since there were no cut marks on any of the heads, scalps seem not to have been the trophies of choice.

The context of these bodies, found randomly tossed into a collapsed and burned pithouse, indicates a single violent episode and thus a substantial number of raiders, at least equal to the number killed, in order to successfully overwhelm the community. The lack of interment for the 11 individuals hints that aside from the probable captives, the community was destroyed. No one returned to bury those slain in the attack.

Claim Date. 1979.

Claimant. Paul R. Nickens, unpublished manuscript (the published account by R. A. Luebben and P. R. Nickens [1982] does not actually claim cannibalism).

Claim Type. Cannibalism (Nickens); violence (Luebben and Nickens).

Other Designations. None given.

Site Location. On the Ray Ismay ranch, 1.66 km (1 mile) southwest of Yucca House National Monument, southwestern Colorado. USGS Towaoc quadrangle (1966), T 34N, R 17W, SE ¼ of Sec. 34.

Site Type. Small village with kivas.

Cultural Affiliation. Mesa Verde Anasazi.

Chronology. On the basis of one tree-ring specimen and architectural features, Luebben (1983:19) suggested a date of late McElmo or early Mesa Verde phase (early Pueblo III, A.D. 1050–1150) for Kiva 2, where the human charnel deposit was found. Kiva 1 was used during the period 1150–1300.

Excavator and Date. Ralph A. Luebben, field director, 1974.

Institutional Storage. Not reported.

Site Reports. Luebben (1982, 1983); Luebben and Nickens (1982).

Osteological Reports. Nickens (1979); Luebben and Nickens (1982).

Skeletal Evidence of Stress. Cribra orbitalia reported.

Burial Context. Bone fragments in Kiva 2 recess pit and fill, in a corrugated vessel, and on the kiva floor. Up to 4.0 cm of ash was beneath the bone deposit.

Associated Artifacts. Mancos Corrugated jar, Mancos Black-on-white bird-form vessel, and two hammerstones. Other artifacts, including manos and an ax, were found on the kiva floor.

Figures. None.

Taphonomy. PRN.

*MNI.* 7.

*Age and Sex.* Two adult males; one adult female; one adult, sex?; one subadult, sex?; two 8- to 10-year-old children.

*Preservation.* Good.

*Bone and Fragment Number.* 380.

*Breakage.* 86.8%.

*Cut Marks.* 1.1%.

Burning. 13.4%.

*Vertebrae Number.* 7.1% of expected (12 of 168).

*Gnawing, Rodent.* 0.5%.

*There is no information for Anvil Abrasions, Polishing, Scalping, Chewing, Insect Parts, or Other Modification.*

Archaeologist's Interpretation. Ralph A. Luebben (1983:24) excavated the site during the summers of 1973 and 1974 with students from Grinnell College—hence the site's name. It contained a large, divided surface structure. Kiva 1 was linked to a one-story circular tower and a subterranean room by a long main tunnel and two short side spurs. Both kivas had burned, but at different times. The presence of bone fragments and artifacts on the floor of Kiva 2 suggested that the structure had been or was about to be abandoned when the bones were deposited. "The desire to bury the partial remains of the individuals in a sacred area may have been a motivating factor in selecting the kiva as a repository" (Luebben and Nickens 1982:78).

Because there were missing skeletal elements, Luebben and Nickens proposed that the individuals died or were "massacred" outside Kiva 2. Independently, Luebben (1983:10, 12) wrote that in Kiva 2 there was

> a mass interment of some disarticulated and largely fragmented bones of at least seven persons of both sexes and varying ages [that] were recovered from a cist situated in the southeast corner of the southern recess. A layer of mixed bones covered the cist bottom and supported a corrugated jar that contained more bones. When these had been transported to the cist, a few had dropped onto and remained on the kiva floor and recess. Some bones demonstrate spiral fracturing, cutting and charring. The fractures and cut marks on long bones and sharp angled breaks on skull fragments are products of human activity and suggest abusive treatment of the dead.

Luebben concluded that the Grinnell architectural features, including the tower, had served as a neighborhood religious center whose inhabitants attended more important ceremonies at nearby Yucca House. He had no idea what the nature of those ceremonies was, and he lamented that 100 years of archaeology had produced little knowledge about Anasazi religion. Because of his explicit concern, it is puzzling that he did not discuss the Kiva 2 human charnel deposit in this context. Surely a site that had primarily a ceremonial function and also a mass of cut, broken, and burned bones from 11 people should have triggered interesting speculation about, if not insight into, the sorts of religious practices that might have been going on. As we write in 1997, however, we know of several sites in the Four Corners area where human remains suggestive of violence and cannibalism have been unearthed. Some of them have been found in kivas, others in storage pits, in refuse, and in habitation structures. Such a distribution strikes us as random, or at least as only weakly correlated with ceremonial architecture.

**Other Interpretations.** Nickens, in his unpublished osteological report (1979), suggested that cannibalism had occurred at the Grinnell site. Apparently Luebben did not agree, or preferred not to raise the issue because of its controversial nature. This reservation seems unnecessarily cautious in light of the fact that the fragmented, cut, and burned human bones were found mixed with obvious nonhuman food refuse—71 small and fragmentary bird, rodent, and other animal bones. One bird bone was said to have had a cluster of five cut marks.

**Discussion.** Luebben and Nickens believed that the Grinnell bone assemblage was very different from both normal Pueblo III inhumations and the other mass burials or charnel deposits known as of 1982. Today we know that this is not the case; similar kiva deposits and taphonomic conditions have been identified at nearby Yellow Jacket ruins (see site 51), at Aztec Wash on the Ute Mountain Indian Reservation, and elsewhere. Less-damaged charnel deposits have also been found in kivas—for example, Snider's Well. Nickens's taphonomic analysis definitely suggests cannibalism. To see whether this suggestion can be raised to a higher level of probability, the series should be reexamined for anvil abrasions and fragment polishing.

## 40
## Mariana Mesa

**Claim Date.** 1980.

**Claimant.** Charles R. McGimsey III.

**Claim Type.** Violence.

**Other Designations.** We have used Mariana Mesa for the name of this site because it is the title of the monograph by Charles R. McGimsey III, wherein the site is reported. There are three other designations: Site 616, Horse Camp Mill Site, and Shipman Site.

**Site Location.** About 29 km (18 miles) southeast of Fence Lake and 24 km (15 miles) northeast of Quemado, New Mexico. USGS Veteado Mountain quadrangle (1967), T 4N, R 15W, NE ¼ of SE ¼, Sec. 36.

**Site Type.** Large site with 500 contiguous surface rooms arranged in a hollow square, with pithouses, kiva, and walk-in well.

**Cultural Affiliation.** Mogollon.

**Chronology.** A.D. 1100–1300.

**Excavator and Date.** Charles R. McGimsey III and members of the Peabody Museum Upper Gila Expedition, 1950.

**Institutional Storage.** Uncertain.

**Site Report.** McGimsey (1980).

**Osteological Report.** McGimsey (1980).

**Skeletal Evidence of Stress.** None reported.

**Burial Context.** In Room C2, the skeleton of a young female was discovered beneath a mass of roof debris. In Room E1, a young adult male skeleton was found on the floor.

**Associated Artifacts.** The female had associated artifacts of stone and pottery near her. They had been burned and buried by the collapsed roof. The male had a small projectile point in his right leg.

**Figures.** None.

**Taphonomy.** CRM.

*MNI.* The two individuals identified above, plus 20 individuals in ten other rooms and two trenches (McGimsey 1980:170).

*Age and Sex.* Besides the adolescent female and young adult male, there were 18 other adults and 2 children.

*There is no information for Preservation, Bone and Fragment Number, Breakage, Cut Marks, Burning, Anvil Abrasions, Polishing, Vertebrae Number, Scalping, Gnawing, Chewing, Insect Parts, or Other Modification.*

**Archaeologist's Interpretation.** McGimsey (1980:16) suggested that conflict arising from escalating problems in agricultural productivity culminated in abandonment of the entire region. At Site 616 he found artifacts of all sorts left behind, which was in marked contrast to the other sites examined on Mariana Mesa, where household artifacts were rare. Site 616 also had some rooms with burned roofs and other conditions indicating violence. These conditions led McGimsey (1980:39) to conclude that "the abandonment of the pueblo was neither gradual nor carefully planned, and that the final exodus was probably made under duress." Moreover, the skeleton of a young girl was found in one room with a broken arm and the head bashed in. The skeleton was also burned, as was the roof material. A young adult male was found sprawled on the floor of another room. McGimsey's findings certainly point to "duress."

Elsewhere McGimsey (1980:73–74) described the female skeleton: "Her right arm had been broken off 9 cm below the shoulder (there was no indication of bone healing) and the lower portion of this arm was not found. In addition, an elongated oval hole (the size and shape of the cross section of the bit of a typical stone axe) in the top of her skull strongly suggested that she met a sudden and violent end."

McGimsey (1980:91) added details about the male skeleton: "A small projectile point was found lying between the tibia and fibula of the right leg midway between the knee and ankle. The occipital region of the skull showed slight evidence of having been battered, but this could have occurred at the time the roof collapsed."

At another site on Mariana Mesa, Site 143, McGimsey (1980:180) found "in the fill of the central area . . . a set of fully articulated lower legs of an adult." And at Site 494 (McGimsey 1980:247), portions of an adolescent male skeleton were recovered just above the floor of Kiva B. "Only the cranium, the clavicles, a fragment of a humerus, and a number of ribs and vertebrae were found, and probably did not represent a formal burial, since no artifacts were demonstrably in association."

**Other Interpretations.** Watson Smith (1992:183), field director for Harvard's Peabody Museum Upper Gila Expedition, but not on the site in 1950, agreed with McGimsey's scenario of the destruction of Site 616: "There was convincing evidence of external hostile attack, as shown by massive burning, dead bodies pierced by projectiles, and the clearly unpremeditated abandonment in situ of all household furnishings."

**Discussion.** As indicated, McGimsey found human skeletal remains in Mariana Mesa sites other than 616. Site 143, excavated in 1950 and 1951, consisted of several hundred rooms arranged in a rough circle around a large central ceremonial structure, approximately 7.6 km (4.75 miles) southwest of Site 616. The site was occupied in the 1200s. Site 494, two miles southwest of Site 616, was occupied earlier, 1100–1150. Site 494 was excavated in 1949 under the direction of Raymond H. Thompson.

If taphonomic analysis of these skeletal remains and of other isolated bones from a number of rooms excavated by McGimsey were to identify any perimortem damage, then the violence that increasingly seems to characterize the Anasazi area could be shown to extend also into the border zone of the adjacent Mogollon area. We are aware that farther south, the large Mogollon village called Point of Pines (Haury 1989) was burned and presumably attacked. However, no skeletal evidence for violence like that discovered in the Mariana Mesa area was reported at Point of Pines, nor have we identified any in our examination of part of that large skeletal series.

**41**
**Monument Valley**

**Claim Date.** 1982.

**Claimants.** G. Gisela Nass and Nicholas Bellantoni.

**Claim Type.** Cannibalism.

**Other Designations.** None known.

**Site Location.** In Monument Valley, between the San Juan River and Oljeto and Gypsum Washes, southern Utah. USGS Oljato quadrangle (1952), T 43S, R 14E, projected Sec. 35.

**Site Type.** Isolated, slab-lined fire pit 30 cm deep and 61 cm wide, near a large slump boulder without any known habitation or other structures or features in the immediate area.

**Cultural Affiliation.** Unknown, but location suggests Kayenta Anasazi.

**Chronology.** Unknown, but A.D. 900–1300 would be a reasonable guess.

**Excavator and Date.** J. Lee Correll, August 12, 1970.

**Institutional Storage.** Connecticut State Museum of Natural History, Storrs.

**Site Report.** None.

**Osteological Report.** Nass and Bellantoni (1982).

**Skeletal Evidence of Stress.** Not reported.

**Burial Context.** Fragmented human bones in a slab-lined pit.

**Associated Artifacts.** None.

**Figures.** 3.165 and 3.166.

**Taphonomy.** GGN and NB.

>*MNI.* 7.

>*Age and Sex.* One old adult male; one adult male; one old adult female; two adolescent females; one adolescent, sex?; one infant.

>*Preservation.* Not discussed, but publication photographs suggest good bone preservation.

>*Bone and Fragment Number.* 644.

>*Breakage.* 80.1%.

>*Cut Marks.* 0.9%.

>*Burning.* 12.6%.

>*Vertebrae Number.* 2.4% of expected (4 of 168).

>*Scalping.* None.

>*Gnawing, Rodent.* None.

>*Chewing, Carnivore.* None.

>*Other Modification.* None.

>*There is no information for Insect Parts, Anvil Abrasions, or Polishing.*

**Archaeologist's Interpretation.** J. Lee Correll excavated the skeletal remains in the summer of 1970 at the request of Navajo Tribal Ranger Wilbur Neez, stationed at Monument Valley Tribal Park. Correll's two-page typewritten report, dated August 12, 1970, says in part:

> Excavation revealed an area approximately 2 feet square containing disarticulated and cracked bones with crania of at least five individuals present—mandibles were not articulated with the crania. The base of the burial was 12 inches below the present surface and was lined with flat stones, with an upright slab on the southeast side of the burial pit. Three slabs covered most of the burial site.

Figure 3.165. Monument Valley, Utah. View of surrounding area from the cannibalized burial site. As at several other sites where cannibalism seems to have occurred, isolation and indefensiveness are evident here. Photograph by J. Lee Correll, 1970; courtesy G. Gisela Nass.

Figure 3.166. Monument Valley. View of location where J. Lee Correll excavated the cannibalized human remains. Correll's undeveloped excavation photographs, still in his camera, were lost when his camera was stolen soon after he completed the excavation. This and the previous view were retakes. Photograph by J. Lee Correll, 1970; courtesy G. Gisela Nass.

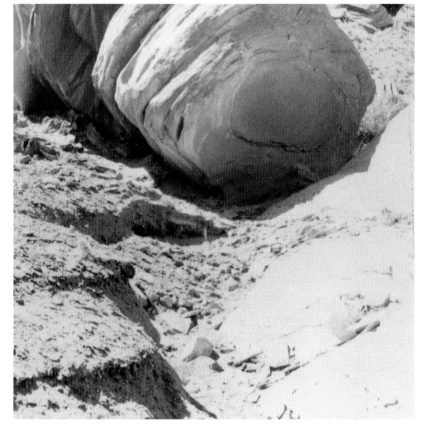

Some of the sandstone slabs indicated evidence of burning. Charcoal was located beneath and above the pile of bones, with some charcoal flakes among the bones. Besides the crania and mandibles, the burial contained numerous disarticulated ribs. The long bones were broken or splintered. There were no vertebrae present.

In a letter dated November 11, 1993, Nass told us how, after learning about the skeletal series, she contacted Correll, drove to Arizona to meet him, collected the skeletons, which he agreed to loan for study, and returned to Wisconsin. Nass also said that during her visit to Arizona, Correll remarked that he suspected the remains had been cannibalized.

**Other Interpretations.** In their published report, Nass and Bellantoni expressed the opinion that various lines of evidence indicated that the bone assemblage was a primary burial, that roasting of human flesh had occurred, and that the fire pit had been constructed for the purpose of roasting the deceased.

**Discussion.** Nass reconstructed the skulls and illustrated three of them. The bone appears to have been well preserved. There was mutilating damage to the faces. Nass and Bellantoni noted that all the crania had lambdoidal flattening, a characteristic of the San Juan Anasazi. Nass loaned us photographs of some of the charnel assemblage. In them, the flattening is evident. We agree, and further note that the facial and vault morphology appears to be more like that of later Pueblos than of earlier Basketmaker Anasazi or historic Navajos.

Nass also related in her 1993 letter that she and Correll had visited the site, examined the remains of the fire pit, and established that the site was just north of the Arizona border in southern Utah. In their published report, Nass and Bellantoni (1982) were unsure whether the site was in Arizona or Utah. Regardless of modern state boundaries, figures 3.165 and 3.166 show the isolation of the site, a characteristic of several of the human charnel deposits with probable cannibalism.

Although we agree with Nass and Bellantoni's cannibalism claim, this series would benefit from additional study to determine whether polishing and anvil abrasions are present.

On June 18, 1998, using Correll's site and site-area photos, the senior author, along with Olga Pavlova and writer-photographer team Douglas Preston and his wife Christine, were able to rediscover the Monument Valley site. It is located at the northwest base of Thunderbird Mesa, on a talus slope about five meters above the valley floor. From Correll's site the Three Sisters buttes can be seen to the northwest on the opposite side of the valley. We saw no indications of any other archaeological remains or structures in the vicinity except for one pottery sherd on the surface near Correll's fire pit location that seemed to be Dogoszhi Black-on-white. This type dates from A.D. 1070–1150. Two small cottonwood trees are located about 20 m east of the site, indicating the presence of a spring or seep. The site is markedly isolated and indefensible.

**42**
**Jones Ranch Road Site 7**

**Claim Date.** 1983.

**Claimant.** Roger Anyon.

**Claim Type.** Violence.

**Other Designations.** NM:12:U2:7.

**Site Location.** In road right-of-way, approximately 3.2 km (2 miles) west of N.M. 32 (now 602), approximately 4.8 km (3 miles) north of Whitewater Arroyo and 4.8 km (3 miles) south of Manuelito Canyon, New Mexico. USGS Vander Wagen quadrangle (1963), T 13N, R 19W, SE ¼ of SE ¼ of Sec. 36.

**Site Type.** Four-room masonry surface building with two subterranean pit structures, a trash midden, and extramural features.

**Cultural Affiliation.** Cibola Anasazi.

**Chronology.** Pit structure 3 had a tree-ring cutting date of A.D. 1214 and was probably in use after most of the rest of the site (dated by ceramics to 1000–1200) had been abandoned.

**Excavator and Date.** James Spain, 1980.

**Institutional Storage.** Skeletal remains were reburied without full professional analysis, 1981.

**Site Report.** Anyon (1983).

**Osteological Report.** Benshoof, Trumble, and Robertson (1983).

**Skeletal Evidence of Stress.** None found.

**Burial Context.** The remains of one individual were found between the floor and the severely burned roof of pit structure 3.

**Associated Artifacts.** Possibly. A Wingate Black-on-red bowl was recovered from the floor.

**Figures.** None.

**Taphonomy.** Lee R. Benshoof.

   *MNI.* 1.

   *Age and Sex.* Young adult female?

   *Preservation.* Poor.

   *Bone and Fragment Number.* Not reported. However, the burial was represented only by the lower extremities, a parietal fragment, and one rib fragment. The missing elements were attributed to backhoe destruction.

   *Breakage.* No perimortem breakage reported.

   *Burning.* Charring and some fracturing that may have been caused by thermal stress.

   *Vertebrae Number.* None.

   *There is no information for Cut Marks, Anvil Abrasions, Polishing, Scalping, Gnawing, Chewing, Insect Parts, or Other Modification.*

**Archaeologist's Interpretation.** Roger Anyon and Ben Robertson (1983:133–134) described the context as follows:

> It appears that the roof did not burn and collapse until sometime after the abandonment of pit structure 3. Directly above the floor, there was a thin (less than 10-cm-thick) layer of fill that appears to have resulted from natural deposition. Before the roof burned and collapsed, an adult female . . . was placed on the fill above floor. Unfortunately, backhoe trench 5 seems to have removed at least the skull. The body appeared to have been partially flexed, lying on its right side, with the skull facing towards the northeast or east.

To the south or southeast side of the probable skull location was an inverted Wingate Black-on-red bowl (item 104), the only item in close enough proximity to the skeleton to be considered a grave good. The roof burned and collapsed on top of these remains. Burned beams were found lying over the human remains, and in fact some of the bones were charred. We have specifically avoided using the term "burial" to describe these human remains because it is not entirely clear that this individual was actually interred. Usually a burial is considered to be a body that was covered after interment. In this case, the covering was a burning roof.

Anyon (1983:757) concluded: "Possible evidence of stress in the Jones Ranch Road sites takes two forms: burned structures and fragmentary human remains. . . . Some of the burned structures . . . may have been the results of violence. Fragmentary human remains were recovered at many of the excavated Jones Ranch Road sites."

**Other Interpretations.** None.

**Discussion.** Anyon and Robertson's Appendix D (1983) lists quantities of human skeletal elements found in the fill of six sites. Some of these are indicated as being fragments. Unfortunately for our purposes, information was not provided about whether any Site 7 breakage was perimortem, and because of reburial, further assessment is impossible. Consequently, the violence claim should be viewed cautiously.

## 43
## Chi Chil Tan Spur Road Site 108A

**Claim Date.** 1983.

**Claimant.** Roger Anyon.

**Claim Type.** Violence.

**Other Designations.** NM:12:U2:108A.

**Site Location.** In road right-of-way, approximately 2.8 km (1.75 miles) northwest of Chi Chil Tan, northwestern New Mexico, on a ridge overlooking the confluence of an unnamed arroyo and White Water Arroyo, which is about 1.2 km (0.75 mile) to the southwest. USGS Vander Wagen quadrangle (1963), T 12N, R 19W, NW ¼ of Sec. 8.

**Site Type.** Small settlement consisting of four pit structures, seven contiguous rooms, one separate surface masonry room, a trash area, storage pits, and other extramural features.

**Cultural Affiliation.** Cibola Anasazi.

**Chronology.** A.D. 1127, the preferred tree-ring date out of 24 that range between 942 and 1142.

**Excavator and Date.** Roger Anyon, 1981.

**Institutional Storage.** Skeletal remains from site presumably were reburied along with those from Jones Ranch Road Site 7.

**Site Report.** Anyon and Robertson (1983).

**Osteological Report.** Benshoof, Trumble, and Robertson (1983).

**Skeletal Evidence of Stress.** None indicated.

**Burial Context.** Bone fragments and loose teeth were recovered from fill in pit structures 1 and 3, in the fill of rooms 3 and 5, and as features in rooms 7 and 9.

**Associated Artifacts.** None reported.

**Figures.** None.

**Taphonomy.** None.

*MNI.* Not reported. Most of the human bone from Site 108A was identified by the faunal analyst, Kathleen M. Trumble, and Ben Robertson assembled a list of whole and fragmentary skeletal elements and teeth from the fill above the roof fall of pit structure 3. We suggest six individuals of unknown age and sex, because the report indicates that human bone was found in six different locations.

*Bone and Fragment Number.* Trumble listed each item from the site, including about two dozen pieces from pit structure 3. Robertson added a list of 40 pieces for the fill above the roof fall of pit structure 3.

*Vertebrae Number.* 4 fragments.

*There is no information for Age and Sex, Preservation, Breakage, Cut Marks, Burning, Anvil Abrasions, Polishing, Scalping, Gnawing, Chewing, Insect Parts, or Other Modification.*

**Archaeologist's Interpretation.** Concerning pit structure 3, Anyon and Robertson (1983:355) remarked: "The roof burned and collapsed directly onto the pit structure floor. The severity of the fire suggests that it was not accidental, but rather it was purposefully set." Trash then washed in quickly and included many small human bone fragments.

**Other Interpretations.** None.

**Discussion.** Our reaction here is the same as that for Jones Ranch Road Site 7. The skeletal remains were reburied before receiving adequate bioarchaeological or physical anthropological analysis.

**44
Ash Creek**

**Claim Date.** 1983.

**Claimant.** Christy G. Turner II.

**Claim Type.** Cannibalism.

**Other Designations.** Tapia del Cerrito; AZ U:3:49 (ASU); AZ U:3:22 (ASM).

**Site Location.** In Tonto Basin, about 8 km (5 miles) south of Punkin Center, on the west side of Ariz. 188, on crest of ridge at base of Mazatzal Mountains, central Arizona. Ash Creek is 1,000 m north of site. USGS Tonto Basin quadrangle (1964), T 5N, R 11E, S ½ of Sec. 7.

**Site Type.** Small pueblo of seven masonry rooms, two masonry granaries, and two ramadas, with two roasting pits, an extensive midden, and a large burial area.

**Cultural Affiliation.** Salado.

**Chronology.** A.D. 1350 (Gila phase).

**Excavator and Date.** John W. Hohmann, prior to and during 1983.

**Institutional Storage.** Department of Anthropology, Arizona State University, Tempe.

**Site Report.** Rice, Hantman, and Most (1982); Hohmann et al. (1985); Rice (1985).

**Osteological Report.** Turner (1983); Bassett and Atwell (1985).

**Skeletal Evidence of Stress.** Only one child from the relatively large cemetery had porotic hyperostosis. Everett J. Bassett and Karen A. Atwell (1985:233–234) judged the cemetery population to be relatively healthy.

**Burial Context.** Bones and bone fragments were found on the floor of

Table 3.42
Bone Elements and Perimortem Damage at Ash Creek

| SKELETAL ELEMENT | WHOLE | FRAGMENT | IMPACT BREAK | CUT MARK | BURN | GNAW/CHEW |
|---|---|---|---|---|---|---|
| Cranial | | | | | | |
| Skull, jaw | 0 | 1 | 1 | 0 | 1 | 0 |
| Postcranial | | | | | | |
| Vertebrae | 0 | 4 | 4 | 0 | 0 | 0 |
| Rib, sternum | 0 | 31 | 31 | 0 | 9 | 1 |
| Long bones | 5 | 117 | 117 | 7 | 29 | 9 |
| Pelvis, sacrum | 0 | 2 | 2 | 0 | 1 | 1 |
| Bone type unknown | 0 | 52 | 52 | 0 | 15 | 0 |
| TOTAL (212) | 5 | 207 | 207 | 7 | 55 | 11 |
| PERCENTAGE | 2.4 | 97.6 | 97.6 | 3.3 | 25.9 | 5.2 |

Percentage of expected vertebrae = <3.3 (4 of 120; MNI = 5).

NOTE: Only summary tabulations are available (Turner 1983). Series is missing. Presence of anvil abrasions and polishing was not determined. Impact breakage, cut marks, and burning represent perimortem damage. Gnawing and chewing are postmortem damage.

burned Room 3, which Hohmann et al. (1985) contended was an elite residence.

Associated Artifacts. On the floor of Room 3 were found metates, jars, bone, shell, turquoise, and other exotic materials, none of which was specifically related to the human skeletal remains.

Figures. 3.167–3.171.

Taphonomy. CGT. Skeletal inventory is in table 3.42.

MNI. 5 (CGT); 7 (EB and KA); 10 (JH et al.).

Age and Sex. CGT. Four adults, sex?; one 13- to 17-year-old, sex?. In addition, a cut fragmentary ulna and a fragment of humerus from an almost dwarf-sized individual was found on the room floor. This exceptional material was considered to be a trophy or heirloom and was not counted for MNI.

Preservation. Poor.

Bone and Fragment Number. 212 (CGT); 223 (Hohmann, personal communication).

Breakage. 97.6%.

Cut Marks. 3.3% (CGT); 0.01% (Hohmann, personal communication).

Burning. 25.9% (CGT); >75.0% (Hohmann, personal communication).

Anvil Abrasions. Not determined.

Polishing. Not determined.

Vertebrae Number. 3.3% of expected (4 of 120; MNI = 5), or 1.2% of expected (3 of 240, MNI = 10).

Scalping. None.

Gnawing, Rodent, and Chewing, Carnivore. 5.2%.

Insect Parts. None identified during skeletal examination.

Other Modification. None.

Archaeologist's Interpretation. Hohmann et al. (1985:239) were impressed by the large quantity of cultural material and human remains

Figure 3.167. Ash Creek, Arizona. Dwarf-sized human ulna with perimortem cut marks. There may be rodent damage also. Specimen was found on floor of Room 3 (CGT neg. 1-12-83:31).

Figure 3.168. Ash Creek. Human distal femur fragment with fine multiple and crisscrossing perimortem cut marks on posterior surface. As with figure 3.167, some of this damage might have been done by rodents. Specimen was found on floor of Room 3 (CGT neg. 1-12-83:27).

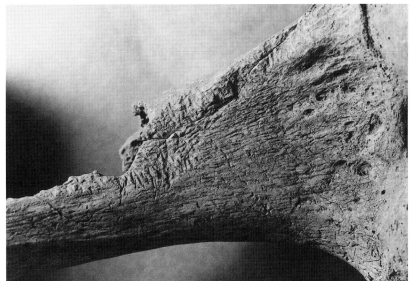

Figure 3.169. Ash Creek. Human long bone fragment with perimortem conchoidal impact breakage and adhering chips. Specimen found on floor of Room 3 (CGT neg. 1-12-83:49).

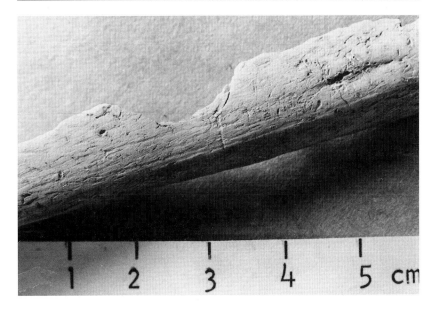

Figure 3.170. Ash Creek. Human rib fragment with probable perimortem carnivore tooth puncture. Specimen found in Room 3, level 2 (near the floor) (CGT neg. 1-12-83:29).

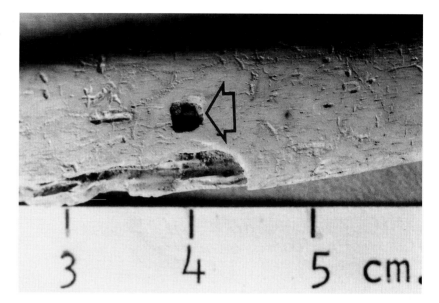

Figure 3.171. Ash Creek. Cut bone fragment (human?) found in Room 3, level 2 (near the floor). It is difficult to tell when this bone was modified. Rodent damage may be present (CGT neg. 1-12-83:33).

on the floor of Room 3. They wrote that "the surface of the floor was littered with human long bones, both clustered and isolated. . . . The position of some of these bones suggests that they had been articulated at the time the room burned and was abandoned." Hohmann (personal communication) suggested that most of the bones were burned on one side only. Such is usually the case for cannibalized assemblages, too. However, without point mapping and field recording of the bone surfaces that faced upward, there is no objective way to determine whether the bones had been burned in a structural fire or earlier.

Hohmann et al.'s figure 9.14 (1985) shows the bone scatter, but in that rough drawing two hearths have been deleted that are shown elsewhere, around which seemingly about half the bones were positioned. There was another "cluster" of bone near a subfloor feature, which also is not shown in their figure 9.14. Their figure 9.13 shows this close relationship of bone concentrations to the hearth and the subfloor feature, which may have been an ash pit. It is curious that Hohmann et al. (1985) did not direct readers to figure 9.13 or discuss these provocative spatial relationships. Moreover, given the uniqueness of this find, it is disappointing that they provided no detailed line drawing or photograph of the bone scatter.

Hohmann et al. (1985:257–261) provided identifications for ten people in Room 3, based on age, side, sex, stature, and bone position in the room. This is twice as many individuals as the senior author could conservatively identify on the basis of side, age, and robusticity. Bassett and Atwell (1985:227) recognized only seven individuals from the floor of Room 3; all had "little" bone, but the bone was in good condition.

In Hohmann et al.'s discussion section (1985:262–264), they proposed that Room 3 was not an ossuary, because of its domestic qualities and lack of a wide range of human bones. We agree. They then asserted that the ten individuals met their deaths "over an extended period of time." We can identify nothing in their article that would form the basis for this statement. They further claimed that the remains were trophy specimens that were bundled as individuals and hung from the roof or upper wall. These bundles fell to the floor surface and near to the floor when Room 3 burned. It is curious that these "bundles" seem to have fallen mainly around the firepit and possible ash pit.

As part of their argument for bundled trophy bones, Hohmann et al. said that there were too few cut marks to support a cannibalism hypothesis; they found only two possible cut marks. The senior author found 7 out of 212 pieces with cut marks (3.3%), very near the mean for all other Southwestern sites where cannibalism has been proposed. Hohmann et al. (1985:262) proposed that "the flesh was intact at the time of deposition," a claim that is clearly at odds with the great amount of perimortem breakage (97.6%). There may indeed have been some flesh still adhering to one or more bones or fragments at the time of incineration, but that does not mean that all or even several bones still had flesh adhering. Had there been adhering flesh, where are the hands and feet?

Hohmann et al. (1985:263) concluded that the "best explanation for these unusual human bone deposits is the argument that these are trophy limbs. Indeed, we argue that these bundles represent the curation of trophy limbs, possibly taken during raids or warfare." Our reaction to this explanation is that the bones may well have been those of captives, perhaps similar to those taken in the raid on Awatovi in 1700. However, inspection of table 3.42 shows that the skeletal remains are not just limb bones; indeed, long bones make up only half (55.2%) of the 212 pieces in this assemblage. Moreover, if the Room 3 human remains represented "trophy limbs," why was there so much perimortem breakage? If the limbs were trophies, then why cut up one or more people in such a strange way that parts of the pelvis wind up in the trophy bundle?

We concur with the suggestion made by Hohmann et al. (1985: 263) that the human remains in Room 3 do not represent some form of ancestor worship, although admittedly we have no empirical basis for predicting what would be the expected bioarchaeological condition. We also allow, for the same reason, that Room 3 was not a specialized structure for storing bones of the elite. Although Hohmann et al. believed Room 3 was an elite residence because of its rather rich yield of jewelry and exotic minerals, we must ask why the elites would have had bones in their house, even if the bones were not the remains of a cannibalistic event? Ethnographically, bones, scalps, and the like were, and still are, considered by most Southwestern Indians to be dangerous objects requiring storage in special or out-of-the-way locations.

Other Interpretations. Glen Rice (1985:141–143), following Hohmann et al. (1985), described the setting well: "The most spectacular of all floor assemblages was found in Room 3. The room had burned catastrophically and the collapse of the roof had sealed an unusually large collection of whole vessels and stone tools. . . . Human bone was found scattered across the floor of Room 3. . . . A number of the bones have spiral fractures indicating they were still green when broken, some burning (which might have happened when the room burned), and some cutting marks. These bones are in a primary cultural context and were not introduced on the floor through post-abandonment mixing."

Rice (1985:154–155) concluded: "Tapia Del Cerrito was a community which served other communities. It produced both plain and decorated ceramics and it functioned as a local burying ground for the dead. At least half of the rooms appear to have been used as storage or production areas, rather than as domiciles. That this service may have been based on some form of coercive control is suggested by the unusual findings in Room 3. Could the burning of the room, the lack of any attempt to remove usable objects (metates, vessels) from the collapsed structure, and the butchering of ten individuals represent a reaction to this coercion?"

Discussion. In addition to our differences with Hohmann et al. regarding the skeletal interpretation, we also have a difference in MNI—five identified by the senior author and ten by Hohmann et al. In an effort to completely reanalyze the human remains for MNI and to check for anvil abrasions and pot-polishing, neither of which was looked for during the initial study, LaJoyce Hall searched thoroughly in all the Department of Anthropology collection storage areas for the assemblage from Room 3. It was not located. The series has disappeared from the department, sometime before March 1993. Thus we may never resolve these differences. However, the MNI may actually be less than ten, because Hohmann et al.'s most frequently described skeletal element was the ulna. They identified two left, one right, and six other ulnae, for a total of nine. If we assume that the six others were half left and half right, then their MNI would be five—that is, five left ulnae. One of them belonged to an adolescent, and the other four represent adults. This is what the senior author found.

The Ash Creek human bone assemblage is relatively far removed from the Anasazi area, where the occurrence of sites with probable cannibalism is heaviest. There may have been an Anasazi link at Ash Creek, however, because Jeddito Black-on-yellow and Sikyatki Polychrome pottery was found at the site, although not in Room 3 (Hohmann et al. 1985:266–275). Ash Creek is also one of the latest of such prehistoric sites. If others can be found in the Salado and Mogollon areas, and if they are of similar late Pueblo III and Pueblo IV times, then a temporal gradient might be proposed for the spread of the practice of cannibalism.

We accept Rice's thinking that there was probably some element of coercion involved in the events that led to the dismemberment of the several people before Room 3 burned. However, the site was not excavated in the kind of microstratigraphic detail that might have turned up streaks of crushed bone flour, and there was no point mapping of the bone fragments for location, surface burning, or orientation, which might have aided the taphonomic interpretation of body processing and related events. Given the small amount of bone recovered—small even for five individuals, let alone seven to ten—the dismemberment seems not to have occurred in Room 3. Perhaps if more of the plaza were tested, the butchering location might be discovered.

In sum, a good case can be made for extramural human body processing at Ash Creek around 1350. The bones found on the floor included more than arms and legs, and perimortem breakage exceeded 95%. Breakage, coupled with cut marks and burning, was enough evidence in 1983 to justify suggesting cannibalism. Since the skeletal assemblage has disappeared and cannot be reexamined for abrasions and polishing, we are unable to validate the earlier claim with the expanded number of criteria. However, in light of the other Southwestern and Mexican charnel deposits we have examined and read about, the case for cannibalism at Ash Creek is, in our view, as strong as the argument for trophy taking, if not stronger.

## 45
## Chaco 1360

**Claim Date.** 1984.
**Claimant.** Peter J. McKenna.
**Claim Type.** Violence.
**Other Designations.** 29SJ1360; Bc240; LA41360.
**Site Location.** About 70 m northeast of Fajada Butte and 1,440 m south of Una Vida great house, Chaco Culture National Historic Park, New Mexico. USGS Pueblo Bonito quadrangle (1966), T 21N, R 10W, SE ¼ of NW ¼ of SW ¼ of Sec. 28.
**Site Type.** Community of 18 masonry surface structures and pithouses, five kivas, and a trash mound. The human remains of concern are from Pithouse B.
**Cultural Affiliation.** Chaco Anasazi.
**Chronology.** Pithouse B, A.D. 950–1030.
**Excavators and Date.** Alden C. Hayes and Charles R. Morrison, 1974.
**Institutional Storage.** Chaco Center, Department of Anthropology, University of New Mexico, Albuquerque.
**Site Reports.** McKenna (1984); LoPiccolo (1992).
**Osteological Report.** McKenna (1984:ch. 7). Other records at the Chaco Center include burial excavation forms and various catalogs.
**Skeletal Evidence of Stress.** Some anemia reported.
**Burial Context.** The largely complete skeletons of two adults and two young children, along with two dog skeletons, were found on the

floor of Pithouse B. The skulls of two additional young children were found in a connecting ventilator shaft.

**Associated Artifacts.** Various household items, many bone tools, but no grave goods. One of the adults had been wearing a long bead necklace, but neither McKenna nor we consider it to have been a mortuary item.

**Figures.** None.

**Taphonomy.** PJM.

    *MNI.* 6 (plus 2 dogs).

    *Age and Sex.* Two adult females, one 39–45 years old and the other 35–39; four children, 2–3.5 years old. As we discuss later, we regard one of the females (Burial 1) to be male and suggest slightly younger ages for the children. The following taphonomic catagories are based on McKenna's report.

    *Preservation.* Excellent.

    *Chewing, Carnivore.* Yes, Burial 1.

    *There is no information for Bone and Fragment Number, Breakage, Cut Marks, Burning, Anvil Abrasions, Polishing, Vertebrae Number, Scalping, Gnawing, Insect Parts, or Other Modification.*

**Archaeologist's Interpretation.** McKenna (1984:66) proposed that Pithouse B was "purposely destroyed without the removal of either portable artifacts or valuable architectural elements. . . . The multitude of utilitarian items of stone and bone, the culinary pottery, the apparent division of storage from living areas, and the presence of two adults, three children, and two dogs on the floor confirm the domestic function of Pithouse B."

Elsewhere McKenna (1984:352) suggested: "The complete undisturbed composure of those on the main floor and the apparently feeble final efforts by those clustered around the ventilator opening suggest asphyxiation. S. Rhine, forensic anthropologist at the University of New Mexico, generally concurs with this assessment." He added, however (1984:353): "Burial 2, the adult female in the main chamber of the pithouse, exhibits ample evidence of having been the victim of violence: two lithic projectile points were found within her torso. These injuries, and a third trauma resulting in the presence of a wooden shaft in her right arm, were all apparently survived, but they obviously suggest violent conflict."

McKenna (1984:362) recognized that the genetic relationships between the women and children might not have been close, and violence might have played a part in the death of at least one of the pithouse occupants:

> Given the ages of the women, it is debatable whether these individuals were the mothers of the infants in Pithouse B, but this assumption has been made throughout this discussion. While it is possible that these individuals were accidentally asphyxiated, the implications of violent trauma in Adult 2 should be underscored. The presence of the projectile points and the degree of healing on the ulna clearly indicate that at least one of the occupants of 1360 had been embroiled in a conflict shortly before her death. The extent to which this event influenced the immediate or long-term lives of the

occupants at the site is unknown, but it is clear the human remains from 1360 do not constitute burials in the normal sense.

**Other Interpretations.** The excavators noted that none of the dead had been buried in a formal fashion.

**Discussion.** The excellent written descriptions, photographic illustrations, and pithouse floor drawing provided by McKenna (1984:347–362) document the unburied and unburned condition of the six individuals and two dogs. Nevertheless, we examined these six for other perimortem damage, especially in light of McKenna's (1984:353) guarded conclusion: "There is no general evidence of serious conflict in Chaco, especially in this early period [950–1030]; however, if the women and children in Pithouse B were indeed the victims of a violent attack, this could have important implications for our understanding of sociopolitical events in Chaco."

We found the existing skeletal element inventory and descriptions curated at the Chaco Center to be quite accurate, so there is no need to present our bone counts and identifications. In effect, they match what is already on record. With the exception of one penetration wound, and ignoring plant root damage, most if not all of the other perimortem damage was caused by carnivore scavenging. There was no rodent gnawing and no burning. Importantly, there are no unequivocal perimortem cut marks that would have to be attributed to inconsiderate human activity. Our key observations include the following:

Burial 1 (CHCU9391). In our opinion this is a 35- to 40-year-old adult male. (Chaco Center records indicate that two other workers also regarded Burial 1 to have been male.) McKenna considered Burial 1 to be a female, and indeed the skeleton is rather gracile, and the pelvis has a slight femalelike quality. Burial 1 was certainly not a powerful, muscular man. Because recent studies of skeletal development and muscle markings have proven to be useful estimators of habitual behaviors, we speculate that in life he could have spent considerable time in mental or light physical tasks rather than in habitual heavy labor. Ethnographic roles for such light activity include religious priests, shamans, older caretakers, the chronically ill, and so forth. Our sex determination does not fit McKenna's hypothesized social context, weakening this aspect of the nonviolent scenario. He believed the two adults were women, and the children were theirs, although he recognized that the women's skeletal ages were rather old relative to those of the children.

There is a vertically oriented, 3.0-cm-long "cut mark" on the left rear parietal of Burial 1. Because the cut is relatively clean and unstained, it cannot be accepted as perimortem without some reservation, although it has none of the usual characteristics of "newness" attributable to excavation or laboratory damage. Most likely it was animal-caused, because there was carnivore chewing on the ends of several bones. There is chewing of the distal end of the right humerus, which left at least one tooth puncture mark. Both distal ends of the femurs have been chewed. The proximal ends of the left tibia and fibula have been completely chewed off, and there is some associated fracture tip polishing. The right lower leg and foot are missing.

The tibia fragment numbered 9355, found in upper fill and believed possibly to belong to Burial 1, does not match the remaining left tibia. Specimen 9355 is significantly smaller and was broken long after death. It does not belong to Burial 1.

Burial 2 (CHCU9326). This 35- to 40-year-old female, whose skeleton is complete, has carnivore chewing of the proximal end and lateral aspect of her right tibia and fibula, on one of her big toes, and at the ends of two other toes. Although McKenna reported some of the carnivore damage for Burial 1, he apparently overlooked the chewing of Burial 2. Inasmuch as the woman's skeleton was found on its right side (McKenna 1984:fig. 7.1), it would have been impossible for a carnivore to have chewed the tibia and fibula after death. The location of the chewing faces downward and would have been in direct contact with the pithouse floor. Hence, the body was in some position other than that illustrated for some time after death and before coming to its final articulated, preexcavation position.

There is a penetration wound on the proximal end of one ulna that is circular and has a entry diameter of 7.0 mm and an exit diameter of 5.0 mm. The penetrating object entered from the back side of the woman's elbow. The wound size is not unlike that which might be caused by bone or wood arrow points, awls, daggers, and other such rounded and pointed man-made and natural objects. While McKenna believed there was some bone reactivity, we found no signs of response, either healing or infection. It is also likely that a blood clot had not formed around the wound, since there is very little iron staining within and around the wound site. The wound could have been caused by either violence or an accidental fall on an object such as a bone awl. In the case of violence, the wound angle would readily fit a situation in which the victim used her arms to protect her face—the classic parry reflex. Given the lack of bone response to this elbow trauma, we feel it safe and parsimonious to interpret the arrow points found in the body cavity also as evidence of penetration wounds, not as mortuary offerings, even though our inspection of the woman's ribs and vertebrae turned up no nicks or other damage. We think the weapon that caused the elbow wound was withdrawn, whereas the points were not. This suggests two assailants—one using a bow and arrow, and the other, a face-to-face assailant, using a dagger or spear.

Burial 3 (CHCU9327). This individual was dentally two years old at the time of death. The child's skeleton is largely complete. It has three short (approximately 3.0 mm) cut marks above the left orbit, and the entire frontal bone has 50 to 60 minute, randomly oriented scratches. There is no carnivore chewing. Although the cuts and scratches might have resulted from stones and soil settling around the infant at some time following natural defleshing, we doubt it, for the simple reason that other cranial elements should also show some scratching. Moreover, Burial 3 was partly beneath the body of the adult male (Burial 1), who lacks similar scratches. Whatever caused the child's frontal bone scratching—and we suspect that excessive field or laboratory dry brushing was responsible—it happened independently of the damage to the overlying adult male. McKenna thought that the adult was trying to place the child in the ventilator shaft to give it air, just before both died. He also felt that the adult

(Burial 1) was stratigraphically related to the head of the child (Burial 7) found in the ventilator shaft near the opening into the pithouse.

**Burial 4.** This is a puppy found near the left knee of Burial 2 that we did not examine.

**Burial 5 (CHCU9393).** This individual was dentally a neonate. The skeleton, which was found lying extended and face up, is complete and has no identifiable perimortem damage. This lack of damage is at odds with the carnivore damage to the right leg of Burial 2, which lay within one meter of the infant. Even if the infant had been bundled up because of winter cold, why did the carnivore(s) not at least chew at the face?

**Burial 6 (CHCU9392).** This is the very fragile skull and a few vertebrae of a neonate. There is no animal damage. Within the cranial vault, where laboratory cleaning has not removed all perimortem taphonomic information, there appears to be some evidence of worm casts and faint possible outlines of fly pupae. The latter suggestion should be verified by a specialist in invertebrate faunal analysis. The skull was found in "Vent X," a location not specified by McKenna, but presumably it was the ventilator shaft opening outside the pithouse wall. Burial 6 could well represent a secondary deposit and have no strong time or event relationship to the occupants of Pithouse B.

**Burial 7 (CHCU9369).** This is the cranial vault of a child whose age was probably around one year. Because the tooth-bearing maxilla and mandible are missing, a dental age cannot be offered. The child, like many others found in Chaco Canyon, had been markedly anemic, as identified by active cribra orbitalia and by moderate to severe porotic hyperostosis on the external aspect of its right parietal bone. There is a faint, 10-mm-long scratch on the right side of the frontal bone. This incomplete skull was found at the bottom of the ventilator shaft, and, like Burial 6, it may have had no temporal or event relationship with burials 1–5, although McKenna felt that Burial 7 was related to the adult (Burial 1) and child (Burial 3) found near the ventilator opening.

**Asphyxiation or Violence?** Peter McKenna offered two reasonable and not mutually exclusive interpretations for the condition and position of the human remains in Pithouse B—asphyxiation (natural or intentional) and violence. Our observations lead us to think that the natural accident scenario rests on several weak assumptions, none of which is fatal alone but which together produce a much less parsimonious explanation than either intentional asphyxiation or violence. Both asphyxiation scenarios have all the individuals dying at the same time on a cold winter night. In all three scenarios, the position of each body indicates what these individuals did during their last moments of life.

The presence of carnivore chewing marks on the underside of the right leg of Burial 2 demonstrates that the woman's body had been moved sometime between death and placement in its final resting position as found by the pithouse excavators. The woman could have been rolled over by the carnivore(s), but if that were the case, then all the other dead would have been exposed to the scavengers as well. Why then, was there no evidence of chewing on the nearby infant (Burial 5)? The same puzzling selective activity by carnivores applies to burials 1 and 3, which were found touching one another, the former with chewing damage, the latter with none. McKenna explained the Burial 1 chewing as due to this adult's having been elevated and more exposed after the bodies were covered by sand and roof debris. However, he did not note the chewing on Burial 2, which weakens the assumption of exposure of only Burial 1. Because all the individuals were contained within the sandy matrix, all must have been exposed to carnivore damage, but not necessarily within the confines of the pithouse. Some individuals may have been dumped into the pithouse following their deaths and scavenging outside. Because water puddling was not observed, the sandy matrix presumably was windblown and so was not an especially sensitive unit for estimating time.

All of these factors—scavenging, body position, and sediments—together suggest that the bodies were exposed for a relatively long time. And they raise the provocative question of why, if the pithouse occupants died an accidental death, their neighbors did not formally bury them. The events that played out in this perimortem episode must have involved more time than the few hours required for asphyxiation.

It is reasonable to question whether the skulls of the two children found at either end of the ventilator system had any close relationship with the event(s) that led to the deaths of the four complete individuals on the pithouse floor. Although the six individuals are linked by both spatial and non-normative "burial" relationships, without complete excavation of the ventilator shaft there is no way to link the skeletons on the floor stratigraphically with the Vent X cranium in the critically important time relationship. Moreover, the incomplete excavation of the ventilator shaft means that no other explanation can be proposed to account for the missing postcranial body parts. Although there is no plausible reason why the postcranial skeletons were not found immediately next to the skulls, there is no physical evidence such as cranial base cut marks to indicate that the children had been decapitated and their heads placed in the ventilator. Patently, excavation of the ventilator shaft would have to be completed before any more could be said about these two children.

Because of the lack of bone response to the elbow penetration wound of the adult woman (Burial 2), it is logical to regard the two arrow points found in her torso as evidence of wounds, not as mortuary offerings. The torso wounds would have been life threatening. The evidence for her having died as the result of a violent encounter is stronger than is the evidence for her having been asphyxiated. Finding her remains on a twilled mat does not exclude death by violence. Furthermore, it is difficult to imagine anyone going to bed wearing a long bead necklace, as this woman apparently was.

Our examination of the perimortem taphonomy of the human skeletal remains found in 29SJ1360 Pithouse B, coupled with contextual information, leads us to accept McKenna's scenario in which violence was partly or wholly responsible for the deaths of the room's occupants. The nonburial of these remains, their damage by carnivores, and similar carnivore damage to human bones found in other parts of this site all suggest that there might have been widespread violence and abandonment of this community between A.D. 920 and 1040. Otherwise, the carnivore activity would have been much less. It was during this period that the Chacoan great houses were beginning to be erected. The perimortem taphonomy of the Pithouse B human remains provides additional evidence that there was violence associated with the rise of the Chaco phenomenon.

## 46 Cottonwood Wash

**Claim Date.** 1988.

**Claimant.** Tim D. White.

**Claim Type.** Cannibalism.

**Other Designations.** 42Sa12209; ML-531; Cottonwood Wash (White 1988); Cottonwood Canyon (White 1992).

**Site Location.** In Cottonwood Canyon, near the forest boundary in the South Cottonwood Creek area of the Monticello Ranger District (Manti-LaSal National Forest), 20.8 km (13 miles) northwest of Blanding, southeastern Utah, approximately 2,000 m (6560 feet) elevation. The site is about 0.8 km (0.5 mile) upstream from the confluence of Cottonwood Canyon with Posey Canyon. USGS Brushy Basin quadrangle (1957), T 35S, R 20E, SW ¼ of SW ¼ of Sec. 11.

**Site Type.** Seven masonry structures with plaza. A kiva was found in 1988 (Wikle 1989), after the main excavation.

**Cultural Affiliation.** Anasazi.

**Chronology.** Pueblo I, A.D. 880–910.

**Excavator and Date.** Jerry Fetterman, Woods Canyon Archaeological Consultants, July 1987.

**Institutional Storage.** Edge of the Cedars Museum, Blanding, Utah (field notes, artifacts, photographic negatives).

**Site Report.** Fetterman, Honeycutt, and Kuckelman (1988).

**Osteological Reports.** White (1988, 1992); White and Folkens (1991).

**Skeletal Evidence of Stress.** None reported.

**Burial Context.** Fragmented bones dumped into surface room 3, concentrated in an area 60 by 70 by 20 cm deep, which was part of the floor fill and of a shallow pit, 10 cm in depth. The only articulated bones were those of one incomplete hand found in the floor fill refuse (White 1992:395).

**Associated Artifacts.** Two stemmed projectile points in refuse.

**Figures.** None.

**Taphonomy.** TDW. (CGT, 6-19-98).

 *MNI.* 4. (4, CGT).

 *Age and Sex.* Two 12-year-old children and two mature adults—a male about 40 and a female of the same age.

 *Preservation.* Good to very poor and friable. White (1988:1) attributed this to "decalcification of the bone brought about primarily by intensive root activity." It is also possible that humic acid was responsible for the "chalky, flaky, intensively etched" condition. White (1992:402) rightly excused his lack of quantified analysis on grounds of poor bone preservation.

 *Bone and Fragment Number.* 691. (457; CGT, 6-19-98).

 *Breakage.* Extensive. (77.5%; CGT, 6-19-98).

 *Cut Marks.* 0.3%. (1.1%; CGT, 6-19-98).

*Burning.* 5.5%. (5.3%; CGT, 6-19-98).
*Anvil Abrasions.* 0.4%. (0.7%; CGT, 6-19-98).
*Polishing.* None reported. (1.7%; CGT, 6-19-98).
*Vertebrae Number.* 9.4% of expected (9 of 96). (0.0%; CGT, 6-19-98).

*Other Modification.* White noted one hammerstone scar, six specimens with adhering bone flakes, and ten examples of crushing.

*There is no information for Scalping, Gnawing, Chewing, or Insect Parts.* (None; CGT, 6-19-98).

Archaeologist's Interpretation. Jerry Fetterman, Linda Honeycutt, and Kristin Kuckelman (1988:42) concluded:

> The condition of the bone varied from very good to extremely friable. While root action had no doubt damaged some of the bone, the extremely fragmentary and splintered state of most of the bone was primarily due to intentional fracturing. These bones are the remains of several cannibalized individuals. The extremely fragmentary condition of the bones is primarily the result of marrow extraction efforts by the cannibal(s); the long bones had been split, the skulls had been broken open, and the spongy bones had been crushed. . . . Lack of articulation proves this is not a primary burial, and the extremely fractured state of the bones proves it is not a secondary burial.

Other Interpretations. White (1988:7) concluded: "The composition and characteristics of the assemblage from Feature #27 of Cottonwood Wash site 42SA12209 are very similar to what is seen in a variety of sites across the prehistoric Southwest, including the assemblage from Mancos Canyon 5MTUMR 2346. These assemblages have been interpreted as evidence of cannibalism and this interpretation is one that I agree with."

Discussion. Because White identified five of the minimal criteria for proposing cannibalism, and because the perimortem damage proportions are in line with those of other series for which cannibalism has been hypothesized, we agree with his interpretation. It is unclear whether White was looking for "pot-polishing" before June 27, 1988, when he submitted his report to Woods Canyon Archaeological Consultants, or whether he began systematically to search for pot-polishing after that date. But because the bone surfaces of the Cottonwood Wash charnel deposit were not well preserved, it is unreasonable to expect White to have found fragment polishing in any case. CGT identified all six minimal criteria and found lambdoidal deformation on solitary cranium, which appears to have been burned on back of head.

**47
Marshview Hamlet**

Claim Date. 1988.
Claimant. C. G. Turner II.
Claim Type. Cannibalism.
Other Designations. 5MT2235.
Site Location. Northwest of Dolores, southwestern Colorado. USGS

Trimble Point quadrangle (1965), T 38N, R 16W, SE ¼ of SE ¼ of NW ¼ of Sec. 36.

**Site Type.** Small farmstead pithouse village.

**Cultural Affiliation.** Anasazi, Sundial phase.

**Chronology.** A.D. 1050–1125, Pueblo III.

**Excavators and Date.** David A. Breternitz, director, Dolores Archaeological Program, and Richard H. Wilshusen, 1981.

**Institutional Storage.** Anasazi Heritage Center.

**Site Report.** Wilshusen (1988).

**Osteological Reports.** Wiener (1988); Turner (1988).

**Skeletal Evidence of Stress.** Porotic hyperostosis is present.

**Burial Context.** Bone fragments in fill immediately above and on floor 2 of abandoned Pithouse 1, mostly from a hearth.

**Associated Artifacts.** Wilshusen (1988:34) listed lithic debitage, utilized flakes, ceramic sherds, and other nonmortuary debris including unworked mammal, bird, and amphibian bones. He illustrated approximately 20 variously complete ceramic vessels, bone awls, and bird bone tubes.

**Figures.** None.

**Taphonomy.** CGT. Skeletal inventory is in table 3.44.

*MNI.* 6 (table 3.43).

*Age and Sex.* One adult male?; one adult female?; one adult, sex?; one subadult, sex?; two 2- to 12-year-old children.

*Preservation.* Good to excellent.

*Bone and Fragment Number.* 528.

*Breakage.* 99.1%.

*Cut Marks.* 2.6%.

*Burning.* 30.7%.

*Anvil Abrasions.* Present.

*Polishing.* Present.

*Vertebrae Number.* 1.1% of expected (2 of 144).

*Scalping.* Possible.

*Gnawing, Rodent, and Chewing, Carnivore.* 7.0%.

*Insect Parts.* None found during skeletal examination.

*Other Modification.* Ann Lucy Wiener (1988:71) reported the presence of a red stain on three bone fragments.

**Archaeologist's Interpretation.** Wilshusen (1988:34–36) reported that the roof had not totally collapsed at the time the human bones were deposited in abandoned Pithouse 1. He felt that the human bone deposit represented a secondary burial because the assemblage was very incomplete, there was evidence of much rodent disturbance (both points confirmed by our taphonomic analysis), and the artifacts were fragmentary and questionable as mortuary offerings. He concluded: "If mass burial does represent the prehistoric inhabitants of the site, then they appear to have been decimated by a disaster and sometime after were buried or reburied by those who thought their interment important" (Wilshusen 1988:50).

**Other Interpretations.** Wiener (1988:71) noted that she examined the human remains with cannibalism in mind, but she did not draw that conclusion. She said that the bone preservation was unlike that known for other cannibalized series in the Mesa Verde region, there

Table 3.43
Minimal Number of Individuals (MNI) at Marshview Hamlet

| SKELETAL ELEMENT | AGE | SEX | NOTES |
|---|---|---|---|
| Mandible, right | 6–8 | ? | FS 184 |
| Burned teeth | 10–12 | ? | FS 187 |
| R scapula, humerus | Subadult | ? | FS 184, 190 |
| Incomplete skull | Adult | M? | FS 184, 186 |
| Teeth, maxilla, other | Adult | ? | FS 184, 186, 190 |
| Orbit, femur fragments | Adult | F? | FS 184, 210 |

SUMMARY: Six individuals. One adult male?; one adult female?; one adult, sex?; one subadult, sex?; two 2- to 12-year-old children.

Table 3.44
Bone Elements and Perimortem Damage at Marshview Hamlet

| SKELETAL ELEMENT | WHOLE | FRAGMENT | IMPACT BREAK | CUT MARK | BURN | GNAW/CHEW |
|---|---|---|---|---|---|---|
| Cranial | | | | | | |
| Skull, jaw | 0 | 84 | 84 | 3 | 10 | 5 |
| Postcranial | | | | | | |
| Vertebrae | 0 | 8 | 8 | 0 | 0 | 3 |
| Scapula, clavicle | 2 | 9 | 9 | 1 | 0 | 4 |
| Rib, sternum | 0 | 6 | 6 | 0 | 0 | 0 |
| Long bones | 0 | 360 | 360 | 10 | 152 | 9 |
| Hand, foot, patella | 3 | 19 | 19 | 0 | 0 | 16 |
| Pelvis, sacrum | 0 | 1 | 1 | 0 | 0 | 0 |
| Bone type unknown | 0 | 36 | 36 | 0 | 0 | 0 |
| TOTAL (528) | 5 | 523 | 523 | 14 | 162 | 37 |
| PERCENTAGE | 0.9 | 99.1 | 99.1 | 2.6 | 30.7 | 7.0 |

Percentage of expected vertebrae = approx. 1.1 (1.6 of 144; MNI = 6).[a]

NOTE: Only elements that were present are listed. Anvil abrasions and polishing were present but not enumerated. Impact breakage, cut marks, and burning represent perimortem damage. Gnawing and chewing are postmortem damage.

a. Fragmentation size suggests that about five fragments could represent one whole vertebra.

was no pattern of spiral fracturing, only one cut mark was observed, and bone burning was infrequent and limited to charring. The last was attributed to the burned bones having been near a hearth and ash pit on floor 2 of the pithouse. From these conditions Wiener concluded that the people had been subjected to some unknown type of violent treatment for an unknown motive.

Discussion. We disagree with Weiner because all six of the minimal criteria for hypothesizing cannibalism are met in this case, and in about the same proportions as at other sites where cannibalism has been hypothesized. We also disagree with Wilshusen on two minor points: (1) How can rodent disturbance account for the great amount of missing bone? Wherever the main mass of bone belonging to six individuals was in the site, it was not recovered inside or outside the pithouse. Much of the perimortem story about the Marshview Hamlet people is missing. (2) In our judgment, based on study of Wilshusen's photograph and line drawings of the human bone deposit in Pithouse 1, the bone fragments were dumped in the room, not interred. There is nothing in the bone scatter pattern, the pattern of the artifacts and other cultural debris, or anything else described in the site report that even hints that this charnel deposit was an intentional interment. Moreover, no pit outline was identified that might have indicated a very simple burial. Charnel pits have been recognized elsewhere— Small House, Leroux Wash, and Monument Valley.

The charnel deposit at Marshview Hamlet illustrates a serious ethical problem that supervisory field personnel will have to address in the future. Discovery of an obviously incomplete mass of fragmented human bones is an unmistakable signal that the remainder of the assemblage is probably elsewhere in the site. Knowing this, is there a professional obligation to search for the missing parts so that the death history can be better understood? Obviously, the question can be answered no, by analogy—if one finds a potsherd, is there an obligation to search for the rest of the pot? We would respond yes, however, if the culture-history study was to be very fine-grained, as would be the situation in any modern forensic or accident case.

## 48
## Rattlesnake Ruin

Claim Date. 1988.

Claimant. Shane A. Baker.

Claim Type. Cannibalism.

Other Designations. 42SA18434.

Site Location. On private land belonging to Kelly and Teri Laws, Mustang Mesa, 4.5 km (2.8 miles) northeast of Blanding, southeastern Utah. USGS Blanding North quadrangle (1985), T 36S, R 23E, NW ¼ of NE ¼ of SE ¼ of Sec. 20.

Site Type. Small masonry field house with exterior storage pit, burial pit, and extramural hearth.

Cultural Affiliation. Anasazi.

Chronology. Ceramic date A.D. 1050–1100 (Baker 1994:35).

Excavators and Date. Bones were excavated by the private landowner who owns the site, 1986; Winston Hurst, Shane A. Baker, and volunteers excavated the remainder of the site, 1987.

Institutional Storage. Edge of the Cedars Museum, Blanding, Utah.

Site Reports. Baker (1988, 1990, 1993, 1994); Hurst (oral report at 1988 Pecos Conference, Dolores, Colorado).

Osteological Report. Baker (1990).

Skeletal Evidence of Stress. Cribra orbitalia present, but Baker (1990:89) felt that health was generally good.

Burial Context. Bone fragments discovered in outside storage pit.

Associated Artifacts. This charnel pit was evidently not a formal burial, and only pottery sherds and stone flake refuse were in the bone-bearing fill.

Figures. None.

Taphonomy. SAB. Skeletal inventory is in table 3.45.

Table 3.45

Bone Elements and Perimortem Damage at Rattlesnake Ruin

| SKELETAL ELEMENT | WHOLE & FRAGMENT | IMPACT BREAK | CUT MARK | BURN | GNAWING |
|---|---|---|---|---|---|
| Cranial | | | | | |
| Maxilla | 33 | 33 | 0 | 1 | 0 |
| Mandible | 38 | 38 | 12 | 1 | 0 |
| Frontal | 45 | 42 | 7 | 0 | 0 |
| Parietal | 265 | 265 | 44 | 3 | 0 |
| Occipital | 37 | 37 | 8 | 0 | 0 |
| Temporal | 46 | 46 | 5 | 2 | 0 |
| Other | 30 | 17 | 1 | 2 | 1 |
| Postcranial | | | | | |
| Cervical vertebrae | 38 | 28 | 0 | 0 | 0 |
| Thoracic vertebrae | 97 | 96 | 2 | 2 | 0 |
| Lumbar vertebrae | 33 | 28 | 0 | 0 | 0 |
| Sacrum-coccyx | 48 | 43 | 0 | 0 | 0 |
| Scapula | 61 | 58 | 7 | 0 | 0 |
| Clavicle | 38 | 27 | 7 | 2 | 0 |
| Rib | 580 | 551 | 23 | 43 | 0 |
| Humerus | 49 | 48 | 4 | 1 | 0 |
| Radius | 32 | 32 | 7 | 0 | 0 |
| Ulna | 32 | 30 | 6 | 2 | 0 |
| Hand | 124 | 81 | 0 | 0 | 0 |
| Pelvis | 60 | 59 | 3 | 0 | 0 |
| Femur | 65 | 65 | 1 | 19 | 1 |
| Tibia | 54 | 54 | 2 | 1 | 0 |
| Fibula | 38 | 38 | 11 | 0 | 0 |
| Patella | 16 | 1 | 12 | 0 | 0 |
| Foot | 295 | 123 | 1 | 1 | 2 |
| Long bone fragments | 829 | 829 | 22 | 8 | 2 |
| Bone type unknown | 1,932 | 1,391 | 0 | 61 | 0 |
| Loose teeth | (100) | (27) | 0 | 0 | 0 |
| TOTAL (5,015; whole 388) | 4,627 | 4,087 | 185 | 149 | 6 |
| PERCENTAGE | | 81.5 | 3.7 | 3.0 | 0.1 |

Percentage of expected vertebrae = 35.0 (168 of 480; MNI = 20).

SOURCE: Baker (1990). Not all catagories are strictly equivalent.

NOTE: Only elements that were present are listed. Anvil abrasions were present but not enumerated; polishing was not reported. Impact breakage, cut marks, and burning represent perimortem damage. Gnawing is postmortem damage.

MNI. 20.

Age and Sex. Two infants (0–2 years); 5 children (3–12 years); 4 adolescents (13–24 years, 1 male, 2 female, 1 sex?); 8 adults (24–39 years, 2 male, 4 female, 2 sex?); 1 old adult, sex?.

Preservation. Good.

Bone and Fragment Number. 5,015 (including teeth).

Breakage. 81.5%.

Cut Marks. 3.7%.

Burning. 3.0%.

Anvil Abrasions. Yes (Baker 1990:74).

Polishing. Not reported.

Vertebrae Number. 35.0% of expected (168 of 480). This is an upper limit estimate; most of the vertebrae had been crushed and broken. Using three fragments as equivalent to one whole vertebra gives a frequency of 11.7% of expected.

*Scalping.* Baker (1988) thought cut marks indicated that several crania, if not all, had been scalped.

*Gnawing, Rodent, and Chewing, Carnivore.* 0.1%.

*Insect Parts.* Not reported.

*Other Modification.* Baker (1990:76) reported a type of cut mark that is exceptionally uncommon in other Southwestern human charnel deposits: heavy, coarse cutting in 12 of the 16 Rattlesnake Ruin patellae. These incisions were inflicted when the patellar ligament was severed, part of the butchering operation to separate the upper and lower leg. Baker (1990:73) also noted that "cut marks were less frequently observed on the back of the skull. In at least one case there were no fine cut marks present, but instead there was a set of heavy coarse chop marks on and inferior to the external occipital protuberance.... Other cut marks occur at various places in the post-cranial skeleton, most frequently around the articular area of joints, indicating that the individuals were dismembered." One bone fragment had a small stone flake in a cut mark (Baker 1990:70).

**Archaeologist's Interpretation.** Winston Hurst reported at the 1988 Pecos Conference that Rattlesnake Ruin contained cannibalized human remains. Shane Baker (1990:53–54) wrote:

> The original burial pit was destroyed completely in the course of the bulldozer work [done by the landowner]. Information from the landowner indicates that the pit was intruded into sterile subsurface sediments, and was not stone lined or otherwise modified. It was approximately 1.2 m long by 1 m wide and about 45 to 60 cm deep. The pit itself, and all the immediately surrounding sediments were removed, making it impossible to establish the stratigraphic relationship between the burial and the rest of the site.... Other data were acquired which suggest that the burial and the structure were probably roughly contemporaneous.

> Baker (1990:172) made a case for social control as the cause of the Rattlesnake Ruin cannibalism on the basis of its taphonomic similarity with Polacca Wash: "The high degree of similarity between the Polacca Wash burial and Rattlesnake Ruin burial suggests that prehistorically there occurred a similar need to control some sort of cultural deviation and to make an example of those who had violated the norms. As in the case at Polacca Wash, the victims may have been killed and mutilated as a part of the punitive sanction."

**Other Interpretations.** None.

**Discussion.** We agree with Baker's interpretation of cannibalism at Rattlesnake Ruin. We note also that his photographic illustrations show very little damage to the ends of long bones (which carnivores quickly consume), a Polacca Wash–like uniformity of broken rib lengths, vertebrae without bodies, and at least one scooplike artifact made from a human parietal bone. Because burning is a critical part of the cannibal signature, it would have been helpful if Baker had illustrated one or two examples of his 149 pieces of burned bone, 43 of which were rib fragments, with 61 unidentifed. Nevertheless, Baker's study is one of the finest and most thorough analyses of cannibalism conducted to date. His idea about social control has much merit but needs some scientific means of testing.

On June 21, 1998, Winston and Kathy Hurst led the senior author and Olga Pavlova to Rattlesnake Ruin. The strongest impression gained from the visit, relative to the charnel deposit, was that the site was very small, isolated, and indefensible. If the human remains Baker analyzed were the site's inhabitants who had been attacked (instead of a group of people who had been rounded up from various settlements in the area and herded to the site for their killing and consumption), there was nothing in the remaining architecture or site location that even hinted the victims might have been worried about the sort of brutality that eventually ended their lives.

## 49
## Fence Lake

**Claim Date.** 1989.

**Claimant.** Sharon S. Grant.

**Claim Type.** Cannibalism.

**Other Designations.** None.

**Site Location.** According to Sharon Grant, who initially studied the human remains, they were dug up by pot hunters, so their exact location is unknown. On the other hand, Tim White (1992:380) claimed that the remains were found "on private land 1 hour W of Grants, New Mexico, off Highway 117 c. 20 minutes from Fence Lake, 1/2 mile from lava flows." This would put the site on the USGS Fence Lake quadrangle (1972), possibly at T 5N, R 17 and 18W, Sec. unknown.

**Site Type.** Surface pueblo.

**Cultural Affiliation.** Site is in a region where Anasazi and Mogollon cultures overlap. Affiliation could be with either one. Tularosa Black-on-white and a corrugated ware were found at the site, but not necessarily in association with the human remains.

**Chronology.** Pottery and known large sites in the area suggested to A. E. Dittert, Jr. (personal communication, September 27, 1988), a probable date of A.D. 1100–1300.

**Excavator and Date.** Pot hunters, 1988.

**Institutional Storage.** Department of Anthropology, San Diego Museum of Man. The bone assemblage was left with the museum in February 1988, according to Rose Tyson, curator of physical anthropology.

**Site Report.** None.

**Osteological Reports.** Grant (1989).

**Skeletal Evidence of Stress.** Adult female occipital has grade 1–2 porotic hyperostosis (CGT).

**Burial Context.** Bone fragments were alleged to have been found in a fire pit. Our examination of the assemblage after it had been cleaned revealed no residual ash.

**Associated Artifacts.** Two manos and two trough metates.

**Figures.** 3.172–3.187.

**Taphonomy.** SSG; CGT. Skeletal inventory is in table 3.47.

  *MNI.* 5 (SSG); 3 (CGT) (table 3.46).

  *Age and Sex.* Two adult males; two adults, female?; one

Table 3.46
Minimal Number of Individuals (MNI) at Fence Lake

| SKELETAL ELEMENT | AGE | SEX | NOTES |
|---|---|---|---|
| Maxilla, whole | Adult | F | Incisors broken but not sockets |
| Mandible, whole | Adult | ? | |
| | Adult | M | Right condyle missing |
| | 16–18 | ? | M3 unerupted, ascending rami gone |
| Left frontal | Adult | ? | Small part of orbit retained |
| Left frontal | Adult | ? | Small part of orbit retained |
| Left frontal | Adult? | ? | Small part of orbit retained |
| Left innominate | Adult | M | Very narrow sciatic notch |
| Left innominate | Adult | M | Very narrow sciatic notch |
| Left innominate | Adult? | F | Very wide sciatic notch |
| Distal fibula | 15–18 | ? | Could belong with 16–18-year jaw |

SUMMARY: Three individuals. Two adult males; one adolescent female.

Table 3.47
Bone Elements and Perimortem Damage at Fence Lake

| SKELETAL ELEMENT | WHOLE | FRAGMENT | IMPACT BREAK | ANVIL ABRASION | CUT MARK | BURN | POLISH | CHEWING |
|---|---|---|---|---|---|---|---|---|
| Cranial | | | | | | | | |
| Maxilla | 1 | 1 | 2 | 0 | 0 | 0 | 0 | 0 |
| Mandible | 1 | 3 | 3 | 1 | 1 | 0 | 0 | 0 |
| Frontal | 0 | 9 | 9 | 0 | 1 | 0 | 0 | 0 |
| Parietal | 1 | 3 | 3 | 2 | 1 | 0 | 0 | 0 |
| Occipital | 0 | 7 | 7 | 1 | 0 | 0 | 0 | 0 |
| Temporal | 0 | 5 | 5 | 0 | 0 | 0 | 0 | 0 |
| Base | 0 | 3 | 3 | 0 | 0 | 0 | 0 | 0 |
| Teeth | 52 | 4 | 4 | 0 | 0 | 1 | 0 | 0 |
| Fragment | — | 16 | 16 | 0 | 1 | 1 | 0 | 0 |
| Postcranial | | | | | | | | |
| Cervical vertebrae | 0 | 1 (C2) | 1 | 0 | 0 | 0 | 0 | 0 |
| Sacrum | 0 | 1 | 1 | 0 | 0 | 0 | 0 | 0 |
| Scapula | 0 | 4 | 4 | 0 | 0 | 0 | 0 | 0 |
| Clavicle | 0 | 2 | 2 | 0 | 0 | 0 | 1 | 0 |
| Rib/sternum | 0 | 2/1 | 2/1 | 0 | 0 | 0 | 0 | 0 |
| Humerus | 0 | 4 | 4 | 1 | 0 | 0 | 1 | 0 |
| Radius | 0 | 2 | 2 | 0 | 0 | 0 | 0 | 0 |
| Ulna | 0 | 4 | 4 | 0 | 0 | 0 | 0 | 0 |
| Hand/foot | 5/5 | 4/6 | 0/5 | 0 | 0/2 | 0/4 | 0 | 4?/0 |
| Pelvis | 0 | 9 | 9 | 0 | 0 | 0 | 0 | 0 |
| Femur | 0 | 13 | 13 | 4 | 1 | 0 | 2 | 0 |
| Tibia | 0 | 14 | 14 | 3 | 1 | 0 | 3 | 0 |
| Fibula | 0 | 9 | 9 | 0 | 1 | 0 | 2 | 0 |
| Patella | 1 | 0 | 0 | 0 | 0 | 0 | 0 | 0 |
| Long bone fragments | — | 61 | 61 | 7 | 0 | 1 | 3 | 0 |
| TOTAL (198)[a] | 14 | 184 | 180 | 21 | 11 | 3 | 12 | 4? |
| PERCENTAGE | 7.1 | 92.9 | 90.9 | 10.6 | 5.6 | 1.5 | 6.1 | 2.0 |

Percentage of expected vertebrae = 1.4 (1 of 72; MNI = 3).

NOTE: Only elements that were present are listed. Impact breakage, anvil abrasions, cut marks, burning and polishing represent perimortem damage. Chewing is postmortem damage.

a. Total does not include teeth.

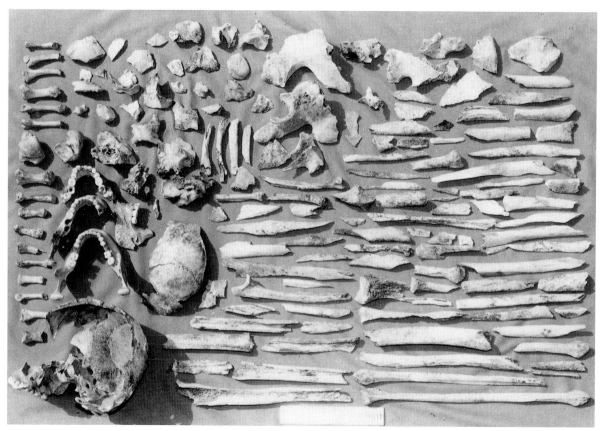

Figure 3.172. Fence Lake, Arizona. Total assemblage for an MNI of three. The remains are said to have been removed from a fire pit by nonprofessionals, and we assume that many small pieces were not collected. Notice that there is only one unbroken long bone, the fibula at lower right. Scale is 15 cm (CGT neg. 5-20-94:2).

Figure 3.173. Fence Lake. The authors examining the assemblage. Note the use of a 75-watt reflector lamp. These lamps are invaluable for long hours of close examination because they are relatively cool and provide the concentrated bright light needed to identify fine cut marks, abrasions, fragment end-polishing, and other minute taphonomic features that are easily missed with more diffused lighting (CGT neg. 5-19-94:13).

Figure 3.174. Fence Lake. Adult female skull with perimortem breakage and some posterior vault damage that might have been caused by burning. There is darkening of the frontal bone and flaking and exfoliation of the back of the head, features common with burning. However, the darkening seems more likely to have been caused by soil staining, and the occipital flaking could have been caused by groundwater. Whatever the taphonomic agency, we have judged the skull unburned (CGT neg. 5-20-94:27).

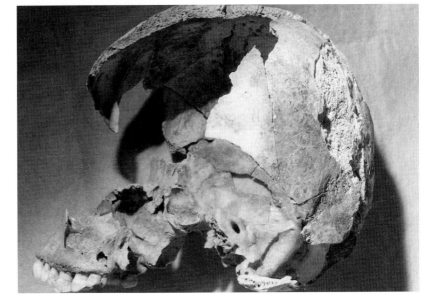

280

Figure 3.175. Fence Lake. Whereas there is uncertainty about the burning of the female skull in figure 3.174, other pieces have unquestionable burning. Shown is a long bone fragment with charring on the right tip, and a burned tooth. Scale in cm (CGT neg. 5-19-94:36).

Figure 3.176. Fence Lake. Perimortem breakage of the adult female anterior teeth and left zygomatic region of maxilla. The lower anterior teeth were undamaged, and there are no anvil or hammerstone abrasions. Altogether, this damage pattern is indicative of violence (CGT neg 5-20-94:25).

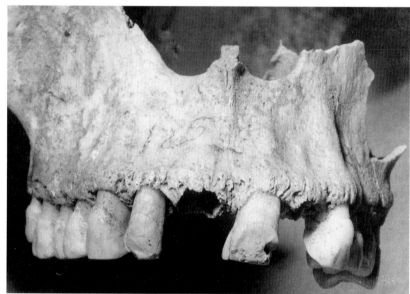

Figure 3.177. Fence Lake. Perimortem cut and chop marks on the anterior border of an adult male mandibular ascending ramus (CGT neg. 5-20-94: 23).

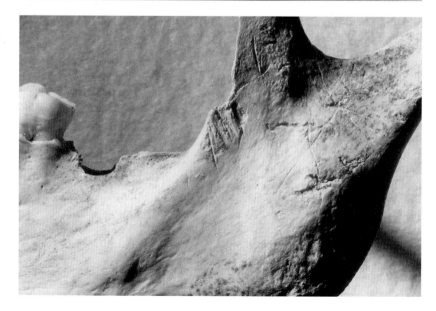

Figure 3.178. Fence Lake. Long bone fragments re-assembled and held together with rubber bands to illustrate the perimortem breakage pattern. Scale in cm (CGT neg. 5-20-94:34).

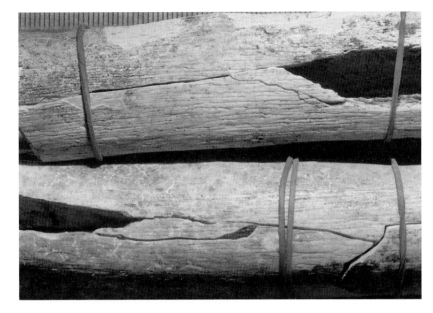

Figure 3.179. Fence Lake. Perimortem cut marks on a toe bone, a very unusual location for cut marks in the human charnel deposits we have reviewed. Scale in cm (CGT neg. 5-19-94:20).

Figure 3.180. Fence Lake. Another toe bone with perimortem abrasions, crushing, and chop marks. Scale in mm (CGT neg. 5-19-94:24).

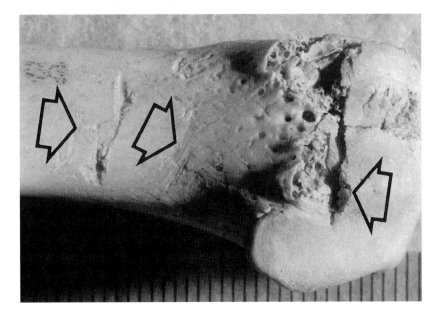

Figure 3.181. Fence Lake.
Long bone fragment with anvil
abrasions and irregular pitting
of undetermined origin. Scale
in mm (CGT neg. 5-20-94:13).

Figure 3.182. Fence Lake.
Perimortem chop marks left by
an indeterminate tool. Compare
with figure 3.207. Scale in mm
(CGT neg. 5-20-94:2).

Figure 3.183. Fence Lake.
Long bone fragment with perimortem chop marks. Photo-
graphed to same scale as
figure 3.182 (CGT neg. 5-
20:94:15).

Figure 3.184. Fence Lake. Perimortem pot-polishing on fragment tip at left. Scale in mm (CGT neg 5-20-94:4).

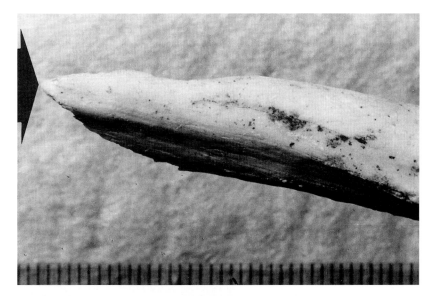

Figure 3.185. Fence Lake. Perimortem pot-polishing on tips of three bone fragments. Scale in mm (CGT neg 5-20-94:9).

Figure 3.186. Fence Lake. Perimortem pot-polishing (at arrow) on a fragment that can be refitted with another fragment. Breakage was for the purpose that indirectly caused the polishing—to extract oil by bone boiling. Scale in cm (CGT neg. 5-19-94:32).

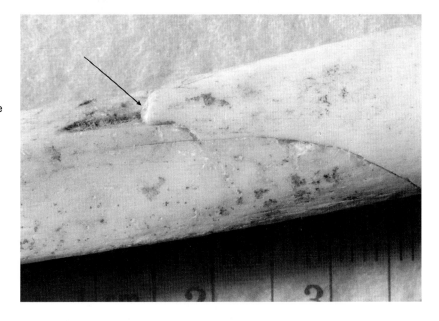

Figure 3.187. Fence Lake. Another pair of refitted fragments with perimortem breakage and polishing (upper right) of one piece after separation. This pair also shows conchoidal breakage at the impact site and the resulting long fracture that separated the two pieces. Scale in cm (CGT neg. 5-20-94:31).

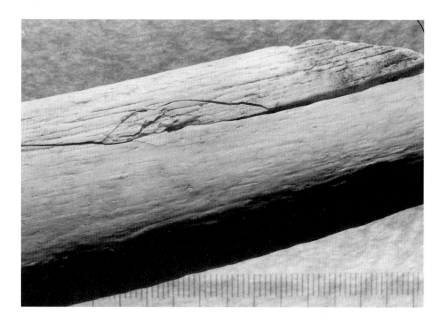

subadult, sex? (SSG). Two adult males; one 16- to 18-year-old female (CGT).

   *Preservation.* Good to excellent.

   *Bone and Fragment Number.* 1,088 (SSG); 198 (CGT).

   *Breakage.* 99.9% (SSG); 92.9% (CGT).

   *Cut Marks.* 0.2% (SSG); 5.6% (CGT).

   *Burning.* 0.5% (SSG); 1.5% (CGT).

   *Anvil Abrasions.* Most bones (SSG); 10.6% (CGT).

   *Polishing.* Not reported (SSG); 6.1% (CGT).

   *Vertebrae Number.* 0.8% of expected (1 of 120) (SSG); 1.4% of expected (1 of 72) (CGT).

   *Scalping.* Uncertain. There are only two cut marks on the 25 cranial vault pieces (CGT).

   *Gnawing, Rodent.* None (CGT).

   *Chewing, Carnivore.* 2.0%? (4? of 198). The apparent gnawing is limited to the ends of fingers, which could just as well have been damaged by perimortem or postmortem smashing (CGT).

   *Insect Parts.* None seen at time of skeletal exam (CGT).

   *Other Modification.* None (CGT).

Archaeologist's Interpretation. None.

Other Interpretations. Grant (1989) was concerned with whether the skeletal remains best fit a model of secondary burial or one of cannibalism. She concluded that cannibalism was the best explanation.

Discussion. Rose Tyson and Sharon Grant permitted us to reexamine the Fence Lake assemblage. As might be expected, some differences turned up, but for the most part we agree reasonably well in our bone and damage counts and identifications. Most importantly, we agree with Grant that the damage pattern best fits that of other assemblages for which cannibalism has been hypothesized. Most, if not all, of the Fence Lake damage was caused by humans.

   The large difference between Grant's total bone count and ours lies mostly in her count of 953 unidentified fragments. We think the 9 in front of the 53 was typed in error and overlooked in the final draft of her manuscript. If so, then her count of 53 is about the same as our count of 61 long bone fragments, and her grand total would be 188 pieces, comparable to our 198.

The difference between our MNI estimates is understandable. Grant was unable to get some mandible and maxilla pieces to fit together, whereas we did get them to fit—so instead of four adults, we recognized two. Grant (1989:2) indicated that "nearly all of the bones exhibit anvil abrasions." Our discussions revealed that this was due to misidentification. Our 10.6% frequency should be used. Finally, Grant found no animal bones in the assemblage, whereas we identified three small animal bone fragments—two bird long bones and one deer-sized rib.

This assemblage has no calcined or charcoaled bone. There are some foot bones with cut marks, which are very rare in Southwestern charnel deposits. The perimortem breakage of the upper incisors in the female has no associated anvil abrasions or alveolar damage, a condition that is believed to represent violence.

## 50
## Yellow Jacket 5MT-1

**Claim Date.** 1989.

**Claimant.** Nancy J. Malville.

**Claim Type.** Cannibalism.

**Other Designations.** Porter Pueblo; Stevenson Site.

**Site Location.** In southwestern Colorado, about 200 m west of Yellow Jacket Canyon and about 1,200 m south of Colo. 666, connecting Monticello, Utah, and Cortez, Colorado. USGS Yellow Jacket quadrangle (1965), T 38N, R 17W, NE ¼ of Sec. 34.

**Site Type.** Residental site associated with large ceremonial center (5MT-5).

**Cultural Affiliation.** Mesa Verde Anasazi.

**Chronology.** A.D. 950–1050, early Mancos period.

**Excavators and Date.** Joe Ben Wheat, principal investigator and director of the Yellow Jacket Project, and University of Colorado Museum archaeological field school students, 1959.

**Institutional Storage.** University of Colorado Museum, Boulder.

**Site Report.** Wheat (1959). Malville (1989:5) noted that J. Andrew Darling was preparing a report on the archaeological context of the 5MT-1 charnel deposit.

**Osteological Reports.** Swedlund (1969); Malville (1989).

**Skeletal Evidence of Stress.** None reported.

**Burial Context.** Fragmented and largely disarticulated human skeletal remains were found mixed with ash, juniper charcoal, animal bone fragments, potsherds, and other debris in a 20-cm-thick layer near the bottom of a storage pit of House II.

**Associated Artifacts.** In the relevant layer were a bifacially flaked stone knife, hammerstones, and bone awls and fleshers (Malville 1989:5).

**Figures.** None.

**Taphonomy.** NJM.

   *MNI.* 4.

   *Age and Sex.* One 17-year-old male; one 4- to 5-year-old child; one 8-year-old child; one 10-year-old child (ages estimated by A. Swedlund, 1969).

*Preservation.* Very good.

*Bone and Fragment Number.* 481, excluding 19 isolated teeth.

*Breakage.* Yes.

*Cut Marks.* 8.9% (43 of 481, excluding isolated teeth).

*Burning.* 2.7% (13 of 481, excluding isolated teeth).

*Vertebrae Number.* 50% of expected (48 of 96).

*Scalping.* Yes, 3 of the 4 crania.

*There is no information for Anvil Abrasions, Polishing, Gnawing, Chewing, Insect Parts, or Other Modification.*

**Archaeologist's Interpretation.** Malville (1989:5) wrote that "the manner in which the bones had been discarded among animal food remains suggested to Wheat (1959) that the human bone fragments represented food remains."

**Other Interpretations.** Malville (1989:6) observed that the bone breakage was seemingly selective, being limited mainly to bones with larger and wider marrow cavities. Furthermore, that the "bones were broken in a manner appropriate for marrow extraction argues against ritual secondary burial" (1989:20). She concluded that the bone damage pattern suggested cannibalism. Alan Swedlund (1969) allowed that the context implied the possibility of cannibalism, but his study of the skeletal remains did not deal with taphonomy. Tim White (1992:370) noted that "the assemblage shares many characteristics [of perimortem damage] with the others described [for the Southwest]."

**Discussion.** We hope Malville will provide additional quantitative taphonomic information on the Yellow Jacket remains, as her report indicates that it is preliminary. Moreover, since 5MT-1 is only about 200 meters from 5MT-3, it would be interesting to know whether any of the 17-year-old male bone fragments from the former fit with adult fragments from the latter, in the manner of Tim White's conjoining efforts at the multiple-room Mancos Canyon charnel deposit. Any matches would suggest that the two Yellow Jacket deposits were part of a single cannibalistic event.

---

**51
Yellow Jacket 5MT-3**

**Claim Date.** 1989.

**Claimant.** Nancy J. Malville.

**Claim Type.** Cannibalism.

**Other Designations.** None.

**Site Location.** About 200 m northwest of previously described 5MT-1. Site 5MT-3 is about halfway between 5MT-5, the large ceremonial center, and 5MT-1. It is also several meters closer to southward-draining Yellow Jacket Canyon than is 5MT-1. USGS Yellow Jacket quadrangle (1965), T 38N, R 17W, NE ¼ of Sec. 34.

**Site Type.** A kiva in a separate residential site.

**Cultural Affiliation.** Mesa Verde Anasazi.

**Chronology.** A.D. 1025–1050; Pueblo II, early to middle Mancos phase.

**Excavators and Date.** Joe Ben Wheat, J. Andrew Darling, and students of the University of Colorado Museum archaeological field school, 1987.

**Institutional Storage.** University of Colorado Museum, Boulder.

**Site Report.** Lange et al. (1988).

Osteological Report. Malville (1989).

Skeletal Evidence of Stress. Not reported.

Burial Context. Bone fragments found on kiva floor and in ventilator shaft, firepit, and fill of an ash pit. Many small fragments were recovered, indicating considerable processing within the kiva (Malville 1989:19).

Associated Artifacts. Not reported.

Figures. None.

Taphonomy. NJM.

*MNI.* 10.

*Age and Sex.* Two adult males; one adult, female?; three adults, sex?; one 18-month-old child; one 2-year-old child; one 4- to 5-year-old child; one 8- to 10-year-old child.

*Preservation.* Very good.

*Bone and Fragment Number.* 1,495, excluding 48 isolated teeth.

*Breakage.* "Massive and nearly total" (Malville 1989:12).

*Cut Marks.* 2.1% (32 of 1,495, excluding isolated teeth).

*Burning.* 11.2% (168 of 1,495, excluding isolated teeth).

*Vertebrae Number.* 13.3% of expected (32 of 240).

*Other Modification.* One long-bone splinter was fashioned into a crude awl.

*There is no information for Anvil Abrasions, Polishing, Scalping, Gnawing, Chewing, or Insect Parts.*

Archaeologist's Interpretation. Frederick Lange and colleagues (1988:39) reported that "during the summer of 1987, excavations on the floor of a Pueblo II kiva at 5MT-3 by J. Andrew Darling, Francis Hayashida, and Susan Converse revealed clusters of charred and fragmented human bone dating to approximately A.D. 1000, which are being studied to evaluate the possibility of cannibalism. . . . Various interpretations for the possibly cannibalized remains have been suggested, including ritual cannibalism, warfare related cannibalism, or the response to food stress during a particularly difficult winter."

Other Interpretations. Malville (1989:16–20) discussed alternatives that might explain the perimortem bone damage. She eliminated natural processes such as rock falls or sediment pressure and movement and argued that multiple secondary burial or ritual secondary burial was not the motive for the damage. She concluded that the bone fragments represented food remains.

Tim White also personally studied 5MT-3. He found that the bone damage signature corresponded closely to that from Mancos Canyon and to artiodactyl bone damage from Badger House in Mesa Verde National Park. This correspondence favored consumption over some form of nonconsumptive mortuary practice (White 1992:343). He apparently did not examine 5MT-3 for pot-polishing, because he did not report having found any (White 1992), nor did Malville.

Discussion. Our comments on 5MT-1 apply here also. We agree with Malville, Wheat, and White that these Yellow Jacket bone assemblages are best explained as examples of cannibalism. There are no clues to why the cannibalism occurred. Malville (1989:12) illustrated a maxilla fragment with the anterior tooth sockets blown out. We believe that this type of damage is evidence of violence when there are no anvil abrasions (see Cave 7 and Largo-Gallina sites). Judging from

Maville's excellent description and White's related comments and comparisons with animal bone food refuse, there seems to be no hint of ritual or sacrifical activity in these two Yellow Jacket human bone assemblages. Malville's (1989:15) photographs of a child's cut clavicle and an adult's ossified thyroid cartilage with multiple cut marks are persuasive evidence of butchering. We agree that at sites 5MT-1 and 5MT-3 together, 14 people were cannibalized during one or more episodes some one thousand years ago at the large Anasazi community we today call Yellow Jacket. Yellow Jacket is within an easy day's walk from other Anasazi sites with cannibalized human bone assemblages.

## 52
## Teec Nos Pos

**Claim Date.** 1989.

**Claimant.** Christy G. Turner II.

**Claim Type.** Cannibalism.

**Other Designations.** NA10674.

**Site Location.** On hillside due west of Teec Nos Pos Wash, Apache County, northeastern Arizona, and 1.6 km (1 mile) south of U.S. 160. USGS Pastora Peak, Ariz.–N.M.–Utah–Colo. quadrangle (1953), T 41N, R 30E, Sec. 27.

**Site Type.** Hillside masonry structure.

**Cultural Affiliation.** Mesa Verde Anasazi.

**Chronology.** A.D. 900–1000, early Pueblo II.

**Excavators and Date.** Peter J. Pilles, Jr., and James W. Mueller, August 19–20, 1969.

**Institutional Storage.** Department of Anthropology, Museum of Northern Arizona, Flagstaff.

**Site Report.** Mueller (1969).

**Osteological Reports.** Stedt (1979); Turner (1989).

**Skeletal Evidence of Stress.** None.

**Burial Context.** Skeleton and fragments on floor of what was reported to have been a burned room. The skeleton did not show extensive burning.

**Associated Artifacts.** Cortez Black-on-white bowl and two bone awls on floor (pottery type identified by David R. Wilcox).

**Figures.** 3.188–3.192.

**Taphonomy.** CGT. Skeletal inventory is in table 3.48.

  *MNI.* 2.

  *Age and Sex.* One adult male about 50 years old; one child or juvenile (immature scapula only).

  *Preservation.* Fair to poor.

  *Bone and Fragment Number.* 102.

  *Breakage.* 3.9%.

  *Cut Marks.* 6.9%.

  *Burning.* 2.9%.

  *Anvil Abrasions.* 0.0%.

  *Polishing.* 0.0%.

  *Vertebrae Number.* 16.7% of expected (8 of 48).

  *Scalping.* Indeterminable (most of skull missing).

  *Gnawing, Rodent.* None.

  *Chewing, Carnivore.* None.

Table 3.48
Bone Elements and Perimortem Damage at Teec Nos Pos

| SKELETAL ELEMENT | WHOLE | FRAGMENT | IMPACT BREAK | CUT MARK | BURN |
|---|---|---|---|---|---|
| Cranial | | | | | |
| Maxilla | 0 | 1 | 1 | 0 | 0 |
| Mandible | 0 | 1 | 0 | 0 | 0 |
| Teeth (18) | | | | | |
| Postcranial | | | | | |
| Cervical vertebrae | 0 | 1 | 0 | 0 | 0 |
| Thoracic vertebrae | 0 | 2 | 0 | 0 | 0 |
| Lumbar vertebrae | 5 | 0 | 0 | 0 | 0 |
| Scapula | 1L | 3 | 0 | 2 | 0 |
| Clavicle | 0 | 2 | 0 | 0 | 0 |
| Rib/sternum | 0 | 46 | 0 | 1 | 0 |
| Radius | 0 | 1 | 0 | 0 | 0 |
| Ulna | 0 | 1 | 0 | 0 | 0 |
| Hand & foot | 11 | 0 | 0 | 0 | 1 |
| Pelvis | 2LR | 0 | 0 | 1 | 2 |
| Sacrum | 1 | 0 | 0 | 0 | 0 |
| Femur | 1R | 1L | 1 | 2 | 0 |
| Fibula | 0 | 1 | 1 | 1 | 0 |
| Long bone fragments | — | 3 | 1 | 0 | 0 |
| TOTAL (102) | 39 | 63 | 4 | 7 | 3 |
| PERCENTAGE | 38.2 | 61.8 | 3.9 | 6.9 | 2.9 |

Percentage of expected vertebrae = 16.7 (8 of 48; MNI = 2).

NOTE: Only elements that were present are listed. No anvil abrasions, polishing, gnawing, or chewing was observed. Impact breakage, cut marks, and burning represent perimortem damage. L denotes left; R denotes right.

Figure 3.188. Teec Nos Pos, Arizona. General view of site area, with "burial" location at arrow. Navajo cornfields and houses are in middle distance beyond the arroyo that was cutting into the site. Isolation and defenselessness characterize this small site. Museum of Northern Arizona Archive photograph by Peter J. Pilles, Jr. (August 20, 1969).

290

Figure 3.189. Teec Nos Pos. Adult male skeleton lying face down on burned room floor. The second individual, a child, is represented only by the scapula indicated by the arrow. Neither individual shows sure evidence of having been burned, so both were probably deposited after the room burned. Museum of Northern Arizona Archive photograph by Peter J. Pilles, Jr. (August 1969); reprinted with permission from *Kiva*.

Figure 3.190. Teec Nos Pos. Perimortem cut marks on proximal end of the adult male's right fibula. Actual width of image in photograph is 3.3 cm (CGT neg. 7-6-88:2; reprinted with permission from *Kiva*).

Figure 3.191. Teec Nos Pos. Perimortem cut marks on a rib of the adult male. Actual width of image in photograph is 3.3 cm (CGT neg. 7-6-88:5; reprinted with permission from *Kiva*).

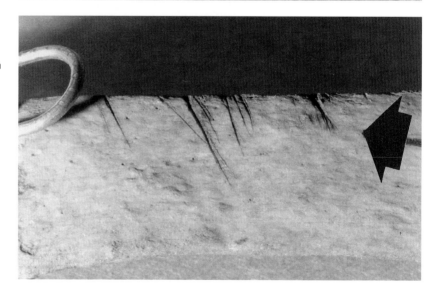

Figure 3.192. Teec Nos Pos. Perimortem cut marks on interior surface and inferior location of the subadult scapula. Actual width of image in photograph is 3.3 cm (CGT neg. 7-6-88:10).

*Insect Parts.* None found at time of skeletal examination.

*Other Modification.* None.

**Archaeologist's Interpretation.** Pilles and Mueller felt that the male could have died as a result of the burning roof's collapsing on him. "The skeleton was face down on a charred occupation surface with two bone awls near the right scapula and to the right of the right knee. It was not an intentional burial" (Mueller 1969:2). They also attributed the missing skeletal elements to their having slid downhill.

**Other Interpretations.** Turner (1989) disagreed with Pilles and Mueller because there was no sign of extensive skeletal burning and because the major missing elements would have lain uphill from the torso and would likely have lodged against the trunk with slopewashing. The cut marks on the two individuals reveal that they had been butchered before the remains were dumped into the room.

**Discussion.** The original report by Turner (1989) gave a date for the site as A.D. 700–900 in the mistaken belief that the bowl found on the room's floor was a Mesa Verde Black-on-white plate. A reexamination of the vessel by David R. Wilcox on June 14, 1990, showed it to be a Cortez Black-on-white bowl, which dates around A.D. 900–1000, a date more in line with the architecture. Fill sherds extended the range to later PII, that is, around A.D. 1000. This correction has also been reported in Turner and Turner (1992a).

## 53 Lake Roosevelt (Grapevine Springs South/Annes)

**Claim Date.** 1991.

**Claimants.** Christy G. Turner II, Marcia H. Regan, and Joel D. Irish.

**Claim Type.** Violence.

**Other Designations.** AZ U:8:221/1576.

**Site Location.** On a ridge overlooking the south shore of the Salt River end of Lake Roosevelt, south of Grapevine Springs, Tonto Basin, central Arizona. USGS Windy Hill quadrangle (1964), T 4N, R 13E, NW ¼ of Sec. 32.

**Site Type.** Agricultural settlement made up of a three-room compound, a granary pedestal, and a walled courtyard.

**Cultural Affiliation.** Salado.

**Chronology.** Roosevelt phase, A.D. 1250–1350.

**Excavator and Date.** Statistical Research, Inc.

**Institutional Storage.** Unknown.

**Site Report.** Shelley and Ciolek-Torrello (1994).

**Osteological Report.** Turner, Regan, and Irish (1994).

**Skeletal Evidence of Stress.** Slight anemia.

**Burial Context.** Two unburied individuals found sprawled on a room floor (Feature 2) that subsequently burned, and another burned and disarticulated individual in a different room (Feature 6) across the courtyard of the compound. The disarticulated young adult male from Feature 6 was not completely excavated (Shelley and Ciolek-Torrello 1994:241), so no bone count is provided here. His disarticulation was probably caused by scavengers.

**Associated Artifacts.** Scattered sherds and a metate were the main items in Feature 2.

**Figures.** None.

**Taphonomy.** CGT, MHR, and JDI.

> *MNI.* 4.
>
> *Age and Sex.* Feature 2: one subadult male (13–15 years) and one 30- to 50-year-old adult male. An unresorbed upper incisor from a 3-year-old child was also recovered. Feature 6: one young adult male.
>
> *Preservation.* Poor.
>
> *Bone and Fragment Number.* Feature 2: subadult, 198 fragments; adult, 680 fragments.
>
> *Breakage.* 1 (depression fracture of vault, subadult).
>
> *Cut Marks.* None.
>
> *Burning.* Considerable, in flesh, dorsal aspect.
>
> *Anvil Abrasions.* None.
>
> *Polishing.* None.
>
> *Vertebrae Number.* Relatively complete except for postmortem diagenic loss.
>
> *Scalping.* None.
>
> *Gnawing, Rodent.* Present.
>
> *Chewing, Carnivore.* None.
>
> *Insect Parts.* None found in laboratory inspection.
>
> *Other Modification.* None.

**Archaeologist's Interpretation.** Steven D. Shelley and Richard Ciolek-Torrello (1994:258–259) concluded: "The weight of the combined evidence [archaeological and physical anthropological] indicates that all three of the individuals found at the site were intentionally killed. After their deaths the site was intentionally burned although whether this was done by the killers or by another party is uncertain. . . . The presence of warfare or other forms of aggression, however, may have been one of the catalysts for the aggregation of small, Roosevelt phase family compounds into larger settlements at the beginning of the Gila phase."

**Other Interpretations.** Turner, Regan, and Irish (1994:582) suggested violence and raiding, on the multiple bases of body positioning (suggesting death prior to burning of the rooms), vault fracturing, absence of females, and animal scavenging. The last indicates inconsiderate treatment of the dead men. Some of the missing body parts could have been taken as trophies.

Discussion. This is surely as unambiguous a case of terminal violence as can be found in a prehistoric context. Making anything else out of it, such as an unusual burial practice, is neither parsimonious nor intuitively satisfying. We are less inclined to view this example of violence as a catalyst for aggregation, as suggested by Shelley and Ciolek-Torrello, because there is solid evidence for violent events as early as Basketmaker II times, at least on the Colorado Plateau. But we do think it a better explanation for aggregation than any violence-free hypothesis.

## 54
## Ram Mesa Kiva

Claim Date. 1992 (unpublished report); 1993 (published report).

Claimants. Marsha D. Ogilvie and Charles E. Hilton (unpublished report); Nicholas P. Hermann, Marsha D. Ogilvie, Charles E. Hilton, and Kenneth L. Brown (published report).

Claim Type. Mixed. Laboratory analysts Ogilvie and Hilton were uncertain about the cause of bone damage and suggested secondary mortuary practices, warfare, and cannibalism as equal possibilities. Archaeologists Richard B. Sullivan and G. Robert Phippen (1994), who excavated the skeletal remains, believed cannibalism had occurred, as did principal investigator Joseph C. Winter (1994).

Other Designations. Transwestern Pipeline Expansion Project Upper Puerco River site OCA 423-124; also LA83500. Herrmann et al. (1993) and Sullivan and Phippen (1994) referred to sites in this area as the Ram Mesa Community. We follow this designation for ease of memory and identification, adding "kiva" to distinguish this charnel deposit site from the West Rio Puerco site OCA 423-131 (Ram Mesa Basketmaker pithouse), which also had damaged charnel deposits.

Site Location. About 23 km (14.3 miles) northeast of Gallup, McKinley County, New Mexico, on the valley floor surface rising below the cliff and boulder talus of Ram Mesa, north of the Rio Puerco. USGS Hard Ground Flats quadrangle (1963), T 16N, R 16W, N ½ of Sec. 11.

Site Type. Charnel deposit found in a kiva associated with a medium-sized, ten-room or more masonry pueblo and midden areas. Great houses (LA89484), great kivas, and a prehistoric road are nearby in the same valley.

Cultural Affiliation. Cibola Anasazi.

Chronology. Pueblo II, about A.D. 1000 (calibrated carbon-14 dates, A.D. 980–1188; ceramic date mean range, A.D. 1004–1081 [Hermann et al. 1993:12–13, 29]).

Excavator and Date. University of New Mexico, Office of Contract Archaeology, for Transwestern Pipeline Expansion Project, 1991.

Institutional Storage. None. Remains were reburied on November 19, 1991, as required by skeletal study restrictions imposed by the Navajo Nation and various Puebloan tribes.

Site Report. Sullivan and Phippen (1994).

Osteological Report. Herrmann et al. (1993).

Skeletal Evidence of Stress. Anemia, dental hypoplasia, and deciduous dental caries.

**Burial Context.** Herrmann et al. (1993:29–31) neatly described what the archaeologists found:

> A [human] bone bed on the kiva bench and floor. . . . Human skeletal material was dispersed throughout 5.88 and 17.81 sq m areas on the Kiva bench . . . and floor . . . respectively. The densest concentration was on the bench (Feature 16). The bone concentration did not extend to the bench edge of the kiva or the southern pilaster; only a few elements were identified on the southeastern bench. These included an articulated talus and calcaneus and immature vertebral fragments. . . . Numerous refits among fragments found on the bench and kiva floor areas suggested a single depositional event. Due to the fact that this material was modified, commingled, and lacked any primary articulation, it was not possible to associate the crania with the postcrania.

**Associated Artifacts.** "Numerous sandstone slabs, hammerstones, lithic debitage, faunal remains, and ceramic sherds were incorporated with the [human] skeletal material. Sherds of a corrugated Cibola Gray Ware [A.D. 575–950] vessel were scattered in the central region of the deposit" (Herrmann et al. 1993:31).

**Figures.** None.

**Taphonomy.** MDO and CEH.

*MNI.* 12.

*Age and Sex.* Two infants (a 1-year-old and a 2.5-year-old); three children (one 4- to 5-year-old, one 4- to 6-year-old, and one 6.5- to 9-year-old); one 12-year-old; one 15-year-old male; one 30-year-old female; two 30- to 35-year-old males; two 30- to 40-year-olds, sex?.

*Preservation.* Good. Hard and dense bone.

*Bone and Fragment Number.* 2,641 (Sullivan and Phippen [1994:390] list 2,845 pieces).

*Breakage.* 99.4% (2,626 of 2,641).

*Cut Marks.* 0.3% (8 of 2,641).

*Burning.* 18.7% (494 of 2,641).

*Anvil Abrasions.* Apparently not searched for, as neither the methodology nor the discussion section by Ogilvie and Hilton (1993) mentioned this taphonomic character. However, Sullivan and Phippen (1994:392) said in their discussion of the kiva bones that anvil/hammerstone abrasions were present, along with other stigmata of intentional perimortem bone damage.

*Polishing.* Ogilvie and Hilton apparently did not study the assemblage for polishing, and Sullivan and Phippen did not mention any.

*Vertebrae Number.* 21.2% of expected (61 of 288).

*Scalping.* Ogilvie and Hilton did not discuss this possibility. Sullivan and Phippen (1994:390) proposed that cut marks on the frontal, temporal, and mandibular bones resulted from scalping and/or "face peeling."

*Gnawing, Rodent.* 0.4% (11 of 2,641).

*Chewing, Carnivore.* None found.

*There is no information for Insect Parts or Other Modification.*

**Archaeologists' Interpretation.** Sullivan and Phippen (1994:386) be-

lieved that the archaeological evidence pointed to the site's having
been "catastrophically abandoned when most of the residents appear
to have been massacred and dismembered in the kiva." Ceramic
analysis by Christine E. Goetze indicates abandonment around
A.D. 1200 (Sullivan and Phippen 1994:361).

In their discussion of probable human marrow extraction at Ram
Mesa Kiva, Sullivan and Phippen (1994:391) reported having found

> at least two concentrations of fragmented human bone, indicating
> possible toss zones [of boiled-out, grease-free bone]. . . . The most
> extensive was on the surface of the eastern bench area, and the
> other was on the floor of the structure in association with a con-
> centration of bone meal and the central hearth. . . . Numerous tab-
> ular rocks, fragments of thermally cracked rocks, hammerstones,
> flaked lithic tools, broken ceramic vessels (jars with soot stains),
> and nonhuman bone tools were identified as point-provenienced
> items in the assemblage associated with the bone bed. Eighteen of
> these items were analyzed for mammalian blood sera [by Kathryn
> Puseman]. Human anti-sera [was] identified on one specimen. . . .
> In addition to the fragmented elements, there were deposits of
> bone so fine that the excavator wrote that it had the consistency of
> "oatmeal."

Sullivan and Phippen (1994:392) concluded that by their calcula-
tions, about half the inhabitants of the Ram Mesa Kiva pueblo had
probably been cannibalized. The problem was not whether "the inhabitants were killed, dismembered, and probably cooked and eaten,
but why and by whom . . . [with five possibilities:] 1. ritual cannibalism; 2. pathological behavior; 3. a border dispute or raiding by
hunters and gatherers, migratory populations, or other sedentary
groups forced to raid because of starvation; 4. emergency cannibalism
by some of the missing site inhabitants (i.e., the young adults); 5. punishment (for witchcraft, a raid, or other misbehavior)."

**Other Interpretations.** Ogilvie and Hilton (1993:128), after reviewing
mortuary and military practices of North American Indians and a few
other death-related anecdotes lacking taphonomic information, concluded that "secondary mortuary and warfare practices offer reasonable alternatives to the cannibalism explanation for the perimortem
modification seen in this assemblage."

Joseph C. Winter (1994:215), principal investigator for the Transwestern Pipeline Expansion Project, favored cannibalism in the final
synthesis and conclusion volume:

> Considering the smashed and sometimes cut and often burned na-
> ture of the bones near a firepit (with some of them in the firepit), it
> is this author's opinion that they were eaten. . . . The inescapable
> fact is that an event of extreme violence occurred in a very sacred
> space, with the likely residents of the site—probably an extended
> family composed of infants, children, teens, men, and women—
> murdered and dismembered, and their bones smashed, cut, and
> burned. . . . It is also this author's opinion that the perpetrators
> were not Anasazi, but instead were members of a non-Puebloid

group, perhaps hunters and gatherers who lived around the edges
of the San Juan Basin.

Discussion. Ogilvie and Hilton's osteological study, conducted in
record time and under pressure of a reburial deadline not of their
making, has substantial merit, but two months (Ogilvie and Hilton
1993:99) did not enable them to study the series adequately. For example, age and sex were based only on cranial elements due to inadequate time to try to refit postcranial fragments into identifiable
elements. They also seemingly had little external consulting help to
guide them in their planning and execution of the osteological and
taphonomic data collecting and analysis. Furthermore, that additional mutilated human skeletal material was found in this site but
was not allowed to be analyzed because of "budgetary and time constraints" is incredible, given the obvious scientific and historical importance of the assemblage (Ogilvie and Hilton 1993:97–98).
However, the study's faults were not all administrative or due to
Indian-archaeologist politics; there were also problems with interpretation, methodology, and communication with the field archaeologists. (Hermann, however, did produce a field inventory of the
assemblage and recognized some burning and much breakage.)

Ogilvie and Hilton did not document in any testable manner the
assertion that there were reasonable alternatives to cannibalism as the
explanation for the Ram Mesa Kiva charnel deposit. Most of the ethnohistoric and prehistoric examples they compiled are irrelevant to
the Southwest or are contextually inappropriate. Moreover, their review of the ethnographic literature failed to include any of the several
examples of cannibalism such as those assembled from early Spanish
chronicles and other sources by Beals (1932 and elsewhere) and others. Their geographic definition of the Southwest stopped at the U.S.
border and therefore did not include any of the ethnographic reports
of cannibalism in western and northern Mexico.

There are more important omissions. Ogilvie and Hilton's analysis
ignored the significance of missing vertebrae, which was not overlooked by Sullivan and Phippen (1994), and they failed to determine
the occurrence of anvil abrasions. Apparently, they did not look for
polishing of any sort—pot-polishing or polishing with expedient
tools. In May 1992, before Ogilvie and Hilton's report was completed—or early enough for them to make revisions before publication—we presented an illustrated lecture to the Office of Contract
Archaeology staff about Southwestern cannibalism. At this time one
of the crew members who excavated the Ram Mesa Kiva charnel deposit said he had seen and saved a mass of bone powder from the kiva
floor. Ogilvie and Hilton were present, heard the remark, and should
have followed up with an examination of the bone powder. Since they
did not, we were subsequently asked for advice by one of the Ram
Mesa archaeologists. I suggested that the bone powder be submitted
to forensic anthropologist Stanley Rhine of the Maxwell Museum of
Anthropology, University of New Mexico, for possible species identification. The results of Rhine's examination are unknown.

In sum, Ogilvie and Hilton's (1993:125) interpretation of the Ram

Mesa Kiva charnel deposit lacks objectivity and seems to have been biased by antipathetic views about Anasazi cannibalism, as evidenced by their stressing the opinion of anticannibalism journalist Paul Bahn (1992). Patently, one cannot reach a conclusion that cannibalism occurred at Ram Mesa Kiva if published key criteria for its identification are overlooked and if well-known ethnohistoric accounts of Greater Southwestern cannibalism are not considered for purposes of analogy.

## 55
## Ram Mesa Pithouse

**Claim Date.** 1992 (unpublished report); 1993 (published report).

**Claimants.** Marsha D. Ogilvie and Charles E. Hilton (unpublished report).

**Claim Type.** Mixed. Claimants were uncertain about the cause of bone damage and suggested secondary mortuary practices, warfare, and cannibalism as equal possibilities.

**Other Designations.** Transwestern Pipeline Expansion Project Upper Puerco River site OCA 423-131. Also LA83507 and OCA 423-101 (the latter number, which is given in Herrmann 1993:50–51, figs. 16a and 16b, may be in error).

**Site Location.** At base of Ram Mesa, McKinley County, northwestern New Mexico, in upper Rio Puerco Valley. Map position is about 3.2 km (2 miles) southwest of Rio Puerco site 423-124 (Sullivan and Phippen 1994:2). USGS Church Rock quadrangle (1963), T 16N, R 16W, N ½ of Sec. 15.

**Site Type.** Residential community with multiple pithouses and associated extramural features, clearly "a substantial BMIII–PI village" (Wellman 1994:159).

**Cultural Affiliation.** Anasazi.

**Chronology.** Basketmaker III–Pueblo I. Kevin D. Wellman (1994:222) thought the pithouse with the deposit of damaged human bones had a terminal occupation date of about A.D. 705. This was a ceramic date averaged from the assemblage in the roof fall, floor, and interior features. Since the bone deposit was in post-abandonment fill, the remains are younger than A.D. 705. Wellman (1994:226) concluded that the two perimortem-damaged people were "interred toward the end of the PI occupation."

**Excavator and Date.** University of New Mexico, Office of Contract Archaeology, for Transwestern Pipeline Expansion Project, 1991.

**Institutional Storage.** None. Remains were reburied on November 19, 1991.

**Site Report.** Wellman (1994).

**Osteological Report.** Herrmann et al. (1993).

**Skeletal Evidence of Stress.** None reported.

**Burial Context.** In pithouse near-floor fill.

**Associated Artifacts.** None reported.

**Figures.** None.

**Taphonomy.** MDO and CEH.

  *MNI.* 1. Another young adult female was represented, but her preservation was poor, indicating a different burial episode (Ogilvie and Hilton 1993:112).

*Age and Sex.* A 30- to 34-year-old female.
*Preservation.* Good. Hard and dense.
*Bone and Fragment Number.* 165.
*Breakage.* 100.0%.
*Cut Marks.* 1.2%.
*Burning.* 0.6%.
*Vertebrae Number.* 25.0% of expected (6 of 24).
*Gnawing, Rodent.* None.
*Chewing, Carnivore.* None.
*There is no information for Anvil Abrasions, Polishing, Scalping, Insect Parts, or Other Modification.*

**Archaeologist's Interpretation.** Wellman (1994:178) described the bone mass as having been "in a circular pile 0.40 m in diameter." Nicholas P. Herrmann (1993:52) noted that additional fragmented human remains were found about 5 m away from the remains just detailed:

> This burial [3-131-30] was similar to the burial from this site analyzed in the laboratory by Ogilvie and Hilton . . . in that perimortem damage was evident. Burial 3-131-30 was not analyzed by Ogilvie and Hilton. . . . This burial consisted of partially disarticulated elements in a 0.20 m diameter circular pile. Elements recovered included only portions of the left scapula, distal left femur, distal left tibia, three thoracic vertebrae, and 12 ribs. Only one right rib was represented while all others were from the left side. One rib and a thoracic vertebra remained articulated. . . . This individual was an adolescent ranging from 13 to 16 years old. . . . Perimortem spiral fractures were evident on the distal femoral midshaft and distal tibia.

> Wellman (1994:226) reviewed environmental changes around Ram Mesa, concluding: "Another indication of a period of environmental stress at or near the time of site abandonment was the partial remains of two individuals recovered from the upper fill of SU 5 [the pithouse with the damaged human bones], who were probably interred toward the end of the PI occupation. The remains were culturally modified in a manner that leads to speculation concerning butchering and subsequent cannibalism."

**Other Interpretations.** On the basis of differential preservation, Ogilvie and Hilton separated out two young to middle-aged adult females. Only the remains that were well preserved (hard and dense bone) had the perimortem damage inventoried above. The friable skeletal material had no identifiable modification and so was considered a disturbed primary burial. Ogilvie and Hilton's interpretations for Ram Mesa I apply here also.

All authors of the 1993 report signed off on the summary and conclusions. Two of their propositions need to be discussed (Herrmann et al. 1993:155):

> Skeletal elements were disproportionally represented with the more dense bone being in good condition. There was little evidence

of weathering, and the state of preservation suggested protection of the bone by adhering soft tissue and/or relatively rapid burial. . . . Given the known cultural continuity in the Southwest, it is noteworthy that there are no ethnographic analogues that suggest cannibalism as an interpretation for the high incidence of perimortem modification. Other possible explanations include warfare, corpse mutilation, and secondary mortuary practices.

Discussion. Our remarks for Ram Mesa Kiva apply equally here. In addition, we note that the osteological analysts were inconsistent in their taphonomic interpretation regarding preservation. Recall that they judged the weathered and poorly preserved burial to be primary. This means that it was by definition not defleshed, and as such the bone was unable to resist microbial and other postmortem diagenic factors. The well-preserved processed bones, stratigraphically identical in the same small pit and therefore about the same age as the primary burial, must have withstood diagenesis better because they lacked the organic substance needed for microbial activity. In other words, defleshing, and probably further processing including roasting and boiling, removed the organic source for microbial metabolism and organic acid production. The lack of acid and enzyme production enabled the superior preservation that all taphonomic analysts have noted for Southwestern charnel deposits suggesting cannibalism. As for their claim that there are no ethnographic analogues for cannibalism, apparently the authors were unaware of various ethnographic accounts of Southwestern cannibalism, especially Gifford's (1936) narrative of cannibalism by Yavapai warriors.

**56**
**Aztec Wash I**

Claim Date. 1992.

Claimants. C. G. Turner and J. A. Turner, but credit for this claim properly belongs to Raymond G. Harriman (field director), Michael H. Dice, Laurens C. Hammack, Nancy S. Hammack, and others of the Complete Archaeological Services Associates (CASA) field crew who excavated and mapped the site in 1990. Dice consulted with C. G. Turner by telephone from Cortez, Colorado, during the several-day excavation period.

Claim Type. Cannibalism.

Other Designations. 5MT10207.

Site Location. Southwest of Cortez, about 14.7 km (9.1 miles) southwest of Towaoc, Ute Mountain Indian community, on the southern foothills of Sleeping Ute Mountain, southwestern Colorado. T 33N, R 18W, NW ¼ of NW ¼ of SE ¼ of SW ¼ of Sec. 29 (Errickson et al. 1993:9–11).

Site Type. Area 1 (of two habitation areas) had at least six separate rooms, a kiva, and other extramural features.

Cultural Affiliation. Anasazi.

Chronology. Early Pueblo III. Kiva 1 had tree-ring dates of A.D. 1021 and 1113, and Room 3, a tree-ring date of 1062. The human bones in Room 4 were deposited at the same time as those in the kiva and Room 3 (Dice 1993c, p. 3-13).

**Excavators and Date.** Michael H. Dice and other CASA field crew members on the Towaoc Canal Reach III project, Bureau of Reclamation, 1990.

**Institutional Storage.** Complete Archaeological Services Associates, Cortez, Colorado.

**Site Report.** Errickson et al. (1993).

**Osteological Report.** Dice (1993c); Turner, Turner, and Green (1993).

**Skeletal Evidence of Stress.** Health said to be good, although some sort of meningeal groove infection was present in three individuals (Dice 1993c, p. 3-14).

**Burial Context.** Bone fragments were encountered on an abandoned kiva floor and on floors of two rooms; Room 3 had burned soon after the human bones were deposited. Dice (1993c, p. 3-14) suggested that the bones in each of the three structures were deposited at the same time, despite his being unable to fit together pieces from different structures.

**Associated Artifacts.** Pottery and ground and chipped stone artifacts, including a metate, were on the kiva floor in close association with the human bone refuse. One flake from the kiva floor tested positive for human blood (Dice 1993c, p. 3-8; Newman 1993). Room 3 had a battered "floor polisher" that fit with one from the kiva floor.

**Figures.** 3.193–3.202.

**Taphonomy.** MHD. Skeletal inventory is in table 3.49.

*MNI.* 13.

*Age and Sex.* Four adults; three age?, sex?; one 13- to 18-year-old; three 7- to 12-year-olds; one 3- to 6-year-old; one neonate. Among these were three males and three females.

*Preservation.* Excellent.

*Bone and Fragment Number.* 1,160.

*Breakage.* 87.5%.

*Cut Marks.* 1.1%.

*Burning.* 16.9%.

*Anvil Abrasions.* 8.3%.

*Vertebrae Number.* 7.1% of expected (22 of 312).

*Scalping.* Possible, but only four cranial cut marks were identified.

*Gnawing, Rodent, and Chewing, Carnivore.* 5.9%.

*Other Modification.* Pulverized bone was found on Kiva 1 floor. An articulated left leg (Feature 18) remained unmodified.

*There is no information for Polishing or Insect Parts.*

**Archaeologists' Interpretation.** Mary Errickson and colleagues (1993:9–11) wrote that "stratigraphic evidence suggests that the roof was dismantled at the time of structural abandonment [of Room 2]. With the exception of a later pit feature containing disarticulated human bones and trash in the fill, the room filled naturally." After abandonment, Room 3 was reentered and a mass of disarticulated human remains and cultural debris was placed on the use surface and within floor features (Errickson et al. 1993:9–12). Stratigraphic data suggested that the wall-supported second roof burned soon after this event. In Kiva 1, human remains were found "on the main floor, [in the] southern recess, and within features. . . . The bone material did not result from secondary deposition but was associated with human

Table 3.49
Bone Elements and Perimortem Damage at Aztec Wash I

| SKELETAL ELEMENT | WHOLE | FRAG-MENT | IMPACT BREAK | ANVIL ABRASION | CUT MARK | BURN | GNAW/CHEW |
|---|---|---|---|---|---|---|---|
| Cranial | | | | | | | |
| Maxilla | 0 | 17 | 17 | 0 | 0 | 3 | 0 |
| Mandible | 1 | 31 | 31 | 3 | 0 | 13 | 0 |
| Frontal | 0 | 13 | 13 | 2 | 0 | 0 | 0 |
| Parietal | 0 | 33 | 33 | 5 | 0 | 4 | 1 |
| Occipital | 0 | 31 | 31 | 2 | 1 | 3 | 0 |
| Temporal | 0 | 27 | 27 | 5 | 1 | 3 | 0 |
| Teeth (44) | | | | | | | |
| Fragment | — | 193 | 193 | 16 | 2 | 37 | 1 |
| Postcranial | | | | | | | |
| Vertebrae | 10 | 35 | 35 | 0 | 0 | 4 | 6 |
| Sacrum | 0 | 4 | 4 | 0 | 0 | 0 | 0 |
| Scapula | 0 | 21 | 21 | 0 | 0 | 2 | 2 |
| Clavicle | 0 | 9 | 9 | 1 | 0 | 2 | 0 |
| Rib | 4 | 120 | 120 | 9 | 0 | 1 | 10 |
| Humerus | 11 | 9 | 9 | 3 | 2 | 2 | 4 |
| Radius | 1 | 12 | 12 | 1 | 0 | 4 | 1 |
| Ulna | 1 | 14 | 14 | 2 | 0 | 3 | 0 |
| Hand & foot | 89 | 34 | 34 | 2 | 0 | 18 | 16 |
| Pelvis | 2 | 23 | 23 | 4 | 0 | 0 | 10 |
| Femur[a] | 7 | 69 | 69 | 22 | 2 | 11 | 8 |
| Tibia | 7 | 19 | 19 | 4 | 0 | 2 | 3 |
| Fibula | 4 | 9 | 9 | 0 | 0 | 0 | 3 |
| Patella | 8 | 0 | 0 | 0 | 1 | 0 | 1 |
| Long bone fragments | — | 187 | 187 | 15 | 3 | 54 | 2 |
| Bone type unknown | 0 | 105 | 105 | 0 | 1 | 30 | 1 |
| TOTAL (1,160) | 145 | 1,015 | 1,015 | 96 | 13 | 196 | 69 |
| PERCENTAGE | 12.5 | 87.5 | 87.5 | 8.3 | 1.1 | 16.9 | 5.9 |

Percentage of expected vertebrae = 7.1 (22 of 312; MNI = 13).[b]

SOURCE: Dice (1993c).

NOTE: Only elements that were present are listed. No polishing was observed. Impact breakage, anvil abrasions, cut marks, and burning represent perimortem damage. Gnawing and chewing are postmortem damage.

a. Dice (1993c, p.3–7) found one bone tool made from human femur that he did not add to the total for femur or site assemblage, nor have we.

b. Assuming that three fragments equal one vertebra.

activities during postoccupation reuse of the structure" (Errickson et al. 1993:9–26).

**Other Interpretations.** None.

**Discussion.** Dice (1993c) made a number of important observations about these charnel deposits. First, on the basis of fitting together two pieces of a stone tool, he was able to suggest that the human bone debris in Room 3 had been initially butchered, broken, and burned in the kiva. Second, thanks to point mapping of each bone fragment, he noted that most of the burned bone was found within and around the central fire pit in the kiva. Last, he reasoned that "if cannibalism did occur, the large numbers of articulated bones in association with processed bones suggests that starvation was not the main motiva-

Figure 3.193. Aztec Wash I,
Colorado. Human bone mass in
place. Pit structure 1, Feature 18.
Field photograph taken in 1990.
Courtesy CASA, Cortez,
Colorado.

Figure 3.194. Aztec Wash I.
The complete charnel assemblage being examined by excavator and analyst Michael A.
Dice (CGT neg. 1-10-91:19).

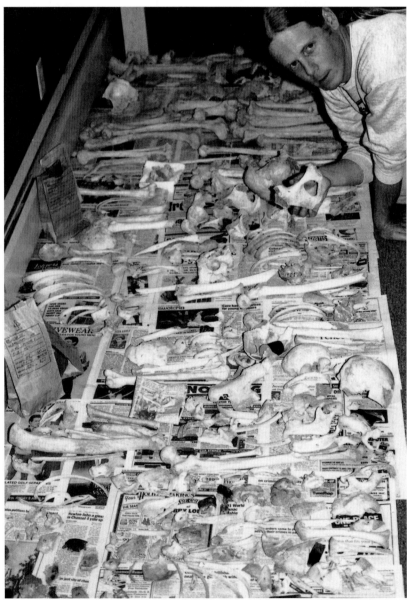

Figure 3.195. Aztec Wash I. Perimortem-fractured adult anterior teeth and blown-out anterior tooth sockets. Specimen 1265 (CGT neg. 1-10-91:10).

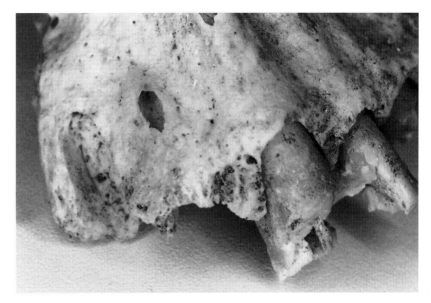

Figure 3.196. Aztec Wash I. Cranial fragment with incomplete perimortem peel fracture. Specimen 1732 (CGT neg. 1-10-91:4).

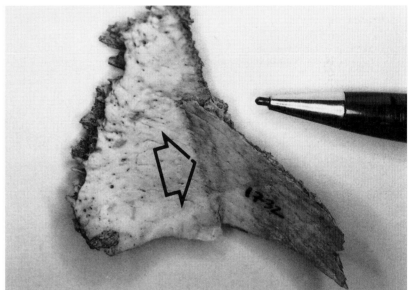

Figure 3.197. Aztec Wash I. Cranial fragment with perimortem breakage and anvil abrasions. Specimen 1648 (CGT neg. 1-10-91:3).

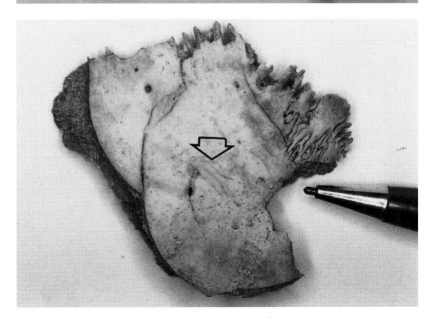

Figure 3.198. Aztec Wash I.
Clavicle fragment with perimortem abrasions (at pencil tip)
and hammerstone impact dent
(at arrow). Specimen 1721
(CGT neg. 1-10-91:8).

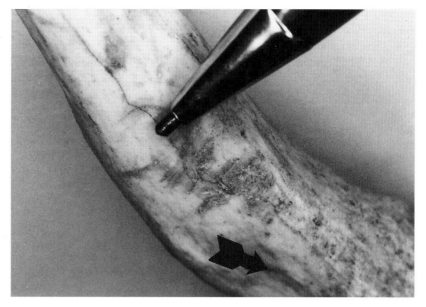

Figure 3.199. Aztec Wash I.
Perimortem crushing of rib fragment, external surface. Specimen 1589 (CGT neg. 1-10-91:1).

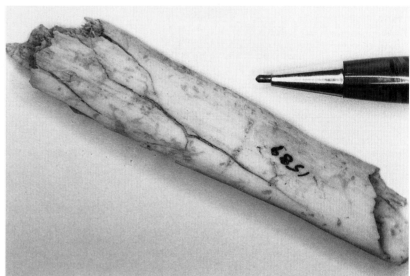

Figure 3.200. Aztec Wash I.
Internal surface of rib fragment
in figure 3.199, showing perimortem crushing. Specimen
1589 (CGT neg. 1-10-91:2).

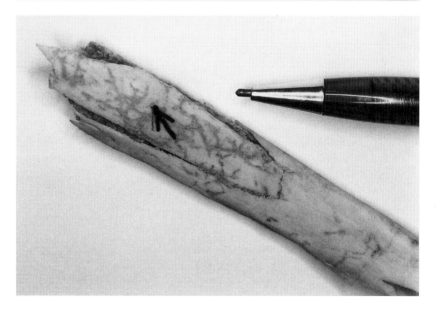

Figure 3.201. Aztec Wash I. Small fragment of long bone with perimortem abrasions at pencil tip and arrow. Specimen 1768 (CGT neg. 1-10-91:7).

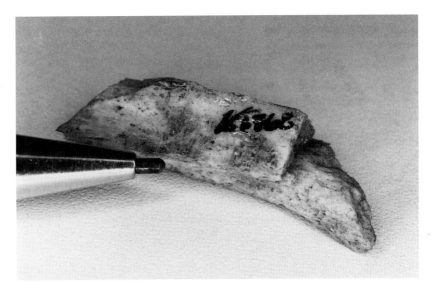

Figure 3.202. Aztec Wash I. Femur head with perimortem breakage and cut marks encircling the neck. Specimen 1160 (CGT neg. 1-10-91:13).

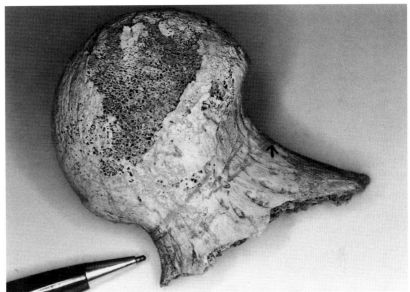

tion. Starving people would probably try to utilize as much of a body as possible, rather than leave prime parts to scavengers" (Dice 1993c, p. 7-7).

At the invitation of CASA's Laurens C. Hammack, we spent January 10, 1991, in Cortez conferring with Dice about the assemblage. It was clear that a great deal of perimortem damage had occurred, and the breaking, cutting, abrading, and burning were identical in kind and similar in amount to that of charnel deposits we had studied previously. In 1991 we were not systematically looking for polishing, but we noticed an example.

This charnel deposit is one of the best excavated to date, and Dice's field methodology should serve as a useful model for future excavations of Southwestern human charnel deposits.

Claim Date. 1992.

Claimants. C. G. Turner and J. A. Turner. The same remarks apply here as for Aztec Wash I.

Claim Type. Cannibalism.

Other Designations. 5MT10206.

Site Location. About 250 m (820 feet) northeast of Aztec Wash I.

Site Type. Two surface rooms, a below-ground storage room, and a kiva.

Cultural Affiliation. Anasazi.

Chronology. Early Pueblo III. Juniper bark dates from kiva beams ranged between A.D. 1129 and 1147.

Excavator and Date. Michael H. Dice, 1990.

Institutional Storage. Complete Archaeological Services Associates, Cortez, Colorado.

Site Report. Errickson et al. (1993).

Osteological Report. Dice (1993c).

Skeletal Evidence of Stress. Unknown.

Burial Context. Bone fragments were found on a kiva floor, in a recess of the kiva, and in bowls on the kiva floor. Human bone was also found in Rooms 1 and 3. Some pieces fit with bone fragments in the kiva. Most of the processing at this site seems to have occurred in the kiva.

Associated Artifacts. To be reported.

Figures. None.

Taphonomy. MHD. Skeletal inventory is in table 3.50.

   *MNI.* 2.

   *Age and Sex.* One adult female; one adolescent, sex?.

   *Preservation.* Excellent in the kiva, poor in Room 1.

   *Bone and Fragment Number.* 566.

   *Breakage.* 97.7%.

   *Cut Marks.* 0.5%.

   *Burning.* 18.6%.

   *Anvil Abrasions.* 4.1%.

   *Vertebrae Number.* 35.4% of expected (17 of 48).

   *Scalping.* Probably not; only one cut mark on the two crania.

   *Gnawing, Rodent, and Chewing, Carnivore.* 1.2%.

   *Other Modification.* None.

   *There is no information for Polishing or Insect Parts.*

Archaeologists' Interpretation. According to the project report (Errickson et al. 1993), excavation showed that the kiva had served both ritual and domestic uses. The human bone deposit was placed on the floor just before the kiva burned, which possibly was intentional; there was no evidence of abandonment before burning. In Room 1, "final events . . . appear to have included the modification and burning of human materials and the deposition of partially burned human material . . . on the floor. The room was then abandoned" (Errickson et al. 1993:8). For Room 2, the authors suggested the possibility that "the placement of human bone on the floor represents the last use of the structure, similar to situations in Room 1 and Kiva 1. Although unburned roof fall materials overlay the floor, the lack of major roof beams suggests that parts of the roof were salvaged" (1993:12). Summing up, Errickson and colleagues proposed

Table 3.50
Bone Elements and Perimortem Damage at Aztec Wash II

| SKELETAL ELEMENT | WHOLE | FRAGMENT | IMPACT BREAK | ANVIL ABRASION | CUT MARK | BURN | GNAW/CHEW |
|---|---|---|---|---|---|---|---|
| Cranial | | | | | | | |
| Maxilla | 0 | 4 | 4 | 0 | 0 | 2 | 0 |
| Mandible | 0 | 2 | 2 | 0 | 0 | 0 | 0 |
| Frontal | 0 | 2 | 2 | 0 | 1 | 0 | 0 |
| Parietal | 0 | 1 | 1 | 0 | 0 | 0 | 0 |
| Occipital | 0 | 4 | 4 | 1 | 0 | 0 | 0 |
| Temporal | 0 | 3 | 3 | 0 | 0 | 0 | 1 |
| Teeth (8) | | | | | | | |
| Fragment | — | 18 | 18 | 1 | 0 | 1 | 0 |
| Postcranial | | | | | | | |
| Vertebrae | 1 | 49 | 49 | 0 | 0 | 3 | 0 |
| Sesamoid | 0 | 1 | 0 | 0 | 0 | 0 | 0 |
| Scapula | 0 | 4 | 4 | 0 | 0 | 0 | 0 |
| Rib | 0 | 25 | 25 | 0 | 0 | 2 | 0 |
| Humerus | 0 | 6 | 6 | 2 | 0 | 0 | 0 |
| Radius | 0 | 6 | 6 | 1 | 0 | 1 | 0 |
| Ulna | 0 | 10 | 10 | 1 | 0 | 2 | 1 |
| Hand & foot | 11 | 47 | 47 | 1 | 0 | 11 | 4 |
| Pelvis | 0 | 2 | 0 | 0 | 1 | 0 | 0 |
| Femur | 0 | 10 | 10 | 3 | 1 | 3 | 0 |
| Tibia | 0 | 13 | 13 | 7 | 0 | 0 | 0 |
| Fibula | 0 | 6 | 6 | 0 | 0 | 1 | 0 |
| Patella | 1 | 0 | 0 | 0 | 0 | 0 | 0 |
| Long bone fragments | — | 85 | 85 | 6 | 0 | 34 | 1 |
| Bone type unknown | — | 255 | — | 0 | 0 | 45 | 0 |
| TOTAL (566) | 13 | 553 | 553 | 23 | 3 | 105 | 7 |
| PERCENTAGE | 2.3 | 97.7 | 97.7 | 4.1 | 0.5 | 18.6 | 1.2 |

Percentage of expected vertebrae = 35.4 (17 of 48; MNI = 2).[a]

SOURCE: Dice (1993c).

NOTE: Only elements that were present are listed. No polishing was observed. Impact breakage, anvil abrasions, cut marks, and burning represent perimortem damage. Gnawing and chewing are postmortem damage.

a. Assuming three fragments equal one vertebra.

that "the activities associated with the human bone deposits constituted the final use of the kiva prior to the burning of the roof and structural collapse. . . . Based on the nature of the final activities occurring within the kiva [that is, cannibalism], the intensity of burning, and rapid deterioration of the walls and ventilator, the roof may have been deliberately set ablaze and collapsed at the time of or soon after abandonment" (1993:29).

Other Interpretations. None.

Discussion. Dice (1993c, p. 4-10a) determined that there were two people deposited in three locations at this site. Burning seems to have occurred in two locations, Kiva 1 and Room 1. He proposed that marrow extraction had occurred as well as other forms of butchering.

The same remarks we made for Aztec Wash I apply to Aztec Wash II. Because the two sites are so close to each other, it is probably useful to combine their perimortem damage frequencies to make a larger sample:

Bone and Fragment Number. 1,726 (158 whole, 1,568 fragmentary).

Breakage. 90.8%.

Cut Marks. 0.9%.

Burning. 17.4%.

Anvil Abrasions. 6.9%.

Vertebrae Number. 10.8% of expected (39 of 360, MNI = 15, assuming three fragments represent one whole vertebra).

Scalping. Probably not.

Gnawing, Rodent, and Chewing, Carnivore. 4.4%.

Other Modification. One polished femur fragment; may have been used as a tool.

Dice (1993a:6–11) reported on another site (5MT7704) lying 500 meters east of Aztec Wash I and 200 meters east of Aztec Wash II. It contained nine human bone fragments with perimortem breakage and burning. They represented at least two individuals and were recovered near the floor of a kiva that also had been abandoned shortly after the bone-discarding event. Despite the proximity of these three sites, Dice concluded that there was too little bone to hypothesize cannibalism for 5MT7704. We agree.

## 58
## Aztec Wash III

Claim Date. 1993.

Claimant. Michael H. Dice.

Claim Type. Cannibalism?

Other Designations. 5MT7723.

Site Location. On the Towaoc Canal, 5.3 km (3.3 miles) southwest of Towaoc, Ute Mountain Indian Reservation, southeastern foothills of Sleeping Ute Mountain. Aztec Wash III lies about 10.6 km (6.6 miles) east-northeast of Aztec Wash I and II.

Site Type. Field houses and two small, circular kivas.

Cultural Affiliation. Anasazi.

Chronology. Late Pueblo II. Tree-ring dates of A.D. 1065, 1048, and 1054 were obtained from kiva roof beams.

Excavator and Date. Michael H. Dice, 1990.

Institutional Storage. Complete Archaeological Services Associates, Cortez, Colorado.

Site Report. Errickson et al. (1993).

Osteological Report. Dice (1993c).

Skeletal Evidence of Stress. None could be found, owing to the small amount of bone and its extensive burning.

Burial Context. Scattered remains on Kiva 2 floor and in floor fill, hearth, and southern recess. Human bones in the hearth were burned and calcined.

Associated Artifacts. Metate fragment.

Figures. None.

Taphonomy. MHD. Skeletal inventory is in table 3.51.

MNI. 1.

Age and Sex. One adult, sex?

Table 3.51
Bone Elements and Perimortem Damage at Aztec Wash III

| SKELETAL ELEMENT | WHOLE | FRAGMENT | IMPACT BREAK | ANVIL ABRASION | CUT MARK | BURN |
|---|---|---|---|---|---|---|
| Cranial | | | | | | |
| Teeth (15) | | | | | | |
| Fragment | — | 1 | 1 | 0 | 0 | 1 |
| Postcranial | | | | | | |
| Humerus | 0 | 4 | 4 | 0 | 0 | 3 |
| Radius | 0 | 3 | 3 | 0 | 0 | 2 |
| Tibia | 0 | 18 | 18 | 0 | 2 | 8 |
| Fibula | 0 | 10 | 10 | 0 | 0 | 10 |
| Long bone fragments | — | 53 | 53 | 1 | 0 | 46 |
| Bone type unknown | 0 | 68 | 68 | 0 | 0 | 51 |
| TOTAL (157) | 0 | 157 | 157 | 1 | 2 | 121 |
| PERCENTAGE | 0.0 | 100.0 | 100.0 | 0.6 | 1.3 | 77.1 |

Percentage of expected vertebrae = 0.0 (0 of 24; MNI = 1).

SOURCE: Dice (1993c).

NOTE: Only elements that were present are listed. No polishing, gnawing, or chewing was observed. Impact breakage, anvil abrasions, cut marks, and burning represent perimortem damage.

*Preservation.* Good.
*Bone and Fragment Number.* 157 (plus 15 teeth).
*Breakage.* 100.0%.
*Cut Marks.* 1.3%.
*Burning.* 77.1%.
*Anvil Abrasions.* 0.6%.
*Vertebrae Number.* 0.0% of expected (0 of 24).
*Scalping.* Not determinable because most of skull is missing.
*Gnawing, Rodent, and Chewing, Carnivore.* None.
*Other Modification.* None reported.
*There is no information for Polishing or Insect Parts.*

**Archaeologists' Interpretation.** Errickson et al. (1993) suggested that the lack of features and remodeling in Kiva 1 indicated that it had not been used for very long. Judging from roof material overlying the human bone refuse, the abandonment of Kiva 1 followed the deposition of the human remains.

**Other Interpretations.** None.

**Discussion.** Dice (1993c, p. 5-4) concluded that this charnel deposit did not meet the multiple criteria test for hypothesizing cannibalism because it lacked anvil abrasions, even though perimortem breakage, burning, cutting, a single anvil abrasion, and an absence of vertebrae characterized the assemblage. He went on to suggest, however, that cooking was possible: "The position of the bones in the central hearth clearly shows that the legs of a single adult may have been roasted, after cutting and breaking." He proposed that these legs might have been brought in from another site, since no disarticulated bone was found anywhere else in Aztec Wash III to help account for the missing body parts.

Dice seems to have overlooked an entry in his table 5.1 of one long bone fragment that he scored as having had anvil abrasions, burning, and a cut mark. Because Dice made his observations before fragment polishing was added to the list of minimal criteria, this site meets the older, five-criteria test, assuming his table 5.1 is correct. Hence, we consider the perimortem taphonomy of Aztec Wash III minimally adequate for hypothesizing cannibalism, especially given the proximity of this site to Aztec Wash I and II, where evidence for cannibalism is well documented by Dice in both his field and laboratory measures and where the excavation methods used by Errickson and associates superbly captured a large mass of contextual information.

**59**
**Hanson Pueblo**

**Claim Date.** 1993.

**Claimants.** James N. Morris, Linda Honeycutt, and Jerry Fetterman; also Michael H. Dice (1993b).

**Claim Type.** Cannibalism.

**Other Designations.** 5MT3876.

**Site Location.** Northwest of Cortez in Montezuma County, southwestern Colorado. According to Morris, Honeycutt, and Fetterman (1993), the site is located in the SE ¼ of SE ¼ of NE ¼ of SE ¼ of an unstated township, range, and section.

**Site Type.** Twenty-five-room pueblo with four kivas and a trash mound to the south.

**Cultural Affiliation.** San Juan Anasazi.

**Chronology.** Pueblo I, II, and III, plus a historic component. The kiva with the human charnel deposit (Structure 3) is dated at A.D. 1134, with only a little postconstruction usage and replastering.

**Excavator and Date.** James N. Morris, 1990.

**Institutional Storage.** Skeletal remains have been reburied (Morris, Honeycutt, and Fetterman 1993:3).

**Site Report.** Morris, Honeycutt, and Fetterman (1993).

**Osteological Report.** Dice (1993b).

**Skeletal Evidence of Stress.** None reported.

**Burial Context.** Scattered remains on kiva floor and in fill of adjacent structures.

**Associated Artifacts.** Artifacts on kiva floor may not have been associated with the hypothesized cannibalism event that immediately preceded abandonment of the structure (Morris, Honeycutt, and Fetterman 1993:30).

**Figures.** None.

**Taphonomy.** MHD.

   *MNI.* 2.

   *Age and Sex.* A subadult (14–20 years) and an adult, both of indeterminable sex.

      *Preservation.* Good.

      *Bone and Fragment Number.* 143.

      *Breakage.* 91.6%.

      *Cut Marks.* 1.4%.

      *Burning.* 45.5%.

      *Anvil Abrasions.* 3.5%.

      *Vertebrae Number.* 14.6% of expected (7 of 48).

      *Scalping.* None.

*Gnawing, Rodent, and Chewing, Carnivore.* Dice found that two fragments were gnawed (1.4%), but he did not identify the animal involved.

*There is no information for Polishing, Insect Parts, or Other Modification.*

**Archaeologists' Interpretation.** Morris, Honeycutt, and Fetterman (1993:30) concluded that

> abandonment activities in the kiva included an apparent act of cannibalism, followed by an unsuccessful attempt to burn the structure by setting fire to the underside of the roof. Evidence for cannibalism consists of charred human bone and teeth fragments in the hearth fill, human bone fragments which were placed along the bench on the east and west sides of the kiva, and human bone fragments in roof fall which could have been displaced from architectural surfaces. . . . Negative evidence indicates that the two individuals may have been butchered outside of the kiva [because no bone chips or splinters were found in the kiva floor fill]. . . . The artifacts on the [kiva] floor do not exhibit any arrangement or patterning that would link them to the human remains either as burial offerings or as butchering tools.

As for explanation, Morris, Honeycutt, and Fetterman (1993:31) wrote: "The circumstances surrounding the cannibalistic event in Structure 3 are difficult to infer from the archaeological record and remain open to speculation. One possibility is that this event reflects a ritual associated with inter-group conflict."

**Other Interpretations.** Dice (1993b:1) suggested that "these persons may have been processed and possibly cannibalized on the [kiva] floor, on the roof, or in an adjacent structure on the site that has not been excavated. A large number of bones were in the central hearth. It is likely that additional body parts will be recovered from the excavated rooms of the pueblo as the excavation progresses."

**Discussion.** We have adjusted Dice's tabulation by randomly moving damaged fragments from his multiple mark class to one of the primary classes. Our copy of Dice's report (1993b) is not a final draft, so some revisions are expected. However, it is a later draft than the 1991 report cited by Morris, Honeycutt, and Fetterman (1993). Dice's written description corresponds closely to descriptions of other assemblages whose perimortem damage supports a cannibalism interpretation, although photographic documentation would be useful. Inasmuch as we have participated directly in Dice's human taphonomy studies elsewhere, we believe that his cannibalism interpretation is correct, as is the cannibalism conclusion reached by Morris, Honeycutt, and Fetterman.

**60**
**La Plata Highway LA37592**

**Claim Date.** 1993.
**Claim Type.** Cannibalism.
**Claimants.** C. G. Turner, J. A. Turner, and R. C. Green (1993).
**Other Designations.** None known.
**Site Location.** North of Farmington, near Jackson Lake, La Plata High-

way, San Juan County, northwestern New Mexico. USGS Farmington North quadrangle (1963), T 30N, R 13W, SE ¼ of NE ¼ of SE ¼ of Sec. 17.

**Site Type.** Pithouse in a farming settlement.

**Cultural Affiliation.** San Juan Anasazi.

**Chronology.** Pueblo II–III, A.D. 1100+. Probably same date as LA65030 but later than LA37593.

**Excavator and Date.** H. Wolcott Toll, principal investigator, La Plata Highway Project, Museum of New Mexico, Office of Archaeological Studies, 1988.

**Institutional Storage.** Office of Archaeological Studies, Museum of New Mexico, Santa Fe, New Mexico.

**Site Reports.** H. Wolcott Toll (in progress); Eric Blinman (in progress).

**Osteological Reports.** Turner, Turner, and Green (1993); Linda Mick-O'Hara (in progress); Debra Martin et al. (in progress).

**Skeletal Evidence of Stress.** None.

**Burial Context.** Fragments of FS229 found on pithouse floor and in fill.

**Associated Artifacts.** None.

**Figures.** None.

**Taphonomy.** CGT and JAT, June 1, 1992. Our observations are not a complete inventory of perimortem damage because the bone was insufficiently cleaned, and at least one set of bones and fragments was not located and examined. Skeletal inventory is in table 3.53.

   *MNI.* 7 (table 3.52).

   *Age and Sex.* Possibly not completely inventoried. One infant; one 4- to 5-year-old; one 6-year-old; one 12-year-old; one adult, male?; one adult, sex?; one old adult, sex?.

   *Preservation.* Fair to good.

   *Bone and Fragment Number.* 291.

   *Breakage.* 64.3%.

   *Cut Marks.* 2.1%.

   *Burning.* 5.5%.

   *Anvil Abrasions.* 1.0%.

   *Polishing.* Uncertain.

   *Vertebrae Number.* 10.7% of expected (12.5 of 168).

   *Scalping.* Uncertain.

   *Gnawing, Rodent, and Chewing, Carnivore.* 5.8%.

   *Insect Parts.* None noted during skeletal examination.

   *Other Modification.* None.

**Archaeologist's Interpretation.** Toll (personal communication, June 1, 1992) thought the bones were deposited as some sort of "intentional event associated with abandonment." The room fill had conspicuous prehistoric rodent activity.

**Other Interpretations.** This assemblage will be reported in greater detail by Alan Swedlund, who, along with Debra Martin and Alan Goodman, contracted with Toll in 1992 to do an osteological analysis.

**Discussion.** Because the bone was not well cleaned, we did not systematically look for polishing, which is difficult to identify even under ideal conditions. Otherwise, the assemblage exhibits the taphonomic signature of cannibalism, which we propose was the cause of the perimortem damage.

Table 3.52
Minimal Number of Individuals (MNI) at La Plata Highway LA37592

| SKELETAL ELEMENT | AGE | SEX |
|---|---|---|
| Maxilla, whole | Adult | M? |
| | 6 | ? |
| | 12 | ? |
| Maxilla, left | Adult | ? |
| Maxilla, right | Old adult | ? |
| Mandible, whole | 4–5 | ? |
| | 6 | ? |
| | Adult | M |
| Mandible, left | Adult | ? |
| Vault | Infant | ? |

SUMMARY: Seven individuals. One infant; one 4- to 5-year-old child; one 6-year-old child; one 12-year-old child; one adult male?; one adult, sex?; one old adult, sex?.

Table 3.53
Bone Elements and Perimortem Damage at La Plata Highway LA37592

| SKELETAL ELEMENT | WHOLE | FRAGMENT | IMPACT BREAK | ANVIL ABRASION | CUT MARK | BURN | GNAW/ CHEW |
|---|---|---|---|---|---|---|---|
| Cranial | | | | | | | |
| Maxilla | 3 | 2 | 5 | 0 | 0 | 0 | 0 |
| Mandible | 3 | 3 | 5 | 0 | 0 | 1 | 0 |
| Frontal | 0 | 6 | 5 | 2 | 1 | 0 | 0 |
| Parietal | 0 | 2 | 2 | 1 | 0 | 0 | 0 |
| Occipital | 1 | 1 | 1 | 0 | 0 | 0 | 0 |
| Temporal | 2 | 2 | 3 | 0 | 0 | 1 | 0 |
| Teeth (not counted) | | | | | | | |
| Fragment | — | 37 | 26 | 0 | 1 | 8 | 0 |
| Postcranial | | | | | | | |
| Cervical vertebrae | 7 | 5 | 0 | 0 | 0 | 0 | 1? |
| Thoracic vertebrae | 0 | 2 | 0 | 0 | 0 | 0 | 0 |
| Lumbar vertebrae | 0 | 4 | 0 | 0 | 0 | 0 | 0 |
| Sacrum | 0 | 2 | 1 | 0 | 0 | 0 | 0 |
| Clavicle | 0 | 6 | 0 | 0 | 2 | 0 | 1 |
| Rib | 1 | 19 | 1[a] | 0 | 0 | 0 | 0 |
| Humerus | 0 | 7 | 8 | 0 | 1 | 0 | 3 |
| Radius | 0 | 3 | 3 | 0 | 0 | 0 | 1 |
| Ulna | 1 | 3 | 4[a] | 0 | 0 | 0 | 0 |
| Hand & foot | 22 | 3 | 5 | 0 | 0 | 0 | 3+1? |
| Pelvis | 0 | 4 | 0 | 0 | 0 | 1 | 1 |
| Femur | 2 | 9 | 7 | 0 | 0 | 1 | 4+1? |
| Tibia | 0 | 13 | 11 | 0 | 0 | 0 | 2 |
| Fibula | 0 | 3 | 3 | 0 | 0 | 0 | 0 |
| Patella | 1 | 1 | 0 | 0 | 0 | 0 | 1 |
| Long bone fragments | — | 111 | 97 | 0 | 1 | 4 | 0 |
| TOTAL (291) | 43 | 248 | 187 | 3 | 6 | 16 | 17+3? |
| PERCENTAGE | 14.8 | 85.2 | 64.3 | 1.0 | 2.1 | 5.5 | 5.8 |

Percentage of expected vertebrae = 7.4 (12.5 of 168; MNI = 7).[b]

NOTE: Only elements that were present are listed. Polishing was not searched for because of limited time and inadequately cleaned bone. Impact breakage, anvil abrasions, cut marks, burning, and polishing represent perimortem damage. Gnawing and chewing are postmortem damage.

a. Includes one "peel" break.
b. Fragmentation size suggests that about two fragments could represent one whole vertebra.

Table 3.54

Minimal Number of Individuals (MNI) at La Plata Highway LA37593

| SKELETAL ELEMENT | AGE | SEX | NOTES |
|---|---|---|---|
| Maxilla, whole | 6–7 | ? | |
| | 11–12 | ? | |
| | 12–15 | ? | |
| | Adult | F | |
| | ? | ? | |
| Maxilla, left | Adult | F | Does not match mandible L |
| Mandible, left | 12–15 | ? | |
| | Adult | F | |
| | ? | ? | |
| | ? | M? | Grade 1 mandibular torus |
| Mandible, right | 12 | ? | |
| | ? | M? | Grade 1 mandibular torus |
| Occipital | Adult | ? | Deformed. |
| Occipital | Adult | ? | Deformed, grade 1 porotic hyperostosis + grade 2 cribra orbitalia |
| L + R femur + L parietal | Adult | M | No deformation, purple bone stain |

SUMMARY: Six individuals. One 6- to 7-year-old; two 12- to 15-year-olds; two adult females; one adult, male?.

## 61
## La Plata Highway LA37593

Claim Date. 1993.

Claimants. C. G. Turner, J. A. Turner, and R. C. Green.

Claim Type. Cannibalism.

Other Designations. Midsummer Site.

Site Location. North of Farmington, San Juan County, northwestern New Mexico. USGS Farmington North quadrangle (1963), T 30N, R 13W, NE ¼ of NE ¼ of SE ¼ of Sec. 17.

Site Type. Cobble roomblocks and pithouse; part of the Jackson Lake community containing LA37594, LA60750, and others.

Cultural Affiliation. San Juan Anasazi.

Chronology. Middle Pueblo II, A.D. 1000–1100 (ceramic date).

Excavators and Date. H. Wolcott Toll, principal investigator, and Charles A. Hannaford, La Plata Highway Project, Museum of New Mexico, Office of Archaeological Studies, 1988.

Institutional Storage. Office of Archaeological Studies, Museum of New Mexico, Santa Fe.

Site Reports. Toll (in progress); Blinman (in progress).

Osteological Reports. Turner, Turner, and Green (1993); Mick-O'Hara (in progress); Martin et al. (in progress).

Skeletal Evidence of Stress. None.

Burial Context. Fragments on pithouse floor and in fill. Fill was natural and contained little trash. Remains were not in a burial pit.

Associated Artifacts. None.

Figures. None.

Taphonomy. CGT and JAT, June 1992. Our perimortem damage inventory is incomplete because bones were insufficiently cleaned and one or more storage boxes had been misplaced and could not be located. Partial skeletal inventory is in table 3.55.

Table 3.55
Bone Elements and Perimortem Damage at La Plata Highway LA37593

| SKELETAL ELEMENT | WHOLE | FRAGMENT | IMPACT BREAK | ANVIL ABRASION | CUT MARK | BURN | GNAW/ CHEW |
|---|---|---|---|---|---|---|---|
| Cranial | | | | | | | |
| Maxilla | 5 | 1 | 2 | 0 | 0 | 0 | 0 |
| Mandible | 0 | 9 | 6 | 0 | 0 | 0 | 0 |
| Frontal | 1 | 3 | 3 | 0 | 0 | 0 | 0 |
| Parietal | 4 | 10 | 6 | 2 | 3 | 0 | 0 |
| Occipital | 1 | 4 | 3 | 0 | 0 | 0 | 0 |
| Temporal | 3 | 5 | 6 | 0 | 0 | 0 | 0 |
| Base | 0 | 1 | 0 | 0 | 0 | 0 | 0 |
| Teeth (not counted) | | | | | | | |
| Fragments | — | 114 | 30 | 1 | 0 | 0 | 0 |
| Postcranial | | | | | | | |
| Cervical vertebrae | 0 | 2 | 0 | 0 | 0 | 0 | 2? |
| Lumbar vertebrae | 2 | 0 | 0 | 0 | 0 | 0 | 0 |
| Sacrum | 1 | 0 | 0 | 0 | 0 | 0 | 0 |
| Rib | 0 | 7 | 2 | 0 | 0 | 0 | 0 |
| Humerus | 1 | 0 | 0 | 0 | 0 | 0 | 0 |
| Radius | 1 | 0 | 0 | 0 | 0 | 0 | 0 |
| Hand & foot | 30 | 0 | 0 | 0 | 0 | 0 | 0 |
| Pelvis | 1 | 2 | 0 | 0 | 0 | 0 | 0 |
| Femur | 3 | 11 | 7 | 0 | 1 | 0 | 1+1? |
| Tibia | 1 | 1 | 1 | 0 | 0 | 0 | 0 |
| Patella | 1 | 0 | 0 | 0 | 0 | 0 | 0 |
| Long bone fragments | — | 7 | 0 | 1 | 0 | 0 | 0 |
| Bone type unknown | 0 | 3 | 0 | 0 | 0 | 3 | 0 |
| TOTAL (235) | 55 | 180 | 66 | 4 | 4 | 3 | 1+3? |
| PERCENTAGE | 23.4 | 76.6 | 28.1 | 1.7 | 1.7 | 1.3 | 0.4 |

Percentage of expected vertebrae = approx. 2.1 (3 of 144; MNI = 6).[a]

NOTE: Only elements that were present are listed. Polishing was not searched for due to limited time and inadequately cleaned bone. Impact breakage, anvil abrasions, cut marks, and burning represent perimortem damage. Gnawing and chewing are post-mortem damage.

a. Fragmentation size suggests that about two fragments could represent one whole vertebra.

*MNI.* 6 (table 3.54).

*Age and Sex.* One 6- to 7-year-old; two 12- to 15-year-olds; two adult females; one adult, male?.

*Preservation.* Fair to good, ivory in color.

*Bone and Fragment Number.* 235.

*Breakage.* 28.1%.

*Cut Marks.* 1.7%.

*Burning.* 1.3%.

*Anvil Abrasions.* 1.7%.

*Polishing.* Uncertain.

*Vertebrae Number.* 2.1% of expected (3 of 144).

*Scalping.* Uncertain. Three parietals have cut marks, but no other cranial bones are cut.

*Gnawing, Rodent, and Chewing, Carnivore.* 0.4%.

*Insect Parts.* None seen during skeletal examination.

*Other Modification.* None.

Archaeologist's Interpretation. H. W. Toll (personal communication, June 1, 1992) believed that kiva structures in the general area were used for burials. The human remains could have been an erosional and/or disturbed accidental deposit. On July 8, 1992, Toll wrote us about the site. Since that date we have been denied permission to quote from written materials prepared by Charles A. Hannaford and supplied by Toll in 1992.

Other Interpretations. A letter dated December 3, 1996, from Toll and Hannaford asserts that Nancy Akins, Debra Martin, Alan Goodman, and Alan Swedlund had concluded that no interpretation of violence and perimortem modification of bone from LA 37593 was warranted.

Discussion. The considerable postmortem damage we found in the human bone assemblage was due to excavation, making MNI, bone element, and damage counts at best only estimates of the prehistoric taphonomic condition. We can easily distinguish between perimortem damage and that caused by recent excavation and archaeological techniques. As was the case for LA37592, polishing was not assessable in a systematic fashion. However, the other criteria for proposing cannibalism are unquestionably present, although in low frequencies. The relatively high frequency of whole bones in this assemblage is misleading because more than half are hand and foot bones, which normally are missing or damaged in assemblages of this sort. It would take only one complete hand or foot to account for just about half of the undamaged bones.

## 62
## La Plata Highway LA65030

Claim Date. 1993.

Claim Type. Cannibalism.

Claimants. C. G. Turner, J. A. Turner, and R. C. Green.

Other Designations. Barker Arroyo.

Site Location. Site is in the vicinity of Earl Morris's La Plata 39. It is 6.4 km (4 miles) north of Jackson Lake, and north of Farmington, San Juan County, northwestern New Mexico. USGS Farmington North quadrangle (1963), T 31N, R 13W, NE ¼ of NE ¼ of NW ¼ of Sec. 33.

Site Type. Multicomponent pithouse farming community.

Cultural Affiliation. Mesa Verde and Chaco Anasazi.

Chronology. Pueblo III, A.D. 1100–1200.

Excavators and Date. H. Wolcott Toll, principal investigator, and Steve Lent, La Plata Highway Project, Museum of New Mexico, Office of Archaeological Studies, 1989.

Institutional Storage. Office of Archaeological Studies, Museum of New Mexico, Santa Fe.

Site Report. Toll (in progress); Blinman (in progress).

Osteological Report. Turner, Turner, and Green (1993); Mick-O'Hara (in progress); Martin et al. (in progress).

Skeletal Evidence of Stress. None.

Burial Context. In pithouse 8, human remains were found in trash, not in a burial pit. Our analysis is limited to pithouse 8 contents.

Associated Artifacts. Unknown.

Table 3.56
Minimal Number of Individuals (MNI) at La Plata Highway LA65030

| SKELETAL ELEMENT | AGE | SEX |
|---|---|---|
| Maxilla, whole | 6 | ? |
| | Adult | F |
| | Adult | F? |
| Mandible, whole | 12–15 | ? |
| | Young adult | F? |
| | Adult | F |
| | Adult | F? |
| Mandible, left | 2–3 | ? |

SUMMARY: Six individuals. One 2- to 3-year-old child; one 6-year-old child; one 12- to 15-year-old adolescent; one young adult female?; one adult female?; one adult female.

Table 3.57
Bone Elements and Perimortem Damage at La Plata Highway LA65030

| SKELETAL ELEMENT | WHOLE | FRAGMENT | IMPACT BREAK | ANVIL ABRASION | CUT MARK |
|---|---|---|---|---|---|
| Cranial | | | | | |
| Maxilla | 3 | 6 | 6 | 1 | 0 |
| Mandible | 4 | 4 | 4 | 0 | 1 |
| Frontal | 4 | 0 | 2[a] | 3 | 1 |
| Parietal | 4 | 13 | 9 | 1 | 1 |
| Occipital | 0 | 3 | 2 | 1 | 1 |
| Temporal | 4 | 2 | 1 | 1 | 1 |
| Teeth (not counted) | | | | | |
| Fragment | — | 43 | 12 | 0 | 0 |
| Postcranial | | | | | |
| Cervical vertebrae | 0 | 6 | 0 | 0 | 0 |
| Clavicle | 0 | 1 | 0 | 0 | 0 |
| Rib | 0 | 10 | 0 | 0 | 0 |
| Hand & foot | 1 | 0 | 0 | 0 | 0 |
| Pelvis | 0 | 1 | 0 | 0 | 0 |
| Long bone fragments | — | 10 | 0 | 0 | 0 |
| TOTAL (119) | 20 | 99 | 36 | 7 | 5 |
| PERCENTAGE | 16.8 | 83.2 | 30.2 | 5.9 | 4.0 |

Percentage of expected vertebrae = approx. 2.1 (3 of 144; MNI = 6).[b]

NOTE: Only elements that were present are listed. No burning, polishing, gnawing, or chewing was observed. Impact breakage, anvil abrasions, and cut marks represent perimortem damage.

a. Includes one "impact dent."
b. Fragmentation size suggests that about two fragments could represent one whole vertebra.

Figures. None.

Taphonomy. CGT and JAT, June 1992. The following is not a complete inventory of perimortem damage because bone was poorly cleaned and one or more storage boxes were not found and examined. Skeletal inventory is in table 3.57.

MNI. 6 (table 3.56).

Age and Sex. One 2- to 3-year-old; one 6-year-old; one 12- to 15-year-old; one young adult, female?; one adult, female?; one adult female.

Preservation. Fair to good.

Bone and Fragment Number. 119.

Breakage. 30.2%.

Cut Marks. 4.0%.

Burning. 0.0%.

Anvil Abrasions. 5.9%.

Polishing. Uncertain.

Vertebrae Number. 2.1% of expected (3 of 144).

Scalping. Uncertain.

Gnawing, Rodent. None.

Chewing, Carnivore. None.

Insect Parts. None noticed during skeletal examination.

Other Modification. None.

Archaeologist's Interpretation. H. W. Toll (personal communication, July 8, 1992) told us by letter that Steve Lent reported: "Pit structure 8 contained several individuals. This structure was found with a backhoe trench, and the burials were disturbed in the process."

Other Interpretations. None.

Discussion. As with the previous two sites, we were unable to look systematically for polishing in this assemblage. Despite the relatively low amount of breakage and the apparent absence of burning, we submit that a provisional claim for cannibalism is in order for LA65030 pithouse 8 because both of these observations are likely a result of small sample size. The excavation record of site damage with a backhoe suggests that small, fragile, darker-colored bone fragments probably were destroyed or missed being collected relative to larger, more obvious, and better preserved pieces. Bioarchaeological expertise would have been valuable under such challenging field conditions.

## 63
## Coyote Village

Claim Date. 1993.

Claim Type. Cannibalism?

Claimant. C. G. Turner, J. A. Turner, and R. C. Green.

Other Designations. 5MV280, CO; Burial 14 (MEVE 525.59/890).

Site Location. Far View area, Mesa Verde National Park, Colorado. USGS Mesa Verde National Park quadrangle (1967), T 35N, R 15W, Sec. 27.

Site Type. Pueblo of 26 rooms and 5 kivas.

Cultural Affiliation. Mesa Verde Anasazi.

Chronology. A.D. 1100–1200, Pueblo II to early Pueblo III.

Excavators and Date. Robert Lister, director, and Jack E. Smith and Al Lancaster, supervisors, 1968 and 1969.

Institutional Storage. Mesa Verde National Park Research Center.

**Site Report.** Jack E. Smith (in progress).
**Osteological Report.** Turner, Turner, and Green (1993).
**Skeletal Evidence of Stress.** None.
**Burial Context.** Bone fragments scattered in trash mound.
**Associated Artifacts.** Unknown.
**Figures.** None.
**Taphonomy.** CGT and JAT, January 11, 1991.
    *MNI.* 1.
    *Age and Sex.* An 8- to 10-year-old child.
    *Preservation.* Good.
    *Bone and Fragment Number.* 45.
    *Breakage.* Yes.
    *Cut Marks.* Yes.
    *Burning.* Yes?
    *Anvil Abrasions.* Yes.
    *Polishing.* Uncertain.
    *Vertebrae Number.* Not determined.
    *Scalping.* Uncertain.
    *Gnawing, Rodent.* Uncertain.
    *Chewing, Carnivore.* Uncertain.
    *Insect Parts.* Not seen during skeletal examination.
    *Other Modification.* Severe skull breakage.
**Archaeologist's Interpretation.** Jack Smith brought this case to our attention when we visited Mesa Verde in 1991 to examine the St. Christopher's Mission series. Smith (personal communication, October 17, 1994) said he had assumed that the broken human remains scattered in the refuse deposit represented simply a burial disturbed by animal burrowing, until Tim White spotted cutting and other perimortem damage during his overview of Mesa Verde faunal and human remains. It was White who separated the child's remains from other human bones found in the refuse.
**Other Interpretations.** In light of the previous comments by Smith, it is curious that White (1992:288) mentioned examining only the mule deer and bighorn sheep remains from Coyote Village, for comparative purposes.
**Discussion.** We can understand White's desire not to be distracted from his main objective of analyzing faunal bone from Coyote Village and making comparisons with the series from Mancos Canyon, adjacent to Mesa Verde. In retrospect, however, White might not have concluded that the Mancos people had been eaten because of starvation had he given thought to the possibility of cannibalism occurring on top of Mesa Verde as well as down below in Mancos Canyon.

For lack of time, we examined the Coyote Village child only briefly for the presence or absence—not frequencies—of damage minutiae. The child and all other human bones from this site need to be reexamined for quantified information. Although most criteria are present, our suggestion that the child could have been cannibalized is made with reservation, because we are less confident of our identification of burned bone than we would like. It is possible that some of the bone fragments belong to other individuals. A more complete study is needed.

**64**
**St. Christopher's Mission**

**Claim Date.** 1993.

**Claim Type.** Cannibalism?

**Claimant.** C. G. Turner, J. A. Turner, and R. C. Green.

**Other Designations.** 42Sa6568. Skeletal series is cataloged in the Mesa Verde National Park archaeological collections as 8337/586.

**Site Location.** On Mission to the Navajo Church land, about 3.2 km (2 miles) east of Bluff, southeastern Utah. USGS Bluff quadrangle (1962), T 40S, R 22E, NE ¼ of Sec. 29.

**Site Type.** Old, open sheet-trash horizon with a buried burned zone unrelated to the human bone deposit.

**Cultural Affiliation.** Anasazi.

**Chronology.** Probably A.D. 1200, Pueblo III, but see "Other Interpretations."

**Excavators and Date.** J. A. Lancaster, A. F. Hewitt, Jr., and J. R. Rudy, February 19, 1961.

**Institutional Storage.** Mesa Verde National Park Research Center.

**Site Report.** Rudy (1961).

**Osteological Report.** Turner, Turner, and Green (1993).

**Skeletal Evidence of Stress.** Cribra orbitalia present in 6-year-old child; porotic hyperostosis occurs in the 10- to 11-year-old.

**Burial Context.** Fragments on old ground surface.

**Associated Artifacts.** Three sherds of a Pueblo III black-on-white bowl and jar, and part of a turkey(?) bone.

**Figures.** 3.203–3.209.

**Taphonomy.** CGT and JAT, January 11, 1991. Skeletal inventory is in table 3.59.

*MNI.* 4 (table 3.58).

*Age and Sex.* Three children (one 6-year-old, one 10- to 11-year-old, and one age?), and one 25- to 30-year-old female.

*Preservation.* Fair to good.

*Bone and Fragment Number.* 176.

*Breakage.* 65.9%.

*Cut Marks.* 5.7%.

*Burning.* 0.0%. There is a possible burn mark on the right side of the adult female mandible, but it may instead be the light purple staining of presumed microbial origin that is occasionally seen on and inside bones of seemingly normal, unburned burials.

*Anvil Abrasions.* 4.0%.

*Polishing.* Uncertain.

*Vertebrae Number.* 10.4% of expected (10 of 96).

*Scalping.* Yes.

*Gnawing, Rodent, and Chewing, Carnivore.* 1.1%.

*Insect Parts.* None noticed at time of skeletal examination.

*Other Modification.* None.

**Archaeologist's Interpretation.** In an area bladed by a bulldozer, Jack R. Rudy (1961) found human bone: "An attempt was made at first to expose the bones *in situ* to determine the burial position. It soon became apparent that the bones did not fall into any pattern but were in a jumbled mess . . . many . . . split lengthwise . . . the only bones found in an articulated position were the left tibia and fibula of an adult. There were no burial offerings." Using skull elements, Rudy suggested five to seven individuals, including at least two children.

Table 3.58
Minimal Number of Individuals (MNI) at St. Christopher's Mission

| SKELETAL ELEMENT | AGE | SEX | NOTES |
| --- | --- | --- | --- |
| Maxilla + mandible | 6 | ? | Cribra orbitalia |
| Maxilla + mandible | 10–11 | ? | Slight occipital deformation |
| R parietal + temporal | Child | ? | Slight occipital deformation |
| Maxilla + mandible | Adult | F | |

SUMMARY: Four individuals. One adult female (25–30); three children (one 6-year-old, one 10- to 11-year-old, one age?).

Table 3.59
Bone Elements and Perimortem Damage at St. Christopher's Mission

| SKELETAL ELEMENT | WHOLE | FRAGMENT | IMPACT BREAK | ANVIL ABRASION | CUT MARK | GNAW/CHEW |
| --- | --- | --- | --- | --- | --- | --- |
| Cranial | | | | | | |
| Maxilla | 3 | 0 | 0 | 0 | 1 | 0 |
| Mandible | 3 | 0 | 0 | 1 | 1 | 0 |
| Parietal | 2 | 0 | 0 | 1 | 1 | 0 |
| Occipital | 1 | 0 | 0 | 0 | 1 | 0 |
| Temporal | 3 | 0 | 0 | 0 | 2 | 1 |
| Teeth (not counted) | | | | | | |
| Fragments | — | 24 | 24 | 0 | 0 | 0 |
| Postcranial | | | | | | |
| Vertebrae fragments | — | 10 | 10 | 0 | 0 | 0 |
| Scapula | 0 | 3 | 3 | 0 | 0 | 0 |
| Clavicle | 0 | 2 | 2 | 0 | 0 | 0 |
| Rib | 0 | 3 | 3 | 0 | 0 | 0 |
| Humerus | 2 | 3 | 3 | 0 | 1 | 0 |
| Radius | 2 | 1 | 1 | 0 | 0 | 0 |
| Ulna | 4 | 0 | 0 | 0 | 1 | 0 |
| Hand & foot | 38 | 0 | 0 | 0 | 0 | 0 |
| Pelvis | 0 | 7 | 7 | 0 | 0 | 0 |
| Femur | 0 | 2 | 2 | 0 | 0 | 0 |
| Tibia | 0 | 4 | 4 | 0 | 1 | 0 |
| Fibula | 2 | 3 | 3 | 0 | 1 | 0 |
| Long bone fragments | — | 54 | 54 | 5 | 0 | 1 |
| TOTAL (176) | 60 | 116 | 116 | 7 | 10 | 2 |
| PERCENTAGE | 34.1 | 65.9 | 65.9 | 4.0 | 5.7 | 1.1 |

Percentage of expected vertebrae = approx. 10.4 (10 of 96; MNI = 4).[a]

NOTE: Only elements that were present are listed. No burning or polishing was observed. Impact breakage, anvil abrasions, and cut marks represent perimortem damage. Gnawing and chewing are postmortem damage.

a. Fragmentation size suggests that about one fragment could represent one whole vertebra.

322

Figure 3.203. St. Christopher's Mission, Utah. Representative perimortem breakage of long bones. Scripto pencil is 13.5 cm long. Mesa Verde National Park 8337/586 (CGT neg. 1-11-91:30).

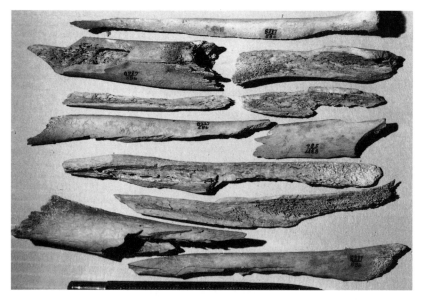

Figure 3.204. St. Christopher's Mission. Perimortem breakage of right half of maxilla and tooth sockets. There is one faint cut mark (arrow) below the broken alveolar bone of the right canine. MVNP 8337/586 (CGT neg. 1-11-91:29).

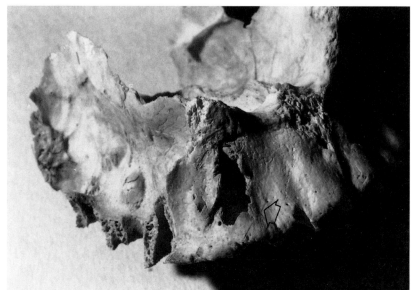

Figure 3.205. St. Christopher's Mission. Perimortem cut marks on occipital bone fragment. MVNP 8337/586 (CGT neg. 1-11-91:23).

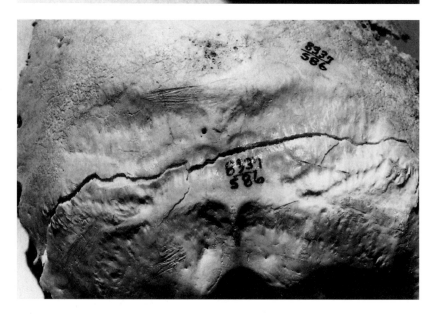

Figure 3.206. St. Christopher's Mission. Perimortem cut marks on cranial vault. MVNP 8337/586 (CGT neg. 1-11-91:28).

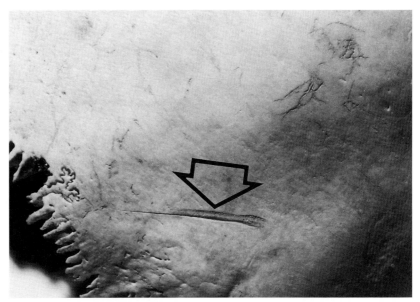

Figure 3.207. St. Christopher's Mission. Perimortem chop marks on right temporal bone. Stone tool type is unknown but damage similar to that in figure 3.182, Fence Lake. MVNP 8337/586 (CGT neg. 1-11-91:24).

Figure 3.208. St. Christopher's Mission. Perimortem cut marks on horizontal ramus of mandible. MVNP 8337/586 (CGT neg. 1-11-91:26).

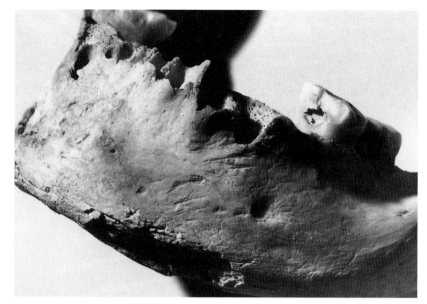

Figure 3.209. St. Christopher's Mission. Perimortem chop marks on ascending ramus of mandible. MVNP 8337/586 (CGT neg. 1-11-91:27).

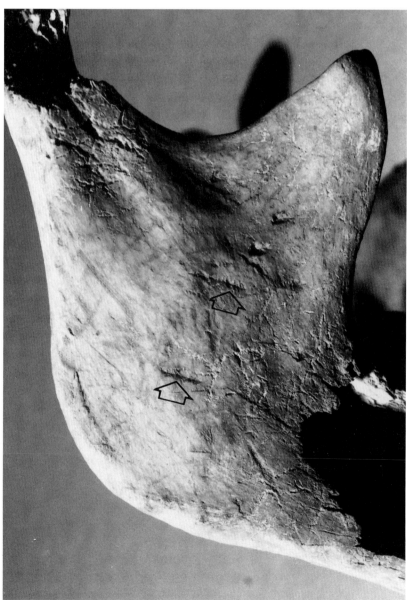

Other Interpretations. Shane Baker (1990:118–120) examined the series in April 1988 at Mesa Verde. He found 176 pieces, all without burning, and noted 4% with cut marks. The majority of the bones were fragmented. He identified five individuals, a 24- to 39-year-old female?, a 24- to 39-year-old, sex?, and three subadults. The ages of the subadults were believed to be 0–2, 6–12, and 13–24. Baker found no evidence of cranial deformation, so he suggested a Basketmaker age for the assemblage. He observed that the human skeletal remains from St. Christopher's Mission had been damaged much like his Rattlesnake Ruin series.

Tim White (1992:371–372) examined the assemblage in 1990, obtaining an MNI of four: an adult female?, a 6-year-old, a 9- to 10-year-old, and a 6- to 10-year-old. His assessments are closer to ours than to Baker's. However, unlike Baker and us, White (1992:372) reported having identified some burning on cranial and postcranial elements, saying "patterning corresponds to soft tissue cover; burning is focused on long-bone ends." White's total bone inventory (202) is higher than ours. He found cut marks and noted that the damage was like that present in the other mass burials.

Nancy Malville (personal communication, August 1992) briefly reviewed this skeletal series, finding five to seven individuals and long bone fragments split lengthwise.

Discussion. Our MNI of four differs by one adult from Baker's, but we share similar inventories for pieces and cut marks. Baker apparently did not look for anvil abrasions. Our respective MNI and age estimates are quite similar to White's. However, White obtained a higher total bone inventory because he counted separately some 25 pieces that had been variously glued together, whereas we and Baker did not. Unlike Baker, we found slight cranial deformation—in the 10- to 11-year-old child and in the child whose age could not be determined. The most significant interanalyst difference has to do with burning. If White is correct about the presence of burned bone, then the St. Christopher's assemblage should be considered as probably having been cannibalized.

Because no well-defined burial pit or grave could be identified, the taphonomy of these remains, with their butchering and subsequent carnivore bite marks, suggests that they had been left out in the open. Rudy's sketch, however, shows the "burial area" at 2.5 feet (0.8 m) below the old surface, which seemed to connect about 45 feet (13.7 m) away with a 10-foot-wide (3.0 m) area of fire-cracked rock, burned clay, and burned reeds, suggesting a burned brush structure. Rudy did not feel that this area of burned materials and the bone deposit were related, but their spatial proximity and similar stratigraphic siting are likely not coincidental. A burned structure and a nearby mass of broken human bones is a fairly good basis for suspecting a raid or attack, with perimortem violence. The soft tissue and fat content of the human bones, if the bones had not been buried, must have been so reduced that carnivores and rodents were not particularly attracted to the bone pile. Altogether, a case for violence and cannibalism could more confidently be proposed if White's finding of burned bone could be verified.

**65**
**Salmon Ruin**

**Claim Date.** 1993.

**Claim Type.** Cannibalism and violence.

**Claimants.** C. G. Turner and J. A. Turner.

**Other Designations.** LA8846.

**Site Location.** Salmon Ruin is near the right bank of the San Juan River, on the south side of U.S. 64, at the western city limit of Bloomfield, northwestern New Mexico. USGS Horn Canyon quadrangle (1965), T 29N, R 11E, NE ¼ of Sec. 30.

**Site Type.** A large, south-facing, E-shaped, two-story masonry pueblo (130 meters long, 250 rooms). Encompasses small kivas, a great kiva on the south edge of the partly enclosed central plaza, and a large, centrally positioned, above-ground tower kiva, Room 64W (10 meters [33 feet] wide). The Chaco Great North Road runs south 97 km (60 miles) from Salmon Ruin to Chaco Canyon. Our concern is only with human skeletal remains from the roof of the burned Tower Kiva.

**Cultural Affiliation.** Early occupation by Chaco Anasazi; Mesa Verde Anasazi were present later.

**Chronology.** Planned Chacoan construction began between A.D. 1088 and 1094. Chacoans abandoned the town around 1140, and it remained deserted until occupied by Mesa Verde people around 1240. In 1263, Tower Kiva caught fire. Consumed in the fire, on the kiva roof, were the bodies of 30 to 35 infants and children, some of whose skeletal remains were intermixed with the apparently butchered remains of two adults. The western end of the town also burned, and the site was totally abandoned by 1300.

**Excavators and Date.** Cynthia Irwin-Williams, director, and Phillip H. Shelly, 1972–1978. Reportedly, more than 750 archaeologists and students helped excavate during these years (San Juan County Museum Association n.d.).

**Institutional Storage.** Salmon Ruin, San Juan County Museum and Archaeological Research Center.

**Site Reports.** Irwin-Williams (1972); Pippin and Irwin-Williams (1973); Irwin-Williams and Shelly (1980).

**Osteological Reports.** J. Shipman (1977, 1980); Turner, Turner, and Green (1993); Lisa Bergschneider (in progress).

**Skeletal Evidence of Stress.** Uncertain. Tower Kiva skeletons were severely burned.

**Burial Context.** Some 30 to 35 highly fragmented and variously burned skeletons, mostly of infants and children, were unearthed from the burned and collapsed Tower Kiva roof.

**Associated Artifacts.** None believed to be associated with the burned Tower Kiva group, but the intense heat of the fire made bone and artifact associations difficult to assess.

**Figures.** None.

**Taphonomy.** Jeff H. Shipman (JHS); CGT and JAT, June 7–8, 1992. Notes on age and damage are in table 3.60.

*MNI.* 35 (mostly children, JHS); in addition to the many children, two adults with perimortem damage could be recognized by JHS, CGT and JAT.

*Age and Sex.* See table 3.60. Our remarks that follow are limited to the two adults.

*Preservation.* The two adults, like all the children, were very

Table 3.60
Salmon Ruin Tower Kiva Human Remains

| SKELETON | AGE | COMMENT | ANALYST |
|---|---|---|---|
| 1(A) | Adult<br>Adult | Female, no postcranial, not burned | JHS<br>CGT & JAT |
| 1(B) | 7–9<br>6 | Head only, not burned | JHS<br>CGT & JAT |
| 1(C) | 5<br>3 | Incomplete, well burned | JHS<br>CGT & JAT |
| 2 | 8<br>7 | No postcranial, charred | JHS<br>CGT & JAT |
| 3A | 7–9<br>Child | No head | JHS<br>CGT & JAT |
| 3B | 4–6<br>Child | Incomplete, charred and calcined | JHS<br>CGT & JAT |
| 4 | 5<br>5 | Incomplete, differentially burned | JHS<br>CGT & JAT |
| 5 | 6<br>4–5 | Incomplete, charred | JHS<br>CGT & JAT |
| 6 | 4<br>5–6 | Incomplete, differentially burned | JHS<br>CGT & JAT |
| 7 | 3<br>5 | Incomplete, differentially burned<br>Anvil abrasions | JHS<br>CGT & JAT |
| 8A | Birth<br>2 | Mostly postcranial, calcined | JHS<br>CGT & JAT |
| 8B | 1–2<br>6–9 | Incomplete, differentially burned | JHS<br>CGT & JAT |
| 9A | 2–3<br>Child | Incomplete, differentially burned<br>Same as JHS + adult bone | JHS<br>CGT & JAT |
| 9B | 4–5<br>5 | Head only, charred | JHS<br>CGT & JAT |
| 10A | 2–3<br>4 | Head only, charred, calcined<br>Same as JHS; mixed with 10B box (#22) | JHS<br>CGT & JAT |
| 10B | —<br>4 | (Unable to read copy) | JHS<br>CGT & JAT |
| 11A | 1–2<br>Child | Incomplete, charred | JHS<br>CGT & JAT |
| 11B | 3–4<br>5 | Incomplete, differentially burned | JHS<br>CGT & JAT |
| 12 | 3–4<br>1–2 | Head unburned, postcranial burned<br>Very large upper first molar | JHS<br>CGT & JAT |
| 14 | 4–5<br>Child | Fairly complete, calcined | JHS<br>CGT & JAT |
| 15 | 3–4<br>Child | Head not burned, postcranial charred | JHS<br>CGT & JAT |
| 18 | 1<br>0.6 | Head slightly burned, no postcranial | JHS<br>CGT & JAT |
| 19 | 2–4<br>4 | Mostly head, well burned<br>Mostly unburned, perimortem rib break | JHS<br>CGT & JAT |
| 20 | Child<br>2–3 | Extremely incomplete | JHS<br>CGT & JAT |
| 21 | 5–7<br>Child | Incomplete, no head | JHS<br>CGT & JAT |
| 22 | Adult<br>Adult | One unburned R femoral diaphysis<br>Female, L femur diaphysis | JHS<br>CGT & JAT |

*Continued on next page*

*Table 3.60 Continued*

| SKELETON | AGE | COMMENT | ANALYST |
|---|---|---|---|
| 23 | 6–8 | Head only, unburned | JHS |
| | 6–7 | | CGT & JAT |
| 24 | 5–7 | Head not burned, body calcined | JHS |
| | 4 | | CGT & JAT |
| 25 | 3 | Incomplete, adult long bone present | JHS |
| | 4 | | CGT & JAT |
| 26 | — | Very incomplete adult and child | JHS |
| | Adult | | CGT & JAT |
| 27A | Birth | Very incomplete, calcined | JHS |
| | Birth | | CGT & JAT |
| 27B | 1–2 | Very incomplete, calcined | JHS |
| | 2 | | CGT & JAT |
| 28 | Child | Extremely incomplete, unburned | JHS |
| | Child | | CGT & JAT |
| 29A | Adult | Very incomplete, charred + calcined | JHS |
| | Adult | | CGT & JAT |
| 29B | Child | Very incomplete, mostly unburned | JHS |
| | Child | | CGT & JAT |
| 30A | Adult | Extremely incomplete, well burned | JHS |
| | Adult | | CGT & JAT |
| 30B | 5–7 | Extremely incomplete, unburned | JHS |
| | 6 | | CGT & JAT |
| 31 | 12–14 | Extremely incomplete, mostly unburned | JHS |
| | Subadult | | CGT & JAT |
| 32 | 3–5 | Extremely incomplete, diff. burning | JHS |
| | Child | | CGT & JAT |
| 33 | Child | Head only, charred | JHS |
| | Child | | CGT & JAT |
| 34A | Adult | Male, well calcined | JHS |
| | | Not located | CGT & JAT |
| 34B | Adult | Female?, well calcined | JHS |
| | | Not located | CGT & JAT |
| 34C | 5–7 | Well calcined | JHS |
| | | Not located | CGT & JAT |
| 35A | 30 | Very incomplete, calcined | JHS |
| | Adult | | CGT & JAT |
| 35B | 5–7 | Very incomplete, calcined | JHS |
| | 5–6 | | CGT & JAT |
| 35C | 0.5 | Very incomplete, calcined | JHS |
| | 1 | | CGT & JAT |
| 36 | Child | Head only, charred | JHS |
| | 4 | | CGT & JAT |
| 37A | Adult | Incomplete, differentially burned | JHS |
| | Adult | Toe bone only | CGT & JAT |
| 37B | 1–3 | Incomplete, charred, some fit with #41 | JHS |
| | 1–2 | | CGT & JAT |
| 38 | 3–5 | Head only | JHS |
| | 3–5 | | CGT & JAT |
| 39 | Adult | Extremely incomplete, charred, calcined | JHS |
| | Adult | Cut marks + anvil abrasions | CGT & JAT |
| 40 | | (Unable to read copy) | JHS |
| | Adult | Unburned mandible with perimortem break | CGT & JAT |
| 41 | 1–3 | Very incomplete and charred, part of #37? | JHS |
| | 1–2 | | CGT & JAT |

*Continued on next page*

*Table 3.60 Continued*

| SKELETON | AGE | COMMENT | ANALYST |
|---|---|---|---|
| 42A | 20 | Adult M? charred, mostly postcranial | JHS |
| | Adult | Adult M? burned, perimortem cuts, anvil abrasions, breakage, percussion spalling | CGT & JAT |
| 42B | Infant | Mostly postcranial, charred | JHS |
| | Child | Anvil abrasion | CGT & JAT |
| 43A | Adult | Cranial fragment only, charred | JHS |
| | | Specimen not located | CGT & JAT |
| 43B | 1–2 | Extremely incomplete, charred | JHS |
| | 2 | Anvil abrasions | CGT & JAT |
| 44 | Adult | Extremely incomplete, unburned | JHS |
| | Adult | | CGT & JAT |
| Quad 3 | | | |
| 7–18–73 | Adult | Cuts or abrasion, charred skull fragment | CGT & JAT |
| 09E/03S | Adult | Cut skull piece, burned on inside | |
| 7–25–73 | | but not on outside | CGT & JAT |

NOTE: Under "Comment," unless added observations are indicated, we agree with the description by Shipman (JHS). Besides the remains listed, there were several excavation units of mixed small bone fragments, mostly found between recognizable individuals and mostly from subadults. These items were provenienced by location, not skeleton number. Most of these fragments could probably be assigned to nearby numbered individuals.

poorly preserved. The bones of each were heavily burned, very fragile, and extremely fragmented.

**Bone and Fragment Number.** Not determined.

**Breakage.** Yes. Some perimortem breaks on burned bones can be unquestionably recognized where calcium salts are present on fractures.

**Cut Marks.** Yes.

**Burning.** Yes.

**Anvil Abrasions.** Yes.

**Polishing.** Storage and handling of the charcoaled bones have damaged most fragment ends.

**Vertebrae Number.** Indeterminable.

**Scalping.** Uncertain.

**Gnawing, Rodent.** None recognized.

**Chewing, Carnivore.** None recognized.

**Insect Parts.** Uncertain.

**Other Modification.** Indeterminable.

**Archaeologist's Interpretation.** On August 3, 1973, summarizing on field data forms about the excavation of the east side of the Tower Kiva roof, an unsigned record noted:

> The heavy human bone scatter is roughly 5.5 m long on its west side, 2 m on its east side, 80 cm wide on its north side, 15 cm wide on its south side and 1.8 m at its widest point. Vertical dimensions vary but it encompasses a range of 35 cm, the SE corner being the highest point and the SW corner the lowest. This feature consists of a very heavy concentration of human bone scatter. The condition of the bone ranges through unburned, unburned but badly deteriorated, varying degrees of burned and totally carbonized. The degree

of burning cannot be correlated with depth. . . . The bone is located either directly on top of or in the level of burnt roof and is mixed in with charcoal, burnt roof adobe, ash and patches of unburnt soil. . . . There is no evidence of burial and very little cultural material was found with this feature. . . . Despite the condition and distribution of the bones, we have designated 18 separate individuals.

In 1974 the west side was excavated. The summary record, dated August 15, 1974, indicated that the "feature covers entire kiva. Vertical range is 1.15 cm and includes bone scatter found above bench and in roof fill which had fallen into ventilator shaft. . . . 26 additional bodies were identified."

**Other Interpretations.** It is interesting that as early as 1897, when Warren K. Moorehead of Phillips Academy, Andover, Massachusetts, and his party spent three days digging in Peter M. Salmon's ruin, violence was considered part of the site's story. Moorehead (1906:53) found "two small buildings that had been destroyed by fire. . . . Apparently, the pueblo was attacked, sacked, and burned while it was still occupied."

In 1972, Tower Kiva had yet to be excavated, but taphonomic signs of chaos were already starting to appear. Lonnie C. Pippin and Cynthia Irwin-Williams (1973:25) mentioned discovering a disarticulated female skeleton in the plaza fronting the central building extension formed by Tower Kiva. According to John W. Hohmann (Hohmann et al. 1985), he was told by George Teague in 1977 that articulated arm bones were found in kiva settings at Salmon Ruin. Hohmann implied that these arm bones were war trophies. Alternatively, they could represent unburied human body parts, similar to the disarticulated plaza female, the remains from the Tower Kiva holocaust, and other, similar finds at sites containing unburied victims of violence.

Shipman's (1980:4–5) Tower Kiva analyses more than hinted at an extremely unusual event. First, he identified about 35 individuals ("no more than"), including only two adults, a man and a woman. The bones of the adults were recovered mixed with the variously complete skeletons of 15 of the infants and children. In other words, the bones of the adults were scattered over the roof of Tower Kiva before the more or less undisturbed bodies of the children were burned in place. Shipman (1980:4) doubted that this burning was accidental: "The osseous remains from the Tower Kiva show all degrees of burning, and this was done when the bones were still "fresh.". . . Although this incineration ostensibly was an accidental situation . . . it is curious that the majority of the remains are those of young children. Only the postcrania of skeletons 15 and 19 [each 2 to 5 years old] were burned. Some individuals had their neurocrania burned, but not their faces. Individuals 6 and 7 showed incineration only on the right sides of their crania."

**Discussion.** This deposit of burned human bones is curious for two additional reasons. First, perimortem taphonomy shows that the two adults had been been butchered, explaining why their remains were found scattered all over the kiva roof, whereas the children were more or less spatially concentrated as specific individuals. That the adult bone fragments were mixed in with bones of several "in-place" children means that the adult remains had been scattered on the roof before the children burned up in the kiva fire. Almost no adult vertebrae were present, so five of the perimortem bone damage requirements for proposing cannibalism are present; polishing could not be reliably identified in this incinerated assemblage. Both of the adults, as well as a few of the children, had preburning perimortem breaks, cut marks, and anvil abrasions in addition to excessive burning.

Second, the simultaneous deaths of many children found together in a Chaco great house is not unique. Earl Morris (1924:51–53) recovered a multiple burial of 15 children at Aztec, a great house only 12 km (7.5 miles) north of Salmon Ruin. Although sacrifice could have been responsible for such deaths, particularly those at Salmon Ruin, other causes need to be considered—such as disease, as suggested by Sheilagh Brooks and Richard Brooks (1978).

During our examination of the Tower Kiva series it became evident that many children had burned in the flesh, not just as fresh or green bone, because there were tiny amounts of shiny, carbonized slag of heat-liquified and frothy tissue (muscle, blood, etc.) adhering on a number of bone fragments; carbonized hair adhering on some charred vault fragments; and one complete carbonized infant brain.

We found no evidence of scavenger damage. This suggests that the burned and scorched bodies and body parts were covered with a protective layer of earth soon after the conflagration of Tower Kiva. Perhaps it was the act of covering the remains that contributed to the extensive commingling of individual skeletal elements. Burning did not prevent the bone from later being damaged by roots. Although a detailed, quantitative taphonomic workup should be done on the Tower Kiva remains, we are convinced that some of the burned individuals, including the two adults, had been butchered, had had their major long bones broken open, and had received facial breakage or mutilation before the kiva burned.

**66**
**San Juan River**

**Claim Date.** 1993.
**Claim Type.** Cannibalism.
**Claimants.** C. G. Turner, J. A. Turner, and R. C. Green.
**Other Designations.** NA7166.
**Site Location.** On north bank of San Juan River at mile 22, southern Utah. Elevation 1,045 m (3,430 feet). USGS Navajo Mountain 4NW quadrangle (1953), T 41S, R 11E, NE ¼ of Sec. 32.
**Site Type.** Slump boulder shelters/rooms.
**Cultural Affiliation.** Kayenta Anasazi.
**Chronology.** Late A.D. 1200s (ceramic date).
**Excavators and Date.** Alexander J. Lindsay, Jr., Paul V. Long, Jr., Michael E. Mosley, and Christy G. Turner II, June 20–21, 1960.
**Institutional Storage.** Department of Anthropology, Museum of Northern Arizona, Flagstaff.
**Site Report.** Lindsay, Turner, and Long (1963).
**Osteological Reports.** Turner, Turner, and Green (1993); Turner and Turner (1997).
**Skeletal Evidence of Stress.** None.

Table 3.61
Minimal Number of Individuals (MNI) at San Juan River

| SKELETAL ELEMENT | AGE | SEX |
|---|---|---|
| Maxilla, left | Adult | ? |
| | Old adult | ? |
| Mandible, left | Adult | ? |
| Mandible, right | Adult | ? |
| Frontal, left | Adult | ? |
| Frontal, left | Adult | ? |
| Frontal, right | Adult | ? |
| Parietal, left | Adult | M? |
| Parietal, right | Adult | M? |
| Occipital, whole | Adult | ? |
| Occipital, whole | Adult | ? |
| Temporal, left | Adult | M |
| Temporal, right | Adult | M |

SUMMARY: Two individuals, both adult males.

Table 3.62
Bone Elements and Perimortem Damage at San Juan River

| SKELETAL ELEMENT | WHOLE | FRAGMENT | IMPACT BREAK | ANVIL ABRASION | CUT MARK | BURN | POLISH | GNAW/ CHEW |
|---|---|---|---|---|---|---|---|---|
| Cranial | | | | | | | | |
| Maxilla | 0 | 2L | ? | 0 | 0 | 0 | 0 | 0 |
| Mandible | 0 | 3 | 3 | 0 | 0 | 2 | 0 | 0 |
| Frontal | 0 | 3 | 3 | 0 | 0 | 1 | 0 | 0 |
| Occipital | 0 | 1 | 1 | 0 | 1 | 0 | 0 | 0 |
| Temporal | 0 | 2 | 2 | 0 | 0 | 0 | 0 | 0 |
| Base | 0 | 2 | 1 | 0 | 0 | 0 | 0 | 0 |
| Teeth (18) | | | | | | | | |
| Fragments | — | 38 | 38 | 1 | 5 | 6 | 0 | 0 |
| Postcranial | | | | | | | | |
| Cervical vertebrae | 4 | 2 | 2 | 0 | 0 | 3 | 0 | 0 |
| Lumbar vertebrae | 0 | 2 | 0 | 0 | 0 | 0 | 0 | 0 |
| Coccyx | 1 | 0 | 0 | 0 | 0 | 0 | 0 | 0 |
| Clavicle | 0 | 1 | 1 | 0 | 0 | 0 | ? | 0 |
| Ribs | 1 | 10 | ? | ? | 0 | 0 | ? | 0 |
| Humerus | 0 | 1 | 1 | 0 | 0 | 1 | 0 | 0 |
| Radius | 1R | 1 | 0 | 0 | 0 | 0 | 0 | 0 |
| Ulna | 0 | 2L | 0 | 0 | 0 | 0 | 0 | 0 |
| Hand | 5 | 0 | 0 | 0 | 0 | 0 | 0 | 0 |
| Foot | 6 | 1 | 0 | 0 | 0 | 0 | 0 | 0 |
| Fibula | 0 | 1 | ? | ? | ? | 0 | ? | ? |
| Long bone fragments | — | 35 | 35 | 0 | 0 | 0 | 0 | 0 |
| TOTAL (125) | 18 | 107 | 88 | 1 | 6 | 13 | 0 | 0 |
| PERCENTAGE | 14.4 | 85.6 | 70.4 | 0.8 | 4.8 | 10.4 | 0 | 0 |

Percentage of expected vertebrae = 16.7 (8 of 48; MNI = 2).

NOTE: Only elements that were present are listed. Impact breakage, anvil abrasions, cut marks, burning, and polishing represent perimortem damage. Gnawing and chewing are postmortem damage. L denotes left; R denotes right.

Figure 3.210. San Juan River (NA7166), Utah. General view of site area and north shore of river. Alexander J. Lindsay, Jr., stands at entrance to slump boulder rock shelter (arrow) where the perimortem-damaged human skeletal remains were found. Isolation and defenselessness characterize this small field house. Expedition camp was located at the white kitchen boat box adjacent to river. Museum of Northern Arizona Archive (Glen Canyon Project) photograph by Christy G. Turner II (June 1960).

Figure 3.211. San Juan River. Complete assemblage for an MNI of two. Mainly long bone and cranial fragments were found (CGT neg. 7-16-93:15).

Figure 3.212. San Juan River. Cranial fragments for one of the adult males reassembled, showing that breakage had occurred before burning of fragment on left (CGT neg. 6-11-92:28).

Figure 3.213. San Juan River. Cranial fragments showing anvil or hammerstone abrasions. Actual width of image in photograph is 3.3 cm (CGT neg. 6-11-92:29).

Figure 3.214. San Juan River. Upper teeth (left) and mandibular fragments and lower teeth (center and right). Weathering makes it difficult to determine whether all the breakage was perimortem, although shapes of fragments suggest it was. Advanced tooth wear suggests an older adult (CGT neg. 6-11-92:30).

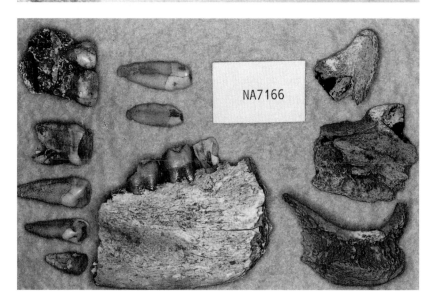

Figure 3.215. San Juan River. Long bone fragments with perimortem breakage. Distal humerus fragment in upper left was burned (CGT neg. 6-11-92:32).

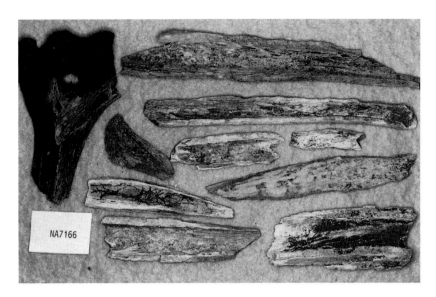

NA7166

**Burial Context.** Bone fragments on slump boulder room floor and in 15 cm of disturbed occupation fill above floor. Bone was concentrated along the east, south, and west room edges.

**Associated Artifacts.** Minor household items, including perishables and fragments of animal bones, none of which were necessarily burial goods or deposited at the same time as the human bones and teeth.

**Figures.** 3.210–3.215.

**Taphonomy.** CGT and JAT, July 2, 1993. Skeletal inventory is in table 3.62.

> *MNI.* 2 (table 3.61).
>
> *Age and Sex.* Two adult males.
>
> *Preservation.* Poor.
>
> *Bone and Fragment Number.* 125.
>
> *Breakage.* 70.4%.
>
> *Cut Marks.* 4.8%.
>
> *Burning.* 10.4%.
>
> *Anvil Abrasions.* 0.8%.
>
> *Polishing.* Uncertain due to poor preservation of bone surfaces.
>
> *Vertebrae Number.* 16.7% of expected (8 of 48).
>
> *Scalping.* Uncertain.
>
> *Gnawing, Rodent.* None.
>
> *Chewing, Carnivore.* None.
>
> *Insect Parts.* None noticed during skeletal examination.
>
> *Other Modification.* None.

**Archaeologist's Interpretation.** Lindsay proposed that the remains represented a disturbed burial.

**Other Interpretations.** None.

**Discussion.** The senior author studied these remains in 1960 but was at that time concerned only with osteometry, dental morphology, and pathology. The perimortem damage indicating cannibalism was not recognized until the 1993 examination.

**67**
**Kin Klethla**

**Claim Date.** 1993.

**Claimants.** Jonathan Haas and Winifred Creamer.

**Claim Type.** Violence.

**Other Designations.** UKV 115.

**Site Location.** Upper Klethla Valley, northeastern Arizona. USGS Shonto quadrangle (1970), not gridded, SE ¼ of SE ¼ of quadrangle. See site report map (Haas and Creamer 1993:52).

**Site Type.** Masonry roomblock and surrounding pithouse village.

**Cultural Affiliation.** Kayenta Anasazi, Tsegi phase.

**Chronology.** A.D. 1250–1300.

**Excavators and Date.** Jonathan Haas and Winifred Creamer, 1986.

**Institutional Storage.** Department of Anthropology, Field Museum of Natural History, Chicago.

**Site Report.** Haas and Creamer (1993).

**Osteological Report.** None.

**Skeletal Evidence of Stress.** Haas and Creamer follow Dennis Ryan's (1977) findings that indicate the Tsegi phase was a period of dietary and general health stress.

**Burial Context.** An isolated skull with perimortem damage in room fill.

**Associated Artifacts.** None.

**Figures.** None.

**Taphonomy.** JH and WC.

> *MNI.* 1.
>
> *Age and Sex.* Adult, probably female.
>
> *Preservation.* Not indicated, but the published photographs of the cranium (Haas and Creamer's figs. 4-27 and 4-28) suggest good preservation.
>
> *Bone and Fragment Number.* Complete skull without mandible.
>
> *Breakage.* Frontal bone missing large circular piece at forehead.
>
> *Cut Marks.* Yes, 2.
>
> *Vertebrae Number.* 0.
>
> *Scalping.* Possible.
>
> *There is no information for Burning, Anvil Abrasions, Polishing, Gnawing, Chewing, Insect Parts, or Other Modification.*

**Archaeologists' Interpretation.** Haas and Creamer (1993:82–84) remarked: "At Kin Klethla, the backhoe cut through one of the burned rooms, and there was an isolated human skull (probably female) in the fill of the room. The forehead of this skull had been bashed in, and there were two clear cut marks on the skull, one at the top and the other at the back. . . . The skull and the burning seen at the site point to some level of violence associated with the occupation and probable abandonment of the site in the second half of the 13th century."

**Other Interpretations.** None.

**Discussion.** Haas and Creamer (1993:85) suggested that the violence at Kin Klethla was caused by conflict between Klethla Valley residents and their neighbors in the Long House Valley to the north. Between the two areas was a zone containing no sites—in other words, a buffer zone or no-man's-land. The illustrated bone damage in the isolated cranium, found in a burned room, does suggest violence, including scalping. One wonders what happened to the rest of the woman's body.

**68
Brown Star Site**

**Claim Date.** 1993.

**Claimants.** Jonathan Haas and Winifred Creamer.

**Claim Type.** Violence.

**Other Designations.** LHV72; NA10,829.

**Site Location.** Long House Valley, northeastern Arizona. USGS Marsh Pass quadrangle (1968), not gridded, S ¼ of quadrangle. See site report map (Haas and Creamer 1993:53–54).

**Site Type.** Small habitation site with four above-ground masonry rooms and a square kiva.

**Cultural Affiliation.** Kayenta Anasazi.

**Chronology.** Tree-ring dates suggest site was contructed in the 1240s and occupied until the 1270s or later. Early Tsegi phase.

**Excavators and Date.** Haas and Creamer, 1984.

**Institutional Storage.** Department of Anthropology, Field Museum of Natural History, Chicago.

**Site Report.** Haas and Creamer (1993).

**Osteological Report.** None.

**Skeletal Evidence of Stress.** See the foregoing remarks for Kin Klethla.

**Burial Context.** Burial was upside-down in a flexed position in a trash area to the south of the kiva, near another burial—a female with nine ceramic bowls.

**Associated Artifacts.** A Tusayan Black-on-white effigy vessel and a projectile point, the latter possibly embedded in the lower abdomen.

**Figures.** None.

**Taphonomy.** JH and WC.

> *MNI.* 1.
>
> *Age and Sex.* Adult male.
>
> *Bone and Fragment Number.* Postcranial skeleton complete, but head missing.
>
> *Vertebrae Number.* Presumably 24.
>
> *Scalping.* Indeterminable.
>
> *There is no information for Preservation, Breakage, Cut Marks, Burning, Anvil Abrasions, Polishing, Gnawing, Chewing, Insect Parts, or Other Modification.*

**Archaeologists' Interpretation.** Haas and Creamer (1993:41) reported finding "a male . . . interred with cranium missing, in a contorted position, and with a projectile point in the vicinity of the pelvis. The projectile point is not characteristic of the Kayenta Tsegi Phase." They said that the upper cervical vertebrae showed no signs of cut marks.

Haas and Creamer (1993:134–135) concluded: "Alternative explanations may be offered for the movement of the population into high redoubts, but none offers the parsimony of warfare. . . . The Kayenta took conscious, deliberate steps to move their residences and stored resources to out-of-the-way, highly defensible locations because they were afraid of being attacked. They were responding to a direct, overt threat of raiding, resources stolen, and people killed or wounded."

**Other Interpretations.** Steadman Upham (1995:370) reviewed Haas and Creamer's monograph and found their views to be "controversial" with respect to changes in Kayenta Anasazi society—namely, that those changes were dependent on cooperation in defense against raiding and warfare due to the deteriorating natural environment. Regardless, Upham acknowledged that the idea of warfare's having influenced group formation among the Anasazi would be the subject of much future study.

Discussion. Haas and Creamer make the most of a modest amount of data to argue for warfare among the Kayenta Anasazi in the late 1200s. Later in this chapter we are able to add another case of probable violence for the Tsegi–Marsh Pass area—one of scalping at Betatakin (site 73) in the same time period. Indeed, we accept Haas and Creamer's argument and go even further to note that violence and conflict do not necessarily need to be limited to local disputes over limited resources. Violence and socially pathological behavior might have been rippling into the Kayenta area from outside the district: it is only 225 km (141 miles) from Marsh Pass to Chaco Canyon, and Houck K, a Chacoan great house in Arizona to be discussed later in this chapter, is only 184 km (115 miles) away.

---

## 69 Wupatki

Claim Date. 1995.

Claimant. C. G. Turner and J. A. Turner.

Claim Type. Violence.

Other Designations. NA405; Wupakihuh (Hopi for "Tall House," Colton 1933:64).

Site Location. About 40 km (25 miles) northeast of Flagstaff and 11.3 km (7 miles) north of the Little Colorado River, at headquarters of Wupatki National Monument, Arizona. USGS Wupatki SE quadrangle (1969), T 25N, R 10E, SE ¼ of NW ¼ of NW ¼ of Sec. 30.

Site Type. Three-story masonry pueblo with 60 to 70 rooms, a ball court, a large, open, kivalike amphitheater, and extramural walls and structures (Colton 1960).

Cultural Affiliation. A limited early Anasazi presence followed by a major Sinagua occupancy and construction phase, then abandonment, and finally a late brief Hopi use. All the perimortem-damaged skeletons are believed to be Sinagua.

Chronology. Pueblo III, A.D. 1100–1200 (tree-rings and ceramics). Harold Colton (1946:62) suggested that the Anasazi were the first to settle at Wupatki, but the Sinagua began the major building around 1137. Final construction occurred between 1190 and 1194. Michael Stanislawski (1963:535) proposed that some Hopis might have briefly reoccupied Wupatki Pueblo in the late thirteenth or early fourteenth century.

Excavators and Dates. Wupatki Pueblo has a long history of archaeological activity, which has been reviewed by Dana Hartman and Arthur H. Wolf (1977) and David R. Wilcox (n.d.). In addition, for human remains discussed in this book, there has been the following activity: In 1926–1927, A. E. Douglass, H. S. Colton, and J. C. Clarke excavated Rooms 35, 36, and 45 in order to collect roof beams for tree-ring dating. In the southeast section of the ruin, workers funded by the Civil Works Administration excavated in 14 rooms and the amphitheater under the direction of Colton and Lyndon L. Hargrave. Other rooms were excavated in 1933–1934 (Colton et al.

Table 3.63
Wupatki Ruin Unrelated Burials with Perimortem Damage

| BURIAL NO. | ROOM NO. | AGE | SEX | PERIMORTEM DAMAGE | GRAVE GOODS | EXCAVATOR & DATE |
|---|---|---|---|---|---|---|
| MNA20[a] | — | A | M | Six broken teeth, full disarticulation | None | Colton, 1934 |
| MNA30 | 28 | YA | ? | Broken jaw + vault (ground pressure?) | None | Colton, 1934 |
| MNA34 | 32 | 6–7 | ? | Broken jaw | Child not mentioned in room report | Colton, 1934 |
| NPS1[b] | 25 | A | M | Cuts, head injuries | Many items | Richert & Mathew, 1952 |
| NPS2 | 25 | A | M? | Midshaft femur breaks | Mass burial | Richert & Mathew, 1952 |
| NPS-x[c] | 73 | 6 | ? | Parietal + jaw injury | | Richert & Mathew, 1952 |
| MNA35[d] | 59 | YA | F | Frontal trauma hole 2.5 x 2.5 cm diameter | None, maybe part of bone mass | Brewers, 1934 |
| MNA35 | 59 | Mixed | — | Carnivore gnawing + tooth marks | None | Brewers, 1934 |
| Trench L | — | J | ? | Femurs with cuts or abrasions | No associations | Colton, 1934 |

NOTE: A denotes adult (18 years or older); F, female; J, juvenile (12–17 years); M, male; and YA, young adult (18–30).

a. The Colton et al. description of Burial 20 (n.d.:n.p.) is remarkably like that of the Room 59 mass burial: "In this burial there was a complete lack of articulation. Judging from the number of rocks scattered with the bones it had been excavated and returned to the crevice [author's query, "Why?"]. The 'grave' is at the edge of the mesa north and east of N.A. 405, in the rim rock. . . . There was so much rock mixed with the bones that not more than one bone was visible at one time . . . and no artifacts, whatever."

b. Richert (n.d.:n.p.) says that "a very complex assemblage of human skeletal material [several individuals] both articulated and scattered, associated with bone awls, a 3/4 groove axe, 3 metates, 3 manos, a long strand of white disk beads, a lump of green paint, hammer stones, conus tinklers and great quantities of potsherds were uncovered. . . . The haphazard position of some of these bones suggests that they may have been exhumed from an earlier grave and thrown into this room."

c. Richert (n.d.) did not mention this child in his discussion of Room 73; he mentioned only the lower body of a young subadult.

d. MNA Site Files record BC35.1 as a formal burial in Room 59, presumably because the young woman was found before and above the bone bed in the bottom of the room. She has undamaged arm and leg bones but lacks shoulder and pelvic bones, ribs, and all vertebrae. Grade 2 porotic hyperostosis is present. There is no cranial deformation. Although the penetrating perimortem frontal wound is irregularly shaped, it is nevertheless a classic internally expanding, cone-shaped impact wound. The tip of her nose may have been broken at the same time.

n.d.). Room 59 was excavated by Sallie P. Brewer and James W. Brewer in 1934, following the end of the Civilian Works Administration excavation and stablization project. In 1952 Roland Richert (n.d.) and Thomas W. Mathews excavated Rooms 25 and 73, recovering human remains with perimortem damage.

**Institutional Storage.** Wupatki National Monument; Department of Anthropology, Museum of Northern Arizona, Flagstaff.

**Site Reports.** Colton (1946); Colton et al. (n.d.).

**Osteological Reports.** Brewer and Brewer (1934); Turner and Turner (1990).

**Skeletal Evidence of Stress.** There is some porotic hyperostosis.

**Burial Context.** There are complete skeletons and isolated bones recovered by Colton's 1933–1934 excavation crews and by Wupatki Pueblo archaeologists in later years that have perimortem cuts, anvil abrasions, and impact fractures but no burning or other damage that would clearly suggest cannibalism. The skeletal remains with human-

Table 3.64
Synoptic Inventory of Wupatki Room 59 Human Remains (MNI = 19)

| SKELETAL ELEMENT | TOTAL NO. | % OF EXPECTED |
|---|---|---|
| Skull & jaw (matching) | 1 | 5.2 |
| Mandible | 16 | 89.5 |
| Hyoid | 2 | 10.5 |
| Clavicle | 28 | 73.7 |
| Scapula | 35 | 92.1 |
| Humerus | 28 | 73.7 |
| Radius | 29 | 76.3 |
| Ulna | 31 | 81.6 |
| Wrist | 84 | 55.3 |
| Hand | 350 | 48.5 |
| Sternum | 13 | 68.4 |
| Ribs | 383 | 84.0 |
| Vertebrae (all) | 167 | 36.6 |
| Cervical 2 | 4 | 21.0 |
| Sacrum | 10 | 52.6 |
| Innominate | 26 | 71.0 |
| Femur | 20 | 52.6 |
| Patella | 5 | 13.3 |
| Tibia | 30 | 78.9 |
| Fibula | 27 | 71.0 |
| Foot | 56 | 42.1 |

SOURCE: Summarized from table 2 in Turner and Turner (1990:194), wherein the values were incorrectly reversed for the first and second vertebrae. The 57.9 expected percentage should apply to the first cervical vertebra, not the second.

inflicted perimortem damage were for the most part spatially unrelated formal burials within rooms.

In addition, Wupatki had a charnel deposit of mixed human remains containing at least 19 individuals whose postcranial bones and lower jaws had been unceremoniously dumped into abandoned Room 59 following a relatively brief exposure to carnivore chewing, disarticulation, weathering, and variable element loss. Only two crania were in the bone bed. The Room 59 bones have no identifiable human-inflicted perimortem damage. Sickness, raiding, and sacrifice are possible causes for these deaths.

Figures. 3.216–3.246.

Taphonomy. CGT and JAT. Because there is no single assemblage of damaged remains at Wupatki, we drop the usual categories for taphonomy in favor of more individual discussion. Skeletal inventories are in tables 3.63–3.65.

Other Interpretations. E. P. Lincoln (1961) suggested that the occurrence in Wupatki refuse of a large skull smashed in the occipital and squamosal regions, and of an adolescent male femur broken in the mid-shaft region, raised the question of cannibalism. Both were found associated with food refuse, and the femur "was broken in the same manner as the bones of deer and antelope" (Lincoln 1961:80). Al-

Table 3.65
Bone Elements and Perimortem Damage at Wupatki, Room 73,
Specimen WUPA 5991

| SKELETAL ELEMENT | WHOLE | FRAGMENT | IMPACT BREAK | ANVIL ABRASION |
|---|---|---|---|---|
| Cranial | | | | |
| Mandible | 0 | 1 | 1 | 1 |
| Frontal | 1 | 0 | 0 | 0 |
| Parietal | 2 | 0 | 1 | 0 |
| Occipital | 1 | 0 | 0 | 0 |
| Temporal | 2 | 0 | 0 | 0 |
| Base | 1 | 0 | 0 | 0 |
| Teeth (not counted) | | | | |
| Postcranial | | | | |
| Clavicle | 0 | 1 | 1 | 0 |
| Humerus | 0 | 1 | 1 | 0 |
| Radius | 0 | 1 | 1 | 0 |
| Hand & foot | Largely all present without damage | | | |
| Pelvis | Whole without damage | | | |
| TOTAL (17)[a] | 7 | 4 | 5 | 1 |
| PERCENTAGE | 41.2 | 23.5 | 29.4 | 5.9 |

Percentage of expected vertebrae = 0.0 (0 of 24).

NOTE: Only elements that were present are listed. No cut marks, burning, polishing, gnawing, or chewing was observed. Impact breakage and anvil abrasions represent perimortem damage.

a. Excluding hand and foot bones.

though neither was burned, Lincoln (1961:80) made the point that burning was rare for most of the animal bones found in the trash.

Discussion. The formally buried skeletons vary in their completeness, but missing bones seem more likely a result of postmortem bioturbation or human disturbance than of prehistoric acts of mutilation or hostility. On the other hand, although we know of no comparable frequency data for random, isolated perimortem damage in another large archaeological site, our experience with large skeletal collections such as those from Point of Pines, the Roosevelt Platform Mound study, and Gran Quivira leads us to believe that the Wupatki taphonomic situation as a whole indeed signals substantial conflict or maltreatment. At least one Wupatki burial, an adult male from Room 25 who probably died from brain damage because his face and head had been beaten so severely, also had had his ears cut off. This could be determined by very fine cut marks around both ear openings.

Elsewhere (Turner and Turner 1990) we discussed the history, taphonomy, and other characteristics of the Room 59 human bone deposit and made a limited qualitative comparison with a sample of prehistoric antelope bones screened by Colton et al. from the Wupatki trash dumps, which are also curated at the Museum of Northern Arizona. Both the Room 59 human bones and the antelope bone refuse have carnivore chewing and tooth marks. Preservation is good in both sets, doubtless because both had been stripped of their soft tissue, greatly reducing the amount of organic matter available for

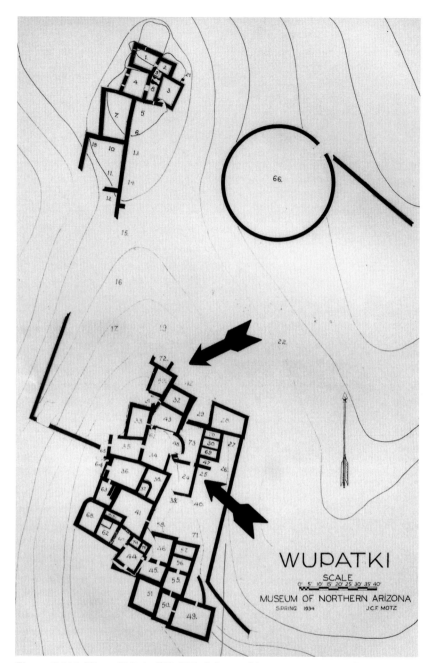

Figure 3.216. Wupatki Ruin (NA405), Arizona. Map prepared by J. C. Fisher Motz, April 1934. The excavation of Room 59, indicated by upper arrow, took place after Civil Works Administration excavations ceased in 1933 and site had been mapped. On this map and in excavation photographs, Room 59 is identified as Room 72. Isolated human skeletal elements with human-caused perimortem damage were found in the trash area in the vicinity of the L-shaped west wall at left center. Lower arrow locates Rooms 25 and 73, where excavations by Richert and Mathews in 1952 also recovered human skeletal remains with human-caused perimortem cutting and breaking. Amphitheater (unroofed great kiva?) is large circular structure in upper right. A large ball court is located off the top of the map. Museum of Northern Arizona Archive photograph (NA405.3).

Figure 3.217. Wupatki. View from the east. Snowfall depth was probably no more than 10 cm. Room 59 is located at the right edge of the main room-block on left. Amphitheater is at extreme right. Museum of Northern Arizona Archive photograph by Milton Snow (1933).

Figure 3.218. Wupatki. Personnel of the Museum of Northern Arizona Civil Works Administration Project. Upper row, left to right: Arthur Fenske, Donald Collier, Ten Broeck Williamson, Dr. Harold S. Colton, Jimmy Kiwaytewa [Kewanwytewa], Grant Tuwayesva. Lower row, left to right: Lyndon L. Hargrave, Pierce Kiwaytewa [Kewanwytewa], J. C. Fisher Motz. Museum of Northern Arizona Archive photograph by Milton Snow (1933).

Figure 3.219. Wupatki. James W. Brewer holding the pelt of a coyote whose carcass hangs from a roof beam in the "patio" of Wupatki Room 36. The animal was trapped and probably skinned on November 31, 1933, by Clyde Pesliki, a Navajo resident of the Wupatki area. The photograph gives some idea of the amount of fat and meat there is in a carcass of this size. Coyotes and village dogs are believed to be the sole cause of the perimortem damage to the human skeletal remains found in Wupatki Ruin Room 59, since no human damage can be found. Museum of Northern Arizona Archive photograph by Milton Snow (1933).

Figure 3.220. Wupatki, Room 25. Adult male skull with peri-mortem vault breakage (WUPA 5993; NPS 475) (CGT neg. 5-10-93:12).

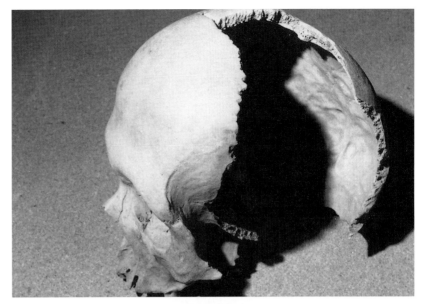

Figure 3.221. Wupatki, Room 25. Adult male of figure 3.220 showing perimortem percussion damage to sockets of anterior teeth (WUPA 5993; NPS 475) (CGT neg. 5-10-93:7).

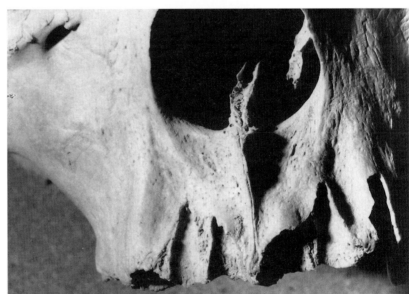

Figure 3.222. Wupatki, Room 25. Adult male of figure 3.220 showing very fine perimortem cut marks that would have been immediately above and to the rear of the right ear (WUPA 5993; NPS 475) (CGT neg. 5-10-93:8).

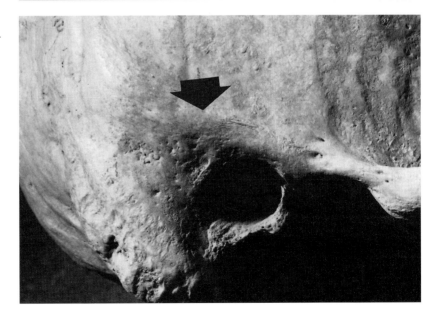

Figure 3.223. Wupatki, Room 25. Adult male of figure 3.220 showing perimortem removal of the mandibular condyle by twisting or smashing (WUPA 5993; NPS 475) (CGT neg. 5-10-93:15).

Figure 3.224. Wupatki, Room 25. Another adult (male?) left and right femurs with perimortem midshaft percussion breakage. This individual was about one-third complete and lacked the cranium and mandible. During their 1952 excavation, Richert and Mathews found the left femur lying southeast of the articulated body. There is no sign of animal damage to this skeleton (WUPA 5994; NPS 476B) (CGT neg. 5-10-93:1).

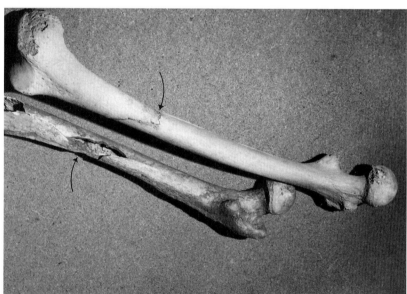

Figure 3.225. Wupatki, Room 25. Close-up of right femur in figure 3.224 showing detail of perimortem midshaft impact breakage (WUPA 5994; NPS 476B) (CGT neg. 5-10-93:3).

Figure 3.226. Wupatki, Room 28. Perimortem breakage of young adult cranial vault and mandible (Burial 30) (CGT neg. 7-16-93:19).

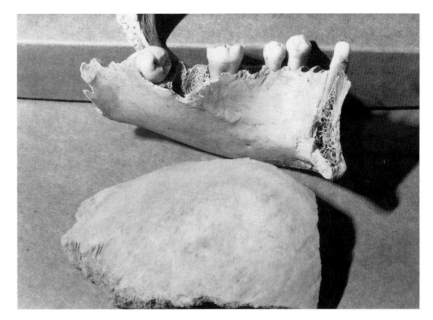

Figure 3.227. Wupatki, Room 32. Perimortem breakage of mandible belonging to six- to seven-year-old child (Burial 34-1) (CGT neg. 7-16-93:18).

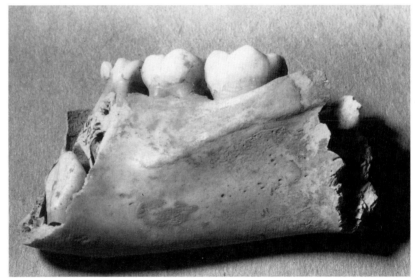

Figure 3.228. Wupatki, Room 59 (identification board indicates Room 72). Largely disarticulated human skeletal remains excavated by 1934 Wupatki Monument caretakers Sallie P. Brewer (Harris) and James W. Brewer. Many of the bones in this photograph were removed from the floor fill before the next stage was photographed. Femur at far left was fused to the pelvic bone (fig. 3.237). Skull at left has perimortem breakage in center of forehead (fig. 3.230). These remains were picked up from somewhere outside and dumped through a roof entrance into the room, where they fell randomly. Museum of Northern Arizona Archive photograph by Milton Snow (1934).

Figure 3.229. Wupatki, Room 59. A slightly later stage in the Brewers' excavation. The skull, mandible, femurs, and other bones that could be seen in the previous figure have been removed. About 1,300 whole and fragmented bones of an MNI of 19 were recovered from the floor and floor fill of this room. There seem to be more articulated elements in this view than in figure 3.228. This difference would be reasonable if whoever dumped the bones into the room had collected the larger, more apparent pieces first, then cleaned up the smaller elements and single fragments. Museum of Northern Arizona Archive photograph by Milton Snow (1934).

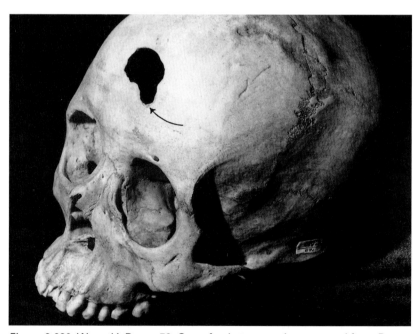

Figure 3.230. Wupatki, Room 59. One of only two crania recovered from Room 59. This is the young adult female skull (Burial 35-1) shown in figure 3.228. A few minute bone chips adhere to the lower border of the perimortem percussion hole. In addition to this breakage, there is an old, completely healed wound at the posterior end and left side of the frontal bone (CGT neg. 7-22-94:3).

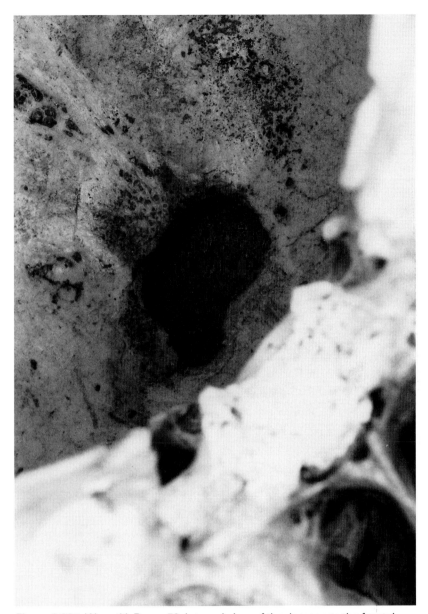

Figure 3.231. Wupatki, Room 59. Internal view of the damage to the frontal bone of Burial 35-1. The conchoidal breakage pattern shows the characteristics of percussion trauma. The wound could have been caused intentionally by an assailant or by the skull's being dropped into the room and landing on a sharp stone. We hesitate to conclude violence in the absence of other recognizable forms of human-inflicted damage (CGT neg. 7-6-88:15).

Figure 3.232. Wupatki, Room 59.
Although the Brewers found
only two crania, they recovered
17 mandibles, all shown here.
We examined them repeatedly
for cut marks and abrasions but
found none. Whoever dumped
the human remains into Room
59 after carnivores had scavenged the bodies must have carried away most of the crania for
deposition elsewhere. With the
possible exception of the mandible on the far left and the damaged forehead of Burial 35-1, all
perimortem damage to the
Room 59 human skeletal remains appears due to carnivore
scavenging (CGT neg. 7-22-94:6).

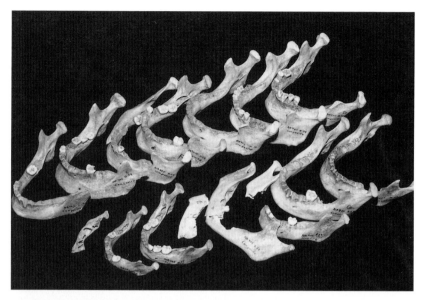

Figure 3.233. Wupatki, Room 59.
One other possible piece of
human-damaged bone from
Room 59 is the previously mentioned mandibular fragment
with its broken-off left ascending ramus (CGT neg. 7-22-94:7).

Figure 3.234. Wupatki, Room 59.
Human vertebrae showing car-
nivore tooth puncture marks
(CGT neg.7-6-88:19).

Figure 3.235. Wupatki, Room 59.
Carnivore chewing and tooth
puncture marks at ends of long
bones (CGT neg. 7-6-88:30).

Figure 3.236. Wupatki, Room 59.
Distal ends of two tibias showing the characteristic pattern of
carnivore hollowing out and
puncturing at the ends of long
bones (CGT neg. 7-6-88:29).

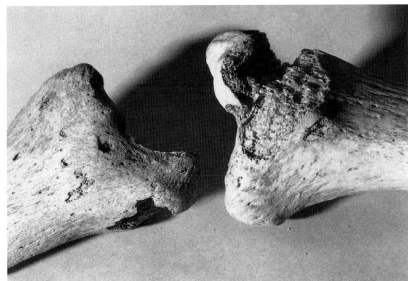

Figure 3.237. Wupatki, Room 59.
This extraordinary specimen is
the hip region of a mature
woman whose femur had fused
to her pelvis. The femur was
frozen in a position approximately like that of lying in bed
with one's legs drawn up toward
the chin. The missing bone at arrow was chewed off by carnivores (CGT neg. 7-6-88:4).

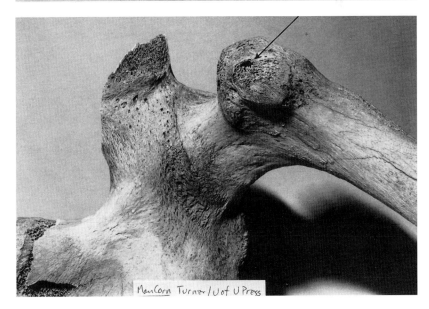

Figure 3.238. Wupatki, Room 59. Human foot bones showing carnivore chewing and tooth puncture marks. None of the Room 59 bones showed any clear-cut damage by humans or rodents (CGT neg. 7-6-88:2).

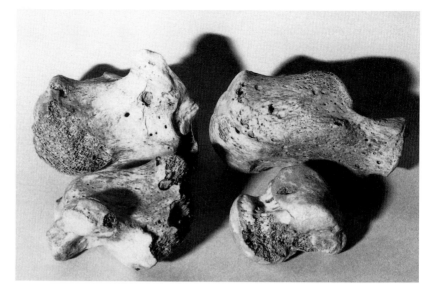

Figure 3.239. Wupatki, Room 59. Ulnas with carnivore chewing at each end; reprinted with permission from *Kiva* (CGT neg. 7-6-88:14).

Figure 3.240. Wupatki, Room 59. Ribs with carnivore tooth puncture marks; reprinted with permission from *Kiva* (CGT neg. 7-6-88:17).

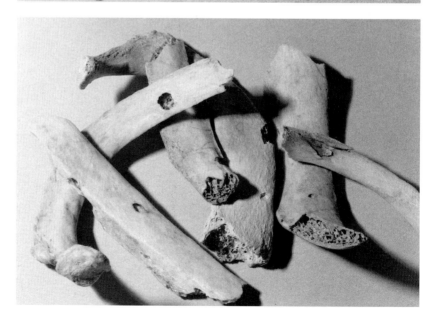

Figure 3.241. Wupatki, Room 73. Mandible of six-year-old child with perimortem breakage at the mandibular symphysis, condyle, and coronoid process. (WUPA 5991; NPS 473) (CGT neg. 5-10-93:17).

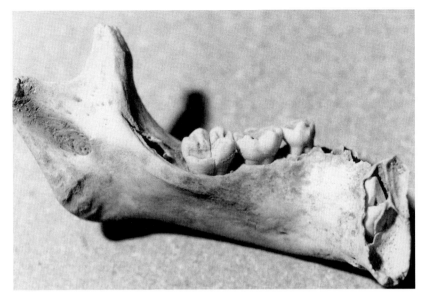

Figure 3.242. Wupatki, Room 73. Perimortem breakage of right parietal of same child as in figure 3.241, external view. Adhering bone chips can be seen at top and bottom of hole (WUPA 5991; NPS 473) (CGT neg. 5-10-93:19).

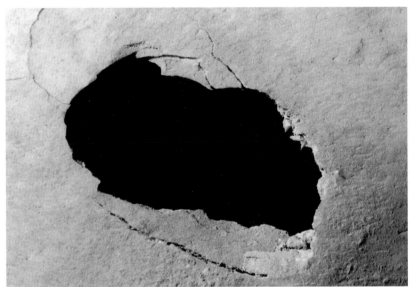

Figure 3.243. Wupatki, Room 73. Right parietal of child in figure 3.241, internal view (WUPA 5991; NPS 473) (CGT neg. 5-10-93:21).

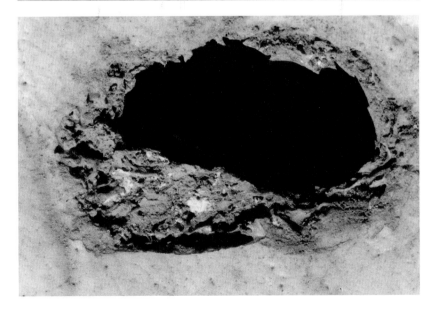

Figure 3.244. Wupatki, Trench L. Isolated fragment of adolescent femur with carnivore chewing and tooth puncture marks. Elsewhere on this fragment there are abrasions and apparent cut marks (CGT neg. 7-16-93:26).

Figure 3.245. Wupatki, Trench L. Long bone fragment with perimortem anvil abrasions. The steplike breakage is postmortem and unrelated to the abrasions (CGT neg. 7-6-88:14).

Figure 3.246. Wupatki, Trench L. Isolated adolescent right humerus with a 5.0-cm (2-inch) cut at arrow (CGT neg. 7-16-93:28).

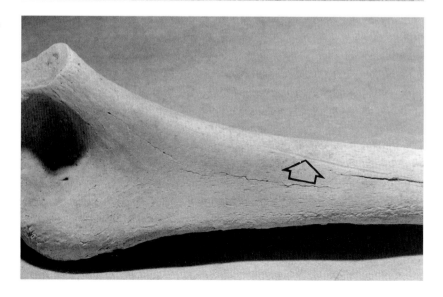

postmortem biochemical breakdown and microbial growth and metabolism. In addition, the antelope bones have incisions from rodent gnawing, stone tool cut marks, perimortem impact fractures, polishing, rough anvil and hammerstone abrasions, and burning, but the Room 59 human bones do not. We have repeatedly examined the Room 59 assemblage, particularly the mandibles and cervical vertebrae, looking for cut marks and any other form of human-caused perimortem damage and have always come up empty-handed. Morover, in July 1995 Shara Bailey examined the Room 59 series independently for a National Park Service NAGPRA inventory and found no signs of human-inflicted perimortem damage.

Another notable difference between the Room 59 human remains and the antelope sample lies in the shortage of human crania. Based on the number of right scapulae, the MNI for Room 59 is 19. There are 17 mandibles, of all ages, but the Brewers found only two crania, and only one of them has been preserved. The postcranial bone frequencies vary from a low of 21.0% of expected for the second cervical vertebra (ignoring the hyoid, which is commonly not recovered in archaeological materials) to 92.1% for the left and right scapulae. Since there are no identifiable cut marks on any of the Room 59 bones, it seems that the crania were not taken as trophies—at least not immediately after death when the mandibles would still have been integral parts of the heads. We do not know what happened to the missing crania. Considering what is known about natural animal diagenesis in the Southwest, the crania were not likely removed by scavengers. Perhaps the heads were buried somewhere in or near Wupatki by whoever dumped the carnivore-ravaged remains in Room 59. But if so, why were the heads treated differently from the rest of the bodies? Perhaps the crania were collected late in the scavenging sequence, after the mandibles were loose or disarticulated, for some sort of ritual or display like the Mesoamerican ceremonial skull racks found from Alta Vista in Zacatecas south to Tlatelolco in Mexico City (Pickering 1985; Pijoan, Pastrana, and Maquivar 1989). Yet even if this were so, we have no taphonomic evidence for how the 19 people died in the first place. An epidemic, distantly followed by raiding or sacrifice, is the most reasonable possibility when all taphonomic and contextual evidence is considered. The isolated examples of probable violence, and especially the strange characteristics of the Room 59 bone assemblage with its relatively large number of carnivore-scavenged but later expediently buried individuals, including children, make Wupatki Pueblo a taphonomic enigma.

Human taphonomy is not the only puzzling aspect of Wupatki. The defensively situated village has masonry construction similar to that in Chaco great houses (Ellis's Chaco style 9, according to Stanislawski 1966:314), but it also possesses a Hohokam-like masonry-walled ball court and a large amphitheater that suggests an unroofed great kiva. This mixture of northern and southern qualities is accentuated by the 41 Mexican macaws whose remains were discovered during Wupatki excavations. How many of these birds had been sacrificed cannot be resolved with certainty, but Hargrave (1970:29) found that Wupatki, with 10 more macaws than Pueblo Bonito's 31, had more of these Mexican imports than any other site in the U.S.

Southwest. Although it can be statistically tricky to extrapolate from cemetery populations to living populations, 41 birds nevertheless suggest a large amount of specialized ritual linked directly with Mexico. Hopis claim that the Parrot clan came from Wupatki.

Mexican copper bells, Pacific marine shells, turquoise, raw and woven locally grown cotton, and other trade items were found during Colton's excavations. If any Southwestern site could be characterized as cosmopolitan, it would have to be Wupatki, with its features of the Sinagua culture and components of Anasazi, Hohokam, and distant Mesoamerica. The human bone refuse of Room 59 would be right at home in a number of Mesoamerican sites, such as the Hall of Columns at La Quemada in Zacatecas, with its mass of headless human remains strewn across the floor (Pickering 1985).

Wilcox (1993) sees Wupatki as a far western outpost of the Chacoan great house sociopolitical network. The considerable and variable perimortem damage to humans at Wupatki, although lacking a sure sign of cannibalism, could easily fit into the sort of militarily backed totalitarian social and religious climate he envisions for the Chaco regional system.

Even though, using our conservative criteria, we cannot identify cannibalism at Wupatki, cannibalism and the site are linked in the minds of some Arizona Indians. Thanks to information provided by Elizabeth Brandt, we obtained a San Juan Southern Paiute story about cannibalism from Evelyn James, the president of that group, who had learned the story from her elderly mother. The story takes place at Willow Springs, 66 kilometers (41 miles) north of Wupatki Ruin. In essence, the story begins when a group of strangers arrives one day at Willow Springs but does not come into the camp. Instead, they halt about a mile away. A day or so later a Paiute adult and a small girl walk out to discover what the strangers are doing. James described the strangers in the following order: They wore large earrings, had bones through their noses, and were dark-skinned. They looked closely at the little girl for a long time, then came into the camp, attacking and killing all the Paiutes except one girl and an infant. The latter ended up hidden in an overturned basket, though wounded with a stone knife embedded in her neck. The strangers then tore the victims apart in order to cook and eat them. James emphasized three times that the strangers came from Wupatki, where they lived in defensive houses. Later, the strangers were driven out of Wupatki and retreated to the Flagstaff area. After a while they left Flagstaff for an unknown location.

This remarkable story of Wupatki cannibals was told to the senior author in Tuba City, Arizona, on March 19, 1997, in the presence of another San Juan Southern Paiute council member, Clyde Whiskers. James, Whiskers, and Turner all personally knew Paiutes, Anglos, and Navajos who had lived or worked around Navajo Mountain. Whiskers remarked that he was named after the anthropologist Clyde Kluckhohn, who in his early Southwestern days had also traveled around Navajo Mountain. Because of the trust engendered by our shared backgrounds and acquaintances, the strange Wupatki cannibal story came across as quite believable. Moreover, the tale has, in common with Hopi legends about the attack on Awatovi and the subsequent mutilation and killing of captives, a substantial credibility owing to its richness of detail, vividness, geographic specificity, and internal consistency. There is even a survivor in the story, corresponding to our assumption that a survivor was responsible for burying some of the charnel deposits described in this chapter, such as those at Leroux Wash and Small House.

There is unquestionably much more to the bioarchaeological story of conflict and suffering at and around Wupatki (and nearby House of Tragedy) than the small segment we have been able to put together. The patchy story that has unfolded so far is mirrored in Chaco Canyon at a series of sites referred to as the Casa Rinconada group. The next site, Bc51, is one of this group.

**70**
**Bc51**

**Claim Date.** 1995.
**Claimants.** C. G. Turner and J. A. Turner.
**Claim Type.** Violence.
**Other Designations.** LA40395; 29SJ395; Casa Rinconada group.
**Site Location.** On south side of Chaco Canyon, 0.8 km (0.5 mile) south of Pueblo Bonito, San Juan County, northwestern New Mexico. USGS Pueblo Bonito quadrangle (1966), T 21N, R 11W, center of Sec. 13.
**Site Type.** Single-story, 45-room, crescent-shaped masonry pueblo with six kivas. Located 30.5 m (100 feet) due east of Bc50 (Tseh So), with which Bc51 shares a common refuse area.
**Cultural Affiliation.** Chaco Anasazi.
**Chronology.** Pueblo III, Hosta Butte phase.
**Excavators and Date.** Clyde Kluckhohn, director, University of New Mexico Archaeological Field School, 1936 and 1937. Some time later, Gordon Vivian excavated and stabilized additional rooms.
**Institutional Storage.** Maxwell Museum of Anthropology, University of New Mexico, Albuquerque.
**Site Reports.** Kluckhohn (1939); Brand et al. (1937).
**Osteological Report.** Senter (1937).
**Skeletal Evidence of Stress.** Donovan Senter (1937:162) did not report on the now well-established nutrition/infection stress known for Chaco Canyon, although he did note that osteoarthritis was common.
**Burial Context.** In a small line-drawing titled "Figure 7—scattered bones in Room 5," Kluckhohn (1939:45) illustrated the plan of Room 5 at a level 6 inches (15 cm) above the floor. This drawing shows the bones (numbered but not identified in the caption), other objects, and pots (all well identified in the caption). Although there is no scale in the figure, judging from the general site map Room 5 was about 2.5 by 1.8 m (8 by 6 feet). Kluckhohn's figure 7 shows 62 numbered whole and broken bones scattered over the northern half of the room. Skeletal elements that can be identified with some certainty include two crania (one broken), three femurs, two articulated feet, and vertebrae and ribs strewn about the bone bed. Except for the undamaged cranium, shown with its mandible attached, and a possibly joined femur-innominate, there are no identifiable articulations.
**Associated Artifacts.** Six ceramic pots (Red Mesa Black-on-white,

McElmo Black-on-white ladle, Red Mesa Black-on-white bird form, McElmo Black-on-white bowl, Deadman's Black-on-red bowl, Wingate Black-on-red bowl), twilled mat, feather cloth, headboard, and two pieces of malachite were identified for Room 5.

**Figures.** None.

**Taphonomy.** CGT and JAT (none by CK).

*MNI.* Kluckhohn's table 3 indicates that three individuals (numbered 60/12, 60/13, and 60/14) were from Room 5. His figure 7 shows no more than two individuals. We found four crania in the collection.

*Kluckholn provided no information for Age and Sex, Preservation, Bone and Fragment Number, Breakage, Cut Marks, Burning, Anvil Abrasions, Polishing, Vertebrae Number, Scalping, Gnawing, Chewing, Insect Parts, or Other Modification.*

**Archaeologist's Interpretation.** Kluckhohn (1939:46) reported: "Some burials, such as those of Room 5 (see Figure 7), were badly scattered. But the fact that some bones were found still in the position of articulation militates against the chance of secondary burial and points rather to disturbance by carnivores or rodents. This alternative gains force from the fact that certain isolated human bones found in the refuse heap appeared gnawed."

**Other Interpretations.** Senter (1937:161) agreed with Kluckhohn, saying: "Most of the graves [at Bc50–51] were disturbed, the bones were out of place, and bones from two skeletons were frequently mixed together. Other skeletons were represented by but a few bones or fragments. Prairie dogs, grave robbers, or superposition of burials may have been responsible for the general state of disturbance of burials."

**Discussion.** Kluckhohn's site map of Bc50–51 shows Room 5 to be due north of a kiva (no. 4), and both are near the center of the largely double row of 24 more or less rectangular rooms and six circular kivas.

Our brief taphonomic survey of Bc51 Room 5 produced an enigmatic picture of skeletal incompleteness without a corresponding amount of perimortem damage. Part of this puzzle may be due to the thick coating of preservative that was put on the incompletely cleaned whole and fragmented bones. On the other hand, incompleteness was probably furthered by methodology, as the following quotation from Senter's discussion of Bc50–51 burials suggests: "Thus one determines just what material should be saved, and the bulk of the 'scrap' can be discarded without first carrying it back into town, thus saving both storage space and shipping expenses" (1937:145).

Specimen 60/12 is an adult of unknown sex. With the exception of a possible broken nose, there is no identifiable perimortem damage to a fragmentary cranial vault, 2 clavicles (of different individuals), 1 rib fragment, 1 cervical vertebra, 11 small indeterminable fragments, 1 patella, 1 radius fragment, 1 fibula fragment, 3 tibia fragments, 1 ulna fragment, and 8 long bone fragments. Some of the postcranial pieces probably belong to the other three individuals, all adult males. They are specimen 60/13a, 35–45 years, represented by a cranium and skull with no perimortem damage; specimen 60/13b, a broken vault with no perimortem damage; and specimen 60/13c, most of a vault with no perimortem damage.

The number of preserved pieces falls short of the 62 numbered bones in Kluckhohn's drawing of Room 5. The absence of unequivocal animal and human perimortem damage to the skeletal remains of the four Room 5 adults, of whom three were males, limits what can be said about disarticulation and scattering by animals, as Kluckhohn suggested, or disturbance by humans. The coating of preservative on most of the bones is also limiting. The presence of six ceramic vessels in Room 5, one of which is shown by Kluckhohn (1939:45) to contain a human bone, would, under most circumstances, indicate that the four sets of remains represent disturbed formal burials. However, the amount of bone recovered is much less than there should be for four adults, so either most of the bones had been removed or the disarticulated skeletal remains must have originated in an old burial site somewhere else and then dumped into Room 5. Kluckhohn's drawing of Room 5 indicates that the human bones were six inches above the floor, another indication of dumping instead of disturbance. There is some suggestion of disrespect signaled by the scattered deposit. The remains do not appear to be a considerate secondary burial. While our examination of the Room 5 bones does not advance the explanation much beyond that which Kluckhohn and Senter suggested more than 50 years ago, it does lead us to other considerations of the Rinconada group.

Besides the unexplainable Room 5 taphonomy, there are other peculiar aspects to Bc50–51. Kluckhohn (1939:39) remarked that one of the most noteworthy facts about the six kivas of Bc51 was the presence of human bones in five of them. "The fill of kivas 3, 4, 5, and 6 contained miscellaneous human bones, while a human mandible and skull were found on the floor of kivas 1 and 6, respectively." The skeletal remains in Kiva 1 included those of "human infants and foetuses" (Kluckhohn 1939:37). At the north end of the pueblo, on the floor of painted Kiva 6, "against the north wall near the deflector was found the skull of an adult male with a fracture (which appeared to be pre-mortem) in the pterion region, anterior to stephanion. . . . There appeared to be the marks of a stone knife on the basilar portion of the occipital. In the room fill, about 1' above the skull, were found the 2nd and 3rd cervical vertebrae in the position of articulation. Within a few inches of these were found the 6th and 7th right ribs" (Kluckhohn 1939:38–39).

At most, five to six miscellaneous adult human bones were found in each of almost all the other rooms: 4, 8 (infant and adult), 9 (infant), 10, 16, 18, and 22. Curiously, only three rooms of the 24 excavated by 1937 were entirely free of human bone. Unfortunately, we were unable to locate or identify these miscellaneous remains in the Maxwell Museum skeletal collection.

Four burials had been recovered during the 1936 excavation of Bc51 Room 1. Senter (1937) recorded three as being adults (male, female, and sex unknown), and one adolescent. All were disturbed (see below).

In addition to Bc51 Room 5, we looked for perimortem damage in human bones from other Casa Rinconada–area sites, all near one another and all dating at about the same time: Bc50 (LA40394, 29SJ394, Tseh So), Bc51 (other than Room 5), Bc53 (LA40396,

29SJ396), Bc57 (LA40397, 29SJ397), and Bc59 (LA40399, 29SJ399). We noted perimortem damage in the following individuals, most of whose bones featured the aforementioned preservative:

Bc50, no. 50. Frontal fragment with breaks and one 1.0-cm-long cut mark, vertical, above nose. Ulna with both ends chewed off and tooth puncture marks on proximal end. Distal end has polishing. Both pieces are well preserved.

Bc50 (x) Trench 3, Level 5, Section 2. Mandible with left condyle chewed off; right condyle has two tooth puncture marks.

Bc51 60/2 Room 1. Adolescent. Chewed distal radius.

Bc51 60/28. Subadult cranial vault with impact blow to top of head, splitting right parietal in half. Maxilla probably broken off at same time.

Bc53 #[no number]. Right tibia with both ends chewed off.

Bc53 a. One chewed toe bone. One chewed rib fragment. One chewed pelvic fragment.

Bc53 b. Eight whole and fragmentary vertebrae with chewing. One severely chewed pelvis fragment. Two chewed rib fragments.

Bc53 c2. All adult pieces. Left scapula with chewing. Another left scapula (labeled Room X Level 4) with chewing. Right humerus with both ends chewed off. Left and right radius with both ends chewed off. Right ulna with both ends chewed off. Left and right femurs with both ends chewed off. Two left tibias, one with proximal end chewed off, the other with distal end chewed off. Right tibia with both ends chewed off. Fibula with both ends chewed off. Two chewed vertebrae. One long bone fragment with breaks. One rib fragment with a tooth puncture mark.

Bc53 60/1a. Cranial base fragment with breaks.

Bc53 60/2a (bones labeled Room 7). Two chewed vertebrae fragments. Two extensively chewed adult pelvis fragments. Left humerus with both ends chewed. Head of humerus with chewing. Left ulna with both ends chewed. Left femur with both ends chewed. Two fibulae with both ends chewed (fig. 3.247).

Bc53 60/2b. Adult thoracic vertebra, chewed. A chewed right adult scapula. Another right scapula with tooth puncture marks. A chewed left adult scapula. At least five chewed rib fragments. One whole rib with chewing. A right adult clavicle chewed on both ends. A subadult female pelvis with chewing and tooth puncture marks. A left adult female femur with both ends chewed off. Two right adult femurs with both ends chewed off. A left adult tibia and fibula with both ends chewed off. A right adult humerus with distal end chewed off. Two left adult humerii with both ends chewed off. A right ulna with both ends chewed off. Distal ends chewed off left and right radius.

Bc57 60/13. Child, 5–6 years. Two rib fragments with cut marks (one with cut marks on internal and external surfaces, the other with 20 cut marks 2 to 5 mm long). One cranial fragment with 5 mm cut mark. Several cranial fragments with light brown burned appearance.

Bc59 60/4. Subadult (dental age 10–11 years). Twenty long bone fragments with spiral fractures. One fragment is burned. Two chewed hand/foot bones. Two maxilla and mandible fragments

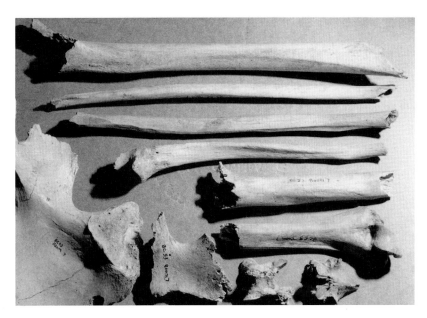

Figure 3.247. Casa Riconada area (Bc53), Chaco Canyon, New Mexico. Carnivore damage to long bones, pelvis, and vertebrae. Note that carnivores damage the ends of bones, not the midshaft areas that are characteristically smashed on anvils by humans. There is no sign of rodent damage. Maxwell Museum of Anthropology 60/2a, Room 7 (CGT neg. 6-30-95:21).

with breaks. Twenty cranial fragments with breaks. Three of the cranial fragments are burned. One cranial fragment has cut marks. Five vertebrae fragments, all with breaks.

Bc59 60/6. Adult female? Distal end right radius chewed off. Tooth scars present on distal end.

Bc59 60/10 and 60/11. Adult male. A nearly complete and largely burned skeleton with some calcining. Some skull fragments burned, especially cranial base. Vault did not burn. About three-fourths of mandible burned. One burned mandible fragment fits with unburned horizontal ramus. The break between these two pieces seems to be postmortem. Skeleton is burned all over. Could have been a cremation. Breakage extensive but attributable to burning.

Bc59 60/4a. Subadult. Two left femurs with breaks at all four ends. One of the left femurs (a.2) has 17 cut marks at midshaft and a mishaft impact fracture area. Proximal end of the cut femur has chewing. Two tibias with all four ends seemingly chewed off. One tibia (a.2) has approximately 20 cut marks in various shaft locations. Shaft of tibia a.2 has long broken attached splinters with impact marks. However, impacts might be carnivore damage, as there are no identifiable anvil abrasions. Fibula with midshaft impact area and spiral fracturing, but with no anvil abrasions. Left and right humerii with both ends chewed off.

Bc59 60/4b. Child. Left humerus fragment with carnivore chewing. Tibia fragment with chewing.

Bc59 60/4c. Adult. Cranial vault fragments (15) are burned. One vault fragment has perimortem breaks. Mandible fragment has breaks and polishing.

In summary, our brief examination of the Casa Rinconada–area skeletons curated at the Maxwell Museum of Anthropology revealed human-caused perimortem damage to nine individuals, as well as extensive carnivore damage. From Bc59, specimen 60/4, a 10- to 11-year-old child, has just enough perimortem damage to be considered cannibalized, and we have classified it that way (see table 3.77). Bc59 had two other specimens with perimortem damage, 60/4a and 60/4c. Finally, two additional sets of bone from Bc59, 60/10 and 60/11, are almost certainly one individual who may have been cremated. The other six individuals with signs of violence were Bc51, Room 5, specimen 60/12 (adult, sex?), and 60/28 from unspecified locations; Bc50, specimen 50; Bc53, specimens c2 and 60/1a; and Bc57, specimen 60/13.

As elsewhere in Chaco Canyon, we do not understand why there is almost no evidence of rodent gnawing, whereas carnivore chewing is unmistakable. Does this perimortem situation support the view that Chaco Canyon had few human inhabitants for parts of the year (reviewed in Sebastian 1992), enabling dogs or coyotes to dig up and damage corpses at their leisure? Could it mean that there were easily scavenged, unburied and mutilated bodies lying about due to violence? Or does it simply mean that carnivores accidently unearthed human remains in their attempts to dig out rodents colonized in Chacoan cemeteries?

Bc51 and the other Casa Rinconada–area sites have a complex human taphonomic picture that corresponds well with that described herein for other Chaco Canyon sites (see also Vivian 1965 for a description of skeletal remains excavated in 1939 at the Three-C Site). Taken as a whole, there was significantly more modification, human and environmental, to Chacoan bodies than has been noted in comparably sized districts of the Mogollon, Classic-period Hohokam, or western Anasazi culture areas. Chaco Canyon is not only architecturally distinctive, it is also taphonomically strange.

## 71
## Guadalupe Ruin

Claim Date. 1995.

Claimants. C. G. Turner and J. A. Turner.

Claim Type. Problematic.

Other Designations. LA2757; ENM838; SDV5.

Site Location. About 56 km (35 miles) northwest of Albuquerque, at the base of and high atop an isolated small mesa in the middle Rio Puerco Valley, southwestern Sandoval County, New Mexico. USGS Guadalupe quadrangle (1961), T 15N, R 3W, NW ¼ of NW ¼ of Sec. 23.

Site Type. Single-story, 50-room masonry pueblo.

Cultural Affiliation. San Juan Mesa Verde Anasazi.

Chronology. The later period of Mesa Verdean occupation (A.D. 1200–1350) pertains to the human remains of interest.

Excavators and Date. Lonnie C. Pippin and field crews, Eastern New Mexico University Rio Puerco Valley Archaeological Project, 1972–1975.

Institutional Storage. Eastern New Mexico University, Portales.

Site Report. Pippin (1987).

Osteological Report. In progress by Lisa Bergschneider (Kathy Roler, personal communication, August 5, 1996). See discussion below.

Skeletal Evidence of Stress. Not reported.

**Burial Context.** Disarticulated human remains found in debris above floors in rooms 15B and 22. Room 15 had burned roof debris.

**Associated Artifacts.** Not reported.

**Figures.** None.

**Taphonomy.** LCP.

   *MNI.* Room 15B, 1; Room 22, human remains present.

   *Age and Sex.* Room 15B, adult male.

   *There is no information for Preservation, Bone and Fragment Number, Breakage, Cut Marks, Burning, Anvil Abrasions, Polishing, Vertebrae Number, Scalping, Gnawing, Chewing, Insect Parts, or Other Modification.*

**Archaeologist's Interpretation.** Pippen (1987:119) described the setting as follows: "Room 15B was divided into two smaller San Juan–Mesa Verde Occupation Rooms (15C and 15D; Figure 52) by the jacal wall described earlier. The floor of the easternmost subdivision (Room 15D) sealed Late Chaco Occupation trash (Stratum C207, Figure 57). The disarticulated skeleton of an adult male was found in a concentration of sandstone rocks above this floor (Figure 58). Burned and fallen roof debris (Stratum F104) was deposited over both room floors. The entire Room 15B was then used for trash disposal (Stratum C103)."

   Trash deposited in Room 22 included "disarticulated human remains . . . throughout the trash deposits."

**Other Interpretations.** Since this site had been excavated as part of the Eastern New Mexico University Rio Puerco Valley Archaeological Project, we asked bioarchaeologist Kathy Roler whether the skeletal remains were curated in her department at that university. They were, and Roler asked graduate student Lisa Bergschneider to do a perimortem taphonomic workup. Bergschneider had previously done human taphonomy analysis with Kirsten Linnea Anderson (1994) on burned and cut human remains exavated many years ago at the Aztalan Site in Jefferson County, Wisconsin. She found little perimortem damage on the Guadalupe Ruin human remains—certainly nothing that would suggest cannibalism.

**Discussion.** Bergschneider found very few burned pieces (seven), almost no cut marks (three or possibly a few more), and no convincing signs of other human-caused perimortem damage types in 1,429 whole and fragmented bones. We consider her observations to be definitive. Nevertheless, there is still a need to explain the small amount of processing she did identify. As illustrated in Pippen's figure 58, labeled "disarticulated skeleton and associated sandstone rock concentration in room 15B," this burial remains enigmatic. In the photo, a broken skull without mandible lies adjacent to a wall, and next to it is a whole humerus. A whole ulna can be identified about 1.0 m (3 feet) away, and there is a headless femur another meter or so away from the skull. In the center of the picture is a nearly whole radius and what appear to be two masses of broken and unidentifiable bones. All the bones and fragments seem to be on the same surface; if so, they were likely deposited at about the same time. Although this "burial" dates to a later time period than the Chacoan heyday of the tenth to eleventh centuries, we remain intrigued about its taphonomic history because it is yet another example of what seems to be a regional tendency to deal with the dead in an apparently dismissive, if not disdainful, manner. We suggest that in future Chacoan archaeology, upon encountering disarticulated, scavenger-damaged, cut-up human remains lacking grave goods, burial pits, or any signs of considerate placement, prudent excavators should pause to explore the contextual setting for taphonomic agencies that might have operated at the time of deposition.

In addition, Kathy Roler (personal communication, August 5, 1996) came across a human temporal bone with cut marks mixed in with nonhuman faunal remains from the Eleanor Ruin (ENM883). According to Roler, Eleanor was the only one of the roomblocks in the Guadalupe community at the base of the small mesa that was even partly excavated. The other roomblocks received only one or two test trenches.

## 72
## Mesa Verde 875

**Claim Date.** 1995.

**Claimants.** C. G. Turner and J. A. Turner.

**Claim Type.** Problematic.

**Other Designations.** Part of Far View group.

**Site Location.** Northern end of Chapin Mesa, due west from the Mummy Lake or Far View group of ruins, Mesa Verde National Park, Colorado. USGS Mesa Verde National Park quadrangle (1967), T 35N, R 15W, Sec. 27.

**Site Type.** Single-story, 17-room pueblo with kiva.

**Cultural Affiliation.** Mesa Verde Anasazi.

**Chronology.** Site was occupied in Pueblo II times for about 50 years. It was then abandoned for some 25 years, after which a late Pueblo II or early Pueblo III, 15-room pueblo and kiva were constructed on the same site. The human remains of interest belong to the first occupation.

**Excavators and Date.** Robert H. Lister and members of the University of Colorado Archaeology Field School, 1955–1956.

**Institutional Storage.** Lister (1965) reported that most specimens and all records went to the Archaeology Laboratory at the University of Colorado. These materials may have since been returned to Mesa Verde National Park.

**Site Report.** Lister (1965).

**Osteological Report.** Wade and Armelagos (1966).

**Skeletal Evidence of Stress.** William D. Wade and George J. Armelagos, specialists in paleopathology, did not indicate any stress out of the ordinary.

**Burial Context.** Disarticulated human remains scattered in the fill of Rooms I, III, and IX of the Pueblo II occupation.

**Associated Artifacts.** Considerable amounts of pottery were found in Room I: 36 whole or fragmentary vessels and sherds of possibly four additional vessels. Room III had artifacts, but none associated with a skull and tibia. Room IX had only two artifacts, neither associated with a cranium and femur.

**Figures.** None.

**Taphonomy.** RHL.

*MNI.* 6 (Room I had 6 right femurs). The femur found in Room IX was said by Wade and Armelagos to be a left one.

*Age and Sex.* Room I, six adults (RHL). Wade and Armelagos (1966:107) said age and sex identifications were impossible because of fragmentation and poor preservation, although they found the Room III individual to be a 35- to 40-year-old male, and the Room IX person, a 30- to 40-year-old male.

*Preservation.* Poor to good.

*Breakage.* Present.

*There is no information for Bone and Fragment Number, Cut Marks, Burning, Anvil Abrasions, Polishing, Vertebrae Number, Scalping, Gnawing, Chewing, Insect Parts, or Other Modification.*

Archaeologist's Interpretation. Room I of the earlier pueblo contained considerable amounts of fragmentary human skeletal material and pottery. Lister (1965:15) believed the skeletal remains had been re-buried:

> There is every reason to believe that the skeletal remains found in Room I represent secondary burials placed there after the structure had been reduced to partial ruin. Their position in the room, between floor level and the surface, demonstrates this fact. The condition and arrangement of the remains, as shown in Figure 6 which illustrates the position of all items found in the room, shows that these are not normal burials. Most bones are disarticulated and randomly scattered. No skeletons are complete or even partially intact. Only pieces of the larger bones, which would have been better preserved in their original graves, were present. Groups of bones sometimes represent more than one individual, and some isolated bones have no relationship to other bones. Much of the pottery is placed in groups which in most instances are not directly related to any of the skeletal remains. All of these factors support the notion that these are secondary burials. . . . The human skeletal remains and artifacts in this room [I] . . . were recovered from the debris which filled the structure. They were concentrated in a horizontal stratum between 10 and 20 inches below the surface and 5 inches above the floor level of the room, and obviously had been placed there sometime after its abandonment. . . . There are two instances of partially articulated bones in the deposit. . . . The individuals buried in the room were former occupants of the first village as shown by the pottery accompanying them. . . . It would appear that these remains were placed in Room I during the construction of the second village when a portion of the refuse deposit of the first village, which lies to the south of the original village, was disturbed by builders of the second village. When burials were encountered the larger bones and burial offerings were removed from the ground and reburied in Room I of the first village—an area not encroached upon by the second village. It appears that in some instances the bones of the exposed burials were so poorly preserved, which is frequently the case in infant burials, that none of the associated artifacts could be removed for reinterment. . . .

Respect for the dead, or a feeling of awe toward the remains, could have accounted for these actions.

Of the human remains in Room III, which was adjacent to and shared a wall with Room I, Lister (1965:20) said: "Five inches above the floor a human skull and a piece of a tibia were exposed. They may represent another case of secondary burial, although no burial furnishings were offered."

In Room IX, separated from I and III by two other rooms, Lister (1965:23) noted: "Two portions of a human skeleton—a cranium and a femur—were found near one another 15 inches deep in the fill of the room. Close by a Mancos Black-on-white ladle was encountered. These also may be the result of secondary burials as were found in Rooms I and III."

Last, Lister (1965:107) described the skeleton found in the refuse area to the south: "Only one burial [7] was found in the refuse deposit of Site 875. It was encountered in Square BL 2, just beneath the surface. A fairly well-preserved adult skeleton—although the right femur and bones of the lower arms, hands, and feet are missing—it had been placed in the grave face down with knees bent to the right of the body in a semi-flexed manner. There were no associated burial offerings."

**Other Interpretations.** Wade and Armelagos (1966:106) said that Burial 7 was a 17- to 23-year-old female with slight but extensive porotic hyperostosis. They offered no taphonomic or forensic interpretation.

**Discussion.** Judging from the photograph of Site 875 Room I and the line drawing of that room, seemingly with some misidentified bones or pots, this series does not appear to be either randomly distributed or laid out in a fashion that supports a secondary burial hypothesis. The human remains definitely should be examined along taphonomic lines.

Wade and Armelagos focused on reconstructing live biological conditions, and Lister considered only the cultural aspects of the Site 875 human remains. No perimortem assessment was given to the ambiguous bone deposit. With so much human bone scattered in three rooms of a small pueblo, and with a face-down "burial" in the refuse missing her hands and feet, we think a taphonomic analysis of these remains might reveal perimortem or postmortem information pointing to a scenario significantly different from that of secondary burial. At the least, the scattering of skeletal remains in Room I, and possibly in Rooms III and IX at the same time, speaks of no obvious respect or awe of the dead. A face-down burial without hands, feet, or grave goods lying in refuse patently should be examined for perimortem trauma.

Just before we wrote this section, our request to reexamine human skeletal remains at Mesa Verde National Park was denied.

73
Betatakin Kiva

Claim Date. 1995.

Claimants. C. G. Turner and J. A. Turner.

Claim Type. Violence.

Other Designations. NA3533; RBMV 593; RBMV 428.

Site Location. In an alcove 60 m long by 15 m deep located about 100 m southwest of Betatakin ruin, in Betatakin Canyon, a side branch of Tsegi Canyon (Laguna Creek), northeastern Arizona. USGS Betatakin quadrangle (1970), not gridded.

Site Type. The main structure is a sunken stone-walled kiva, plus an adjacent surface room and an outside work area, all within the alcove.

Cultural Affiliation. Kayenta Anasazi.

Chronology. Late Pueblo III (ceramics); tree-ring dates of A.D. 1267–1286 were obtained for the contemporaneous Betatakin ruin (K. Anderson 1966:67).

Excavator and Date. Milton Wetherill, March 1935.

Institutional Storage. Department of Anthropology, Museum of Northern Arizona, Flagstaff.

Site Report. None. MNA site files have a letter dated March 21, 1938, from Wetherill to "Lyn" (Lyndon Hargrave) describing the structure and what was found.

Osteological Report. None.

Skeletal Evidence of Stress. None.

Burial Context. A flexed "burial" on kiva floor next to north wall, head to west.

Associated Artifacts. A plain gray jar and Tusayan Polychrome and Tsegi Black-on-orange sherds on kiva floor.

Figures. 3.248–3.250.

Taphonomy. CGT and JAT.

MNI. 1.

Age and Sex. Young adult male.

Preservation. Good.

Bone and Fragment Number. Complete except for ribs and sternum.

Breakage. Breaks and holes in back of head seem perimortem but could be otherwise, as suggested in Wetherill's letter.

Cut Marks. Yes. Mainly on right side of head.

Burning. None.

Anvil Abrasions. None.

Polishing. None.

Vertebrae Number. All present.

Scalping. Yes.

Gnawing, Rodent. None.

Chewing, Carnivore. None.

Insect Parts. None noted at time of skeletal observations.

Other Modification. None.

Archaeologist's Interpretation. Wetherill's letter described the scene: "The face was up. The body had been moved by the falling of heavy rocks from above. A part of a p[l]ain gray jar was found mashed on the floor at the feet."

Other Interpretations. Keith M. Anderson (1966:62) reviewed Wetherill's work, writing: "In 1935, Milton Wetherill, then custodian of

368

Figure 3.248. Betatakin Kiva, Arizona. Adult skull, probably male, with scalping cut marks on right side (CGT neg. 8-5-86:10).

Figure 3.249. Betatakin Kiva. Detail of upper, longer scalping cut marks on the adult's cranium. Note the characteristic stone tool pattern of striations within individual cuts. Actual width of image in photograph is 3.3 cm (CGT neg. 6-26-86:3).

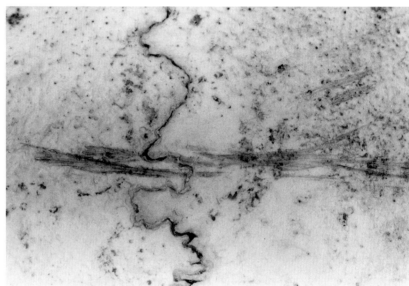

Figure 3.250. Betatakin Kiva. Detail of lower, shorter scalping cut marks on the adult's cranium. Actual width of image in photograph is 3.3 cm (CGT neg. 6-26-86:5).

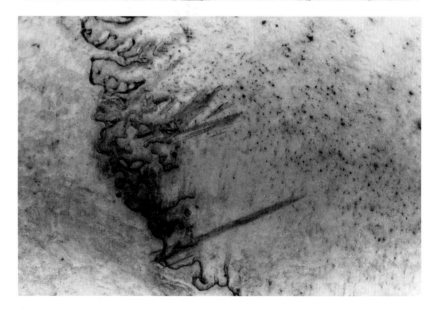

Navajo National Monument, excavated a rectangular kiva at this site, finding two burials within the structure, one adult on the floor and a mummified infant leaning against the east wall (Milton Wetherill, personal communication)." Anderson (1966:69) went on to say, "It is reasonable to assume that this [ceremonial] site represents a necessary expansion out of the village proper at the time of maximum population in Betatakin."

**Discussion.** Wetherill did not comment on the cut marks. They were made around the time of death, with a stone knife, and are old and discolored. They are not tool marks from Wetherill's excavation. We doubt that this young adult male with pronounced and asymmetrical cranial deformation had been formally buried, even though Wetherill described the skeleton as a flexed burial. Given the cranial cut marks and the rare use of kivas for burial, a more plausible scenario would be a violent encounter in which the man was attacked and scalped in or near the kiva. He might have been left in the kiva or might have sought it for shelter before he died. The rocks atop the body could have been thrown on it instead of having fallen naturally. Wetherill's notes indicate that the kiva was abandoned after the body was on the floor. Sometime later, a baby that subsequently mummified was buried about 6 inches above the floor on top of collapsed roof material. There was no associated cultural material buried with the infant, so it could have been interred sometime after Betatakin was abandoned, assuming that the scalped man died before the abandonment.

Betatkin was a short-lived settlement, constructed in a location as suitable for defense as for any other consideration. The combination of apparent traumatic death, scalping, and unceremonious abandonment of a young adult male adds support to the views of Jonathan Haas, Winifred Creamer, David Wilcox, and others who envision later Tsegi Anasazi settlements as having been sited defensively.

## 74
## Houck K

**Claim Date.** 1995.

**Claimants.** C. G. Turner and J. A. Turner.

**Claim Type.** Cannibalism.

**Other Designations.** NA8440.

**Site Location.** Between Interstate 40 and the Puerco River, at the entrance to Tegakwitha Catholic Mission, near Houck, northeastern Arizona. USGS Houck quadrangle (1971), T 22N, R 29E, SW ¼ of NE ¼ of Sec. 25.

**Site Type.** A great-house masonry pueblo with at least two kivas.

**Cultural Affiliation.** Chaco Anasazi. A letter from A. P. Olson to L. L. Hargrave, dated April 24, 1967, states explicitly that Houck K is a Chacoan site. The dressed, 0.5-m-thick walls and very large rooms were unlike any other of the sites excavated during this salvage project.

**Chronology.** A.D. 1150–1200. The letter from Olson to Hargrave gives the date as approximately 1250, based on floor sherds of Gallup, Puerco, and Walnut Black-on-whites, Houck, Pinto, Querino, and St. Johns Polychromes, and Puerco Black-on-red. Most of these types date prior to 1200, so we do not understand why Olson used the 1250 date. At our request, David R. Wilcox and Kelley Hays-Gilpin reexamined the Room 2 sherds on August 3, 1995, and agreed on a date of 1150–1200, allowing that the site does have ceramics with longer life spans, such as Pinto Polychrome (1100–1300).

**Excavator and Date.** Alan P. Olson, 1962.

**Institutional Storage.** Department of Anthropology, Museum of Northern Arizona, Flagstaff.

**Site Report.** We have found only a broad overview by George Gumerman and Alan Olson (1968) on the culture history of the Houck area. We can find no records on the excavation of Houck K Room 2 in the MNA site files.

**Osteological Report.** Several biological studies have been conducted on the four formal burials of two adults and two infants from NA8440, Broadside 1. In 1967 Stephen Kunitz collected cancellous bone from Burials 3 and 4 for a fluorescent antibody study; also in 1967 E. Zaino studied Burials 1–4 for osteoporotic pitting of orbits and/or parietal bones. William Wade (1970) wrote his Ph.D. dissertation on the human skeletal remains from the Puerco Valley, and Dana Hartman studied Burial 3 to determine presence of teeth. In 1972 John Winter wrote an M.A. thesis that included the pathology of Burials 1–4. In 1974 Dana Hartman filled out MNA skeletal analysis forms for Burials 1–4. At an unknown date someone, presumably Hartman, prepared a miscellaneous human bone inventory for NA8440. This inventory lists 100 items. Some are multiple entries, such as "4 adult scapulae." Marcia Regan (1988) included the Houck series in her M.A. thesis research on bone growth and diet.

**Skeletal Evidence of Stress.** Mild porotic hyperostosis is present.

**Burial Context.** Our concern with Houck K is only with the damaged bone assemblage that Olson recovered from the "fill" of small, west-facing Room 2.

**Associated Artifacts.** None, although Hargrave identified golden eagle, sandhill crane, and turkey bones from Room 2 fill. The room fill also contained a large number of variously processed rodent bones and a few bones of other animals.

**Figures.** 3.251–3.271.

**Taphonomy.** CGT and JAT, June 3, 1994; 36 additional human elements were found by Shara Bailey in faunal remains storage boxes and were examined by CGT on July 2, 1997. Skeletal inventory is in table 3.67.

*MNI.* 7 (table 3.66).

*Age and Sex.* One adult, male?; one adult female; one young adult, male?; one young adult, sex?; two juveniles, 15 to 16 years old; one child, 3 years old.

*Preservation.* Good, but with a small amount of rotten bone caused by either preservation conditions or exposure to fire.

*Bone and Fragment Number.* 326.

*Breakage.* 62.9%.

*Cut Marks.* 30.1%.

*Burning.* 2.8%.

*Anvil Abrasions.* 7.1%.

*Polishing.* 3.4%.

*Vertebrae Number.* 1.8% of expected (3 of 168).

*Scalping.* Yes.

Table 3.66
Minimal Number of Individuals (MNI) at Houck K, Room 2

| SKELETAL ELEMENT | AGE | SEX | NOTES |
|---|---|---|---|
| Maxilla, whole | Adult | M? | Belongs with whole jaw #1; 6 front teeth blown out; cuts across nose |
| Maxilla, left | 3 | ? | Belongs with 3-year mandible parts |
| | 15 | ? | |
| | YA | M? | Not same person as maxilla R YA One tooth blown out, cut teeth |
| Maxilla, right | YA | ? | Not same person as maxilla L YA |
| Mandible, whole | Adult | M? | Belongs with whole maxilla; one tooth blown out |
| | YA | M? | Cut teeth, 6 blown out; belongs with L maxilla YA |
| | YA | M? | Does not fit with any maxilla |
| Mandible, left | 3 | ? | Belongs with 3-year L maxilla |
| Mandible, right | 3 | ? | Fits with 3-year L mandible |
| Mandible, center | 15–16 | M | Does not fit with any maxilla |
| Frontal & orbit, right | 3 | ? | |
| Frontal & orbit, right | YA | ? | |
| Frontal & orbit, right | Adult | M? | |
| Frontal & orbit, right | YA | F | Burning on frontal |
| Frontal & orbit, right | YA | F | Burning on frontal |
| Frontal & orbit, right | Adult | ? | |
| Frontal & orbit, left | Adult | ? | |
| Frontal & orbit, left | YA | ? | |
| Frontal & orbit, left | 3 | ? | |
| Frontal & orbit, left | 3 | ? | |
| Frontal & orbit, left | Adult | F | Probably belongs with 1 R YA F |
| Temporal, right & left | Adult | ? | |
| Temporal, right & left | Adult | ? | |
| Temporal, right & left | Adult | ? | |
| Temporal, right & left | Adult | ? | |
| Pelvis | Middle A | F | Very wide sciatic notch |

SUMMARY: Seven individuals. One adult male?; one adult female; one young adult, male?; one young adult, sex?; two juveniles (15–16); one 3-year-old child.
NOTE: YA denotes young adult.

*Gnawing, Rodent.* 0.3%.

*Chewing, Carnivore.* 1.0%.

*Insect Parts.* None found during skeletal examination.

*Other Modification.* The perimortem breakage and nearly complete absence of articular ends of all the adolescent and adult ribs suggests that the chests of all except the child were disarticulated by prying and bending their rib cages until the ribs snapped off near the vertebral column (figs. 3.264, 3.265). The proximal (articular) ends must have remained connected with the columnar elements. Because no proximal rib fragments are present in this assemblage, they presumably were smashed and destroyed along with the vertebrae when the latter were crushed and boiled to extract fat. Uniform perimortem proximal rib breakage and missing articular ends are more suggestive

Table 3.67
Bone Elements and Perimortem Damage at Houck K, Room 2

| SKELETAL ELEMENT | WHOLE | FRAGMENT | IMPACT BREAK | ANVIL ABRASION | CUT MARK | BURN | POLISH | GNAW/ CHEW |
|---|---|---|---|---|---|---|---|---|
| Cranial | | | | | | | | |
| Maxilla | 1 | 5 | 5 | 0 | 4 | 0 | 0 | 0 |
| Mandible | 3 | 3 | 0 | 1 | 4 | 1 | 0 | 1R |
| Frontal | 0 | 10 | 4 | 0 | 5 | 2 | 0 | 0 |
| Parietal | 3 | 5 | 3 | 2 | 6 | 0 | 0 | 0 |
| Occipital | 0 | 3 | 2 | 1 | 2 | 0 | 0 | 0 |
| Temporal | 2 | 6 | 6 | 0 | 4 | 0 | 0 | 0 |
| Base | 0 | 1 | 0 | 0 | 0 | 0 | 0 | 0 |
| Teeth | 71 | 10 | 0 | 0 | 4 | 0 | 0 | 0 |
| Fragment | — | 34 | 34 | 3 | 4 | 3 | 0 | 0 |
| Postcranial | | | | | | | | |
| Cervical vertebrae | 1 | | | | | | | |
| Vertebrae fragments | — | 4 | 3 | 0 | 0 | 0 | 0 | 0 |
| Scapula | 0 | 14 | 2 | 1 | 0 | 0 | 0 | 0 |
| Clavicle | 4 | 2 | 0 | 0 | 4 | 0 | 0 | 0 |
| Rib | 0 | 99 | 97a | 0 | 43 | 0 | 7 | 0 |
| Humerus | 0 | 8 | 5 | 3 | 2 | 1 | 0 | 1C |
| Radius | 0 | 7 | 7 | 5 | 0 | 0 | 0 | 0 |
| Ulna | 0 | 8 | 5 | 2 | 1 | 0 | 1 | 0 |
| Hand & foot | 24 | 9 | 0 | 0 | 0 | 0 | 0 | 2C |
| Pelvis | 0 | 3 | 2 | 0 | 3 | 0 | 0 | 0 |
| Femur | 0 | 19 | 9 | 2 | 8 | 0 | 0 | 0 |
| Tibia | 2 | 11 | 6 | 2 | 2 | 1 | 0 | 0 |
| Fibula | 0 | 6 | 4 | 0 | 2 | 0 | 2 | 0 |
| Patella | 2 | 0 | 1 | 0 | 0 | 0 | 0 | 0 |
| Long bone fragments | — | 9 | 9 | 1 | | | 1 | |
| Bone type unknown | 0 | 18 | 1 | 0 | 0 | 1 | 0 | 0 |
| TOTAL (326) | 42 | 284 | 205 | 23 | 98 | 9 | 11 | 4 |
| PERCENTAGE | 12.9 | 87.1 | 62.9 | 7.1 | 30.1 | 2.8 | 3.4 | 1.2 |

Percentage of expected vertebrae = 1.8 (3 of 168; MNI = 7).b

NOTE: Only elements that were present are listed. Impact breakage, anvil abrasions, cut marks, burning and polishing represent perimortem damage. Gnawing and chewing are postmortem damage.

a. Eight rib fragments also have peeled breakage.

b. Fragmentation size suggests that about two fragments could represent one whole vertebra.

of processing for consumption than of random body mutilation or esoteric ceremonialism.

We recognize that this butchering scenario may be unconvincing to some readers because of the poorly recorded depositional context, but it is supported by additional evidence. Had the ribs been pounded apart from the vertebral columns, there should be at least a few anvil or hammer abrasions at or near the fractures, but none occurs. Had the ribs been partly cut first and then snapped, we would expect cut marks at or near the perimortem breaks, but not a single rib has any cut mark at the breakage location. Nor is there any identifiable thermal weakening that might be recognized by changes in bone color, texture, or density, such as were observed in two crania that seem to have been roasted. The absence of evidence for rib cage roasting, along with the relatively large amount of rib fragment end-polishing, indicates that the rib fragments had been boiled.

We propose that the ribs and other fragmented bones were

Figure 3.251. Houck K, Arizona. General view of the Chaco outlier located at the entrance to the Tegakwitha Catholic Mission. A portion of the structure has been destroyed by the road on the left. The Puerco River is out of sight about 1.5 km (1 mile) away to the south in the left background (CGT neg. 8-13-94:35).

Figure 3.252. Houck K. Gerald A. Bair and Jacqueline A. Turner examining Room 2, where Alan P. Olson found the human charnel deposit in 1962. Note the characteristic Chacoan style of rubble-filled masonry walls with neatly laid layers of small surface-facing flat stones (CGT neg. 8-13-94:28).

boiled after most of the adhering flesh had been cut away. There are quite a few cut marks elsewhere on the ribs (table 3.67): almost half (43 of 99) have one or more cut marks, and several have many. Because the lengths of the Houck K rib fragments are greater than those found in other assemblages, separation of the individual ribs must have been done beforehand in order to fit them into an average-size cooking vessel. Finally, as table 3.67 indicates, the perimortem rib damage cannot be attributed to carnivore or rodent activity; there was very little gnawing and chewing in the entire assemblage. The Houck K rib-cage damage alone indicates carcass processing for consumptive ends. If the primary objective of this processing had been ceremonialism, violence, mutilation, or simple disarticulation for secondary burial, the amount, location, and types of perimortem damage should have been entirely different. At the least there should have been no polishing.

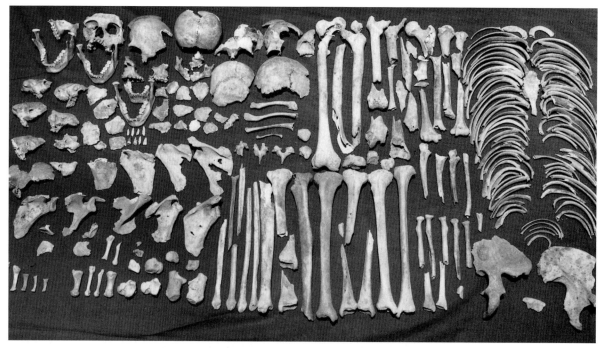

Figure 3.253. Houck K. The complete bone assemblage from the fill of Room 2. The MNI is 7. As at other sites with hypothesized cannibalism, the number of vertebrae is very low—only three fragments, shown in center. However, Houck K has many more nearly complete ribs, shown at right (CGT neg. 6-6-94:25).

Figure 3.254. Houck K, Room 2. Adult female (faint supraorbital ridges) frontal bone with perimortem cut mark (at arrow) and burning of vault (CGT neg. 6-6-94:29).

Figure 3.255. Houck K, Room 2. Another adult female (faint supraorbital ridges) frontal bone with numerous perimortem cut marks, suggesting that the entire head had been flayed. This extensive cutting of the head and face is similar to the treatment of crania belonging to the skull rack deposit at Tlatelolco, Mexico City (CGT neg. 6-6-94:27).

Figure 3.256. Houck K, Room 2. Adult male? maxilla with all anterior tooth sockets blown out by perimortem impact injuries. Multiple cut marks, some visible on border of nasal opening (on viewer's left) (CGT neg. 6-6-94:17).

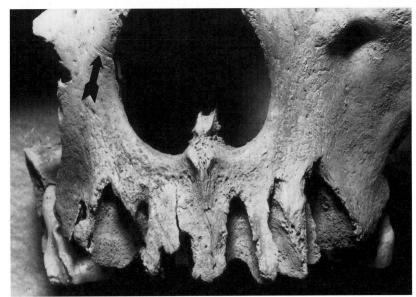

Figure 3.257. Houck K, Room 2. Adult skull with extensive perimortem cutting of temporal bone. The deeper cut marks run from top to bottom, which for a right-handed person would mean that the victim's head was being held upright, assuming that the end of a slice is shallower than the beginning (CGT neg. 6-6-94:32).

Figure 3.258. Houck K, Room 2.
Occipital bone with perimortem
scalping or flaying cut marks.
Individual has grade 2 porotic
hyperostosis (the pitting visible
on both parietal bones) (CGT
neg. 6-6-94:30).

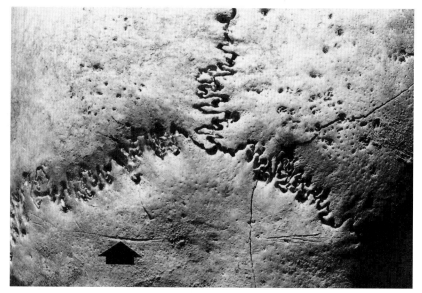

Figure 3.259. Houck K, Room 2.
Left maxilla fragment with perimortem cut marks on face (at arrows) and on buccal surfaces of
anterior teeth. The left central
incisor had also been blown out
by impact injury (CGT neg.6-6-
95:15).

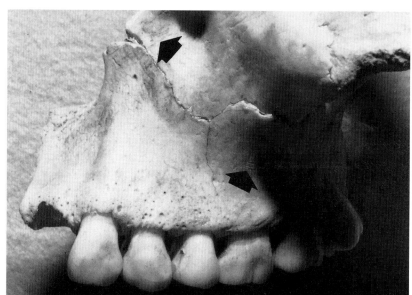

Figure 3.260. Houck K, Room 2.
Left side of young adult male?
mandible that belongs with the
maxilla of figure 3.259. Perimortem cut marks can be seen
on the crowns of the second
premolar and first molar, at the
base of the canine socket, on the
anterior border of the ascending
ramus, and near the gonial
angle (CGT neg. 6-6-94:7).

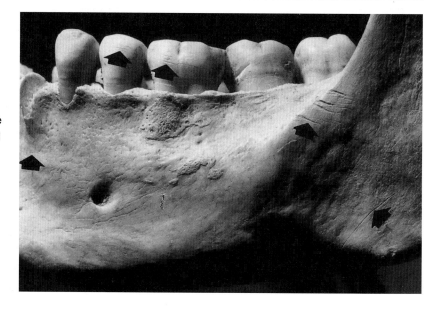

Figure 3.261. Houck K, Room 2. Detail of cutting in figure 3.260. The pattern of cut marks suggests a back-and-forth cutting motion, with greater pressure being applied from left to right and simple dragging of the cutting tool from right to left. It appears that the cutting began from the top and worked downward in a sawing fashion. For a right-handed person, the cranium would have to have been lower than the jaw. Hence, the dead man would likely have been on his back, head still attached to his body, when the cutting was done (CGT neg. 8-6-86:8).

Figure 3.262. Houck K, Room 2. Mandible of figure 3.260 showing perimortem cut marks on right ascending ramus and below canine socket (CGT neg. 6-6-94:10).

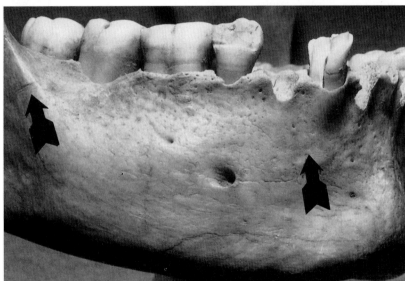

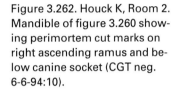

Figure 3.263. Houck K, Room 2. Mandible of figure 3.260 showing cut marks on internal surface of horizontal ramus. Similarly placed cut marks frequently occur on the skull rack mandibles at Tlatelolco and were present at La Plata 23 (fig. 3.95) (CGT neg. 6-6-94:19).

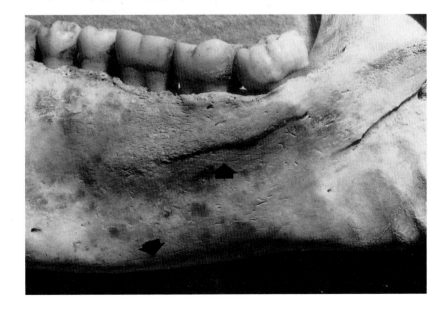

378

Figure 3.264. Houck K, Room 2. All the proximal ends (heads) of the right ribs were broken off around the time of death. No rib heads were recovered in the excavation. An undamaged lab specimen is in lower right for comparison. Scale is 15 cm (CGT neg. 6-6-94:6).

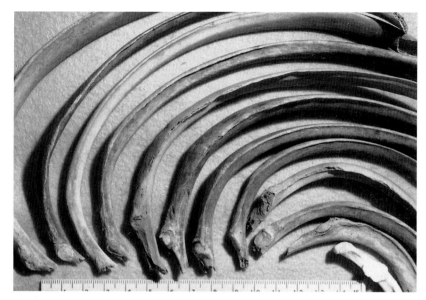

Figure 3.265. Houck K, Room 2. All the proximal ends of the left ribs were broken off, and as with the right ribs, none were recovered. An undamaged lab specimen is in lower right for comparison. Scale is 15 cm (CGT neg. 6-6-94:3).

Figure 3.266. Houck K, Room 2. Humerus fragments showing perimortem midshaft breakage. Scale is 15 cm (CGT neg. 6-6-94:9).

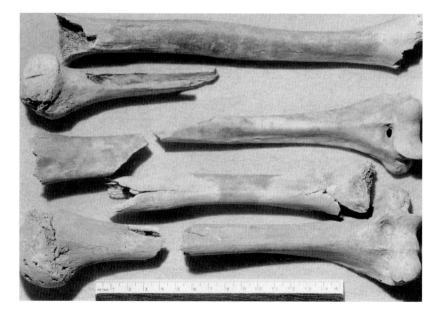

Figure 3.267. Houck K, Room 2. Perimortem midshaft breakage of radius and ulna elements. Scale is 15 cm (CGT neg. 6-6-94:36).

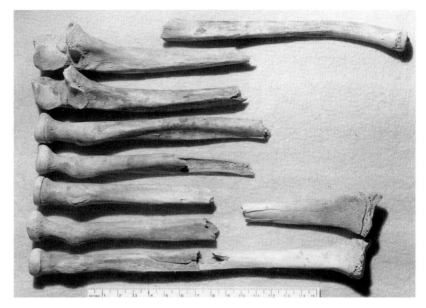

Figure 3.268. Houck K, Room 2. Rib fragment with perimortem peel breakage and polishing of the tiny tip on right. Scale in mm (CGT neg. 6-6-94:24).

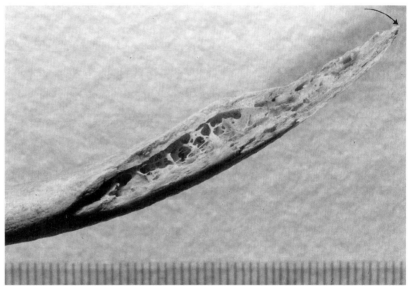

Figure 3.269. Houck K, Room 2. Rib fragment with perimortem peel break and polishing of tip at far right. Actual width of image in photograph is 3.3 cm (CGT neg. 6-6-94:21).

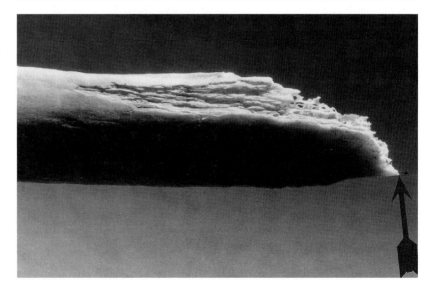

Figure 3.270. Houck K, Room 2. Rib fragment with perimortem snap break and polishing of tip on left. Scale in mm (CGT neg. 6-6-94:22).

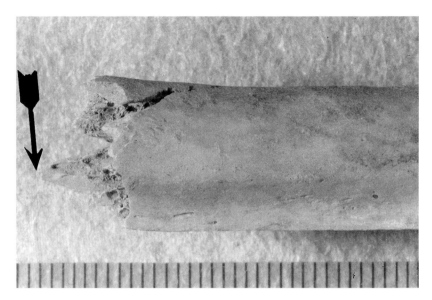

Figure 3.271. Houck K, Room 2. Right proximal ulna fragment with perimortem polishing of the tip on left. Actual width of image in photograph is 3.3 cm (CGT neg. 6-6-94:35).

In addition to the unexpectedly large amount and unusual type of rib processing, there is a damage feature in the Houck K assemblage that so far is unique among Southwestern charnel deposits. When the fleshy sides of the face of one of the adults were stripped away from the skull, the operator's stone knife went so deep and so powerfully that it cut into the buccal surfaces of some of the left and right mandibular molars (figs. 3.259, 3.260). This suggests to us flaying of the entire head, not just scalping. Another piece of an adult Houck K face (fig. 3.259)—possibly the same adult with the cut teeth—had received horizontal cut marks across the upper nose. This degree of facial cutting exceeds the scalp and ear trophy-taking found in other human charnel deposits. Such facial mutilation could represent either socially pathological violence to the victim or, more likely to our minds, ceremonial flaying like that done to Mesoamerican Tlaloc or Xipe Totec sacrificial victims. Moreover, the blown-out anterior teeth of two or more individuals suggests violence. The overall perimortem taphonomy of the Houck K assemblage has no simple, single explanation, but it represents our strongest case for some manner of ritual processing along with consumption.

**Archaeologist's Interpretation.** No documentation has been found for Room 2 except excavation photographs. The only remark known for Houck K is Gumerman and Olson's (1968:124) summary interpretation: "One site excavated at Houck is so distinctive in its architecture that we consider it evidence of a migration of a group from the central Chaco Basin. This intrusion is equated with Gladwin's (1945) Bonito Phase. The probable span of occupation of this pueblo was for two or three decades in the middle of the 13th century." Although the architecture may suggest a migration, David Wilcox (personal communication, August 3, 1995) notes that the sherd collection indicates a preponderance of locally made pottery.

**Other Interpretations.** None of the physical anthropologists identified earlier did any analysis of the Houck K Room 2 charnel deposit.

**Discussion.** A search through the MNA archaeological site files, library, and photo archives turned up no notes or exact dates for the Room 2 excavation. Olson took excellent field notes in all his other MNA work, so those he made at Houck must be misfiled somewhere. There is no way to know whether the human bone was found randomly distributed in the room fill, which would suggest a repeated and relatively long period of deposition, or concentrated in one or a few places, suggesting a single short-term event. Judging from the average size of the bone fragments, we are even unsure whether or not the Room 2 fill was screened, and if it was, what the mesh size was and how experienced the screener.

With the help of Gerald A. Bair, we relocated Houck K on August 13, 1994. It was clear that the fill depth of Room 2 probably did not exceed two meters, and near the west wall not more than one meter. Given the heights of the wall remnants, we suspect that the charnel deposit was concentrated near the floor, which suggests that the remains had been dumped into the room rather than being the leftovers of a cannibal event within the room. A haul road from Interstate 40 to a sand quarry on the Puerco River has cut through the eastern end of the site, but the western side, toward the Catholic mission, including Room 2, is the same as when Olson photographed the excavations in 1962 (fig. 3.252). Houck K has Chacoan style masonry with small, tightly fitted, rectangular sandstone exterior blocks and rubble-filled wall interiors. The site was larger—maybe 30 to 40 meters in length—before the haul road was built. Although Houck K seems to have been a great house, there were no signs of berms or prehistoric roads, perhaps owing to the considerable historic use of the site area. Contemporary roads and cornfields surround the site; to the south a large highway borrow pit has been excavated, and to the west is the Catholic mission.

J. W. Fewkes (1904) thought that all the ruins in the Puerco River region from Navajo railroad station to the eastern Arizona border were related more to Zuni than to Hopi, because of ceramic similarities. Houck is within a day's walk of Zuni. It is only a few kilometers from Houck to great houses farther west called Navajo Springs, Padres Mesa, Sanders, and Navajo Springs South.

The previously described Chacoan sites with charnel deposits of perimortem-damaged human bones suggesting cannibalism and violence are replicated in the Houck K assemblage. Here, however, the apparent flaying of at least one head provides the first direct taphonomic evidence of possible ritual use of the human body, followed by the now familiar processes of butchering, roasting, and boiling.

## 75
## Pueblo del Arroyo

**Claim Date.** 1995.

**Claimants.** C. G. Turner and J. A. Turner.

**Claim Type.** Violence.

**Other Designations.** 29SJ1947; Bc254.

**Site Location.** On the north bank of Chaco Wash, about 0.5 km (0.8 mile) downstream from Pueblo Bonito, Chaco Canyon, San Juan County, northwestern New Mexico. USGS Pueblo Bonito quadrangle (1966), T 21N, R 11W, SE ¼ of SW ¼ of Sec. 12.

**Site Type.** Three-story, 284-room great house with probably 16 kivas.

**Cultural Affiliation.** Chaco Anasazi; later, Mesa Verde.

**Chronology.** A.D. 1052–1117, based on tree-rings (Judd 1959:172).

**Excavator and Date.** Neil M. Judd, Smithsonian Institution and National Geographic Society, 1923–1926; Karl Ruppert, supervisor; 44 rooms and 8 kivas opened up. In the 1950s Gordon Vivian excavated and stabilized some units for the National Park Service. The human remains of concern here were recovered by Judd.

**Institutional Storage.** Department of Anthropology, National Museum of Natural History, Smithsonian Institution, Washington, D.C.

**Site Report.** Judd (1959).

**Osteological Report.** Akins (1986).

**Skeletal Evidence of Stress.** Porotic hyperostosis on left and right parietals and occiput of one adult male (327139).

**Burial Context.** Disarticulated and scattered individuals were found on room floors or in room and kiva fill and in trash of later McElmo Tower construction to the west and outside of the main D-shaped pueblo. The following notes are extracted from Judd's (1959) burial descriptions.

Room 3 (p. 108), right half adult maxilla (FS89) in middle of room, 1.5 feet above floor in construction debris. Left half found in similar debris in Room 9, which is adjacent to Room 3 but has "no direct connection."

Room 4 (p. 108), bundled infant (FS90) in windblown sand 4 inches above floor. Higher up, in construction debris, two adult and one infant mandibles were recovered.

Room 9 (p. 11), disarticulated adult male with crushed skull (327141) in trash, without mortuary offerings. Later (p. 109) Judd noted finding the left half of the Room 3 maxilla at 1.5 feet above the floor of Room 9. At the west end of this long room (about 10 by 60 feet), most of a disarticulated adult male skeleton (FS91) was unearthed.

Room 10 (p. 15), trash-filled room with a disarticulated adult male skeleton (327139), slightly above the floor. Skull had been crushed, and there were no mortuary offerings.

Room 11 (p. 16), adolescent (334890; FS154) without mortuary offerings.

Room 13 (p. 18), 15- to 16-year-old on mat in middle of room. Body had been partly "disarticulated by vandals."

Room 15 (p. 18), two femur fragments (FS118) and, among other things, a pendant made of shell from the west coast of Mexico.

Room 16 (p. 21), bone fragments that Judd thought possibly belonged with those found in adjacent Room 24.

Room 21 (pp. 18, 21), the scattered skeleton of an adult female in construction debris two to three feet above the floor.

Room 24 (p. 21), a "number of miscellaneous human bones." Judd suggested that some of these may have belonged with the skeleton of Room 16.

Room 40 (p. 27), young man buried on the floor in a flexed position, along with a bowl and pitcher, after abandonment of room.

Kiva H (p. 79), a shattered adult skull (FS465) at bench level in wind-blown sand, and parts of a child's skeleton (FS466) above bench level.

Kiva I (p. 81), part of an infant skeleton in construction debris about 15 inches above the floor.

McElmo tower area (p. 119), portions of several skeletons (FS596; 327137) buried without mortuary offerings.

These useful burial descriptions do not match perfectly the cataloged Pueblo del Arroyo skeletal remains. Museum records do not indicate why bone lots were assigned a given catalog number. Furthermore, during cataloging, bones from different rooms may have been mixed together. All Pueblo del Arroyo skeletons transferred in 1924 possess the same accession number (85084; Nov. 20, 1924). Thus, the catalog card indicates that 327138 was originally numbered "R[oom] 4A no. 87," whereas Judd indicates that Room 4 had FS90. The catalog number 327138 also applies to the remains from Room 11A FS154, and it notes that this lot was found scattered throughout the fill of a room. Judd wrote that the remains from Room 11 were cataloged as 334890. Rooms 4 and 11 are not actually connected in the pueblo. Judd described the Room 4 remains as an infant plus three mandibles, two of which were from adults. For Room 11, he described having found an adolescent. We found 327138 to consist of one adult, sex?, two adolescents, a six-year-old child, and a one- to two-year-old child. Lot 327139 had an original number of R10A no. 149 and was said to have been found in the northeast quarter 6 inches to 1.5 inches above the floor. Judd indicated that he had found a disarticulated adult male. We also identified an adult male for 327139. Lot 327141 had original numbers of R9A no. 91 and R15A no. 118 and was recorded as having been found in the west end of a long room. Judd found an adult in Room 9 and two femurs in Room 15. We found two adults and an adolescent. Because of the lack of complete agreement, and because it is uncertain whether or not these bone lots represent three temporal units, we deal with them sepa-

Table 3.68
Minimal Number of Individuals (MNI) at Pueblo del Arroyo,
Unit 327138

| SKELETAL ELEMENT | AGE | SEX |
|---|---|---|
| Vault | 1–2 | ? |
| Mandible, whole | 1–2 | ? |
| Mandible, fragment | 6 | ? |
| Clavicle | Adult | ? |
| Cervical vertebrae (3) | Adolescent | ? |
| Cervical vertebra | Older adolescent | ? |

SUMMARY: Five individuals. One adult; two adolescents, two children (one 6-year-old, one 1- to 2-year-old).

Table 3.69
Minimal Number of Individuals (MNI) at Pueblo del Arroyo,
Unit 327139

| SKELETAL ELEMENT | AGE | SEX |
|---|---|---|
| Maxilla, right | Adult | M |

SUMMARY: One adult male.

Table 3.70
Minimal Number of Individuals (MNI) at Pueblo del Arroyo,
Unit 327141

| SKELETAL ELEMENT | AGE | SEX | NOTES |
|---|---|---|---|
| Maxilla, whole | Old adult | M? | Only 3 teeth remain |
| Mandible, whole | Old adult | M? | Teeth very worn |
| Femur, left (2) | Adult | ? | |
| Humerus, left (2) | Adult | ? | |
| Vertebrae (2) | Juvenile | ? | |

SUMMARY: Three individuals. Two adults (one male, one sex?); one juvenile, sex?

rately, even though an adolescent right humerus in lot 327139 matches perfectly the size, form, and color of a left humerus in lot 327138, neither of which number is mentioned in Judd's report.

**Associated Artifacts.** In Room 4, an infant was wrapped in textiles. Room 9 had discarded fabricational materials along with turquoise and shell chips. Judd mentioned a few other items, but on the whole the Pueblo del Arroyo series had very few grave offerings.

**Figures.** 3.272–3.283.

**Taphonomy.** CGT and JAT. Skeletal inventories are in tables 3.71–3.74.

*MNI.* Lot 327138, 5; lot 327139, 1; lot 327141, 3; combined total, 9 (tables 3.68–3.70).

*Age and Sex.* Lot 327138, one adult, sex?; two adolescents; one 6-year-old child; one 1- to 2-year-old child. Lot 327139, one adult

Table 3.71
Bone Elements and Perimortem Damage at Pueblo del Arroyo, Bone Lot
SI 327138

| SKELETAL ELEMENT | WHOLE | FRAGMENT | IMPACT BREAK | ANVIL ABRASION | POLISH | CHEWING |
|---|---|---|---|---|---|---|
| **Cranial** | | | | | | |
| Mandible | 1 | 1 | 0 | 0 | 0 | 1 |
| Frontal | 1 | 0 | 0 | 0 | 0 | 0 |
| Parietal | 1 | 0 | 0 | 0 | 0 | 0 |
| Occipital | 1 | 0 | 0 | 0 | 0 | 0 |
| Temporal | 1 | 0 | 0 | 0 | 0 | 0 |
| Base | 1 | 0 | 0 | 0 | 0 | 0 |
| Teeth (not counted) | | | | | | |
| **Postcranial** | | | | | | |
| Cervical vertebrae | 5 | 0 | 0 | 0 | 0 | 1 |
| Thoracic vertebrae | 3 | 0 | 0 | 0 | 0 | 2 |
| Scapula | 0 | 1 | 0 | 0 | 0 | 1 |
| Clavicle | 1 | 1 | 1 | 0 | 0 | 0 |
| Rib/sternum | 2/1 | 6 | 6 | 0 | 0 | 0 |
| Humerus | 0 | 1 | 1 | 0 | 0 | 0 |
| Radius | 0 | 2 | 2 | 0 | 0 | 0 |
| Ulna | 0 | 1 | 1 | 0 | 0 | 0 |
| Pelvis | 0 | 2 | 0 | 0 | 0 | 2 |
| Femur | 0 | 1 | 0 | 1 | 1 | 1 |
| Tibia | 0 | 1 | 0 | 0 | 0 | 1 |
| TOTAL (35)[a] | 18 | 17 | 11 | 1 | 1 | 9 |
| PERCENTAGE | 51.4 | 48.6 | 31.4 | 3.0 | 3.0 | 25.7 |

Percentage of expected vertebrae = 6.7 (8 of 120; MNI = 5).

NOTE: Only elements that were present are listed. No cut marks or burning was observed. Impact breakage, anvil abrasions, and polishing represent perimortem damage. Chewing is postmortem damage.

a. Long bones of the 1- to 2-year-old child were not counted.

male. An adolescent humerus in this lot is considered to belong with lot 327138. Lot 327141, one old adult male?; one adult, sex?; one adolescent.

*Preservation.* Good to excellent. Most bones are creamy white in color, ivorylike in hardness.

*Bone and Fragment Number.* Combined lots, 118 (60 whole, 58 fragments). See tables 3.71–3.73 for individual lots.

*Breakage.* Lot 327138, 31.4%; lot 327139, 47.1%; lot 327141, 34.8%; total, 41.5%.

*Cut Marks.* Lot 327138, 0.0%; lot 327139, 5.9%; lot 327141, 0.0%; total, 0.8%.

*Burning.* None.

*Anvil Abrasions.* Lot 327138, 3.0%; lot 327139, 17.6%; lot 327141, 0.0%; total, 3.4%.

*Polishing.* Lot 327138, 3.0%; lot 327139, 0.0%; lot 327141, 0.0%; total 0.8%.

*Vertebrae Number.* Lot 327138, 6.7% of expected (8 of 120); lot 327139, 12.5% (3 of 24); lot 327141, 25.0% (18 of 72); total, 13.5% (29 of 216).

*Scalping.* None certain, but young female 331212 is a possible case.

Table 3.72
Bone Elements and Perimortem Damage at Pueblo del Arroyo, Bone Lot
SI 327139

| SKELETAL ELEMENT | WHOLE | FRAGMENT | IMPACT BREAK | ANVIL ABRASION | CUT MARK | CHEWING |
|---|---|---|---|---|---|---|
| Cranial | | | | | | |
| Maxilla | 0 | 1 | 1 | 0 | 0 | 0 |
| Frontal | 0 | 1 | 1 | 1 | 0 | 0 |
| Parietal | 0 | 2 | 2 | 1 | 0 | 0 |
| Base | 0 | 1 | 1 | 0 | 0 | 0 |
| Teeth (not counted) | | | | | | |
| Postcranial | | | | | | |
| Cervical vertebrae | 3 | 0 | 0 | 0 | 0 | 3 |
| Rib | 0 | 4 | 0 | 0 | 0 | 4 |
| Humerus | 0 | 1 | 1 | 1 | 1 | 1 |
| Radius | 0 | 1 | 1 | 0 | 0 | 1 |
| Pelvis | 0 | 1 | 0 | 0 | 0 | 1 |
| Femur | 0 | 1 | 1 | 0 | 0 | 1 |
| Tibia | 0 | 1 | 0 | 0 | 0 | 1 |
| TOTAL (17) | 3 | 14 | 8 | 3 | 1 | 12 |
| PERCENTAGE | 17.6 | 82.4 | 47.1 | 17.6 | 5.9 | 70.6 |

Percentage of expected vertebrae = 12.5 (3 of 24; MNI = 1).

NOTE: Only elements that were present are listed. No burning or polishing was observed. Impact breakage, anvil abrasions, and cut marks represent perimortem damage. Chewing is postmortem damage.

*Gnawing, Rodent.* None.

*Chewing, Carnivore.* Lot 327138, 25.7% (9 of 35); lot 327139, 70.6% (12 of 17); lot 327141, 18.2% (12 of 66); total 28.0% (33 of 118).

*Insect Parts.* None found during skeletal examination.

*Other Modification.* The cranially deformed adult male of lot 327139 had received heavy perimortem blows to the head and face, resulting in the alveolar bone's being blown out at the sockets of the right first incisor and right canine. The nasal bones were also broken. There are no anvil or coarse stone weapon abrasions on the maxilla, but at least three of the nine perimortem-fractured pieces of the cranium have abrasions—on the left, right, top, and back of the vault. There is no mandible for this cranium.

The old adult male (327141) had a healed 18-mm-long cut and percussion wound on his frontal bone (fig. 3.283). We are convinced that this cut is exactly that and not an embedded vein track because the line is exceptionally straight and terminates or begins at an obvious healed percussion wound. The frontal may have had some abrasion scars near the healed wound, although the scars might have been made during excavation because they are somewhat lighter in color than the surrounding bone. This man's nose, like that of 327139, was broken. His cranium had been broken into 18 pieces. There were five perimortem breaks on the left and right ascending rami of the mandible alone. Neither 327139 nor 327141 had a burned or scavenger-modified skull. The human-induced damage was limited mainly to perimortem breakage.

Table 3.73
Bone Elements and Perimortem Damage at Pueblo del Arroyo, Bone Lot
SI 327141

| SKELETAL ELEMENT | WHOLE | FRAGMENT | IMPACT BREAK | CUT MARK | CHEWING |
|---|---|---|---|---|---|
| Cranial | | | | | |
| Maxilla | 0 | 1 | 1 | 0 | 0 |
| Mandible | 0 | 1 | 1 | 0 | 0 |
| Frontal | 0 | 1 | 1 | 1 | 0 |
| Parietal | 0 | 2 | 2 | 0 | 0 |
| Occipital | 0 | 1 | 1 | 0 | 0 |
| Temporal | 0 | 1 | 1 | 0 | 0 |
| Teeth (not in total) | 0 | (9) | 0 | 0 | 0 |
| Postcranial | | | | | |
| Cervical vertebrae | 6 | 0 | 0 | 0 | 0 |
| Thoracic vertebrae | 9 | 0 | 0 | 0 | 0 |
| Lumbar vertebrae | 3 | 0 | 0 | 0 | 0 |
| Sacrum | 1 | 0 | 1 | 0 | 0 |
| Scapula | 1 | 0 | 0 | 0 | 1 |
| Clavicle | 0 | 1 | 0 | 0 | 1 |
| Rib | 15 | 10 | 5 | 0 | 5 |
| Humerus | 1 | 2 | 2 | 0 | 1 |
| Radius | 0 | 2 | 2 | 0 | 1 |
| Ulna | 0 | 1 | 1 | 0 | 1 |
| Pelvis | 2 | 0 | 1 | 0 | 0 |
| Femur | 0 | 3 | 3 | 0 | 0 |
| Tibia | 1 | 0 | 0 | 0 | 1 |
| Fibula | 0 | 1 | 1 | 0 | 1 |
| TOTAL (66) | 39 | 27 | 23 | 1 | 12 |
| PERCENTAGE | 59.1 | 40.9 | 34.8 | 1.5 | 18.2 |

Percentage of expected vertebrae = 25.0 (18 of 72; MNI = 3).

NOTE: Only elements that were present are listed. No anvil abrasions, burning, or polishing
was observed. Impact breakage and cut marks represent perimortem damage. Chewing
is postmortem damage.

Finally, there are individuals cataloged as Pueblo del Arroyo but
with higher catalog numbers than those previously discussed. The
reason for this could not be determined. Number 331212 (A466 in
catalog, but Judd refers to it as A465) is a 17- to 18-year-old female
skull lacking the face. It has a 20-mm-long cut mark on the left parietal. This skull was found in the clay fill of Kiva H. Number 331215
is a mixed lot of adult and subadult long bone and vertebrae fragments, some with chewing marks on the ends and processes.

**Archaeologist's Interpretation.** Judd (1959:172–173) determined that
the entire Pueblo del Arroyo occupation lasted for only a few generations (A.D. 1052–1117). He believed that northern migrants soon
settled into the town, as was evidenced by the lower-quality masonry
of the later occupation, changes in pottery, and the construction of a
three-walled McElmo tower. Judd's settlement reconstruction did not
consider the skeletal remains.

In his foreword to the Pueblo del Arroyo study, Judd (1959:iii)
wrote that he expected there to be subsequent reports, including one
on the skeletal remains from Pueblo del Arroyo and Pueblo Bonito.
Perhaps because such reports were to be prepared, he did not try to

Table 3.74
Bone Elements and Perimortem Damage at Pueblo del Arroyo, Pooled
Accession Lots

| SKELETAL ELEMENT | WHOLE | FRAGMENT | IMPACT BREAK | ANVIL ABRASION | CUT MARK | POLISH | CHEWING |
|---|---|---|---|---|---|---|---|
| Cranial | | | | | | | |
| Maxilla | 0 | 2 | 2 | 0 | 0 | 0 | 0 |
| Mandible | 1 | 2 | 1 | 0 | 0 | 0 | 1 |
| Frontal | 1 | 2 | 2 | 1 | 1 | 0 | 0 |
| Parietal | 1 | 4 | 4 | 1 | 0 | 0 | 0 |
| Occipital | 1 | 1 | 1 | 0 | 0 | 0 | 0 |
| Temporal | 1 | 1 | 1 | 0 | 0 | 0 | 0 |
| Base | 1 | 1 | 1 | 0 | 0 | 0 | 0 |
| Teeth (9) | | | | | | | |
| Postcranial | | | | | | | |
| Cervical vertebrae | 14 | 0 | 0 | 0 | 0 | 0 | 4 |
| Thoracic vertebrae | 12 | 0 | 0 | 0 | 0 | 0 | 2 |
| Lumbar vertebrae | 3 | 0 | 0 | 0 | 0 | 0 | 0 |
| Sacrum | 1 | 0 | 0 | 0 | 0 | 0 | 0 |
| Scapula | 1 | 1 | 0 | 0 | 0 | 0 | 2 |
| Clavicle | 1 | 2 | 1 | 0 | 0 | 0 | 1 |
| Rib | 18 | 20 | 11 | 0 | 0 | 0 | 9 |
| Humerus | 1 | 4 | 4 | 1 | 1 | 0 | 2 |
| Radius | 0 | 5 | 5 | 0 | 0 | 0 | 2 |
| Ulna | 0 | 2 | 2 | 0 | 0 | 0 | 1 |
| Pelvis | 2 | 3 | 1 | 0 | 0 | 0 | 3 |
| Femur | 0 | 5 | 3 | 1 | 0 | 1 | 2 |
| Tibia | 1 | 2 | 0 | 0 | 0 | 0 | 3 |
| Fibula | 0 | 1 | 1 | 0 | 0 | 0 | 1 |
| TOTAL (118)[a] | 60 | 58 | 40 | 4 | 2 | 1 | 33 |
| PERCENTAGE | 50.8 | 49.1 | 33.9 | 3.4 | 1.7 | 0.8 | 28.0 |

Percentage of expected vertebrae = 13.4 (29 of 216; MNI = 9).

NOTE: Only elements that were present are listed. No burning was observed. Impact breakage, anvil abrasions, cut marks, and polishing represent perimortem damage. Chewing
is postmortem damage.

a. Long bones of the 1- to 2-year-old child were not counted.

explain the disturbed burials other than to repeat his belief that vandals had been at work (see Pueblo Bonito).

**Other Interpretations.** Nancy J. Akins and John D. Schelberg (1984),
and later Akins alone (1986), drew together and synthesized the
Chaco Canyon skeletal and mortuary data—which is sparse and un-
even at best, considering the thousands of hours of private, institutional, and federally supported excavation that has been carried out
there (see Akins 1986:7). However, like Judd, Akins and Schelberg
did not make a point of considering human taphonomy as a resource
for explaining some of the Pueblo del Arroyo "burial disturbance,"
skeletal element scatter, and natural and human damage.

As a final example, Erik K. Reed (1962:247) noted an unusual
modification to a Pueblo del Arroyo skull in the possession of the National Park Service: "A cut-out place 20 mm long on the right parietal
of adult male from Pueblo del Arroyo (Room 82-A) looks pre-
mortem, rather than administered in finding; and a smaller cut on the
left portion of the frontal might also be. These do not represent fracturing blows with the traditional blunt instrument, they are not in the

Figure 3.272. Pueblo del Arroyo,
Chaco Canyon, New Mexico.
Room 13A showing "disturbed"
burial on room floor. Photo-
graph by O. C. Havens, 1923.
National Anthropological
Archives, Judd papers 94-7835.

Figure 3.273. Pueblo del Arroyo.
Total assemblage of a one-
year-old child plus the chewed
mandible of an eight- to nine-
year-old child (left) and the
chewed first cervical vertebra of
an adult (lower right). NMNH
327138 (CGT neg. 4-27-94:3).

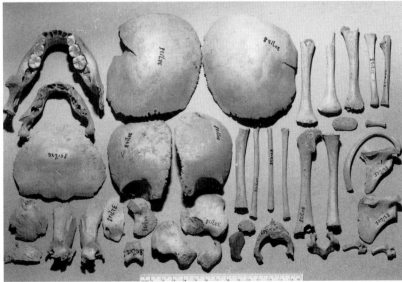

390

Figure 3.274. Pueblo del Arroyo. Detail of carnivore chewing and tooth puncture marks on mandible of eight- to nine-year-old child in figure 3.273. NMNH 327138 (CGT neg. 4-27-94:4).

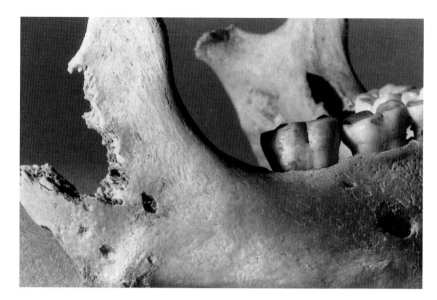

Figure 3.275. Pueblo del Arroyo. Detail of carnivore chewing on first cervical vertebra in figure 3.273. NMNH 327138 (CGT neg. 4-27-94:7).

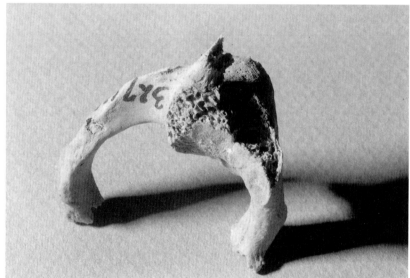

Figure 3.276. Pueblo del Arroyo. Total assemblage of a subadult with carnivore chewing on most pieces. Also in this lot are an adult ulna and clavicle (top) with perimortem breakage. NMNH 327138 (CGT neg. 4-27-94:2).

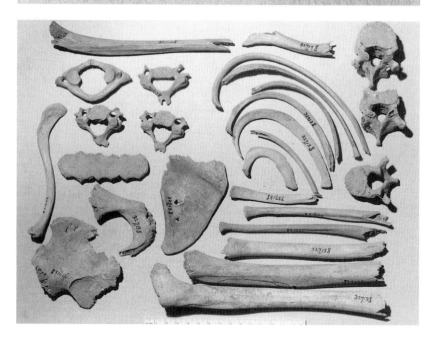

Figure 3.277. Pueblo del Arroyo. Adult male skull with perimortem breakage of frontal and left parietal bones. The skull shows lambdoidal cranial deformation, which was common in the Chaco Canyon area. NMNH 327139 (CGT neg. 4-27-94:11).

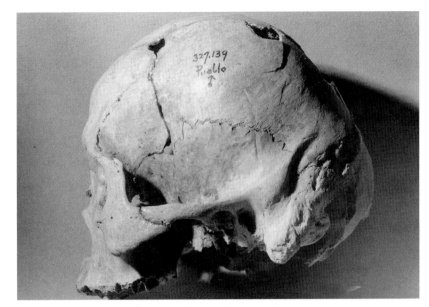

Figure 3.278. Pueblo del Arroyo. Adult male cranium of figure 3.277 showing additional perimortem breakage to frontal bone and right side of face. Anterior tooth sockets were blown out and nose was broken. NMNH 327139 (CGT neg. 4-27-94:13).

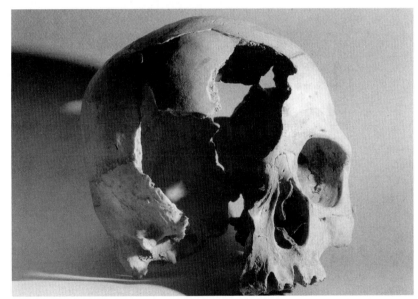

Figure 3.279. Pueblo del Arroyo. Detail of blown-out sockets in figure 3.278. The breaking away of a socket's external border, most marked on the right, is a frequent perimortem feature of human remains with taphonomic indications of violence and cannibalism. Force was applied to the crown, the lingual or back border of the socket served as the fulcrum, and the end of the root tip was the lever that broke away the buccal socket wall. NMNH 327139 (CGT neg. 10-12-94:26).

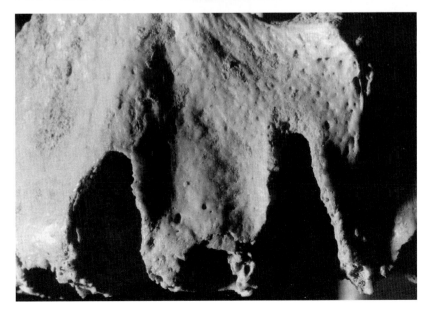

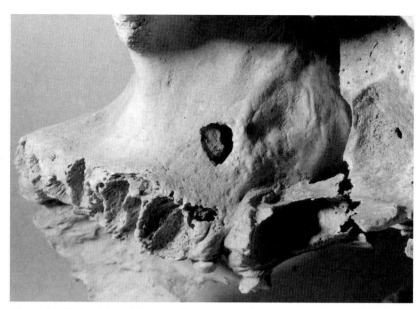

Figure 3.280. Pueblo del Arroyo. Circular maxillary puncture wound in the adult male of previous figures. Diameter of the perimortem wound is about 5 mm. There is no infection or healing. The lack of tooth scratching decreases the possibility that the injury was caused by a carnivore; the causal agency was more likely human. NMNH 327139 (CGT neg. 4-27-94:17).

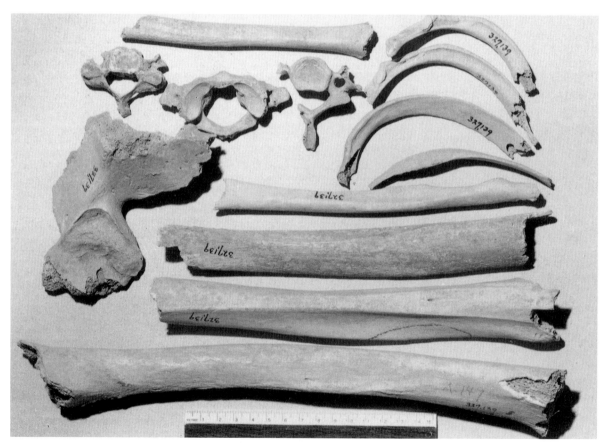

Figure 3.281. Pueblo del Arroyo. Two individuals are mixed in this lot. One is a subadult represented by a right humerus (upper left) that matches a left humerus in a different lot (327138). The second is an adult male. Carnivore chewing is evident in most of these pieces, especially the long bones. NMNH 327139 (CGT neg. 4-27-94:8).

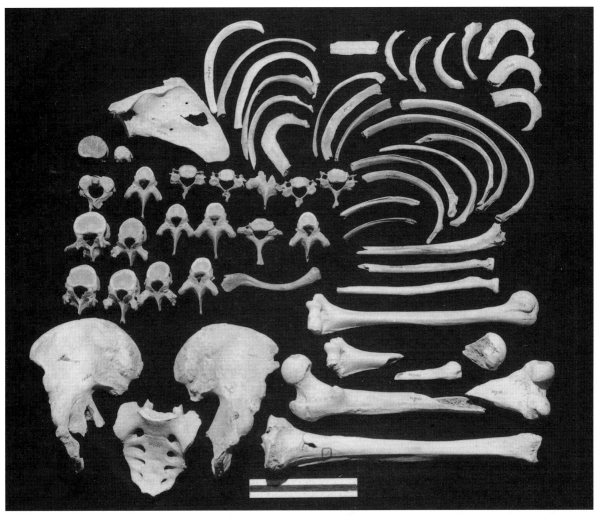

Figure 3.282. Pueblo del Arroyo. Postcranial assemblage of adult male with perimortem breakage of long bones and ribs. Several elements are missing. Two immature vertebrae (upper left) do not belong. NMNH 327141 (CGT neg. 4-27-94:8).

Figure 3.283. Pueblo del Arroyo. Perimortem breakage of an old adult male cranium. There is lambdoidal cranial deformation and a healed wound on the frontal bone. NMNH 327141 (CGT neg. 4-27-94:10).

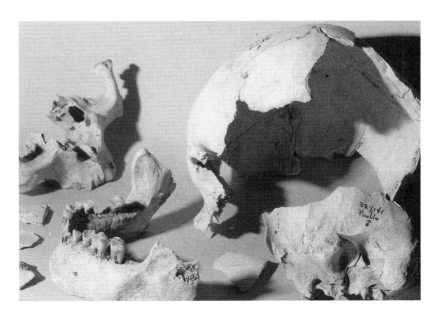

right locations to have any connection with scalping, and they do not closely resemble trepanation." Recall that similar examples were found at Polacca Wash (fig. 3.126) and Casas Grandes.

Discussion. Judd seems to have lost interest in the burials, and he showed no real concern with the large amount of disarticulation and scattering of human bones in Pueblo del Arroyo. He fell back on scenarios of the occasional vandal or grave robber as facile explanations for the burial "disturbances." Judd found most of the skeletons scattered, broken up, or largely incomplete. Our examinations show that not all of this damage was due to room reuse, grave robbing, or re-burial.

The strong perimortem breakage forces that had been applied to the heads, faces, and long bones of the individuals itemized in the taphonomy section were greater than the force one might expect to have been applied by carnivores that subsequently chewed on the remains, especially the ends of long bones. Tooth puncture marks on ribs and other bones suggest that these carnivores were about the size of foxes, coyotes, badgers, medium-sized dogs, or perhaps skunks. None of the bones shows excessive chewing, suggesting that the animals did not have time to more completely reduce the bones. Nevertheless, 28% of all pieces evidence some scavenger damage. This is a high value—not much less than perimortem breakage at 33.9%—which, on a quantitative basis alone, makes scavengers about as destructive a force as the humans who damaged these individuals at or around the time of their deaths.

Undoubtedly most of the perimortem breakage was done by humans. However, because the total amount of other damage (anvil abrasions, cut marks, and polishing) is so low, it is probably safest to allow that some of these damage minutiae are scavenger damage mimicry and that some portion of the perimortem breakage was done by animals.

We do not consider these remains to represent cannibalism, but we do view some of the perimortem damage as episodic, intentional, and violent. The occurrence of considerable perimortem carnivore damage suggests that the remains were left exposed in the open or not securely buried. As at Wupatki Room 59, the absence of gnawing indicates that carnivores stayed near the Pueblo del Arroyo human remains, prohibiting rodent access.

We are uncertain how to model the scenario that best fits this combination of human and animal damage, other than to suggest that the victims were first fatally injured by human assailants and their bodies were then left exposed to scavenging animals for a relatively short time, either in the rooms where Judd found them or outside in the open. Viewed in the context of what is now substantial taphonomic evidence for violence and cannibalism in Chaco Canyon, we look upon the Pueblo del Arroyo human remains as part of the undefined phenomenon that caused what appears to be Chaco terrorism and possible social pathology. We believe that much of the perimortem damage of the Pueblo del Arroyo remains represents something other than postinterment disturbance.

76
Black Mesa

Claim Date. 1995.

Claimants. C. G. Turner and J. A. Turner.

Claim Type. Uncertain.

Other Designations. D:7:262.

Site Location. On the second terrace of a large tributary of Moenkopi Wash, 2,036 meters in elevation, in the N-14 Mining Area (eastern half of the Peabody Coal Company lease area), north end of Black Mesa, northeastern Arizona.

Site Type. A large, multiple-occupation site with four masonry roomblocks, pithouses, kivas, and a trash midden. The skeletal remains in question were found in the (incompletely excavated) fill of a burned, D-shaped, slab-lined pithouse (Structure 33), 4.7 by 4.5 by 1.75 m in size.

Cultural Affiliation. Basketmaker and Kayenta Anasazi.

Chronology. A.D. 600–1100. Skeletal remains may postdate the initial site occupation, 600–850.

Excavators and Date. Report indicates that 25 people were involved in 6.5 weeks of site excavation during 1980.

Institutional Storage. School of Natural Science, Hampshire College, Amherst, Massachusetts.

Site Report. Sink et al. (1982).

Osteological Report. None prepared (Debra Martin, personal communication, November 21, 1994).

Skeletal Evidence of Stress. None.

Burial Context. Disarticulated and scattered bones found in the fill of a pithouse (Burial 5, Feature 115, Structure 33). The bones were not considered to be associated with the pithouse.

Associated Artifacts. None.

Figures. None.

Taphonomy. CGT. Skeletal inventory is in table 3.76.

    *MNI.* 3 (table 3.75).

    *Age and Sex.* Two adults, sex?; one subadult, sex?.

    *Preservation.* Good to fair. Most bones are creamy white in color and light in weight.

    *Bone and Fragment Number.* 103 (25 whole; 78 fragments).

    *Breakage.* 2.9%.

    *Cut Marks.* None.

    *Burning.* 17.5%.

    *Anvil Abrasions.* None.

    *Polishing.* None.

    *Vertebrae Number.* 16.7% of expected (12 of 72).

    *Scalping.* None.

    *Gnawing, Rodent.* None.

    *Chewing, Carnivore.* None.

    *Insect Parts.* None found during skeletal examination.

    *Other Modification.* None.

Archaeologists' Interpretation. Clifton W. Sink and colleagues (1982:99) reported that "the fill of Structure 33 contained a series of well-stratified midden deposits. There was a layer of roof fall approximately 20 cm above the floor. Charcoal recovered from this layer and oxidation of the walls of the structure indicates that the structure had

Table 3.75
Minimal Number of Individuals (MNI) at Black Mesa D:7:262

| SKELETAL ELEMENT | | AGE | SEX |
|---|---|---|---|
| Clavicle, | left (1) | Adult | ? |
| | right (2) | Adult | ? |
| Tibia | | Subadult | ? |

SUMMARY: Three individuals. Two adults, sex?; one subadult, sex?.

Table 3.76
Bone Elements and Perimortem Damage at Black Mesa D:7:262

| SKELETAL ELEMENT | WHOLE | FRAGMENT | IMPACT BREAK | BURN |
|---|---|---|---|---|
| Cranial | | | | |
| Fragment | — | 13 | 0 | 8 |
| Postcranial | | | | |
| Thoracic vertebrae | 12 | 0 | 0 | 0 |
| Scapula | 0 | 1 | 0 | 0 |
| Clavicle | 3 | 0 | 0 | 0 |
| Rib/sternum | 7/0 | 49/1 | 3/0 | 0 |
| Ulna | 0 | 1 | 0 | 0 |
| Hand & foot | 3 | 1 | 0 | 2 |
| Tibia | 0 | 2 | 0 | 0 |
| Long bone fragments | — | 8 | 0 | 6 |
| Bone type unknown | 0 | 2 | 0 | 2 |
| TOTAL (103) | 25 | 78 | 3 | 18 |
| PERCENTAGE | 24.3 | 75.7 | 2.9 | 17.5 |

Percentage of expected vertebrae = 16.7 (12 of 72; MNI = 3).

NOTE: Only elements that were present are listed. No anvil abrasions, cut marks, polishing, gnawing, or chewing was observed. Impact breakage and burning represent perimortem damage.

burned. The fill contained a large amount of human bone. Although no formalized burial was uncovered, there was enough bone present to warrant the assignment of a feature number (Feature 115)." Despite the stratification, Sink et al. (1982) did not say whether the bone was found in one or more strata. In their discussion of burials (1982:100) they said, "Burial 5 (Feature 115) consists of a large amount of human bone that was recovered from the fill of Structure 33 (a pithouse). The skeletal remains appear to represent two adult individuals. Evidence of burning on several of the bones may indicate interment prior to the burning of the structure, or entrapment of these individuals during this event."

Other Interpretations. None.

Discussion. We include the Structure 33 human remains in this study for three reasons. First, the assemblage illustrates how a brief published description in an archaeological site report, without taphonomic analysis, can raise questions about violence or an unusual death context—in this case by mentioning structure burning, a "large amount of human bone," and the "entrapment" of two individuals on the basis of some burned bone.

Second, whereas the skilled team of Martin et al. (1991) studied other skeletons from the Black Mesa archaeological project, they passed over the remains from Structure 33. Apparently these were not considered useful in a major monograph on the Black Mesa skeletal remains because the bones were believed to be disturbed. This inference is substantiated by the fact that Martin et al. (1991) conducted no perimortem taphonomic examinations in their Black Mesa study, or at least did not discuss any such work. An assumption of disturbance without taphonomic analysis probably underlies the fact that the Houck K remains, too, were never studied by the physical anthropologists who used the Houck series for various biological investigations. Just as archaeologists have jumped to the conclusion that disarticulated and fragmented human remains represent nothing other than disturbed burials, so, too, have a number of physical anthropologists working with Southwestern human skeletal remains.

Third, incomplete excavation severely limits any taphonomic interpretation. Study of the Structure 33 human remains shows that three individuals were represented, but burning can be demonstrated for no more than one of them, along with the burning of a few bones of a deer-sized animal. Several of the vertebrae, none burned, fit together, suggesting they had been articulated around the time of final deposition. Most of the bone fragmentation was postmortem, and no burned fragment had with any certainty been broken before it burned. Lacking point-mapping, we are unable to tell from the bones themselves when the burning occurred. Because of the incomplete excavation we are also unable to tell whether the limited amount of bone recovered—far less than expected for three individuals—is taphonomically meaningful.

Thus, here is a case in which scientifically valuable human skeletal remains played second fiddle to moving dirt: "Due to time constraints, only part of the structure was excavated" (Sink et al. 1982:99). The unfortunate result is a bone assemblage almost useless for taphonomic interpretation. The lesson for future excavation policy should be obvious. When a mass of human bones is found in a structure, the entire structure and surrounding old ground surface should be sampled further. Human bone should receive at least as much attention in mapping and data recording as a pot scatter or a deflector slab.

## Other Cases of Possible Violence or Cannibalism

WE STOPPED COLLECTING data in August 1995. At that time there were sets of human remains that we had seen only briefly, were trying to locate, or had simply heard or read about. Had there been more time for laboratory analysis, some of the following 10 finds would surely have been added to the 76 just reviewed.

**Cave 11 (Green Mask Cave).** The collection made by Richard Wetherill during the 1897 Hyde Exploring Expedition in southeastern Utah included human remains. We determined that an incomplete skeleton of old adult female? (AMNH H/16034) from the floor of room 1 in Cave 11 had perimortem and postmortem breakage of her cranium. Most of her cervical vertebrae were present and undamaged. In addition, there were arm and leg bone fragments with perimortem mid-

Figure 3.284. Red Canyon, Utah. Adult male Basketmaker skull with circular perimortem impact wound to left side and broken left zygomatic arch. Right side undamaged. AMNH H/12657 (CGT neg. 6-26-78:4).

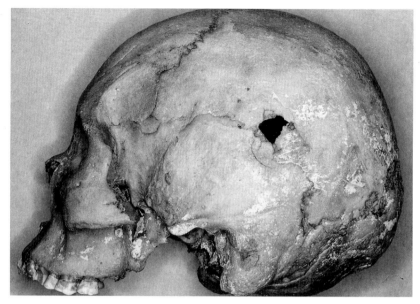

Figure 3.285. Red Canyon. Detail of head wound in figure 3.284. Circularity of wound is more suggestive of perimortem human action than of accident or postmortem burial damage (CGT neg. 6-26-78:1).

shaft breakage and end-of-bone carnivore chewing, along with other chewed bones. A detailed study is in order, and a search should be made for more contextual information and other Green Mask Cave skeletal remains. Recently, Sally J. Cole (1993) has argued convincingly that the Green Mask pictograph, for which the cave is named, depicts a flayed and painted Basketmaker face and head (i.e, whole face and hair scalp).

Red Canyon. An adult male Basketmaker (AMNH H/12657) with an impact wound to the left side of the head is another Wetherill find made between 1893 and 1895 for the Hyde expedition in southeastern Utah (figs. 3.284–3.285).

42Sa554. Working in Lake Canyon, a left-bank tributary to the Colorado River between miles 114 and 113, Floyd W. Sharrock et al. (1961:74) reported that all the bones excavated at Rogers House, a Pueblo II–III site, "had been scattered from their original locus."

Turner (1961b) indicated that the University of Utah Glen Canyon Project excavators had found a mass of broken and burned human bones. None of the bone fragments exhibited "checking," suggesting that the bone burning had occurred in the flesh, not as defleshed green bone or dry bone. In this bone mass four individuals could be identified—an old female?, based on fragments of mandible, femur, mastoids, and pieces of pelvis; a child, based on the size of a temporal bone mastoid process; another child of about 5 to 6 years, based on the development of scapula and cranial fragments; and tiny bones representing an infant. Burned pieces of bone could be fitted with unburned fragments. There were no obvious skeletal pathologies, and enough vertebrae were found for one of the children. There was a sagittal section of anterior cranium with the face but no mandible. As in the case of the San Juan River charnel deposit, the senior author was entirely unable to see the unexpected in 1961. This bone lot is presumably at the Utah Natural History Museum, University of Utah, Salt Lake City.

**White House.** In the fall of 1926, Earl Morris and A. V. Kidder excavated in Canyon de Chelly, Arizona. The human remains they recovered are curated at AMNH. At White House Overhang they recovered human remains that Morris felt had been treated violently. We briefly examined part of this collection. One of the specimens, a young adult male (AMNH 99/9105, Morris's burial 49), is of special interest. Like one individual at Houck K, this male has a broken mandible with many fine cut marks along the inferior and interior border of the right horizontal mandibular ramus (none on left side). He also has a 2 by 2 cm wound on the right temporal bone. There are no recognizable cut marks or abrasions on the cranium (figs. 3.286–3.290). Morris (n.d.*b*) thought the individual had been killed by a blow to the right side of the head. Two other individuals had one or more types of perimortem damage, but burning was not evident.

This site, with its Chacolike masonry, is considered to have been occupied during Pueblo III times. However, tree-ring dates indicate that it was in use during the last half of the eleventh century—somewhat early for Pueblo III. Morris (n.d.*b*) noted: "The graves were extraordinarily prolific in pottery, as many as nineteen vessels accompanying one body. To judge from the wares, the White House was a shrine or mart, visited from all parts of the surrounding country: Kayenta, Mesa Verde, Chaco, and Little Colorado vessels being easily recognizable." Given such apparent cosmopolitanism, a thorough taphonomic examination could fill out the White House story.

**Mummy Cave.** Earl Morris (1938:134) reported that Mummy Cave in Canyon del Muerto may have been abandoned because of violence. On the tower floor he found human skeletons with fractured skulls and broken long bones, which suggested victims of clubbing. Mummy Cave is a Pueblo III site with Mesa Verde–style masonry. It is thought that a Mesa Verde group migrated to Mummy Cave and built the three-story tower, leaving by 1300. We did not locate the Mummy Cave human remains.

**LA2675 and LA2699.** Alan P. Olson and William W. Wasley (1956) reported on their 1953 pipeline excavations for the El Paso Natural Gas Company. At LA2675, a nine-room Pueblo II "Chaco frontier

Figure 3.286. White House, Canyon de Chelly, Arizona. Perimortem damage to skull of young adult male, AMNH 99/9105. This view shows a 2-cm-wide impact wound on the right temporal bone. Because the cranial vault lacks deformation, the man could have lived during Basketmaker times (CGT neg. 5-6-94:2).

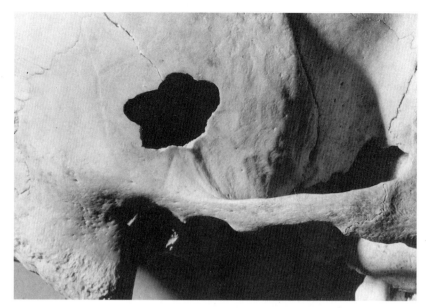

Figure 3.287. White House. Perimortem breakage of mandible belonging to the young man in figure 3.286. There are several very fine cut marks along the inferior border of the right horizontal ramus (CGT neg. 5-6-94:1).

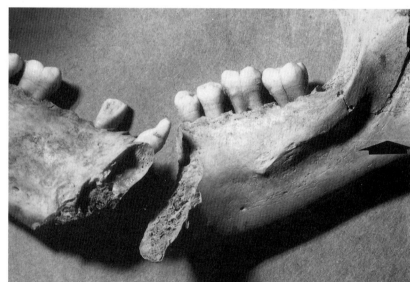

Figure 3.288. White House. Perimortem impact wound measuring 2.5 by 1.5 cm on right parietal of middle-aged adult male. There is a healed wound directly below the perimortem wound. AMNH 99/9109 (CGT neg.5-6-94:3).

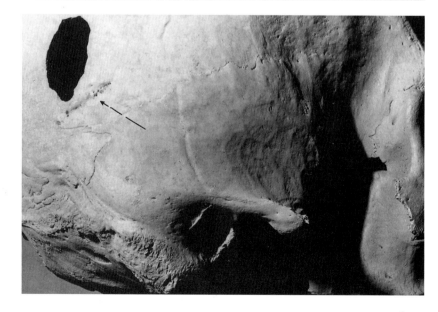

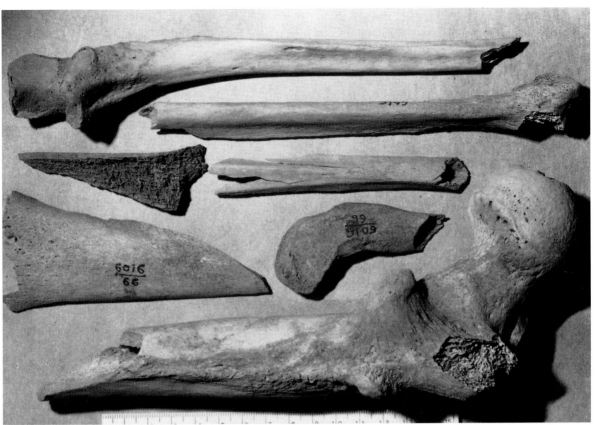

Figure 3.289. White House. Perimortem breakage of some postcranial bones of a middle-aged male, AMNH 99/9109. Most of the skeleton had been preserved. There are hammerstone or anvil abrasions on the lateral aspect of the femur near the midshaft break, but no burned bones or animal damage is evident (CGT neg. 5-6-94:5).

Figure 3.290. White House. Detail of perimortem anvil or hammerstone abrasions of femur in figure 3.289 (AMNH 99/9109). Actual width of image in photograph is 3.3 cm (CGT neg. 5-6-94:6).

village" with two kivas located between Prewitt and Thoreau, north-western New Mexico, they found scattered human remains: "Isolated bones, disarticulated skulls, and missing bones were common. . . . It would appear that the inhabitants of the pueblo had neither much fear nor respect of the dead, nor were they particularly conscientious about providing the deceased with burial furniture" (Olson and Wasley 1953:357). The skeletal remains received a preliminary examination by Daniel J. Scheans (1956:392), who worked out an MNI of 18, three being adolescents represented only by mandible fragments found in Kiva 2.

At LA2699, 5.7 km (3.6 miles) north of Gallup, New Mexico, they excavated another small Chaco Anasazi pueblo with a deep kiva. They dated the site at A.D. 1000–1050. In the kiva firepit "were found a human parietal fragment and a burned section of a mandible. An explanation for the presence of these bones is lacking" (Olson and Wasley 1956:365). Scheans (1956:393) examined these remains too, but added no further information.

**Two Kivas Ruin and Turkey Hill Pueblo.** On August 3, 1995, David R. Wilcox requested our help in identifying the sex and possible scalping of two skulls in the MNA physical anthropology collections. These indeed had multiple cut marks indicating scalping, and both adult men had, in addition, perimortem trauma wounds to the sides of their heads. Cuts and blows were unhealed and uninfected. Both skulls had been excavated from Sinagua sites in the Flagstaff area—one from Two Kivas Ruin (NA700, Burial 2), the other from Turkey Hill Pueblo (NA660, Burial 15). Violence was unquestionably involved in the deaths of these two men.

**McKinley Mine.** On June 29, 1995, Marsha D. Ogilvie and Charles E. Hilton showed us the remains of a child with cut marks and perimortem breakage. The child had been recovered several years earlier in the vicinity of Gallup, New Mexico, by archaeologists conducting salvage excavations for the McKinley Mine project. The bones had been studied, and an unpublished report had been prepared by David Eck. They are today curated in the Maxwell Museum of Anthropology, University of New Mexico. Like Ogilvie and Hilton, we recognized some perimortem cut marks on one rib, a few anvil abrasions, and breakage, notably of the vertebrae. There was no sign of burning. The overhead fluorescent lighting was too diffused to tell whether any pot-polishing was present, but it should be looked for.

**Gomero Project.** On June 30, 1995, Richard C. Chapman told us about finding parts of at least six individuals years ago in a firepit on the Gomero Project. These remains had been submitted to Mahmoud El-Najjar for analysis and then sent to the University of New Mexico for curation. No skeletal report was published. Cherie Schieck (1983) provided a site report.

**Cowboy Wash.** At the 1996 Pecos Conference, Brian Billman reported on his excavations for Soil Systems, Inc., at a late Pueblo II to early Pueblo III (A.D. 1100–1150) site near Cortez, Colorado. His crew found human remains with the taphonomic signature of cannibalism. The site, 5MT10,010, had damaged bone distributed in three pit structures. Billman said one contained five individuals on the floor with cut marks, breakage, and "boiling" but no burning. He referred

Figure 3.291. David A. Breternitz and Korri Dee Turner examine perimortem damage to human remains from Indian Camp Ranch. Breternitz has been directly or indirectly involved with at least four sites for which claims of cannibalism have been made—Mancos Canyon, Marshview Hamlet, 5MT10,010 and Indian Camp Ranch (CGT neg. 10-95:4).

to the breakage as "symbolic." The vent shaft for this room contained additional bones. On the floor of the second pit structure he found the broken, cut, and burned remains of two people. The third structure contained one bone in the vent shaft.

Billman said that architectural and other features indicated the body processing took place at the time of abandonment and was done for ritual purposes, although he offered no evidence to support this explanation. In addition, he maintained that the processing was neither a daily activity nor nutritionally driven. He linked the episode, and others in the Cortez area, to a "great drought and the collapse of Chaco." Additional reporting of this cannibalized assemblage was presented on April 3, 1997, at the Society for American Archaeology meeting in Nashville, Tennessee, by Billman, Banks L. Leonard, and Patricia M. Lambert. The cannibalism was attributed to environmental stress. On June 5, 1997, the senior author showed Lambert examples of fragment end polishing in the Chaco Canyon Small House assemblage curated at NMNH. Lambert had not systematically searched for polished fragments in the Cowboy Wash series because she was unfamiliar with their definition and appearance.

Indian Camp Ranch. One of the series of broken and burned human remains alluded to by Billman was excavated from a pit structure on the Indian Camp Ranch near Cortez, Colorado. This series was recently analyzed by Korri Dee Turner, who is preparing a taphonomic analysis for the excavators, Jerry Fetterman and Linda Honeycutt of Woods Canyon Archaeological Consultants, Inc., Yellow Jacket, Colorado (fig. 3.291).

## Some Statistical Analyses

BECAUSE THE 76-site inventory incorporates so much physical, temporal, behavioral, and analytical variation—for example, in excavators, their experience, their excavation methods, chronologies, preservation, osteological and taphonomic methods, soil conditions, bioturbation, and the almost unknowable motives and actions of prehistoric people—we are reluctant to aggregate the sites and skeletal remains for statistical comparisons. Yet there is no way to make scientific generalizations except by pooling the available information. With this strong reservation, we offer a few simple statistical analyses.

Beginning with sex differences, a chi-square comparison of the aggregated demographic summaries shown in tables 3.77 and 3.78 produced a statistically significant difference between sites with violence and sites with cannibalism in terms of the frequencies of recognizable adult males and females ($\chi^2 = 8.53$, 1 d.f., $p < .01$). Sites with cannibalism have nearly identical frequencies of adult males and females, whereas sites with violence have more than twice as many adult males as adult females. This comparison suggests that when violence occurred, either more men were slaughtered, more women were spared or taken captive, or women were less involved in the male-dominated conflict than would have been expected on the basis of chance alone. Another interpretation might be that Southwestern cannibalism was not strictly linked with practices of human sacrifice in which adult males or females were differentially selected for special ceremonies, as was reported for Mexican rituals at the time of European contact. Moreover, if Southwestern cannibalism had been strongly linked to ritual, we might expect an age difference between victims in sites that had violence and victims in sites that had cannibalism.

To test this proposition, we made a chi-square comparison for the ratio of individuals over and under 18 in the two types of sites (excluding individuals for whom age could not be identified). There was no statistically significant difference ($\chi^2 = 2.04$, 1 d.f., $p < .10$). This indicates that the aggregated age ratios in sites with evidence of cannibalism and sites with evidence of violence are no more different than would be expected on the basis of chance alone. Unlike the case for gender, the same frequency of adults relative to subadults died in each of the two types of sites.

Sample size permitted us to expand the previous test to four age classes—infant, child, subadult, and adult—again ignoring individuals whose age was indeterminable (table 3.79). Again, there was no statistically significant difference ($\chi^2 = 1.5$, 3 d.f., $p > .50$). This lack of signifi-

Table 3.77
Individuals with Evidence of Cannibalism in Southwestern Sites, by Age Group and Sex

| SITE | >18 MALE | >18 FEMALE | >18 SEX? | 12–18 SUBADULT | 3–12 CHILD | 0–3 INFANT | AGE? SEX? | TOTAL |
|---|---|---|---|---|---|---|---|---|
| Canyon Butte 3 | 1 | 1 | 1 | 1 | | | | 4 |
| Peñasco Blanco | 1 | 1 | 4 | 1 | | 1 | | 8 |
| Pueblo Bonito | | | | | | | 2 | 2 |
| Comb Wash | | | 1 | | | | | 1 |
| La Plata 23 | | 1 | 1 | 2 | | 1 | | 5 |
| La Plata 41 | | | 4 | 1 | 1 | | | 6 |
| House of Tragedy | | 1 | | | | | | 1 |
| Small House, Chaco | | | 2 | 4 | 1 | | 1 | 8 |
| Sambrito Village | 1 | 1 | 4 | 2 | 3 | | | 11 |
| Polacca Wash | 1 | 2 | 13 | 4 | 6 | 2 | 2 | 30 |
| Leroux Wash | | | 21 | 5 | 9 | | | 35 |
| Mancos Canyon | | | 15 | 8 | 5 | | 1 | 29 |
| Burnt Mesa | 4 | 2 | 1 | 1 | 2 | 1 | | 11 |
| Grinnell | 2 | 1 | 1 | 1 | 2 | | | 7 |
| Monument Valley | 2 | 1 | | 3 | | 1 | | 7 |
| Ash Creek | | | 4 | 1 | | | | 5 |
| Cottonwood Wash | 1 | 1 | | 2 | | | | 4 |
| Marshview Hamlet | 1 | 1 | 1 | 1 | 2 | | | 6 |
| Rattlesnake Ruin | 2 | 4 | 3 | 4 | 5 | 2 | | 20 |
| Fence Lake | 2 | | | 1 | | | | 3 |
| Yellow Jacket 5MT-1 | | | | 1 | 3 | | | 4 |
| Yellow Jacket 5MT-3 | 2 | 1 | 3 | | 2 | 2 | | 10 |
| Teec Nos Pos | 1 | | | | 1 | | | 2 |
| Ram Mesa Kiva | 2 | 1 | 2 | 2 | 3 | 2 | | 12 |
| Ram Mesa Pithouse | | 1 | | | | | | 1 |
| Aztec Wash I | | | 4 | 1 | 4 | 1 | 3 | 13 |
| Aztec Wash II | | 1 | | 1 | | | | 2 |
| Aztec Wash III | | | 1 | | | | | 1 |
| Hansen Pueblo | | | 1 | 1 | | | | 2 |
| La Plata Hwy. LA37592 | 1 | | 2 | 1 | 2 | 1 | | 7 |
| La Plata Hwy. LA37593 | 1 | 2 | | 2 | 1 | | | 6 |
| La Plata Hwy. LA65030 | | 3 | | 1 | 1 | 1 | | 6 |
| Coyote Village | | | | | 1 | | | 1 |
| St. Christopher's Mission | | 1 | | | 3 | | | 4 |
| Salmon Ruin | | | 2 | | | | | 2 |
| San Juan River | 2 | | | | | | | 2 |
| Houck K | 2 | 1 | 1 | 2 | 1 | | | 7 |
| Casa Rinconada Bc59 | | | | | 1 | | | 1 |
| TOTAL | 29 | 28 | 92 | 54 | 59 | 15 | 9 | 286 |
| PERCENTAGE | 10.1 | 9.8 | 32.2 | 18.9 | 20.6 | 5.2 | 3.1 | |

All adults as percentage of total individuals = 52.1.

NOTE: Four sites have evidence of cannibalism and violence in different individuals: Pueblo Bonito, House of Tragedy, Salmon Ruin, and Bc59 of the Casa Rinconada group.

Age-class definitions differ between analysts, as does their bioarchaeological experience. To capture the maximum amount of information between analysts, we use broad age (dental) categories. An infant is 0 to 3 years (all deciduous teeth in occlusion). A child is 3 to 12 (eruption of second permanent molar). A subadult is 12 to 18 (eruption of third permanent molar). An adult is 18 or older (eruption of third permanent molar or fusion of the basisphenoid suture). Age unknown is indeterminable, but in almost all cases is older than 6–12 years. The values in this table should be viewed relatively.

Table 3.78

Individuals with Evidence of Violence in Southwestern Sites, by Age Group and Sex

| SITE | >18 MALE | >18 FEMALE | >18 SEX? | 12–18 SUBADULT | 3–12 CHILD | 0–3 INFANT | AGE? SEX? | TOTAL |
|---|---|---|---|---|---|---|---|---|
| Cave 7 | 34 | 9 | 9 | 9 | | | | 61 |
| Snider's Well | | | | | | | 25 | 25 |
| Long House | 2 | | | | | 1 | | 3 |
| Awatovi | | 1 | | | | | 1 | 2 |
| Pueblo Bonito | 2 | 1 | | | | | | 3 |
| Battle Cave | 5 | 1 | 1 | 1 | 1 | 2 | | 11 |
| Charnel House Tower | | 3 | 8 | | | 3 | | 14 |
| Jack Smith's Houses | 1 | 1 | | | | | | 2 |
| Whitewater District | | | | | | | 3 | 3 |
| Alkali Ridge | 2 | | | 1 | | | | 3 |
| House of Tragedy | 1 | 2 | 1 | | | | | 4 |
| Te'ewi | | | | 24 | 6 | | | 30 |
| Coombs Site | 4 | 2 | 1 | 2 | | 3 | | 12 |
| Mesa Verde 499 | 1 | | | | | | | 1 |
| Casas Grandes | | | | | | | 127 | 127 |
| Huerfano Mesa | 1 | | 1 | | 1 | | | 3 |
| Llaves-Alkali Spring | 1 | | | | | | | 1 |
| Llaves-Alkali Spr. 2 | 1 | 1 | | | | | | 2 |
| Llaves-Alkali Spr. 12 | | 1 | | | 1 | | | 2 |
| Largo-Gallina Bg2 | 7 | 4 | 4 | 1 | | | | 16 |
| Largo-Gallina Bg3 | 4 | 2 | 1 | 1 | 3 | | | 11 |
| Largo-Gallina Bg20 | 8 | 2 | 1 | | 2 | | | 13 |
| Largo-Gallina Bg51 | 1 | | 2 | | | | | 3 |
| Largo-Gallina Bg88B | 8 | | | 2 | 1 | | | 11 |
| Mariana Mesa | 1 | | | 1 | | | | 2 |
| Jones Ranch Road 7 | | 1 | | | | | | 1 |
| Chi Chil Tan 108A | | | | | | | 6 | 6 |
| Chaco 1360 | | 2 | | | | 4 | | 6 |
| Lake Roosevelt | 2 | | | 1 | | 1 | | 4 |
| Salmon Ruin | | | | | 30 | | | 30 |
| Kin Klethla | | 1 | | | | | | 1 |
| Brown Star | 1 | | | | | | | 1 |
| Wupatki | 1 | 1 | 1 | 1 | 2 | | | 6 |
| Bc51 Chaco[a] | | | 3 | 2 | 1 | | 2 | 8 |
| Guadelupe Ruin | 1 | | | | | | | 1 |
| Mesa Verde 875 | 2 | | 4 | | | | | 6 |
| Betatakin Kiva | 1 | | | | | | | 1 |
| Pueblo del Arroyo | 2 | | 2 | 3 | 1 | 1 | | 9 |
| TOTAL | 94 | 35 | 39 | 49 | 49 | 15 | 164 | 445 |
| PERCENTAGE | 21.1 | 7.9 | 8.8 | 11.0 | 11.0 | 3.4 | 36.8 | |

All adults as percentage of total individuals = 37.7.

NOTE: Four sites have evidence of cannibalism and violence in different individuals: Pueblo Bonito, House of Tragedy, Salmon Ruin, and Bc59 of the Casa Rinconada Area.

Age-class definitions differ between analysts, as does the amount of bioarchaeological experience. To capture the maximum amount of information between analysts, we use broad age (dental) catagories. An infant is 0 to 3 years (all deciduous teeth in occlusion). A child is 3 to 12 (eruption of second permanent molar). A subadult is 12 to 18 (eruption of third permanent molar). An adult is 18 and older (eruption of third permanent molar or fusion of the basisphenoid suture). Age unknown is indeterminable, but in almost all cases is older than 6–12 years. The values in this table should be viewed relatively.

a. Includes other Casa Rinconada-area sites Bc50, Bc53, Bc57, and Bc59.

Table 3.79
Summary of Individuals with Evidence of Violence or Cannibalism in
Southwestern Sites, by Age Group

| AGE GROUP | Violence | | Cannibalism | | TOTAL | PERCENT |
|---|---|---|---|---|---|---|
| | NO. | % | NO. | % | | |
| Infant (0–3 years) | 15 | 3.4 | 15 | 5.2 | 30 | 4.1 |
| Child (3–12) | 49 | 11.0 | 59 | 20.6 | 108 | 14.8 |
| Subadult (12–18) | 49 | 11.0 | 54 | 18.9 | 103 | 14.1 |
| Adult (18 or over) | 168 | 37.7 | 149 | 52.1 | 317 | 43.4 |
| Age? Sex? | 164 | 36.8 | 9 | 3.1 | 173 | 23.6 |
| TOTAL (MNI) | 445 | | 286 | | 731 | 100.0 |

cant age difference between aggregated sites with cannibalism and those with violence can, like the sex ratio, be interpreted in various ways. Foremost, it suggests that the cause of the killings could have been the same or similar in the two types of sites. In the case of violence, the objective seems to have been to kill without regard to age. The four age classes for sites with violence shown in table 3.79 have frequencies similar to the well-known age pyramids that characterize many prehistoric Southwestern cemeteries (briefly summarized in Turner and Turner 1990:200), which suggests that assailants paid little attention to the ages of those they killed. This lack of age discrimination for violent death also applies to the cannibalized individuals. Inasmuch as the cannibalized remains often exhibit violence in the form of facial mutilation and scalping, we propose that the previous chi-square results can be interpreted as meaning that Southwestern cannibalism usually followed acts of violence.

Turning to temporal relationships, tables 3.80 and 3.81 reveal large differences between the frequencies of violence and cannibalism through time, especially a marked increase in cannibalism from A.D. 900 to 1300 and its return to the pre-900 level after 1300. A chi-square comparison for the number of individuals showing evidence of violence or cannibalism in the three time periods shows the differences to be highly significant ($\chi^2 = 104.3$, 2 d.f., $p < .001$). Even if we allow for some dating error and for unequal sampling of the three time periods, it is unreasonable to conclude that the high incidence of cannibalism between 900 and 1300 was due to chance alone.

Finally, even though it would be desirable to formally evaluate the relationship between contextual location and time period for these charnel deposits (table 3.82), some of the sample sizes in the 6-by-3 matrix are too small to provide even suggestive results. Although some cells could be collapsed into others, there is no behavioral or other basis for doing so. For example, would it be meaningful if the tower assemblage at Salmon Ruin were pooled with the assemblages from refuse or kiva locations? The most we can say is that there are no obvious temporal trends in the locations in which charnel deposits were placed or abandoned.

408

Table 3.80
Individuals Showing Evidence of Violence or Cannibalism, by Site and
Time Period

| | | No. Individuals | | |
| SITE | STATE | VIOLENCE | CANNIBALISM | TOTAL |
|---|---|---|---|---|
| Pre–A.D. 900 (BMII–PI) | | | | |
| Cave 7 | UT | 61 | — | 61 |
| Battle Cave | AZ | 11 | — | 11 |
| Ram Mesa Pithouse | NM | — | 1 | 1 |
| Whitewater District | AZ | 3 | — | 3 |
| Cottonwood Wash | UT | — | 4 | 4 |
| Small House | NM | — | 8 | 8 |
| *Subtotal* | | 75 | 13 | 88 |
| *Mean per site* | | 25.0 | 4.3 | 14.7 |
| A.D. 900–1300 (PII–III) | | | | |
| Snider's Well | CO | 25 | — | 25 |
| Long House | CO | 3 | — | 3 |
| Canyon Butte 3 | AZ | — | 4 | 4 |
| Peñasco Blanco | NM | — | 8 | 8 |
| Pueblo Bonito | NM | 3 | 2 | 5 |
| Comb Wash | UT | — | 1 | 1 |
| Charnel House | CO | 14 | — | 14 |
| Jack Smith's Houses | AZ | 2 | — | 2 |
| La Plata 23 | CO | — | 5 | 5 |
| La Plata 41 | NM | — | 6 | 6 |
| Alkali Ridge | UT | 3 | — | 3 |
| House of Tragedy | AZ | 4 | 1 | 5 |
| Coombs | UT | 12 | — | 12 |
| Mesa Verde 499 | CO | 1 | — | 1 |
| Sambrito Village | NM | — | 11 | 11 |
| Leroux Wash | AZ | — | 35 | 35 |
| Mancos Canyon | CO | — | 29 | 29 |
| Burnt Mesa | NM | — | 11 | 11 |
| Huerfano Mesa | NM | 3 | — | 3 |
| Llaves-Alkali Spring | NM | 1 | — | 1 |
| Llaves-Alkali Spring 2 | NM | 2 | — | 2 |
| Llaves-Alkali Spring 12 | NM | 2 | — | 2 |
| Largo-Gallina Bg2 | NM | 16 | — | 16 |
| Largo-Gallina Bg3 | NM | 11 | — | 11 |
| Largo-Gallina Bg20 | NM | 13 | — | 13 |
| Largo-Gallina Bg51 | NM | 3 | — | 3 |
| Largo-Gallina Bg88B | NM | 11 | — | 11 |
| Grinnell | CO | — | 7 | 7 |
| Mariana Mesa | AZ | 2 | — | 2 |
| Monument Valley | UT | — | 7 | 7 |
| Jones Ranch Road 7 | NM | 1 | — | 1 |
| Chi Chil Tan 108A | NM | 6 | — | 6 |
| Ash Creek | AZ | — | 5 | 5 |

*Continued on next page*

*Table 3.80 Continued*

| SITE | STATE | No. Individuals | | TOTAL |
|------|-------|-----------------|--------------|-------|
| | | VIOLENCE | CANNIBALISM | |
| Chaco 1360 | NM | 6 | — | 6 |
| Lake Roosevelt | AZ | 4 | — | 4 |
| Marshview Hamlet | CO | — | 6 | 6 |
| Rattlesnake Ruin | UT | — | 20 | 20 |
| Fence Lake | NM | — | 3 | 3 |
| Yellow Jacket 5MT-1 | CO | — | 4 | 4 |
| Yellow Jacket 5MT-3 | CO | — | 10 | 10 |
| Teec Nos Pos | AZ | — | 2 | 2 |
| Ram Mesa Kiva | NM | — | 12 | 12 |
| Aztec Wash I | CO | — | 13 | 13 |
| Aztec Wash II | CO | — | 2 | 2 |
| Aztec Wash III | CO | — | 1 | 1 |
| Hansen Pueblo | CO | — | 2 | 2 |
| La Plata Hwy. LA37592 | NM | — | 7 | 7 |
| La Plata Hwy. LA37593 | NM | — | 6 | 6 |
| La Plata Hwy. LA65030 | NM | — | 6 | 6 |
| Coyote Village | CO | — | 1 | 1 |
| St. Christopher's Mission | UT | — | 4 | 4 |
| Salmon Ruin | NM | 30 | 2 | 32 |
| San Juan River | UT | — | 2 | 2 |
| Kin Klethla | AZ | 1 | — | 1 |
| Brown Star | AZ | 1 | — | 1 |
| Wupatki | AZ | 6 | — | 6 |
| Bc51 Chaco[a] | NM | 8 | 1 | 9 |
| Guadelupe Ruin | NM | 1 | — | 1 |
| Mesa Verde 875 | CO | 6 | — | 6 |
| Betatakin Kiva | AZ | 1 | — | 1 |
| Houck K | AZ | — | 7 | 7 |
| Pueblo del Arroyo | NM | 9 | — | 9 |
| *Subtotal* | | 211 | 243 | 454 |
| *Mean per site* | | 6.6 | 7.1 | 7.3 |
| A.D. 1300–1900 (PIV–V) | | | | |
| Awatovi | AZ | 2 | — | 2 |
| Te'ewi | NM | 30 | — | 30 |
| Polacca Wash | AZ | — | 30 | 30 |
| Casas Grandes | MEX | 127 | — | 127 |
| *Subtotal* | | 159 | 30 | 189 |
| *Mean per site* | | 53.0 | 30.0 | 47.2 |
| TOTAL | | 445 | 286 | 731 |
| MEAN PER SITE | | 11.7 | 7.5 | |

NOTE: Four sites have cannibalism and violence in different individuals: Pueblo Bonito, House of Tragedy, Salmon Ruin, and Bc59 of the Casa Rinconada group.

a. Includes sites Bc50, Bc53, Bc57, Bc59 in the Casa Rinconada area.

Table 3.81

Summary of Individuals Showing Evidence of Violence or Cannibalism, by Time Period

| | Violence | | Cannibalism | | TOTAL VICTIMS | TOTAL SITES |
|---|---|---|---|---|---|---|
| TIME PERIOD | NO. | % | NO. | % | | |
| Pre–A.D. 900 (BMII–PI) | 75 | 85.2 | 13 | 14.8 | 88 | 6 |
| A.D. 900–1300 (PII–III) | 211 | 46.4 | 243 | 53.5 | 454 | 69 |
| A.D. 1300–1900 (PIV–V) | 159 | 84.1 | 30 | 15.9 | 189 | 4 |
| TOTAL | 445 | 60.9 | 286 | 39.1 | 731 | 79 |

NOTE: Excludes 90 cases of "probable violence" for A.D. 900–1300: 65 from Snider's Well, 20 from Mariana Mesa, and 5 from Salmon Ruin, none of which we can verify. If these additional cases were included, the overall frequencies would be 65.2% violence and 34.8% cannibalism.

Table 3.82

Individuals with Evidence of Cannibalism or Violence, by Time Period and Depositional Context

| | Pre–A.D. 900 BMII–PI | | 900–1300 PII–III | | 1300–1900 PIV–V | | Total | |
|---|---|---|---|---|---|---|---|---|
| CONTEXT | NO. | % | NO. | % | NO. | % | NO. | % |
| Room or pithouse | 14 | 15.9 | 229 | 50.4 | 2 | 1.0 | 245 | 33.5 |
| Kiva | 1 | 1.1 | 107 | 23.6 | 30 | 15.9 | 138 | 18.9 |
| Tower | 0 | 0.0 | 19 | 4.2 | 0 | 0.0 | 19 | 2.6 |
| Refuse | 1 | 1.1 | 3 | 0.7 | 0 | 0.0 | 4 | 0.5 |
| Extramural pit | 72 | 81.8 | 88 | 19.4 | 30 | 15.9 | 190 | 26.0 |
| Throughout pueblo | 0 | 0.0 | 8[a] | 1.8 | 127[b] | 67.2 | 135 | 18.5 |
| TOTAL INDIVIDUALS | 88 | 100.0 | 454 | 100.0 | 189 | 100.0 | 731 | 100.0 |
| TOTAL SITES | 6 | | 62 | | 4 | | 72 | |

a. All from sites in the Casa Rinconada area.
b. All reported from Casas Grandes, Chihuahua (Di Peso, Rinaldo, and Fenner 1974).

The Chaco Connection

CANNIBALISM IN THE Southwest had a restricted distribution: it occurred primarily in or near Chacoan sites, both within Chaco Canyon proper (Pueblo Bonito, Peñasco Blanco, Small House, Bc59) and in Chacoan outliers (Salmon Ruin, Houck K, La Plata sites). As evidence of the relationship between things Chacoan and Anasazi cannibalism we offer the strongly correlated mapping of David Wilcox's (1993) Chacoan spheres of influence and the locations of Southwestern cannibalized human assemblages (fig. 3.292). We discuss this spatial pattern and other Chaco considerations in more detail in chapter 5; at this point we simply want to draw attention to the nonrandom distribution and make three other observations.

First, Southwestern sites evidencing cannibalism are also linked to the so-called Chaco phenomenon temporally. Although taphonomic and diagenic processes make dating skeletal assemblages tricky, the great majority of the cannibalized assemblages appear to postdate A.D. 900, and

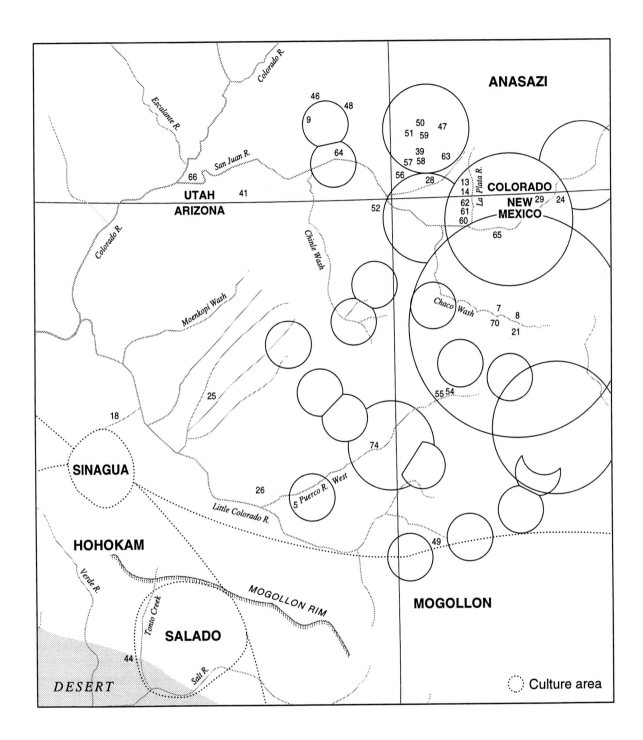

Figure 3.292. Locations of Southwestern sites where cannibalism is believed to have taken place and their correspondence to spheres of influence around Chacoan great houses and outliers as mapped by David Wilcox (1993). The spheres of influence are shown on the map as circles. Site numbers correspond to those in chapter 3, table 3.1, and figure 3.1.

only one, Polacca Wash, is dated later than 1300 (table 3.80). Second, there has long been controversy over how much Mesoamericans influenced the rise and fall of Chaco. If we understand the Chaco literature correctly, most workers agree that there was some Mexican influence, but few agree on the amount or how the influence took place. The occurrence of Chacoan cannibalism suggests an additional element of Mexican influence. Third, Mesoamerican cannibalism is historically tied to ritualized body processing, especially human sacrificial ceremonies involving enormous numbers of individuals (although Mexican archaeological findings hint at the eating of human flesh far beyond the exclusivity of ceremonial participation). The perimortem damage pattern of the Houck K human remains suggests that at least one of the Southwestern cannibalized assemblages could have resulted from ritual processing like that practiced in Mesoamerica.

MOST ANTHROPOLOGISTS and regional historians believe that modern Pueblo Indians are related to the Anasazi, as do the Puebloans themselves. (Leigh Jenkins [1991:32–33], a Hopi, wrote, "I would prefer that you know the Hopi word *Hisatsinom,* to the Navajo word *Anasazi* . . . [which] literally means 'people of long ago.'") One would think that the vast storehouse of information about modern Pueblo culture would provide powerful insight into Anasazi values relative to violence and cannibalism. Yet the long-standing debate about the fundamental nature of Pueblo culture still has not been resolved. John W. Bennett (1946) discussed the two major views held early in the twentieth century—the view represented by Laura Thompson and others versus the view held by Esther S. Goldfrank and others. Bennett (1946:362–363) summarized these views, first Thompson's, then Goldfrank's:

> [Thompson feels that] Pueblo culture and society are integrated to an unusual degree. . . . [There is] an ideal personality type which features the virtues of gentleness, non-aggression, cooperation, modesty, tranquillity, and so on. . . . [On the other hand, Goldfrank believes that] Pueblo society and culture are marked by considerable *covert* tension, suspicion, anxiety, hostility, fear, and ambition. Children, despite a relatively permissive . . . early training, are later coerced subtly and (from our viewpoint) brutally into behaving according to Pueblo norms. The ideals of free democratic election and expression are conspicuously lacking in Pueblo society, with authority in the hands of the group and chiefs, the latter formerly holding the power of life and death over his "subjects." The individual is suppressed and repressed.

Goldfrank's view of Pueblo culture corresponds better than Thompson's with the evidence for cannibalism and violence presented in this chapter. Thompson's view is so lacking in any qualities that might be associated with Anasazi violence and cannibalism that it would be difficult to incorporate our findings into her perspective. Hence, Goldfrank's characterization of Pueblo culture might be the better of the two to project back into the Anasazi past, at least as a working scenario that probably fits reality better than does the model of the environmentally harmonious and peaceful farmer that has evolved since the 1950s, becoming firmly entrenched during the "Age of Aquarius."

It should be remembered, however, that the skeletal assemblages from the 76 sites reviewed are far from representative of Anasazi burials. The vast majority of all Southwestern burials, including those of the Anasazi, show abundant evidence of consideration and concern for the dead. Still, this does not mean that people given considerate burials always died of natural causes. For instance, we reported earlier (Turner and Turner 1992a:677) that our inventory of the human remains at the Museum of Northern Arizona tallied 870 individuals from the Cibola, Kayenta, Mesa Verde, and Virgin branches of the Anasazi culture area. Of these, at least 68, or about 8%, appeared to have been cannibalized. Said another way, 1 out of 12 Anasazi individuals represented in this collection, mainly from northeastern Arizona, shows evidence of cannibalism. The 870 individuals were recovered from 165 sites, and the site frequency for cannibalism in the sample was 2.4% (4 of 165 sites). In inventorying these remains we made no attempt to determine the number of considerately buried individuals who had died violently, because of the difficulty of distinguishing trauma caused by accident from trauma caused by violence. Nevertheless, there were several individuals among the 870 who showed severe perimortem trauma.

We hope the empirical documentation provided in this chapter for Southwestern violence and cannibalism is sufficient to allow the following minimal summary conclusions to be tendered:

First, the perimortem taphonomic signatures of violence and cannibalism are distinct. Cannibalism involves a greater amount and different types of body processing than are present in examples of violence. Contextual information, when available, enhances the distinction.

Second, unlike the perimortem characteristics of violence, the taphonomic signature of Southwestern cannibalism is effectively the same as that found in contemporary and prehistoric processed game animals of both large and small species. Parsimony and Occam's razor, as well as common sense, dictate that similarity in processing equates with similarity in purpose. This is an extraordinarily clear example of the principle of *sufficient reason*. Any alternative explanation flies in the face of this principle and must be considered conjecture, fiction, guessing, or make-believe.

Third, our search through the Southwestern archaeological literature and skeletal collections has identified claims for cannibalism and new examples of it almost exclusively in the Anasazi culture area. The sites where cannibalism has been or can be hypothesized are strongly linked with the Chaco phenomenon, both in physical proximity to great houses within and outside the canyon and in time—that is, the period from A.D. 900 to 1300.

Fourth, although violence can be demonstrated to have existed centuries before the construction of the great Chaco towns and buildings, Southwestern cannibalism seems to have begun with Chacoan development and areal expansion.

Fifth and last, our criteria for hypothesizing cannibalism are probably too rigorous, but given the extraordinarily controversial nature of the topic, we believe it is best to err on the side of conservatism. We feel confident that at least 38 Southwestern episodes of cannibalism took place that involved the eating of at least 286 persons of all ages and both sexes. Had a simple, inexpensive, and nondestructive way been found to resolve the major source of taphonomic difficulty—that of identifying threshold levels of bone burning—it is likely that the number of sites and individuals would have been even greater.

Although the evidence presented in this chapter for assessing claims of violence and cannibalism seems self-evident, to rejoin any remaining critics of the cannibalism hypothesis we demonstrate in the next chapter that the Southwestern cannibal signature corresponds well with prehistoric human body processing in Mexico. There, one finds both ethnohistoric acceptance that cannibalism took place and archaeological charnel deposits indicating a wide variety of body processing, including abundant cannibalism.

# Comparative Evidence

## Cannibalism and Human Body Processing in Mexico

◆ And the body was divided, and a thigh sent to Mochteczoma for him to eat, the rest being distributed to other chieftains or relatives, who went to eat it in the house of the man who had captured the victim. They cook that meat with corn.
—Fray Bernardino de Sahagún, *A History of Ancient Mexico 1547–1577*, volume 1

The vast ethnohistoric literature from Mesoamerica, along with abundant archaeological finds, leaves no doubt that violence and cannibalism—part of an interwoven complex of warfare, religion, and human sacrifice—were common features of the sociopolitical landscape, especially in central Mexico. As two recent symposia attest (Pijoan 1993; Malvido, Tiesler, and Pereira 1995), Mexican scholars, among others, generally believe that at European contact in 1519, Aztecs and other Mesoamerican peoples performed massive human sacrifice and ritually consumed human flesh. Although scholars debate the magnitude of Aztec cannibalism and the reasons for it, we believe it is unnecessary to argue that the practice existed. Instead, in this chapter we offer merely a brief glimpse into the ethnohistoric evidence and then turn to the archaeological record for comparative data on cannibalism and human body processing in Mexico.

We wanted to compare human bone deposits from the U.S. Southwest that we interpret as having been cannibalized with Mexican bone deposits known more securely to have cannibalized. To that end, in 1993 we began at every opportunity to examine archaeologically derived human skeletal assemblages excavated in Mexico. Our studies of such assemblages demonstrate the applicability of the minimal taphonomic signature outside the Southwest and show that in Mexico, cannibalism and human sacrifice are minimally 2,500 years old and possibly as much as 6,000.

### Ethnohistoric Evidence for Cannibalism in Mexico

OF ALL URBAN American Indian groups, the Aztecs are universally regarded as having been the most bloodstained and violent, performing sacrificial killings, victim mutilation, and cannibalism on a scale known nowhere else in the Americas (see, among many others, Anaya Monroy 1966; Carrasco 1982; Cook 1946; González Torres 1985; Hassig 1988; Ilia Najera 1993; Keegan 1993). According to the ethnographer Paul Kirchhoff (1943:106), cannibalism and the taking and displaying of trophy heads were two of the key elements that defined ancient Mesoamerican culture. Although some scholars maintain reservations about the reliability of early accounts of Aztec and Mesoamerican life (for example, Parry and Keith 1984), the consensus view grants the chronicles a core of accuracy despite European ethnocentrism and exaggeration.

415

Perhaps the lengthiest, best-known, and most highly respected ethno-historic records for central Mexico are those compiled by Fray Bernar-dino de Sahagún (1932), who arrived in Mexico in 1529. Collecting descriptions in words and pictures from Nahuatl-speaking informants and then translating them into Spanish, Sahagún portrayed, among many other things, the major ceremonies the Aztecs observed during their 18-month year. To a modern reader, his repetition of gruesome detail conveys in striking fashion the enormity of Aztec sacrificial cere-monies. In the first month, for example, a ceremony was performed in honor of the rain god Tlaloc and probably also Quetzalcoatl, the god of winds. "In this month they killed many children; they sacrificed them in many places on the top of mountains" (Sahagún 1932:51). At one hill called Tepepulco, "they killed a large number of infants each year, and once dead they cooked and ate them" (Sahagún 1932:72). Cannibalism of sacrificial victims, often following flaying, also figured prominently in ceremonies in which the gods Xipe Totec and Huitzilopochtli were hon-ored (Sahagún 1932:74–75).

During the second month, according to Sahagún (1932:52), captives were sacrificed this way:

> Captives were killed by scalping them, taking the scalp off the top of the head. . . . When the masters of these captives took their slaves to the temple where they were to be killed, they dragged them by the hair. As they pulled them up the steps of the Cú, some of these cap-tives would faint, so their owners had to drag them by the hair as far as the block where they were to die. . . . After thus having torn their hearts out, and after pouring their blood into a jacara (bowl made of a gourd), which was given to the master of the dead slave, the body was thrown down the temple steps. From there it was taken by cer-tain old men called Quaquaquilti, and carried to their calpul (or chapel), cut to pieces, and distributed among them to be eaten. Be-fore cutting them up they would flay the bodies of the captives; others would dress in their skins and fight sham battles with other men.

For month 10, Sahagún (1932:111) described the grisly ceremony for Xiutecutli, the god of fire, in which naked captives were burned at a temple dedicated to Paynal. The parenthetical additions are those of the translator, Fanny Bandelier:

> As soon as they reached the top they threw them [the captives] into that fire. As they were thrust in, a great cloud of ashes arose (from the fire) and wherever anyone of them fell, a deep hole (hollow) was made (by the body) in the fire because it was ablaze with embers and live coal. The poor captives at once began to twist and turn in that fire and to suffer from nausea (have vomiting spells), his body begin-ning to squeak (I think sizzle would be better), as does the body or part of an animal when roasting, and big blisters would rise all over the body. While in this (infernal) agony, the priests called Quaqua-cuiltin pulled him (or them) out with gambrels (grappling irons) and placed, one after the other on the block they called techcatl, and at once cut the breast from nipple to nipple or a little below, and tore the

heart out and threw (the body) at the feet of the statue of Xiuhtecutli, god of the fire.

Sahagún was not alone among the Spanish chroniclers to record cannibalism in central Mexico. Fray Diego Durán (1993) also spoke Nahuatl and wrote about the Aztec world shortly after the conquest began. Though repulsed by Aztec human sacrifice and cannibalism, he nevertheless wrote much about the former and a few passages about the latter (e.g, Durán 1993:192–193, 233, 474). "I am not exaggerating," he said; "there were days in which two thousand, three thousand, five thousand, or eight thousand men were sacrificed. Their flesh was eaten and a banquet was prepared with it after the hearts had been offered to the devil" (Durán 1993:407).

And there are many others. The historian David Carrasco (1987:124), for instance, cited an eyewitness account given by Bernal Díaz del Castillo, a sergeant in Cortés's army, in which the Aztecs sacrificed captured Spanish soldiers during the lengthy Spanish attack on the capital, Tenochtitlan. Christopher L. Moser (1973:26–27), citing the same chronicler, wrote: "Bernal Díaz . . . describes two *tzompantli* [skull racks], one in Xocotlan with over one hundred thousand skulls and the other in the central square of Tenochtitlan. The latter was also described by Durán."

Some scholars (e.g., Castile 1980) have questioned others' uncritical acceptance of the early Spanish chronicles that mention cannibalism. But there are other ethnographic lines of evidence, too. Surviving pre-Hispanic or early Hispanic codices, for example, contain drawings of human body parts being cooked or feasted upon. One such manuscript preserved in Florence, Italy, shows food offerings to a deity that include a human arm (Nuttall 1903:60), as well as a complex feast scene with pots of human body parts (Nuttall 1903:73). The Codex Hall (Dibble 1947) also depicts human body parts being cooked in a large pot. The Codex Borgia (Díaz and Rodgers 1993), painted in southern or central Puebla at the time of the Spaniards' arrival or a few years before, portrays many examples (figs. 4.1, 4.2). It is not for the fainthearted.

Adela Fernández's *Diccionario ritual de voces nahuas* (1992) offers a fascinating line of evidence for human sacrifice and cannibalism in the form of Nahuatl (Aztec) words. For example, she defines the name Acatlayacapan this way (our translation from Fernández's Spanish text): "'At the summit of the cane field,' name of the seventy-sixth building of the ceremonial center of Tenochtitlán. In it reside the slaves who are supposed to be immolated in honor of the Tlaloques. Afterward, the sacrificed person is quartered and the meat is prepared as a meal with squash flowers for the gentlemen and principals, who eat it in a ritual manner." Another example is the word *tlacatlaolli,* which lends this book its title: "'Man corn,' invariable sacred meal of sacrificed human meat, cooked with corn. The sacrificed bodies are returned to their relatives or rulers so that upon consuming their meat, they are nurtured of their spirit. This type of cannibalism is eminently religious in character."

After the physical conquest of Mexico, the Catholic church continued the cultural conquest, which did not proceed as quickly or smoothly as hoped. Even in 1537, everywhere don Juan de Zumárraga, the bishop of

Figure 4.1. One of the Aztec symbols for Xolotl, the evil twin of Quetzalcoatl, is a dismembered person being carried in a cooking pot. From the Codex Borgia. (Courtesy Archivio Fotografico, Biblioteca Apostolica Vaticana.)

Mexico, looked "he saw heinous practices, at one time suppressed, coming back stronger than ever; human sacrifice and cannibalism were almost common again" (Padden 1967:251).

Teresa Piossek Prebisch (1991) noted that Spanish law in the New World dealt with cannibalism as a serious moral, if not practical, problem. She pointed out (1991:1) that in a sixteenth-century legal text titled "Libro Primero de la Recopilación de Leyes de Indias, Título Primero de la Santa Fé Católica," law VII prohibited, among other activities, "comer carne humana, aunque sea de los prisioneros, y muertos en la guerra" (to eat human meat, even if it be of prisoners and war dead). This law was announced on June 23, 1523, by Emperor Carlos V and was repeated in 1538 and again in 1551. Piossek thinks that legal restatement each generation indicates the magnitude and persistence of the New World cannibalism problem for Spain.

The Aztecs may be the best-known practitioners of the sociopolitical complex linking warfare, religion, human sacrifice, and cannibalism,

Figure 4.2. Another of the Aztec symbols for Xolotl is a dismembered person being cooked in a pot over a fire. Flames and steam indicate that cooking was in progress. From the Codex Borgia. (Courtesy Archivio Fotografico, Biblioteca Apostolica Vaticana.)

but they certainly were not alone. The Tlaxcalans to the east, for example, at the time of European contact practiced human sacrifice and cannibalism on a similarly terrifying scale (Thomas 1993:240). The list could continue with ethnohistoric examples from Michoacán (Seler 1993:24–25, 44), Jalisco (Baus Czitrom 1985), and Durango (Moser 1973:7; Ramírez M. 1988:311). Here, however, we call attention only to some ethnographic references to cannibalism in northern Mexico, because of its proximity to the present-day U.S. Southwest and to the prehistoric Greater Southwest.

In their description of Tarahumara fiestas in southwestern Chihuahua, Wendell C. Bennett and Robert M. Zingg (1935:288) noted that there might once have been cannibalism: "The sacrifice of animals is an invariable part of the native *fiesta* . . . [and] our Tarahumara informants stated, independent of one another, that there was a time when children were sacrificed . . . in place of animals."

In the *Handbook of the North American Indians,* T. B. Hinton

(1983:323) discussed the southwestern periphery of the U.S. Southwest: "The Spaniards found the western parts of the Sierra and the barrancas of Durango and Sinaloa west of the Tepehuan occupied by two closely related tribes, the Acaxee and the Xixime. These peoples lived in scattered rancherias and engaged in endemic warfare with frequent cannibalism." In the same volume, W. B. Griffen (1983:335–336) related that cannibalism and human sacrifice also existed in the southeastern periphery: "In ceremonies associated with war, some testimonies noted that the flesh of captives was often eaten or their ground bones consumed with peyote. On an occasion or two the meetings of bands to cement alliances were accompanied by the sacrifice of human beings, whose bodies were eaten with peyote. . . . [In addition] endocannibalism, the eating of deceased kinsmen, was practiced in Nuevo Leon."

Fray Vicente de Santa María (1973) wrote in the eighteenth century about aboriginal conditions in northeastern Mexico and southwestern Texas, a vast tract dominated by a Spanish colony called Nuevo Santander. He mentioned cannibalism, violence, and mutilation of prisoners by the region's Indians.

Ralph L. Beals (1943:40–43), referring to the Cáhita Indians of Sinaloa, wrote: "The treatment of warfare and cannibalism under a single heading seems warranted by their close linkage in aboriginal life. . . . As a rule, cannibalism was limited to the eating of valiant enemies in war, the belief existing that the valor of the victim was translated to those who partook of the flesh." Earlier, Beals (1932:114) had provided a masterful synthesis of the warfare-religion-sacrifice complex in his ethnohistoric study of northern Mexico before 1750:

> Organized warfare in the sense that the fighting men were divided into divisions, usually of definite numbers, with a leader for each division, seems to have been general in the western part of the area. It is probable that this distribution should be extended to the Yuman tribes of the Colorado river and perhaps the Maricopa and Pima. There was among these peoples at least a division of the fighting men on the basis of the weapons used and a great formalization in the style of fighting. . . . The taking of trophies in warfare presents several formalized aspects of wide distribution found in northern Mexico. Both scalping and head taking were practiced. . . . Head taking seems primarily western in its distribution. The preservation of the skull has a more limited but also western distribution. . . . Cannibalism, usually ceremonial in nature, and involving the eating of war captives or the bodies of slain enemies, occurred widely in northern Mexico and to the north and south.

Later in the same work, Beals (1932:129–130) went on to compare practices in northern and central Mexico:

> Human sacrifice rarely occurs in Mexico without an association of cannibalism. Cannibalism in much of our area [northern Mexico] was ceremonial in nature, even where not associated with human sacrifice. . . . In practically all cases it was connected with the celebration of war victories and in many cases with the preservation of the bones

and skulls of enemies (suggestive of the Mexican skull rack). Among the Acaxee, where cannibalism was probably most highly developed in our area, the bones and skulls were presented to an idol or deity on certain occasions, and the first portion of human flesh prepared for eating was placed on the altar. . . . [Among the Aztecs] the sacrifices were in most cases associated with ceremonial cannibalism, and the heart of the victim was usually "fed" to the god. There exists, then, a roughly continuous series starting on the one hand with the human sacrifice of Mexico, with the heart and other foods fed to the god (a rather direct manifestation of the widespread idea of food offerings to the supernatural), and cannibalism. Next is the ceremonial cannibalism of the Acaxee (the first portion given to the god, the second to the slayer of the enemy being eaten) and the preservation of bones and skulls. Finally, there are the less specialized methods of the Sinaloans and the peoples of Nuevo Leon and elsewhere, and the apparently simple ceremonial cannibalism of the Yavapai and perhaps Karankawa.

Many more comparable ethnographic and historic accounts are available, but these few serve to illustrate that cannibalism, with or without ritual sacrifice, was widely if not frequently practiced in Mexico. In our view, the accounts suggest that it was both an instrument for social control and an expression of social pathology. The Aztec world, especially, seems to have crossed a threshold into what we consider pathological—as did the archaeologist Richard E. W. Adams (1991:401): "The Aztec state by . . . [the late 1400s] had also become a mad world of bloody terrorism based on the cynical, psychopathic policies of the high imperial rulers. Coronation ceremonies of the later kings were accompanied by the offering of fantastic quantities of human victims to the gods. These victims were purchased slaves from Aztec society itself, and the collected captives from the constant foreign campaigns of the Aztec armies."

Bioarchaeological findings from Mexico, to which we turn next, are consistent with the historic accounts and illustrate, where ethnography cannot, that Adams's "mad world" went back much further in time.

The Archaeological Record

ARCHAEOLOGY PROVIDES its own account of warfare, ritual human sacrifice, and cannibalism in central Mexico. Where taphonomic analyses have been carried out there, cases of probable cannibalism inevitably show up. Christine Niederberger (1987:674), for example, has suggested for the Valley of Mexico that damaged human bones found in various archaeological sites indicate that cannibalism was once widely, if not frequently, practiced.

At the great complex of Teotihuacan in the Valley of Mexico (fig. 4.3), where overall dates ranged from 200 B.C. to A.D. 600, Richard E. W. Adams (1991) told of the thousands of figurines and large number of broken human bones found in contexts dating from at least A.D. 400 to 600. Among the figurines were representations of the deities Xipe Totec, Tlaloc, Quetzalcoatl, and Xiuhtecuhtli, all of which were to be worshipped a thousand years later by the Aztecs. Adams (1991:224) allowed that the "same association of religion with warfare and ritual cannibalism was present in the final stages of Teotihuacan as in Aztec times.

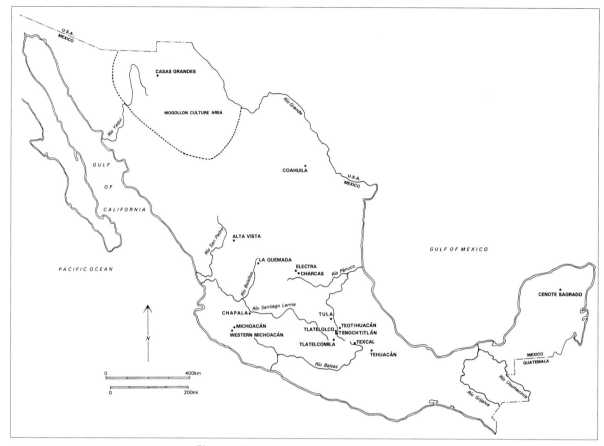

Figure 4.3. Locations of selected Mexican sites and studied human skeletal assemblages. Map by Alison Dean.

Maquixco, for example, produced large quantities of split and splintered human bone fragments in general garbage and trash heaps, indicating that humans were being used for food."

Even during the building phase of the public structures of Teotihuacan there occurred slayings, torture, sacrifice, and other violence. Rubén Cabrera Castro (1993:106) outlined the considerable evidence showing that "large-scale human sacrifice was practiced in the early phases of Teotihuacan, confirming the despotic character of the Teotihuacan state. Human sacrifice . . . [was] an instrument of repression on the part of the state to consolidate and preserve its power. This act is a means of social control."

Carlos Serrano Sánchez (1993) noted examples of perimortem treatment including dismemberment, cutting, and burning at Teotihuacan—for example, in the habitation zone north of the Old Temple of the Feathered Serpent. In the Plaza of the Moon and Zone of the Caves have been found parts of skulls used as containers, as well as burials of decapitated heads (Lagunas and Serrano 1993). Saburo Sugiyama (1995) described the mass sacrifice of more than 137 richly attired men and women whose deaths at A.D. 200 were associated with the building of the Feathered Serpent pyramid. It is not unlikely that construction of all the large public structures at Teotihuacan involved involuntary human death.

Writing about human skeletal remains in Teotihuacan's apartment compound Tlajinga 33, occupied from A.D. 200 to 650, Rebecca Storey (1992:78) reported:

> [Human] refuse interments are all disarticulated, very fragmentary remains that were numbered and excavated as burials only because they formed a concentration of human bone identifiable during general excavation. These remains have no recognizable pit and are never accompanied by offerings. The bones are usually somewhat scattered and often turn out to consist of skeletal fragments from several individuals. They show little evidence of care in placement and are usually found in trash pits or fill layers, mixed up with other artifacts in these secondary contexts. A few also have butchering or cut marks. . . . Although excavated as burials, these secondary-context individuals are found in an archaeological context that is quite different from that of primary and secondary interments; they more closely resemble the faunal bones found in trash pits and middens. . . . Although many bones are poorly preserved, there is no evidence of calcined, warped, or cracked bones, as is found in cremated material. It should be noted that much of the faunal remains are burned and calcined, and so the lack of human skeletal material so treated is indeed a clear pattern.

The lack of burned human bone at Tlajinga 33 is not out of line with historic accounts that human flesh was prepared as a stew (*posoli*). All of the glyphs in published codices that we have examined show human parts cooking in large pots, never directly over a fire (see Díaz and Rodgers 1993; Dibble 1947; Nuttall 1903).

Storey (1992:129–130) identified human bones with cut marks that were recovered from excavations in refuse middens. These bone fragments undoubtedly represent the carrying of human flesh to the residential districts of Teotihuacan after sacrifice, decapitation, and dismemberment at the ceremonial centers:

> A small percentage of the bones in middens have cut marks or some sort of deliberate modification for decoration or use. There is no evidence on any of the formal-grave individuals that defleshing, which would produce cut marks, was a specialized burial treatment at Tlajinga 33. Cut marks are found on a few adult or late adolescent bones. These bones apparently represent pieces of humans that were deliberately dismembered and then ultimately discarded with little care. . . . It seems that these bones and their treatment can best be explained as pieces of human sacrifices. There is evidence for human sacrifice at Teotihuacan in the form of skeletal finds. . . . Most of these skeletal finds consist of just heads or whole skeletons whose context indicates they were sacrificed. At Tlajinga 33 the cut marks are mostly on femurs, humeri, and ribs and do not appear to make up one, or most of one, dismembered skeleton. . . . It is probable that only pieces of a victim would be present in the compound and that perhaps several compounds would have parts of the same individual.

Figure 4.4. Carmen María Pijoan
Aguadé, INAH physical anthro-
pologist who pioneered human
taphonomy research in Mexico.
Photograph by Ramon Enriquez,
Laboratorio DAF-INAH,
Mexico City.

Figure 4.4. Carmen María Pijoan Aguadé, INAH physical anthropologist who pioneered human taphonomy research in Mexico. Photograph by Ramon Enriquez, Laboratorio DAF-INAH, Mexico City.

> Although this treatment resembles the later Aztec practice of dismem-
> berment, partitioning, and eating of sacrificial victims . . . none of the
> bones with cut marks at Tlajinga appear to have been burned or
> boiled.

Storey did not say what her criteria were for recognizing bone boiling
or threshold burning. Given what we have seen of bone preservation in
Mexico, cut marks on bone fragments generally preserve best when boiling, roasting, or defleshing have occurred before deposition.

The pioneer in Mexican human taphonomy is Carmen María Pijoan
Aguadé (fig. 4.4). Working with her associates, Pijoan has examined
previously excavated collections of damaged human remains from a
number of sites in and outside Mexico City that are curated in the Department of Physical Anthropology at the National Museum of Anthropology and History (INAH) in Mexico City. Pijoan and Alejandro
Pastrana C. (1985) have definitely identified cannibalism. Pijoan has
published on two sets of human remains from Tlatelolco, the second
Aztec ceremonial center in what is today Mexico City. One studied assemblage was a group of 170 heads of sacrificial victims whose precise
and orderly arrangement in the ground indicated they had been on a
skull rack (Pijoan, Pastrana, and Maquivar 1989). We, too, examined
this collection and will discuss both studies shortly.

The other Tlatelolco series, called Burial 14, was a mass grave of dismembered body parts of 153 individuals excavated in 1961 near the
structure called Templo Redondo by Francisco González Rul (Pijoan
1997; Pijoan, Mansilla, and Pastrana 1993). González was able to determine that the temple had been built between A.D. 1400 and 1420, and

Burial 14 occurred between 1418 and 1427 (Pijoan 1997:278). Pijoan, Pastrana, and Maquivar's analysis of femurs and tibias showed a strong pattern of cut marks in specific locations on these two skeletal elements. The pattern indicated not only that bodies had been dismembered but also that flesh had been removed. In this study, the most numerous bone was the left femur. Young men, women, and a few children were involved in the sacrificial event.

Pijoan (1997:278) concluded that large amounts of muscle tissue belonging to the Burial 14 victims had been removed for consumption, but not because of inadequate protein. The bodies had been extensively butchered, but articulated elements and the complete absence of processing marks on some bones indicated that considerable amounts of edible tissue must have remained on the corpses.

Pijoan (1997) wrote her doctoral dissertation after analyzing the entire Burial 14 series for perimortem damage, using a system she and Josefina Mansilla Lory (1993) had developed earlier. Compatible with the mass grave's being located near a temple, the skeletal remains showed no signs of cooking or marrow extraction. However, the individuals were surely sacrificed for their hearts, inasmuch as a majority of the sternal bones had been cut in half. Her frequencies of bones present in the mass grave showed that some 10–25% of the appendicular skeletons were missing. We suggest that wherever those bones went, there the cooking occurred. Vertebrae, ribs, hands, and feet were the most commonly missing elements.

Looking north of the Valley of Mexico, we turn next to Tula, capital of the Toltecs until it was sacked around A.D. 1170. The Toltecs are often portrayed as peaceful philosopher-farmers. Ross Hassig (1992:112) will have none of this, not only because the Toltecs developed the side-bladed and curved "short sword," an excellent slashing weapon for hand-to-hand combat, but also because "much of Tollan's [Tula's] prominence was the result of warfare, for which there is ample evidence in the city. . . . Human bone fragments are also common in the archaeological ruins, suggesting human sacrifice and cannibalism."

Richard A. Diehl (1983:27–29) summarized the history of archaeological investigations at Tula, the most recent of which were conducted by the University of Missouri in the 1970s under the direction of Diehl and Robert A. Benfer. These excavations recovered animal and human bones, both of which Diehl (1983:98) thought were "rare festival food."

In a work in progress on the faunal remains from Tula, Diehl (n.d.: 8–9) offered the kinds of insights that only field excavators can make: "There are no indications of significant [bone] losses due to rotting or disintegration. . . . [B. Miles] Gilbert and Robert A. Benfer identified 320 fragmented human remains not associated with recognizable burials, which I will argue came from cannibalized individuals." He added, "Several long bones were broken longitudinally in a manner suggesting human breakage while extracting the marrow, and Benfer . . . believes that the breaks were not caused by carnivores or other non-human agents. Six human bones showed evidence of burning" (Diehl n.d.:14). However, Diehl reported that neither Benfer nor Gilbert found any butchering marks.

Despite the foregoing suggestions of cannibalism, Tula has not yet produced clear-cut osteological evidence of sacrifice such as that discov-

ered at Teotihuacan, Tenochitlan, Tlatelolco, Cacaxtla, and other great
Mesoamerican ceremonial centers. In April 1994 we examined human
skeletons from single, multiple, and secondary Tula burials excavated in
1980 and 1981 from habitation areas called Malinche and Charnoy,
across the river from the great ceremonial buildings of Tula Grande.
These skeletons are curated at INAH's Physical Anthropology Department in Mexico City. According to Mansilla and Pompa (1990), these
are the only known skeletons from Tula; all the others from previous excavations have been lost. We found no identifiable perimortem processing damage except for possible leg breaking in a secondary burial.
Screened refuse from the two burial areas produced well-preserved rodent and deer bones, all heavily processed but without burning or roasting damage.

Moving from Tula to western Michoacán, we call attention to an
almost unknown aspect of Mesoamerican body processing—the use of
human skeletal elements to make a wide variety of artifacts. We first
learned of this prehistoric practice in March 1994 when we examined in
Zápopan-Guadalajara, Jalisco, at least 2,000 objects made from human
bones that Federico Solórzano Barreto of INAH had recovered from
pot-hunted late Classic to Postclassic burials in western Michoacán. Figures 4.5–4.7 show a very small sample of this immense collection. Such
production, which might or might not have followed ritual sacrifice and
consumption of a victim's flesh, strikes us as novel evidence for gaining
further insight into the ancient Mexican Indian mind—a mind whose
worldview embraced both noble religious thoughts about the processing
of humans (ritual sacrifice and cannibalism) and an ignoble, if not socially pathological, attitude toward the use and treatment of people.
This latter attitude, which permitted human bones to be turned into
utilitarian artifacts, would agree well with a mindset that saw humans as
edible.

Turning our attention eastward, we note that Michael D. Coe and
Richard A. Diehl (1980) reported discarded human bone refuse at San
Lorenzo Tenochtitlan, a group of Olmec sites in Vera Cruz. The main
Olmec occupation there lasted from 1100 to 900 B.C. Olmec human
remains are quite rare, so when fragments of human bone were discovered, they were considered very important. These turned out to be not
from burials but from refuse containing pottery sherds, animal bones,
and other items. Coe and Diehl (1980:390) judged that "the evidence
that the San Lorenzo Olmec were cannibals is overwhelming: of the
human skeletal remains in culinary debris, some show the same signs of
burning and breaking that any other animal bones would. Most of these
individuals were adults, presumably war captives."

Finally, we turn to northern Mexico. In 1994 Robert B. Pickering and
Michael S. Foster published a review of prehistoric disease and trauma
in northwestern and western Mexico, which they defined as including
western Coahuila, Chihuahua, Sonora, Durango, Zacatecas, Jalisco,
Sinaloa, and Nayarit. They noted that little was known about the archaeology of the region and even less about the physical anthropology.
Culling all their cases that could be attributed to violence, warfare,
conflict, sacrifice, or cannibalism, we found only the following few examples; there were none for Sonora, Durango, Nayarit, or Coahuila.

In the state of Chihuahua, human remains from the site of Casas

Figure 4.5. Michoacán, late Classic to Postclassic. Deeply incised and carved musical rasps made from human long bones. Scale is 15 cm. Federico Solórzano Barreto collection, Zápopan-Guadalajara, Jalisco (CGT neg. 3-31-94:24).

Figure 4.6. Michoacán, late Classic to Postclassic. Flat daggers and other artifacts made from human long bones. Scale is 15 cm. Federico Solórzano Barreto collection, Zápopan-Guadalajara, Jalisco (CGT neg. 3-31-94:18).

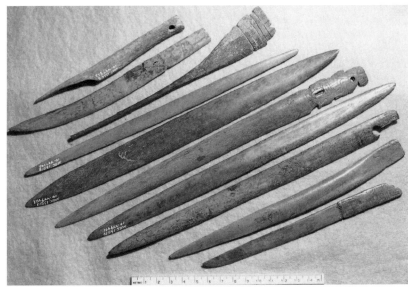

Figure 4.7. Michoacán, late Classic to Postclassic. Awls, barbed points, daggers, and other artifacts made from human long bones. Scale is 15 cm. Federico Solórzano Barreto collection, Zápopan-Guadalajara, Jalisco (CGT neg. 3-31-94:21).

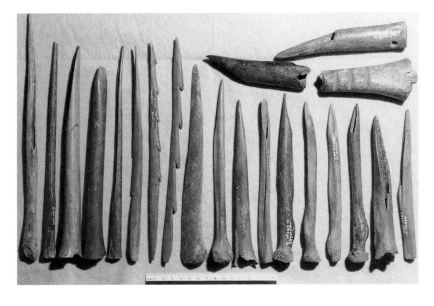

Grandes had little direct evidence for trauma, although the archaeological contexts of many skeletons showed clearly that those individuals had died violent deaths. One female from a cave near Santa Ana, also in Chihuahua, had a head injury. In Sinaloa, the site of Guasave produced trophy heads. In Jalisco, Tizapán el Alto, which dates from A.D. 1000 to 1220, had five male skeletons without heads or upper cervical vertebrae. At Cerro del Huistle in northern Jalisco, Pickering and Foster noted that six deposits of crania and long bones were found in the main plaza. One deposit may have included up to 60 individuals, mostly adult males. Some bones displayed burning and cutting, and many of the skulls were perforated at the apex. In Zacatecas, at the ceremonial center of Alta Vista (A.D. 450–1000), numerous isolated bones and bone fragments with cut marks were found near the pyramid. Thirty skulls with holes drilled at the top were probably part of a trophy skull display.

Again in Zacatecas, the late Preclassic to Classic site of La Quemada (A.D. 100–300 to 900) yielded many human remains, some in apparent ritualistic contexts suggesting "human sacrifice, possible ancestor worship, and cannibalism" (Pickering and Foster 1994:4). Pickering (1985:323) wrote that "on the floor of the Hall of Columns at La Quemada, a mass of human remains lacking heads and feet was deposited and covered with post-abandonment debris." More recently, Ben A. Nelson (1995) reported that the human bones found on the floor of the Hall of Columns were the remains of 400 cut, burned, and disarticulated young adult males. Nelson had no doubt about the occurrence of institutionalized violence at La Quemada, noting in addition that there were six known skull and long bone racks at the site.

Finally, in a study from the state of Chihuahua, Sheilagh T. Brooks and Richard H. Brooks (1990) suggested that some type of Tarahumara Indian ceremonial or culinary activity might account for the condition of human remains they found in a cave about 105 km (65 miles) southwest of Chihuahua City. They identified 15 almost completely intermixed and incomplete individuals. Some bones showed rodent gnawing, and others, the evident burning of more than one individual. One 25-year-old female skull was cut near the base. "There was no evidence of any type of intensive fire within the midden to account for the numerous charred human bones. The burnt bones apparently were not part of a cremation as there was no actual fire lens or accumulation of ash" (Brooks and Brooks 1990:261). "It is possible that some of these were token burials and the entire body or skeleton was not brought here for interment" (Brooks and Brooks 1990:263). Speaking of one skull, "Arturo Romano [personal communication, 1957] suggested that this skull [the 25-year-old female] might have been placed on a skull rack, which would have involved widening the foramen magnum. . . . Romano also mentioned (1957) that he had encountered similarly cut skulls from a cave, La Cueva de la Paila, near Parras in Coahuila" (Brooks and Brooks 1990:270). The form of this rack must have differed from the fencelike rack of the Aztecs, on which skulls were mounted by passing a pole through holes punched in the sides.

Mexican Skeletal Assemblages
Examined for Perimortem
Damage

ARCHAEOLOGICAL AND osteological analyses by other scholars offer
ample evidence for the antiquity and wide geographical spread of ritual
human sacrifice and cannibalism in Mexico. In order to begin compiling
a systematic comparative data base against which to assess our Southwestern evidence, we recently began examining Mexican skeletal collections firsthand. The characteristics of some of these assemblages
compare well with the minimal taphonomic signature we have proposed
for cannibalism in the Southwest. Others differ usefully in ways that
reflect differences in ritual context, practices, and attitudes about the
human body. And one site—the first to be discussed in this section—
extends the evidence for ritual cannibalism far back into the past.

In the early 1960s, at Coxcatlan Cave in the Tehuacán Valley in the
state of Puebla, Melvin L. Fowler and Richard S. MacNeish excavated
the burned cranium of a five-year-old child (B2, Tc50). The find suggested sacrifice and cannibalism (MacNeish 1962:9): the child's head
had been placed on the body of a six-month-old infant, and the infant's
head, unburned, had been placed on the body of the five-year-old. Neither child had any burning of its postcranial body parts. They had been
buried side by side. The stratum containing these two skeletons, and
other burials, was minimally 6,000 years old (El Riego phase), a date estimated from carbon-14 assays on materials in upper and lower strata
dating 5200–4800 B.C. (Fowler and MacNeish 1972). Even if the burials had been intrusive, an undisturbed overlying stratum (XII) dated at
4700–4300 B.C.; hence the 6,000 year minimum.

Because these authors suggested that the child's skeleton represented
some sort of "purposeful killing," we examined the remains for perimortem damage (see also J. Anderson 1965, 1967). As figures 4.8–4.17
show, the child's head had been cut off and then set facing upward on a
fire for roasting. There were many cut marks, indicating that the head
had been skinned, but we could not determine whether this took place
before or after roasting. The interior of the vault had shiny, carbonized
adhesions, indicating that the brain and other tissue were present at the
time of roasting. Perimortem breakage and chipping indicated that the
cranium was then broken open in order to gain access to the cooked
brain. If this processing sequence represents cannibalism—and we agree
with NacNeish that it does—then it likely represents some manner of ritual rather than emergency cannibalism, because only one head of two
complete children was cooked.

As we and our coworkers in this case determined (Turner et al. n.d.),
the older child had been ill at the time of its death. Figures 4.8 and 4.13
show the severely infected upper incisor abscess area. There were signs
of possible brain infection as well. What was there about a sick, possibly
feverish child that made someone cut off, roast, and break open its head
and seemingly eat its brain? Were the children captives, and if so, why
were they given considerate burials? If not as trophies, why else might
the two deciduous upper first molars have been removed forcefully
from the jaw and not buried with the burned and misplaced head?

The burned head of the Tehuacán child is a strange candidate for the
oldest known case of sacrifice and cannibalism in the Americas. Because
of its unusual burial context and its types of damage, we can say that the
processing was probably motivated by something other than hunger.

430

Figure 4.8. Coxcatlan Cave, Tehuacán Valley. Skull of Burial 2, a five-year-old child. Frontal view shows intentionally broken sockets of missing left and right deciduous first molars, large abscess of left incisors, and asymmetrical nasal aperture. Rear of head is burned but face is not, nor is the postcranial skeleton, indicating that the head had been cut off and then roasted. Arrows point to cut marks on frontal and maxillary bones that seem to have been made after burning (CGT neg. 4-8-94:34).

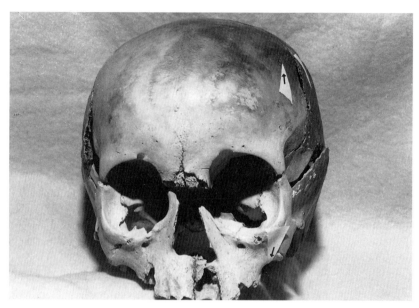

Figure 4.9. Coxcatlan Cave, Burial 2. Left side of skull showing differential burning from back to front. Arrows point to cut marks (CGT neg. 4-8-94:28).

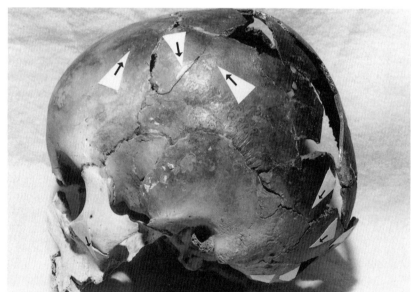

Figure 4.10. Coxcatlan Cave, Burial 2. Back of skull showing severe burning. Arrows point to cut marks (CGT neg. 4-8-94:36).

Figure 4.11. Coxcatlan Cave, Burial 2. Base of skull showing differential burning from back to front of head. Note that left temporal bone is heat-discolored, whereas the right is not, suggesting that the cranium had been crushed on the right side and the right temporal bone pushed into the vault and protected from thermal alteration. Arrows point to cut marks (CGT neg. 4-8-94:31).

Figure 4.12. Coxcatlan Cave, Burial 2. Right side of face showing burning of back of head and mandible, but no burning of face and right temporal bone. The latter must have been driven internally and protected from the roasting fire. Arrow points to polishing of tip of zygomatic process of temporal bone, which may have been produced by the impact that displaced the temporal bone. Arrow at occiput points to cut marks. Intentionally broken alveolar socket and missing deciduous right upper first molar shows directly above the lower second molar. The lack of perfect occlusion is due to ground pressure deformation (CGT neg. 4-8-94:8).

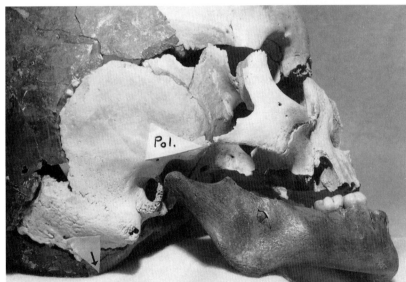

Figure 4.13. Coxcatlan Cave, Burial 2. Detail of left side of maxilla showing large severe abscess of incisor region and intentionally damaged socket of first deciduous molar. Arrow points to cut marks (CGT neg. 4-8-94:6).

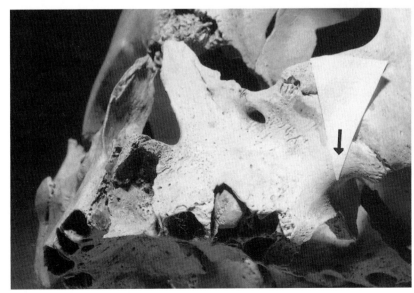

432

Figure 4.14. Coxcatlan Cave, Burial 2. Detail of right side of maxilla showing intentionally damaged socket of first deciduous molar (CGT neg. 4-8-94:3).

Figure 4.15. Coxcatlan Cave, Burial 2. Detail of external surface of parietal fragment showing perimortem damage sequence: burning, followed by breakage, then chipping along fracture plane (at arrow), and subsequent deposition of caliche in some chipping sites. Scale shows mm (CGT neg. 4-6-94:18).

Figure 4.16. Coxcatlan Cave, Burial 2. Detail of cranial vault fragment with film of carbonized organic matter adhering to internal surface, supportive of an interpretation of perimortem head roasting. Note chipping along upper internal fracture plane, which is believed to have resulted when cranium was opened to extract the cooked brain. Actual width of image in photograph is 3.3 cm (CGT neg. 4-6-94:20).

Figure 4.17. Coxcatlan Cave, Burial 2. Detail of burned parietal fragment showing abrasion on internal surface (CGT neg. 4-6-94:23).

Perhaps Aztec sacrifice and cannibalism were rooted in antecedent cultures as far back as the middle Holocene.

*Tlatelcomila*

The next earliest site whose human skeletal remains we have personally examined is that of Tlatelcomila in Tetelpan, Mexico, D.F., south of the floating gardens of Xochimilco. The human bone assemblage came from four stratigraphic pits excavated in 1972 by Rosa María Reyna Robles. The human remains date to the upper Preclassic phases of Cuatepec (Zacatenco) and Ticomán I, or 700–500 B.C. Reyna's excavations were only tests, and only her Pit D produced black, burned materials; there is no way to estimate how much more human bone was left in the ground.

Pijoan and Pastrana (1985, 1987) used this assemblage to develop their methodology for analyzing and replicating cut marks in bone. Importantly, they distinguished cut marks *on* bone from the cutting *of* bone, a distinction that could lead to different explanations. The former suggests defleshing, whereas the latter points more toward the use of bone as raw material for artifact production.

Further analysis of the Tlatelcomila series by Pijoan and Pastrana (1989) led to well-founded interpretations of ritual use of humans and their consumption by at least 500 B.C. Pijoan and Pastrana (1989:302) estimated that about 90% of the postcranial bones had been exposed to heat. They further suggested that *tzompantli* were in use by 500 B.C., since at least one skull had been broken open on the sides for mounting on a horizontal pole. There is no reason to believe that Tlatelcomila was unique or even the center of public human sacrifice and cannibalism in Mesoamerica at 700–500 B.C.

In August 1993 we studied the Tlatelcomila assemblage in the National Museum of Anthropology and History, Mexico City (figs. 4.18–4.30). As table 4.1 shows, we obtained an MNI of 18, as did Pijoan and Pastrana (1989). Given the preliminary nature of the archaeology, there likely are more unexcavated individuals with perimortem bone damage in this site. The youngest child we could identify was about three years old at death. There were other children and adults of various ages.

Figure 4.18. Tlatelcomila, Mexico, D.F. Horizontal ramus of mandible with internal cut marks (arrow) (CGT neg. 4-8-94:26).

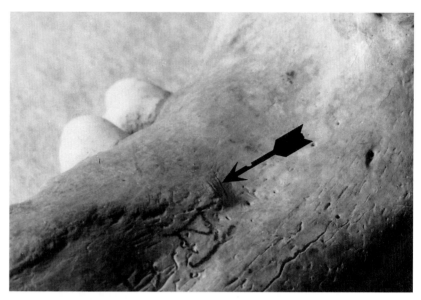

Figure 4.19. Tlatelcomila. All the remaining vertebrae for an MNI of 18. This is about 10% of expected. Only four are minimally broken. Scale is 15 cm (CGT neg. 4-7-94:15).

Figure 4.20. Tlatelcomila.
First cervical vertebra (shown in
figure 4.19 at upper right) with
fine multiple perimortem cut
marks (CGT neg. 4-7-94:13).

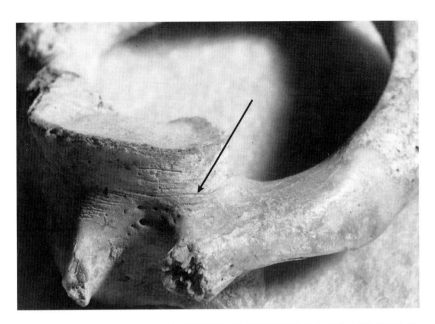

Figure 4.21. Tlatelcomila. Entire assemblage of perimortem long bone fragments without ends. Many have cut marks, abrasions, and fragment end-
polishing, and some are burned. Scale is 15 cm (CGT neg. 4-7-94:36).

436

Figure 4.22. Tlatelcomila. Femur fragments of adults, a child, and a fetus. Short fetal femur at left center is 5.8 cm long, a length indicating death at about 8 months prenatal age (CGT neg. 4-7-94:6).

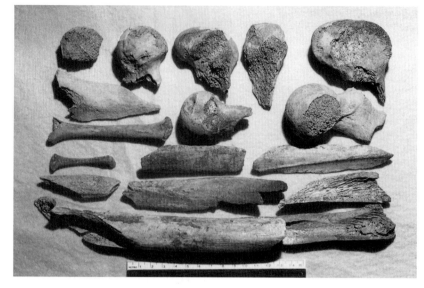

Figure 4.23. Tlatelcomila. Tibia fragments with perimortem breakage and other damage. Scale is 15 cm (CGT neg. 4-7-94:1).

Figure 4.24. Tlatelcomila. Detail of femur head showing perimortem breakage of shaft and cut marks on neck (CGT neg. 4-7-94:9).

Figure 4.25. Tlatelcomila. Detail of another femur head showing perimortem breakage and cut marks (CGT neg. 4-7-94:10).

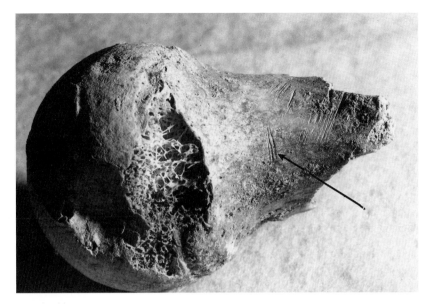

Figure 4.26. Tlatelcomila. Detail of distal end of subadult tibia showing perimortem breakage and cut marks (CGT neg. 4-7-94:34).

Figure 4.27. Tlatelcomila. Detail of distal end of femur showing perimortem breakage and crushing of cortex fragments into the cancellous bone (CGT neg. 4-7-94:35).

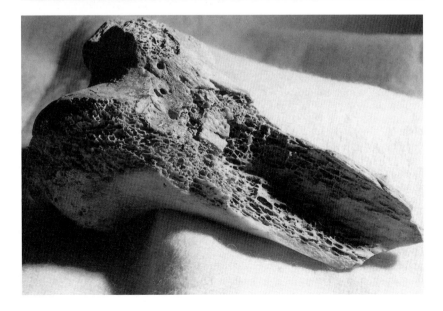

438

Figure 4.28. Tlatelcomila.
Detail of long bone fragment
showing perimortem breakage
and roughly hammered area of
cortex. Tip of bone spur on far
right has pot-polishing (CGT
neg. 4-8-94:21).

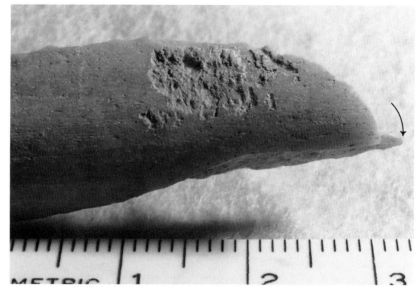

Figure 4.29. Tlatelcomila.
Detail of long bone fragment
showing perimortem breakage
and anvil abrasions interrupted
by subsequent fracture (CGT
neg. 4-8-94:23).

Figure 4.30. Tlatelcomila.
Detail of humerus fragment
showing perimortem breakage
and pot-polishing at tip on right.
Actual width of image in photograph is 3.3 cm (CGT neg.
4-7-94:4).

Table 4.1
Minimal Number of Individuals (MNI) at Tlatelcomila, Tetelpan,
Mexico, D.F.

| SKELETAL ELEMENT | AGE | SEX | NOTES |
|---|---|---|---|
| Maxilla, whole | Old adult | ? | Matches right mandible |
| | Old adult | ? | Matches whole mandible |
| Maxilla, left | 12–13 | ? | Matches whole mandible |
| | 9–10 | ? | |
| | 7 | ? | |
| | 5–6 | ? | Matches whole mandible |
| | 5 | ? | |
| Maxilla, right | 15 | ? | Matches right mandible |
| | 12–13 | ? | Matches whole mandible |
| | 11–12 | ? | No match with left maxilla |
| | 5 | ? | No match with left maxilla |
| Mandible, whole | Old adult | M | No match with maxilla |
| | Old adult | M? | No match with maxilla |
| | Old adult | ? | |
| | 12–13 | ? | |
| | 12–13 | ? | |
| | 5–6 | ? | |
| | 3 | ? | |
| Mandible, left | Adult | M? | |
| | 6 | ? | |
| Mandible, right | Old adult | ? | |
| | YA | ? | |
| | 15 | ? | |
| | 12–13 | ? | |

SUMMARY: 18 individuals. One old adult male; two adults, male?; two old adults, sex?; one young adult, sex?; five 11- to 15-year-old adolescents; seven 3- to 10-year-old children. The MNI of 18 is the same as that obtained by Pijoan and Pastrana (1989).

Table 4.2 inventories the assemblage and its perimortem damage. The cannibal signature is evident. All six minimum perimortem damage criteria are present. There was no identifiable animal damage. Here as elsewhere, we identify less burning than have other analysts. Nevertheless, we are certain that 70 pieces were burned. The relatively large number of cut marks suggests that some sort of ritual was involved, especially because so many cranial pieces were cut.

Tables 4.3 and 4.4 provide two data sets for long bone and rib fragment lengths. These are discussed in the last section of this chapter; here we note only that the lengths are remarkably similar to those of other sets. For example, the lengths of long bone fragments in different units at Leroux Wash averaged 5.7, 7.9, 2.9, 6.7, and 5.5 cm, respectively. At Tlatelcomila, they averaged 6.0 cm. For the lengths of rib fragments, the former site averaged 5.7, and the latter, 7.1 cm.

The Tlatelcomila charnel deposit is scientifically and historically important for several reasons: (1) It exhibits the taphonomic signature of cannibalism without ambiguity. The six minimal criteria are present and easy to recognize. Sample size is quite sufficient. (2) The series originates in a region of the world where ethnographic and linguistic evidence for institutionalized cannibalism is irrefutable, even by the most demanding standards of evidence. (3) The dating for Tlatelcomila is well accepted, showing that cannibalism in Mesoamerica goes back at least 25 cen-

Table 4.2
Bone Elements and Perimortem Damage at Tlatelcomila

| SKELETAL ELEMENT | WHOLE | FRAGMENT | IMPACT BREAK | ANVIL ABRASION | CUT MARK | BURN | POLISH |
|---|---|---|---|---|---|---|---|
| Cranial | | | | | | | |
| Maxilla | 2 | 9 | 9 | 0 | 1 | 0 | 0 |
| Mandible | 7 | 6 | 7 | 0 | 8 | 2 | 0 |
| Frontal | 5 | 4 | 4 | 0 | 7 | 3 | 1 |
| Parietal | 13 | 14 | 14 | 3 | 8 | 4 | 1 |
| Occipital | 1 | 10 | 10 | 0 | 4 | 2 | 0 |
| Temporal | 13 | 4 | 11 | 1 | 8 | 2 | 0 |
| Base | 0 | 11 | 10 | 0 | 1 | 2 | 0 |
| Teeth (150) | | | | | | | |
| Fragments | — | 61 | 62 | 0 | 5 | 13 | 2 |
| Postcranial | | | | | | | |
| Cervical vertebrae | 6 | 2 | 1 | 0 | 1[a] | 0 | 0 |
| Lumbar vertebrae | 0 | 1 | 1 | 0 | 1 | 0 | 0 |
| Vertebrae fragments | — | 30[b] | 25 | 0 | 1 | 0 | 0 |
| Scapula | 0 | 12 | 9 | 0 | 4 | 0 | 1 |
| Clavicle | 1 | 5 | 6 | 0 | 2 | 0 | 0 |
| Rib | 1 | 111 | 108 | 1 | 17 | 9 | 4 |
| Humerus | 0 | 4[c] | 4 | 0 | 0 | 0 | 0 |
| Radius | 1 | 2 | 2 | 0 | 1 | 0 | 0 |
| Ulna | 2 | 1 | 0 | 0 | 1 | 0 | 0 |
| Hand | 9 | 8 | 2 | 0 | 1 | 0 | 0 |
| Pelvis | 0 | 34 | 34 | 1 | 1 | 1 | 0 |
| Femur | 2 | 16 | 16 | 2 | 12 | 2 | 0 |
| Tibia | 0 | 13 | 13 | 0 | 4 | 1 | 2 |
| Fibula | 0 | 7 | 6 | 0 | 1 | 4 | 1 |
| Patella | 0 | 1 | 1 | 0 | 0 | 0 | 0 |
| Foot | 8 | 7 | 6 | 0 | 1 | 1 | 0 |
| Long bone fragments | — | 321 | 321 | 10 | 38 | 24 | 9 |
| Bone type unknown | 0 | 5[d] | 5 | 0 | 1 | 0 | 0 |
| TOTAL (770) | 71 | 699 | 687 | 18 | 129 | 70 | 21 |
| PERCENTAGE | 9.2 | 90.8 | 89.3 | 2.3 | 16.8 | 9.1 | 2.7 |

Percentage of expected vertebrae = 4.9 (21 of 432; MNI = 18).

NOTE: Only elements that were present are listed. No gnawing or chewing was observed. Impact breakage, anvil abrasions, cut marks, burning, and polishing represent perimortem damage.

a. There are at least 16 cut strokes on the left side of one first cervical vertebra. All cut marks were made with a very sharp stone tool, presumably of obsidian.
b. There are no vertebral bodies, only arches and spines. The 33 fragments equal about 15 whole vertebrae.
c. One 16.1-cm-long humerus fragment had been used as an probelike expedient tool. It had 1.2 cm of polishing on the pointed tip.
d. In addition, there are 2 burned deer-sized scapula fragments.

Table 4.3
Lengths (cm) of Unidentifiable Human Long Bone Fragments with Perimortem Breakage, Tlatelcomila

| | | | | | | |
|---|---|---|---|---|---|---|
| 6.0 | 6.6 | 8.7 | 12.1 | 11.6 | 11.6 | 11.2 |
| 17.3 | 4.1 | 2.8 | 5.9 | 2.9 | 6.2 | 3.6 |
| 9.1 | 4.9 | 5.1 | 2.9 | 3.5 | 4.0 | 8.9 |
| 3.7 | 20.8 | 7.5 | 3.2 | 3.0 | 5.6 | 5.3 |
| 2.5 | 4.5 | 4.7 | 4.4 | 4.0 | 3.5 | 2.2 |
| 3.8 | 3.8 | 8.5 | 8.6 | 7.4 | 4.4 | 5.0 |
| 6.3 | 11.9 | 10.5 | 8.7 | 7.5 | 5.2 | 4.4 |
| 7.5 | 8.4 | 4.2 | 7.7 | 11.4 | 9.6 | 6.6 |
| 4.2 | 5.4 | 3.6 | 4.8 | 3.0 | 4.2 | 4.9 |
| 4.7 | 6.8 | 4.3 | 3.0 | 4.0 | 3.0 | 2.9 |
| 3.6 | 3.5 | 3.6 | 5.8 | 4.5 | 9.5 | 4.1 |
| 15.5 | 4.6 | 4.0 | 9.3 | 9.0 | 3.8 | 9.7 |
| 8.5 | 8.8 | 13.5 | 12.5 | 11.3 | 9.0 | 9.6 |
| 10.9 | 3.2 | 3.9 | 7.1 | 4.5 | 3.0 | 3.2 |
| 2.0 | 3.3 | 3.1 | 3.0 | 4.2 | 6.9 | 5.2 |
| 8.5 | 7.5 | 8.3 | 5.6 | 3.2 | 2.5 | 3.3 |
| 4.2 | 4.8 | 7.5 | 7.3 | 9.2 | 10.8 | 10.8 |
| 10.2 | 8.2 | 3.1 | 1.9 | 3.5 | 2.1 | 2.5 |
| 3.5 | 4.9 | 3.7 | 2.6 | 3.0 | 5.9 | 4.1 |
| 4.6 | 5.4 | 5.5 | 11.0 | 9.8 | 7.0 | 11.5 |
| 4.5 | 4.3 | 5.2 | 5.7 | 7.3 | 12.8 | 12.9 |
| 14.5 | 7.0 | 2.8 | 4.1 | 2.5 | 1.5 | 2.7 |
| 2.7 | 5.1 | 2.7 | 3.5 | 4.3 | 4.6 | 2.8 |
| 5.1 | 7.1 | 5.2 | 7.8 | 6.8 | 9.4 | 5.2 |
| 3.8 | 5.2 | 7.1 | 9.2 | 8.0 | 4.6 | 7.2 |
| 5.6 | 8.6 | 3.9 | 3.0 | 2.6 | 2.5 | 3.2 |
| 2.2 | 5.9 | 3.4 | 4.6 | 4.7 | 1.8 | 4.2 |
| 4.3 | 11.9 | 7.6 | 6.7 | 5.6 | 8.0 | 3.0 |
| 8.2 | 6.1 | 6.8 | 2.6 | 10.3 | 4.4 | 12.4 |
| 3.0 | 7.1 | 14.1 | 3.7 | 6.5 | 5.0 | 8.1 |
| 6.7 | 7.4 | 12.2 | 7.4 | 5.0 | 3.9 | 7.9 |
| 3.8 | 6.5 | 3.5 | 4.1 | 9.1 | 8.0 | 7.6 |
| 5.2 | 9.0 | 12.8 | 18.4 | 9.7 | 3.3 | 6.9 |
| 8.2 | 8.4 | 11.3 | 3.6 | 4.4 | 5.9 | 4.0 |
| 8.9 | 6.5 | 5.4 | 3.3 | 4.4 | 5.0 | 3.5 |
| 4.6 | 4.2 | 5.3 | 7.4 | 9.5 | 4.9 | 8.6 |
| 10.5 | 4.6 | 7.6 | 4.1 | 3.8 | 4.6 | 4.2 |
| 5.9 | 3.5 | 3.6 | 4.2 | 4.3 | 3.8 | 3.9 |
| 7.3 | 6.0 | 4.2 | 3.8 | 6.7 | 3.9 | 4.9 |
| 2.8 | 5.2 | 4.5 | 3.8 | 4.5 | 8.0 | 4.9 |
| 4.8 | 5.3 | 4.4 | 5.7 | 5.3 | 6.6 | 3.5 |
| 5.6 | 5.6 | 5.2 | 3.0 | 4.5 | 3.8 | 4.1 |
| 2.8 | 4.0 | 3.4 | 7.9 | 4.4 | 4.4 | 7.9 |
| 3.5 | 8.7 | 8.2 | 7.2 | 5.2 | | |

N = 306.   Range = 1.5–20.8.   Mean = 6.0.   S.D. = 3.0.

NOTE: Measurements are for a sample of 306 out of 321 fragments.

Table 4.4
Lengths (cm) of Human Rib Fragments with Perimortem Breakage,
Tlatelcomila

| | | | | | | |
|---|---|---|---|---|---|---|
| 16.5 | 6.6 | 15.3 | 7.0 | 7.7 | 5.9 | 6.5 |
| 3.3 | 3.8 | 3.8 | 2.1 | 5.2 | 5.5 | 15.0 |
| 9.2 | 2.9 | 3.5 | 6.6 | 14.6 | 6.4 | 11.9 |
| 8.6 | 6.0 | 6.9 | 4.4 | 5.1 | 3.5 | 9.3 |
| 4.6 | 14.0 | 13.7 | 11.9 | 9.3 | 13.7 | 5.6 |
| 3.4 | 13.7 | 6.5 | 7.3 | 7.0 | 2.7 | 6.3 |
| 13.2 | 11.1 | 14.5 | 12.5 | 12.4 | 7.9 | 15.2 |
| 6.6 | 7.0 | 6.5 | 11.0 | 4.3 | 3.8 | 9.9 |
| 8.0 | 6.9 | 7.2 | 7.8 | 12.4 | 11.6 | 7.4 |
| 9.3 | 5.8 | 6.3 | 3.6 | 4.7 | 6.3 | 3.8 |
| 5.8 | 8.0 | 3.7 | 5.3 | 4.5 | 8.0 | 7.4 |
| 4.1 | 4.1 | 3.4 | 10.6 | 3.6 | 5.8 | 2.1 |
| 3.6 | 3.5 | 4.4 | 3.4 | 5.4 | 7.0 | 4.7 |
| 2.7 | 3.7 | 3.0 | 3.3 | 6.0 | 3.4 | 4.1 |
| 3.3 | 3.9 | 3.0 | 5.6 | 2.7 | 5.6 | 10.1 |
| 8.5 | 6.2 | 7.0 | 16.7 | 8.7 | 10.9 | 4.7 |
| 5.5 | 6.2 | 6.5 | 3.0 | 9.3 | 2.8 | 3.5 |
| 3.8 | 4.8 | 6.2 | 2.9 | 4.4 | 3.3 | 5.4 |
| 11.0 | 11.1 | 13.7 | 6.7 | 9.2 | 3.5 | 4.7 |
| 3.2 | 13.2 | 15.4 | 6.2 | 13.7 | 6.7 | 10.3 |
| 11.1 | 10.0 | 11.0 | 6.7 | 4.0 | 4.9 | 11.1 |
| 9.4 | 2.8 | | | | | |

N = 149.    Range = 2.1–16.7.    Mean = 7.1.    S.D. = 3.6.

NOTE: Measurements are for a sample of 149 fragments. An additional small package of
  bones was found for measurement, including 38 more rib fragments, so the total is not
  the same as the figure for ribs in table 4.2.

turies. (4) The assemblage has been studied independently by two teams
of analysts, and both reached the same conclusion: the perimortem damage resulted from ritual and cannibalism.

*Electra*

Another site that may meet the minimal taphonomic signature of cannibalism is that of Electra, located relatively far north in Mexico—in Villa
de Reyes, about 40 km (25 miles) south of San Luis Potosí. Béatriz
Braniff C. (1975, 1992) found damaged human remains there in 1966
during her excavation of a large enclosure or ceremonial patio that
dated between A.D. 350 and 800 (Classic period; San Luis phase of Tu-
nal Grande subarea). The stratum containing the human remains also
had the bones of hares, a large number of pottery sherds, charcoal, ash,
and other refuse.

Years later, Pijoan and Mansilla (1990a, 1990b) studied the human
remains, finding an MNI of 10: two children 0–6 years of age, two
13–20, and six adults, among whom Pijoan and Mansilla identified
three males and two females. They recognized, but did not enumerate,
perimortem breakage, burning, cut marks, and a low number of vertebrae.

In August 1993 we examined this series at INAH in Mexico City.
Nine individuals could be identified, seven of whom were adults (>18

Table 4.5
Minimal Number of Individuals (MNI) at Electra, Villa de Reyes, San
Luis Potosí, Mexico

| SKELETAL ELEMENT | AGE | SEX | NOTES |
|---|---|---|---|
| Maxilla, whole | 12–14 | ? | Matches whole mandible below |
|  | 25–30 | ? |  |
| Mandible, whole | 12–14 | ? |  |
|  | 20 | M |  |
| Mandible, left | 6 | ? |  |
| 8 L scapula | Adult | ? |  |
| 8 R scapula | Adult | ? |  |
| R scapula | Child | ? |  |

SUMMARY: Nine individuals. One adult, probable male; six adults, sex?; one 6-year-old
child; one 12- to 14-year old adolescent.

Table 4.6
Bone Elements and Perimortem Damage at Electra

| SKELETAL ELEMENT | WHOLE | FRAGMENT | IMPACT BREAK | ANVIL ABRASION | CUT MARK | POLISH | GNAWING |
|---|---|---|---|---|---|---|---|
| Cranial |  |  |  |  |  |  |  |
| Maxilla | 2 | 0 | 2 | 0 | 2 | 0 | 0 |
| Mandible | 2 | 1 | 2 | 0 | 3 | 0 | 0 |
| Frontal | 1 | 2 | 1 | 0 | 2 | 0 | 0 |
| Parietal | 2 | 5 | 2 | 0 | 4 | 0 | 0 |
| Occipital | 0 | 4 | 2 | 0 | 2 | 0 | 0 |
| Temporal | 2 | 5 | 5 | 0 | 4 | 0 | 0 |
| Base | 0 | 2 | 2 | 0 | 1 | 0 | 0 |
| Teeth (51) |  |  |  |  |  |  |  |
| Fragments | — | 13 | 13 | 0 | 2 | 0 | 0 |
| Postcranial |  |  |  |  |  |  |  |
| Cervical vertebrae | 4 | 2 | 0 | 0 | 6 | 0 | 0 |
| Lumbar vertebrae | 0 | 1 | 0 | 0 | 0 | 0 | 0 |
| Vertebrae |  |  |  |  |  |  |  |
| fragments | — | 2 | 1 | 0 | 0 | 0 | 0 |
| Scapula | 0 | 22 | 6 | 1 | 11 | 0 | 0 |
| Clavicle | 2 | 7 | 2 | 0 | 9 | 0 | 0 |
| Rib | 2 | 26 | 10[a] | 0 | 16 | 2 | 0 |
| Sternum | 0 | 3 | 0 | 0 | 1 | 0 | 0 |
| Humerus | 2 | 4 | 0 | 0 | 6 | 0 | 0 |
| Radius | 2 | 8 | 0 | 0 | 5 | 0 | 0 |
| Ulna | 1 | 7 | 0 | 0 | 6[b] | 0 | 0 |
| Pelvis | 0 | 20 | 0 | 0 | 9 | 0 | 0 |
| Femur | 0 | 12 | 11 | 2 | 12 | 1 | 0 |
| Tibia | 0 | 4 | 2 | 1 | 3 | 0 | 0 |
| Fibula | 0 | 15 | 2 | 0 | 12 | 0 | 0 |
| Foot | 4 | 1 | 2 | 0 | 0 | 0 | 1 |
| Long bone |  |  |  |  |  |  |  |
| fragments | — | 16 | 16 | 5 | 6 | 2 | 0 |
| TOTAL (208) | 26 | 182 | 81 | 9 | 122 | 5 | 1 |
| PERCENTAGE | 12.5 | 87.5 | 38.9 | 4.3 | 58.6 | 2.4 | 0.5 |

Percentage of expected vertebrae = 4.2 (9 of 216; MNI = 9).

NOTE: Only elements that were present are listed. No unequivocal signs of burning were
observed. Impact breakage, anvil abrasions, cut marks, and polishing represent perimortem damage. Gnawing is postmortem damage.

a. Ten of the 26 ribs had "snap" breakage.
b. One ulna fragment had at least 55 cut marks. These are short, delicate (made with an
obsidian tool?), and repetitious and show "no sign of anger."

Table 4.7
Lengths (cm) of Human Bone Fragments with Perimortem Breakage,
Electra

| Long Bones | | | | | | |
|---|---|---|---|---|---|---|
| 6.3 | 7.1 | 14.6 | 6.1 | 10.8 | 14.7 | 7.2 |
| 7.9 | 14.8 | 8.3 | 11.3 | 7.2 | 11.6 | 7.0 |
| 5.1 | 7.9 | | | | | |
| Ribs | | | | | | |
| 22.1 | 19.2 | 20.6 | 20.1 | 18.0 | 15.7 | 10.4 |
| 15.3 | 16.0 | 7.5 | 8.4 | | | |

Long Bones: N = 16.   Range = 5.1–14.8.   Mean = 9.2.   S.D. = 3.3.
Ribs: N = 11.   Range = 7.5–22.1.   Mean = 15.7.   S.D. = 5.0.

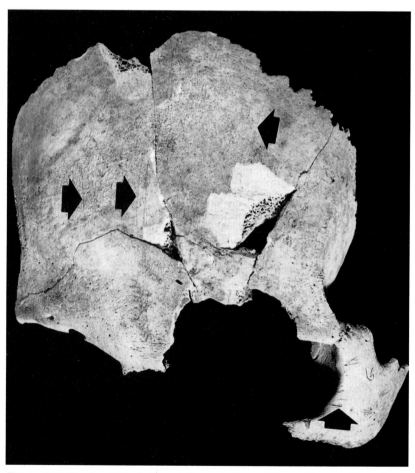

Figure 4.31. Electra, Villa de Reyes, San Luis Potosí. Frontal bone with perimortem cut marks and breakage. (Photograph by R. Enríquez, Laboratorio
DAF-INAH, Mexico City; courtesy Carmen María Pijoan Aguadé, April 1994.)

years). We could confidently identify the sex of only one male (table 4.5). As table 4.6 shows, most of the assemblage was fragmentary, and there were many pieces with cut marks (fig. 4.31). One ulna fragment had as many as 55 very fine cut marks. The assemblage was generally well preserved. All of the minimal criteria for hypothesizing cannibalism were present except for unequivocal signs of burning. Pijoan and Mansilla (1990a:90, 94), however, said they identified burning based on modification of the trabeculae and the appearance of cuts and fractures, which they believed indicated cooking. As we mentioned in chapter 3, we have difficulty identifying threshold levels of burning, and such is the situation for Electra.

On average, the lengths of broken long bones and ribs were greater at Electra than at Tlatelcomila. The Electra sample size, however, is very small (table 4.7), and collecting procedures for the two sites probably differed to some degree. Small pieces of burned bone could have been missed at Electra or misidentified as faunal remains. All things considered, including depositional context, we are inclined to agree with Pijoan and Mansilla that some cooking of one or more Electra individuals probably took place. Considering the many, often delicate cut marks, there probably was ritual processing of the bodies as well.

*Alta Vista*

Another site in northern Mexico displays, in our opinion, no firm evidence of cannibalism—though it remains a strong possibility—but instead provides a great deal of useful comparative data on sacrificial body processing. Alta Vista, a ceremonial complex of the Chalchihuites culture, is located in the state of Zacatecas, about 95 km (60 miles) southeast of Durango. It encompasses several large constructions including a sunken plaza, a pyramid, a columned hall, an astronomical observatory, and two long, low, undulating walls that form feathered serpents. It also had a temple skull rack. These and other features give Alta Vista a strong albeit rough Mesoamerican quality.

Ellen A. Kelley (1978) described Alta Vista architectural and human skeletal finds made in the mid-1970s at the Temple of the Skulls. Carbon-14 dates suggested that the temple was built around A.D. 652 and used until 756 or 860, in the early Alta Vista phase (late Classic to early Postclassic). Use of the temple ceased before Alta Vista was abandoned around 1050.

Kelley found disarticulated human bones directly on the plastered floor in the northern corner of the approximately 5 by 5 m (16 by 16 feet) temple room. She recovered 21 crania (of which at least one seemed to be female), 14 mandibles, 9 femurs, 1 tibia, 1 humerus, 11 probable arm bone shaft fragments, 4 innominate bones, and 1 vertebra, probably cervical. She reported (1978:109) that many of the crania had holes drilled "postmortem" at their apexes. Several mandibles were tentatively identified as having belonged to young and middle-aged adult males; one was believed to have been about 17 years old, on the basis of minimal third molar eruption. Kelley (1978:115) thought the bones had not simply been scattered on the floor:

> The bones and skulls, however, had been positioned very carefully in the locations in which they were found. Lastly, unlike many other areas of the site, this temple showed no evidence of burning. . . . The

conclusion is inescapable that trophy heads (probably defleshed skulls) and long bones are represented in this collection and that they were suspended from a bone rack or from the roof or walls of the temple. At the time of abandonment of the temple, or subsequently, the bone rack was dismantled and the skulls were taken down and neatly arranged on the floor.

Kelley concluded that cannibalism had occurred at Alta Vista, because it was thought by the Spaniards to have been associated with the saving of skulls and bones of enemies in ceremonial houses. She noted that the distribution of skull and long bone suspension was poorly known for northwestern Mesoamerica. Her only other cited bone-suspension site was Casas Grandes, where Di Peso and his associates believed scalped, drilled, and undrilled trophy heads to have been part of a Mesoamerican ritual complex, possibly that of Xipe Totec and possibly linked with cannibalism.

Like La Quemada, Alta Vista has a Hall of Columns. In the Alta Vista hall, below the floor, excavators found a strongly Mesoamerican-like burial dating A.D. 300–500. It consisted of the headless skeleton of a 16- to 22-year-old covered with many other human bones, including two rows of four skulls each, all about the same age as the principal burial. J. Charles Kelley (1974:34) described it this way: "The status burial found in our 1971 excavations at Alta Vista . . . consisted of one relatively intact skeleton covered by the sorted and stacked bones of several young adults. A broken flute, decorated in paint cloisonné technique, lay at the top of the stack of bones and the mid-section of a sacrificial knife of red obsidian lay a few feet away. Obviously human sacrifice is indicated, probably in honor of Tezcatlipoca, in view of the flute."

On the floor of a structure (No. 3) located south of the Hall of Columns was found a mass of disarticulated adult long bones showing cut marks and burning. The context and bone types suggested to Robert B. Pickering (1974:242–246) that the bones might represent cannibalism or that structure 3 was a depository for defleshed bones.

Thomas Holien and Robert Pickering (1978) reviewed the young headless male burial in the Hall of Columns, noting an extra pair of disarticulated legs. The primary burial was capped with earth and then overlaid by a deposit of long bones and skulls with the disarticulated mandibles of eight young males, also 16 to 22 years old. Concerning the extra pair of legs in the primary burial, Holien and Pickering (1978:148) wrote: "In view of what appears to have been common practice at this ceremonial center, [the legs] probably constituted ritual food. . . . The Alta Vista attendants, disarticulated and with small bones apparently discarded, may have constituted the provision for ritual feasting."

With respect to other human remains found at Alta Vista, Holien and Pickering (1978:146) noted that "there is a variety of burial types elsewhere at the site, including an infant urn burial, cremations in a cyst, and ossuary caches of selected bones, some of which show cutting marks at the muscle attachments. Butchering for food is our present supposition."

Later Pickering (1985:322) published a paper supportive of E. Kelley's previously mentioned views on mortuary practices and cannibalism, saying: "The [taphonomic] data strongly indicate that systematic

Table 4.8
Skeletal Elements from Alta Vista, by Age Group

| AGE | NUMBER OF ELEMENTS | PERCENT |
|---|---|---|
| Infant | 327 | 5.5 |
| Child | 805 | 13.5 |
| Adult | 4,620 | 77.5 |
| Unknown | 206 | 3.5 |

SOURCE: Pickering (1985).
NOTE: Ages in years were not specified.

Table 4.9
Damage Frequencies for Skeletal Elements from Alta Vista

| BODY PART | Burned | | Cut | | Perforated | |
|---|---|---|---|---|---|---|
| | NO. | % | NO. | % | NO. | % |
| Skull | 225 | 27.5 | 42 | 5.2 | 33 | 4.1 |
| Thorax | 89 | 7.8 | 11 | 1.0 | 0 | — |
| Pectoral Girdle | 215 | 18.1 | 96 | 8.1 | 0 | — |
| Pelvic Girdle | 176 | 19.1 | 66 | 7.2 | 0 | — |
| Foot | 64 | 8.7 | 28 | 3.8 | 0 | — |
| Hand | 40 | 6.3 | 2 | 0.3 | 0 | — |
| Teeth | 12 | 2.3 | 17 | 3.2 | 0 | — |

TOTAL ISOLATED BONES = 5,949.

SOURCE: Pickering (1985).

Table 4.10
MNI Count for Alta Vista Skeletal Elements

| ELEMENT | SIDE | INFANT | CHILD | ADULT |
|---|---|---|---|---|
| Humerus | L | 3 | 11 | 83 |
| | R | 1 | 12 | 72 |
| Femur | L | 5 | 6 | 49 |
| | R | 7 | 7 | 52 |
| Cranium | | 2 | 2 | 35 |

SOURCE: Pickering (1985).

dismemberment of the bodies was being practiced but the problem of who was receiving this dubious honor is still unclear. . . . There is strong evidence for the curation of remains from members of the Alta Vista population at the same time that there is evidence [from size and form] that head taking included people from within and outside the society. Similarly, it appears that sacrifice also affected Alta Vistans and their neighbors."

Tables 4.8–4.10 provide observations made by Pickering (1985) that succinctly characterize the Alta Vista perimortem human taphonomic situation. In sum, they show that all ages are represented, the MNI is 95, burned bones and cut marks are abundant (even some teeth are cut), and skulls have been perforated for suspension.

Pickering (1985:314) provided a line drawing of a skeleton that showed the locations of all the Alta Vista cut marks. They were limited to the distal ends of the lower leg, distal and proximal ends of the femur, distal end of the humerus, and lower cervical vertebrae. His figure 12.2 shows a cranium without its mandible. Cuts occur on the side of the frontal and parietal, more or less following the temporal muscle line. There also are cuts above and slightly posterior to the external auditory meatus, and the drawing shows a coronal arc of cuts on the parietals about two-thirds of the distance back from the front of the skull. No cuts are indicated for the face or occipital areas.

Pickering (1985:321) addressed four research questions about the Alta Vista human remains. First, why were so many bones found as isolated specimens instead of as articulated skeletons? He answered that the area excavated was a ceremonial precinct, not a mortuary site, and human bodies were used in religious functions, including postmortem curation. Second, were the isolated bones distributed randomly with respect to age and sex? He found a definite excess of adults and a possible excess of males. Body parts were also nonrandomly selected (table 4.9).

Third, what sorts of cultural modifications did the bones receive? Pickering found, on the basis of cut locations, that bodies had been systematically dismembered. The cut marks on the crania indicated beheading and probably skinning. Cranial vault perforation was fairly common. Most perforated skulls seem to have been those of adult males, although one female was identified. Only adults had their skulls perforated. Bone burning seemed to have occurred when some buildings burned, but certain elements were burned more often than others. Some type of cultural selection was operating that favored skulls and long bones, similar perhaps to the situation in the Hall of Columns at La Quemada, where a mass of human bones lacking heads and feet was deposited and covered with post-abandonment debris.

Fourth, what was the relationship between mortuary practice and social organization? Pickering (1985:323) felt that the osteological, mortuary, and other data pointed to a "high degree of organization and sophistication on the part of the Alta Vista residents." Nothing in the processing, however, helped to identify who the victims were—Alta Vistans or their neighbors. Pickering pointed out that Moser (1973) cited what Santaren, a missionary among the Acaxee in the early seventeenth century, had noted: namely, that enemies were cooked and the bones saved as trophies. Pickering also cited Beals (1932, 1943) as saying that the Acaxee, Xixime, Tepehuane, Cora, and Cahita cannibalized the remains of "valiant warriors" killed or captured in combat.

In 1994, with help from Olga Villanueva Sánchez, Peter Jiménez Betts, and Baudelina Lydia García Urouga, we examined a sample of the Alta Vista skeletal collection curated in the INAH Franciscan Monastery Museum in Guadalupe, Zacatecas. The human remains had been excavated in the 1970s by Ellen Kelley (1978) as formal burials, sacrifices, and a large number of isolated, randomly occurring bones in various locations among the buildings, pyramids, great plaza, and other features, including her Temple of the Skulls. Most of the sample had been exam-

Table 4.11
Numbers of Bones or Pieces with Perimortem Damage in a Selected
Sample of Skeletal Remains from Alta Vista (including Temple of
Skulls), Mexico

| SKELETAL ELEMENT, BY BAG | BREAK | BURN | CUT | GNAW/ CHEW | PROVENIENCE |
|---|---|---|---|---|---|
| Skull[a] | 1 | — | 1 | — | LCBJ 3-A 1975 |
| Skull[a] | — | — | 1 | — | LCBJ 3-A Str.4 1975 |
| Skull[b] | — | — | 1 | — | LCBJ 3-A Str.3 1975 |
| Mandible | — | — | 1 | 1R | LCBJ 3-1 Str.2C 1975 |
| Mandible | — | — | 1 | — | LCBJ 3-1 Str.2C 1975 |
| Occipital frag. | — | — | 1 | — | LCBJ 3-1 Str.2C 1975 |
| Parietal frag. | 1 | — | 1 | — | LCBJ 3-1 Str.2C 1975 |
| Vault frag. | 1 | — | — | — | LCBJ 3-1 Str.2C 1975 |
| Temporal frag. | — | — | 1 | — | LCBJ 3-1 Str.2C 1975 |
| Mastoids | 5 | — | 5 | — | LCBJ 3-1 Str.2C 1975 |
| Maxilla frags. | — | — | 4 | — | LCBJ 3-1 Str.2C 1975 |
| Vault frags. | 40 | — | 15 | — | LCBJ 3-1 Str.2C 1975 |
| Zygomatic frags. | 6 | — | 3 | — | LCBJ 3-1 Str.2C 1975 |
| Radius | 2 | — | 2 | — | LCBJ 3-1 Str.2C 1975 |
| Tibia | — | — | 1 | — | LCBJ 3-1 Str.2C 1975 |
| Femurs | 2 | — | 2 | — | LCBJ 3-1 Str.2C 1975 |
| Tibias | — | 2 | 2 | — | LCBJ 3-1 Str.2 1974 |
| Tibia | — | — | 1? | — | LCBJ 3-1 Str.2 1974 |
| Tibia, frag. | — | 1[c] | — | — | LCBJ 3-1 Str.2 1974 |
| Tibia, frags. | 11 | — | — | — | LCBJ 3-1 Str.2 1974 |
| Tibia, frags. | 6 | 6 | — | — | LCBJ 3-1 Str.2 1974 |
| Tibia, frags. | 4 | — | 4 | — | LCBJ 3-1 Str.2 1974 |
| Tibia, frags. | 2 | 2 | 2 | — | LCBJ 3-1 Str.2 1974 |
| Tibia | — | — | — | 1C | LCBJ 3-1 Str.2 1974 |
| Tibia | — | — | 1[d] | — | LCBJ 3-1 Str.2 1974 |
| Long bone frags. | 24 | 24 | — | — | LCBJ 3-1 A.V.Str.2V74 |
| Long bone frags. | 4 | 4 | 4 | — | LCBJ 3-1 A.V.Str.2V74 |
| Long bone frags. | 6 | 6 | — | — | LCBJ 3-1 A.V.Str.2V74 |
| Long bone frags. | Many | Many | — | — | LCBJ 3-1 1974 |
| Long bone frag. | — | 1 | 1 | — | LCBJ 3-1 1974 |
| Small frags. | Many | — | — | — | No number on bag |

SOURCE: Observations by authors, April 13, 1994, in Guadalupe, Zacatecas.
NOTE: In column 5, R denotes rodent; C, carnivore.

a. Two holes also drilled near apex of skull.
b. Skull has severe frontal deformation.
c. Burned in mid-shaft region, after flesh had been removed.
d. Abrasions are also present, but they seem to be more the result of rubbing than of striking, possibly due to the bone's having been cleaned instead of smashed.

Figure 4.32. Alta Vista, Zacatecas. Internal view of cranium showing small perimortem hole at apex. It appears to have been punched from the inside. The hole would have served to attach a cord to hang the skull in a shrine or on a skull rack. (Courtesy Robert B. Pickering, Denver Museum of Natural History.)

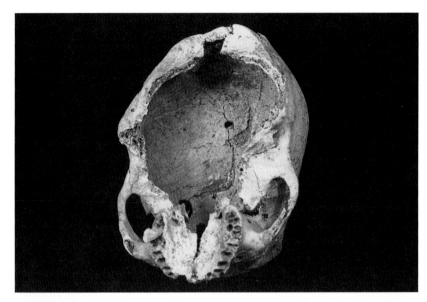

Figure 4.33. Cerro el Huistle, Huejuquilla, Jalisco (southwest of Alta Vista). This is another location where skulls were perforated for hanging in shrines or on skull racks. Shown is an external view of the apex perforation. The spalling shows clearly that the perforation was punched from the inside. (Photograph by R. Enríquez, Laboratorio DAF-INAH, Mexico City; courtesy Carmen María Pijoan Aguadé, April 1994).

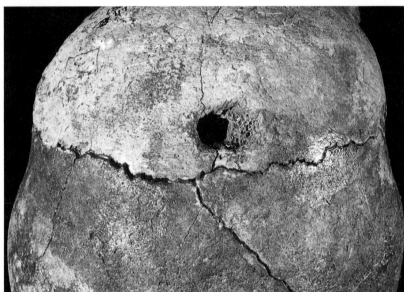

Figure 4.34. Alta Vista, Zacatecas. Distal humerus showing perimortem cut marks suitably located for cutting the arm in half at the elbow joint. The midshaft break appears to be postmortem because of its lack of spiraling. (Courtesy Robert B. Pickering, Denver Museum of Natural History.)

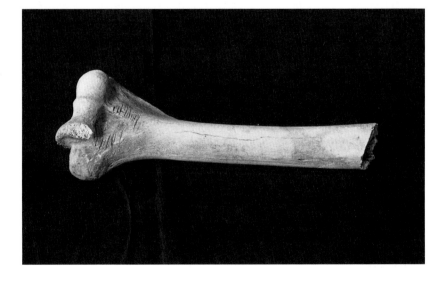

ined previously by Pickering (1985). Our observations are presented in table 4.11.

Comparing our data with Pickering's, there is excellent agreement on the kinds of body parts discarded inside the ceremonial center—mainly cranial and long bone fragments. In addition to Pickering's examples of joint dismemberment, decapitation, head flaying, and skull apex drilling (figs. 4.32–4.34), we also found perimortem long bone breakage. By identifying "spot burning" and bone surface checking we determined that some limbs had been defleshed, perhaps only by natural decay, before exposure to heat. Some of the bone burning was postmortem and perhaps was associated with burned building materials that Pickering (1985:301) said were carbon-14 dated at A.D. 525. The roasting pattern found in Anasazi charnel deposits was not evident in the pattern of burned Alta Vista bones.

Overall, preservation was fair to poor, although some fragments were very well preserved, retaining ivory hardness and color—a condition we and others have suggested can result from bone boiling. Most bones evidenced a flaky-to-checked surface weathering, signaling exposure to sunlight and repeated changes in temperature, humidity, and microbe activity. If there had been anvil abrasions or polishing on the specimens we examined, weathering had since obliterated them.

The possibility of cannibalism at Alta Vista, which Pickering (1985) hinted at by citing Spanish accounts for regional ritual cannibalism of enemy warriors and the curation of their bones, is not demonstrable using the Anasazi taphonomic signature. The Alta Vista and Anasazi damage characteristics are different. If cannibalism occurred at Alta Vista, then the body processing pathway differed from that of the Anasazi sites, where roasting and boiling signs can be identified. The Alta Vista sample has taphonomic characteristics more like many of the human remains found in ceremonial centers farther south in Mesoamerica (Pijoan and Pastrana 1985). Nevertheless, Alta Vista, like those southern centers, provides unquestionable proof of body processing on a substantial scale.

The unanswered question is, where did all the flesh go that apparently was stripped from these individuals? In the seven structural excavation units with disarticulated and isolated human skeletal and dental remains, Pickering (1985:312) obtained an MNI of 97 (3 infants, 11 children, 83 adults). This would be a minimum of 2,430 kg (5,400 pounds) of edible protein and fat (90 persons × 27 kg). Excavation and food refuse recovery from residential areas in or near Alta Vista are needed to better assess the question of whether cannibalism was practiced there. However, given the previously mentioned apparent sacrifice to Tezcatlipoca, the two snake wall structures that seemingly symbolize Quetzalcoatl, and two recently discovered snake and bird petroglyphs in the observatory structure—all ideological elements associated with later Aztec cannibalism—it would be surprising if excavations in refuse areas away from the ceremonial complex failed to turn up human remains with the taphonomic signature of cannibalism.

*Tlatelolco*

The last site we discuss for which we have personally examined human skeletal remains is the ceremonial center of Tlatelolco in Mexico City. It exemplifies the importance of context in ruling cannibalism *out*. In

1962, Francisco González Rul (1963) conducted excavations in the area northwest of the main pyramid. An orderly mass of 170 crania was found in front of a low platform with west-facing stairs. A few of the crania were each associated with two or three cervical vertebrae. These skulls were the in situ remains of a *tzompantli,* or skull rack. Its chronological age has not been precisely determined, but bone preservation was very good, suggesting no great antiquity.

Years later, Pijoan, Pastrana, and Maquivar (1989) carried out a detailed study of cut marks on 100 of the crania. They first determined that their sample contained 42 female crania, 55 male, and three whose sex could not be determined. The last three were from subadults. Out of the 100 crania, only one had no cut marks or holes on either side of the head through which the rack pole was inserted. The rack holes were generally circular, having been produced with a sharp-pointed punch or chisel. The holes varied in diameter from about 5 to 10 cm (2 to 4 inches).

The cut marks were generally quite delicate and very numerous, suggesting to Pijoan, Pastrana, and Maquivar the use of razor-sharp obsidian blades. A few cut marks had a saw-toothed edge, which might have been produced by a knife or scraper. Cut marks were most frequently found above and below the orbits, above the upper teeth, along the back of the head, along the temporal area and mastoids, and along the crest of the head from front to rear. About 5% of the crania had cut marks around the distal border of the foramen magnum. The majority of the cut marks that Pijoan, Pastrana, and Maquivar found were in appropriate locations for severing the head and then removing its skin and attached muscle tissue. The Tlatelolco mandibles had many cut marks, particularly on the posterior border of the ascending ramus but also on the inner surface of the horizontal ramus. These interior surface cut marks suggested removal of the tongue. Mandibles with interior surface cut marks suggesting tongue removal have turned up in the U.S. Southwest at Houck K, White House, and La Plata 23.

In August 1993 we studied the Tlatelolco series in the National Museum of Anthropology and History, coming up with 136 crania, almost that many mandibles, and a few vertebrae (table 4.12). Like Pijoan and her associates, we found many cut marks—more than 90% of the skulls and vertebrae had one or more. In addition, 12.5% of the skulls had anvil abrasions, and five (1.8%) showed unequivocal burning. Facial mutilation included the blowing out of one or more alveolar tooth sockets and the crushing or breaking of a large part of the maxilla, usually in association with damage to the nasal bones. Some of this mutilation, if not all, could have occurred when the rack holes were being punched through the sides of the head. The same explanation probably underlies the occurrence of anvil abrasions.

If damage type frequencies alone were used to hypothesize cannibalism at Tlatelolco, this series would almost meet the minimal test, lacking only pot-polishing. Even the amount of breakage (though not the type) could be used in the cannibal argument. However, context carries the day here, as does the high frequency of whole pieces and the high frequency of cut marks. Hence, this skull rack series provides a useful baseline for identifying intensive special processing associated with sacrifice,

Table 4.12
Bone Elements and Perimortem Damage in Human Remains from the
Skull Rack at Tlatelolco, Mexico, D.F.

| SKELETAL ELEMENT | WHOLE | FRAGMENT | IMPACT BREAK | ANVIL ABRASION | CUT MARK | BURN |
|---|---|---|---|---|---|---|
| Cranium | 136 | 0 | 133 | 33 | 135 | 5 |
| Mandible | 125 | 0 | 3 | 2 | 124 | 0 |
| Cervical vertebrae | | | | | | |
| C-1 | 4 | 7 | 0 | 0 | 2 | 0 |
| C-2 | 1 | 2 | 0 | 0 | 1 | 0 |
| Fragments | — | 6 | 0 | 0 | 0 | 0 |
| TOTAL (281) | 266 | 15 | 136 | 35 | 262 | 5 |
| PERCENTAGE | 94.7 | 5.3 | 48.4 | 12.5 | 93.2 | 1.8 |

NOTE: Only elements that were present are listed. No polishing, gnawing, or chewing was observed. Impact breakage, anvil abrasions, cut marks, and burning represent perimortem damage.

flaying, decapitation, flesh removal, and the mounting of crania for public exhibit.

**Some Statistical Comparisons**

AS WE REMARKED for the Southwest at the end of chapter 3, we doubt whether the various ways in which the Mexican human charnel assemblages were generated, deposited, excavated, and preserved were sufficiently similar to warrant formal statistical comparisons. We do, however, want to attempt some "scientific generalization," so we make a few comparisons, largely between Tlatelcomila and Electra, on one hand, and U.S. Southwestern sites on the other.

We first ran chi-square comparisons (table 4.13) between pairs of bone assemblages, both human and nonhuman, for the frequencies of different types of perimortem damage: anvil abrasions, burning, cut marks, and polishing (3 d.f.). We excluded breakage because of potential sampling problems due to the lack of screening.

The relatively small human bone sample from Electra was compared only with the pronghorn antelope series. The very large chi-square value (138.1) is due mainly to the Electra sample's lacking burning and having much more cutting than the pronghorn sample. These comparisons support the view already expressed that there might have been ritual processing at Electra; cannibalism might have been only a minor component of the perimortem damage (the Mesoamerican ethnohistoric literature is nearly silent about the roasting of human flesh). Another possibility is that the increased cutting may be related to the greater abundance and availability of razor-sharp obsidian for fine cutting tools in Mesoamerica than in the U.S. Southwest.

The comparison between Tlatelcomila and antelope also produced a significant difference, but a smaller one than that between Electra and antelope. Again, ritual cutting of the humans is possible, although the cannibal signature is patently evident at Tlatelcomila.

Most of the comparisons between Tlatelcomila and human bone samples from the U.S. Southwest yielded significant differences. In the cases of Canyon Butte 3, Leroux Wash, and Small House, the differences

Table 4.13
Chi-Square Comparisons of Frequencies of Perimortem Damage Types in U.S. and Mexican Large Animal and Human Bone Assemblages (3 d.f.)

| PAIR | X² | P |
|---|---|---|
| Electra + Antelope | 138.1 | <0.01 |
| Tlatelcomila + Antelope | 59.1 | <0.01 |
| Tlatelcomila + Canyon Butte 3 | 188.7 | <0.01 |
| Tlatelcomila + Sambrito | 94.9 | <0.01 |
| Tlatelcomila + Polacca Wash | 82.8 | <0.01 |
| Tlatelcomila + Leroux Wash | 114.8 | <0.01 |
| Tlatelcomila + Peñasco Blanco | 72.7 | <0.01 |
| Tlatelcomila + La Plata 23 | 65.7 | <0.01 |
| Tlatelcomila + Small House | 38.6 | <0.01 |
| Tlatelcomila + Fence Lake | 65.2 | <0.01 |
| Tlatelcomila + Teec Nos Pos | 0.5 | >0.80 |
| Tlatelcomila + La Plata Hwy. 37592 | 13.7 | <0.01 |
| Tlatelcomila + La Plata Hwy. 37593 | 7.6 | >0.05 |
| Tlatelcomila + San Juan River | 10.4 | <0.05 |
| Tlatelcomila + Houck K | 30.0 | <0.01 |

were mainly because the Tlatelcomila sample displayed much more cutting. In the cases of Sambrito, Polacca Wash, La Plata 23, and San Juan River, the differences were largely a result of Tlatelcomila's having both more cutting and less burning. We have no way to evaluate whether the burning frequency at Tlatelcomila is relatively low due to sampling and excavation procedures or for some other reason.

Tlatelcomila and Peñasco Blanco differ significantly; cutting is once again responsible, but in this case so also is the *greater* amount of burning in Tlatelcomila.

Tlatelcomila and Fence Lake differ significantly because cutting is very high and anvil abrasions are low in the former. In the significant difference between Tlatelcomila and La Plata Highway LA37592, small sample size in the latter is probably a contributing factor. The final significant difference, that between Tlatelcomila and Houck K, is interesting because the cutting frequency in the former is relatively low and the amount of burning high. As discussed in chapter 3, the large amount of cutting on the Houck K crania may be evidence for some sort of ritual flaying.

Finally, two pairs showed no significant difference. In the case of Tlatelcomila and Teec Nos Pos, this is attributable to small sample size and to the absence of anvil abrasions and polishing in the latter. For Tlatelcomila and La Plata Highway LA37593, the small sample size of the latter makes any interpretation doubtful.

In sum, the Tlatelcomila series has all of the perimortem damage features of the cannibal signature, but it differs significantly from most of the U.S. assemblages because of its greater amount of cutting. This attribute may be due to some ritual processing beyond simple butchering and flesh removal. It might also be due to the abundance of obsidian in the Valley of Mexico—an excellent material for very sharp knives and blades.

Besides testing for differences and similarities in the frequencies of damage types, we compared assemblages in terms of lengths of bone fragments. For many years analysts have observed that long bones and ribs found in human charnel deposits were broken into rather uniform lengths (Turner and Morris 1970). This observation suggested some underlying reason such as the breaking of bones with their adhering bits of flesh and marrow in order to fit them into a cooking vessel. Despite this apparent uniformity, fragment length has never been considered a strong candidate for an attribute required to be present before cannibalism can be suggested for a charnel deposit. One reason has been the lack of published measurements of fragment length. Hence, we made measurements for six assemblages—four of human and two of nonhuman animal bone—to see whether there was sufficient uniformity to propose length as an additional criterion. These measurements have been presented in various tables in this book. The *t*-test results for differences between the means of long bone fragment lengths in various sample pairs are given in table 4.14, and for rib fragment lengths in table 4.15. Table 4.16 gives the measurements we made in April 1994 of some nonhuman long bone fragments from the Mexican site of Tula; these were used in the *t*-tests summarized in table 4.14.

Of 15 possible comparisons between long bone samples, 9 were significantly different and 6 were not (table 4.14). This is more than would have been expected on the basis of chance alone had there been no underlying singular cause for the length—that is, had breakage been determined by the universe of possible agencies that could have affected these assemblages. Of the six groups used here, Tlatelcomila and Leroux Wash have the lowest, and nearly identical, average fragment lengths (5.9 and 6.0 cm, respectively), whereas Electra has the largest average (9.2 cm). The unweighted mean for the six groups is 7.5 cm (ca. 3 inches). Although there probably is a bone property or mechanical component to this apparent uniformity, we tentatively propose that a mean long bone fragment length of between 6.0 and 9.0 cm be added to the list of criteria for hypothesizing cannibalism. However, breakage length and breakage frequency are surely interdependent to some extent, so adding fragment length as a criterion is not adding a completely independent variable. Breakage length is a more qualitative aspect of these bone assemblages. Note also that fragment length as referred to here is based on fragments that lacked ends, which, had they been present, would have made the bone elements easy to identify. The fragments measured for this exercise were those that were unidentifable or not easily identifiable.

Rib fragment length was not measured for Tula nonhuman animals because sample size was too small. Thus, there are ten possible comparisons of rib fragment measurements (table 4.15). Much to our surprise, all but one pair (Peñasco Blanco and Tlatelcomila) showed statistically significant *t* values. These nine significant values suggest that average rib fragment length lacks sufficient universality to be considered a cross-cultural and interspecies criterion for the taphonomic definition of cannibalism in the U.S. Southwest and Mexico. Nevertheless, we remain struck by the intraseries uniformity. Average rib fragment length and

Table 4.14
Results of *t*-Tests for Mean Long Bone Fragment Lengths in U.S. and Mexican Large Animal and Human Assemblages

| PAIR | T | P | SIGNIFICANT |
|------|---|---|-------------|
| Leroux Wash + Antelope | 10.32 | <.01 | Yes |
| Leroux Wash + Peñasco Blanco | 8.56 | <.01 | Yes |
| Leroux Wash + Tlatelcomila | 0.37 | >.50 | No |
| Leroux Wash + Electra | 4.90 | <.01 | Yes |
| Leroux Wash + Tula animal | 2.18 | <.05 | Yes |
| Antelope + Peñasco Blanco | 1.69 | >.05 | No |
| Antelope + Tlatelcomila | 9.04 | <.01 | Yes |
| Antelope + Electra | 0.84 | >.40 | No |
| Antelope + Tula animal | 2.11 | >.02 | Yes |
| Peñasco Blanco + Tlatelcomila | 7.62 | <.01 | Yes |
| Peñasco Blanco + Electra | 1.06 | >.30 | No |
| Peñasco Blanco + Tula animal | 1.81 | >.05 | No |
| Tlatelcomila + Electra | 3.90 | <.05 | Yes |
| Tlatelcomila + Tula animal | 1.41 | >.10 | No |
| Electra + Tula animal | 2.01 | >.02 | Yes |

Table 4.15
Results of *t*-Tests for Mean Rib Fragment Lengths in U.S. and Mexican Large Animal and Human Assemblages

| PAIR | T | P | SIGNIFICANT |
|------|---|---|-------------|
| Electra + Antelope | 2.87 | <.01 | Yes |
| Electra + Peñasco Blanco | 5.45 | <.01 | Yes |
| Electra + Leroux Wash | 6.61 | <.01 | Yes |
| Electra + Tlatelcomila | 5.48 | <.01 | Yes |
| Antelope + Peñasco Blanco | 7.24 | <.01 | Yes |
| Antelope + Leroux Wash | 12.36 | <.01 | Yes |
| Antelope + Tlatelcomila | 8.32 | <.01 | Yes |
| Peñasco Blanco + Leroux Wash | 3.69 | <.01 | Yes |
| Peñasco Blanco + Tlatelcomila | 0.35 | >.50 | No |
| Leroux Wash + Tlatelcomila | 3.92 | <.01 | Yes |

Table 4.16
Lengths (cm) of Animal Long Bone Fragments with Perimortem Breakage, from Bone Refuse, Tula, Mexico

| | | | | | | |
|-----|-----|-----|------|-----|-----|-----|
| 7.8 | 5.0 | 9.1 | 6.8 | 7.2 | 3.7 | 5.9 |
| 9.5 | 4.0 | 6.8 | 11.1 | | | |

N = 11.   Range = 3.7–11.1.   Mean = 7.0 cm.

SOURCE: Data collected by authors, April 5, 1994.

NOTE: As part of the Tula Project, in July 1980, Susana Gómez S. excavated in the habitation area at Charnay. Fill was screened. Remains are well preserved and exhibit fragment end-polishing. Refuse includes deer bones, shell, potsherds, stone flakes, rodent bones, and bone with considerable processing, but no burning. Boiling, not roasting, is indicated. Possible dog burial present. All bones appear cooked.

standard deviation are both less than the comparable statistics for natural breakage in considerate burials or in the early stages of the surface diagenesis of dead animals. Means for rib fragment length ranged from a low of 5.7 cm for Leroux Wash to a high of 15.7 cm for Electra. The unweighted mean for the five groups is 9.4 cm (ca. 3.75 inches).

These exercises provide a good way to make a final point about culturally determined perimortem taphonomy. It is an anthropological dictum that groups of people display cultural differences in their minor, day-to-day activities as well as in their major metaphysical principles, and that these differences are related to environmental, historical, evolutionary, and chance considerations. Highly specific behavioral universals among humans are few. Finding similarities between groups, such as the proposed cannibalism signature, is truly the exception. When the cannibalism signature is considered cross-culturally, some allowances need to be made for the multiple factors, other than the processing "directive," that affect the types and frequencies of damage. But having found substantial cross-cultural regularity in the cannibal signature of the Southwest and Mexico, we must ask: Will this signature apply elsewhere in the world and farther back in time, excluding pot-polishing where ceramics are lacking? Only future research will tell.

Summary

ETHNOHISTORIC ACCOUNTS and archaeologically derived human skeletal remains speak in unison about large-scale human sacrifice and cannibalism in central Mexico at and before historic contact. Although ethnographic accounts indicate that there was cannibalism in northern Mexico as well, the skeletal evidence there is underdeveloped. When one looks at the entire picture of Mexican warfare, religion, human sacrifice, public and private trophy taking, and cannibalism, one senses that a very powerful, dehumanizing sociopolitical and ideological complex had evolved in central Mexico even before the time of the monumental constructions at Teotihuacan, at least 2,500 years ago. Time and again this complex was overthrown or collapsed, only to arise again and grow ever more powerful. Its icons, ideology, and sacrificial themes spread throughout the central plateau and into the jungle world of the Mayas and the desert world of Chichimeca. Elements of Mesoamerican culture reached Alta Vista, La Quemada, and other northern sites, along with Casas Grandes—only a few days' walk from the modern New Mexico border. It takes nearly blind faith in the effectiveness of geographical distance and the nonreceptivity of provincialism to believe that this complex and its adherents failed to reach the American Southwest.

Charnel deposits in the Southwest and Mexico that have been independently assessed as having resulted from cannibalism are similar not only in their types of perimortem damage but also in their preservation and contexts. The range of types of charnel deposits in Mexico, however, is much greater than that in the Southwest, owing to the greater amount of body processing associated with many different forms of ritual human sacrifice in Mexico. Human sacrifice and cannibalism are also much older in Mesoamerica than in the Southwest.

Additional taphonomic considerations involving bone fragment length show enough similarily in the processing of humans and animals that long bone fragment length—though not that of ribs—can be tentatively added to the list of taphonomic features minimally required in order for cannibalism to be hypothesized for a given human charnel deposit.

In short, human body processing in Mexico provides powerful independent, extraregional evidence for explaining human bone damage in the U.S. Southwest.

## ◆ 5

# Conclusion

*Explaining*
*Southwestern*
*Cannibalism*

◆ Why had they ceased? . . . Any epidemic would have
left unburied bodies. Father Duchene suggested . . .
that the tribe had been exterminated.
—Willa Cather, *The Professor's House*

UNTIL NOW we have focused on narrowing down the number of
possible explanations for the perimortem taphonomic conditions of prehistoric human charnel deposits in the American Southwest.
We have excluded natural causes of damage as the primary agents, leaving anthropogenic mechanisms. A review of Southwestern mortuary behavior has shown that the charnel deposit signature lies far beyond the
known range of considerate burial practices, disturbed burials, and even
violent mutilation. The Southwestern human charnel deposits have their
strongest perimortem taphonomic correspondences with the bones of
large and small game animals that were butchered and cooked, and with
skeletal assemblages in Mesoamerica where cannibalism was linked to
ceremonies of human sacrifice. Hence, on the basis of both exclusion
and correspondence, we propose cannibalism as the primary explanation for the human perimortem bone damage.

Evidence for cannibalism in the U.S. Southwest is, with one or two
possible exceptions, concentrated in the Anasazi culture area. In our several years of examining skeletal collections from across the Southwest,
including the very large Grasshopper and Point of Pines assemblages and
all of the human remains at the Museum of Northern Arizona, we have
come across the cannibalism signature nowhere except in the sites discussed in chapter 3. It is within the Chacoan sphere of influence that
cannibalized human remains occur most often, although the archaeology of western Arizona is less well sampled to date. But why did cannibalism occur there? Did these episodes represent a local development or
an introduced, exotic behavior? Who were the cannibals? Why did they
feed on men, women, and children alike?

Hermann Helmuth (1973) prepared a brief but comprehensive,
worldwide ethnographic review of cannibalistic motivations, in the hope
of explaining prehistoric cannibalism. He ignored emergency cannibalism on the grounds that anyone starving could eat human flesh out of
simple necessity, without any ideological, cultural, or behavioral motivation. Helmuth found that numerous explanations for cannibalism had
been identified and recorded, not all of them involving human aggression or violence: "Even though the belief of the transmission of qualities
was undoubtedly the most widespread, completely different concepts,
often between neighboring tribes, also played a role. Mockery, con-
tempt, revenge, fury and hate, fear of the return and revenge of the
dead man, punishment for a crime, as well as feelings of friendship and
belonging together, resulted in anthropophagy. Also, the attempt to pre-

serve a continuity, an already existent order, lay behind the eating of human flesh" (Helmuth 1973:248).

We resist the temptation to recite Helmuth's many examples and individual explanations for tribal, local, and regional cannibalism, but we note that he found endocannibalism (eating members of one's own group) much more common among South American hunters and gatherers than exocannibalism (eating of outsiders), which was more frequent among that continent's agriculturalists. Given these relationships, he proposed that in South America endocannibalism, with its positive, friendly attitude and motivations, was older than exocannibalism, with its hostile and magical feelings.

Helmuth's multiple motivation conclusion does not make our task of explaining Southwestern cannibalism any easier—although it does nudge our thinking in the direction of hostile exocannibalism, since all Anasazi cannibalized remains found to date have been in agricultural settings. His review, however, makes it evident that ethnographic analogy, even where there are accounts of cannibalism (which are uncommon but not absent in the Southwest) may not be as useful a source of explanation as what can be learned from a well-excavated charnel assemblage and a detailed taphonomic study of its perimortem bone damage.

Considering the many reasons for cannibalism offered by Helmuth and others, we suggest that most can be lumped into one or another of five basic but not mutually exclusive explanations: (1) emergency, or starvation, (2) sociobiology and evolutionary psychology, (3) social control, (4) ritual human sacrifice, and (5) social pathology. Of these five, we reject the emergency explanation for Southwestern cannibalism except perhaps in a very few cases, and we find sociobiology too much an ultimate, rather than proximate, explanation to be very useful at the local or regional level. Instead, we offer a hypothesis that combines the last three categories in a scenario involving the actual intrusion of Mexican Indians into the American Southwest. Before outlining that hypothesis, we offer a few more remarks on starvation and sociobiology.

We reject starvation as a general explanation for Southwestern cannibalism because of the near absence of examples in the Mogollon area, where winters would have been harsher than in the other culture areas of the Southwest and where one might therefore expect many starvation emergencies to have occurred. There are no known claims for Mogollon cannibalism, nor have we found any Mogollon skeletal series that suggests cannibalism except possibly for the Fence Lake site, whose exact location and cultural affiliation are unknown. A majority of the cannibalized assemblages are located in or near Chacoan great houses, so the distribution of cannibalized remains is neither random nor environmentally correlated with the worst winter conditions. Cannibalized assemblages with only one or two individuals would be the logical candidates for starvation events, if such ever occurred. To explain assemblages with 10, 20, 30, or more individuals as the result of emergency cannibalism stretches credulity too far.

Except possibly in the worst of Southwestern winter blizzards, food of some sort could have been found at least every few days. Starvation could have been avoided by catching and eating invertebrates, small reptiles, and mice and other rodents, or by eating the village dogs or making broth out of bones and scraps from previous meals. Although we can well imagine that prehistoric Indians felt real hunger at times each year, we question how serious a threat starvation really was in the past. The average human can survive without eating for many days, and going without some type of food for a week or so was unlikely anywhere in the Southwest except during unusually severe winters that might have restricted travel in the high mountain Mogollon country of central Arizona and New Mexico.

Looking at Chaco Canyon itself, we believe it is unlikely that the apparent cannibalism there was caused by starvation, because, first, the abundant faunal remains suggest a fair amount of available food. Nancy Akins (1984:234) estimated that 1.75 million animal bones had accumulated over a period of 70 years in just one Chacoan trash mound—the one associated with Pueblo Alto. She numerically transformed this estimated bone mass into meat, producing an estimated consumption of about 40% of a cottontail rabbit per day for 26 people for 70 years, assuming an average daily meat intake amounting to 200 calories. That is the equivalent of approximately half a small turkey breast per day.

Second, to date there are ten known sites in Chaco Canyon with taphonomic evidence of probable cannibalism and violence. For cannibalism, these are Peñasco Blanco (eight individuals), Pueblo Bonito (two), Small House (eight), and Bc59 (one). For violence, Pueblo Bonito has at the very least three individuals; Chaco 1360, six; Bc50, one; Bc51, two; Bc53, two; Bc57, one; Bc59, two; and Pueblo del Arroyo, nine. Had starvation been the root cause of the apparent cannibalism, then why weren't the 26 other individuals evidencing perimortem trauma not eaten as well?

Although we do not subscribe to starvation as the single best explanation for Anasazi cannibalism, we are aware that there are Hopi, Zuni, and other Pueblo Indian oral traditions regarding famine and starvation (e.g., Hodge, in Smith et al. 1966; Parsons, ed., 1936; Wallis and Titiev 1945). Richard B. Brandt (1974:359) wrote: "Some Hopi say that there are children's bones at Old Oraibi and Hotevilla (in a cave) and that these are from children kidnapped and eaten during famine times. . . . The most interesting thing about these beliefs is that Hopi consider them credible." When food supplies ran low, however, most people simply moved away.

Perhaps more plausible in a broad sense are theories derived from sociobiology and evolutionary psychology. If one assumes that cannibalism (or at least exocannibalism) is part of a larger pattern of human violence and aggression, then the evolutionary view is that cannibalistic behavior can be adaptive under certain conditions, as it is in the reproductive strategies of some species of beetles, bees, and other invertebrates and of various fishes, amphibians, birds, rodents, and nonhuman primates (Elgar and Crespi 1992).

Lee Ellis (1989, 1990a, 1990b) reviewed several contemporary theories about the ultimate cause of violence, murder, and rape. He felt that the sociobiology paradigm provided the best overall explanation. Evolutionary theory predicts that violence between males should be much more frequent than that between females: "Males who failed either to maintain a fairly high degree of credibility in their threats of violence, or to challenge the credibility of other males, would both be likely to reproduce less well than males who did" (Ellis 1990a:70). It is well known that fighting between males over females is common in other animal species.

Gerard G. Neuman (1987) reviewed past and recent thinking about human aggression. Noteworthy in his review is the intimate linkage of three behavioral categories: violence, warfare, and cannibalism. The three frequently happen together. Although nearly, if not completely, universal, this trinity is morally bad only when practiced against one's own group, a fact well in line with the sociobiological concept of genetic success through kin-oriented altruism. Outward-directed cannibalism not only destroys an external enemy but also provides a hefty food dividend.

Paul D. MacLean (1987:37) developed a universal, evolutionary, and neurological basis for aggression:

> The close relationship of oral and genital functions in this part of the brain [the limbic system] is apparently due to the olfactory sense which, dating far back in evolution, plays a primary role in both feeding and mating. By electrical stimulation, we have traced neural circuits involving the mouth and genitals lying side-by-side right down through the brainstem. Activity in one spills over into the other, and both may be elicited in angry, combative responses. We therefore can see here a close tie-in of oral and sexual functions in aggression.

From this evolutionary viewpoint, rape, mutilation, and eating the flesh of violently killed victims are understandable acts in a species with a nervous system in which sex, feeding, and aggressive signals can be mixed together as a result of neural anatomy and unusual stimuli. Konrad Lorenz (1967:114) noted that livestock breeders were well aware of how slight disturbances could cause failure of inhibition mechanisms, citing a case he knew of "where an airplane, flying low over a silver-fox farm, caused all the mother vixens to eat their young." We suggest that human intraspecies killing, like the universals of disposing of the dead in some manner, language, and the nuclear family, is a species characteristic the origin of which must reside in faraway prehistory.

We feel that the sociobiology and evolutionary psychology paradigms provide a thought-provoking explanatory substrate for Southwestern violence and cannibalism. Yet they cannot be applied to the Southwest in any specific way because it is impossible to distinguish kinship relations with the prehistoric Southwestern data base. That is, it cannot be determined whether enemies were eaten but kin were not, because there is no way at this time to determine who did the eating or who was eaten—friends, relatives, slaves, strangers, or enemies. Hence, sociobiological hypotheses cannot be evaluated from the archaeologically derived materials. Sociobiology and evolutionary psychology may offer an ultimate explanation for Southwest cannibalism, but for a proximate explanation we are logically bound to take primarily a cultural-historical approach.

A Proximate Explanation for Anasazi Cannibalism

OUR PROPOSED explanation for Anasazi cannibalism combines the last three of our five categories—social control, ritual human sacrifice, and social pathology—in a scenario that begins in prehistoric Mexico. Around 200 B.C. the centralized and stratified Teotihuacan culture developed, with human sacrifice associated minimally with the Pyramid of the Sun. By A.D. 300 Teotihuacan dominated much of central Mexico, but in about 650 it was looted and violently destroyed (Adams 1991: 256–257). The Toltecs then emerged all powerful, but around 1000 their tribute-demanding militaristic theocracy collapsed in turn. There was civil war among the Toltecs, and with the fall of their capital, Tula, in about 1170, anarchy reigned in central Mexico until about 1325, when the Aztecs established their capital at Tenochtitlan.

Bertha Dutton (1964:490–491) suggested that with the breakup of Teotihuacan and later the Toltec city-state, vanquished warrior-cultists might have migrated northward, explaining the arrival of warrior priest-hoods in the Southwest. We agree that during this protracted period of Toltec cultural strife, between roughly A.D. 800 and 1000, waves of diverse Mexican traits were carried into the American Southwest by cultists, priests, warriors, pilgrims, traders, miners, farmers, and others fleeing or displaced by the widespread unrest and civil war in central Mexico. In this chaos-driven refugee scenario, a mishmash of Meso-american culture and language features would be expected to have reached the Southwest, not some integrated biocultural system.

Specifically, we think some of these immigrants might have been warrior-cultists dedicated to gods of the Tezcatlipoca–Xipe Totec complex, with its human sacrifice and cannibalism. We propose that in the Chaco area, some such group of Mexicans was able to use these practices for social control, terrorizing the local populace into submission and developing the hierarchical social system we see reflected in the region's architecture. To some extent, their practice of violence and cannibalism, effective as it may have been for social control, veered into social pathology, which we believe characterized these cults in Mexico itself.

As we discussed in chapter 4, there is abundant and convincing evidence for human sacrifice and cannibalism in Mesoamerica, correlated practices that extended back in time at least 2,500 years. Such great time depth for these widespread, institutionalized practices points to their having been fundamental elements of Mesoamerican belief and ritual. If Chacoan cannibalism was *not* due to the presence of Mexican cultists or warriors, then the occurrence within the Chacoan sphere of the remains of nearly 300 people with perimortem damage featuring the taphonomic signature of cannibalism has to be one of the more remarkable parallelisms in New World prehistory.

Why did the same thing not happen in the Mogollon area, through which the Mesoamericans probably traveled to reach Chaco Canyon, or in the Hohokam region, where Mexican influence was especially pronounced? We believe the Mogollon people were too scattered and "wild" and their natural resources insufficiently concentrated to make them easy targets for subjugation under centralized control. Conversely, the Hohokam were already so centrally controlled that a relatively small force of immigrants stood little chance of conquering them. The Chaco Anasazi sphere, however, offered abundant natural resources (water, arable land, timber, game animals, easily worked building materials, etc.) and a relatively large population whose social organization, it seems to us, had so little central control that an effective defense could not be roused against even a small group of organized warrior-cultists.

To muster evidence for this explanation requires us to revisit a venerable debate in Southwestern archaeology—the debate over whether, and to what degree, Mesoamerican "influence" can be recognized in the Southwest. We look first at evidence for Mesoamerican traits, including features related to ritual or religious ideology, in the Anasazi region and in Chaco Canyon particularly. Moroever, we need to demonstrate that Mexicans were actually in the Southwest, which we do by using intentional dental modification as a Mesoamerican biocultural marker. Finally, we take a brief look at cannibalism as an aspect of social control and as an expression of social pathology, and we assess some interpretations of the Chaco system in light of the practice of cannibalism there.

## Mesoamerican Influence on the Anasazi

THE APPARENT LACK of Southwestern cannibalism before A.D. 900—the date often cited for the earliest construction of great houses in Chaco Canyon—its occurrence largely in Chacoan Anasazi sites, and the similarities in the taphonomic signatures of Mesoamerican and Southwestern cannibalism suggest diffusion. Some form of religious or military complex involving cannibalism, perhaps in conjunction with ritual human sacrifice, might have been introduced from Mexico by actual practitioners. This possibility is consistent with a variety of other evidence for contact, migration, and bidirectional trade and exchange. The evidence we cite here is drawn from only a few among many works by researchers who have thought about the problem of interaction between the Southwest and Mesoamerica—a topic of long debate and disagreement in Americanist archaeology. Because we hypothesize that immigrant Mexicans reached the Anasazi region before 1300, we omit the enormous amount of literature on the Aztecs, who postdated the phenomenon we want to explain. And although there is abundant evidence for Mesoamerican traits in the Mogollon and Hohokam areas, we ignore it as well, because of the apparent absence of cannibalism there.

Some of the most basic features of Anasazi economy and culture originated in Mesoamerica—corn and corn culture, pottery, and cotton, for example. Emil Haury (1945), although he focused on the Hohokam region, listed other Mesoamerican features that eventually reached the Anasazi as well: ball courts, which reached the Flagstaff area by A.D. 1050; copper bells, carried to both Hohokam and Anasazi by 1100; Mexican macaws, known so far primarily among the Anasazi, by 1100; and textile techniques, gauze weave, weft-wrap openwork, and tie-dying. Haury (1945:65) thought that the elements did not all move north at the same time, travel over the same route, or come from the same source.

Richard E. W. Adams (1991:285) recognized considerable Mexican influence on the American Southwest:

> The Toltec expanded into the northern frontier zone, or Gran Chichimeca, about A.D. 900 [making contact] with the cultures of what is now the southwestern United States . . . [and] trading copper bells and other items for turquoise, slaves, peyote, salt, and other commodities that the northerners provided. Cultural influences followed commerce, and it is believed that many traits in ethnographic religions of the U.S. Southwest derive from Mesoamerican influence. Murals from Awatowi [sic] in the Hopi area seem to show regional versions of Tlaloc, Quetzalcoatl appears in several areas, and Chaco

Canyon in far-off northwestern New Mexico shows impressive architectural parallels with Toltec building.

Erik K. Reed (1964:183–184) noted both the absence of some typical Mesoamerican features and the presence of others:

> Contact with Mexican cultures cannot, however, have been very close or continuous, for there are many cultural elements known in Mexico that never spread north to our area, such as chili peppers, legged (tripod) metates, polished stone-celts, dental mutilation, to name a few. . . . [Nevertheless] in the time between about A.D. 1150, or shortly after, and A.D. 1275 or 1300 . . . in the eastern San Juan region . . . we find triple-walled "towers" and other structures of bizzare ground plan. A number of detailed architectural features that appeared in the San Juan after A.D. 1050 seem to be of Mexican derivation and may well represent the arrival in the northern Southwest of the cult of Quezalcoatl.

Bertha P. Dutton (1964) prepared an inventory of Mesoamerican culture traits found in the Southwest. Besides maize, it included pottery forms and finishes that extended into the Four Corners area, among them polished red vessels, hobnail and punctate decoration, duck vessels, clay figurines, and other effigy forms (Dutton 1964:482–483). Referring specifically to Chaco Canyon, she listed cylindrical jars and effigy vessels, rattle-handled dippers and handled fumigators, trays, pottery stamps, and stirrup jars, all found in Mexico. Copper bells were present, too.

Dutton also pointed out architectural similarities between Chacoan and Mesoamerican sites. She noted that around A.D. 950 people at Chaco began to build more elaborate surface structures—a Mexican idea—and then galleries with masonry colonnades at Chetro Ketl and Bc-51. These were similar to Casas Grandes constructions (Dutton 1964:485). Massive two-story platforms or towers appeared at Chaco in the 1000s. The Chaco style of masonry (rubble core with a veneer of well-laid stone) is found in Mexico, at La Quemada, for example. Great kivas at Chaco had massive roof supports resting on thick circular stone wheels, a technique found also at Tula.

Robert H. Lister and Florence C. Lister (1981:174–175) reviewed Chaco archaeology for Mesoamerican ties. They proposed that the following features had their origins in Mexico: rubble-cored masonry, square columns used in colonnades, circular structures in the form of tower kivas and tri-walled units, the practice of seating discs beneath roof support posts, T-shaped doorways, cylinder jars, effigy vessels, incense burners, stamps or seals, alien design motifs, copper bells, iron pyrite mosaics, shell trumpets, shell beads, shell bracelets, macaws and parrots, turkey burials, bone pins, ceremonial wooden canes, altar components of wood, turquoise beads and pendants, turquoise mosaic sets, decorative techniques of cloisonné and mosaics, water control means such as dams, canals, and reservoirs, the roads and signal stations, and alignments of architectural and other features for the purpose of observing and recording astronomical data (on the last point see Sofaer, Marshall, and Sinclair 1989).

Charles D. Trombold (1991:154–155) compared the Chacoan and La Quemada road systems, concluding: "A general Mesoamerican presence seems evident at Chaco based on (among other things) the comparatively widespread occurrence of earlier road networks in north-central Mexico. . . . It may be more than just coincidence, then, that formal routes were constructed at La Quemada between *c.* A.D. 600 and 800; at Schroeder between *c.* A.D. 900 and 1100; and at Chaco between *c.* A.D. 1050 and 1100. At the very least, this may indicate the spread of Mesoamerican symbolism to demonstrate elite power and legitimacy." Trombold (1991:164) proposed on diverse grounds that "one of the primary functions of the [La Quemada] causeways was military"—more likely for ensuring subjugation of the local population than to guard against external enemies.

There is good archaeological as well as ethnographic evidence that Southwestern Indians received, imported, adopted, or adapted elements of Mexican Indian religion or cosmology. Generalizing about such connections, Carroll L. Riley (1987:322) visualized that "large increments of Mesoamerican religion including specific deities were brought to the Southwest at various times through what were fundamentally trade contacts. By the sixteenth century this religion had been reinterpreted so that obvious Mesoamerican elements such as human sacrifice had been removed, except for echos in the mythology. However, there is a strong possibility that human sacrifice was practiced at Chaco Canyon as late as the eleventh or twelfth century."

In particular, scholars have remarked on Southwestern rock art, scenes on Mimbres pottery, religious paraphernalia and practices, and kiva paintings that appear to represent aspects of two ancient Mesoamerican deities, Quetzalcoatl and Xipe Totec (e.g., Di Peso 1974; Ellis and Hammack 1968; Fewkes 1893b, 1920, 1923; Schaafsma and Schaafsma 1974). Both gods were important members of the pantheon at Teotihuacan early in the first millenium A.D. and continued to be worshipped by the Toltecs and later the Aztecs. Among the Toltecs, however, they were eclipsed in importance by the violent and evil god Tezcatlipoca, who in turn was superseded in importance by the Aztecs' dominant god, Huitzilopochtli. There are no recognizable images of Tezcatlipoca in prehistoric Southwestern art, but Quetzalcoatl is represented as the horned or plumed serpent, and Xipe Totec may have been represented as Maasaw.

The feathered serpent appears in Anasazi rock and kiva art by sometime after A.D. 900. There are numerous rock art depictions of the feathered serpent in the Four Corners area by at least A.D. 1200, although the designs are probably more often associated with later Style 2 rock art (1300–1600; Turner 1963). That the serpent was associated with Quetzalcoatl is based on the fact that this god was similarly represented in Toltec carved stone panels and even earlier carvings, particularly those for which the feathered serpent pyramid at Teotihuacan is named, and on ethnographic evidence from the historic Southwest. For example, J. W. Fewkes (1914:44) learned that "the horned serpent cult at Walpi is said to have been introduced from the south." Earlier (1897:188–194) he claimed that the Hopi Water House and Squash "families" came from the south, bringing with them the feathered serpent cult and many words of Nahuatl root. Fewkes (1920:511) proposed that "Quetzalcoatl symbolizes the same conception as the plumed serpent of the Hopi."

There is in one of Fewkes's collections of Hopi myths an item of much interest: a legendary linkage between the feathered serpent and human sacrifice. The legend of the great snake who causes a momentous flood has the snake telling a village chief that he will eliminate the flood if the chief will "sacrifice to me your son," which the chief did (Fewkes 1920: 507). Buried beneath the feathered serpent temple at Teotihuacan were many sacrificial victims.

J. J. Brody (1983:115) illustrated a prehistoric Mimbres bowl depicting a man wearing a plumed serpent outfit and cutting off the head of a sacrificed victim. He wrote: "On examining this painting, the Hopi artist, Fred Kabotie, recalled that his people traditionally practiced human sacrifice as supplication on very rare occasions, under extreme stress of famine due to drought."

Randall McGuire (1980:24–25) argued that the Toltecs and Aztecs associated their feathered serpent, Quetzalcoatl, not with water, as the Pueblo Indians do, but with sky, so that there is a functional difference between them. (Fewkes, however [1920:500], proposed "that the Hopi horned serpent is a sky god, and appears during the winter solstice rite, which is a prayer to the sky god to return and renew life.") McGuire acknowledged that the feathered serpent and the Zuni new-fire ceremony were Mesoamerican-derived beliefs, but he thought they were in the Southwest not because of direct influence by foreigners but because the area was the "northernmost extent of a basic set of beliefs and symbols that were variously combined in different cults."

Far more directly associated with human sacrifice than Quetzalcoatl was Xipe Totec, "Our Lord the Flayed One," the war and fertility god who wore the flayed skins of his sacrificed victims. Victims to Xipe Totec were killed by having their hearts torn out; then, after being flayed, their skins were worn by Xipe impersonators for a period of days or weeks. The victim's flesh was eaten. Roberta H. Markman and Peter T. Markman (1992:40) described pottery icons of Xipe Totec as usually a simple smooth face with three indentations, two for eyes and one for the mouth, encircled by a band of clay—in all, symbolic of a flayed head.

The Hopi deity Maasaw, the most dreaded entity in the Hopi spirit world, shares many features with Xipe Totec, including a major ceremony in February. Oral traditions invariably attribute human sacrifice to Maasaw, and Hopi clan totems connected with the deity are "rooted in Maasaw's close affiliation with death, war, and fire" (Malotki and Lomatuway'ma 1987:191–194). Two petroglyphs of a Hopi clan symbol called Maasaw turned up in a survey of rock art in Petrified Forest National Park (Patricia McCreery, personal communication, 1989). These glyphs are very similar to the many ceramic figurines of Xipe Totec found at Teotihuacan and elsewhere in Mesoamerica. Although said to be a clan symbol, the glyph for Maasaw seems not to be a locally evolved design.

Ekkehart Malotki and Michael Lomatuway'ma (1987) assembled several of many tales about Maasaw. "His head was of colossal size and his face was covered with blood. Sores infested his head, from which sprouted only a sparse covering of hair. . . . His body was clearly in a state of putrefaction, so offensive was the stench he emitted. His shins were clearly visible, spotted with boils from which dripped pus" (Malotki and Lomatuway'ma 1987:45). Elsewhere in the same book (1987:23–25) they portrayed Maasaw as

> the owner of fire. Maasaw sits at an unknown place and constantly stokes his fire, causing a wave of searing heat to be emitted from it. In spite of this intense heat radiation, his face never gets burned. This is because the god, who is reputed to be a very capable hunter, makes it a habit to pour the blood of his prey on his head whenever he slays a jack rabbit. As layer upon layer of this blood is baked by the fire and builds up in thickness, his head grows larger and larger. These layers of encrusted blood are so dense that the heat from the fire cannot penetrate them and thus does not reach his face. . . . People say that Maasaw is a repulsive being. His head is so enormous and so bloody that it shines a little when light falls on it. His mouth is round and his eyes are hollow. Furthermore, his forehead bulges out in a large ridge. . . . Maasaw's dress basically constitutes a death shroud and must be obtained directly from the dead.

Maasaw "primarily (and aboriginally) . . . is the deity in control of the earth and of crops" (Malotki and Lomatuway'ma 1987:14). "According to Hopi lore, Maasaw wears a belt fashioned of purple corn around his waist symbolizing his power of maize fecundity" (Malotki and Lomatuway'ma 1987:119).

Maasaw's eyes, mouth, dress (including the belt of corn and the garb of the dead), bloody body, putrefaction, and stench correspond to elements of the flayed Xipe Totec. Xipe sacrifice was much involved with fertility, especially of maize. Although Mesoamerican deities are unsettlingly transformable, the correspondences between Maasaw and Xipe Totec are not easily dismissed as owing solely to chance.

Not only are there common elements of form in Maasaw and Xipe, there are also shared purposes. A parallel with human sacrifice in Mexico has to do with Maasaw's duty to maintain the working order of the universe (Malotki and Lomatuway'ma 1987:91–96):

> Keeping the sun going will be possible only at the expense of human life. Only by flaming with human grease can the sun burn. . . . For this reason people will have to die from now on. . . . Maasaw suggested [to the Hopi chief] human sacrifice to keep the sun rotating at its proper speed. Ultimately, man would have to die to guarantee the perpetual movement of the sun. . . . Then Maasaw said, "As you recall, I suggested we daub this [sun disk] hide with grease. . . . You'll have to sacrifice the niece who is most dear to you. I'm afraid we'll have to kill her. The girl must die so that the disk can spin with her grease.". . . [The chief said] "I suppose I have no choice but to sacrifice her." . . . And so they applied the girl's fat to the buckskin. When the hide was really greasy, Maasaw said, "Well then, let's try again." With that he hurled the disk out with such vehemence that it emitted an odd sound. Before long a faint light began to appear and then it manifested itself in brilliant brightness.

There is even a Maasaw story involving flaying: "The Navajo woke up and to his horror beheld a grotesque-looking figure. However, at the instant he set eyes on the monster he died of fright. This is how Maasaw's terrible appearance affected the man. With some skill Maasaw managed to remove the man's skin. Then, ever so carefully, he rolled up the skin, tucked it under his arm and left the hogan. The skinless body of the Navajo man remained inside, a mere red lump, and horrid to look at" (Malotki and Lomatuway'ma 1987:113).

The human charnel deposit from Houck K provides our most likely case of ceremonial flaying and cannibalism. Recall also the unique rib breakage at Houck K and the considerable head processing, including cutting out of the tongue of at least one individual. We speculate that this Mexican-like processing could represent the Xipe Totec flaying ceremony or a derived analogue. Recall too, however, that decapitation and the skinning of partial and whole human heads occurred in Basketmaker times. This is not the same as flaying of the entire body, but it leads us to consider the possibility that Maasaw and Xipe Totec were northern and southern manifestations of an ancient common ancestral deity. Although that is possible, we believe it preferable to envision Maasaw as derived from Xipe Totec—that is, as having a more recent origin. All known rock art depictions of Maasaw are post-Basketmaker; the deity seems to be absent in Southwestern rock art until around A.D. 1000. Maasaw or Maasaw-like depictions are seemingly rare in the Southwest outside the Anasazi culture area.

Mexican Influence: Direct or Diffused

IF WE ACCEPT that elements of Mesoamerican culture, whether material or ideological, reached the U.S. Southwest before or during the period of interest here—A.D. 900 to 1300—then we are left with the question, how did they get there? Like the degree of Mexican influence itself, this question has prompted sharp differences of opinion (for a summary, see McGuire et al. 1994). Many researchers (e.g., Di Peso 1974; Kelley and Kelley 1975) have attributed the spread of Mesoamerican traits to the arrival of actual people, especially the ubiquitous traveling merchants previously called by their Nahuatl name, *pochteca,* and now more commonly by the term *trocadores* ("mobile merchants"). Others doubt that the direct entry of persons from Mexico into the Southwest was necessary. Randall McGuire and colleagues (1994), for example, rejected the idea that Southwestern and Mesoamerican relations were due to actual intrusions of southern people. Lister and Lister (1981:175) expressed an apparent middle position:

Realistically viewed, Chaco Canyon need not have been an actual cog in the Toltec organization of trading outposts to have been influenced by Mexican cultures, for shock waves emanating from an advanced epicenter have a way of reverberating outward to engulf otherwise removed entities. . . . News, ideas, and technological knowledge undoubtedly passed along the trade routes as readily as did material things, and the traveling salesmen of the times most likely played important roles in cultural diffusion. By that means, eyewitness accounts of Mesoamerican religious rituals, irrigation schemes, architectural embellishments, communication means, and other strange wonders may have reached Chaco. The descriptions may have inspired and encouraged local technicians and leaders to adopt those measures that would be beneficial to the Chacoans.

Bertha Dutton (1964:487) proposed the arrival of a religious contingent in a scenario not unlike our own:

> That ceremonial figures were being depicted [in the Southwest], and these associated with sacred accoutrement, bespeaks the arrival of religious officers in the Southwest, so organized as to manipulate personages and paraphernalia with increasing efficiency. Until the 1000s, no central control had been recognized. It is at this time that the Mogollon and the Chaco peoples evidence striking religious evolution and development, mirroring the promotion of priesthoods and sacred societies. In order to control expanding populations, the priests had to concentrate the people, to assure manpower for the construction of buildings, the production of ample food, and to enact ceremonial duties; for such a social organization, there had to be successful hunters to augment the horticultural products, and warriors to guard the fields and the villages—thus making necessary warrior societies to function in conjunction with the sacerdotal.

Edwin N. Ferdon (1955:24–25), after examining architectural parallels between Mexico and the Southwest, suggested:

> The means by which these traits were introduced may never be determined, but a review of the conditions attending in the Chaco Anasazi and the River Hohokam at the time of these introductions [A.D. 1050–1300] may cast some light on the subject. If we regard as probable the direct culture-to-culture hypothesis for the introduction of these traits, we have three reasonably possible means by which this could have been accomplished: (1) knowing that in both Toltec and Aztec times widespread trading activity was common, it is possible that these new features were introduced by trading parties from Mexico; (2) it is equally possible, though not as probable, that small trading groups from the Southwest got down into Mexico and returned with new ideas; and (3) the introduction could have been accomplished by a small, well organized force of Mexicans, as was apparently the case at Chichen Itza.

Obviously we prefer Ferdon's third option, the arrival of a Mexican force that we think used cannibalism not only for ritual purposes but also, as in their homeland, as an element of intimidation and social control. We speculate that this force consisted of cultists and warriors of the Quetzalcoatl–Xipe Totec–Tezcatlipoca deity complex who overwhelmed the local residents, much the way the soldiers led by Cortés fell upon Mexico.

Objections have repeatedly been raised against the hypothesis of a strong Mesoamerican influence on the development of the Chaco system. Isolated artifacts such as copper bells and macaws are looked up only as transfers, not as commuters. Most objectors want to see a coherent Mexican presence. But discounting the direct-influence hypothesis because, for example, very little in the way of Mesoamerican goods reached Chaco Canyon, overlooks the fundamental issue of how one recognizes a small but powerful amount of direct influence in contrast to less palpable interaction. Steven LeBlanc (1989) has pointed out that the archaeological evidence for Mimbres warfare is almost invisible but still is sufficient to conclude that it did occur (see also Jelinek 1961). Archaeological near-invisibility would also be the case for a few but powerful Mesoamerican warrior-priests if any had directed the Chaco system.

Edward H. Spicer's (1962:283–284) examination of the historic Spanish conquest and incoherent cultural exchange provides an impeccable analogy for accepting weak signals for strong influences. Spicer's example quashes the claim that strong and coherent signals must be evident before acknowledging a significant Mesoamerican presence in Chaco:

> To assume that Spanish culture of the 1500s in all its European complexity was somehow transported to America and the Indians made aware of it is quite unjustified. . . . [Nor] was church life and organization of old Spain . . . duplicated. Only a portion of the rich variety of observances of a Spanish parish was brought by any missionary or secular priest, and for long years the missionaries concentrated only on what they regarded as the few minimum essentials of doctrine and ritual in teaching the Indians. This same condition obtained also for tools; it has been shown that of the large variety of plows developed in Spain only one of the simpler forms was introduced into Mexico, and in fact in all Latin America.

Jonathan Reyman (1995) pointed out that the volume of trade need not be as great as some archaeologists would require in order to verify direct Mesoamerican influences on the Southwest. He determined the recent value of macaw feathers through a feather exchange project, finding that their worth was substantial, analogous to the weight-volume-value ratio of diamonds or certain illegal drugs. He proposed that turquoise had a similarly high value, and, like feathers, a small load of Southwestern turquoise could have produced a substantial profit in Mexico.

Although there is little evidence for prehistoric trade in macaw feathers, there is good evidence for trading of live birds. Lyndon Hargrave (1970:32) proposed that trafficking in macaws began about A.D. 1100 and declined after 1375. Of his total sample, 71% (83 of 117) were fledglings (11–12 months old). There were no nestlings or juveniles that might have hatched in the Southwest, so he felt they were transported from their home in tropical Mexico. The earliest dated sites with macaws are in Chaco Canyon—Pueblo del Arroyo, Pueblo Bonito, and Kin Kletso, where they had been buried. Room 38 in Pueblo Bonito had at least 12.

Birds buried in the Southwest but born in tropical Mexico hint at a significant Southwest-Mesoamerica ritual or commercial connection. We wonder, however, how the transporters protected themselves against the perils of traveling through Chichimeca? Perhaps they traveled in armed groups, additionally protected by dangerous and powerful deities such as Tezcatlipoca or Xipe Totec. We believe a new sort of evidence for the presence of Mexicans in the Southwest has recently begun to appear—evidence in the form of deliberately modified teeth.

Dental Evidence for Mexicans
in the Southwest

DENTAL TRANSFIGUREMENT is a term we coin to avoid the ethnocentricity of "dental mutilation" (Milner and Larsen 1991) in referring to intentional chipping, notching, filing, inlaying, ablating, coloring, and other nontherapeutic alteration of the labial and occlusal surfaces of anterior teeth. Prehistoric dental transfigurement was probably done for the same reasons as those identified by Eurasian, African, Pacific, and New World ethnographers: cosmetic enhancement, individual choice, group and human identification, rituals of puberty and entry into adulthood, indication of status, and many others. All can be reduced to a single theme—the signaling of membership. Tooth enamel is hard and lifeless, so dental modification, like tatooing of the skin, is long-lasting. It probably carries with it about the same degree of health risk as tatooing.

The extensive variation in Mesoamerican anterior tooth transfigurement has been described and classified by Javier Romero Molina (1958, 1960, 1970, 1986). From his work and that of others (Fastlicht 1971; Gill 1985; José Antonio Pompa, personal communication, 1994; Powell and Powell 1992; Romero and Fastlicht 1951), it is evident that dental transfigurement is an old and distinguishing characteristic of Mesoamerican culture, even though frequencies and styles varied through time and space and no one has estimated the overall amount of dental transfigurement for the region.

A few examples of dental transfigurement have been described for prehistoric Indians in the midwestern United States, all relatively late in prehistory (Milner and Larsen 1991), and for two undated sites in northwest Texas (Willey and Ubelaker 1976). Although George R. Milner and Clark Spencer Larsen favor an independent origin for the midwestern cases of dental transfigurement, the numerous correspondences between Mississippian culture elements and those of Mesoamerica, and the absence of such in most of the rest of the United States—except the Southwest—are difficult to reconcile without invoking some degree of shared cultural relationships. The northward spread of maize out of Mesoamerica patently involved more than just germ plasm (Hall 1993; Kehoe 1993).

North of the Valley of Mexico, dental transfigurement has been found in crania dating around A.D. 200 in Nuevo León (Powell and Powell 1992) and around 1350 in Guasave, Sinaloa (Ekholm 1942). The former area included Romero's type A modification, notched occlusal surfaces, and the latter, mostly type C, corner chipped or filed. The Guasave finds included crania with blackened teeth (Ekholm 1942:120); these are the only ones we have seen in all of North and South America. Isabel Kelly (1945) reported finding three crania from Culiacan, Sinaloa, in 1939 that had filed lower incisors. W. J. McGee (1898) noted that the married Seri Indian women of Rancho Costa Rica, Sonora, had no upper lateral incisors, whereas the unmarried women had theirs, facts he attributed to tooth removal connected with marriage.

Dental transfigurement has not so far been reported for Alta Vista, La Quemada, Casas Grandes, or other large northern sites with Mesoamerican monumental architecture and other characteristics. There are not enough examples of dental transfigurement in northern Mexico to determine which of Romero's seven main types was most common in the region.

José Antonio Pompa, currently Mexico's leading authority on dental transfiguration, has found no examples at Alta Vista. He believes there may be examples at the northern frontier site of Cerro de Huistle, Huejuquilla, northern Jalisco, excavated by Ann Maria Hers (Pompa, personal communication, 1994).

Between 1967 and 1976, Stuart D. Scott conducted excavations in six Postclassic sites in the Teacapan estuary, a Pacific Ocean lagoon-swamp wetland on the border between southern Sinaloa and northern Nayarit. Carbon-14 dates for these sites ranged between A.D. 965 and 1273 (Gill 1985:195). Among the physical anthropological studies of the human remains by George Gill and his students was a detailed analysis of the Teacapan dental and cranial modifications. For the former, Gill found that of 43 crania with observable anterior teeth, 44.2% had at least one filed or notched tooth. The Teacapan types of modification included heavily filed and pointed incisors, which were also present in skulls excavated by Gordon Ekholm at Guasave (figs. 5.1–5.3), and simple, laterally notched specimens like those from Arizona (fig. 5.4–5.6).

In the American Southwest, dental transfiguration was unknown until Marshall H. Saville (1913) mentioned in passing and T. D. Campbell (1944) later described in detail the filed teeth of a skull Fewkes had excavated in the early 1890s at an unnoted location in Sikyatki ruin (figs. 5.4 and 5.5). The skull had been sent by Aleš Hrdlička as an exchange item to the South Australian Museum in Adelaide where Campbell worked (NMNH Physical Anthropology card catalog record). When Campbell published his description of the Sikyatki dental transfiguration, the Smithsonian requested and got the return of the skull, because it was the only one then known from the Southwest with dental transfiguration.

After 1944, no published reports on dental transfiguration in the Southwest appeared until very recently (Burnett 1997 [Pecos]; Regan, Turner, and Irish 1996 [Salado]; Turner and Turner 1995 [Hohokam]). The last example cited is from a rich Classic-period burial at the Grand Canal village site in Phoenix, Arizona, excavated by Gerald A. Bair for Soil Systems, Inc. (fig. 5.6). Lorrie Babb reported at the 1996 Pecos Conference that two Hohokam males at Las Acequias had modified teeth. As of this writing, the few examples of Southwestern dental transfiguration include labial surface polishing, mesial and distal edge notching, and filed labial-occlusal notching at the crown midpoint.

Most of the Southwestern examples of culturally-modified teeth presumably belong in the late prehistoric time period. One, however, likely falls within the range that concerns us here. This example of intentionally chipped teeth occurs in a 45 to 60 year-old adult male that Neil M. Judd (1954) uncovered in Room 330 of Pueblo Bonito, a room he firmly believed had been built by the "Old Bonitans" of Pueblo 11 times (A.D. 900–1100). Judd's workers found the floor of Room 330 strewn with the remains of at least 23 individuals, of whom most were adult men and women. In addition to the extraordinary mortuary situation suggestive of episodic burial, which speculatively may well have been due to sacrificial proceedings given the large number of bodies, one of these individuals was the male whose upper anterior teeth we discovered to have Mesoamerican-like transfiguration (fig. 5.7). The death of this unique individual may have been the stimulus for the burial of the

474

Figure 5.1. Guasave, Mexico. Notched and filed upper and lower anterior teeth. Labial view. AMNH 99.1/974 (CGT neg. 6-30-89:7).

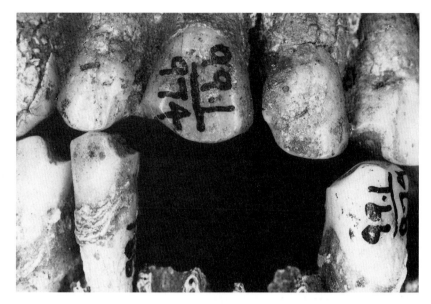

Figure 5.2. Guasave. Notched teeth and filed upper incisors and canine (at right). Lingual view. AMNH 99.1/995 (CGT neg. 6-30-89:24). Sometime following the dental treatment, the exposed pulp chamber of each incisor became necrotic.

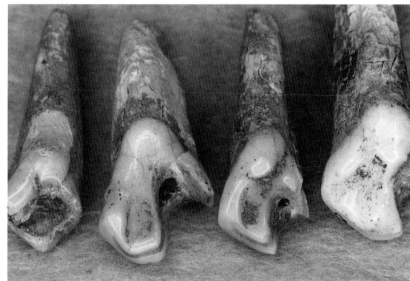

Figure 5.3. Guasave. Notched and filed upper and lower anterior teeth. Labial view. The horizontal groove on the upper incisor is not cosmetic but from developmental hypoplasia. Male? AMNH 99.1/998 (CGT neg. 6-30-89:25).

Figure 5.4. Sikyatki, Arizona. Labial view of notched upper and lower incisors in a middle-aged adult male found by J. W. Fewkes. Notching is present on the upper left and right central incisors and on the upper left lateral incisor. All four of the lower incisors are notched. Because the skull is somewhat chalky and brachycranic and has slight asymmetrical right occipital and parietal cradleboard deformation, we presume it to be prehistoric. There are no cut marks or abrasions anywhere on the skull, which lowers the probability that it was a trophy skull carried to Sikyatki from Mexico. NMNH 156318 (CGT neg. 4-29-94:19).

Figure 5.5. Sikyatki. Lingual view of teeth in the individual shown in figure 5.4. NMNH 156318 (CGT neg. 6-10-78:19).

Figure 5.6. Grand Canal Ruin, Phoenix, Arizona. Notched upper anterior teeth of a high-status male buried in this Hohokam site. Excavated by G. A. Bair for Soil Systems, Inc., Feature 90 (CGT neg. 7-10-90:4).

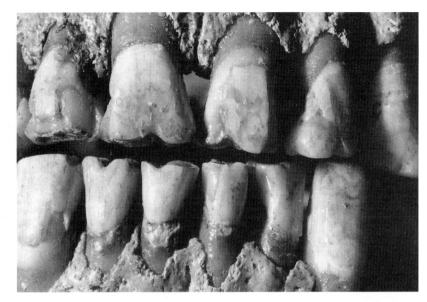
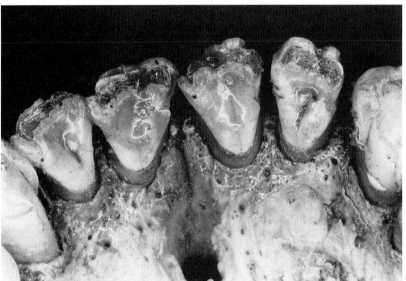
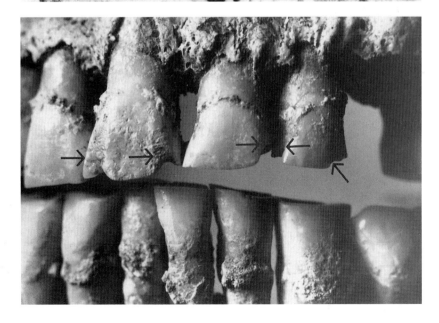

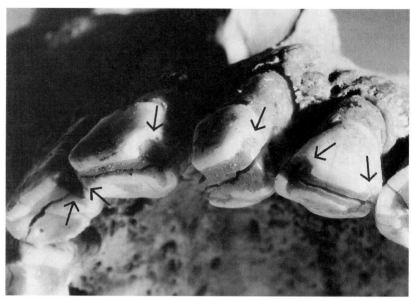

Figure 5.7. Pueblo Bonito, Room 330, Chaco Canyon, New Mexico. Dental transfiguration (multiple notching type) of several upper anterior teeth in a robust old man. The far left arrow points to notching on the mesial border of a rare congenitally-fused right lateral incisor and canine. Other arrows point to additional notches on other teeth. As there was no notching on the lower teeth, accidental transfiguration can be ruled out. No other examples of dental modification were observed in any other of some 100 Chaco Canyon crania. In Mesoamerica, the practice of dental transfiguration was relatively common. NMNH 327099, Judd's skeleton 22, FS#1947 (CGT neg. 6-3-97:34).

others. Adding to speculation, we cannot help but wonder whether his motherland more likely had been in Mexico than in Chaco Canyon because of the episodic burial context and extreme rarity of intentionally modified teeth in the Southwest, whereas such teeth were relatively common in prehistoric Mesoamerica. It is unfortunate that every one of the high-status Chaco burials excavated by Richard Wetherill and George Pepper had advanced anterior tooth wear or antemortem or postmortem loss, preventing our learning whether one or more of these "elite" persons had dental transfiguration.

Because dental transfiguration has no ethnographic or archaeological foundation in the Southwest—or in California, the Great Basin, or the Great Plains—whereas it is ancient and widespread in Mesoamerica, it is more parsimonious to believe that human remains with dental modification in the Southwest were in life from Mexico than to propose that the treatment arose independently. Since the number of Southwestern individuals with modified teeth is very small compared with the thousands of studied crania without such treatment, we propose that not only did the idea of transfiguration originate in Mexico but so did the treated individuals found in Arizona and New Mexico. These people did not necessarily have to have been traders but might also have included consorts of Mexican travelers, pilgrims or other religious sorts, slaves traded northward, curiosity seekers, or even bandits or members of small Mexican warrior bands.

Our purpose here is to initiate a new line of evidence for suggesting that Mexicans were physically present in the Southwest. Heretofore, evidence of Mesoamerican influence has been restricted to trade goods, architectural forms, and other such features. The occurrence of individuals with dental transfigurement supports the idea that actual Mexicans moved among the Anasazi, Hohokam, and Salado communities. How they managed to do so without armed guards is a mystery. Perhaps some of these travelers used cannibalism for terrorism as well as ritual.

Social Control and Social
Pathology

SHANE A. BAKER (1990) suggested that Anasazi cannibalism might have been used as a form of social control. We, too, see this is as a plausible motive, although we acknowledge that the taphonomic and contextual evidence presently available for each cannibalized assemblage is no more discriminating of a social control hypothesis than it is of hypotheses of revenge, non-Anasazi raiders, ritual, psychopathy, or other taphonomically invisible possibilities. Yet we find it quite plausible that a few score or hundred well-organized and fanatical warrior-cultists using rule-breaking but example-setting cannibalism and human sacrifice as conspicuous elements of terrorism might quickly and easily dominate small farming communities. Recall that some Southwestern charnel assemblages include as many as 35 individuals: we cannot simply average the total over three or four centuries and then dismiss the terrifying impact of such acts because they occurred less than once a year.

Referring to Aztec human sacrifice, David Carrasco (1987:154–155) concisely described its effectiveness toward social control, albeit on a much larger scale than anything we see in the Southwest: "At these ceremonies of massive human sacrifice, the kings and lords from allied and enemy city-states were invited to the ceremonial center to witness the spectacular festival. The ritual extravaganza was carried out with maximum theatrical tension, paraphernalia, and terror in order to amaze and intimidate the visiting dignitaries, who returned to their kingdoms trembling with fear and convinced that cooperation, and not rebellion, was the best response to Aztec imperialism."

Hypothesizing the use of cannibalism in the Southwest as a means of social control does not necessarily mean there had to be a direct link with the Mesoamerican central plateau, where Toltec and other city-state leaders enforced their will and tribute demands through brutality, terrorism, and ritual cannibalism. A scenario could be developed that envisioned either Mesoamerican warrior-cultists from the northern frontier moving into the Southwest or some such locally evolved group taking over. In the latter case, one would want to see evidence for the evolution of perimortem body processing, something we have not yet recognized in the bioarchaeological record. We favor the first scenario.

The use of cannibalism as a short-term mechanism for social control fits the sociobiological paradigm well. Terrorizing, mutilating, and murdering might be evolutionarily useful behaviors when directed against unrelated competitors. And what better way to amplify opponents' fear than to reduce victims to the subhuman level of cooked meat, especially when they include infants and children from whom no power or prestige could be derived but whose consumption would surely further terrorize, demean, and insult their helpless parents or community. Logically, cannibalism could have adaptive potential that in Anasazi times required no new technology, no increase in the number of warriors or assailants, and no new skills. The benefits would be threefold: community control, control of reproductive behavior (that is, dominating access to women), and food.

From the standpoint of sociobiology, then, cannibalism could well represent useful behavior done by well-adjusted, normal adults acting out their ultimate, evolutionarily channeled behavior. On the other hand, one can easily look upon violence and cannibalism as socially pathological—that is, as behavior variably expressed, depending on circumstances, as deviant, disruptive, hurtful, contagious, and even maladaptive. Each perspective has its own logic; what may be harmful at one level of biological organization may be beneficial at another. What is bad for one group (those eaten and intimidated) is good for another (the well-fed winners). We do not intend to resolve what is obviously a paradox, but we do want to explore the topic of social pathology a bit further. Even if the prehistoric Southwestern killer-cannibals are not viewed as socially pathological, the consumption of nearly 300 men, women, and children is not the sort of behavior that leads to trust, cooperation, and sharing, the positive behavioral components of all human societies.

Frank J. MacHovec's (1989:68) study on cults provides some useful definitions with which to begin:

> *Psychopaths* are, directly or indirectly, impulsive thrill seekers who ignore or violate societal and legal standards. They are uncivilized, undersocialized, and have somehow never learned to care about others. They seem to have a predatory instinct, totally selfish and without conscience. Their ruthlessness is vented through ambition and avarice or violence and crime, in a cult, business, politics, even religion. . . . Violence and crime are especially exciting to the psychopath, to have an innocent person under total control with power over life and death. Frequently insensitive to pain themselves, ritual abuse can be an obsessive preoccupation, even humorous to them in a sordid, gruesome way, a vehicle for imaginative and macabre "fun." *Sociopaths* also disregard or violate social norms or laws, but they do so less directly than the psychopath. . . . Usually, they are what many call "losers" and "loners" who live and work in the shadows, indirectly, passively self-destructive.

All well-founded claims of cannibalism in contemporary society pertain to persons who clearly fit MacHovec's description of psychopaths. Most such killers are loners, so analogues based on modern killer-cannibals such as Albert Fish (Wertham 1949), Edmund Kemper (Lunde 1976), or Jeffrey Dahmer (Ressler and Schachtman 1992) are probably not applicable to the violent episodes represented by the Southwestern cannibalized assemblages, where multiple assailants were surely involved. Instead, we look at the sort of social pathology that arises in individuals but can spread as mob behavior or as cultism under the influence of sociopathic leaders.

Social psychologists have long entertained a theory of social pathology. Basically, it reduces to the commonly made observation that the socially disruptive behavior of one individual can spread to others. Examples include spontaneous and deadly behavior by gang members, mob behavior at sporting events and lynchings, and probably episodes such as multiple killings of noncombatants in war zones. Although the theory cannot predict specific outcomes, we find it useful as a counter to the undifferentiated normative view of behavior that characterizes much prehistoric research.

The social pathology hypothesis is based on a number of psychological and criminological findings, especially those dealing with antisocial events involving groups rather than single individuals. In H. E. Lehmann's (1980) review of unusual psychiatric disorders, he discusses collective mental disorders involving many persons. One type of collective mental disorder "is represented by the sudden release of irrational and unusually aggressive behavior. It is observed in lynching and looting mobs when large numbers of people, under the influence of a strong emotion and what may be thought of as the herd instinct, temporarily lose rational and moral control and indulge in violent behavior that is entirely foreign to their normal personalities" (Lehmann 1980:1989).

A consideration of pathological group behavior inevitably leads to considerations of cultism. Cults can be nasty, as is clear from Mac-Hovec's (1989:118) grisly generalizations about cultist child abuse:

> Physical abuse is in most cases sadistic and painful, to degrade and evoke terror, by being thrown, repeatedly spun around, beaten, or ritually cut. The child is abused directly by one or more adults, forced to attack another child or watch another victim being abused. Reported degrading practices are being smeared with blood, feces and urine, forced to eat or drink these or human flesh, being placed inside a dissected animal, in a casket with a corpse, in a garbage can or closet, electric shock, "Russian roulette," or the child's hand is placed on the knife used by an adult to kill an animal or human sacrifice. . . . Sexual abuse is most frequently done forcibly, violating the person by anal, vaginal, or oral penetration by person or objects (pencils, sticks, penis, or animal or human body parts) adult to child, forced child to child, or adult to adult witnessed by the child.

MacHovec proposed and defined a scale for cult involvement. The strongest stage he called "delusional, with psychopathy." There is high risk due to ritual abuse, mutilation, murder: "These are the hardcore cultists with psychopathic or sociopathic commitment to the cult. . . . Criminal cultists at this level can decompensate to a delusional or psychotic degree dangerous to self and others. Regularly repeated ritual abuse suggests psychopathy not unlike serial killers, an addictive hunger for violence, sadism, and excitement" (MacHovec 1989:135–136).

Ken Levi (1982:18) provides valuable insight into socially pathological cults: "Learning violence is crucial to its (intentional) performance. And we might expect that religions which specifically condone and engage in either homicide or suicide also teach violence. . . . Jim Jones [instigator of the Jonestown mass suicide], as well as Charles Manson, dwelt on the imagery of race war. . . . Manson saw the coming of war as a time of 'Helter Skelter,' which his 'family' would cleverly manipulate by turning blacks against whites."

Levi suggests that cults can provide a breeding ground for socially pathological persons: "Inclination to participate in violence may be a condition for membership in cults already established as violent. The more common occurrence seems to be that a cult originally was not vio-

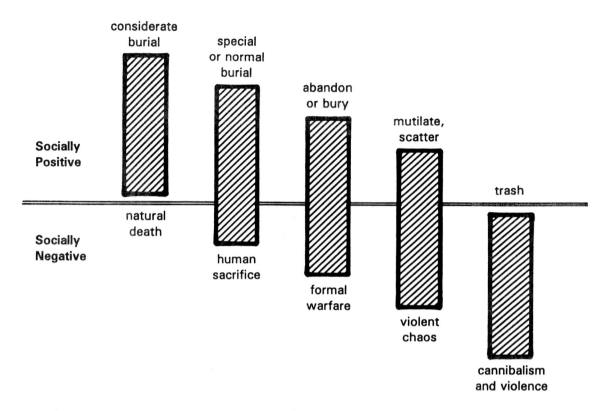

Figure 5.8. Hypothetical relationship between social pathology and treatment of the dead. The scheme envisions social health as a continuum along which different forms of burial treatment provide an estimate of the degree of social pathology linked to the burial or skeletal assemblage.

lent but becomes so. Recruits had initially no proclivity for violence as a strategy. Leaders may deliberately have desensitized members to violence against themselves or others by drills and rehearsals (example, the suicide drills in Jonestown)" (Levi 1982:70).

Florence Hawley Ellis (1951:177) surveyed the literature on historic Pueblo Indians looking for evidence of aggression and the war cult. She found throughout a "definite underlying stratum of personal aggression," and she saw warfare and violence as ways to release the accumulations of hostility and irritation that went with agriculturally bound village life requiring conformity for economic goals. She concluded that this aggression was channeled into intra- and intervillage warfare and capital punishment against individuals or groups who appeared to be nonconformists or overly competitive. Those who were perceived as "bad" were targeted for destruction by their war priest, who infected his warrior followers with his murderous command. Scalps, heads, and other trophies were carried back to the community, which celebrated and released emotional pressure by dancing, yelling, and insulting the trophies for days.

If the concept of social pathology is modified to include *institutionalized* violence, one expectation could be a cannibal warrior cult. Such a cult might have initially evolved along purposeful lines like those of the ogre kachinas of Hopi and Zuni, who function to train and control children; in tales and kiva ceremonies the ogres threaten to eat children if they do not behave (Green 1979; Parsons 1939; Titiev 1944). The power of such psychological terrorism could have been used on adults as well, as stories of Maasaw clearly indicate.

Led by a psychopath like Charles Manson (Sanders 1971), cannibal warriors with a collective mental disorder would have been a rough bunch to deal with (recall Awatovi–Polacca Wash). The 450-year written ethnohistoric record is silent on the possibility of such a group, perhaps because of Spanish and later Mexican and American prohibitions against Pueblo warfare, which drove any such organizations underground (Ellis 1951:200). Nevertheless, the remains of the many individuals seemingly cannibalized in the Anasazi area show enough patterning and correspondence of perimortem damage to make the notion of a cannibal warrior cult not unreasonable. In sum, as we discover and learn more about episodic mass human destruction in the prehistoric Southwest, we may have to allow that some form of institutionalized sociopathic behavior existed. Gangs and cult behavior provide potential analogues. The way in which such behaviors might be inversely correlated with considerate treatment of the dead is shown in figure 5.8.

## Cannibalism and the Chaco System

THE SOCIOPOLITICAL structure of the Chacoan world remains almost as much a question mark today as it was in Richard Wetherill and George Pepper's time. How might acknowledging the practice of cannibalism in the Chacoan sphere influence contemporary thought on this question?

One prominent view of Chaco Canyon is that of a "vacant ceremonial center" in which the great houses were occupied mainly on a temporary basis (Judge 1989). This view was based partly on the limited recovery of human burials—Chaco Canyon archaeology has a long history of excavator puzzlement about the scarcity of burials. James Judge (1989:251) used low burial number to support his thesis for seasonal occupation of the great houses and their rule by elite personages: "Akins (1986) . . . questions the long-held concept that Chaco lacks sufficient numbers of burials, noting in particular that the recent estimates of reduced population also require reduced expectations of burial populations. Akins . . . [also] endorses the concept of elites in Chaco Canyon and, in her view, the mortuary data provide the strongest evidence of social stratification." Judge (1989:250) also cited Stephen H. Lekson, who, on other grounds, suggested as few as 2,100–2,700 residents, about half the population traditionally believed to have occupied the canyon.

Adding to this perspective, Thomas Windes (1984:84) proposed that the small number of rooms with fire pits meant that the canyon population was perhaps 2,000 or less, and the many rooms without fire pits pointed to the Chaco towns' having been "occupied by small numbers of elite with differential access to resources and power."

Joseph A. Tainter and Fred Plog (1994:180) took Judge, and others they refer to as "Chaco revisionists," to task, objecting to interpretations of Chaco Canyon as a nearly vacant ceremonial center and to views of Chacoan society as not distinctively ranked. They noted that the empty ceremonial center idea is an old one in American archaeology; it was applied, for example, to the great lowland Mayan centers now known to have been actual cities. The use of Chaco great houses primarily as pilgrim quarters instead of for housing canyon residents did not fit the general world pattern for local exploitation of pilgrims. Wilcox (n.d.*b*) thinks that there were "elite rulers and commoners" in the Chacoan system and that by the early part of the eleventh century the system had turned into a tribute-extracting state. Although this sounds Mesoamerican, Wilcox views it largely as a local evolutionary development.

Tainter and Plog (1994:180–181) also noted that "the roads, great houses, [and] transport of commodities [at a minimum, 150,000 wooden roof beams, 40,000 pottery vessels, and the latter's possible contents to Pueblo Alto alone] . . . indicate a level of labor investment in the Chacoan system well above the norm for the Puebloan Southwest." This is hardly the sort of effort any Puebloan would voluntarily make to get a few pieces of turquoise or some small transportable lucky charm. Log-carrying pilgrims are not intuitively satisfying, either. Moreover, Tainter and Plog point out that the revisionist view of fewer people in Chaco favors Judge's position of a less hierarchical and less complex system.

We agree with Tainter and Plog because of the neglect by Judge and associates to consider the social implications of cannibalism in Chaco Canyon. These charnel deposits were extraordinary discoveries that should have been considered in evaluating the idyllic "beau ideal" model of canyon life. Integrating cannibalism into an alternative model for the Chaco phenomenon suggests something that might be called "intrusive terrorism": enter a place uninvited, often by force, and coerce by use of systematic violence and intimidation. Adding cannibalism to the Chaco explanatory mix points to a strong hierarchy, one whose power and control can more hardheadedly be hypothesized as based on brutality rather than benevolence.

John D. Schelberg (1984:5) has for more than a decade favored a more complex social structure: "Reconstruction of the social complexity and organization of the prehistoric inhabitants of Chaco Canyon places too much emphasis on arguments of analogy with the Pueblo Indians of the ethnographic present. . . . At its most complex, the Chacoan society implies a hierarchy of sites with three distinct levels of complexity, perhaps related to specialized administrative control activities. This is reflected in the settlement systems and the internal organization of the sites." Schelberg (1984:18) concluded that the Chacoans had a "complex chiefdom."

However many levels of hierarchy the Chaco system encompassed, there seems to be no correlation between size of great house and the presence or absence of cannibalism and violence. Schelberg (1984:11–12) listed 67 great houses ranked by surface area, not by number of rooms. The largest was Chetro Ketl at 23,395 square meters. The sites where we know or suspect that violence or cannibalism took place cover almost the entire areal size range of great houses (table 5.1).

The Chacoans apparently had different values regarding the consumption of humans from those prevailing before, and elsewhere at the same time, in the prehistoric Southwest. The interregional contrast in Southwestern cannibalism seems to fit the idea of an actual Mexican Indian presence stimulating or even directing the Chaco phenomenon. We propose that these southerners were practitioners of the Xipe Totec (or Maasaw) and the Tezcatlipoca-Quetzalcoatl (plumed serpent) cults.

Table 5.1

Relationship Between Great House Size and Perimortem Activity

| SIZE RANK | SITE | AREA (M²) | KIVAS | ROOMS | CANNIBALISM | VIOLENCE |
|---|---|---|---|---|---|---|
| 2 | Pueblo Bonito | 18,530 | 3 | 695+ | Yes | Yes |
| 4 | Penasco Blanco | 15,010 | 4 | 215+ | Yes | Yes |
| 5 | Pueblo del Arroyo | 8,990 | 1? | 290+ | No | Yes |
| 7 | Salmon Ruin | 8,320 | 1 | 175+ | Yes | Yes |
| 27 | Guadalupe | 1,400 | 0 | 25+ | ? | Yes? |
| 30 | Yucca House | 1,190 | Yes | 40+ | No | Yes |
| 65 | Houck K | 200 | ? | 9+ | Yes | Yes |

SOURCE: Size ranks, areal estimates, and kiva and room counts are from Schelberg (1984).

They entered the San Juan basin around A.D. 900 and found a suspicious but pliant population whom they terrorized into reproducing the theocratic lifestyle they had previously known in Mesoamerica. This involved heavy payments of tribute, constructing the Chaco system of great houses and roads, and providing victims for ceremonial sacrifice. The Mexicans achieved their objectives through the use of warfare, violent example, and terrifying cult ceremonies that included human sacrifice and cannibalism. After the abandonment of Chaco, human sacrifice and cannibalism all but disappeared, suggesting some kind of prehistoric discontinuity.

Summary

OUR STORY OF Southwestern cannibalism and violence began with the remarkable discoveries in Cave 7 by rancher-archaeologist Richard Wetherill and associates in 1893. Their discoveries were quickly followed by similar ones made by Jesse Walter Fewkes, George H. Pepper, Walter Hough, and other pioneers of Southwestern prehistory. We have, so far as possible, evaluated by taphonomic analysis the cannibalism or violence claims made by these early workers and found them to be credible. We acknowledge and pay homage to the insight of these talented pioneers.

The taphonomic findings provide a wealth of information that points to a more violent prehistoric Southwest than has commonly been recognized—one whose inhabitants in the Chaco region were processing humans in the same manner as game animals and in the same way in which Mesoamericans prepared both game and people. Unbiased analysts who have worked directly with human charnel deposits that exhibit the taphonomic signature of cannibalism conclude that the victims had been cooked.

Our study of human perimortem skeletal damage has revealed nonrandom spatial and temporal distributions for what we and other workers believe to be the taphonomic signature of Southwestern cannibalism. This signature occurs in no other mortuary, violence, abandonment, or diagenic context, each of which can be readily distinguished by taphonomic and contextual analysis. The cannibalism signature is also present in human bone assemblages in Mesoamerica, where cannibalism undoubtedly occurred, and some of those assemblages exhibit extensive ritual and other forms of processing. In Mexico, the level of ritual body processing, consumption, and display far exceeded anything known for the Southwest, as would be expected if the stimulus flow was strongly from south to north. Considering the distance between the Southwest and central Mexico, the lesser amount of ritual body processing in the former—a peripheral manifestation of the relevant Mexican cults—is only to be expected.

There are ethnohistoric suggestions of cannibalism throughout the Greater Southwest, but mostly in low frequency relative to Mesoamerica. Some cases involve starvation; some, other reasons. However, the mutilated and cooked human charnel deposits found so far in the U.S. Southwest are strongly correlated with the Chaco sphere of influence during its heyday, A.D. 900–1200. The earliest sites with cannibalized human remains date around 900, and so far only the Awatovi–Polacca Wash episode is known to have occurred after historic contact in 1539. With contact, the register between prehistoric and ethnographic practices involving warfare, violence, and religion quickly weakens.

By exclusion, correspondence, analogy, and distribution evidence, we propose that the majority of Chaco Anasazi cannibal episodes resulted from acts of violent terrorism, possibly combined with ritual, incited by a few zealous cultists from Mexico and their descendant followers who possessed the deadly ceremonial knowledge of certain Mexican socio-religious and warfare practices. If we are right, then it follows that the strong spatial and temporal concordance between Anasazi cannibalism and Chacoan great houses points also to a Mexican stimulus for the rapid development of things Chacoan. That Mexicans were actually in Arizona and New Mexico can be hypothesized on the basis of a few human skeletal remains with dental transfigurement, including one individual from Pueblo Bonito. We suggest that these cultists were maniacally concerned with Xipe Totec and/or the Tezcatlipoca-Quetzalcoatl complex. The Hopi spirit-being called Maasaw has several functional and physical features of Xipe Totec, including legendary association with warfare, human sacrifice, and fertility.

Southwestern cannibalism seems to be explainable, at least for the moment, by a hypothesis that combines social control, social pathology, and ritual purpose within the Chacoan sphere of influence. Each of these classes of explanation is evident as well in the intertwined Mesoamerican psychosocial, economic, and cosmological beliefs that were acted out through interminable warfare, unimaginable amounts of human sacrifice, and centuries of cannibalism—all carried out on the orders of tyrannical rulers with unlimited authority over the lives of their people. It appears to us that this harsh, totalitarian, and fatalistic Mesoamerican worldview was carried to the San Juan basin by actual immigrants from Mexico and imposed on a resident population that earlier had received only bits and snatches of Mexican culture from itinerant traders, explorers, and wanderers. The extraordinary quality of the Southwestern cannibal events should make us think more about what *individuals* did in the past, rather than focusing entirely on abstractions such as cultures, systems, spheres of influence, and traditions, which obscure the chains of events that can stem from a single individual's actions.

FOR THIS STUDY we used the four data-collecting forms reproduced in this appendix. We structured chapter 3 according to the categories listed on forms 1 and 2. The tables presented in chapter 3 are based on data recorded on forms 3 and 4.

The first form focuses on provenience and basic background information about a site. The second summarizes the perimortem characteristics of the skeletal assemblage and the reporting archaeologist's opinion about what was involved in its formation. It is largely the archaeological interpretation of bone distribution, deposition, and other associations and spatial limits that defines the charnel deposit and determines whether it was formed in a single event or in a series of depositional events over time. On occasion, some temporal information can be obtained from bone weathering.

The third form inventories perimortem damage. It does not include all the bones that exist in the skeleton, but its categories catch more than 99.9% of those that have been preserved in the charnel deposits examined to date. On the form, *base* refers to small fragments of connected elements that occur frequently in charnel deposits. Rather than expend time allocating the attached pieces to their respective skeletal elements, scoring such pieces simply as "base" is practical and detracts nothing from the skeletal analysis. The same comment applies to *ribs/sternum;* usually the sternum is not preserved, so we have pooled it with ribs.

Adult cranial bones are seldom broken exactly on a suture line. For example, a piece of frontal bone may have adhering to it a small piece of parietal or maxilla. We refer to any bone, whole or fragmentary, as a *piece.* An anatomically recognized and defined separate bone is an *element,* whether whole or fragmentary. When muliple element fragments occurred, as in the frontal-maxilla example, we scored them only once, for the element with the greatest area.

Teeth are a special problem. They are often found separately, but because single-rooted teeth loosen and fall out of their sockets easier than multiple-rooted teeth, counting loose teeth as part of the total pieces of an assemblage makes little practical or processual sense. Therefore we counted all teeth, in and out of their sockets, but did not use the number of teeth for computing the bone total. Because teeth might have been removed from a victim's head as small trophies (Knowles 1940:197), it could prove helpful to know the number and types of teeth present as well as missing.

The fourth form is a worksheet for computing the minimal number of individuals (MNI), which, in our studies, is frequently based on the maxilla or mandible. The notes column helps in sorting beyond the information that side, age, and sex can provide. For example, an assemblage might have five whole, two left, and five right maxillae, all from adults. The left and right sides might be too fragmentary to reassemble, but a very large left maxilla might be considered to match with a very large right maxilla because of their size, because both were calcined near the palatine suture, and because they had identical nonmetric molar crown and root morphology. The other left maxilla, however, might have teeth much smaller and more worn than those belonging to any of the right maxillae. Thus, instead of an MNI of twelve (five whole, five right, and two left maxillae) or ten (five whole and five right maxillae), the match and the small unmatched maxilla indicate that the MNI is eleven.

The same sorts of information are often helpful in matching maxillary and mandibular fragments where teeth have been lost and a match cannot be made by occlusal fit. Occasionally another skeletal element such as a fetal long bone demonstrates that a second individual was present, even if (in this example) the fetus had no other skeletal element representation. The safest approach to determining MNI is to use only the most frequently occurring skeletal element, which is generally one of the tooth-bearing bones. Analysts can, however, usually make slightly more accurate MNI estimates if they attempt the kinds of matching and subsorting just described. The significance of MNI accuracy, aside from professional conscientiousness, depends on the problems at hand.

There are a number of other ways to make bone and bone fragment counts for different kinds of taphonomic analyses (e.g., Lyman 1994; P. Shipman 1981; White 1992). We have not used these because they shed little light on the two central problems we address: was there cannibalism in the Southwest, and if so, why? We also illustrate in chapter 3 some examples of bone element reconstruction. This refitting or conjoining can be useful in considerations of processing and activity when bone fragments are scattered over a relatively wide area or are found in more than one feature or structure. Refitting can help in deciding whether a site had one or more episodes of body processing.

Finally, as a general recommendation for data recording, we summarize and add to Kenneth A. R. Kennedy's (1994:247–248) thoughtful protocol for standard field and laboratory study of trauma and violent death in human skeletal assemblages:

1. Make detailed written, photographic, and cartographic records of the skeletal remains before they are removed from their provenience. This is especially important if there is disarticulation and commingling. Identify and describe the embedding sediments and all related statigraphy from a datum point.

2. Identify and count the number of individuals. Confirm these field observations with laboratory analysis.

3. Identify and record all artifacts associated with the skeletal remains. Record all contextual signs of violence such as fire or intentional destruction of artifacts.

4. Examine all surfaces of the remains for trauma marks with at least a ten-power hand lens.

5. When trauma is evident, determine whether it could have been involved in the cause of death.

6. Search for any historic records, oral traditions, witnesses, monumental inscriptions, or other lines of evidence for violence at the site under investigation.

PROVENIENCE SHEET (Site Name):                                1994 P.1

| CLAIM DATE. |
| CLAIMANT. |
| CLAIM TYPE. |
| OTHER DESIGNATION(S). |
| SITE LOCATION. |
| SITE TYPE. |
| CULTURAL AFFILIATION. |
| CHRONOLOGY. |
| EXCAVATOR AND DATE. |
| INSTITUTIONAL STORAGE. |
| SITE REPORT. |
| OSTEOLOGICAL REPORT. |
| SKELETAL EVIDENCE OF STRESS. |
| BURIAL CONTEXT. |
| ASSOCIATED ARTIFACTS. |

488

| |
|---|
| TAPHONOMY<br>  MNI. |
| AGE AND SEX. |
| PRESERVATION. |
| WHOLE BONE AND FRAGMENT NUMBER. |
| BREAKAGE. |
| CUT MARKS. |
| BURNING. |
| ANVIL ABRASIONS. |
| POLISHING. |
| VERTEBRAE NUMBER. |
| SCALPING. |
| GNAWING, RODENT. |
| GNAWING, CARNIVORE. |
| INSECT PARTS. |
| OTHER MODIFICATION. |
| ARCHAEOLOGIST'S INTERPRETATION. |
| OTHER INTERPRETATIONS. |
| REMARKS. |

TAPHONOMY  Site:                    Unit:        Date:        1994 P.3

| Element | Whole | Frags | Smash | Peel | Anvil | Cut | Burn | Polish | Gnaw |
|---|---|---|---|---|---|---|---|---|---|
| Maxilla | | | | | | | | | |
| Mandible | | | | | | | | | |
| Frontal | | | | | | | | | |
| Parietal | | | | | | | | | |
| Occipital | | | | | | | | | |
| Temporal | | | | | | | | | |
| Base | | | | | | | | | |
| Teeth | | | | | | | | | |
| Skull Frags | | | | | | | | | |
| Cervical V. | | | | | | | | | |
| Thoracic V. | | | | | | | | | |
| Lumbar   V. | | | | | | | | | |
| Sacrum | | | | | | | | | |
| Scapula | | | | | | | | | |
| Clavicle | | | | | | | | | |
| Ribs/stern. | | | | | | | | | |
| Humerus | | | | | | | | | |
| Radius | | | | | | | | | |
| Ulna | | | | | | | | | |
| Hand | | | | | | | | | |
| Pelvis | | | | | | | | | |
| Femur | | | | | | | | | |
| Tibia | | | | | | | | | |
| Fibula | | | | | | | | | |
| Patella | | | | | | | | | |
| Foot | | | | | | | | | |
| LB Frags | | | | | | | | | |
| Unknown | | | | | | | | | |
| **Total** | | | | | | | | | |
| Percent | | | | | | | | | |

MNI SHEET (Site):                                    Unit:        1994 P.4

| Skeletal element | Age | Sex | Notes (color, burns, etc.) |
|---|---|---|---|
| Maxilla whole | | | |
| Maxilla left | | | |
| Maxilla right | | | |
| Mandible whole | | | |
| Mandible left | | | |
| Mandible right | | | |
| Other MNI element | | | |
| | | | |
| | | | |
| | | | |
| Animal bones | | | |
| Remarks | | | |

# ACKNOWLEDGMENTS

MANY PEOPLE AND institutions contributed to the production of this monograph. Although some are no longer living or affiliated with their respective institutions, we refer to them as of the time of our research. Acknowledgment of their assistance should not be viewed as suggesting in any way that they endorse what we have studied or what we believe we have learned. We are solely responsible for our findings and interpretations.

We deeply appreciate the help and access to collections we received from many scientists, museum staff members, other professionals, graduate students, and other interested persons. Because our research depended entirely on museum collections, we are grateful for the thousands of hours given by excavators, catalogers, and curators in recovering and maintaining the skeletal remains and associated records. It is because of the philosophy of fiduciary responsibility that these remains have been curated at private, state, and federal expense. Without such concern for preserving the past as national heritage, this book would have been impossible.

The oldest Southwestern skeletal series evidencing violence—the one Richard Wetherill and associates found in southeastern Utah in 1893— has been curated for more than 100 years at the Department of Anthropology of the American Museum of Natural History. It is fitting, then, to begin by thanking the museum's staff for its tremendous help, especially Jaymie L. Brauer, Barbara Conklin, Anibal Rodriguez, and Gary Sawyer. Permission to study the collections in various years was granted by Ian Tattersall.

Our interest and research in Southwestern human taphonomy began with the Polacca Wash series curated at the Museum of Northern Arizona (MNA). It was excavated by the late Alan P. Olson, and permission to study it was first granted by Alexander J. Lindsay, Jr. Funds to date some of the bones were made available by Edward B. Danson, director. Restudy of Polacca Wash and other series with perimortem damage in the MNA collections was later granted by David R. Wilcox, curator of anthropology, who also helped us better understand the so-called Chaco phenomenon, made possible the correlative mapping of great houses and cannibal sites, and provided many other forms of assistance. Phil C. Weigand bettered our understanding of Mexican and Southwestern connections as these became more important to our developing ideas about the causes of Southwestern cannibalism. Paul Drummond, Gwen Gallenstein, Elaine Hughes, Noland Wiggins, and a host of student assistants helped with access to the human and comparative faunal collections and site records and with similar aid.

In the early 1980s a brief examination of the Leroux Wash series at the Museum of Northern Arizona was granted by Robert Bowen, director. Dana Hartman and Peter Pilles, excavators of the Leroux Wash se-

491

ries, provided helpful comments and recollections of their archaeological work at this important site. Laura Graves Allen located bone for the carbon-14 dating of the Leroux Wash series, and the dating was freely provided by Robert Stuckenrath of the Smithsonian Institution's Radiation Biology Laboratory.

As life fellows of the Museum of Northern Arizona, we received housing during several summers under the directorships of Philip Thompson and Michael J. Fox. Their respective adminstrative assistants, Judy Burke and Shirley Groenhout, handled many details of these summer visits. As always, Dorothy A. House, librarian, helped find needed references. Barbara Thurber, library manager, was similarly helpful. Carol Burke allowed us to range freely in the photographic archives and made her darkroom available for many weeks of developing film and printing negatives. Holly Emerick's analysis of the Wupatki pottery showed that Room 59 had none. Truly, this monograph could not have been written had it not been for the vision of Harold S. and Mary-Russell F. Colton that created the Museum of Northern Arizona.

Colleagues at many other institutions and organizations in the Southwest offered generous assistance as well. At the Arizona State Museum, we owe thanks to Raymond H. Thompson, director, Walter H. Birkby of the Human Identification Laboratory, and Alexander J. Lindsay, Jr. At the Utah State Museum of Natural History in Salt Lake City, we thank Ann Hanniball, Colleen Hennessy, and Laurel Casjens. Help was generously provided in Blanding, Utah, by Renee Barlow, Curator, Edge of the Cedars Museum, and Winston Hurst. We are also grateful to Signa Larralde of the Bureau of Reclamation, Upper Colorado Regional Office, Salt Lake City, Utah; David A. Breternitz of the University of Colorado's Delores Archaeological Program; Jack Smith of Mesa Verde National Park; and Laurens C. Hammack, Nancy S. Hammack, and (in 1991) Michael H. Dice of Complete Archaeological Services Associates (CASA) in Cortez, Colorado.

In New Mexico, our thanks go to Stanley Rhine, Marsha D. Ogilvie, Gerald A. Bair, Charles Hilton, and Bradley J. Vierra of the University of New Mexico's Maxwell Museum of Anthropology and Office of Contract Archaeology; to David Simons of the Bureau of Land Management, Farmington District Office; to C. T. Wilson, Dabny Ford, Philip LoPiccolo, and Sara Kuhnle of Chaco Culture National Historical Park and the Chaco Center, Department of Anthropology, University of New Mexico; to David A. Phillips, Jr., director, and H. Wolcott Toll of the Museum of New Mexico's Laboratory of Anthropology and Office of Archaeological Studies; and to Byron P. Johnson and Penelope Whitten of the San Juan County Museum at Salmon Ruin, New Mexico.

Among staff members of other museums around the country, we owe our gratitude to Lane Beck and Alan Brew of the Peabody Museum, Harvard University, Cambridge; Rose Tyson of the San Diego Museum of Man; and John L. Cotter, curator emeritus of American historical archaeology, and Lucy F. Williams, keeper of the American section collections, at the University Museum, University of Pennsylvania, Philadelphia. In the Department of Anthropology at the Smithsonian Institution's National Museum of Natural History, permission to study and photograph several skeletal series was granted by Donald J. Ortner, past chairman, and Dennis Stanford, current chairman. Assistance was generously provided by David R. Hunt, manager of the physical anthropology collections, and by Bruno Frolich, Neil Houck, James Krakker, and William L. Merrill. Staff of the National Anthropological Archives were also very helpful, especially James Glen.

Many colleagues in Mexico at the various museums of the Instituto Nacional de Antropología e Historia (INAH) gave generously of their time and expertise. At the Museo de Las Culturas de Norte, Paquime, Casas Grandes, Chihuahua, we thank Béatriz Braniff; at the Chihuahua Centro Regional, Ben Brown; at the Zacatecas Centro Regional, Olga Villanueva Sánchez, Peter Jiménez Betts, and Baudelina Lydia García Urouga; at the Guadalajara Centro Regional, Federico A. Solórzano Barreto, Mrs. Solórzano, and Enrique González Rubio Barreto; in Hermosilla, Elisa Villapando C.; and at INAH's Department of Physical Anthropology, Ramon Enríquez, Josefina Mansilla Lory, Loudres Márquez Morfín, Patricia Ochoa Castilla, Carmen María Pijoan Aguadé, Jose Antonio Pompa, María Elena Salas, and María Carmen Serra Puche, president of the INAH Archaeological Council. We also appreciate the assistance of Jaime Litvak King at the Instituto de Investigaciones Antropológicas of the Universidad Nacional Autónoma de México in Mexico City.

Special credit is due the students in my spring 1996 physical anthropology seminar at Arizona State University (ASU), who devoted a large part of the semester to reading and discussing the manuscript for this book. They included Annalisa Brigitte Alvrus, Gregory E. Berg, Starletta Brown, Scott E. Burnett, Christine Lee, and Nicole Jean Silverman. Also at ASU, help was given by James Ayres, Donald M. Bahr, Roy Barnes, Elizabeth Brandt, Christopher Carr, George L. Cowgill, Michael H. Dice, Alfred E. Dittert, Jr., Sharon S. Grant, William Haeussler, Diane Hawkey, Sharon Hurlbut, Rhea Jacanin, Trinkle Jones, Penny D. Minturn, Donald H. Morris, Charles L. Redman, Glen E. Rice, Katherine Spielmann, Lyle B. Steadman, Korri Dee Turner, and all the students over several years of the bioarchaeology core course. Seed money was made available by the department's Research and Development Committee, John Martin, chairman. Leonard Bloom of Sponsored Projects helped us manage our finances.

A great deal of correspondence and discussion was involved in this project. We made inquiries related to locating collections, tracking down people and identifying officials, checking records and experiences, following leads, questioning identifications, and much more. The following people responded generously and helpfully: Bruce Anderson, Wupatki National Monument; Victoria Atkins, Anasazi Heritage Center, Dolores, Colorado; Gerald A. Bair, Office of Navajo and Hopi Indian Relocation, Sanders, Arizona; Nicolas Bellantoni, Office of the State Archaeologist, Storrs, Connecticut; Robert A. Black, University of California, Berkeley; David A. Breternitz, University of Colorado; William P. Cheshire, *Arizona Republic,* Phoenix Newspapers, Inc.; John L. Cotter and Rebecca Buck, University Museum, University of Pennsylvania, Philadelphia; Winifred Creamer, Northern Illinois University; Richard Diehl, University of Alabama, Tuscaloosa; Michael Eastman, Department of Chemistry, Northern Arizona University, Flagstaff; Jeffrey Eighmy, Department of Anthropology, Colorado State University, Fort Collins; Michael Foster, Soil Systems, Inc., Phoenix, Arizona; Roger C. Green, Department of Anthropology, University of New Zealand, Auckland; George Gumerman, Department of Anthropology, Southern Illinois University, Carbondale; Jonathan Haas, Field Museum of Natural History, Chicago; William Haeussler, Phoenix, Arizona; Robert L. Hall, Department of Anthropology, University of Illinois at Chicago; Dan M. Healan, Department of Anthropology, Tulane University, New Orleans; the late Carle Hodge; Kali T. Holtschlag, Adams Ranch–Texas Canyon, Dragoon, Arizona; Art Hutchinson and Linda Towle, Mesa Verde National Park; Evelyn James, tribal president, San Juan Southern Paiute Tribe, Tuba City, Arizona; Errol G. Jensen, Bureau of Reclamation, Durango, Colorado; Jane Holden Kelly, Department of Archaeology, University of Calgary; Anthony L. Klesert, Navajo Nation Archaeology Department, Window Rock; Pamela Kogler, Department of Anthropology, University of New Mexico, Albuquerque; Richard S. MacNeish, Andover Foundation for Archaeological Research; Ekkehart Malotki, Department of Modern Languages, Northern Arizona University, Flagstaff; Nancy J. Malville, Department of Anthropology, University of Colorado, Boulder; Debra Martin, School of Natural Science, Hampshire College, Amherst; Elizabeth A. Morris, Tucson; G. Gisela Nass, San Francisco State University; Ben A. Nelson, Department of Anthropology, Arizona State University, Tempe; Robert B. Pickering, Department of Anthropology, Denver Museum of Natural History; Jonathan E. Reyman, Springfield, Illinois; Michael Schultz, Zentrum Anatomie, Universitat Göttingen, Germany; Lucy Cranwell Smith, Tucson, Arizona; Cookie Stephan, New Mexico State University, Las Cruces; Alan Swedlund, Department of Anthropology, University of Massachusetts; Korri Dee Turner, Department of Anthropology, Arizona State University, Tempe; Margaret Van Ness, Colorado State Archaeology and Historic Preservation Office; Albert E. Ward, Center for Anthropological Studies, Albuquerque; and Tim D. White, Department of Anthropology, University of California, Berkeley. We also would like to thank Patricia and Jack McReary of San Luis Obispo, California, J. Lee Young of Holbrook, Arizona, Raymond Fitzgerald of Holbrook, and Joan G. Olson of Littleton, Colorado, for their valuable help.

We are grateful to Roger C. Green for permission to quote from his unpublished field notes, to Richard A. Diehl for permission to quote from his unpublished manuscript, and to G. Gisela Nass for permission to quote from an unpublished report by J. Lee Correll.

For editorial assistance, we thank first and foremost Jeffrey L. Grathwohl, director of the University of Utah Press, for inviting us to write this monograph, offering valuable editorial advice, and selecting two very helpful peer reviewers. For catching errors in some of our quotations we thank Kristine A. Haglund of the Denver Museum of Natural History and Cheryle M. Mitchell of *El Palacio*. We particularly thank Gerald A. Bair for reading the entire manuscript and providing many helpful comments and corrections, some uplifting drollery, and unwavering support. The immense help given by manuscript editor Jane Kepp not only reduced an excessively long manuscript but also turned the remainder into a much more readable work. Reading page proofs was greatly aided by Olga Pavlova.

Finally, we deeply appreciate the generous support provided by the National Geographic Society (grant 5135-93) on the advice of its Exploration and Research Committee, which made possible much of the data collecting and related travel, analysis, and photography for this project and assisted in the preparation and publication of this monograph.

# FIGURES

# TABLES

503

# REFERENCES CITED

Adams, Richard E. W.
1991    *Prehistoric Mesoamerica*. Rev. ed. University of Oklahoma Press, Norman.

Ager, Derek
1993    *The New Catastrophism: The Importance of the Rare Event in Geological History*. Cambridge University Press, New York.

Akins, Nancy J.
1984    Temporal Variation in Faunal Assemblages from Chaco Canyon. In *Recent Research on Chaco Prehistory*, edited by W. J. Judge and J. D. Schelberg, pp. 225–240. Reports of the Chaco Center, no. 8. National Park Service, Albuquerque, New Mexico.
1986    *A Biocultural Approach to Human Burials from Chaco Canyon, New Mexico*. Reports of the Chaco Center, no. 9. National Park Service, Santa Fe, New Mexico.

Akins, Nancy J., and John D. Schelberg
1984    Evidence of Organizational Complexity as Seen from the Mortuary Practices in Chaco Canyon. In *Recent Research on Chaco Prehistory*, edited by W. J. Judge and J. D. Schelberg, pp. 89–102. Reports of the Chaco Center, no. 8. National Park Service, Albuquerque, New Mexico.

Alexander, George
1974    New Discoveries Indicate Widespread Cannibalism in Early Pueblos. *Los Angeles Times*, September 15, pp. 1, 5.

Anaya Monroy, Fernando
1966    La antropofagia entre los antiguos mexicanos. *Estudios de Cultura Nahuatl* 7:211–218. Instituto de Investigaciones Históricas, Universidad Nacional Autónoma de México.

Anderson, James E.
1965    Human Skeletons of Tehuacán. *Science* 148:496–497.
1967    The Human Skeletons. In *The Prehistory of the Tehuacan Valley, vol. 1: Environment and Subsistence*, edited by D. S. Byers, pp. 91–113. University of Texas Press, Austin.

Anderson, Keith M.
1966    NA 3533: A Second Kiva for Betatakin. *Plateau* 39(1):61–67.

Anderson, Kirsten Linnea
1994    The Aztalan Site: A Human Skeletal Inventory and Excavation History. Master's thesis, Department of Anthropology, University of Chicago, Chicago, Illinois.

Anyon, Roger
1983    Site Description NM:12:U2:7. In *Archaeological Investigations between Manuelito Canyon and Whitewater Arroyo, Northwest New Mexico*, vol. 1, edited by R. Anyon, S. M. Collins, and K. H. Bennett, pp. 117–150. Report no. 185, Zuni Archaeology Program, Pueblo of Zuni, New Mexico.

Anyon, Roger, and Ben Robertson
1983    Site Description NM:12:U2:108A. In *Archaeological Investigations between Manuelito Canyon and Whitewater Arroyo, Northwest New Mexico*, vol. 1, edited by R. Anyon, S. M. Collins, and K. H. Bennett, pp. 282–370. Report no. 185, Zuni Archaeology Program, Pueblo of Zuni, New Mexico.

Arens, William
1979     *The Man-Eating Myth: Anthropology and Anthropophagy.* Oxford
         University Press, Oxford.
Bahn, Paul
1991     Is Cannibalism Too Much to Swallow? *New Scientist* 130(1766):38–40.
1992     Ancestral Cannibalism Gives Us Food for Thought. Review of *Prehis-
         toric Cannibalism* by T. D. White. *New Scientist* 134(1816):40–41.
Bahti, Thomas N.
1949     A Largo-Gallina Pit House and Two Surface Structures. *El Palacio*
         56(1):52–59.
Bair, Gerald A., Christy G. Turner II, and Jacqueline A. Turner
n.d.     A Mesoamerican Abroad: Reconsidering Pochtecas/Trocadores in the
         American Southwest. Manuscript in preparation.
Baker, Shane A.
1988     Rattlesnake Ruin and Anasazi Cannibalism. *Newsletter of BYU An-
         thropology and Archaeology* 4(1):n.p.
1990     Rattlesnake Ruin (42SA18434): A Case of Violent Death and Peri-
         mortem Mutilation in the Anasazi Culture of San Juan County, Utah.
         Master's thesis, Department of Anthropology, Brigham Young Univer-
         sity, Provo, Utah.
1993     Rattlesnake Ruin: The Question of Cannibalism and Violence in
         Anasazi Culture. *Canyon Legacy* 17:2–10.
1994     The Question of Cannibalism and Violence in the Anasazi Culture: A
         Case Study from San Juan County, Utah. *Blue Mountain Shadows: The
         Magazine of San Juan County History* 13:30–41.
Baldwin, Gordon C.
1948     Lake Mead Recreational Area: Archeological Surveys and Excavations
         in the Davis Dam Reservoir Area. Unpublished manuscript on file in
         Harold S. Colton Research Center Library, Museum of Northern
         Arizona, Flagstaff.
Bartlett, Katharine
1934     *The Material Culture of Pueblo II in the San Francisco Mountains, Ari-
         zona.* Museum of Northern Arizona Bulletin no. 7, Flagstaff.
Bassett, Everett J., and Karen A. Atwell
1985     Osteological Data on the Ash Creek Population. In *Studies in the Ho-
         hokam and Salado of the Tonto Basin,* edited by G. Rice, pp. 221–236.
         Office of Cultural Resource Management Report no. 63. Arizona State
         University, Tempe.
Baus Czitrom, Carolyn
1985     The Tecuexes: Ethnohistory and Archaeology. In *The Archaeology of
         West and Northwest Mesoamerica,* edited by M. S. Foster and P. C.
         Weigand, pp. 93–115. Westview Press, Boulder, Colorado.
Beaglehole, Ernest, and Pearl Beaglehole
1935     *Hopi of the Second Mesa.* Memoirs of the American Anthropological
         Association no. 44, Menasha, Wisconsin.
Beals, Ralph L.
1932     *The Comparative Ethnology of Northern Mexico before 1750.* Ibero-
         Americana no. 2. University of California, Berkeley.
1943     *The Aboriginal Culture of the Cáhita Indians.* Ibero-Americana no. 19.
         University of California, Berkeley.
Benfer, Robert A., Jr.
1968     An Analysis of a Prehistoric Skeletal Population, Casas Grandes, Chi-
         huahua, Mexico. Ph.D. dissertation, University of Texas, Austin.
Bennett, John W.
1946     The Interpretation of Pueblo Culture: A Question of Values. *South-
         western Journal of Anthropology* 2(4):361–374.
Bennett, Kenneth A.
1966     Appendix B: Analysis of Prehistoric Human Skeletal Remains from the
         Navajo Reservoir District. In *Prehistory in the Navajo Reservoir Dis-
         trict, Northwestern New Mexico,* edited by F. W. Eddy, pp. 523–546.
         Museum of New Mexico Anthropological Papers no. 15, part 2, Santa Fe.

Bennett, Wendell C., and Robert M. Zingg
1935 *The Tarahumara: An Indian Tribe of Northern Mexico.* University of Chicago Press, Chicago.

Benshoof, Lee, Cathleen M. Trumble, and Ben Robertson
1983 Appendix D: Human Osteology. In *Archaeological Investigations between Manuelito Canyon and Whitewater Arroyo, Northwest New Mexico,* vol. 2, edited by R. Anyon, S. M. Collins, and K. H. Bennett, pp. 833–859. Zuni Archaeology Program Report no. 185, Pueblo of Zuni, New Mexico.

Bernheimer, Charles L.
1929 Unpublished diary of 1929 Bernheimer Expedition. Copy in Harold S. Colton Research Center Library, Museum of Northern Arizona, Flagstaff.

Binford, Lewis R.
1981 *Bones: Ancient Men and Modern Myths.* Academic Press, New York.

Blackburn, Fred M., and Victoria M. Atkins
1993 Handwriting on the Wall: Applying Inscriptions to Reconstruct Historic Archaeological Expeditions. In *Anasazi Basketmaker: Papers from the 1990 Wetherill–Grand Gulch Symposium,* edited by V. M. Atkins, pp. 41–100. Bureau of Land Management, Cultural Resource Series no. 24. Salt Lake City, Utah.

Blackburn, Fred, and Ray Williamson
1997 *Cowboys and Cave Dwellers: Basketmaker Archaeology in Utah's Grand Gulch.* School of American Research Press, Santa Fe, New Mexico.

Blom, Frans
1924 Field Notes. Neil M. Judd Papers, National Anthropological Archives, Smithsonian Institution, Washington, D.C.

Blumenthal, E. H., Jr.
1940 An Introduction to Gallina Archaeology. *New Mexico Anthropologist* 4(1):10–13.

Brand, Donald D., Florence M. Hawley, Frank C. Hibben, et al.
1937 *Tseh So: A Small House Ruin, Chaco Canyon, New Mexico (Preliminary Report).* University of New Mexico Bulletin 308, Anthropological Series vol. 2, no. 2. University of New Mexico Press, Albuquerque.

Brandt, Richard B.
1974 *Hopi Ethics: A Theoretical Analysis.* University of Chicago Press, Chicago.

Braniff, Béatriz C.
1975 *La estratigrafía arqueológica de Villa de Reyes, SLP: Un sitio en la frontera mesoamericana.* Cuadernos de los Centros no. 17, Dirección de Centro Regionales, INAH. México.
1992 *La estratigrafía arqueológica de Villa de Reyes, San Juan Potosí.* INAH, México.

Brew, John Otis
1937 The First Two Seasons at Awatovi. *American Antiquity* 3(2):122–137.
1939 Preliminary Report of the Peabody Museum Awatovi Expedition of 1937. *American Antiquity* 5(2):103–114.
1941 Preliminary Report of the Peabody Museum Awatovi Expedition of 1939. *Plateau* 13(3):37–48.
1946 *Archaeology of Alkali Ridge, Southeastern Utah.* Papers of the Peabody Museum of American Archaeology and Ethnology, no. 21. Harvard University, Cambridge, Massachusetts.
1949 Part I: The History of Awatovi. In *Franciscan Awatovi: The Excavation and Conjectural Reconstruction of a Seventeenth-Century Spanish Mission Establishment at a Hopi Indian Town in Northeastern Arizona,* by R. G. Montgomery, W. Smith, and J. O. Brew, pp. 1–43. Papers of the Peabody Museum of American Archaeology and Ethnology, vol. 36 (Reports of the Awatovi Expedition no. 3). Harvard University, Cambridge, Massachusetts.

n.d.     Preliminary Report of the Peabody Museum Awatovi Expedition of 1938. Mimeographed. Copy in Harold S. Colton Research Center Library, Museum of Northern Arizona, Flagstaff.

Brewer, Sallie P., and Jim W. Brewer

1934     Excavation of Wupatki Room 59 Human Remains. Manuscript on file in Department of Anthropology, Archaeological Site Archives, Museum of Northern Arizona, Flagstaff.

Brody, J. J.

1983     *Mimbres Pottery: Ancient Art of the American Southwest.* Hudson Hills Press, New York.

Brooks, Sheilagh T., and Richard H. Brooks

1990     Skeletal Remains from La Cueva de Dos Cuchillos, San Francisco de Borja, Chihuahua, Mexico. In *Para conocer al hombre: Homenaje a Santiago Genoves a los 33 años como investigador en la UNAM,* edited by L. Lara Tapia, pp. 261–271. Universidad Nacional Autónoma de México, México, D.F.

Brown, Marie E.

1993     Natural History and Ethnographic Background. In *Across the Colorado Plateau: Anthropological Studies for the Transwestern Pipeline Expansion Project, vol. 15, Subsistence and Environment,* by J. Gish et al., pp. 275–326. Office of Contract Archaeology and Maxwell Museum of Anthropology, University of New Mexico, Albuquerque.

Brown, Marie E., and Kenneth L. Brown

1993     Subsistence and Other Cultural Behaviors as Reflected by the Vertebrate Faunal Remains. In *Across the Colorado Plateau: Anthropological Studies for the Transwestern Pipeline Expansion Project, vol. 15, Subsistence and Environment,* by J. Gish et al., pp. 327–381. Office of Contract Archaeology and Maxwell Museum of Anthropology, University of New Mexico, Albuquerque.

Brues, Alice

1946     Appendix B: Alkali Ridge Skeletons, Pathology and Anomaly. In *Archaeology of Alkali Ridge, Southeastern Utah,* by J. O. Brew, pp. 327–329. Papers of the Peabody Museum of American Archaeology and Ethnology, no. 21. Harvard University, Cambridge, Massachusetts.

Bullock, Peter Y.

1991     A Reappraisal of Anasazi Cannibalism. *Kiva* 57(1):5–16.

1992     A Return to the Question of Cannibalism. *Kiva* 58(2):203–205.

Burgh, Robert F.

1957     Earl Halstead Morris, 1889–1956. *American Anthropologist* 59(3):521–523.

Burnett, S. E.

1997     Dental Mutilation at Pecos Pueblo, New Mexico: Two Cases Dating from 1400–1600 A.D. *American Journal of Physical Anthropology* Supplement 24, pp. 84–85.

Butler, Barbara H.

1971     The People of Casas Grandes: Cranial and Dental Morphology through Time. Ph.D. dissertation, Southern Methodist University, Dallas, Texas.

Cabrera Castro, Rubén

1993     Human Sacrifice at the Temple of the Feathered Serpent: Recent Discoveries at Teotihuacan. In *Teotihuacan: Art from the City of the Gods,* edited by K. Berrin and E. Pasztory, pp. 101–107. Thames and Hudson, New York.

Campbell, T. D. (communicated by T. D. Stewart)

1944     The Dental Condition of a Skull from the Sikyatki Site, Arizona. *Washington Academy of Sciences* 34(10):321–322.

Carle, Peggy

1941     Burial Customs of the Indians of the Southwest. Master's thesis, Texas Technological College, Lubbock.

Carrasco, David

1982    *Quetzalcoatl and the Irony of Empire: Myths and Prophecies in the Aztec Tradition.* University of Chicago Press, Chicago.

1987    Myth, Cosmic Terror, and the Templo Mayor. In *The Great Temple of Tenochtitlan: Center and Periphery in the Aztec World,* edited by J. Broda, D. Carrasco, and E. Matos Moctezuma, pp. 124–162. University of California Press, Berkeley.

Castile, George Pierre

1980    Purple People Eaters? A Comment on Aztec Elite Class Cannibalism a la Harris-Harner. *American Anthropologist* 88(2):389–391.

Cather, Willa

1925    *The Professor's House.* Alfred A. Knopf, New York.

Cattanach, George S., Jr. (with contributions by R. P. Wheeler et al.)

1980    *Long House.* Mesa Verde National Park, Colorado, Publications in Archeology 7H, Wetherill Mesa Studies. National Park Service, Washington, D.C.

Chase, James E.

1976    Deviance in the Gallina: A Report on a Small Series of Gallina Human Skeletal Remains. In *Archeological Excavations in the Llaves Area, Santa Fe National Forest, New Mexico, 1972–1974,* by H. W. Dick, pp. 67–106. USDA Forest Service, Southwestern Region, Archeological Report no. 13, Albuquerque.

Clary, Karen Husum

1984    Anasazi Diet and Subsistence as Revealed by Coprolites from Chaco Canyon. In *Recent Research on Chaco Prehistory,* edited by W. J. Judge and J. D. Schelberg, pp. 265–279. Reports of the Chaco Center no. 8, National Park Service, Albuquerque.

Coe, Michael D., and Richard A. Diehl

1980    *In the Land of the Olmec, vol. 1: The Archaeology of San Lorenzo Tenochtitlán.* University of Texas Press, Austin.

Cole, Sally J.

1993    Basketmaker Rock Art at the Green Mask Site, Southeastern Utah. In *Anasazi Basketmaker: Papers from the 1990 Wetherill–Grand Gulch Symposium,* edited by V. M. Atkins, pp. 193–220. Bureau of Land Management, Cultural Resources Series no. 24. Salt Lake City, Utah.

Colton, Harold S.

1933    Wupatki, the Tall House. *Museum Notes* (Museum of Northern Arizona) 4(11).

1946    *The Sinagua: A Summary of the Archaeology of the Region of Flagstaff, Arizona.* Museum of Northern Arizona Bulletin no. 22, Flagstaff.

1960    *Black Sand: Prehistory in Northern Arizona.* University of New Mexico Press, Albuquerque.

Colton, Harold S., Lyndon L. Hargrave, James W. Brewer, Jr., et al.

n.d.    Scientific Report on the Excavation of Wupatki. F-68 CWA Work Project no. 10, Wupatki National Monument. Manuscript on file in Harold S. Colton Research Center Library, Museum of Northern Arizona, Flagstaff.

Cook, Sherburne F.

1946    Human Sacrifice and Warfare as Factors in the Demography of Pre-Colonial Mexico. *Human Biology* 18(2):81–102.

Cordell, Linda S.

1989    Northern and Central Rio Grande. In *Dynamics of Southwest Prehistory,* edited by L. S. Cordell and G. J. Gumerman, pp. 293–335. Smithsonian Institution Press, Washington, D.C.

Courlander, Harold

1971    *The Fourth World of the Hopis.* Fawcett Publications, Greenwich, Connecticut.

Cushing, Frank H.

1896    Outlines of Zuñi Creation Myths. *Thirteenth Annual Report of the Bu-

*reau of Ethnology, 1891–1892*, pp. 325–447. Smithsonian Institution, Washington, D.C.

1979    On the Trail. In Zuñi. *Selected Writings of Frank Hamilton Cushing*, edited by J. Green, pp. 308–314. University of Nebraska Press, Lincoln.

Danson, Edward B.

1965    *Thirty-seventh Annual Report of the Museum of Northern Arizona and Research Center*, pp. 1–31. Flagstaff.

Dean, Jeffrey S., and John C. Ravesloot

1993    The Chronology of Cultural Interaction in the Gran Chichimeca. In *Culture and Contact: Charles C. Di Peso's Gran Chichimeca*, edited by A. I. Woosley and J. C. Ravesloot, pp. 83–103. Amerind Foundation, Dragoon, Arizona, and University of New Mexico Press, Albuquerque.

Díaz, Gisele, and Alan Rodgers

1993    *The Codex Borgia: A Full-Color Restoration of the Ancient Mexican Manuscript*. Dover Publications, New York.

Dibble, Charles E.

1947    *Codex Hall: An Ancient Mexican Hieroglyphic Picture Manuscript*. Monographs of the School of American Research no. 11. University of New Mexico Press, Albuquerque.

Dice, Michael H.

1993a    A Disarticulated Human Bone Assemblage from Leroux Wash, Arizona. Master's thesis, Department of Anthropology, Arizona State University, Tempe.

1993b    Disarticulated Human Remains from the Hanson Pueblo, 5MT3976, Cortez, Colorado. Manuscript on file at Woods Canyon Archaeological Consultants, Yellow Jacket, Colorado.

1993c    Disarticulated Human Remains from Reach III of the Towaoc Canal, Ute Mountain Ute Reservation, Montezuma County, Colorado. Report prepared for Bureau of Reclamation, Upper Colorado Region, Salt Lake City, Utah, by Complete Archaeological Services Associates, Cortez, Colorado.

Dick, Herbert W.

1976    *Archeological Excavations in the Llaves Area, Santa Fe National Forest, New Mexico, 1972–1974, Part 1: Architecture*. USDA Forest Service, Southwestern Region, Archeological Report no. 13. Albuquerque.

Diehl, Richard A.

1983    *Tula: The Toltec Capital of Ancient Mexico*. Thames and Hudson, London.

n.d.    Faunal Remains from Tula, Hidalgo, Mexico. Manuscript in preparation.

Di Peso, Charles C.

1974a    *Casas Grandes, a Fallen Trading Center of the Gran Chichimeca, vol. 1: Preceramic, Plainware, and Viejo Periods*. Edited by G. J. Fenner. Amerind Foundation, Dragoon, Arizona, and Northland Press, Flagstaff.

1974b    *Casas Grandes, a Fallen Trading Center of the Gran Chichimeca, vol. 2: Medio Period*. Amerind Foundation, Dragoon, Arizona, and Northland Press, Flagstaff.

Di Peso, Charles C., John B. Rinaldo, and Gloria J. Fenner

1974    *Casas Grandes, a Fallen Trading Center of the Gran Chichimeca, vol. 8: Bone, Economy, Burials*. Amerind Foundation, Dragoon, Arizona, and Northland Press, Flagstaff.

Dittert, A. E., Jr., F. W. Eddy, and B. L. Dickey

1966    LA 4195, Sambrito Village. In *Prehistory in the Navajo Reservoir District, Northwestern New Mexico*, edited by F. W. Eddy, pp. 230–254. Museum of New Mexico Papers in Anthropology no. 15, part 1. Santa Fe.

Douglass, A. E.

1935    *Dating Pueblo Bonito and Other Ruins of the Southwest*. National Geographic Society, Contributed Technical Papers, Pueblo Bonito Series, no. 1. Washington, D.C.

Durán, Fray Diego

1993    *The History of the Indies of New Spain.* Translated, annotated, and with an introduction by D. Heyden. University of Oklahoma Press, Norman.

Dutton, Bertha P.

1964    Mesoamerican Culture Traits which Appear in the American Southwest. *Proceedings of the Thirty-fifth Congress of Americanists, 1962,* vol. 1, pp. 481–492. Instituto Nacional de Antropología e Historia, México, D.F.

Eddy, Frank W.

1977    *Archaeological Investigations at Chimney Rock Mesa, 1970–1972.* Memoirs of the Colorado Archaeological Society no. 1, Boulder, Colorado.

1993    History of Research at Chimney Rock. In *The Chimney Rock Archaeological Symposium. October 20–21, 1990, Durango, Colorado,* edited by J. McK. Malville and G. Matlock, pp. 10–13. USDA Forest Service, Fort Collins, Colorado.

Efremov, I. A.

1940    Taphonomy: New Branch of Paleontology. *Pan-American Geologist* 74(2):81–93.

Ekholm, Gordon F.

1942    *Excavations at Guasave, Sinaloa, Mexico.* Anthropological Papers of the American Museum of Natural History, no. 38, part 2. New York.

Elgar, Mark A., and Bernard J. Crespi, editors

1992    *Cannibalism: Ecology and Evolution among Diverse Taxa.* Oxford University Press, New York.

Ellis, Florence Hawley

1950    The Mechanics of Perpetuation in Pueblo Witchcraft. In *For the Dean: Essays in Anthropology in Honor of Byron Cummings on His Eighty-Ninth Birthday,* edited by E. Reed and D. King, pp. 143–158. Hohokam Museums Association and Southwest Monuments Association, Tucson and Santa Fe.

1951    Patterns of Aggression and the War Cult in Southwestern Pueblos. *Southwestern Journal of Anthropology* 7(2):177–201.

Ellis, Florence H., and L. C. Hammack

1968    The Inner Sanctum of Feather Cave, a Mogollon Sun and Earth Shrine Linking Mexico and the Southwest. *American Antiquity* 33(1):25–44.

Ellis, Lee

1989    *Theories of Rape: Inquiries into the Causes of Sexual Aggression.* Hemisphere Publishing, New York.

1990a   The Evolution of Violent Criminal Behavior and Its Nonlegal Equivalent. In *Crime in Biological, Social, and Moral Contexts,* edited by L. Ellis and H. Hoffman, pp. 61–80. Praeger, New York.

1990b   Conceptualizing Criminal and Related Behavior from a Biosocial Perspective. In *Crime in Biological, Social, and Moral Contexts,* edited by L. Ellis and H. Hoffman, pp. 18–35. Praeger, New York.

Ennis, George

1952    Appendix 3: Human Skeletal Remains from Big Hawk Valley. In *Excavations in Big Hawk Valley,* by W. Smith, pp. 184–188. Museum of Northern Arizona Bulletin no. 24, Flagstaff.

Errickson, Mary M., with C. B. Brandt et al.

1993    *Prehistoric Archaeological Investigations on Reach III of the Towaoc Canal, Ute Mountain Ute Reservation, Montezuma County, Colorado.* Four Corners Archaeological Project Report no. 21, prepared for Bureau of Reclamation, Upper Colorado Region, Salt Lake City, Utah, by Complete Archaeological Services Associates, Cortez, Colorado.

Ezell, Paul H., and Alan P. Olson

1955    An Artifact of Human Bone from Eastern Arizona. *Plateau* 27(3):8–11.

Fastlicht, Samuel
1971    *La odontología en el México prehispánico.* Privately printed, México,
        D.F.
Fay, Patricia M., and Pamela Y. Klein
1988    A Reexamination of the Leroux Wash Skeletal Material for Evidence of
        Human Modification. Paper prepared for Museum of Northern Ari-
        zona and Northern Arizona University Summer Field School,
        D. Wilcox, director. Manuscript on file at Museum of Northern Ari-
        zona, Flagstaff.
Ferdon, Edwin N., Jr.
1955    *A Trial Survey of Mexican-Southwestern Architectural Parallels.*
        Monographs of the School of American Research and Museum of New
        Mexico, no. 21, Santa Fe.
Ferguson, William M., and Arthur H. Rohn
1987    *Anasazi Ruins of the Southwest in Color.* University of New Mexico
        Press, Albuquerque.
Fernández, Adela
1992    *Diccionario ritual de voces nahuas: Definiciones de palabras que ex-
        presan el pensamiento mítico y religioso de los Nahuas prehispánicos.*
        Panorama Editorial, México, D.F.
Fetterman, Jerry, Linda Honeycutt, and Kristin Kuckelman
1988    *Salvage Excavations of 42SA12209, a Pueblo I Habitation Site in Cot-
        tonwood Canyon, Manti-LaSal National Forest, Southeastern Utah.*
        Report to USDA Forest Service, Monticello, Utah, by Woods Canyon
        Archaeological Consultants, Yellow Jacket, Colorado.
Fewkes, Jesse Walter
1893a   A-wa'-to bi: An Archeological Verification of a Tusayan Legend. *Amer-
        ican Anthropologist* 6:363–375.
1893b   A Central American Ceremony which Suggests the Snake Dance of the
        Tusayan Villages. *American Anthropologist* 6:284–306.
1895    Fewkes Files 4408:4, 11, 13, 21, 22, Fewkes Archive, National Anthro-
        pological Archives, Smithsonian Institution, Washington, D.C.
1897    The Sacrificial Element in Hopi Worship. *Journal of American Folk-
        Lore* 10(38):187–201.
1899    Archeological Expedition to Arizona in 1895. In *Seventeenth Annual
        Report of the Bureau of American Ethnology, 1895–96,* part 2,
        pp. 519–744. Smithsonian Institution, Washington, D.C.
1904    Two Summers' Work in Pueblo Ruins. In *Twenty-second Annual Re-
        port of the Bureau of American Ethnology, 1900–1901,* part 1,
        pp. 3–195. Smithsonian Institution, Washington, D.C.
1911    *Antiquities of the Mesa Verde National Park: Cliff Palace.* Bureau of
        American Ethnology Bulletin 51. Smithsonian Institution, Washington,
        D.C.
1914    Archeology of the Lower Mimbres Valley, New Mexico. *Smithsonian
        Miscellaneous Collections* (Publication 2316) 63(10):1–53. Washing-
        ton, D.C.
1920    Sun Worship of the Hopi Indians. *Smithsonian Report for 1918,*
        pp. 493–526. Publication 2571. Washington, D.C.
1923    Designs on Prehistoric Pottery from the Mimbres Valley, New Mexico.
        *Smithsonian Miscellaneous Collections* (Publication 2713) 74(6):1–47.
        Washington, D.C.
n.d.    J. W. Fewkes File 4408. National Anthropological Archives, Smithson-
        ian Institution, Washington, D.C.
Fink, T. Michael
1989    *Analysis of the Human Remains from site 42SA3724, Southeastern
        Utah.* Soil Systems Technical Reports 89–104. Phoenix, Arizona.
1996    Current Issues in Cremation Analysis: A Perspective from the American
        Southwest. Master's thesis, Department of Anthropology, Arizona
        State University, Tempe.
Fink, T. Michael, and K. J. Schroeder
1994    Human Remains. In *Pioneer and Military Memorial Park Archae-*

*ological Project in Phoenix, Arizona, 1990–1992, vol. 1: Project Parameters and the Prehistoric Component,* edited by K. J. Schroeder, pp. 246–253. Roadrunner Publications in Anthropology 3. Phoenix.

Fink, T. Michael, and Korri Dee Turner
n.d.     The Human Skeleton from NA 20,700. Manuscript in authors' possession.

Flannery, Kent V.
1967     Vertebrate Fauna and Hunting Patterns. In *The Prehistory of the Tehuacan Valley, vol. 1: Environment and Subsistence,* edited by D. S. Byers, pp. 132–177. University of Texas Press, Austin.

Flinn, Lynn, Christy G. Turner II, and Alan Brew
1976     Additional Evidence for Cannibalism in the Southwest: The Case of LA4528. *American Antiquity* 41(3):308–318.

Food and Agriculture Organization of the United Nations
1991     *Guidelines for Slaughtering, Meat Cutting and Further Processing.* FAO Animal Production and Health Paper 91, Rome.

Forsyth, Donald W.
1983     The Beginnings of Brazilian Anthropology: Jesuits and Tupinamba Cannibalism. *Journal of Anthropological Research* 39(1):147–178.
1985     Three Cheers for Hans Staden: The Case for Brazilian Cannibalism. *Ethnohistory* 32(1):17–36.

Fowler, Melvin L., and Richard S. MacNeish
1972     Excavations in the Coxcatlan Locality in the Alluvial Slopes. In *The Prehistory of the Tehuacan Valley, vol. 5: Excavations and Reconnaissance,* edited by R. S. MacNeish et al., pp. 219–340. University of Texas Press, Austin.

Frisbie, Theodore R.
1978     High Status Burials in the Greater Southwest: An Interpretative Synthesis. In *Across the Chichimec Sea: Papers in Honor of J. Charles Kelley,* edited by C. L. Riley and B. C. Hedrick, pp. 202–227. Southern Illinois University Press, Carbondale.

Gibbons, Ann
1997     Archaeologists Rediscover Cannibals. *Science* 277:635–637.

Gifford, E. W.
1936     Northeastern and Western Yavapai. *University of California Publications in American Archaeology and Ethnology,* vol. 34, pp. 247–354. Berkeley.

Gill, George W.
1985     Cultural Implications of Artificially Modified Human Remains from Northwestern Mexico. In *The Archaeology of West and Northwest Mesoamerica,* edited by M. S. Foster and P. C. Weigand, pp. 193–215. Westview Press, Boulder.

Gilmore, M. R.
1933     The Plight of Living Scalped Indians. *Papers of the Michigan Academy of Science, Art and Letters* 19:39–45.

Gladwin, Harold S.
1945     *The Chaco Branch: Excavations at White Mound and in the Red Mesa Valley.* Medallion Papers no. 33. Gila Pueblo, Globe, Arizona.

González Rul, Francisco
1963     Un tzompantli en Tlatelolco. *Boletin del Instituto Nacional de Antropología e Historia* 13:3–5.

González Torres, Yolotl
1985     *El sacrificio humano entre los Mexicas.* Instituto Nacional de Antropología e Historia, México, D.F.

Grant, Sharon S.
1989     Secondary Burial or Cannibalism? An Example from New Mexico. *American Journal of Physical Anthropology* 78:230–231.

Green, Jesse
1979     Introduction. In *Selected Writings of Frank Hamilton Cushing,* edited by J. Green, pp. 3–34. University of Nebraska Press, Lincoln.

Greene, Jerry L., and Thomas W. Mathews
1976    Appendix 5: Faunal Study of Unworked Mammalian Bones. In *The Hohokam, Desert Farmers and Craftsmen: Excavations at Snaketown, 1964–1965,* edited by E. W. Haury, pp. 367–373. University of Arizona Press, Tucson.

Griffen, William B.
1983    Southern Periphery: East. In *Handbook of North American Indians, vol. 10: Southwest,* edited by A. Ortiz, pp. 329–342. Smithsonian Institution Press, Washington, D.C.

Gumerman, George J., and Jeffrey S. Dean
1989    Prehistoric Cooperation and Competition in the Western Anasazi Area. In *Dynamics of Southwest Prehistory,* edited by L. S. Cordell and G. J. Gumerman, pp. 99–148. Smithsonian Institution Press, Washington, D.C.

Gumerman, George J., and Alan P. Olson
1968    Prehistory in the Puerco Valley, Eastern Arizona. *Plateau* 40(4):113–127.

"H"
1894    Recent Finds in Utah. *Archaeologist* 2:154–155.

Haas, Jonathan, and Winifred Creamer
1993    *Stress and Warfare among the Kayenta Anasazi of the Thirteenth Century A.D.* Field Museum of Natural History Fieldiana Anthropology, New Series, no. 21, Publication 1450. Chicago.

Hagberg, Elizabeth Boies
1939    Southwestern Indian Burial Practices. Master's thesis, University of Arizona, Tucson.

Haglund, William D., Donald T. Reay, and Daris R. Swindler
1988    Tooth Mark Artifacts and Survival of Bones in Animal Scavenged Human Skeletons. *Journal of Forensic Sciences* 33:985–997.
1989    Canid Scavenging/Disarticulation Sequence of Human Remains in the Pacific Northwest. *Journal of Forensic Sciences* 34(3):587–606.

Hall, Robert
1993    A Green Card for the Green Corn Goddess, or, Acknowledging Xilonen's Legitimate Residence in the U.S. *Abstracts of the Thirteenth International Congress of Anthropological and Ethnological Sciences, Mexico City,* pp. 183–184. Mexico City.

Hamperl, H., and W. S. Laughlin
1959    Osteological Consequences of Scalping. *Human Biology* 31(1):80–89.

Hargrave, Lyndon Lane
1933    *Pueblo II Houses of the San Francisco Mountains, Arizona.* Museum of Northern Arizona Bulletin no. 4, pp. 15–75. Flagstaff.
1970    *Mexican Macaws: Comparative Osteology and Survey of Remains from the Southwest.* Anthropological Papers of the University of Arizona no. 20. Tucson.

Hartman, Dana
1975    Preliminary Assessment of Mass Burials in the Southwest. *American Journal of Physical Anthropology* 42(2):305–306.

Hartman, Dana, and Arthur H. Wolf
1977    *Wupatki: An Archeological Assessment.* Museum of Northern Arizona Research Paper no. 6. Flagstaff.

Hassig, Ross
1988    *Aztec Warfare: Imperial Expansion and Political Control.* University of Oklahoma Press, Norman.
1992    *War and Society in Ancient Mesoamerica.* University of California Press, Berkeley.

Haury, Emil W.
1945    The Problem of Contacts between the Southwestern United States and Mexico. *Southwestern Journal of Anthropology* 1(1):55–74.
1989    *Point of Pines, Arizona: A History of the University of Arizona Archaeological Field School.* Anthropological Papers of the University of Arizona no. 50. University of Arizona Press, Tucson.

Haury, Emil W., editor
1976    *The Hohokam, Desert Farmers and Craftsmen: Excavations at Snake-town, 1964–1965.* University of Arizona Press, Tucson.

Hayes, Alden C.
1964    *The Archeological Survey of Wetherill Mesa. Mesa Verde National Park, Colorado.* Archeological Research Series no. 7A. National Park Service, Washington, D.C.

Haynes, Gary
1983    Frequencies of Spiral and Green-Bone Fractures on Ungulate Limb Bones in Modern Surface Assemblages. *American Antiquity* 48(1):102–114.

Hegler, Roger
1984    Burned Remains. In *Human Identification: Case Studies in Forensic Anthropology,* edited by T. A. Rathburn and J. F. Buikstra, pp. 148–158. Charles C. Thomas, Springfield, Illinois.

Helmuth, Hermann
1973    Cannibalism in Paleoanthropology and Ethnology. In *Man and Aggression,* 2d ed., edited by A. Montagu, pp. 229–253. Oxford University Press, New York.

Herrmann, Nicholas P.
1993    Burial Descriptions. In *Across the Colorado Plateau: Anthropological Studies for the Transwestern Pipeline Expansion Project, vol. 18, Human Remains and Burial Goods,* by N. P. Herrmann et al., pp. 11–75. Office of Contract Archaeology and Maxwell Museum of Anthropology, University of New Mexico, Albuquerque.

Herrmann, Nicholas P., Marsha D. Ogilvie, Charles E. Hilton, and Kenneth L. Brown
1993    Summary and Conclusions. In *Across the Colorado Plateau: Anthropological Studies for the Transwestern Pipeline Expansion Project, vol. 18, Human Remains and Burial Goods,* by N. P. Herrmann et al., pp. 153–157. Office of Contract Archaeology and Maxwell Museum of Anthropology, University of New Mexico, Albuquerque.

Hewett, Edgar L.
1936    *The Chaco Canyon and Its Monuments.* Handbooks of Archaeological History. University of New Mexico Press, Albuquerque.

Hibben, Frank C.
1944    The Mystery of the Stone Towers. *Saturday Evening Post,* December 9, pp. 14–15, 68–70.

Hill, W. W.
1938    *The Agricultural and Hunting Methods of the Navaho Indians.* Yale University Publications in Anthropology no. 18. New Haven, Connecticut.

Hinton, Thomas B.
1983    Southwestern Periphery: West. In *Handbook of North American Indians, vol. 10: Southwest,* edited by A. Ortiz, pp. 315–328. Smithsonian Institution Press, Washington, D.C.

Hodge, Frederick Webb
1912    Awatobi. In *Handbook of American Indians North of Mexico,* pp. 119–120. Bureau of American Ethnology Bulletin no. 30. Smithsonian Institution, Washington, D.C.
1918    Excavations at Hawikuh, New Mexico: Explorations and Field-Work of the Smithsonian Institution in 1917. *Smithsonian Miscellaneous Collections* 68(12):61–72.
1920    *Hawikuh Bonework.* Indian Notes and Monographs, vol. 3, no. 3. Museum of the American Indian, Heye Foundation, New York.
1937    *History of Hawikuh, New Mexico: One of the So-Called Cities of Cíbola.* Frederick Webb Hodge Anniversary Publication Fund vol. 1, Southwest Museum and Museum of the American Indian, Heye Foundation. Los Angeles.

Hoffman, J. Michael
1990    Final Report: The Human Skeletal Remains from the Duckfoot Site

(5MT3868). Report Submitted to Crow Canyon Archaeological Center, Cortez, Colorado.

1993     Human Skeletal Remains. In *The Duckfoot Site, vol. 1: Descriptive Archaeology,* edited by R. R. Lightfoot and M. C. Etzkorn, pp. 253–296. Crow Canyon Archaeological Center, Cortez, Colorado.

Hogg, Gary

1966     *Cannibalism and Human Sacrifice.* Citadel Press, New York.

Hohmann, John, Paul Fortin, Jerry Howard, and Helen O'Brien

1985     Site AZ U:3:49 (ASU). In *Hohokam and Salado Hamlets in the Tonto Basin: Site Descriptions,* by J. W. Hohmann, pp. 216–290. Office of Cultural Resource Management Report no. 64, Arizona State University, Tempe.

Holien, Thomas, and Robert B. Pickering

1978     Analogues in Classic Period Chalchihuites Culture to Late Mesoamerican Ceremonialism. In *Middle Classic Mesoamerica: A.D. 400–700,* edited by E. Pasztory, pp. 145–157. Columbia University Press, New York.

Holmes, William M.

1878     Report on the Ancient Ruins of Southwestern Colorado Examined during the Summers of 1875 and 1876. *Tenth Annual Report of the United States Geological and Geographical Survey of the Territories, Embracing Colorado and Parts of Adjacent Territories, Being a Report of Progress of the Exploration for the Year 1876,* by F. V. Hayden, pp. 383–408. Washington, D.C.

Hough, Walter

1902     Ancient Peoples of the Petrified Forest of Arizona. *Harper's Monthly* 105:897–901.

1903     Archeological Field Work in North-eastern Arizona: The Museum-Gates Expedition of 1901. *Report of the United States National Museum for 1901,* pp. 279–358. Smithsonian Institution, Washington, D.C.

1932     Biographical Memoir of Jessie Walter Fewkes, 1850–1930, Presented to the Academy at the Autumn Meeting, 1932. *National Academy of Sciences of the United States of America Biographical Memoirs,* vol. 15, ninth memoir, pp. 261–283. National Academy of Sciences, Washington, D.C.

Hrdlička, Aleš

1931     Catalogue of Human Crania in the United States National Museum Collections: Pueblos, Southern Utah Basket-Makers, Navaho. *Proceedings of the U.S. National Museum,* vol. 78, article 2, pp. 1–95. Washington, D.C.

Hurst, Winston B., and Christy G. Turner II

1993     Rediscovering the "Great Discovery": Wetherill's First Cave 7 and Its Record of Basketmaker Violence. In *Anasazi Basketmaker: Papers from the 1990 Wetherill–Grand Gulch Symposium,* edited by V. M. Atkins, pp. 143–191. Bureau of Land Management, Cultural Resources Series no. 24. Salt Lake City, Utah.

Ilia Najera, Martha

1993     El sacrificio humano: Alimento de los dioses. *Revista de la Universidad Nacional Autónoma de México* 515:24–28.

Irwin-Williams, Cynthia, editor

1972     *The Structure of Chacoan Society in the Northern Southwest: Investigations at the Salmon Site, 1972.* Eastern New Mexico University Contributions in Anthropology no. 5, part 1. Portales, New Mexico.

Irwin-Williams, Cynthia, and Phillip H. Shelly

1980     Investigations at Salmon Ruin: Methodology and Overview. In *Investigations of the Salmon Site: The Structure of Chacoan Society in the Northern Southwest,* vol. 1, part 2, edited by C. Irwin-Williams and P. H. Shelly, pp. 107–170. Eastern New Mexico University, Portales.

James, George Wharton

1901     The Storming of Awatobi. *Chautauquan* 33(5):497–500.

1917     *Arizona the Wonderland.* Page Company, Boston.

James, Harry C.
1974    *Pages from Hopi History.* University of Arizona Press, Tucson.
James, Steven R.
1994    Hohokam Hunting and Fishing Patterns at Pueblo Grande: Results of
        the Archaeofaunal Analysis. In *The Pueblo Grande Project, vol. 5: En-*
        *vironment and Subsistence,* edited by S. Kwiatkowski, pp. 249–318.
        Soil Systems Publications in Archaeology 20(5). Phoenix, Arizona.
Jeançon, Jean Allard
1922    *Archaeological Research in the Northeastern San Juan Basin of Col-*
        *orado during the Summer of 1921.* State Historical and Natural His-
        tory Society of Colorado and University of Denver.
Jelinek, Arthur J.
1961    Mimbres Warfare? *Kiva* 27(2):28–30.
Jenkins, Leigh
1991    The Hopi View. In *The Anasazi: Why Did They Leave? Where Did*
        *They Go?* edited by J. G. Widdison, pp. 31–33. Southwest Natural and
        Cultural Heritage Association, Albuquerque.
Jennings, Jesse D.
1966    *Glen Canyon: A Summary.* Anthropological Papers no. 81 (Glen
        Canyon Series no. 31), Department of Anthropology. University of
        Utah Press, Salt Lake City.
Johnson, Eileen
1985    Current Developments in Bone Technology. In *Advances in Archaeo-*
        *logical Method and Theory,* no. 8, edited by M. B. Schiffer, pp. 157–
        235. Academic Press, New York.
Jones, W. P.
1972    A Probable Example of a Massacre and/or Cannibalism from the
        Navajo Reservoir District, Northwestern New Mexico. Graduate re-
        search paper, Department of Anthropology, Arizona State University,
        Tempe. Manuscript in authors' possession.
Judd, Neil M.
1936    Walter Hough: An Appreciation. *American Anthropologist*
        38(3):471–481.
1954    The Material Culture of Pueblo Bonito. *Smithsonian Miscellaneous*
        *Collections* 124 (Publication 4172). Washington, D.C.
1959    Pueblo del Arroyo, Chaco Canyon, New Mexico. *Smithsonian Miscel-*
        *laneous Collections* 138(1) (Publication 4346). Washington, D.C.
Judge, W. James
1989    Chaco Canyon–San Juan Basin. In *Dynamics of Southwest Prehistory,*
        edited by L. S. Cordell and G. J. Gumerman, pp. 209–261. Smithson-
        ian Institution Press, Washington, D.C.
Keegan, John
1993    *A History of Warfare.* Hutchinson, London.
Kehoe, Alice B.
1993    Cohokia as a Mesoamerican City. In *Abstracts of the Thirteenth Inter-*
        *national Congress of Anthropological and Ethnological Sciences, Mex-*
        *ico City,* p. 220. Mexico City.
Kelley, Ellen A.
1978    The Temple of the Skulls at Alta Vista, Chalchihuites. In *Across the*
        *Chichimec Sea: Papers in Honor of J. Charles Kelley,* edited by C. L.
        Riley and B. C. Hedrick, pp. 102–126. Southern Illinois University
        Press, Carbondale.
Kelly, Isabel
1945    *Excavations at Culiacan, Sinaloa.* Ibero-Americana 25. University of
        California Press, Berkeley.
Kelley, J. Charles
1974    Speculations on the Culture History of Northwestern Mesoamerica. In
        *The Archaeology of West Mexico,* edited by B. Bell, pp. 19–39. West
        Mexican Society for Advanced Study, Ajijic, Jalisco, Mexico.
Kelley, J. Charles, and Ellen Abbott Kelley
1975    An Alternative Hypothesis for the Explanation of Anasazi Culture His-

tory. In *Collected Papers in Honor of Florence Hawley Ellis*, edited by
T. R. Frisbie, pp. 178–223. Papers of the Archaeological Society of
New Mexico no. 2, Santa Fe.

Kennedy, Kenneth A. R.

1994    Identification of Sacrificial and Massacre Victims in Archaeological
Sites: The Skeletal Evidence. *Man and Environment* 19:247–251.

Kidder, Alfred Vincent

1932    *The Artifacts of Pecos.* Yale University Press, New Haven.

1958    *Pecos, New Mexico: Archaeological Notes.* Papers of the Robert S.
Peabody Foundation for Archaeology no. 5. Phillips Academy, Andover, Massachusetts.

Kidder, Alfred Vincent, and Samuel J. Guernsey

1919    *Archaeological Explorations in Northeastern Arizona.* Bureau of
American Ethnology Bulletin no. 65. Smithsonian Institution, Washington, D.C.

Kirchhoff, Paul

1943    Mesoamerica: Sus limites geográficos, composición étnica y carácteres
culturales. *Acta Americana* (Sociedad Inter-Americana de
Antropología y Geografía) 1(1):92–107.

Kluckhohn, Clyde

1939    The Excavation of Bc 51 Rooms and Kivas. In *Preliminary Report on
the 1937 Excavations, Bc 50–51, Chaco Canyon, New Mexico,* edited
by C. Kluckhohn and P. Reiter, pp. 30–48. University of New Mexico
Bulletin 345, Anthropological Series vol. 3, no. 2. Albuquerque.

Knowles, Nathaniel

1940    The Torture of Captives by the Indians of Eastern North America. *Proceedings of the American Philosophical Society* 82(2):151–225.

Koch, Christopher P., compiler

1989    *Taphonomy: A Bibliographic Guide to the Literature.* Center for the
Study of the First Americans, Orono, Maine.

Kroeber, A. L.

1927    Disposal of the Dead. *American Anthropologist* 29(3):308–315.

Lagunas R., Zaid, and Carlos Serrano S.

1993    Los restos oseos humanos excavados en la Plaza de la Luna y Zona de
las Cuevas, Teotihuacan, Mexico (Temporada V, 1963). *UNAM Notas
Antropológicas* 2(5):28–60.

Lang, Richard W., and Arthur H. Harris

1984    *The Faunal Remains from Arroyo Hondo Pueblo, New Mexico: A
Study in Short-Term Subsistence Change.* Arroyo Hondo Archaeological
Series 5. School of American Research Press, Santa Fe, New Mexico.

Lange, Charles H.

1940    A Brief Summary of a Cranial Series from North Central New Mexico.
*New Mexico Anthropologist* 4(1):13–17.

Lange, Frederick, Nancy Mahaney, Joe Ben Wheat, et al.

1988    *Yellow Jacket: A Four Corners Anasazi Ceremonial Center.* Rev. ed.
Johnson Books, Boulder, Colorado.

LeBlanc, Steven A.

1989 Cultural Dynamics in the Southern Mogollon Area. In *Dynamics of Southwest Prehistory,* edited by L. S. Cordell and G. J. Gumerman, pp. 179–
207. Smithsonian Institution Press, Washington, D.C.

Lekson, Stephen H. (with contributions by William B. Gillespie and Thomas C.
Windes)

1986    *Great Pueblo Architecture of Chaco Canyon, New Mexico.* University
of New Mexico Press, Albuquerque.

Leechman, Douglas

1951    Bone Grease. *American Antiquity* 16(4):355–356.

Lehmann, H. E.

1980    Unusual Psychiatric Disorders, Atypical Psychoses, and Brief Reactive
Psychoses. In *Comprehensive Textbook of Psychiatry III,* vol. 2,
3d ed., edited by H. F. Kaplan, A. M. Freedman, and B. J. Sadock.
Williams and Wilkins, Baltimore.

Levi, Ken

1982    *Violence and Religious Commitment: Implications of Jim Jones's People's Temple Movement.* Pennsylvania State University Press, University Park.

Lightfoot, Ricky R.

1993    Synthesis. In *The Duckfoot Site, vol. 1: Descriptive Archaeology,* edited by R. R. Lightfoot and M. C. Etzkorn, pp. 297–302. Crow Canyon Archaeological Center Occasional Paper 3. Cortez, Colorado.

Lincoln, Edward P.

1961    A Comparative Study of Present and Past Mammalian Fauna of the Sunset Crater and Wupatki Areas of Northern Arizona. Master's thesis, Department of Zoology, University of Arizona, Tucson.

Lindsay, Alexander J., Jr., Christy G. Turner II, and Paul V. Long, Jr.

1963    Excavations along the Lower San Juan River, Utah, 1958–1960. Unpublished report on file in Harold S. Colton Research Center Library, Museum of Northern Arizona. Flagstaff.

Lister, Robert H.

1959    *The Coombs Site.* Anthropological Papers of the University of Utah no. 41 (Glen Canyon Series 8). University of Utah Press, Salt Lake City.

1964    *Contributions to Mesa Verde Archaeology, I: Site 499, Mesa Verde National Park, Colorado.* University of Colorado Studies, Anthropology Series no. 9. University of Colorado Press, Boulder.

1965    *Contributions to Mesa Verde Archaeology, II: Site 875, Mesa Verde National Park, Colorado.* University of Colorado Studies. Anthropology Series no. 11. University of Colorado Press, Boulder.

Lister, Robert H. (with collaborators E. Anderson et al.)

1966    *Contributions to Mesa Verde Archaeology, 3: Site 866, and the Cultural Sequence at Four Villages in the Far View Group, Mesa Verde National Park, Colorado.* University of Colorado Studies, Anthropology Series no. 12. University of Colorado Press, Boulder.

Lister, Robert H., J. Richard Ambler, and Florence C. Lister

1960    *The Coombs Site, Part 2.* Anthropological Papers of the University of Utah no. 41 (Glen Canyon Series no. 8). University of Utah Press, Salt Lake City.

Lister, Robert H., and Florence C. Lister

1961    *The Coombs Site, Part 3: Summary and Conclusions.* Anthropological Papers of the University of Utah no. 41 (Glen Canyon Series 8). University of Utah Press, Salt Lake City.

1968    *Earl Morris and Southwestern Archaeology.* University of New Mexico Press, Albuquerque.

1981    *Chaco Canyon: Archaeology and Archaeologists.* University of New Mexico Press, Albuquerque.

Long, Paul V., Jr.

1960    Archaeology of Curtain Cliff Site. *Plateau* 33(1):17–18.

LoPiccolo, Philip

1992    National Park Service Accession Receiving Report Chaco Culture NHP Collection CHCU Acc. no. 269, CHCE Acc. no. 15. Chaco Center, Department of Anthropology, University of New Mexico, Albuquerque.

Lorenz, Konrad

1967    *On Aggression.* Translated by M. K. Wilson. Bantam Books, New York.

Luebben, Ralph A.

1982    The Grinnell Site: A Small Ceremonial Center near Yucca House, Colorado. Manuscript on file in the Department of Anthropology, Grinnell College, Iowa.

1983    The Grinnell Site: A Small Ceremonial Center near Yucca House, Colorado. *Journal of Intermountain Archeology* 2:1–26.

Luebben, Ralph A., and Paul R. Nickens

1982    A Mass Interment in an Early Pueblo III Kiva in Southwestern Colorado. *Journal of Intermountain Archeology* 1:66–79.

Lumholtz, Carl

1889     *Among Cannibals: An Account of Four Years' Travels in Australia and of Camp Life with the Aborigines of Queensland.* John Murray, London. Reprint, Caliban Books, Sussex, England, 1979.

1902     *Unknown Mexico: A Record of Five Years' Exploration among the Tribes of the Western Sierra Madre; in the Tierra Caliente of Tepic and Jalisco; and among the Trascos of Michoacan.* 2 vols. C. Scribners, New York. Reprint, Rio Grande Press, Glorieta, New Mexico, 1973.

Lunde, Donald T.

1976     *Murder and Madness.* The Portable Stanford Series, San Francisco Book Co., San Francisco.

Lyman, R. Lee

1994     *Vertebrate Taphonomy.* Cambridge University Press, Cambridge.

MacHovec, Frank J.

1989     *Cults and Personality.* Charles C. Thomas, Springfield, Illinois.

Mackey, James, and R. C. Green

1979     Largo-Gallina Towers: An Explanation. *American Antiquity* 44(1):144–154.

MacLean, Paul D.

1987     On the Evolution of the Three Mentalities of the Brain. In *Origins of Human Aggression: Dynamics and Etiology,* edited by G. G. Neuman, pp. 29–41. Human Sciences Press, New York.

MacNeish, Richard S.

1962     *Second Annual Report of the Tehuacan Archaeological-Botanical Project.* Robert S. Peabody Foundation for Archaeology, Phillips Academy, Andover, Massachusetts.

Malotki, Ekkehart, and Michael Lomatuway'ma

1987     *Stories of Maasaw, a Hopi God.* University of Nebraska Press, Lincoln.

Malotki, Ekkehart, Michael Lomatuway'ma, Lorena Lomatuway'ma, and Sidney Namingha, Jr.

1993     *Hopi Ruin Legends Kiqötutuwutsi.* Northern Arizona University and University of Nebraska Press, Lincoln.

Malvido, Elsa, Vera Tiesler, and Grégory Pereira, coordinators

1995     *El cuerpo humano y su tratamiento mortuorio.* Program, Simposio Internacional. Museo del Carmen, México, D.F.

Malville, Nancy J.

1989     Two Fragmented Human Bone Assemblages from Yellow Jacket, Southwestern Colorado. *Kiva* 55(1):3–22.

Mansilla, Josefina, and José Antonio Pompa

1990     Los restos oseos de los Toltecas. In *Mesoamerica y Norte de México, Siglo IX–XII,* coordinated by F. Sodi Miranda, pp. 565–574. Tercer Seminario de Arqueología, vol. 2. Museo Nacional de Antropología e Historia, México, D.F.

Markman, Roberta H., and Peter T. Markman

1992     *The Flayed God. The Mesoamerican Mythological Tradition: Sacred Texts and Images from Pre-Columbian Mexico and Central America.* HarperCollins, New York.

Martin, Debra L.

1994     Patterns of Diet and Disease: Health Profiles for the Prehistoric Southwest. In *Themes in Southwest Prehistory,* edited by G. J. Gumerman, pp. 87–108. School of American Research Press, Santa Fe, New Mexico.

Martin, Debra L., Alan H. Goodman, George J. Armelagos, and Ann L. Magennis

1991     *Black Mesa Anasazi Health: Reconstructing Life from Patterns of Death and Disease.* Occasional Papers no. 14. Center for Archaeological Investigations, Southern Illinois University, Carbondale.

Martin, Paul S.

1929     The 1928 Archaeological Expedition of the State Historical Society of Colorado. *Colorado Magazine* 6(1):1–35.

Martin, Paul S., John B. Rinaldo, and Ernst Antevs
1949   *Cochise and Mogollon Sites, Pine Lawn Valley, Western New Mexico.* Fieldiana: Anthropology, vol. 38, no. 1. Chicago Natural History Museum, Chicago.

Matos Moctezuma, Eduardo
1984   The Templo Mayor of Tenochtitlan: Economics and Ideology. In *Ritual Human Sacrifice in Mesoamerica,* edited by E. H. Boone, pp. 133–164. Dumbarton Oaks, Washington, D.C.

McCreery, Patricia, and Ekkehart Malotki
1994   *Tapamveni: The Rock Art Galleries of Petrified Forest and Beyond.* Petrified Forest Museum Association, Petrified Forest, Arizona.

McDonald, James A.
1976   *An Archeological Assessment of Canyon de Chelly National Monument.* Western Archeological Center Publications in Anthropology no. 5. National Park Service, Tucson.

McGee, W. J.
1898   *The Seri Indians.* Reports of the Bureau of American Ethnology, no. 17, part 1. Smithsonian Institution, Washington, D.C.

McGimsey, Charles R. III
1980   *Mariana Mesa: Seven Prehistoric Settlements in West-Central New Mexico. A Report of the Upper Gila Expedition.* Papers of the Peabody Museum of Archaeology and Ethnology no. 72. Harvard University, Cambridge, Massachusetts.

McGregor, John C.
1943   Burial of an Early American Magician. *Proceedings of the American Philosophical Society* 80(2):270–298. Philadelphia.
1965   *Southwestern Archaeology.* University of Illinois Press, Urbana.

McGuire, Randall H.
1980   The Mesoamerican Connection in the Southwest. *Kiva* 46(1):3–38.

McGuire, Randall H., E. Charles Adams, Ben A. Nelson, and Katherine A. Spielmann
1994   Drawing the Southwest to Scale: Perspectives on Macroregional Relations. In *Themes in Southwest Prehistory,* edited by G. J. Gumerman, pp. 239–265. School of American Research Press, Santa Fe, New Mexico.

McKenna, Peter J.
1984   *The Architecture and Material Culture of 29SJ1360 Chaco Canyon, New Mexico.* Reports of the Chaco Center 7. Division of Cultural Research, National Park Service, Albuquerque.

McNitt, Frank
1966   *Richard Wetherill: Anasazi.* Rev. ed. University of New Mexico Press, Albuquerque.

Micozzi, Marc S.
1991   *Postmortem Change in Human and Animal Remains: A Systematic Approach.* Charles C. Thomas, Springfield, Illinois.

Miles, James S.
1975   *Orthopedic Problems of the Wetherill Mesa Populations, Mesa Verde National Park, Colorado.* Publications in Archeology no. 7G, Wetherill Mesa Studies. National Park Service, Washington, D.C.

Milner, George R., and Clark Spencer Larsen
1991   Teeth as Artifacts of Human Behavior: Intentional Mutilation and Accidental Modification. In *Advances in Dental Anthropology,* edited by M. A. Kelley and C. S. Larsen, pp. 357–378. Wiley-Liss, New York.

Milner, George R., and Virginia G. Smith
1989   Carnivore Alteration of Human Bone from a Late Prehistoric Site in Illinois. *American Journal of Physical Anthropology* 79(1):43–49.

Mindeleff, Cosmos
1891   *A Study of Pueblo Architecture: Tusayan and Cibola.* Bureau of American Ethnology Annual Report no. 8. Smithsonian Institution, Washington, D.C.

Minturn, Penny Dufoe

1994    A Study of Perimortem Damage to Human Bone from Sambrito Village, Northwestern New Mexico. Master's thesis, Department of Anthropology, Arizona State University, Tempe.

Mitchell, Douglas R.

1992    Explorations of Spatial Variability in Hohokam and Salado Cemeteries. In *Proceedings of the Second Salado Conference, Globe, Arizona, 1992,* edited by R. C. Lange and S. Germick, pp. 191–200. Arizona Archaeological Society, Phoenix.

Moorehead, Warren K.

1906    *A Narrative of Explorations in New Mexico, Arizona, Indiana, Etc. Together with a Brief History of the Department.* Bulletin 3, Department of Archaeology, Phillips Academy. The Andover Press, Andover, Massachusetts.

Morlan, Richard E.

1984    Toward the Definition of Criteria for the Recognition of Artificial Bone Alterations. *Quaternary Research* 22:160–171.

1987    Archaeology as Palaeobiology. *Transactions of the Royal Society of Canada* (Series 5) 2:117–124.

Morris, Ann Axtell

1933    *Digging in the Southwest.* Cadmus Books. E. M. Hale and Co., Chicago.

Morris, Earl H.

1924    *Burials in the Aztec Ruin.* Anthropological Papers of the American Museum of Natural History no. 26, part 3. New York.

1925    Exploring in the Canyon of Death. *National Geographic* 48(3):263–300.

1938    Mummy Cave. *Natural History* 42(2):127–138.

1939    *Archaeological Studies in the La Plata District, Southwestern Colorado and Northwestern New Mexico.* Carnegie Institution of Washington, Publication 519. Washington, D.C.

n.d.*a*   Field Notes, Bernheimer Expeditions of 1921, 1922, 1929, and 1930. Copy in the Harold S. Colton Research Center Library, Museum of Northern Arizona, Flagstaff.

n.d.*b*   Field Notes: Canyon del Muerto. Copy at the Western Archeological Center, National Park Service, Tucson.

Morris, Elizabeth Ann

1956    A Bibliography of Earl H. Morris. *Southwestern Lore* 22(3).

1980    *Basketmaker Caves in the Prayer Rock District, Northeastern Arizona.* Anthropological Papers no. 35. University of Arizona Press, Tucson.

Morris, James N., Linda Honeycutt, and Jerry Fetterman

1993    *Preliminary Report on 1990–1991 Excavations at Hanson Pueblo Site 5MT3876.* Indian Camp Ranch Archaeological Report no. 2. Woods Canyon Archaeological Consultants, Yellow Jacket, Colorado.

Morse, Dan

1984    The Time of Death. In *Handbook of Forensic Archaeology and Anthropology,* rev. ed., edited by D. Morse, J. Duncan, and J. Stoutamire, pp. 124–144. Rose Printing Co., Tallahasee, Florida.

Moser, Christopher L.

1973    *Human Decapitation in Ancient Mesoamerica.* Studies in Pre-Columbian Art and Archaeology no. 11. Dumbarton Oaks. Trustees for Harvard University, Washington, D.C.

Mueller, James W.

1969    Burial Salvage and Reconnaissance in the Four Corners Area. Unpublished report on file in Department of Anthropology site records, NA10674, Museum of Northern Arizona, Flagstaff.

Narváez Valverde, Fray José

1937    Notes upon Moqui and Other Recent Ones upon New Mexico (written by Fray José Narvares [Narváez] Valverde, Senecú, October 7, 1732). In *Historical Documents Relating to New Mexico, Nueva Vizcaya, and the Approaches Thereto, to 1773,* edited by C. W. Hackett, vol. 3, pp. 385–387. Carnegie Institution of Washington, Washington, D.C.

Nass, G. Gisela, and Nicholas F. Bellantoni

1982    A Prehistoric Multiple Burial from Monument Valley Evidencing Trauma and Possible Cannibalism. *Kiva* 47(4):257–271.

Nelson, Ben A.

1995    Complexity, Hierarchy, and Scale: A Controlled Comparison of Chaco Canyon and La Quemada. Arizona State University, Department of Anthropology Colloquium, April 11.

Neuman, Gerard G.

1987    Past and Present Thinking on Aggression: An Introductory Overview. In *Origins of Human Aggression: Dynamics and Etiology,* edited by G. G. Neuman, pp. 17–28. Human Sciences Press, New York.

Neumann, Georg K.

1940    Evidence for the Antiquity of Scalping from Central Illinois. *American Antiquity* 5(3):287–289.

Newman, Margaret E.

1993    Appendix A: Immunological Analysis, Site 5MT10207. In Disarticulated Human Remains from Reach III of the Towaoc Canal, Ute Mountain Ute Reservation, Montezuma County, Colorado, by M. H. Dice. Report prepared for Bureau of Reclamation, Upper Colorado Region, Salt Lake City, Utah, by Complete Archaeological Services Associates, Cortez, Colorado.

Nickens, Paul R.

1974    *Analysis of Prehistoric Human Skeletal Remains from the Mancos Canyon, Southwestern Colorado.* Report prepared in conjunction with Bureau of Indian Affairs Contract no. MOOC14201337. Department of Anthropology, University of Colorado, Boulder.

1975    Prehistoric Cannibalism in the Mancos Canyon, Southwestern Colorado. *Kiva* 40(4):283–293.

1979    Osteological Analysis of Human Skeletal Material from the Grinnell and Ismay Sites, Montezuma County, Southwestern Colorado. Manuscript in authors' possession.

Niederberger, Christine

1987    Le developement de sociétés complexes. 4 Cannibalisme. *Etudes Mesoamericaines. Paleopaysages et Archeologie Pre-Urbaine du Bassin de Mexico (Mexique)* 11(2):674–677. Centre d'Etudes Mexicaines et Centraamericaines. México.

Noe-Nygaard, Nanna

1977    Butchering and Marrow Fracturing as a Taphonomic Factor in Archaeological Deposits. *Paleobiology* 3(2):218–237.

Nordby, Larry V.

1974    *The Excavation of Sites 5MTUMR 2343, 5MTUMR 2345 and 5MTUMR 2346, Mancos Canyon, Ute Mountain, Ute Homelands, Colorado.* Bureau of Indian Affairs, Contract MOOC14201337 Report.

Nordenskiöld, Gustaf E. A. von

1973    *The Cliff Dwellers of the Mesa Verde, Southwestern Colorado: Their Pottery and Implements.* Translated by D. L. Morgan. Antiquities of the New World, vol. 12. AMS Press, New York. (Originally published 1893.)

Nuttall, Zelia

1903    *The Book of the Life of the Ancient Mexicans Containing an Account of Their Rites and Superstitions.* Part 1, Introduction and Facsimile. University of California, Berkeley.

Ogilvie, Marsha D., and Charles E. Hilton

1992    Analysis of Selected Human Skeletal Material from Sites 423–124 and –131. Unpublished report.

1993    Analysis of Selected Human Skeletal Material from Sites 423–124 and –131. In *Across the Colorado Plateau: Anthropological Studies for the Transwestern Pipeline Expansion Project, vol. 18, Human Remains and Burial Goods,* by N. P. Hermann et al., pp. 97–128. Office of Contract Archaeology and Maxwell Museum of Anthropology, University of New Mexico, Albuquerque.

Olsen, Sandra L., and Pat Shipman

1994    Cutmarks and Perimortem Treatment of Skeletal Remains on the
        Northern Plains. In *Skeletal Biology in the Great Plains: Migration,
        Warfare, Health, and Subsistence,* edited by D. W. Owsley and R. L.
        Jantz, pp. 377–387. Smithsonian Institution Press, Washington, D.C.

Olson, Alan P.

1966    A Mass Secondary Burial from Northern Arizona. *American Antiquity*
        31(6):822–826.

1971    *Archaeology of the Arizona Public Service Company 345KV Line.* Mu-
        seum of Northern Arizona Bulletin 46. Flagstaff.

Olson, Alan P., and William W. Wasley

1956    An Archaeological Traverse Survey in West-Central New Mexico. In
        *Pipeline Archaeology: Reports of Salvage Operations in the Southwest
        on El Paso Natural Gas Company Projects, 1950–1953,* edited by
        F. Wendorf, N. Fox, and O. L. Lewis, pp. 256–390. Laboratory of An-
        thropology, Santa Fe, and Museum of Northern Arizona, Flagstaff.

Owsley, Douglas W.

1994    Warfare in Coalescent Tradition Populations of the Northern Plains. In
        *Skeletal Biology in the Great Plains: Migration, Warfare, Health, and
        Subsistence,* edited by D. W. Owsley and R. L. Jantz, pp. 333–343.
        Smithsonian Institution Press, Washington, D.C.

Padden, R. C.

1967    *The Hummingbird and the Hawk: Conquest and Sovereignty in the
        Valley of Mexico, 1503–1541.* Ohio State University Press, Columbus.

Palkovich, Ann M.

1984    Disease and Mortality Patterns in the Burial Rooms of Pueblo Bonito:
        Preliminary Considerations. In *Recent Research on Chaco Prehistory,*
        edited by W. J. Judge and J. D. Schelberg, pp. 103–113. Reports of the
        Chaco Center, no. 8. National Park Service, Albuquerque, New Mex-
        ico.

Parry, John H., and Robert G. Keith, editors and commentators

1984    1502? Amérigo Vespucci to Lorenzo di Pier Francesco de Medici, from
        Lisbon. In *New Iberian World: A Documentary History of the Discov-
        ery and Settlement of Latin America to the Early Seventeenth Century.
        vol. 5: Coastlines, Rivers, and Forests,* pp. 15–17. Times Books and
        Hector & Rose, New York.

Parsons, Elsie Clews

1939    *Pueblo Indian Religion.* University of Chicago Press, Chicago.

Parsons, Elsie Clews, editor

1936    *Hopi Journal of Alexander M. Stephen.* Columbia University Contri-
        butions to Anthropology, vol. 23. New York.

Peckham, Stewart

1963    A Basket Maker III Site near Tohatchi, New Mexico. In *Highway Sal-
        vage Archaeology,* vol. 4, assembled by S. Peckham, pp. 73–82. New
        Mexico State Highway Department and Museum of New Mexico,
        Santa Fe.

Pepper, George H.

1906    Human Effigy Vases from Chaco Cañon, New Mexico. In *Anthropo-
        logical Papers Written in Honor of Franz Boas,* pp. 320–334. G. E.
        Stechert, New York.

1909    The Exploration of a Burial-Room in Pueblo Bonito, New Mexico. In
        *Putnam Anniversary Volume: Anthropological Essays,* edited by
        F. Boas, pp. 196–252. G. E. Stechert, New York.

1920    *Pueblo Bonito.* Anthropological Papers of the American Museum of
        Natural History no. 27. New York.

Pickering, Robert B.

1974    A Preliminary Report on the Osteological Material from Alta Vista,
        Zacatecas. In *The Archaeology of West Mexico,* edited by B. Bell,
        pp. 240–248. West Mexican Society for Advanced Study, Ajijic,
        Jalisco, México.

1985    Human Osteological Remains from Alta Vista, Zacatecas: An Analysis of the Isolated Bone. In *The Archaeology of West and Northwest Mesoamerica,* edited by M. S. Foster and P. C. Weigand, pp. 289–325. Westview Press, Boulder.

Pickering, Robert B., and Michael S. Foster

1994    A Survey of Prehistoric Disease and Trauma in Northwest and West Mexico. *Proceedings of the Denver Museum of Natural History* 3(7):1–15.

Pijoan Aguadé, Carmen María

1997    *Evidencias de sacrificio humano y canibalismo en restos oseos: El caso del entierro número 14 de Tlatelolco, D.F.* Doctoral thesis in anthropology, Universidad Nacional Autónoma de México, México, D.F.

Pijoan Aguadé, Carmen María, coordinator

1993    Un enfoque interdisciplinario de los sacrificios humanos y el canibalismo. Symposium at the Thirteenth International Congress of Anthropological and Ethnological Sciences, Mexico City.

Pijoan Aguadé, Carmen María, and Josefina Mansilla Lory

1990a   Prácticas rituales en el norte de Mesoamerica: Evidencias en Electra, Villa de Reyes, San Luis Potosí. *Arqueologia* 4:87–96.

1990b   Evidencias rituales en restos humanos del norte de Mesoamerica. In *Mesoamerica y Norte de México, Siglo IX–XII,* coordinated by F. Sodi Miranda, pp. 467–478. Tercer Seminario de Arqueología, vol. 2. Museo Nacional de Antropología e Historia, México, D.F.

1993    Las marcas de golpes sobre los huesos largos del entierro 14 de Tlatelolco, D.F. *Abstracts of the Thirteenth International Congress of Anthropological and Ethnological Sciences, Mexico City,* p. 350.

Pijoan Aguadé, Carmen María, Josefina Mansilla, and Alejandro Pastrana C.

1993    Un caso de desmembramiento, Tlatelolco, D.F. *Estudios de Antropología Biológica* 5:89–100. INAH/UNAM, México.

Pijoan Aguadé, Carmen María, and Alejandro Pastrana C.

1985    Evidencias de antropofagia y sacrificio humano en restos oseos. *Avances en Antropología Física* 2:37–45. INAH, México.

1987    Método para registro de marcas de corte en huesos humanos: El caso de Tlatelcomila, Tetelpan, D.F. *Estudios de Antropología Biológica* 3:561–583. INAH/UNAM, México.

1989    Evidencias de actividades rituales en restos oseos humanos en Tlatelcomila, D.F.:El Preclasico o Formativo. *Avances y Perspectivas,* pp. 287–307. MNA/INAH, México.

Pijoan Aguadé, Carmen María, Alejandro Pastrana C., and Consuelo Maquivar M.

1989    El tzompantli de Tlatelolco: Una evidencia de sacrificio humano. *Estudios de Antropología Biológica, 4: Coloquio de Antropología Física Juan Comas, 1986,* pp. 561–583. UNAM/INAH, Mexico.

Pilles, Peter J.

1974    The Leroux Wash Excavation. Report presented at the Pecos Conference, Mesa Verde National Park, Colorado.

Piossek Prebisch, Teresa

1991    *Ensayo sobre la antropofagia en América de la conquista: A desafío para España.* Privately printed. Argentina.

Pippin, Lonnie C.

1987    *Prehistory and Paleoecology of Guadalupe Ruin, New Mexico.* University of Utah Anthropological Paper 112. University of Utah Press, Salt Lake City.

Pippin, Lonnie C., and Cynthia Irwin-Williams

1973    *Excavations at the Salmon Ruin.* San Juan County Museum Association, San Juan Archaeological Research Center and Library, Bloomfield, New Mexico, and Eastern New Mexico University.

Powell, Joseph F., and Leah Carson Powell

1992    The Oldest Example of Dental Filing North of the Valley of Mexico. *Dental Anthropology Newsletter* 7(1):4–6.

Ramírez M., Axel

1988    La Antropología en Durango. In *La antropología en México.*

*Panorama histórico, 12: La antropología en el norte de México,* edited by C. García Mora and V. M. Rojo Leiva, pp. 309–344. Instituto Nacional de Antropología e Historia, México, D.F.

Ravesloot, John C.
1988     *Mortuary Practices and Social Differentiation at Casas Grandes, Chihuahua, Mexico.* University of Arizona Press, Tucson.

Ravesloot, John C., and Patricia M. Spoerl
1989     The Role of Warfare in the Development of Status Hierarchies at Casas Grandes, Chihuahua, Mexico. In *Cultures in Conflict: Current Archaeological Perspectives,* edited by D. C. Tkaczuk and B. C. Vivian, pp. 130–137. Proceedings of the Twentieth Annual Chacmool Conference, University of Calgary Archaeological Association, Calgary, Canada.

Reed, Erik K.
1949a    Fractional Burials, Trophy Skulls, and Cannibalism. *Region 3 Anthropology Notes* 79:1–2. National Park Service, Southwestern Region, Santa Fe.
1949b    The Significance of Skull Deformation in the Southwest. *El Palacio* 56(4):106–119.
1953     Appendix III: Human Skeletal Remains from Te'ewi. In *Salvage Archaeology in the Chama Valley, New Mexico,* assembled by F. Wendorf, pp. 104–118. School of American Research Monograph no. 17, Santa Fe, New Mexico.
1955     Human Skeletal Remains from the Turner-Look Site. In *A Reappraisal of the Fremont Culture with a Summary of the Archaeology of the Northern Periphery,* by H. M. Wormington, pp. 38–43. Proceedings no. 1, Denver Museum of Natural History, Denver.
1962     Human Skeletal Material from Site 59, Chaco Canyon National Monument. *El Palacio* 69(4):240–247.
1963     Occipital Deformation in the Northern Southwest. Regional Research Abstract 310. Santa Fe.
1964     The Greater Southwest. In *Prehistoric Man in the New World,* edited by J. D. Jennings and E. Norbeck, pp. 175–191. University of Chicago Press, Chicago.

Regan, Marcia H.
1988     Methodological and Nutritional Correlates of Long Bone Growth in Two Southwestern Prehistoric Skeletal Samples. Master's thesis, Department of Anthropology, Arizona State University, Tempe.

Regan, Marcia H., Christy G. Turner II, and Joel D. Irish
1996     Physical Anthropology of the Schoolhouse Point Mound, U:8:24/13A. In *The Place of the Storehouses. Roosevelt Platform Mound Study: Report on the Schoolhouse Point Mound, Pinto Creek Complex,* part II, by O. Lindauer (with P. H. McCartney et al.), pp. 787–840. Roosevelt Monograph Series 6, Anthropological Field Studies 35. Arizona State University, Department of Anthropology, Office of Cultural Resource Management, Tempe, Arizona.

Reiter, Paul
1938     *The Jemez Pueblo of Unshagi, New Mexico, with Notes on the Earlier Excavations at "Amoxiumqua" and Giusewa.* University of New Mexico Bulletin nos. 326 and 327, Monograph Series nos. 5 and 6. Parts I and II. Monographs of the University of New Mexico and School of American Research. University of New Mexico Press, Albuquerque.

Ressler, Robert K., and Tom Schachtman
1992     *Whoever Fights Monsters.* St. Martin's, New York.

Retzius, G.
1973     Human Remains from the Cliff Dwellings of the Mesa Verde. In *The Cliff Dwellers of the Mesa Verde, Southwestern Colorado: Their Pottery and Implements,* by G. von Nordenskiöld, pp. 1–11. Translated by D. L. Morgan. AMS Press, New York. (Originally published 1893.)

Reyman, Jonathan E.
1995     Value in Mesoamerican-Southwestern Trade. In *The Gran Chichimeca:*

*Essays on the Archaeology and Ethnohistory of Northern Mesoamerica,* edited by J. E. Reyman, pp. 271–280. Avebury Worldwide Archaeology Series, Aldershot, Hampshire, England.

Rice, Glen

1985    The Organization of Work Space in a Small Salado Compound Site. In *Studies in the Hohokam and Salado of the Tonto Basin,* edited by G. Rice, pp. 133–155. Office of Cultural Resource Management Report no. 63, Arizona State University, Tempe.

Rice, Glen, Jeffrey Hantman, and Rachel Most, editors

1982    *The Ash Creek Archaeological Project: Preliminary Field Report.* Office of Cultural Resource Management Report no. 56. Department of Anthropology, Arizona State University, Tempe.

Richert, Roland

n.d.    Untitled manuscript on 1952 excavations at Wupatki. On file in Western Archaeological Center Archives, National Park Service, Tucson.

Riley, Carroll L.

1987    *The Frontier People: The Greater Southwest in the Protohistoric Period.* University of New Mexico Press, Albuquerque.

Roberts, Frank H. H., Jr.

1929    *Shabik'eshchee Village: A Late Basket Maker Site in the Chaco Canyon, New Mexico.* Bureau of American Ethnology Bulletin no. 92. Smithsonian Institution, Washington, D.C.

1939    *Archeological Remains in the Whitewater District, Eastern Arizona, Part 1: House Types.* Bureau of American Ethnology Bulletin no. 121. Smithsonian Institution, Washington, D.C.

1940    *Archeological Remains in the Whitewater District, Eastern Arizona, Part 2: Artifacts and Burials.* Bureau of American Ethnology Bulletin no. 126. Smithsonian Institution, Washington, D.C.

n.d.    Roberts Archive: Box 2, Folder 4; Box 4; Box 7, Folder 4. National Anthropological Archives, Smithsonian Institution, Washington, D.C.

Roberts, Heidi

1991    A Comparative Analysis of Human Skeletal Remains from Parowan Fremont, Virgin Anasazi, and Kayenta Anasazi Archaeological Sites. Master's thesis, Department of Anthropology, University of Nevada, Las Vegas.

Robinson, William J., and Bruce G. Harrill

1974    *Tree-Ring Dates from Colorado, 5: Mesa Verde Area.* Laboratory of Tree-Ring Research, University of Arizona, Tucson.

Robinson, William J., and Roderick Sprague

1965    Disposal of the Dead at Point of Pines, Arizona. *American Antiquity* 30(4):442–453.

Rohn, Arthur H.

1989    Northern San Juan Prehistory. In *Dynamics of Southwest Prehistory,* edited by L. S. Cordell and G. J. Gumerman, pp. 149–177. Smithsonian Institution Press, Washington, D.C.

Romero Molina, Javier

1958    *Mutilaciones dentarias prehispánicas de México y América en general.* Instituto Nacional de Antropología e Historia, México, D.F.

1960    Ultimos hallazgos de mutilaciones dentarias en México. *Anales del Instituto Nacional de Antropología e Historia* 12:151–215.

1970    Dental Mutilation, Trephination, and Cranial Deformation. In *Handbook of Middle American Indians, vol. 9: Physical Anthropology,* edited by T. D. Stewart, pp. 50–67. University of Texas Press, Austin.

1986    *Catálogo de la colección de dientes mutilados prehispánicos,* part 4. Instituto Nacional de Antropología e Historia. Colección Fuentes, México, D.F.

Romero Molina, Javier, and Samuel Fastlicht

1951    *El arte de las mutilaciones dentarias.* Enciclopedia Mexicana de Arte no. 14. Ediciones Mexicanas, México, D.F.

Rudy, Jack R.

1961    Investigation of a Site at Bluff, Utah. Unpublished report to Mesa

Verde National Park Superintendent, on file in Mesa Verde National Park Archives.

Ryan, Dennis J.

1977    The Paleopathology and Paleoepidemiology of the Kayenta Anasazi Indians in Northeastern Arizona. Ph.D. dissertation, Department of Anthropology, Arizona State University, Tempe.

Sadek-Kooros, Hind

1972    Primitive Bone Fracturing: A Method of Research. *American Antiquity* 37(3):369–382.

Sahagún, Fray Bernardino de

1932    *A History of Ancient Mexico 1547–1577*, vol. 1. Translated by F. R. Bandelier from the Spanish version of C. M. de Bustamante. Fisk University Press, Nashville.

Sanders, Ed

1971    *The Family: The Story of Charles Manson's Dune Buggy Attack Battalion.* E. P. Dutton, New York.

San Juan County Museum Association

n.d.    *Salmon Ruin Trail Guide.* San Juan County Archeological Research Center and Library, Bloomfield, New Mexico.

Santa María, Fray Vicente de

1973    *Relación histórica de la colonia del Nuevo Santander.* Introduction and notes by E. de la Torre Villar. Nueva Biblioteca Mexicana 27. Instituto de Investigaciones Bibliográficas, Universidad Nacional Autónoma de México, México, D.F.

Saville, Marshall H.

1913    Precolumbian Decoration of the Teeth in Ecuador with Some Account of the Occurrence of the Custom in Other Parts of North and South America. *American Anthropologist* 15:377–394.

Schaafsma, Polly, and Curtis F. Schaafsma

1974    Evidence for the Origins of the Pueblo Katchina Cult as Suggested by Southwestern Rock Art. *American Antiquity* 39(4):535–545.

Scheans, Daniel J.

1956    Human Skeletal Material from Pipeline Excavations: Skeletal Remains from the Archaeological Survey of West Central New Mexico. In *Pipeline Archaeology: Reports of Salvage Operations in the Southwest on El Paso Natural Gas Company Projects, 1950–1953*, edited by F. Wendorf, N. Fox, and O. L. Lewis, pp. 256–390. Laboratory of Anthropology, Santa Fe, and Museum of Northern Arizona, Flagstaff.

Schelberg, John D.

1984    Analogy, Complexity, and Regionally Based Perspectives. In *Recent Research on Chaco Prehistory,* edited by W. J. Judge and J. D. Schelberg, pp. 5–21. Reports of the Chaco Center no. 8, National Park Service, Albuquerque.

Schieck, Cherie L.

1983    *The Gomero Project: Flexibility as an Adaptive Response.* School of American Research, Santa Fe, New Mexico.

Schultz, Michael, Carmen Pijoan Aguadé, and Peter Schwartz

1993    Results of Microscopic Research on Bones from Preclassic Tetelpan, Mexico. *Abstracts of the Thirteenth International Congress of Anthropological and Ethnological Science, Mexico City,* p. 411.

Sebastian, Lynne

1992    *The Chaco Anasazi: Sociopolitical Evolution in the Prehistoric Southwest.* Cambridge University Press, Cambridge.

Seler, Eduard

1993    *Collected Works in Mesoamerican Linguistics and Archaeology.* English translations of German papers made under supervision of C. P. Bowditch. Edited by J.E.S. Thompson and F. B. Richardson. Vol. 4. Labyrinthos, Culver City, California.

Senter, Donovan

1937    Appendix II: Burials from Mound 50 and Mound 51. In *Tseh So: A Small House Ruin Chaco Canyon, New Mexico,* edited by D. D. Brand et al., pp. 140–162. University of New Mexico Bulletin 308, Anthropological Series vol. 2, no. 2. University of New Mexico Press, Albuquerque.

Serrano Sánchez, Carlos

1993    Funerary Practices and Human Sacrifice in Teotihuacan Burials. In *Teotihuacan: Art from the City of the Gods,* edited by K. Berrin and E. Pasztory, pp. 108–115. Thames and Hudson, New York.

Sharrock, Floyd W., Keith M. Anderson, Don D. Fowler, and David S. Dibble

1961    *1960 Excavations, Glen Canyon Area.* Anthropological Papers of the University of Utah no. 52 (Glen Canyon Series no. 14). University of Utah Press, Salt Lake City.

Shelley, Steven D., and Richard Ciolek-Torrello

1994    Grapevine Recreation and Stockpile Areas. In *The Roosevelt Rural Sites Study, vol. 2: Prehistoric Rural Settlements in the Tonto Basin, Part 1,* edited by R. Ciolek-Torrello, S. D. Shelley, and S. Benaron, pp. 223–259. Statistical Research Technical Series no. 28, Tucson.

Shipman, Jeff H.

1977    Preliminary Data on Skeletal Remains from the Salmon Site (LA 8846), New Mexico. Unpublished inventory, 7 pp. On file at Salmon Ruin, San Juan County Archeological Research Center and Library, Bloomfield, New Mexico.

1980    Part 10: Human Skeletal Remains from the Salmon Ruin (LA 8846), and Appendix 10.1: Basic Data on Skeletal Remains from the Salmon Site (LA 8846), New Mexico: Statewide and Room 64W. In *Investigations at the Salmon Ruins: The Structure of Chacoan Society in the Northern Southwest.* vol. 4, edited by C. Irwin-Williams and P. H. Shelly, pp. 47–58. Eastern New Mexico University, Portales.

Shipman, Pat

1981    *Life History of a Fossil.* Harvard University Press, Cambridge.

Shipman, Pat, Alan Walker, and David Bichell

1985    *The Human Skeleton.* Harvard University Press, Cambridge.

Shipman, Pat, Giraud Foster, and Margaret Schoeninger

1984    Burnt Bones and Teeth: An Experimental Study of Color, Morphology, Crystal Structure, and Shrinkage. *Journal of Archaeological Science* 11(4):307–325.

Simmons, Marc

1974    *Witchcraft in the Southwest: Spanish and Indian Supernaturalism on the Rio Grande.* Northland Press, Flagstaff, Arizona.

Sink, Clifton W., Douglas M. Davy, A. Trinkle Jones, Laura Michalik, and Diane Pitz

1982    Arizona D:7:262. In *Excavations on Black Mesa, 1980: A Descriptive Report,* edited by P. P. Andrews et al., pp. 86–108. Research Paper 24, Southern Illinois University at Carbondale Center for Archaeological Investigations, Carbondale.

Smith, Anthony

1969    *The Body.* Avon Books, New York.

Smith, Watson

1952    *Excavations in Big Hawk Valley, Wupatki National Monument, Arizona.* Museum of Northern Arizona Bulletin 24, Flagstaff.

1992    One Man's Archaeology. *Kiva* 57(2):101–191.

Smith, Watson, Richard B. Woodbury, Nathalie F. S. Woodbury, and Ross G. Montgomery

1966    *The Excavation of Hawikuh by Federick Webb Hodge: Report of the Hendricks-Hodge Expedition, 1917–1923.* Contributions from the Museum of the American Indian, Heye Foundation, no. 20. New York.

Snow, Clyde Collins, and John Fitzpatrick

1989    Human Osteological Remains from the Battle of the Little Bighorn. In *Archaeological Perspectives on the Battle of the Little Bighorn,* edited by D. Scott et al., pp. 243–282. University of Oklahoma Press, Norman.

Sofaer, Anna, Michael P. Marshall, and Rolf M. Sinclair
1989      The Great North Road: A Cosmographic Expression of the Chaco Culture of New Mexico. In *World Archaeoastronomy,* edited by A. F. Aveni, pp. 365–375. Cambridge University Press, Cambridge.

Spicer, Edward H.
1962      *Cycles of Conquest: The Impact of Spain, Mexico, and the United States on the Indians of the Southwest, 1533–1960.* University of Arizona Press, Tucson.

Stanislawski, Michael B.
1963      Extended Burials in the Prehistoric Southwest. *American Antiquity* 28(3):308–319.

Stedt, Pauline Gertrude
1979      Trace Element Analysis of Two Prehistoric Populations: The Fremont and the Anasazi. Master's thesis, Department of Anthropology, San Diego State University, San Diego.

Stevenson, Matilda Coxe
1904      *The Zuñi Indians: Their Mythology, Esoteric Fraternities, and Ceremonies.* Twenty-third Annual Report of the Bureau of American Ethnology, 1901–1902. Washington, D.C.

Stewart, Kenneth M.
1968      Culinary Practices of the Mohave Indians. *El Palacio* 75(1):26–37.

Stewart, T. D.
1937      Different Types of Cranial Deformity in the Pueblo Area. *American Anthropologist* 39:169–171.
1940      Appendix B: Skeletal Remains from the Whitewater District, Eastern Arizona. In *Archeological Remains in the Whitewater District Eastern Arizona, Part 2: Artifacts and Burials,* by F. H. H. Roberts, Jr., pp. 153–166. Bureau of American Ethnology Bulletin 126. Smithsonian Institution, Washington, D.C.

Storey, Rebecca
1992      *Life and Death in the Ancient City of Teotihuacan: A Modern Paleodemographic Synthesis.* University of Alabama Press, Tuscaloosa.

Sugiyama, Saburo
1995      Mass Human Sacrifice and Symbolism of the Feathered Serpent Pyramid in Teotihuacan, Mexico. Ph.D. dissertation, Department of Anthropology, Arizona State University, Tempe.

Sullivan, Richard B., and G. Robert Phippen
1994      Site 423–124. In *Across the Colorado Plateau: Anthropological Studies for the Transwestern Pipeline Expansion Project, vol. 10, Excavations at Anasazi Sites in the Upper Puerco River Valley,* by R. B. Sullivan (with contributions by M. Binford et al.), pp. 306–392. Office of Contract Archaeology and Maxwell Museum of Anthropology, University of New Mexico, Albuquerque.

Sumner, William Graham
1906      *Folkways: A Study of the Sociological Importance of Usages, Manners, Customs, Mores, and Morals.* Ginn and Co., Boston.

Swanton, John R., and Frank H. H. Roberts, Jr.
1931      Obituary: Jesse Walter Fewkes. *Smithsonian Report for 1930* (Publication 3105), pp. 609–616. Washington, D.C.

Swedlund, Alan C.
1969      Human Skeletal Material from the Yellow Jacket Canyon Area, Southwestern Colorado. Master's thesis, Department of Anthropology, University of Colorado, Boulder.

Tainter, Joseph A., and Fred Plog
1994      Strong and Weak Patterning in Southwestern Prehistory: The Formation of Puebloan Archaeology. In *Themes in Southwest Prehistory,* edited by G. J. Gumerman, pp. 165–181. School of American Research Press, Santa Fe, New Mexico.

Titiev, Mischa
1943      Notes on Hopi Witchcraft. *Papers of the Michigan Academy of Sciences, Arts, and Letters* 28(1942):549–557.

1944      *Old Oraibi: A Study of the Hopi Indians of Third Mesa.* Papers of the Peabody Museum of American Archaeology and Ethnology 22(1). Harvard University, Cambridge, Massachusetts.

1956      Shamans, Witches, and Chiefs among the Hopi. *Tomorrow* 4(3):51–56.

Thomas, Hugh

1993      *The Conquest of Mexico.* Hutchinson, London.

Trombold, Charles D.

1991      Causeways in the Context of Strategic Planning in the La Quemada Region, Zacatecas, Mexico. In *Ancient Road Networks and Settlement Hierarchies in the New World,* edited by C. D. Trombold, pp. 145–168. University of Cambridge Press, Cambridge.

Turner, Christy G. II

1960      Physical Anthropology of Curtain Cliff Site. *Plateau* 33(1):19–23.

1961a      Appendix II, Human Skeletons from the Coombs Site: Skeletal and Dental Aspects. In *The Coombs Site, Part 3: Summary and Conclusions,* by R. H. Lister and F. C. Lister, pp. 117–136. Anthropological Papers of the University of Utah no. 41 (Glen Canyon Series no. 8). University of Utah Press, Salt Lake City.

1961b      Appendix III: Human Skeletal Material. In *1960 Excavations, Glen Canyon Area,* by F. W. Sharrock et al., pp. 338–360. Anthropological Papers of the University of Utah 52 (Glen Canyon Series 14). University of Utah Press, Salt Lake City.

1963      *Petrographs of the Glen Canyon Region: Styles, Chronology, Distribution, and Relationships from Basketmaker to Navajo.* Museum of Northern Arizona Bulletin no. 38 (Glen Canyon Series no. 4). Flagstaff.

1983      Taphonomic Reconstructions of Human Violence and Cannibalism Based on Mass Burials in the American Southwest. In *Carnivores, Human Scavengers, and Predators: A Question of Bone Technology,* edited by G. M. LeMoine and A. S. MacEachern, pp. 219–240. Archaeological Association of the University of Calgary, Calgary, Canada.

1988      Appendix 2H, Another Prehistoric Southwest Mass Human Burial Suggesting Violence and Cannibalism: Marshview Hamlet, Colorado. In *Dolores Archaeological Program: Aceramic and Late Occupations at Dolores,* compiled and edited by G. T. Gross and A. E. Kane, pp. 81–83. Bureau of Reclamation, Engineering and Research Center, Denver.

1989      Teec Nos Pos: More Possible Cannibalism in Northeastern Arizona. *Kiva* 54(2):147–152.

1992      Anasazi Cannibalism: Review of Tim D. White's *Prehistoric Cannibalism at Mancos 5MTUMR-2346. Review of Archaeology* 13(2):7–13.

1993      Cannibalism in Chaco Canyon: The Charnel Pit Excavated in 1926 at Small House Ruin by Frank H. H. Roberts, Jr. *American Journal of Physical Anthropology* 91(4):421–439.

Turner, Christy G. II, and Nancy T. Morris

1970      A Massacre at Hopi. *American Antiquity* 35(3):320–331.

Turner, Christy G. II, Marcia H. Regan, and Joel D. Irish

1994      Physical Anthropology and Human Taphonomy. In *The Roosevelt Rural Sites Study, vol. 2: Prehistoric Rural Settlements in the Tonto Basin, Part 2,* edited by R. Ciolek-Torrello, S. D. Shelley, and S. Benaron, pp. 559–583. Statistical Research Technical Series 28, Tucson.

Turner, Christy G., II, and Jacqueline A. Turner

1990      Perimortem Damage to Human Skeletal Remains from Wupatki National Monument, Northern Arizona. *Kiva* 55(3):187–212.

1992a      The First Claim for Cannibalism in the Southwest: Walter Hough's 1901 Discovery at Canyon Butte Ruin 3, Northeastern Arizona. *American Antiquity* 57(4):661–682.

1992b      On Peter Y. Bullock's "A Reappraisal of Anasazi Cannibalism." *Kiva* 58(2):189–201.

1993    Cannibalism in the American Southwest. Paper presented at the Thir-
        teenth International Congress of Anthropological and Ethnological Sci-
        ences, Mexico City.

1995    Cannibalism in the Prehistoric American Southwest: Occurrence,
        Taphonomy, Explanation, and Suggestions for Standardized World
        Definition. *Anthropological Science* (Tokyo) 103(1):1–22.

1997    Looking but Not Seeing: Reexamination of Some Glen Canyon Skeletal
        Remains Thirty-five Years Later. Paper presented at the annual meeting
        of the Society for American Archaeology, Nashville, Tennessee.

Turner, Christy G. II, Jacqueline A. Turner, and Roger C. Green

1993    Taphonomic Analysis of Anasazi Skeletal Remains from Largo-Gallina
        Sites in Northwestern New Mexico. *Journal of Anthropological Re-
        search* 49(2):83–110.

Turner, Christy G. II, Jacqueline A. Turner, Carmen María Pijoan Aguadé, et al.

n.d.    Human Perimortem Bone Damage Suggests Ritual Cannibalism in
        Central Mexico 7000–8500 Years Ago. Manuscript in preparation.

Ubelaker, Douglas H., and Bradley J. Adams

1995    Differentiation of Perimortem and Postmortem Trauma Using Tapho-
        nomic Indicators. *Journal of Forensic Sciences* 40(3):509–512.

Upham, Steadman

1995    Review of *Stress and Warfare among the Kayenta Anasazi of the Thir-
        teenth Century A.D.*, by J. Haas and W. Creamer. *American Antiquity*
        60(2):369–370.

Villa, Paola

1992    Cannibalism in Prehistoric Europe. *Evolutionary Anthropology*
        1(3):93–104.

Villa, Paola, Claude Bouville, Jean Courtin, et al.

1986    Cannibalism in the Neolithic. *Science* 233(4762):431–437.

Vivian, R. Gwinn

1965    *The Three-C Site: An Early Pueblo II Ruin in Chaco Canyon, New
        Mexico.* University of New Mexico Publications in Anthropology
        no. 13. University of New Mexico Press. Albuquerque.

Volhard, Ewald

1939    *Kannibalismus.* Strecker und Schroder Verlag, Stuttgart.

Voth, H. R.

1905    *The Traditions of the Hopi.* Stanley McCormick Hopi Expedition.
        Field Columbian Museum Publication 96, Anthropological Series
        no. 8. Chicago.

Wade, William D.

1970    Skeletal Remains of a Prehistoric Population from the Puerco Valley,
        Eastern Arizona. Ph.D. dissertation, Department of Anthropology,
        University of Colorado, Boulder.

Wade, William D., and George J. Armelagos

1966    Anthropometrical Data and Observations upon Human Skeletal Ma-
        terial. In *Contributions to Mesa Verde Archaeology, 3: Site 866, and
        the Cultural Sequence at Four Villages in the Far View Group, Mesa
        Verde National Park, Colorado,* by R. H. Lister et al., pp. 97–112. Uni-
        versity of Colorado Studies, Series in Anthropology no. 12. University
        of Colorado Press, Boulder.

Walker, Phillip L.

1989    Tool Marks on Skeletal Remains from Aaunatuk (NgTN-1). Report to
        the Prince of Wales Heritage Center, Yellowknife, NWT. Manuscript in
        authors' possession.

Wallis, Wilson D., and Mischa Titiev

1945    Hopi Notes from Chimopovy. *Papers of the Michigan Academy of Sci-
        ence, Arts and Letters* 30:523–555.

Ward, Albert E.

1975    *Inscription House: Two Research Reports.* Museum of Northern Ari-
        zona Technical Series no. 16. Flagstaff.

Waters, Jennifer

1995    Rodent Consumption among the Late Classic Hohokam at Pueblo

Grande. Master's thesis, Department of Anthropology, Arizona State University, Tempe.

Wellman, Kevin D.

1994    Site 423–131. In *Across the Colorado Plateau: Anthropological Studies for the Transwestern Pipeline Expansion Project, vol. 10, Excavations at Anasazi Sites in the Upper Puerco River Valley,* by R. B. Sullivan (with contributions by M. Binford et al.), pp. 159–226. Office of Contract Archaeology and Maxwell Museum of Anthropology, University of New Mexico, Albuquerque.

Wendorf, Fred

1953    Excavations at Te'ewi. In *Salvage Archaeology in the Chama Valley, New Mexico,* assembled by F. Wendorf, pp. 34–98. School of American Research Monograph 17, Santa Fe, New Mexico.

Wertham, Fredric

1949    *The Show of Violence.* Doubleday, Garden City, New York.

Wetherill, Richard

1893a    Letters from Richard Wetherill to B.T.B. Hyde and Fred Hyde Jr. from 1893 to 1902. Copies on file in Harold S. Colton Research Center Library, Museum of Northern Arizona, Flagstaff.

1893b    Letter to Gustaf Nordenskiöld, December 31. Copy on file in Wetherill–Grand Gulch Archives, Edge of Cedars State Park Museum, Blanding, Utah.

1894    Letter to editor about Snider's Well, from Mancos, Colorado, June 24, 1894. *Archaeologist* (Ohio Archaeological and Historical Society) 2(9):288–289.

Wheat, Joe Ben

1959    The Architecture of Porter Pueblo. Manuscript on file at the University of Colorado Museum, Boulder.

1972    *The Olsen-Chubbuck Site: A Paleo-Indian Bison Kill.* Memoirs of the Society for American Archaeology no. 26. *American Antiquity* 37:1 (part 2).

White, Theodore E.

1952    Observations on the Butchering Technique of Some Aboriginal Peoples: I. *American Antiquity* 17(4):337–338.

White, Tim D.

1988    Appendix C, Cottonwood Wash, Southeastern Utah: The Human Osteology of Feature 3, FS#27, Site 42SA12209. In *Salvage Excavations of 42SA12209,* edited by J. Fetterman, L. Honeycutt, and K. Kuckelman, pp. 1–7. Woods Canyon Archaeological Consultants, Yellow Jacket, Colorado.

1992    *Prehistoric Cannibalism at Mancos 5MTUMR-2346.* Princeton University Press, Princeton, New Jersey.

White, Tim D., and Pieter Arend Folkens

1991    *Human Osteology.* Academic Press, San Diego.

Whiteley, P.

1988    *Bacavi: Journey to Reed Springs.* Northland Press, Flagstaff, Arizona.

Whittemore, Mary

1939    Artifacts of Bone, Antler, and Shell. In *Preliminary Report on the 1937 Excavations, Bc50–51, Chaco Canyon, New Mexico,* edited by C. Kluckhohn and P. Reiter, pp. 131–146. University of New Mexico Bulletin 345, Anthropology Series vol. 3, no. 2. University of New Mexico Press, Albuquerque.

Wiener, Ann Lucy

1988    Appendix 2D: Human Remains from Marshview Hamlet. In *Dolores Archaeological Program: Aceramic and Late Occupations at Dolores,* compiled by G. T. Gross and A. E. Kane, pp. 71–72. Bureau of Reclamation, Engineering and Research Center, Denver, Colorado.

Wikle, Les

1989    Possible Cannibalism Found at Anasazi Village. *Forest News,* Feb.–Mar., p. 11. Intermountain Report, Department of Agriculture.

Wilcox, David R.

1993     The Evolution of the Chacoan Polity. In *The Chimney Rock Archaeo-
         logical Symposium, October 20–21, 1990, Durango, Colorado,* edited
         by J. McK. Malville and G. Matlock, pp. 76–90. USDA Forest Service
         General Technical Report RM-227. Fort Collins, Colorado.

n.d.     Wupatki Archaeological Inventory. Work in progress. National Park
         Service and Museum of Northern Arizona, Flagstaff.

Willey, P., and D. H. Ubelaker

1976     Notched Teeth from the Texas Panhandle. *Journal of the Washington
         Academy of Sciences* 66:239–246.

Wilshusen, Richard H.

1986     The Relationship between Abandonment Mode and Ritual Use in
         Pueblo I Anasazi Protokivas. *Journal of Field Archaeology*
         13:245–254.

1988     Excavations at Marshview Hamlet (Site 5MT2235), a Pueblo III Habi-
         tation Site. In *Dolores Archaeological Program: Aceramic and Late
         Occupations at Dolores,* compiled by G. T. Gross and A. E. Kane,
         pp. 17–53. Bureau of Reclamation, Engineering and Research Center,
         Denver, Colorado.

Wilson, John P.

1972     Awatovi: More Light on a Legend. *Plateau* 44(3):125–130.

Windes, Thomas C.

1984     A New Look at Population in Chaco Canyon. In *Recent Research on
         Chaco Prehistory,* edited by W. J. Judge and J. D. Schelberg, pp. 75–87.
         Reports of the Chaco Center no. 8. National Park Service, Albu-
         querque, New Mexico.

Winter, Joseph C. (with contributions by Rick Morris et al.)

1994     *Across the Colorado Plateau: Anthropological Studies for the Trans-
         western Pipeline Expansion Project, vol. 20, Conclusions and Syn-
         thesis: Communities, Boundaries, and Cultural Variation.* Office of
         Contract Archeology and Maxwell Museum of Anthropology, Univer-
         sity of New Mexico, Albuquerque.

Woodbury, Richard B.

1959     A Reconsideration of Pueblo Warfare in the Southwestern United
         States. *Proceedings of the Thirty-third International Congress of Amer-
         icanists, San Jose, Costa Rica, 1958,* vol. 2, pp. 124–133. San Jose: Ed-
         itorial Lehmann.

1979     Prehistory: Introduction. In *Handbook of North American Indians,
         vol. 9: Southwest,* edited by A. Ortiz, pp. 22–30. Smithsonian Institu-
         tion Press, Washington, D.C.

1993     *Sixty Years of Southwestern Archaeology: A History of the Pecos Con-
         ference.* University of New Mexico Press, Albuquerque.

Wormington, H. Marie

1955     *A Reappraisal of the Fremont Culture, with a Summary of the Archae-
         ology of the Northern Periphery.* Denver Museum of Natural History
         Proceedings no. 1, Denver.

Yava, Albert

1978     *Big Falling Snow: A Tewa-Hopi Indian's Life and Times and the His-
         tory and Traditions of His People.* Edited and annotated by H. Cour-
         lander. Crown Publishers, New York.

Young, Gwen

1980     Analysis of Faunal Remains. In *Tijeras Canyon: Analyses of the Past,*
         edited by Linda S. Cordell, pp. 88–120. Maxwell Museum of Anthro-
         pology and University of New Mexico Press, Albuquerque.

Zierhut, N. W.

1967     Bone Breaking Activities of the Calling Lake Cree. *Alberta Anthropol-
         ogist* 1:33–36.

## A

acid, and breakdown of bone, 16–17

Adams, Richard E. W., 421–22, 464–65

age, ratios of in sites with evidence of cannibalism and of violence, 404, *405, 406, 407. See also* children

aggression: and explanations for cannibalism, 461–62; and literature on historic Pueblo, 480

agriculture, and cultural history of Southwest, 3

Akins, Nancy J., 126, 127, 130, 131, 316, 388, 461

Alexander, George, 205

Allen, Robert, 60

Ambler, J. Richard, 178–82

American Museum of Natural History, 111, 112, 132

analogy, and interpretations of prehistoric violence, 50

Anasazi: and considerate mortuary practices, 39–50; cultural history of, 3, *4;* evidence for frequency of cannibalism among, 413; explanations for and interpretations of cannibalism among, 451, 459–84; and modern Pueblo, 412; and sites reviewed, 81, 146, 151, 184, 262–63, 269, 276, 299, 306, 308, 320, 338. *See also* Basketmaker cultures

Chaco: and sites reviewed, 95, 111, 153, 172, 263, 316, 326, 357, 369, 382

Cibola: and sites reviewed, 255, 256, 293

Gallina: and sites reviewed, 232

Kayenta: and sites reviewed, 161, 178, 331, 336, 337, 367, 395

Largo-Gallina: and sites reviewed, 227, 228, 229, 230, 236, 239, 242, 244

Mancos Mesa: and sites reviewed, 158

Mesa Verde: and sites reviewed, 65, 78, 132, 142, 182, 220, 248, 285, 286, 316, 318, 362, 364

Piedra: and sites reviewed, 223

San Juan: and sites reviewed, 310, 312, 314, 362

Sundial phase,: and sites reviewed, 271

Tsegi: and defensive siting of settlements, 369

Winslow: and sites reviewed, 200

Anderson, Keith M., 367

Anderson, Kirsten Linnea, 363

animals: archaeological evidence for processing of, 35–38; ethnographic accounts of processing of, 31–34, 54; taphonomic analysis and damage to human bones by, 12–16; taphonomy and butchering/cooking process for, 24–31. *See also* carnivores; rodent gnawing

anvil abrasions: as evidence of violence or cannibalism, *88, 99, 106–107, 110, 139–140, 166, 177, 185, 211–214, 282, 285, 303, 310, 334, 354, 401–402, 438;* human damage to bones and, 18; and taphonomic signature of cannibalism, 24; use of term, 7. *See also* hammerstone

Anyon, Roger, 255–56, 256–57

Apaches, 90

archaeology: and evidence for animal processing, 35–38; and evidence for cannibalism in Mexico, 421–28, 457–58; violence and cannibalism in history of, 55; Wetherill and, 60

architecture, and similarities between Chacoan and Mesoamerican sites, 465

Arens, William, 2, 8, 90

Arikaras (Nebraska/Kansas), 52

Armelagos, George J., 182, 183, 364, 365, 366

arrows, and projectile points as evidence of violence, 50, 235, 266, 268. *See also* projectile points

artifacts. *See* tools

asphyxiation, and violence as cause of death, 267–68

Atwell, Karen A., 257, 261

Awatovi, oral traditions and folklore concerning attack on, 6, 51, 52–53, 71–72, 189–90, 197–98